GROUP

Theory and Experien

GROUPS
Theory and Experience

Fifth Edition

Rodney W. Napier

Matti K. Gershenfeld
Temple University

HOUGHTON MIFFLIN COMPANY　Boston　Toronto
Dallas　Geneva, Illinois　Palo Alto　Princeton, New Jersey

To the support and affection I feel from my loving daughters, Amma, Laura, Tori. *R. W. N.*

To the continuing support and affection from my caring sons, Beryl, Howard, Richard, Ken, and their families. *M. K. G.*

Senior Sponsoring Editor: Loretta Wolozin
Senior Development Editor: Susan Granoff
Project Editor: Jean Levitt
Production/Design Coordinator: Caroline Ryan
Senior Manufacturing Coordinator: Marie Barnes
Marketing Manager: Katie Griffin

Cover design by Perennial Design.

Chapter opening photo credits:
Chapter 1: Jean-Claude Lejeune
Chapter 2: Fredrik Bodin/Stock Boston
Chapter 3: Spencer Grant/Stock Boston
Chapter 4: Owen Franken/Stock Boston
Chapter 5: Mike Boroff/TexaStock
Chapter 6: Jean-Claude Lejeune
Chapter 7: Photo Researchers, Inc.
Chapter 8: Addison Geary/Stock Boston
Chapter 9: COMSTOCK INC./Robert Hauser
Chapter 10: Elizabeth Crews/Stock Boston
Chapter 11: Bill Bachman/Photo Researchers, Inc.
Chapter 12: Jim Davis

Excerpt on p. 116 by Claude Haberman, copyright © 1988 by The New York Times Company. Reprinted by permission.
Excerpt on p. 160 by Peter Waldman, reprinted by permission of *The Wall Street Journal,* © Dow Jones & Company, Inc., 1987. Reprinted by permission.

Printed in the U.S.A.

Library of Congress Catalog Number: 92-72385

ISBN: 0-395-63869-0

3456789-AH-96 95 94

Contents

Preface

One of the original reasons we wrote *Groups: Theory and Experience* was to bring the literature of group dynamics to life. Until then, readers had to deal with books that focused strictly on theory and research. This book became a helpful alternative resource in the area of group processes because it was the first to combine a rigorous empirical approach with a highly readable and practical orientation. This balanced focus on research, theory, *and* application continues to separate our book from others in the market.

Through the years, instructors and readers have told us that they have benefited from using previous editions of this textbook as a "tool" in their own work with groups and organizations. Our new edition continues our commitment to this practical approach—to the translation of theory and research into useful methods of application.

Audience

Since the publication of our first edition, interest in group function has expanded, as has the diversity of our readers. The text has been adopted in departments of psychology, education, communication, speech, social work, business, and management, and it continues to find new audiences with each edition. Organizations and groups that are interested in human relations training, planned change, organizational development, problem solving, leadership, or team development have been able to increase both their theoretical understanding and their operational effectiveness by using this text as a resource and guide. Although the text attracts a varied readership and uses examples from all walks of life, it remains focused on the characteristic features found in virtually all groups.

Features of the New Edition

The fifth edition of *Groups: Theory and Experience* reflects the many developments that the field of group dynamics has experienced in recent years.

An especially noteworthy change in this edition is an *innovative new chapter,* "Making Large Groups More Effective." Here we present eight real-life cases involving groups ranging in size from thirty to several hundred members. The cases are drawn from an extraordinarily wide variety of settings, including a major American university, the Nicaraguan national government, a large midwestern corporation, and an inner-city school. Each case focuses on a specific intervention that was carefully designed to solve a particular problem and to move the large group forward toward achieving its goals. By examining the theoretical concepts underlying each intervention, the cases help readers gain a unique understanding of how theory can be utilized as part of a strategy to make groups function more effectively.

Another significant change is the *expansion of Chapter 11,* "Small Group Proc-esses: Three Contemporary Applications." We have extensively revised the section on quality circles to present an in-depth analysis and assessment of the movement to Total Quality Management. Additionally, we have added a major new section on focus groups and new coverage of therapeutic self-help groups.

A third highlight of the fifth edition is our *increased coverage of issues related to gender and cultural diversity.* For example, Chapter 1 has a new section on gender differences in communication, Chapter 3 includes new coverage of cultural norms, and Chapter 5 contains new material on gender differences in leadership styles. In addition, we have tried to incorporate a richer array of culturally diverse examples and cases throughout the book.

In addition to the changes noted above, *every chapter has been thoroughly updated and revised* to take account of the most recent developments in this dynamic field of study. We have substantially revised our chapter on norms, group pressures, and deviancy (Chapter 3) and have continued to revise our understand-ing of the rapidly changing field of leadership and its relation to group processes (Chapter 5). Among other key changes are a new section on strategic plans (Chap-ter 4), new coverage of Pareto analysis and new methods of group problem solving (Chapter 7), and new sections on the FIRO theory of interpersonal behavior and the recurring phase theory of group development (Chapter 10).

Content

We begin by exploring the observable and predictable communication patterns that tend to develop in every group. An awareness of these patterns is crucial for understanding the group and raising the level of effective interaction among group members. In addition, understanding one's own perception of the group and its members can dramatically improve communications within the group. Thus, per-ception and communication are the topics of Chapter 1.

A second critical aspect for the success of a working group is an understanding of what makes individuals feel as though they belong to the group. One's feeling of belonging is directly related to the amount of cohesion found in a group and the ability of individuals to work effectively together. The concept of membership is explored fully in Chapter 2.

Chapter 3, "Norms, Group Pressures, and Deviancy," is closely related to Chap-ter 4, "Goals." Because norms can be both constructive and destructive in terms of a group reaching its goals, understanding what norms and goals are, how they develop, and how they can be changed is essential.

Leadership is central to the success of virtually any group. Our premises are that *any* group member can perform leadership functions, that appropriate leadership is determined by the needs of a group, and, because those needs change, so will leadership behavior and strategies. To be successful as a leader demands flexibility of role, a willingness to share authority when appropriate, and an interest in making the most of the resources of other group members, even when this calls for reducing one's own leadership role. Such is the dynamic role of leadership discussed in Chapter 5.

Chapter 6, "A Systems View of Small Group Behavior," explores the small group as a system, providing the opportunity to view group dynamics from a new and more integrative perspective. It links much of the information concerning issues of maintenance and group process in a holistic and integrative fashion.

A critical aspect of any working group is that of problem solving and decision making. Techniques for improving the problem-solving capabilities of a group and various methods of reducing group conflict and reaching consensus are outlined in Chapter 7.

In Chapter 8 we look at the use of humor in groups. Humor plays many roles in the life of a group. When deliberately introduced into a group that is defensive or even hostile, humor can reduce tension, provide a more constructive and positive climate, and thus help move a group toward its goals.

The next chapter makes the assumption that meetings represent the opportunity to apply group process skills in practical ways. Thus, we explore what hinders groups and why so many meetings fail, along with solutions to make them more effective. Special attention is given to the concept of design.

Chapter 10, "The Evolution of Groups," integrates much of the material presented in the earlier chapters by describing the developmental characteristics of working groups. Armed with an understanding of the stages of development, group needs, and the critical events in the life of a group, group members can increase the possibility that they will respond in appropriate and constructive ways and thereby contribute to the group's effectiveness. Attention is given to the family as a small group and the relevance of family therapy to group development.

In Chapter 11, concepts examined earlier in the text are applied to three contemporary group forms: self-help groups, quality circles and Total Quality Management, and focus groups. These types of small groups have become increasingly popular and influential in recent years. This chapter explores the practical application of group theory to types of groups that many of us may encounter at work or in our personal lives.

Chapter 12, our new chapter, offers a perspective on how group theory can be utilized with large groups. Through the eight real-life case studies it presents, the chapter examines specific intervention strategies that were designed to improve the functioning of the groups in question. Here, too, readers are offered an opportunity to see how group theory can be put to use to solve real problems in the real world of groups.

A Final Word

The fifth edition of *Groups: Theory and Experience* represents our continued effort to make our text:

- Accessible and appealing to students
- Comprehensive and current in its review of the literature
- Useful in its methods and tools of application
- An accurate reflection of the complex and diverse society in which we live
- Balanced in its presentation of research, theory, and practical applications.

We feel this fifth edition is our best effort to date in meeting this challenge.

Acknowledgments

Amma Napier brought a refreshing perspective to the review, selection, and integration of critical research to this edition. Carolyn Perks and Sigrid Burns were of great assistance throughout the course of this extensive revision. Esther Rubenstein typed the manuscript and was a "perfectionist" and a helpful critical reviewer. Jean Levitt, our project editor, provided the support and encouragement necessary to organize successfully a complex revision such as this. Finally, Susan Granoff and Loretta Wolozin have continued their strong leadership, which over the past twenty years has helped us maintain our consistently good relations with Houghton Mifflin.

We would also like to thank the following academic reviewers for their helpful suggestions and constructive criticism at various stages in the development of this latest revision: Ernestyne J. Adams, *Temple University;* Mary Anne Fitzpatrick, *University of Wisconsin, Madison;* Barbara Herlihy, *U. of Houston–Clear Lake;* Michael Naumes, *Southern Oregon State College;* Celeste A. Ridgeway, *La Guardia Community College;* and Bruce Tuckman, *Florida State University, Tallahassee.*

R. W. N.
M. K. G.

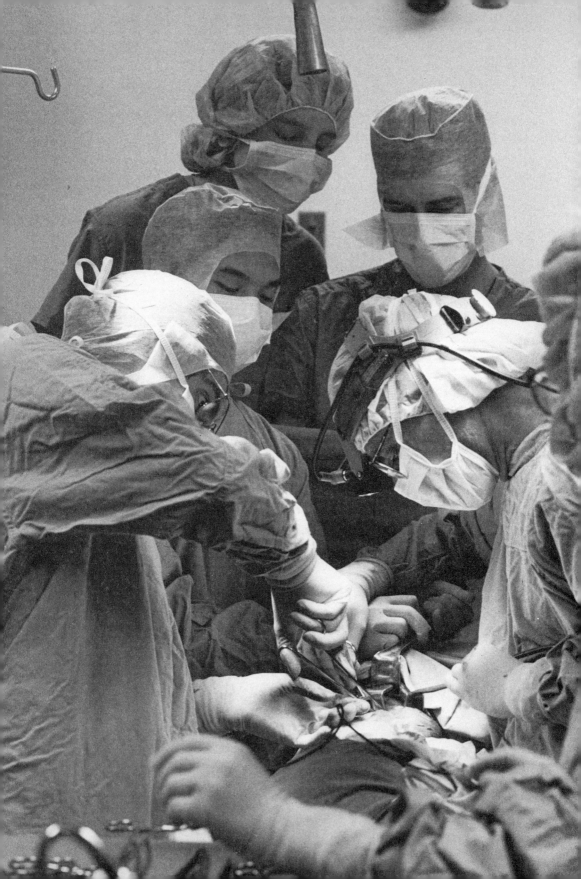

◆ 1 ◆

Perception and Communication

T wenty-four people from various places and walks of life come to a remote island in Canada to learn how to become leaders and build a sense of community. They are psychologists, businesspeople, workers, students, teachers, and community leaders. They come from metropolitan centers and small towns and from all socioeconomic levels. They range in age from twenty-seven to fifty-five.

All have decided on their own to take part in the Temagami experience. They are expecting to learn leadership and community building by using parts of themselves they have never had time to focus on before. For example, advance materials have explained that they will learn about leadership by listening to the silence within themselves as some Native American cultures teach.

On the first day of the program, the twenty-four participants are in a shuttle bus on the island. Somewhat self-consciously, they are preparing to follow the instructions they received before they left home: "Remain completely silent. When you arrive, decide where in the complex you want to live for the three weeks: go to the men's, women's, or mixed dorms, but do not speak. If your spouses come, do not identify them as such. They are to make their own decisions about where they want to stay."

Once the participants arrive at the community center, they are instructed to explore and to get to know the environment. Again, they are asked to refrain from speaking.

After lunch, the group gathers in a teepee. The participants are directed to sit in a circle. As the leader begins to talk of the group's goals, the participants realize that their traditional philosophies and norms do not apply here. Not the Judeo-Christian ethics they are used to, but a Native American cultural orientation, with which most are unfamiliar, is the norm.

Imagine yourself as one of the twenty-four, alone on this faraway island with the crutches of familiar society taken away. What do you see? What do you project? What messages do you hear in the words of others? What will you learn about the group and about yourself, and how will the group respond to your presence?

We have all stood on the threshold of a new group, in this way, carefully screening our own behavior and trying to communicate what we believe will be most acceptable. And, in turn, we select from the narrow world of experience what we believe is truth, selectively perceived information about the group facing us. We take the data we pick up from others, and after a process of filtering, sifting, and refining, we respond to our particular personal understanding of the situation— often a distortion of our own creation. The ideas and information become alloys of our own making. Thus one new member of a group may see twenty-three potential friends while another sees twenty-three sources of potential rejection. One may observe dress, tone of voice, age, sex, posture; another may focus immediately on evidence of influence and power, indicated perhaps in the direction of word flow or the movement of eyes toward the source of approval. Whatever the processes and needs of the individual, the view that eventually enters the mind's eye will be, to some degree, a distorted vision of what actually is taking place, reduced by some and expanded by others.

Our objective in this chapter is to dispel a stubborn, enduring myth: the myth that we see objectively, hear objectively, and speak in ways that are instantly understood and that people—if they have half a mind to—have no difficulty communicating. Not so.

We see selectively as individuals, and our culture affects how we see and what we see. Selective perception not only influences us as individuals, but it is further complicated in a group.

To be more specific, in this chapter we will discuss the nature of communication that goes beyond words. We will discuss factors that inhibit communication in a group even when all the members want that communication to be effective. Beyond these basics, we will move on to understanding communication in groups and, finally, to examining factors that influence group communication. Expressing what you want to say and having it understood is, to say the least, a complicated, difficult process.

Selective Perception and the Individual

That we see what we need to see is not merely a psychologist's whim; it is reality. An ink blot reveals how an ill-defined or nebulous stimulus can elicit a wide range of responses from different individuals. Each perception and its interpretation of virtually any event are based on a combination of historical experiences, present needs, and the inherent properties of the scene being perceived. Because what we see is always a combination of what is actually occurring and what is happening within us at that moment, it is unlikely that two people will ever perceive the same thing in exactly the same way (Harrison, 1976; Wrench, 1964).

It is necessary to base our understanding of how we perceive our experience on the assumption that we distort; then we can proceed to build on these distortions. Even with the most objective task, it is nearly impossible to keep our subjective views from altering our perception of what really exists.

◆ Reader Activity

Before reading any further, look at the figure that follows. Count the number of triangles in this diagram.

Write your number here _____ before reading on.   ◆

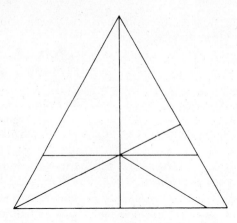

If this diagram is presented to a group of fifty people and they are asked to count the number of triangles, it is almost certain there will be anywhere from ten to eighteen different responses; at most, ten of the fifty people will agree to one number.

How is this possible among a representative group of normal, well-adjusted, intelligent people? The task is clear and easy enough (a fifth grader could handle it), yet rarely does one find more than 20 percent agreement on one response. The following are only a few of the possible reasons for the differences in the perceived realities of this group.

1. One individual vigorously defends the perception that there is only one triangle in the diagram. Somewhere in the far reaches of her memory, she sees a triangle as having to have three equal sides.
2. Another person somehow discovers forty-three by counting every possible angle as a triangle.
3. A number of people, counting from left to right around the diagram but not counting the figure in the lower right-hand corner, report six triangles.
4. Others find seven; they assume the figure in the lower right-hand corner is a triangle.
5. Some people find seven, eight, or nine triangles by combining a few of the lines to form other triangles. Others push on and discover thirteen, fourteen, fifteen, or twenty triangles.

Later, it is learned that some who stopped short of discovering all the possible combinations did not like puzzles or did poorly in geometry and still carried that fear with them. Others saw the whole thing as a game, perhaps a trick, and so felt it was a fruitless exercise. Still others felt that they were being tested and thought it wiser to find fewer triangles and be correct (as on the SATs or Graduate Record Exams, with their penalties for guessing) than to find many and be wrong. Then, of course, there were the competitors, some of whom managed to see triangles that were not even there. Some people assume that they missed some (nobody's perfect) and added from five to ten to their findings just be on the "safe" side (thinking that, as in a jellybean contest, the number closest wins). Still others noticed who put up their hands at which numbers; if they perceived the hand-raisers as smart, they gave up their own findings and voted in accordance with the "smart" ones, for to be aligned with talent was to experience a fleeting moment of being a winner. So even in a simple, straightforward task among a responsible group of participants, one is able to ferret out unreasonable suspicion, fear of inadequacy, competitiveness, distortion of the instructions, and perhaps ten or twenty other variables that make such an enormous variety of responses predictable. (What was your own result?) Because there are so many factors involved in solving even such a simple problem, imagine what happens when we add the additional variables that pertain whenever the choice involves another human being.

Individual Insecurity

Why is the accurate perception of experience so difficult in groups? What is it in a group that alters our behavior and interferes with our ability to behave as we would individually?

One startling yet powerful insight pervades the literature on groups: when individuals join a group, they change; they are no longer the same people they were before becoming group members. Once within a group, individuals display and express behaviors that differ remarkably from their out-of-group behaviors. It seems that in a group, people's individuality—the sum of qualities that characterize and distinguish them from all others—somehow becomes warped, unsettled, and distorted. Factors operate both in the group and in the members that distract and/or subtract from their individuality.

The most powerful factor altering people's individuality in groups is anxiety (Bennis and Shepard, 1987), a feeling of uneasiness, ranging from mild to extreme, that is brought about by a conscious or unconscious feeling of danger, not necessarily real, and a readiness or preparation to meet that danger (Brill, 1972).

When people enter a group, anxiety is the first apparent behavioral symptom— that is, change in their actions. Accurately or not, they feel endangered by the other members. They feel self-doubt about how the others perceive them—and about how they perceive the others—and their behavior is based on these feelings. At the base of the anxiety are internal uncertainties, such as feelings of self-doubt and the fear of the unknown dangers the other members pose. Because most people feel such uncertainties in new situations involving strangers, anxiety is to one degree or another the prevailing emotion at the start of any group setting.

A second prevalent experience involves the role shift from individual to group member. This sudden role shift creates conflicts: between the person's wish to belong and his or her self-protective impulse to withdraw, between the wish to interact with others and the need to protect his or her individuality, and between the wish to contribute to the group's task and self-doubts regarding his or her *ability* to contribute (Turquet, 1978). These conflicts are experienced as ambivalence.

To sum up, then, anxiety rooted in internal uncertainties and ambivalences springing from the sudden role shift are major sources for distortions, misperceptions, and miscommunication (Bennis and Shepard, 1987; Miller and Rice, 1975; and Rioch, 1978). Our individual insecurities alter our individual behavior when we are struggling to merge countless external stimuli with often conflicting internal impulses.

Life Positions

Often, past distortions are infused into the present and compounded in such a way that the real and imagined and the past and present intertwine and form the present reality (Nidorf, 1968; Nidorf and Crockett, 1964). Some distortions in perception stem from our early experiences with family and friends.

Transactional Analysis (Berne, 1976; Woollams and Brown, 1978) provides insight into the important influence of our past on our current behavior, both individually and in groups. It suggests that on the basis of early experiences, people decide on a *life position*. Henceforth, they are influenced by their life positions in how they think, feel, act, perceive, and relate to others.

The theory of Transactional Analysis (TA) essentially goes like this. We were all once children and, in the course of life's experiences, developed a concept of self-worth by the time we were six years old. While we were formulating a sense of our own worth, we were also formulating a sense of the worth of others, especially those around us. We did this by crystallizing our experiences and making decisions about the kind of a life we would have (sad, happy); what parts we would play (strong hero, loner); and how we would act out the parts of our life scripts (adventurously, in fear, slowly, with permission). These early days in life are our days of decision—a time when we commit ourselves to acting in ways that become part of our character. These decisions may be quite unrealistic, although they seem logical and make sense to us at the time we make them.

For example, if as children we are ridiculed and regularly called stupid, we may decide we are stupid and that other people "know it all." We will thus begin to think of ourselves that way and act that way; we will base our life scripts on the conclusions that "I'm not O.K., but you (other people) are O.K." When we go to school, we may fail. As we grow older, we will further fulfill our own prophecies by constantly asking advice, doing what "they're" doing, and fearing being different. We will often make mistakes, for which we will be reprimanded, and then we will feel stupid—thereby maintaining our status quo in our chosen life position.

According to TA theory, even as we think we are listening intently and being objective, we are screening out information that conflicts with our chosen life positions. It is not surprising, therefore, that in a group situation with a tremendous amount of incoming stimuli to be screened, we are unable to interpret the experience accurately.

Perception and Development

Developmental theory provides another way to understand how we view and interpret the world. Although people's characters are created in the early years of life, developmental theory suggests that our perception of the world continually changes throughout our entire life span. Piaget (1952, 1954) discovered that the views of children differ fundamentally from adult views and that cognition (thinking) and perception develop in sequential stages throughout childhood and adolescence. Each stage has certain general characteristics that determine how the individual understands and perceives the world. Consider the example of two brothers looking down from the Empire State Building. The younger brother said, "Look at the toy cars," and the older brother said simultaneously, "Look at the cars. They look like toys." The older brother had learned about the effect of distance on apparent size. The younger brother, perceiving the same scene differently, actually mistook the cars for miniatures.

Other developmental theorists (Kegan, 1982; Kohlberg and Gilligan, 1972) have expanded Piaget's findings to include the individual's identity and relationships with other people. This process of constructing a "self" or a "reality" involves putting the perceptual pieces together into a total picture that makes sense to us. We naturally construct a consistent world view that allows us to make sense of the world and function in it with others. Meaning making (or constructing an identity and reality) is a natural process that evolves over time in stages parallel to Piaget's stages. If you asked a young child, a high school student, and a college student what is important about the Golden Rule, you would get three very different answers reflecting three different ways of perceiving the world. The young child might say, "If he hit me then I can hit him." The high school student might say, "It's important to be a good friend or neighbor and to consider what the other person feels." The college student might say, "It's like a moral code or contract that allows the whole society to get along." The three answers reflect different constructions of "fairness" based on normal developmental stages in making meaning.

It is clear from this example that our behavior in groups is affected by our development. We perceive groups differently at different ages and as the time we spend in them goes by (Abraham, 1983–1984). As an example of how such perceptions change in our lifetimes, Selman (1980) reports on conceptions of friendship. A young child assumes that a friend thinks and feels just as he or she does. An older child realizes that other people think and feel differently but still doesn't think about the friendly interactions between two people. By adolescence, people have learned how to take another's perspective and are able to think about the interaction between individuals.

Selective Perception and Culture

The culture and particular environment in which we develop also affect our perception of reality. And the cultural *context* in which the group experience takes place also has profound effects. Consider this first-person account from a college teacher of English:

> Having taught basic English to American and foreign college students for
> many years, I noticed something I had not witnessed before: Korean and
> Japanese students strictly avoided each other, even moved desks away so
> as to avoid any contact, particularly physical proximity and eye contact.
> Another time, when the class discussion focused on the pros and cons
> of capital punishment, students of Arabic descent clamored not only for
> capital punishment, but also its televising. American students, on the other
> hand, abhorred the idea.

Cultural factors profoundly affect how we think about groups and behave in them. When we enter a group, do we expect everyone to think as we do, based on past experience? Will we be able to understand the differing opinions and views of people from other backgrounds? Will we value and understand the group interactions as a whole, separate from our experience in the culture we grew up in? As research confirms (Varghese, 1982), we cannot understand the group experience without making reference to the cultural and personal backgrounds of the members.

Unconscious Factors

Many of us never realize that these powerful influences are at work on our perception. A group of people represents various degrees of acceptance and rejection, likes and dislikes, and pleasant and distasteful memories; it is from this complex assortment of stimuli that we conjure up a picture of our reality and respond, as we believe, appropriately to maintain our own positions and integrity within the group. We begin early. Boulton and Smith (1990) studied two classes of eight-year-olds and two classes of eleven-year-olds. Each child ranked all members of his or her class in terms of the degree to which a classmate was liked. Children consistently overestimated their place in the hierarchy in relation to peers' perceptions.

Our personal needs remain consistently present, nearly every one of our perceptions is affected by them, and these needs affect behavior in turn. The needs are often unconscious and completely hidden from us. For example, people who have limited tolerance for ambiguity create a simple structure for reality as they perceive it, no matter how accurate or faulty that picture is (Livesley and Bromley, 1973). Those who are especially sensitive to whether they are liked and to cues regarding their acceptance are likely to be more hampered in communicating freely than those who care little about how others accept them (Winthrop, 1971). Those who make immediate decisions about liking or not liking someone and believe that they can size a person up and be right, do just that in a group. They make a decision on limited information and stay with it. They are "right," and they are consequently resistant to change when presented with new information (Ehr-lich, 1969; Johnson and Ewens, 1971; Reid and Ware, 1972). Similarly, those individuals who focus on feelings and emotions and those who prefer logical thinking and reason evaluate their participation in groups on the basis of their own particular orientation (Pratt, Uhl, and Little, 1980).

The U.S. visit in 1988 of Mikhail Gorbachev, then Secretary General of the U.S.S.R., illustrates how unconscious factors shape our views without our knowledge. Since World War II, many Americans had perceived the former Soviet Union as a world aggressor and champion of communism. But Gorbachev arrived on his visit smiling, charming everyone, and making jokes. The media spotlight focused on him for the entire trip. At the end of the visit, many Americans were left with a new impression of Gorbachev—one shaped by euphoria and media attention. Critics met that change of opinion with continued skepticism. "You can't trust the Russians. Gorbachev's visit is just another ploy and another Russian strategy." They noted that Gorbachev was working hard to create a favorable image in the United States and concluded that what was presented was only window-dressing.

What was the reality with respect to this question? Many people argued strongly for each interpretation, backing up their arguments with data and information, intuition, and common sense. Gorbachev's actions became food for thought—and for interpretations based on selective perceptions.

Although much has happened since that initial visit by Gorbachev, including the breakup of the Soviet Union itself, the point of this example is that world events are very much influenced by people's perceptions, whether conscious or not, and further influence people's decisions and actions.

The Halo Effect

When they make decisions, most people believe they make judgments based on facts and information. They believe that in a particular situation, given specific, relevant information, they can render impartial judgments uninfluenced by their personal knowledge of the people involved.

Nisbett and Wilson, from the Institute of Social Research at the University of Michigan, were staunch believers that people could do just that until they conducted an experiment testing the psychological phenomenon known as the *halo effect* (Nisbett and Wilson, 1978). As a result, Nisbett was convinced that "one's objectivity is not to be trusted."

The experiment is an interesting one. The investigators described the halo effect as simply "the power of an overall feeling about an individual to influence evaluations of the person's individual attributes." For example, if you are usually annoyed when someone is consistently late but find lateness charming in a friend whom you like, you have experienced the halo effect.

To test the extent of the halo effect and people's awareness of its influence, Nisbett and Wilson showed college students one of two videotaped interviews with a college professor. In the first interview, the professor appeared to be quite likable, expressing warm attitudes about his students and teaching. In the other, he conveyed the unlikable attitude of distrust of his students and rigidity in his teaching. Half the students saw the warm interview and half the cold interview. In addition, some of each half saw the interviews without the audio portion.

The students were then asked to rate how much they liked the teacher, his physical appearance, his mannerisms, and his distinct French accent. Now, for the special part. To determine whether the subjects were aware of the cognitive processes underlying their evaluations, the researchers asked some of the students (as part of the design) whether their liking or disliking of the professor had influenced their evaluations of his personal characteristics. At the same time, they asked others the reverse question: had their ratings of individual characteristics influenced their overall liking?

Regardless of whether they had seen the warm or the cold professor, the subjects who had been asked the first question said their evaluations of individual attributes had not been influenced by their liking of the man. When the question was reversed however, the subjects who saw the cold professor believed their negative evaluations of the individual traits had been responsible for their not liking the man. In the face of additional questioning, most of the students held firmly to these beliefs.

To summarize, the students were not aware of how they had arrived at their evaluations. This finding parallels results from similar experiments conducted by the researchers. In all such experiments, subjects' explanations differed regarding what factors affect their judgment. Nisbett and Wilson observe, "People tend to rely on their prior assumptions about the causes of behavior instead of direct introspections." Therefore, they conclude, the validity of self-reporting is questionable, because people do not know why they do what they do.

We often admit to not knowing how we arrived at a judgment. But even when we think we *are* making objective judgments, research shows we are not. Given this fact, is it any wonder that opinion among many observers may differ even where "objective" evidence is available for analysis?

Selective Perception and Group Behavior

Groups as well as individuals are affected by unconscious factors and inaccurate assumptions. Consider an example involving the particularly volatile topic of AIDS, where objective information had no weight in the face of the selective perception of the group.

In October of 1986, nearly thirty fearful and disgruntled employees of New England Bell walked off the job en masse (with camera crews from the local television station there to record the event) when they discovered that one of their company workers had AIDS. Epidemics have almost always sparked irrationality and superstition, and AIDS has been no exception. Many workers react to news of a co-worker's infection with panic, anger, and cruelty. "There is something about the topic of AIDS that can cause otherwise intelligent and rational people to lose their basic common sense" (Puckett, 1988).

Public health officials, including the National Academy of Sciences, the Surgeon General of the United States, and the Centers for Disease Control, assure us that AIDS is spread only by the *direct exchange* of infected bodily fluids through sexual contact, the sharing of contaminated needles, contaminated-blood transfusions, or the exchange of maternal/fetal blood in pregnancy. It is not possible to get AIDS through casual contact, by sharing telephones or equipment, by being sneezed or coughed on, or simply by working near someone. As a result, guidelines from the Centers for Disease Control say that people diagnosed with the disease may continue on the job without endangering their co-workers.

However, despite extensive information and assurances, in the heat of the moment these startled and frightened New England Bell employees reacted with panic. It is within this environment of irrationality that public health officials are attempting to campaign for communication and education about AIDS. What is the likelihood of the facts being heard? Given the selective perception of groups and the many factors, unconscious as well as conscious, driving their behavior, it is likely that rumors and misinformation will continue to have much greater potency than facts, information, and data.

Problems in perception and communication cut across every group. Each group and each individual must justify its existence, it seems, at the expense of truth and reason.

The Influence of Stereotypes

In a group, individual stereotypes—preconceived notions of how individuals from certain groups think, feel, and act—feed on themselves, and as group members, we rapidly turn for support to those we believe share our own views (Kelley, 1951; Slater, 1955). We seek to affirm our personal construction of reality in any situation we fail to understand or control. Especially in a group in which our roles are not determined clearly in advance, it is natural to seek confirmation that we are not alone, that there are potential allies among the strange faces (Festinger, 1950; Loomis, 1959). It takes but a few minutes to scan the superficial cues and identify those with whom we can feel either safe or threatened, who have energy, anger, insecurity, power, softness, frayed nerves, or humor. We make our predictions and then spend a good part of our energy proving that we are correct (Ehrlich, 1969; Johnson and Ewens, 1971; Reid and Ware, 1972). The tapping fingers, nervous smile, loud talk, tightly folded arms, cultivated friendliness, seeming indifference, unabashed openness—these and a thousand pieces of instant information are sifted, labeled, and shelved for later use in our effort to confirm our own identities and understand others in the group. They are used as evidence and, in the long run, can be destructive as well as helpful in the development of the group and our relationships within it.

Groups of people, too, form stereotypes about the "in-ness" or "out-ness" of other groups of people. People are discriminated against or accepted because of their membership in a particular group (Locksley, Ortiz, and Hepburn, 1980). The more the makeup of a group is perceived by an outsider to be the same, or homogeneous, the more likely that outsider is to generalize one member's behavior to the whole group (Quattrone and Jones, 1980). For example, if 90 percent of all fraternity members are big, blond, and sports-minded, then an outsider to that group would be quite likely to assume that "They're all alike. They look alike, think alike, and do the same things."

People form stereotypes in this way not only about primary groups but also about subgroups within them. For example, subjects who were asked to rate decisions made by three nations (the United States, Holland, and the U.S.S.R.) and to predict whether citizens of those nations concurred made inferences about the citizens' attitudes that were based on stereotypes of the nations (Allison and Messick, 1985).

In another study by the same researchers, subjects were asked to attribute attitudes to jurors after reading a vignette about a court case and the final decision of guilt or innocence. The results indicated that subjects attributed attitudes to jurors based on both the final jury vote and the decision of guilt or innocence (Allison and Messick, 1985).

The data of these studies indicate that people commit what the authors call attribution error. This they define as "a tendency to assume a correspondence between a group decision and members' preferences" even when the assumption may be unwarranted. In other words, people committing attribution error assume that the actions of the group reflect the particular attitudes of individual members and that knowing something about how a group behaves tells us something significant about subgroups or individuals within it.

Consider the relationships between Americans and Japanese. The torrent of retrospectives at the 50th anniversary of Pearl Harbor showed how the Americans and the Japanese still see each other through propagandized eyes. *The New York Times* (December 1991) notes:

> In the United States, the images of Japan as sneaky, threatening, and unfair, that were flash-frozen by Pearl Harbor, resurface now in talk of Japanese as Samurai in business suits, out to do economically what they could not do militarily. In Japan, where any sense of responsibility for the aggression of Pearl Harbor is dwarfed by the horror of Hiroshima and Nagasaki,

America now seems more like the decadent superpower once portrayed in Japanese wartime propaganda. . . . [B]oth countries remain trapped by history and their selective memories. In the United States, for example, the sense of treachery at Pearl Harbor and the racist depictions of Japanese continue to resonate today. . . . Many Japanese still believe racism motivates much American behavior toward Japan, from the internment of Japanese–Americans during the war to the decision to drop the bomb.

Stereotypes of more than 50 years ago persist.

Unless we are ready to challenge our own untested assumptions about individuals and groups, we can expect that there will be many breakdowns in communications. The problem, of course, is that if we attempted to test many of our assumptions about people, we would find it very hard to classify them, stereotype them, or pigeonhole them, and thus we would find it difficult if not impossible to understand and interpret reality. The resulting confusion would make our lives much less secure and more complex than that based on our assumptions.

The fact is that people are a thousand things, but first and foremost in our effort to understand reality, they are what we want them to be in relation to our own need for a clear simple interpretation. We tend to see a person as fat, hostile, irrational, Jewish, lethargic, smart, African–American, paranoid, handsome, homosexual, or militant—with all that these labels connote to us. We take a very specific term with a very narrow definition and try to frame a whole, complex human being in it.

◆ Individual Experiment

List all the stereotypes about your family background, both good and bad. What are the stereotypes about your race? About your ethnic background? About your religion? About your father's occupation? About your mother's occupation? What are your feelings about each of those stereotypes? How do they affect you? (For example, are you supposed to reach out, or to overachieve, or to work hard, given the stereotypes you cite?) How do these stereotypes affect your personality? Are they a help or a hindrance?   ◆

◆ Reader Activity

Think back on some of your own experiences with others. How have you been "labeled" in a way that you did not like?

Label _____

Why didn't you like it?

_____

_____

_____

What do you wish had happened instead?

_____

_____

_____

How did that label influence you?

_____

_____

_____

◆

◆ Individual Experiment

Choose a subgroup of people within your school, dormitory, neighborhood, or place of employment. What common characteristic do they all have? List as many attributes of this group as you can. Ask your friends how they would characterize the individuals within this group. Carefully compare your list and your actual experience with a member of the group. Is it accurate? Are some characteristics exaggerated and others minimized? Is the list of characteristics helpful in understanding the behavior of the group members or knowing how to interact with them? Does the list constitute a stereotype that is used by society to belittle, disqualify, or oppress the group as a whole? Or does it idealize, empower, and assist the group? You may find your list useful in dealing with others, or you may find it destructive because it creates negative expectations of the individuals in a group.   ◆

In the past, many whites thought of blacks as a separate and inferior species. The word *Negro* called up images and elicited behavior among whites that caused tremendous psychological and physical suffering. Judge Leon Higgenbotham of the U.S. Court of Appeals, Third Circuit, writes of his experience during World War II:

> In 1944, I was a 16-year-old freshman at Purdue University—one of twelve black civilian students. If we wanted to live in West Lafayette, Indiana, where the university was located, solely because of our color the twelve of us at Purdue were forced to live in a crowded private house rather than, as did most of our white classmates, in the university campus dormitories. We slept barracks-style in an unheated attic.

One night, as the temperature was close to zero, I felt that I could suffer the personal indignities and denigration no longer. The United States was more than two years into the Second World War, a war our government had promised would "make the world safe for democracy." Surely there was room enough in that world, I told myself that night, for twelve black students in a northern university in the United States to be given a small corner of the on-campus heated dormitories for their quarters. Perhaps all that was needed was for one of us to speak up, to make sure the administration knew exactly how a small group of its students had been treated by those charged with assigning student housing.

The next morning, I went to the office of Edward Charles Elliot, president of Purdue University, and asked to see him. I was given an appointment.

At the scheduled time I arrived at President Elliot's office, neatly (but not elegantly) dressed, shoes polished, fingernails clean, hair cut short. Why was it, I asked him, that blacks—and blacks alone—had been subjected to this special ignominy? Though there were larger issues I might have raised with the president of an American university (this was but ten years before *Brown v. Board of Education*) I had not come that morning to move mountains, only to get myself and eleven friends out of the cold. Forcefully, but none the less deferentially, I put forth my modest request; that the black students of Purdue be allowed to stay in some section of the state-owned dormitories; segregated, if necessary, but at least not humiliated.

Perhaps if President Elliot had talked sympathetically that morning, explaining his own impotence to change things but his willingness to take up the problem with those who could, I might not have felt as I did. Perhaps if he had communicated with some word or gesture, or even a sigh, that I had caused him to review his own commitment to things as they were, I might have felt I had won a small victory. But President Elliot, with directness and with no apparent qualms, answered, "Higginbotham, the law doesn't require us to let colored students in the dorm, and you either accept things as they are or leave the University immediately."

As I walked back to the house that afternoon, I reflected on the ambiguity of the day's events. I had heard, on that morning, an eloquent lecture on the history of the Declaration of Independence, and of the genius of the founding fathers. That afternoon I had been told that under the law the black civilian students at Purdue University could be treated differently from their 6,000 white classmates. Yet I knew that by nightfall hundreds of black soldiers would be injured, maimed, and some even killed on far-flung battlefields to make the world safe for democracy. Almost like a mystical experience, a thousand thoughts raced through my mind as I walked across campus. I knew then I had been touched in a way I have never been touched before, and that one day I would have to return to the most disturbing element in this incident—how a legal system that proclaims "equal justice for all" could simultaneously deny even a semblance of dignity to a 16-year-old boy who had committed no wrong.[1]

Being black meant being outside the system. That perception applied to the president and the newest freshman. It was viewed as the norm, beyond change, and despite its incongruity with the Declaration of Independence, it was steadfastly upheld.

The word *black* is not the only label that elicits assumptions about a group that are untested and stereotypic. A host of untested assumptions are elicited by the words *Arab, Jew, labor, management, male,* and *female.* But in our day and age, attitudes about maleness and femaleness, about age, and about modesty and appropriateness have been uprooted. Traditional stereotypes instructing us about the "right" way to act as women and men no longer hold true. Men have learned that they can be emotional and caring. Women have learned that they can assert their opinions and rights. People are confused about what was once the most standardized and secure set of relationships. It is difficult at this time to point to rights and wrongs. Rules and stereotypes once helped us keep our bearings; now, we don't know what to do.

Gestalt Theory

We select and organize physical stimuli in the manner that is easiest and most convenient for us, and we organize the complexities of human behavior in similar ways. A number of simple concepts developed by the Gestalt psychologists in relation to physical stimuli can help us understand what occurs when people get together in a group (Kohler, 1947). For example, we tend to create figure–ground relationships. In any one perceptual field (all the stimuli we are able to perceive at one time), certain figures are drawn forward into positions of dominance and others recede to form the background of the scene. In many cases, those objects that are reduced to the background and those that are drawn forward are dependent on the immediate needs of the viewer. For example, in the following classic picture of the two profiles–goblet configuration, some viewers see a goblet in the foreground and not the people. Others see two faces and not the goblet.

Gestalt theory also helps us understand how experience organizes itself irrespective of the perceiver. In a group, for example, certain individuals will be a clear part of the foreground whose presence is easily noted (in Gestalt terms, they are figures), whereas others, for a variety of reasons, remain part of the ground.

1. From *In the Matter of Color: Race and the American Legal Process: The Colonial Period* by A. Leon Higginbotham, Jr. Copyright © 1978 by Oxford University Press, Inc. Reprinted by permission.

◆ Reader Activity

There is a tendency to place objects in a natural order, thus making it easier to establish relationships in a scene. The mind struggles to achieve order by grasping similarities that appear to be present or by perceiving certain continuities in the stimuli presented. This exercise illustrates how we organize dots. Below are nine dots, arranged three dots per row in three rows. Connect the nine dots with four lines so that the end of one line is the beginning of the next. It can be done. Turn to page 19 for the answer.   ◆

•   •   •

•   •   •

•   •   •

Similarly, using arrangement, size, sex, clothes, tone of voice, posture, and many other cues, we proceed to subtly break down a group of people into a variety of component groups. This ordering is how we manage to deal with complexity without being overwhelmed, a way of handling the enormous amount of data that suddenly confront us at any one moment.

Another concept discussed originally by Gestaltists concerns the tendency to take incomplete data and organize them into a meaningful whole. By that process, people more often than not see an incomplete circle as a full circle rather than a curved line. Apparently, we have a need to bring closure to objects within our perceptual field—thus we use the word *Gestalt,* meaning "form" or "shape."

In looking at the participants in a group, we take the data they put forth in such a voice, verbal gestures, and dress, then add our own stereotypes, and in this way develop a complete picture of a group member. We bring closure to what is incomplete and, in a sense, fill in the missing pieces so that we can more easily be content with the previously unknown commodity. By putting all the clues together into a meaningful package, we are better able to have a relationship that is consistent and comfortable for us. It provides a means of gaining a measure of safety for us in what is, perhaps, an incomplete, strange, and uncomfortable situation.

According to Gestalt theory, people have a tendency to take the various stimuli and focus on one set of stimuli that appears to be "good" in terms of similarity, continuity, closure, and symmetry. According to this concept, for example, we are immediately attracted to those in a group who tend to fit our perception of a "good" group member, those who are least threatening to us and tend to create the least dissonance in terms of our own values and goals within the group.

If we were not able to impose this kind of order on the group and on certain of its members, the situation might prove unbearably tense and difficult. Thus if we are quiet and shy, we may seek order and some relief in the group by discovering those who are the least abrasive or dominating and those who show the greatest restraint. In this way, we can bring harmony to a dissonant situation; we can seek allies and support in fact or in fantasy.

Selective Perception and Communication

Our propensity to organize a group in the manner that is most comforting to us can prove to be a distinct liability to effective communication. It often generates inflexibility, restricted routes of information, and a need to verify and then justify our initial perception. As a result, we often begin with two strikes against us in our efforts to achieve understanding and insight into group processes.

Consider the importance we place on grades. We often believe that the grade someone earns is an accurate indication of that person's level of knowledge. In reality, though, grading is a result of selective perception and communication on the grader's part.

Research has shown that if twenty-five English teachers administer the same test and use the same clear criteria for grading it, the scores for that test will range along the normal distribution curve, because even with a clear set of criteria,

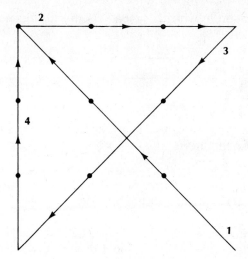

subjectivity enters into grading. Where twenty-five *geometry,* as opposed to English, teachers administer and grade a test, there will be an even wider distribution. The reason is that math teachers give more points for effort and partial answers than English teachers do. Grading, then, is highly biased; personal needs, factors of background, and experience affect teachers' choices. Given this fact, the grades students earn in school may reveal more about their teachers than about their own levels of knowledge.

◆ Reader Activity

When someone claims to have a 2.3 grade point average, what assumptions would you make about that person?

_____

_____

_____

When someone claims to have a 3.9 grade point average, what assumptions would you make about that person?

_____

_____

_____

How have grades influenced your perception of yourself?

_____

_____

_____

Describe one situation in which a grade very much influenced your behavior. What was the effect?

_____

_____

_____   ◆

◆ Individual Experiment

In a group situation, such as a class or meeting, choose one person whom you do not know well and watch his or her behavior for a few minutes. Then briefly write a story about that person, including your assumptions about why he or she behaved in a certain manner, what he or she might have been feeling and thinking, and your general description of the person. Create a story about that person based on the limited information you perceive. Test the accuracy of your story by gathering information from that person about his or her intentions, perception of the situation, thoughts, and feelings.   ◆

The Nature of Communication

Verbal language is only one aspect of the ongoing communication that occurs in all human behavior. In fact, communications theory (Watzlawick, 1977; Watzlawick, Beavin, and Jackson, 1967) postulates that "one cannot not communicate." Every action, even silence, is a communication. What that means in day-to-day life is that we are actually aware of only a small part of our communication with others. Body language, such as eye contact, gestures, posture, and proximity between individuals as they talk, is an important part of the complex process of communication of which individuals are rarely aware.

We can think of communication as having three aspects: the nonverbal aspect (which, like the verbal aspect, is determined to a large degree by the cultural and personal backgrounds of the communicator); the emotional aspect (the mood or feeling being expressed), and the content or verbal aspect. These three aspects combine to form the total message given *and* the total message received. Obviously, someone communicating anger will convey a different message from a person who delivers the same words in a very calm manner. Likewise, someone in a sad or depressed state will give a different meaning to, say, "I'd like to apply for the job" than someone excited and motivated by a career change. But emotional state has an equally potent effect on the message as it is received. Research by Bower (1981) identifies what the investigator calls the mood-congruity effect, whereby people tend to hear and learn information that matches their emotional states. A related phenomenon is mood-state-dependent retention, whereby people recall events better if their emotional states during recall match those they experienced during learning. Furthermore, when the emotional tone of a story matches the mood of the reader, the significance and memorability of events in the story increase for the reader. Sad readers thus tend to choose sad materials, identify with sad characters, and recall more about those characters.

Another, perhaps more subtle, influence shaping a communication is the particular *style* in which a message is conveyed. Style can have an important effect on what we hear and communicate. Consider a teacher inexperienced in black English who hears one boy saying to another, "You're *bad! Too* bad for this school, man." She worries that the receiver of this message might suffer from such obvious rejection and is surprised to see him grin with pleasure. The teacher is responding to the verbal message alone, but the real meaning is the product of the culture, personal style, and words of the message giver.

According to communication theory, communication has two aspects, the content aspect and the relationship aspect. The content aspect of a message conveys information of some sort or another, regardless of whether the particular information is true or false. The relationship aspect of a message includes how the content aspect should be taken. It is the attempt of the communicator to define the relationship. For example, when a mother tells her son, "This is your last warning—clean up your room or you can't go out to play," or "It's important that I get the house clean today. Please clean your room before you go out to play," the content information is the same but the relationships differ. This process of defining the relationship is an ongoing process, and the relationship gets defined and redefined with every bit of communication. In our example, if the son replies, "Come on, Mom, how come you want me to clean my room every time I have something to do? I'll clean it after," or "I wanted to see Jeffrey this afternoon. Do you think I can clean it when I come in before dinner?" he is implying two different types of relationships. In each communication there is an implicit arrangement between the individuals concerning how they mutually define the relationship and thus set up an expectation of how their next interaction will be. It is important to remember that this process generally goes on outside the communicators' awareness: that is, individuals rarely deliberately define the relationships they are in. Using Gestalt terms, the relationship aspect of communication is the perceptual ground and the content aspect is the figure.

The continual communication and interaction between individuals in a group, whether in a meeting, classroom, family, or entire school, involves an ongoing process of defining the relationships within the group and the development of a set of arrangements between group members. This set of arrangements is a system that has certain rules, norms, and a regularity to it. The system of interaction and communication, like the relationship aspect of communication, exists outside of group members' awareness.

Language Equals Words; Communication Equals People

A famous adage states that "the pen is mightier than the sword." In other words, language is power. In Britain's Victorian era, parliamentary procedures were governed by eloquence, loquaciousness, dramatic flair, and wit, and language was a tool for clarifying, addressing, and reshaping social and political issues. In our society today, language is often a tool for creating confusion, ambiguity, doubt, and uninformed judgments.

What is puzzling and fascinating about words is that as we hear or read them, we apply connotations. That is, we attach our own meaning or interpretation and add to it our own "baggage" of perceived experiences that we have accumulated over the years.

It has often been said that today only people, and not words, have any meaning in our attempts to communicate. Unless we are able to probe behind the easily flowing façade of words that screen us from one another, we will remain confused and out of touch. So often it is gesture, tone, inflection, posture, or eye contact that holds the key to the real message, while the clear, seemingly unambiguous words merely subject the unwary listener to false starts and dead ends. Even when we think we understand the meaning behind a word, there are usually three or four possible variations in meaning that could fit nicely into the sentence. Usually, we draw on the intent we believe the speaker has in mind. It's hard to imagine that a simple word such as *hard* has more than twenty-six possible definitions (*American Heritage Dictionary,* 1973). Among other things, that one word can describe the solidity of coal, the difficulty of a test, the type of binding on a book, the ability of a person to maintain his or her position despite pressure, the penetrating power of an x-ray, and the parsimony of an elderly person. Many subtle innuendos flavor language and require a personal definition before they can be translated into the context of a particular statement.

In some cases, even the dictionary may not help where an individual or a group has invented new meanings for words and phrases.

> Have you ever been to a *Valium picnic?* Or been guilty of *scoodling?* Or yearned for *warm fuzzies?* If these terms are totally bewildering, you may need a crash course in "Biz Speak," the colorful language of the business world, described by R. S. Epstein and N. Liebman (1986). These authors explain that a Valium picnic is a slow day on the stock market. Warm fuzzies are praise from the boss. And scoodling is the unauthorized duplication of prerecorded music. Wall Streeters talk about fallen angels (out-of-favor stocks at bargain prices), shark repellents (strategies used by companies to ward off takeover attempts), and fill or kill (an order to a broker that must be canceled if it cannot be completely and immediately executed). Management experts speak of tin-cupping (when one corporate division begs for management support) and dead-heading (by-passing a senior employee to someone more junior). Advertisers refer disparagingly to white bread (consumers with bland taste). Business executives try to avoid a Mickey Mouse (a major effort that produces minimum results).

The use of this sort of jargon—other examples of which might not be so playful as the above—has the effect of confusing and even excluding those not in the know. And yet it is commonplace for us to use words and phrases whose meaning is unclear to us, depending more on their feel and emotional tone than on their precise meaning.

Often, what we end up with is nothing more than a makeshift assemblage of words spiced with half-known definitions and a variety of feelings. What eventually transpires depends on the web created out of past experience, definitions, language skills, expectations, speed, clarity of the words spoken, and the general psychological climate that exists. How often are we led off the trail because we do not have enough information and drift further away rather than closer to the actual meaning? On the other hand, when history and experience are on our side, when we are familiar with the nonverbal communication that accompanies the words, then the group in which we are participating may respond in near unison to a message that to the casual listener may mean just the opposite.

There are other words that, when we hear them, evoke a special meaning for us depending on our context, our experience, and our culture. One such word is *management*. To much of American labor, the word *management* is adversarial; to the union member it means "I have to get what I can get. Management is only concerned with profits and couldn't care less about me." In Japan, however, management is thought of as a caring father. Workers assume that they can trust management and can expect it to take care of them for their lifetime. These are two very different perceptions of management.

Communication: The Gender Difference

It was once assumed that because boys and girls grow up in the same households and later attend the same schools, they communicate in the same way. Recent studies, however, suggest that boys and girls grow up in what are essentially different cultures, so talk between men and women is cross-cultural communication. Linguist Deborah Tannen in "You Just Don't Understand: Women and Men in Conversation" (1990) builds a strong case for her hypothesis that boys and girls grow up in different worlds of words. Her analysis, research, and myriad illustrations had such impact that the book became a number-one national best seller.

Building on the work of Maltz and Borker (1982), she notes that boys and girls play differently, usually in same-sex groups, and that their ways of using language in their games are separated by a world of difference.

> Boys tend to play outside, in large groups that are hierarchically structured. Their groups have a leader who tells others what to do and how to do it, and resists doing what other boys propose. It is by giving orders and making them stick that high status is negotiated. Another way boys achieve status is to take center stage by telling stories and jokes, and by sidetracking or challenging the stories and jokes of others. Boys' games have winners and losers and elaborate systems of rules that are frequently the subjects of arguments. Finally, boys are frequently heard to boast of their skill and argue about who is best at what.

Girls, on the other hand, play in small groups or in pairs; the center of a girl's social life is a best friend. Within the group, intimacy is key: Differentiation is measured by relative closeness. In their most frequent games, such as jump rope and hopscotch, everyone gets a turn. Most of their activities (such as playing house) do not have winners or losers. Though some girls are certainly more skilled than others, girls are expected not to boast about it, or show that they think they are better than the others. Girls don't give orders; they express their preferences as suggestions, and suggestions are likely to be accepted. Whereas boys say, "Gimme that!" and "Get outta here!" girls say, "Let's do this," and "How about doing that?" Anything else is put down as "bossy." They don't grab center stage—they don't want it—so they don't challenge each other directly. And much of the time, they simply sit together and talk. Girls are not accustomed to jockeying for status in an obvious way; they are more concerned that they be liked.

These differences cast a long shadow into adulthood. When men and women talk to each other about troubles, there is a problem because each expects a different response. The men's approach seeks to deal with feelings indirectly by attacking their cause. The women, expecting to have their feelings supported, misconstrue the men's approach and feel they themselves are being attacked.

Whereas men seek status, women seek connection. In one illustration that Tannen offers, a man and woman were standing beside the information booth at a sprawling complex of booths and displays. The man said to the woman, "You ask for directions. I don't want to ask." The woman was angry. Because asking for directions would not make the woman uncomfortable, his refusing to ask made no sense to her. For the man, asking for information sends a metamessage of inferiority. If relationships are inherently hierarchical, then the one who has more information is higher up on the ladder by virtue of being more knowledgeable and competent. From this point of view, to request information is to give up an essential part of one's independence.

More of the differences get expressed around the question of whether men or women talk more. According to the stereotype, women talk more. Throughout history, women have been punished for talking too much or in the wrong way. In colonial America, there were a variety of physical punishments: women were strapped to dunking stools and held under water, they were put into stocks with signs pinned to them, they were gagged and silenced by a cleft stick applied to their tongues.

Women are believed to talk too much, yet study after study shows that it is men who talk more—at meetings, in mixed group discussions held in classrooms where girls or young women sit next to boys or young men. Communication researchers B. W. and R. G. Eakins (1978) tape-recorded and studied seven university faculty meetings. They found that with one exception, men spoke more often and spoke for a longer period of time. Not only did men speak for a longer time, but the women's longest turns were shorter than the men's shortest turns. Tannen found that regardless of the proportion of women and men in the audience, men almost invariably asked the first question, asked more questions, and asked longer questions.

Who talk more, then, women or men? The seemingly contradictory evidence is reconciled by the differences between what are called public speaking and private speaking.

Men feel more comfortable doing "public speaking," whereas women feel more comfortable doing "private speaking." Another way of capturing these differences is by using the terms *report talk* and *rapport talk*. For most women, the language of conversation is primarily a language of rapport; for most men, talk is primarily a means of preserving independence and negotiating and maintaining the status in a hierarchical social order.

To the man, talk is for information. To the woman, talk is for interaction. Telling things is a way to show involvement, and listening is a way to show interest and caring.

There are scores of examples of how men and women speak differently because they are operating within different systems; each is speaking a different "genderlect." In conversation, then, men and women need to learn how to interpret each other's messages and grasp what the other is saying so that they can understand and accept each other.

The Tannen theory is extensively supported in research focusing on how men and women talk. Jose and McCarthy (1988) divided 26 male and 26 female undergraduates into 4-person mixed-sex discussion groups. Each was administered the BEM Sex-Role Inventory. After each discussion, each participant rated the other group members on degree of talkativeness, quality of expressed ideas, and degree of concern for others' feelings. Those who scored highest on masculinity in the BEM Inventory were perceived to have talked more and to have had good ideas. Females and subjects with high femininity scores were judged to have had more concern about group members' feelings.

Apparently, men and women communicate differently, and this is a significant factor in understanding, listening to, and responding to communications.

Reward-Seeking Behavior and Communication Patterns

People want to be liked and accepted, as well as to be separate and unique. In some ways, that desire is our Achilles' heel, because it leaves us vulnerable to the subtle influence and control of those from whom we seek approval. Often, the pressures pushing us to adjustment, compliance, and eventual favor in the eyes of another are not even discernible by us or the other person (see Chapter 3 on group norms). In our efforts to be accepted, we become sensitive to the minute behavioral clues that suggest the degree of approval on the part of the other persons; as we know them better or are in a group longer, we base how we act on those clues (Greenspoon, 1955; Sorensen and McCroskey, 1977; Verplanck, 1955). Indeed, we are as keen as any bloodhound in ferreting out and following these clues to acceptance.

If the need is to be accepted by seven or eight people instead of only one, it is quite possible that we will work overtime to discover the sources of reward in the group, as well as the favored behavior. This, in turn, alters communication patterns and overt behavior within the group, as we see in the following example.

> A first meeting was being held with six women college faculty and a consultant to discuss relationship problems among departments and members of the faculty. Each of the women introduced herself by her first name. They ranged in age from twenty-eight to fifty. Each was well-educated, articulate, conservatively dressed, and committed to the success and growth of the college. The consultant asked that each describe one incident that would illustrate the present problem of the college. All eyes gazed in the direction of the twenty-eight-year-old woman, the youngest of the group. She began by presenting an incident, and the others elaborated on it. No new incidents were described. The consultant then asked what was the one problem that they thought had to be resolved. This time the consultant called on the person to her left. There was a long pause, and finally she said, "I need time to think about it." A similar reply came from the next person, and the next. Again, the twenty-eight-year-old stated a problem of concern to her, and the others added information on that problem. The consultant was aware that something was happening, but what? How could the twenty-eight-year-old have such influence and, without admonishing a person or saying a word, control the group so effectively? There was an answer. The consultant looked at the youngest, most powerful member and said, "Are you the newly appointed president of the college?" She was surprised and flustered; the others were incredulous that the consultant "somehow" knew.

It was clear that members of the committee were more influenced by the impression they wanted to make on the new president than by the goal of resolving the college's problems. Acceptance was at issue, not the ostensible business of the day.

Factors That Inhibit Communication in a Group

Previous Experience of Group Members

Two of the greatest factors inhibiting communication in groups are the previous experience of members with groups and skepticism that success in a group is even possible. We remember conflicts in our families as we grew up, in which it seemed our parents represented their values and we were supposed to "be seen and not heard," and we recall our days as adolescents, when we had constant arguments with our parents and made exasperated, futile attempts to be understood. In school, we saw groups as problems as we struggled for acceptance by powerful cliques on campus.

Past experience leaves many of us with the expectation that a group experience in the present will be equally unrewarding. Unfortunately, this negative expectation creates a self-fulfilling prophecy in which we tend to perceive what we expect to perceive. As we begin to learn more about the complexities of human communication and perception, it becomes increasingly clear why we have tended to experience groups as frustrating and unsatisfying.

False Assumptions

False assumptions held by members inhibit communication in a group. Such assumptions are pervasive, and they must be brought to consciousness to be examined and, with understanding, rejected. However, they are not readily cast aside. In order to recognize these assumptions as false, we need to bring them regularly back into the glare of consciousness, and to make the decision again and again.

One faulty assumption is that we know what others mean; another is that they know what we mean.

People assume that verbal communication is straightforward. They think that all they need to do is to express what they want to say in words and that the message sent is the message received. This is not so. The meaning one person has is never identical to that which another person has, because meanings are in people's minds, not in the words they use. Some people readily say, "I love you." They love their friends, their dogs, their schools, certain movies, and their favorite recording stars. For them to say "I love you" to a date is an indicator of having had a pleasant evening. For another, who has been going with one woman exclusively for over a year, the words are hard to say. To him, these words reflect an intent to marry, and he is not sure he is ready for such a commitment.

◆ *Reader Activity*

Words evoke meaning in us in a special, very individual way. What is difficult for you to express? _____

For those feelings difficult to express, how do you do it? What is your special way (a way that those who know you well may understand but that others may not)?

Anger _____

Jealousy _____

Unfairness _____

Gratitude _____

Resentment _____

A terrific idea _____

A ridiculous idea _____

Affection _____

Sadness _____

What words do some people use that you think are phony _____

Overbearing _____

That stick in your throat (you don't seem to be able to say them, but you wish you could) _____

_____ ◆

◆ *Individual Experiment*

Attend a group situation (a meeting or work group) where you know the others present. Watch for an incident—perhaps one person speaking strongly on behalf of some action, someone remaining quiet throughout a heated discussion, someone supporting a particular person in an unpopular opinion. In writing, describe the specific incident and your assumptions about what the people involved were communicating—their intentions, thoughts, and feelings. After the meeting, ask several other participants how they perceived the people involved in the incident. Compare your assumptions with theirs.   ◆

   Total accuracy in communication would require that two persons have an identical history of shared experiences, along with identical perceptual abilities. Only then could they perceive exactly the same meaning for a given message. Given the reality of different life experiences, such a situation is impossible (Chartier, 1976).

   We have other false assumptions about communication (Coan, 1968; Luft, 1969; Watson, 1967):

   1. That persons respond to each other objectively, listening only to the information conveyed. The key to what is happening in a group or between persons is not what is happening objectively but what is going on subjectively, what each person's feelings are. Subjective factors such as attitudes and values tell how people see themselves and others and how they order their world. The prime aim of most people is to survive in the group and, if possible, to enhance themselves in their own eyes and in the eyes of others. Each of us is forever bound up in the issue

of our own personal needs and goals within the group, but unless the group can provide a means of personal self-fulfillment, we will move from the group either psychologically, with reduced participation, or physically.

2. That what happens in a group is rational and easily understood as the group proceeds in an orderly, sequential manner to solve a problem or convey and receive information. Though some of the events in groups can be viewed as being orderly and making good sense, behavior is influenced more by emotions and by largely irrational strivings: logic and reason play relatively minor roles in human interaction. There are questions of identity: "Who am I to be in this group? What image am I going to project to these people?" and "What roles will I undertake to project this image?" In some cases, our response to these questions is very natural, but in others it is strategic and is geared toward establishing an identity and a power base. Other questions relate to power, control, and influence. Who has it, and how much will be shared? Whether an individual's behavior will be facilitative or destructive to the group process will depend on that person's particular needs and the realities of that particular group.

3. That the individual, like the group of which he or she is a part, is fully aware of the sources of his or her behavior and of the effects of his or her behavior on others. Parts of our behavior are unknown to us; it is often a surprise to find ourselves doing things that are difficult for us to understand or to make sense of. (We may have fantasized about being invited to become an officer of a professional group, yet when we are asked, we hear ourselves making an excuse about being too busy. Afterwards, it is difficult to understand how that happened.)

We want to be accepted by other members, yet we have limited information on how they perceive us. We may be shy and frightened; they may perceive us as snobbish and aloof. We may want to be involved and see ourselves as offering suggestions that are helpful; we may be perceived as behaving in a highly dictatorial manner. We have very limited understanding of how our behavior influences others.

These false assumptions greatly reduce our ability to communicate in a group or even to understand what seems to be happening around us.

Understanding Communication in Groups

How Tension and Defensiveness Arise in the Communication Process

If individuals wish to create problems in communication, there seem to be certain tried and true behaviors that will most assuredly help them on their way (Gibb, 1961; Rogers and Roethlisberger, 1952). A first step would be to keep other people from expressing their own ideas. People have a simple need to be heard, to have their ideas made visible. To have them accepted is desirable, yet not always possible. However, not even to be recognized or heard is an intolerable situation for most of us. Thus there will be tension in a group if it is dominated by a few vociferous individuals while others listen passively.

Closely linked to this situation is one in which individuals respond with such certainty and force that only a full-scale verbal war would change their opinions. People naturally don't like to be pushed. Sometimes individuals in a group will attack a position in which they basically believe merely because someone has taken a "too certain" opposing viewpoint. In that situation, passive participants have just as much to do with the group tone as the active participants.

Even though we spend much time and energy evaluating people and events, if there is one thing that puts us on guard, it is the feeling that *we* are being evaluated by *others*. We are so used to judging the person along with the idea that we tend to become supersensitive to the same treatment. It is such a short step from hearing "Do you really believe that idea?" to the translation in one's mind: "How could you possibly be so stupid as to believe that idea?" In a group where our need for acceptance increases, the feeling that we are being personally judged is a sure way of developing internal friction. Similarly, if we feel someone is placing himself or herself above us in some sort of superior position, an immediate response is to prove to the world that this individual is "not that good." Quite often we find ourselves responding on the inside to the sharp but barely perceptible cues of superiority from another person.

Communication is damaged when individuals do not trust the group enough to share what they really feel or think. The problem, of course, is that when we fail to express our feelings, others tend to read into this lack of expression what they *believe* we are feeling or thinking. More often than not, our need to be liked leads us to fear potential rejection, which translates this neutral behavior into a negative perception. This behavior as well as other strategies that hide one's real self from the group predictably result in defensive reactions by those on the receiving end. The outline of feelings on page 31 reveals the subtleties involved in this complex process.

Bill's response to John's statement is partly the result of the selection of words, the context in which they are spoken, and his image of John, as well as of all the nonverbal cues he gets from tone of voice, gestures, and posture. Also, the nature of the statement is partly the result of John's response to Bill's particular behavioral strategy with him (in this case, neutrality). The result is a predictable increase in what Jack Gibb (1961) would call "defensive communication." Part of the problem obviously lies in John's insensitivity to Bill and in Bill's tendency to read more into the words than was actually intended. Worse than this is the fact that the underlying issues build in a cumulative fashion, which results in increased tension, deteriorated communication, greater polarization among group members, and less inclination to remove these emotional roadblocks.

Statement by John: "Yes, but Bill, that's impossible. I've been here for five years, and I've never known that to work. Have you thought of the fact that . . ."

John feels:		*John as perceived by Bill*
Reasonable.	———————→	Evaluative, judging.
Correct.	———————→	Superior.
Having heard Bill.	———————→	Certain.
I've got him backing up.	———————→	Controlling.
The group is with me.		
He's probably angry; you never know with Bill.		

Bill feels:		*Bill's eventual response:*
What's he mean "yes"?	———————→	Withdrawal.
He never even heard me.	———————→	Neutrality.
If it's impossible, I wouldn't have said it.	———————→	Passive hostility.
Big deal—five years—he doesn't know everything.		
It's impossible to be right against him.		
He can sure make a person feel stupid.		
Obviously I've thought about it.		
It's always a fact coming from him.		
I'll bet everyone agrees with him.		
I should just keep quiet—that's better than looking stupid.		

Impact on Group:	
	Unresolved hostility.
	Other members afraid to venture out against John.
	Those sympathetic to Bill strengthen their protective subgroup.

Gibb found that defensiveness increases when a person feels that he or she is being evaluated or controlled or is the butt of a strategy (a plan or maneuver to accomplish an unknown outcome). A large part of the adverse reaction to many personal growth groups is a feeling against what are perceived gimmicks or tricks to involve people and have them think they are really participating in a decision or to make listeners think someone is really interested in them as people. Defensiveness also arises when a person feels that another is reacting to him or her "clinically" or as a case (neutrally), from a superior position, or from a position of certainty. Defensiveness interferes with communication and then makes it difficult, and sometimes impossible, for anyone is convey ideas clearly and to move toward a solution.

Feedback: A Means of Reducing Distortions in the Communication Process

We like to think that we are effective in our efforts, and it can be quite threatening to discover that often we are not. Thus, in groups we are frequently torn between a real desire to confront how we are actually perceived (at both content and image levels) and our desire to live with the image we would like to think we are projecting.

Feedback is the process by which we find out whether the message intended is the message actually received. In the simplest sense, feedback refers to the return to you of behavior you have generated. A mirror gives one kind of feedback, as does a tape recorder, a camera, and a videotape machine.

However, the most powerful form of feedback is the human response. Optimal learning requires sensitivity and judgment in the feedback process, and for this reason, human response remains the most powerful instrument. Machines are limited to interaction that has been programmed into them, and people have limitations also. A person is always faced with a choice of behavior from which to extract pertinent messages, and even the simplest communication may be misinterpreted and misunderstood. The same may be said for every silence, because silence is communication too. Even the simplest question can be transformed into a challenge or an attack.

The antidote is feedback. In a group, honest feedback can increase accuracy, instill a sense of being understood, and promote closeness and a sense of confidence. It can also increase defensive communication and the level of guardedness.

Feedback is most effective when it is asked for (in contrast to the unsolicited "I'm telling you for your own good"); when it is descriptive rather than evaluative; when it is behavioral rather than global; when it occurs soon after the behavior occurs rather than after a long time; and when it is positive rather than negative (Campbell and Dunnette, 1968; Jacobs et al., 1973; Yalom, 1970).

What is useful feedback? Consider an example involving two colleagues at a conference. One has just given a presentation; the other rushes up to congratulate him. "You were terrific," he says with enthusiasm. "Don't give me that," retorts the other. "I need to know what exactly you liked and didn't like about what I did. What I want to know is, How did I deal with the subject? How did I come across?" He was proving (though not very tactfully) that useful feedback is nonjudgmental, descriptive information geared to the specific situation at hand.

◆ Individual Experiment

Giving feedback is difficult; it is a skill that requires practice. Here are two practice exercises:

1. At lunch or dinner with a friend, feed back a response to something that is said. Remember, your response should be descriptive and specific. Take note of your friend's response. What did you learn from the experience?

2. At a meeting or in a group, give feedback on an incident that occurs during the session. Remember, be nonjudgmental and descriptive. Note the response and analyze its relationship to your feedback.   ◆

Besides allowing members to ascertain whether what was intended was actually received, feedback also plays a crucial role in reducing distortions in the communication process. And the impact of feedback, or how it is perceived by the members, affects members' personal and interpersonal development. Gordon (1983) studied interpersonal feedback to determine how much of it was perceived as being useful. Members of a group were asked to rate feedback as either beneficial or harmful, useful or useless, and valuable or worthless; subjects rated about 90 percent of the received feedback as beneficial, useful, and valuable.

Jacobs and her associates (1973) and Snyder and Newburg (1981) found that positive feedback was rated as more credible, as more desirable, and as having greater impact than negative feedback. They further found that negative feedback that is behavioral was more credible than negative feedback that was emotional. Either way, people are less satisfied with their jobs and how they perform their jobs when they get negative feedback from their peers (Denisi, Randolph, and Blencoe, 1983). We change by hearing (and seeking out) positive information on ourselves. And, in fact, we are more likely to accept feedback when it's given as a consensus from a group of people (Wimer and Derlega, 1983) or when it comes from the leader of the group (Snyder et al., 1981). Think about your response when another student tells you what a good job you did on that last paper, as opposed to having your professor compliment your work. We are most likely to hear negative information when it is behavioral and we can think about and modify the behavior to which it refers; we protect ourselves from others' judgments of ourselves, even to the point of not believing those judgments.

In most groups, the feedback process can be used to best advantage as a means of clearing the air, providing an opportunity to shift course or procedures, and raising important issues that could not easily be explored during the give-and-take of the meeting.

Groups do better, more effective jobs when they get feedback on how they're doing (Jorgenson and Papciak, 1981). It is possible to begin the process gently. For example, after a meeting the participants can spend a few minutes discussing what went well and what could be improved the next time in order to ensure a more effective meeting. In this way the process can focus on future behavior and events and not just on the behavior that hindered the present meeting. It requires the participants to develop effective modes of future behavior and a constructive attitude toward their own efforts. Similarly, without becoming too personal, the participants might jot down on a piece of paper a specific type of behavior they feel was facilitative in the meeting as well as one that inhibited the progress of the group. The use of such immediate information can prepare a group to accept more readily specific information related to individual behaviors. It can also increase the members' desire to solicit information about their own effectiveness. It is out of this search for personal learning and improvement that a climate of increasing support and openness evolves. Eventually the group may develop enough trust so that the feedback process becomes an integral and unobtrusive part of the entire meeting, with members responding at both a feeling level and a content level and checking out their own perceptions with others in the group.

There is, of course, the possibility that feedback can come to be of greater importance to the members than the task facing the group. There is no doubt that the process can, if mishandled, become distorted, inappropriately personal, and an actual imposition. One way to control this situation is occasionally to appoint a member of the group as observer and nonparticipant. Examining this individual's brief descriptive report after the meeting can provide a stimulus for the group to reassess its own working goals and priorities. Another approach is to develop a clear group contract about feedback expectations. Of greatest importance is that the use of feedback not be imposed, because it will inevitably create even more tensions and divisiveness and clog the very communication channels the group is attempting to open.

Poor Communication: The Rule, Not the Exception

If one were to take a cross section of American institutions, one would probably find that breakdowns in communication are a primary source of internal conflict and stress. Spend a day in a mental health institution and you may observe that the administration communicates poorly with the staff, psychiatrists with psychologists, doctors with nurses, and nurses with day-care workers. Somewhere in the labyrinth of statuses, roles, job descriptions, and the multitude of internal conflicts that exist, help is given to the resident patient. There are, of course, those exceptional institutions where hierarchical power struggles are minimized, where role differentiation in terms of status is limited, and where, as a result, communication channels remain relatively uncluttered.

Perhaps nowhere is there a better example of tensions that exist because of the communication process than in our schools, particularly the classrooms. Most of us have had firsthand experience with the following problems pervading our schools:

1. Communication is one-way—from a source of information to the receiver who can ask for clarification. The latter is seldom in a position to transfer his or her learnings to others, be they younger students or age peers.
2. In the classroom group, the goals of learning are seldom established by the participants or even with them, but by an outside power source instead.
3. Rather than being shared, leadership is usually held tightly in the hands of the "responsible" person.
4. The participants are held accountable only for content information—usually in the form of an evaluative examination that labels individuals according to performance in terms of discrete letters or numbers.
5. Although held accountable in content areas, the participants are seldom held accountable in other areas that are relevant to them, such as discipline and decision making.
6. The faculty are not held highly accountable for their performance in terms of the student participants. This lack of a two-way evaluation increases distance between student and teacher.
7. Rather than being perceived as *an* important resource to be used effectively by the classroom group, the teacher is established as the *only* resource person.
8. Often the internal climate is highly competitive and sets student against student rather than stressing the educational venture as a cooperative one.
9. The communication of information from the students to the teacher is usually, for a variety of reasons, through a relatively small number of students. Learning is passive, low-interactive communication.

With a very slight shift in titles and in certain terms, the situation described here could easily be transferred to small groups within a variety of institutions. Obviously, it would be simplistic to say that changing communication patterns would change all these conditions. Nevertheless, research in the area of small groups suggests a variety of logical alternatives that could make for more open communication.

Factors That Influence Group Communication

Group leaders are often hesitant to spend (waste) time developing interpersonal relations in a group where the goals are clearly defined in terms of specific tasks (Grace, 1956; Slater, 1955). Thus a program director may have a regularly scheduled 3-hour meeting every week (150 hours over a year) for his or her staff and never spend any time strengthening the communication process or exploring ways to improve interpersonal relations within the group. Similarly, a high school history teacher may spend from 3 to 5 hours a week with the same students for an entire year.

Almost any new group is charged with tension (Crook, 1961) as individuals test out their environment and observe the various personalities involved. It is in this early period when most communication patterns develop. But research has shown that time spent initially and periodically in improving the communication process will pay dividends in terms of greater work efficiency (see also decision making and problem solving in Chapter 7).

Research shows, too, that when people enter into a task with a predefined need to be cooperative and interdependent, there is more listening, more acceptance of ideas, less possessiveness of ideas and, in general, more communication. Within such an atmosphere, the group also tends to create achievement pressure itself. Furthermore, there seems to be more attentiveness to members' ideas and a friendlier climate than in groups where interpersonal competition is stressed. As suggested earlier, all these conditions help to make a group more attractive to its participants and generally lead to greater group productivity.

Size of Group

There is no exact specification of how large a group may be before it is no longer appropriate to call it a small group. The usefulness of the designation rests on the fact that size is a limiting condition on the amount and quality of communication that can take place among members as individual persons. This then affects the interpersonal relations among members (Hare, 1976).

Size is a factor in group relationships because, as the size increases, the number of relationships possible among members increases even more rapidly. Kephart (1950) has demonstrated how that increase in the number of relationships becomes almost astronomical with the addition of a few more people. Note in Table 1.1 how the addition of a person vastly increases the number of possible relationships.

The number of potential relationships among group members increases rapidly as a group grows larger, so a large group tends to break into subgroups. Communication then takes on another dimension as subgroups relate to each other.

Aside from communication, group size also affects group members' self-awareness and sense of how to behave in front of the group. Mullen, Chapman, and Salas (1989) studied the effects of large and small groups on the individual. They concluded that in small groups, people are more self-aware and more likely to regulate their behavior. People in large groups are less self-aware and less concerned about their behavior. In fact, their behavior can border on the bizarre. For example, one Temple University graduate student, who participated in the "Large Group" event at a Temple University Tavistock Conference attended by about 50 professionals and faculty, behaved very oddly. While everyone else was sitting, he

Table 1.1 Increase in Potential
Relationships with an
Increase in Group Size[2]

Size of Group	Number of Relationships
2	1
3	6
4	25
5	90
6	301
7	966

[2]Reprinted from "A Quantitative Analysis of Intragroup Relationships" by William M. Kephart, *American Journal of Sociology* 60 (1950), by permission of The University of Chicago Press.

lay down on the floor in the spread-eagled position and announced that he was Christ on the cross.

In a small work group, only a few possible relationships exist. Yet it is easy to understand that in a discussion group, when time is limited, the average member has fewer chances to speak and intermember communication becomes difficult. Morale declines, because the former intimate contact among members is no longer possible. With a larger group, there are greater member resources for the accomplishment of problem solving, the average contribution of each member diminishes, and it becomes more difficult to reach agreement on a group solution.

◆ Individual Experiment

People who talk a lot are perceived as having a lot of influence whether they say anything of value or not.

In a group of twenty people, how many people do you think would talk and dominate the conversation?

In a group of ten, how many would dominate?

In a group of eight?

In a group of five?

_____

In a group of three?

_____

In a group of two?

_____

What are the implications of group size for *how many will participate and be actively involved?*

_____

_____

_____ ◆

People can usually answer the questions in the foregoing experiment from experience. In a group of twenty, the number will be five or fewer. In a group of ten or eight, it will be three. In a group of five, it is likely to be two. In a group of three, interestingly, it is hard for one person to dominate, and two or all three will speak often. In a group of two, one will dominate. Thus the size of the group has a strong influence on the number of people who become actively involved in its activities. Small groups encourage proportionally more participation than large ones. It is no accident that today, with a very limited time available for volunteer activities, members of large boards report minimal satisfaction with board meetings, whereas members of small task forces or small specific projects have more satisfaction (Huberman, 1987).

Size influences communication and behavior. Two-person groups often result in considerable tension, because a dominant–submissive relationship inevitably develops. When one member does not feel that he or she has power over the other, he or she will tend either to fight the other person and his or her ideas or to withdraw into a passive pattern of behavior. Each member will use whatever behavior is required to balance the control component within the group. However, in the dyad, obviously the possibility also exists for the greatest degree of intimacy. Pearson (1981) found that women talk more about themselves in dyads and that men talk more about themselves in groups of three or more.

A three-person group may have less tension, but only because two people usually join forces and push their ideas into acceptance. The recognition of power through numbers decreases the resistance of the third member and allows a quicker resolution of the problem under consideration. The person in the minority may not feel good about it (in one study, the odd person out in a three-person roommate situation was dissatisfied, felt sick, and was less confident in social situations [Reddy et al., 1981]) but is better able to rationalize away his or her own impotence, given the obvious power of the opposition. Similarly, communication in odd-number groups tends to be smoother because the possibility of an equal split of opinion and the resulting struggle for power does not exist.

Above the size of five, members complain that a group is too large, and this may be due to the restriction on the amount of participation (Gentry, 1980). Beyond a certain size, groups tend to split up and form cliques (Mamali and Paun, 1982). A five-person group eliminates the possibility of a strict deadlock because of the odd number of members; the group tends to split into a majority and a minority, but being in the minority of two does not isolate an individual; the group is large enough for people to be able to shift roles.

There appears to be no magic number for a successful working group. However, in general, as the size of the group increases, the affectional tie among members decreases (Berelson and Steiner, 1964; Kinney, 1953; Schellenberg, 1959), as does motivation to do certain tasks (Kerr and Bruun, 1981). Pantin and Carver (1982) and Latané and Nida (1981) found that people were slower to respond to medical emergencies when they were part of a larger group. Much depends on the topic and on the individual personalities, motivations, and past experience of group members; nevertheless, a group of five seems to be optimal in a number of situations. It is large enough to allow for diversity of opinions and ideas, yet small enough to allow everyone to be heard (Hackman and Vidmar, 1970).

Physical Attractiveness

What role does physical attractiveness play in interaction? On that question, debate continues (Heilman, 1980). Although people are attracted to and react more favorably toward individuals who are physically attractive, the effect of that perception is varied (Brehm and Kassin, 1993). It is not that being more attractive is an indication of greater talent or virtue (Hatfield and Sprecher, 1986). Nor is it clear that physically attractive people have greater social skills. In one study, only physically attractive *men* perceived themselves as having greater social skills than their less attractive peers (Reis et al., 1982); and in another, only physically attractive *women* perceived themselves as having greater social skills (O'Grady, 1989).

The effect of our expectations may be one of the reasons why research results on the role played by physical attractiveness in communication are so mixed. We respond in kind to the images we conjure up that relate to attractiveness. In a recent Yale study (Heilman, 1980), participants were asked to decide who should be hired for a management job. Attractive male applicants were considered strong and competent, and they were more likely to be hired. Attractive female applicants were judged more feminine, a quality associated with helplessness and high emotionality, and were not named to the position. The issue raises all kinds of questions about our objectivity and the relationship between physical attractiveness and our communication patterns, as well as the assumptions we have about gender-related work roles.

Time for Communication

As group size increases, the time for overt communication during a meeting of any given length decreases. Each member has a more complicated set of social relationships to maintain and more restricted resources with which to do it. In larger groups, a few members do most of the talking. Members of groups are aware of this, and an increased number of members of discussion groups report feelings of threat and inhibition about participating as group size increases. The effect of increasing size is to reduce the amount of participation per member. As the group size increases, a larger and larger proportion of members have less than their share of participation time—that is, under the group mean (Shaw, 1981; Seaman, 1981; Hare, 1982).

Crowding

Crowding is another factor in communication, as are heat and cold. Crowding does not just pertain to the number of people in physical space; it is also a psychological factor. Gender seems to make a difference in the perception of crowding: females find smaller rooms more comfortable and are more likely to engage in intimate positive conversation; males prefer larger rooms (Freedman, 1971).

Raising the temperature of a room tends to create an effect of crowding, as does decreasing the distance between people conversing (Smith, Reinheimer, and Gabbard, 1981). Under conditions of crowding and increased (or varying) temperatures, people tend to react negatively to each other (Griffitt, 1970; Griffitt and Veitch, 1971).

Other Factors

A few other generalizations can be made (Bavelas, 1950; Shaw, 1964).

1. Morale is higher in groups in which there is more access to participation among those involved—the more open the participation, the higher the morale.
2. Efficiency tends to be lowest among groups that are the most open. Because more wrong ideas need to be sifted out, more extraneous material is generated and more time is "wasted" listening to individuals even when a point has been made.
3. Groups that are most efficient tend to be those in which all members have access to a central leadership figure who can act as an expediter and clarifier as well as keep the group on the right track in working through the problem.
4. Positions that individuals take can have a definite influence on leadership in the group as well as on potential conflict among group mem-

bers. In the process of performing communication functions—such as deciding on goals, giving directions, summarizing, and being self-assured—groups can predict potential leaders who may be chosen for positive and/or negative qualities (Schultz, 1986).

5. Groups with centralized leadership (see item 3) tend to organize more rapidly, be more stable in performance, and show greater efficiency. However, morale also tends to drop, and this decline can, in the long run, influence their stability and even their productivity (Glazer and Glazer, 1961; Hearn, 1957).

6. Leaders in groups without strong identities (low cohesion) do best to direct and run things, but in groups that have high cohesion, leaders are more effective when they take group members' needs into account and work in a more collaborative way (Schriesheim, 1980).

7. The group leaders' gender can affect the members' perceptions of them. In an investigation of this issue, females were perceived as less competent and less potent leaders than males (Morrison and Stein, 1985). Investigating how female instructors are perceived, Gilbert, Holt, and Long (1988) surveyed 128 female and 138 male college students. In one condition, students were in a same-sex group; in the other, they were the only male or female in the group. Findings indicate that the sex composition of the group affected person perception.

Groups in which the lines of communication are clear from the beginning and in which relations with authority are specified tend to be more productive in terms of completing task objectives. The price for this, of course, is a reduction in the amount of information shared and a subsequent increase in dependence on the person(s) in authority. In the short run, it is doubtful that tension and resentment in such groups would be inhibiting when the concern for completing a task is greatest. In the long run, however, such communication patterns may well create numerous problems as individual frustrations build up with no legitimate ways for venting them.

Thus, a dilemma. One may choose greater leader control and efficiency at the price of lower morale and participation. Or it is possible to choose higher morale and group satisfaction at the price of efficiency. The answer would seem to be a combination of the two, but it is the rare person who can encourage sharing and full participation and still impose the restrictions desired to help maximize the operation of the group. Playing such a role *is* possible if the individual is aware of the many difficulties and traps when, for example, some individuals demand more structure and guidance while others seek absolute freedom from restrictions.

Physical Environment

The physical environment, like the social environment, has a significant impact on communication and interaction in groups. In one study of the effects of different physical settings and seating arrangements, the results suggest that communication and productivity are enhanced when participants operate in a circle—for example, at circular tables (Key, 1986).

Such knowledge can help the teacher or group leader "set the stage" for the type of group interaction he or she desires.

A meeting was planned for about 40 individuals to help introduce them to one another as well as to orient them for a large convention involving 20,000 people the next day. The room was capable of seating nearly 250 people, and chairs were arranged in rows. In order to alter the sterile environment, the program director changed the chairs around in a manner that would be more conducive for informal talking and getting to know one another. Thus the chairs in the front of the room were rearranged to form loosely grouped circles of about five chairs each. Barriers were then arranged so that the chairs in the back of the room could not be reached.

When the director arrived five minutes before the meeting was scheduled to begin, he found his efforts had been futile. No one was sitting in the front of the room, and, as a result of much effort on the part of a number of individuals, the chairs in the back were now accessible and occupied. It was clear that the participants came to be talked *to* and that they felt more comfortable in straight rows and with a minimum of contact with one another. Their desires to meet and listen in straight rows, not to interact, to remain strangers in the group until drawn together by the force of a task, and to remain "comfortable" while being fed information are all the result of past conditioning. For the director to have allowed the situation to remain as it was would probably have resulted in many of the participants' leaving dissatisfied with the formal and structured nature of the program. To have moved them out of their security would have risked incurring a negative reaction as individuals became less secure and more dependent on themselves and not the authority.

Status and Power

In any group there will be both high-status members who have the power to influence others and low-status members who are less influential. Status is partly determined by a person's role in the group. It has been shown that when high-status individuals are present in a group, both high- and low-status individuals direct their communication to them (Hurwitz et al., 1968). Not only that, but Kashyap (1982) has shown that a group member who is perceived either as wealthy or as an an expert on some topic exerts more influence in changing others' opinions. It is the high-status individuals who tend to be accepted more, and they find it easier and to their advantage to speak more. Similarly, because low-status participants don't value acceptance by their own status peers, they often avoid association with one another during the meeting. Rather, they wait until later to express their own feelings and attitudes concerning the proceedings. Also, because there is a general fear of evaluation by those with power, those who lack power take few risks, generally speak inconsequentially, and avoid candidness in their statements. Because of this expected trend in behavior, it becomes even more difficult to contribute if one lacks power; considerably more attention is given to each contribution by a low-status person, and this increases his or her fears of intimidation and critical evaluation. The cycle is further extended by the probability that those with influence will hesitate to reveal any of their limitations or personal vulnerability among those with lesser influence, thus lending an artificial quality to the whole proceeding.

Juries are a good example of status in action. As Christian (1978) points out, "A jury is not an aggregate of twelve autonomous individuals. Leaders will emerge; some people may try to become leaders and be rebuffed; some will fit passively into the group structure; and some will become isolates."

Christian found in his study of juries that in general an individual's status and power in the jury group mirror his or her status and power in the real world. This means that men, people with higher education and prestigious occupations, whites, and older individuals will have more status than others.

Christian also found that people of similar status will form friendships and become cliques. These cliques become especially formidable. For example, in the trial of the Gainesville Eight, he found that the clustering of jury members was the most important factor in the understanding of the group dynamics and decision-making process of the jury. The key to clustering, he found, was power—the ability to convince other jurors of one's viewpoint. The person who could sway the other jury members had influence even outside the group, because the jury's decision had to be unanimous.

Status and power talk to status and power, while others tend to become observers in the process. What appears to be voluntary silence may be subtly imposed by the group. Unless it is legitimate to "draw in" those pushed to the periphery by the sheer power present, they will tend to feel an increasing sense of impotence. This may not occur if the individual is able to share vicariously the ideas and influence of a person with high status. But even the individual who participates least in the group has feelings about what is going on, has ideas that could contribute to the discussion, and, most of all, a desire to feel worthwhile. However, he or she may also lack the skills, trust, and energy to overcome the obstacles to his or her communication.

Interestingly, the power distribution in a group displays itself in the way the group physically arranges itself. When members of the board come into the boardroom, typically the boss either sits in the center of the short end of a rectangular table farthest from the door or at the head of the table; his or her cronies usually flank the boss on the left and right. Those either disinterested in the issue or powerless to influence the outcome generally sit at the opposite end or foot of the table and cluster together there. Where will the adversarial combatants sit? Typically they sit opposite each other on the long sides of the table—arrayed for combat.

◆ Reader Activity

If you wanted to enhance communication, how would you redesign the seating arrangement described above?

_____

_____

_____   ◆

Predictably, after three or four high-status individuals in a group have been involved in heated discussion and someone suggests breaking up into groups of two and three, the noise level in the group goes up tenfold as individuals who have been silent up to that point realize they have a chance to express themselves. It is not that they had nothing to say before; rather, the atmosphere in the group simply did not allow free expression of their ideas. Even among individuals skilled in working with groups, it takes a concerted effort to push beyond immediate needs and sources of gratification to seek and actually cultivate opportunities for participation. This process does not seem to evolve naturally—there are too many personal needs in the way.

The purpose of this chapter has been to increase awareness of the *process* underlying group endeavors. It is not necessary to print long lists of "how tos"; awareness of what is happening is the first and largest step in correcting some of the obvious problems that exist. It is an awareness of ourselves at both a feeling and a behavioral level and then an awareness of what is happening among other group members that are most important. Communication problems that exist reflect our own fallibility and the extent of our needs whenever we get together with others. For that very reason communication is difficult, but for the same reason it is possible to improve.

◆ ◆ EXERCISE 1

The Three-Stage Rocket: An Exercise in Listening and Speaking Precisely

Objectives

- To stimulate participants to listen more carefully
- To develop skills in the feedback of verbal content
- To help in the clear and succinct expression of ideas
- To increase one's awareness of nonverbal cues in the communication process

Rationale

We are forever in a hurry to say what must be said and to be listened to in return. We expect instant attention on the part of others and an alert response to *our* responses. However, we are so busy formulating our own ideas, preparing rebuttals, and thinking beyond the person who is speaking (with the same expectations) that we often fail to hear the message he or she is sending our way. As a result, some people feel that expending energy in the conversation is senseless and withdraw; others try to make their point by overwhelming the other person with words. Neither response is very effective.

Setting

The group is divided into sets of three persons. The facilitator may want this group to be with participants who are unfamiliar with one another or with individuals who communicate regularly. There is a tendency for a structured activity to be more effective if the individuals who are working together in the skill session are not close friends. (Among strangers the norm is usually to participate, whereas among friends it is easy to become sidetracked.) Individuals within the three-person groups are labeled *A, B,* and *C.* The three stages of this session can easily take between forty-five minutes and an hour, including discussion. It is assumed that the participants have been having some difficulty communicating or in some other way have been readied for the exercise. This might be nothing more than talking with the group about the factors that make simple verbal communication such a difficult task (for example, poor speech, saying too much, not listening). The facilitator then asks for two participants to demonstrate an activity that will help them all focus more directly on the problem, and a topic is selected in which they can comfortably take opposite sides. He or she then establishes the rule that each individual must recapitulate what the other has said to that other's satisfaction before he or she is able to express an idea or opinion of his or her own. Thus person *A* opens with a statement, and person *B* must capture the essence of the message and feed it back to *A* to *A*'s satisfaction (a nod of the head is sufficient). If the feedback is not satisfactory, *B* must try again until *A* is certain that he or she has grasped the message. *C* (in this case the facilitator) acts as a moderator to make sure both participants are listening and recapitulating before injecting their own ideas into the conversation.

Action

Stage One   *As* and *Bs* in all the trios now begin talking (it may facilitate things if a common topic is selected) with *C* as the moderator. The facilitator should float and see that the instructions are understood. After five minutes, *B* talks to *C,* and *A* becomes the moderator. This continues for another five minutes (if there is time, the facilitator may want *A* and *C* to have a chance to converse with *B* as the moderator).

Stage Two   Another rule is imposed on the participants. The process is to continue, but a time limit is added. *A* makes a statement to *B*. Now *B* must reflect
the essence of the message to *A's* satisfaction and introduce his or her own idea
in no more than twenty-five seconds. If he or she is unable to do so, *B* forfeits
the chance to add his or her own idea. The aim is to sharpen listening and
recapitulating and, at the same time, to reduce *B's* input to what is essential. It
is important that *C* be a strict referee or else this stage of the exercise will prove
ineffective. After five minutes or so, *B* and *C* interchange in this manner and *A*
is the referee. It is possible during this second interchange (and perhaps during
a third—between *C* and *A*) for the facilitator to have the participants sit on their
hands, thus adding another restriction.

At this point, it is helpful to have a brief discussion among the members of the
trio concerning what has occurred up to that moment. Some facilitators, however,
do not like to break up the sequence of the activity and hold off the discussion
until after the third stage.

Stage Three   Now the time restriction is removed and all three participants take
part equally. They are all to discuss a particular topic (by this time they will easily
select a topic of interest by themselves). They must, however, still reflect on what
the speaker has said and recapitulate to the speaker's satisfaction. The new restriction is that all the participants must keep their eyes closed during this entire
stage. The conversation should be relatively natural because the recapitulating
will be fairly natural by then. The rationale for this stage is to make the participants
aware of their dependence on many nonverbal cues in the process of normal
conversation.

Discussion

The participants may talk together within their own trios about their learnings and
the implications of the Three-Stage Rocket in their efforts to communicate. Or,
it is sometimes helpful to establish new trios for the discussion with members
from different groups helping them to focus on specific questions such as

> At which point in the exercise did you feel least comfortable? Why
> should this be?
>
> What did you learn about yourself from this exercise that may have
> implications for you in your future efforts to communicate?
>
> Did the exercise prove annoying to you at any time? Why?
>
> What did the time restriction do to you? Was it helpful?
>
> What did you learn about yourself with your eyes closed and about
> how you listen and how you communicate?

With these types of questions in mind, the discussion should be profitable. It
may be helpful to have the groups report specific findings to the entire group in

an effort to begin closure to the exercise. Also, although feedback is held strictly to the verbal content level, it may be worthwhile to use this exercise as a first step in readying the group for a more in-depth analysis of the subject.

◆ ◆ *EXERCISE 2*

Communication Role Reversal

Objectives

- To make group members aware of how easily they "tune out" one another
- To force people into a position in which listening becomes expected at both an emotional (affective) level and a content level

Setting

The large group is divided into subgroups or sets of four or five participants. Each person is given a rather large name tag that is pinned on him or her or placed in his or her lap so that every other person can clearly see it. This is to be done even if members know one another's names. Again, it is probably helpful if the members are not too familiar with one another, because lack of familiarity usually requires greater concentration and ensures greater involvement (unless the members are voluntarily together where familiarity is one of the aims of that particular program).

Action

The subgroups are given a topic that ensures some involvement on the part of all the participants. If possible, the topic should be of such a nature that opposing views will be presented. After five or ten minutes—at a point when the discussion has developed to a considerable degree—the facilitator requests that each individual give his or her name tag to the person across from him or her. They are then asked to continue the discussion as if they were the person whose name tag they now have. After another five minutes, the facilitator asks the group members to begin expressing the views of the person on their right (another exchange of tags).

Discussion

If the participants have really been listening to one another and the discussion is moving with most individuals participating, the exercise will not prove difficult. However, if a person has not been participating for some reason, this poses questions for the person playing him or her, and it poses questions for the group.

Why was he or she not involved in a topic about which he or she must have ideas? The group is also asked to discuss whether the switch made them uncomfortable or made the task particularly difficult. Also, what was present in this situation that is present in most group communication? Was it easy to pick up the emotional as well as the content information of the person you were playing? Did the learnings from the first switch carry over into the second switch?

◆ ◆ *EXERCISE 3*

The Blind Builder: A Task in Interdependent Communication

Objectives

- To observe how different individuals give direction
- To observe how different individuals receive direction
- To gain a better understanding of what happens when communication occurs under stress conditions

Setting

This exercise is limited to some extent by the availability of materials and space. Groups consisting of four participants are established. Two of the four are to be observers. Each group must have the following materials:

A blindfold

A backsaw or other small handsaw

Odd-sized pieces of wood board (perhaps five or six)

A hammer

Ten to twenty tacks or small nails

A three-foot piece of rope or twine

The participants are told the following story:

Two people flying across a group of islands in the South Pacific were forced to crash-land on a small, uninhabited island. The temperature is extremely hot and, although the land is quite arid, it appears that there will be rain sometime during the day. The two fully expect to be rescued in a few days, and they have enough food for five days. However, their water supply was lost in the crash and they don't even have a container for holding water should it rain. Because of the heat and their fear of dehydration, the two survivors feel it is essential to build a water container and then wait for what looks like an inevitable thunderstorm. They find some wood and tools and are ready to set about their task. The only problem is that during the crash one of the two received a heavy blow on the head and is now both blind and mute. The second person burned both hands while pulling the tools from the burning wreckage and is not able to use them at all. But together they must build the container—and before the rain comes. A few drops begin to fall.

Thus the hands of one individual are to be tied with the twine securely behind his or her back, and the other is to be blindfolded.

Observer Roles

Both observers are to take notes on the more general aspects of the activity, but each is responsible for a more detailed observational report concerning one of the people taking part. How does the second person give directions? Is it possible for the blind person to understand him or her? Do they establish a basic nonverbal system of communication so that the blind person can communicate? What signs do each of the people reveal as the task becomes increasingly difficult? How is this frustration communicated to the other, and what is the other's response? What could have been done to facilitate their communication?

Action

The task will take between fifteen and thirty minutes. The observers may wish to observe other groups for the sake of contrast. When the task is completed (or not completed), the facilitator consolidates the two groups of four into one group of eight for a discussion of (a) the observers' data and (b) the feelings of the two participants. He or she then has the group of eight try to pull together some general learnings and implications to be shared with the large group.

◆ ◆ *EXERCISE 4*

One-Way Versus Two-Way Communication[3]

Objectives

- To illustrate problems in communication between one person and another
- To show the value of clarification through a question-and-answer process

---

3. A workshop demonstration of this exercise was given by Hugh Stephans of Victoria, Texas, at the National Council on Family Relations Annual Conference in Dallas, Texas (1985).

■ To explore the feelings of the recipient of a communicated message under two conditions

Materials

Three dominoes for each person

Action

Two group members sit in chairs with their backs to each other. Each holds three dominoes and, on his or her lap, something with a smooth, firm surface, such as a book or magazine. Other group members must look on without comment.

Round 1   Person A constructs a design with the three dominoes. Person B must try to construct an exact duplicate of person A's design by asking questions that can be answered with yes or no only. When person B feels the design is complete, the participants compare and discuss the designs.

Round 2   Person A again constructs a design. This time, person A instructs person B on how to construct a duplicate design. Person B may not ask any questions. When person A feels that the design has been adequately described, person B must try to duplicate it. Then the two may compare and discuss the designs.

Round 3   Person A makes another design. Now each person may give and take information. At the completion, they compare and discuss.

Discussion

In a discussion following the activity, the group considers the elements needed for effective communication. Some examples are

The frustration of a one-sided dialogue

The need for clarifying questions

The importance of common terminology

The advantage of give and take

Variations

The exercise can be done in groups of two, allowing everyone to participate. Another variation is to have the leader turn his or her back to the group; in this situation the leader is person A and the group is person B.

◆ ◆ EXERCISE 5

An Introductory Micro-Laboratory Experience

Objectives

- To hasten the development of interpersonal communication within a group
- To help establish a norm of openness within a group in which both content-level and feeling-level statements are appropriate
- To begin exploring perceptions of one another among the participants

Rationale

A micro-experience is designed to move group members through a variety of activities in a relatively short period of time (one or two hours). By reducing the amount of time spent on any one activity, the group can develop a wide range of ideas and experiences and then build upon them later. The objectives of each micro-lab will differ according to the aims of the facilitator and the needs of the group. This particular design is directed at helping to open channels of communication in a new group of individuals or in a group where channels of communication have been restricted or narrowly defined. Of course, a key in this approach is the participants' knowledge that they are free to communicate at any level that is comfortable for them and that the various activities are merely meant to help provide a structure within which to relate. This approach has met with considerable success; people basically desire to be known and enjoy talking about themselves and others. An opportunity to do this in an atmosphere of fun and goodwill can be most satisfying and may build innumerable personal bridges among individuals in the group.

For the facilitator, it is important that the activities build on one another in a sequential fashion and make sense in terms of the stated objectives. If the approach is misused, individuals may be submerged too rapidly into personal areas that bring on later feelings of guilt or anger.

The following design sequence lasts about ninety minutes but could easily be extended to two or three hours by adding other activities. (Many of the exercises in the section on Selective Perception could be integrated with little difficulty if they proved appropriate in terms of the aims of the program.)

1. Getting to Know You

(Time: 15–20 min.) The group divides itself into pairs, each person with someone she or he does not know. They have five minutes to get to know each other in any way they wish. The facilitator has a blackboard or newsprint available and, after five minutes, asks members of the group to call out the topical areas that were being discussed. He or she posts these quickly.

He or she then says something like this to the group: "In each of our lives there are usually a handful of individuals that we can call true friends. These are the people in whom we could have complete and ultimate trust. If this person to whom you are now talking were to become one of these very special friends, what would you have to know about him? What would be the most important thing to discover before you could have a relationship with the kind of trust necessary to sustain it?" The group members discuss this for about five minutes with their "potential" friend.

Again, after five minutes or a bit longer, the facilitator asks the group to share the topical areas they were exploring together. He or she lists these next to the original list developed after the first talk. The difference should be apparent. The second list should be much less superficial, more personal, and with much more involvement. In this period of ten minutes, the participants will probably have shared more about themselves than they ever have in many of the "friendly" relationships they now enjoy. How simple it is to go a little deeper, if only the two participants agree that it is all right to venture into these areas. Both usually like the experience. There is no need for much discussion of the data outside, only perhaps a few expressions of feelings from the group. The point is too self-evident to lose in a superficial discussion.

2. Discussion of Communication with a Person Like Yourself

(Time: 15–20 min.) The facilitator has the members of the group look around and find someone who, for some reason, they believe is like themselves. He or she has each of them sit with that person. This may take a little encouragement and pushing on the part of the facilitator, but once individuals see others doing it, it becomes much easier. These new pairs are to spend a few minutes discussing what it was about themselves that caused them to get together and what else they have in common. (5–10 min.)

At this point, the group is asked to listen carefully to a record (for example, "Thunder Road" by Bruce Springsteen) and discuss the implications it has for their own participation in a group. The aim is to get the individuals involved at a content level, thus using different behaviors from those they used when they first began talking. (5–10 min.)

The pairs are to discuss some dissimilarities they have now noticed about themselves, things that were not apparent when they first began to talk, and also whether the original similarities were just as apparent at this point. (5– 10 min.)

3. Discussing a Critical Event in Life with a Person Unlike Yourself

(Time: 15–20 min.) The facilitator now has the members of the group look around and find someone who, for some reason, they believe is unlike themselves. Again, the new pairs are to spend five to ten minutes discussing what it is about themselves that they perceive as probably different.

Then the facilitator asks the two individuals to share an experience in their lives that proved absolutely crucial in shaping "who they are" today. The experience can be positive or negative but must have been essential in their development as a person.

The participants discuss once more the initial differences they perceived. Are they the same? Are there others that they have since noticed during the course of their conversation?

4. Childhood Fantasy with a Person You Would Like to Know

(Time: 20–30 min.) This particular experience can be rich in a variety of learnings and, if taken naturally along with the other events, will not be perceived as threatening to the participants. Evaluation or analysis is not the key. Rather it is the pulling together of a wide variety of verbal and nonverbal cues that can communicate to each of us an enormous amount of information about the other person.

The facilitator might introduce this section by giving everyone a final chance to meet someone else in the group. He or she has all the members seek out another person they would simply like to get to know better and gives them five minutes or so to talk about the kinds of things that usually keep people from getting to know others. What keeps people from being personal with one another and allowing much more information to come to the surface? (5 min.)

The facilitator continues: "Now, knowing just what you have been able to learn in these few minutes, let's see how much more we can discover about the person with us. Think for a few.minutes about this person and imagine him or her when he or she was an eight-year-old. Try to draw a picture of him or her at that time in his or her life. For example, try to imagine him or her at play, how he or she played, with whom, his or her types of friends in school, how he or she enjoyed it, what he or she liked about it, his or her family, wealthy or poor, how many children, oldest, youngest, his or her relations with his or her family, how he or she expressed anger, and so forth."

The facilitator can close by saying: "There are a thousand possible avenues you might want to focus on. Try to be as thorough as you can so as to obtain a complete picture. Now, after thinking about all this, share it with the individual.

Then let him or her share his or her picture with you. After that, tell him or her how accurate he or she was and what the *real* picture was. You may want to know why certain things were pictured."

It should be stressed that the most a person can be is absolutely wrong. After at least fifteen minutes or when it appears that most of the pairs are through conversing, it might be useful to have two groups of pairs come together and explain why they believe they were able to be so accurate or why they were so inaccurate. Also, why go through this exercise in the first place among relative strangers? It is always interesting to have a show of hands among the total group to discover how many individuals were very accurate in their descriptions. Often as many as 80 percent feel their partner hit the mark. Why? Because we are the product of our past. For most of us, our behaviors at age thirty are remarkably similar to those at age eight. We are open books to the world, though we seldom realize it.

A general discussion of the significance of the micro-experience for the participants and its relation to the rest of the program can provide a useful conclusion to the total experience.

◆ ◆ *EXERCISE 6*

Communication: A New Symbol of the City

Objectives

- To highlight the problems involved in getting people to listen when members of a group are advocating their individual points of view
- To demonstrate how much information is retained under situations of personal advocacy
- To show some of the common problems in communication from different perspectives

The Situation

Each of you, as a recognized leader of your local community, has been selected by the mayor to sit on the board of directors of the municipally sponsored zoo. Because the zoo is the pride of the community and is nationally known, membership on the board is publicly recognized as a position of trust and responsibility.

Last week the mayor asked you, the board, to meet in special session to choose an animal to represent the city. This is not unusual. Many cities are represented by animals that symbolize some characteristic that the city leaders find appropriate. Each member will meet with his or her constituency to decide on a choice and will then be a proponent for that animal.

The Problem

You will be separated into dyads (pairs). Each pair will favor and promote a different animal at the board meeting, as if this is what the local community preferred. One member of each dyad will be the spokesperson and the other the resource person. You will be given ample time to confer prior to the meeting to plan strategies for getting your points communicated and accepted.

Each resource person will receive a sheet of paper naming the animal his or her dyad is to support and listing the reasons for supporting it (this material is supplied in the accompanying table).

Your task is to convince the board to select your animal by presenting the reasons clearly.

Planning

(Time: 10 min.) The dyads meet to discuss the strategy the spokesperson will adopt.

The Meeting

(Time: 10 min.) Spokespeople meet to select the city's new symbol. Spokespeople present their cases for their animals to the rest of the group. If there is no decision, the facilitator announces that the board will meet for five more minutes.

(Time: 5 min.) The board continues the decision-making process. At the end of five minutes the facilitator stops the group.

Discussion

As a group, discuss the following questions:

1. Do you feel that you were personally successful in getting your ideas communicated and accepted? Why or why not? What could you have done to get your ideas accepted by more people on the board?

2. Consider the other dyads. What could board members have done to make themselves more aware of their positions? Do you feel that you yourself really communicated with these groups?

3. Thinking back on the exercise, what were some of the communication skills that were or were not used? What helped board members communicate successfully with some dyads? Why did they not communicate effectively with others?

Group	Animal	Reason
1	Fox	a. Is associated with the "chases" at the Radnor Hunt
		b. Provides foxtails
		c. Is clever, like us

2	Dove	a. Is associated with the City of Brotherly Love b. Coos quietly c. Is peaceful, like us
3	Wild turkey	a. Was eaten by early settlers b. Is a big bird c. Is indomitable, like us
4	Raven	a. Edgar Allen Poe wrote about it here b. Has a sharp beak c. Enjoys collecting, like us
5	Steer	a. Is the basis for meat-packing industry in the city b. Has horns c. Suffers, like us
6	Owl	a. Is intelligent and wise b. Eats mice c. Is a "night person," like us
7	Elephant	a. Is a noble worker and the children's friend b. Carries trees c. Has a long memory, like ours
8	Pilot whale	a. Is a mascot at Aquarama b. Is big and heavy c. Is unique, like us
9	Gorilla	a. Bamboo, a gorilla, made our zoo famous b. Has no tail c. Is strong, like us
10	Cardinal	a. Has a beautiful voice and appearance b. Marries for life c. Loves his home, like us

1. Please list the number of the dyads whose animals you remember, and enter the names of the animals they proposed.
2. Under each dyad number and animal name, please list the reasons that the group gave in support of their choice.

Group	Animal	Reasons
_____	_____	a. _____ b. _____ c. _____
_____	_____	a. _____ b. _____ c. _____

_____ _____   a. _____
                   b. _____
                   c. _____

_____ _____   a. _____
                   b. _____
                   c. _____

_____ _____   a. _____
                   b. _____
                   c. _____

_____ _____   a. _____
                   b. _____
                   c. _____

_____ _____   a. _____
                   b. _____
                   c. _____

_____ _____   a. _____
                   b. _____
                   c. _____

_____ _____   a. _____
                   b. _____
                   c. _____

_____ _____   a. _____
                   b. _____
                   c. _____

_____ _____   a. _____
                   b. _____
                   c. _____

_____ _____   a. _____
                   b. _____
                   c. _____

◆ ◆ EXERCISE 7

Do You See What I See?

Objectives

- To experience perception in a novel way
- To build skills in perception
- To experience perception, creativity, and pleasure in an introductory exercise

Setting

Divide the class into groups of three.

Rationale

Your brain, like the rest of your body, occasionally needs a break—a time for fun and relaxation. Brain teasers offer the mind an opportunity to be playful. One of the most popular brain teasers involves creative new ways to express familiar words, phrases, and titles. For example,

We shall
come

is a playful way of expressing "We shall overcome" that incorporates the concept *over* in visual rather than verbal terms.[4]

Action

You will be working in groups of three. Your job in the groups will be to figure out what each of the eleven brain teasers says. This is a cooperative exercise; members of the group are to help each other. It is also a competitive exercise; the first group to complete all eleven brain teasers wins.

A leader distributes one sheet containing brain teasers to each group (see the accompanying box) and notes the order in which the groups complete the task.

Discussion

After the exercise, identify in discussion what helped you get the answers. What blocked you? Did it get easier as you continued to figure out the brain teasers?

---

4. This and the other teasers in this exercise are from Charles E. Ross, "What's in a Word?" *Reader's Digest* (June 1982): 126–127, 136. Reprinted by permission of the author.

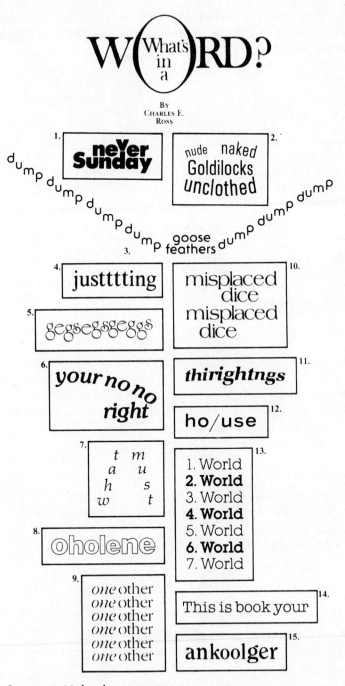

W(What's in a O)RD?

By
CHARLES E.
ROSS

1. neVer Sunday

2. nude naked Goldilocks unclothed

dump dump dump dump dump dump dump dump dump

3. goose feathers

4. justtttting

5. gegsegssgeggs

6. your no no right

7.
t	m
a	u
h	s
w	t

8. oholene

9.
one other
one other
one other
one other
one other
one other

10. misplaced dice misplaced dice

11. thirightngs

12. ho/use

13.
1. World
2. World
3. World
4. World
5. World
6. World
7. World

14. This is book your

15. ankoolger

Answers   See page 60 for the answers.

Did you develop a sense of how to solve the teasers as you went along? Did your group come up with a method of working together? What in particular did you learn from this experience?

Answers to "What's in a word?"

1. Never on Sunday
2. Goldilocks and the Three Bears
3. Down in the dumps
4. Just teasing
5. Scrambled eggs
6. Right under your nose
7. What goes up must come down
8. A hole in one
9. Six of one, half-dozen of the other
10. Paradise Lost
11. Right in the middle of things
12. A house divided
13. World Series
14. You're out of order
15. Look back in anger

◆ ◆ *EXERCISE 8*

A Portrait Plus

Objectives

- To observe differences in interpersonal communication between men and women
- To observe how men and women work differently
- To recognize different patterns of relationships between men and women

Rationale

Do men and women take the same task and work differently? Do they, in fact, communicate in a different style? Are men more achievement-oriented and women more relationship-oriented? This exercise will enable participants to answer these questions and to discuss their objectives.

Materials

Large sheets of newsprint, one for each group, mounted on a wall

A set of multicolored finger paints or crayons for each group

Aprons, or some covering, to keep participants clean when using finger paints

A set of instructions for each group

Setting

The group is divided into sets of between two and four persons. One set should be all females, one set should be all males, and one set should be mixed. Depending on the number involved, there can be multiple groups in each category (male, female, or mixed). Two people are assigned to be observers of each group. Observers will focus on how the group works, how they give each other instructions, and how they divide the task, paying attention to the words used by members doing the task.

Action

Each group goes to a sheet of newsprint with their paints. They are instructed to create a portrait of the class instructor (or any other person known to all), but they must include the items on the instruction sheet:

1. a ring
2. a mushroom
3. a cup
4. a flower
5. jewelry

6. a butterfly
7. eye glasses
8. an animal
9. something made from a circle
10. shoes

The groups then create their portraits. Allow about 20 minutes.

Discussion

Do the men's, the women's or the mixed group's pictures look different? Can you tell which is a woman's picture, which a man's picture, and which a mixed-group picture? How?

Observers report how women's groups worked; other observers report how men's groups worked; a final observer reports on how mixed groups worked. Discussion then continues with all participants.

Questions

1. Women's Group: How did it feel to be in a women's group? How is it different from being in a mixed group?
2. Men's group: How did it feel to be in a men's group? How is it different from being in a mixed group?
3. Do men and women communicate differently?
4. Do men and women work on a task differently?
5. What are the implications?

References

Abraham, A. "Le groupe en images. Le test: 'Dessinez un Groups' " [The group in pictures: The draw-a-group (DAG) Test]. *Bulletin de Psychologie,* 37, Nos. 1–5, (1983–84), 177–191.

Allison, S. T., and D. M. Messick, "The attribution of attitudes to groups." Paper presented at the 65th Annual Meeting of the Western Psychological Association, San Jose, Calif., April 18–21, 1985.

The American Heritage Dictionary of the English Language. Ed. W. Morris. New York: American Heritage Publishing Co. and Houghton Mifflin, 1969, p. 600.

Asch, S. E. "Studies of independence and conformity: I. A minority of one against a unanimous majority." *Psychological Monographs 70,* 9, Whole No. 416 (1956).

Back, K. "Influence through social communication." *Journal of Abnormal and Social Psychology,* 46, No. 9 (1951).

Bales, R. F., F. L. Strodtbeck, T. M. Mills, and M. E. Roseborough. "Channels of communication in small groups." *American Sociological Review,* 16 (1951), 461–468.

Bavelas, A. "Communication patterns in task oriented groups." *Journal of the Acoustical Society of America,* 22, No. 725 (1950).

Bennis, W. G., and H. A. Shepard. "A theory of group development." In *Analysis of Groups,* edited by G. S. Gibbard, J. J. Hartman, and R. D. Mann. San Francisco: Jossey-Bass, 1987.

Berelson, B., and C. A. Steiner. *Human Behavior.* Short ed. New York: Harcourt, Brace and World, 1964.

Berne, E. *Beyond Games and Scripts.* New York: Grove Press, 1976, pp. 44–53, 123–135.

Bower, G. S. "Mood and memory." *American Psychologist,* 36, No. 2 (February 1981), 129–148.

Boulton, M. J., and P. K. Smith. "Affective bias in children's perceptions of dominance relationships." *Child Development,* 61, (February 1990), 221–229.

Brand, D. "Here comes Gorbachev." *Time,* 130, No. 25 (December 21, 1987), 17–22.

Brehm, S. S., and S. M. Kassin, *Social Psychology.* 2nd ed. Boston: Houghton Mifflin, 1993.

Brill, A. A. *Freud's Contribution to Psychiatry,* Gloucester, Mass.: Peter Sanith Publishing Company, 1972.

Campbell, H. P., and M. D. Dunnette. "Effectiveness of T-group experiences in managerial training and development." *Psychological Bulletin 70* (1968), 73–104.

Chartier, M. R. "Clarity of expression in interpersonal communication." *The 1976 Annual Handbook for Group Facilitators.* La Jolla, Calif.: University Associates, 1976, pp. 149–156.

Christian, R. "Probability vs. precedence: The social psychology of jury selection." In *Psychology and Law,* edited by G. Bermant. Springfield, Mass.: Thomas, 1978.

Coan, R. W. "Dimensions of psychological theory." *American Psychologist* 23 (1968), 715–722.

Codol, J. P. "On the system of representations in a group situation." *European Journal of Social Psychology,* 4, No. 3 (1974), 343–365.

Crook, R. "Communication and Group Structure." *Journal of Communication,* 11 (1961), 136.

Denisi, A., W. Randolph, and A. Blencoe, "Potential problems with peer ratings." *Academy of Management Journal,* 26 (1983), 457–464.

Deutsch, M. "The effects of cooperation and competition upon group process." In *Group Dynamics.* 2nd ed. Ed. D. Cartwright and A. Zander. New York: Harper & Row, 1960, pp. 414–448.

Eakins, B. W., and R. G. Eakins. "Sex Differences in Communication." Boston: Houghton Mifflin, 1978.

Ehrlich, H. J. "Affective style as a variable in person perception." *Journal of Personality,* 37 (1969), 522–539.

Ekman, P., W. V. Friesen, and J. Bear. "The international language of gestures." *Psychology Today* (May 1984), 64–69.

Epstein, R. S., and N. Liebman. "Biz speak: A dictionary of business terms, slang, and jargon." *Time,* 128, No. 18 (November 3, 1986), 31.

Fabun, D., ed. "Communications." *Kaiser Aluminum,* 23, No. 3 (1965).

Festinger, L. "Informal social communication." *Psychological Review,* 57 (1950), 271.

Festinger, L., and J. Thibaut. "Interpersonal communication in small groups." *Journal of Abnormal and Social Psychology,* 56 (1951), 92.

Freedman, J. L. "The crowd: Maybe not so madding after all." *Psychology Today,* 5, No. 4 (September 1971), 58–61.

Freedman, J. L., S. Klevansky, and P. R. Ehrlich. "The effect of crowding on human task performance." *Journal of Applied Social Psychology,* 1, No. 1 (January 1971), 7–25.

Gentry, G. "Group size and attitudes toward the simulation experience." *Simulation and Games,* 11 (1980), 451–460.

Gerard, H. "The effect of different dimensions of disagreement on the communication process in small groups." *Human Relations,* 6 (1953), 249.

Gibb, J. "Defensive communications." *Journal of Communication,* 11 (September 1961), 141–148.

Gibbs, *Time,* (October 21, 1991), 35.

Gilbert, L. A., R. W. Holt, and K. M. Long. "Teaching gender-related material: The effect of group sex composition on perceptions of a female instructor." *Sex Roles,* 19, Nos. 3–4 (August 1988), 241–254.

Glazer, M., and R. Glazer. "Techniques for the study of group structure and behavior: Empirical studies of the effects of structure in small groups." *Psychological Bulletin,* 58 (1961).

Goffman, E. *Asylums.* Garden City, New York: Doubleday-Anchor, 1961.

Goffman, E. *The Presentation of Self in Everyday Life.* Garden City, New York: Doubleday-Anchor, 1959.

Goffman, E. *Stigman: Notes on the Management of Spoiled Identity.* Englewood Cliffs, N.J.: Prentice-Hall, 1963.

Gordon, R. "An investigation of the giving and receiving of interpersonal feedback within the human relations group." Paper presented at the Annual Conference of the Communication Association of the Pacific America, Honolulu, August 1983.

Grace, H. "Confidence, redundancy and the purpose of communication." *Journal of Communication,* 6 (1956), 16.

Greenspoon, L. "The reinforcing effect of two spoken sounds on the frequency of two responses." *American Journal of Psychology,* 68 (1955), 409–416.

Griffitt, W. B. "Environmental effects on interpersonal affective behavior: Ambient effective temperature and attraction." *Journal of Personality and Social Psychology,* 15, No. 3 (1970), 240–244.

Griffitt, W. J., and R. Veitch. "Hot and crowded: Influence of population density and temperature on interpersonal affective behavior." *Journal of Personality and Social Psychology,* 17, No. 1 (January 1971), 92–98.

Hackman, J. R., and N. Vidmar, "Effects of size and task characteristics on group performance and member reactions." *Sociometry,* 33, No. 1 (March 1970), 37–54.

Hare, P. *Handbook of Small Group Research.* New York: Free Press, 1976, p. 214.

Hare, P. *Creativity in Small Groups.* Beverly Hills, Calif.: Sage Publications, 1982, p. 141.

Harrison, A. A. *Individuals and Groups.* Monterey, Calif.: Brooks/Cole, 1976, pp. 100–107.

Hatfield, E., and S. Sprecher. *Mirror, Mirror . . . The Importance of Looks in Everyday Life.* Albany, N.Y.: State University of New York Press, 1983.

Hearn, G. "Leadership and the spatial factor in small groups." *Journal of Abnormal and Social Psychology,* 54 (1957), 219–272.

Heilman, M. E. "Sometimes beauty can be beastly." *New York Times,* Business and Finance, June 22, 1980, p. 8.

Heise, G. A., and G. Miller. "Problem solving by small groups using various communication nets." *Journal of Abnormal and Social Psychology,* 46 (1951), 327.

Huberman, S. "Making Jewish leaders." *The Journal of Jewish Communal Service,* 64, No. 1 (Fall 1987), 32–41.

Huff, F. W., and T. P. Piantianida. "The effect of group size on group information transmitted." *Psychonomic Science,* 11, No. 10 (1968), 365–366.

Hurwitz, J., A. Zander, and B. Hymovitch. "Some effects of power on the relations among group members." In *Group Dynamics.* 3rd ed. Eds. D. Cartwright and A. Zander. New York: Harper & Row, 1968, pp. 291–297.

Jacobs, M., A. Jacobs, G. Feldman, and N. Cavior. "Feedback II—the credibility gap: Delivery of positive and negative and emotional and behavioral feedback in groups." *Journal of Consulting and Clinical Psychology,* 41, No. 2 (1973), 215–223.

Jacoby, J., M. C. Nelson, and W. D. Hoyer. " 'Plain English' not that plain." *The Wharton Magazine,* 7, No. 1 (Fall 1982), 9–10.

Johnson, M. P., and W. L. Ewens. "Power relations and affective style as determinants of confidence in impression formation in a game situation." *Journal of Experimental Social Psychology,* 78, No. 1 (1971), 98–110.

Jorgenson, D., and A. Papciak. "The effects of communication, resource feedback, and identifiability on behavior in a simulated commons." *Journal of Experimental Social Psychology,* 17 (1981), 373–385.

Jose, P. E., and W. J. McCarthy. "Perceived agentic and communal behavior in mixed-sex group interactions." *Personality and Social Psychology Bulletin,* 14, No. 1 (March 1988), 57–67.

Kashyap, A. "Differential efficacy of power base in opinion change in group discussion." *Journal of Psychological Researches,* 26 (1982), 9–12.

Kegan, R. *The Evolving Self.* Cambridge, Mass.: Harvard University Press, 1982.

Kelley, H. "Communication in experimentally created hierarchies." *Human Relations,* 4 (1951), 39.

Kephart, W. M. "A quantitative analysis of intragroup relationships." *American Journal of Sociology,* 60 (1950), 544–549.

Kerr, N., and S. Bruun. "Ringelmann revisited: Alternative explanations for the social loafing effect." *Personality and Social Psychology Bulletin,* 7 (1981), 224–231.

Key, N. "Abating risk and accidents through communication." *Professional Safety,* 31, No. 11 (November 1986), 25–28.

Kinney, E. E. "A study of peer group social acceptability at the fifth-grade level in a public school." *Journal of Educational Research,* 47 (1953), 57–64.

Kohlberg, L., and C. Gilligan. "The adolescent as a philosopher." In *Twelve to Sixteen: Early Adolescence.* Eds. J. Kagan and R. Coles. New York: Norton, 1972.

Kohler, W. *Gestalt Psychology.* New York: A Mentor Book—The New American Library, 1947.

Laing, R. D. *The Politics of the Family and Other Essays.* New York: Vintage Books, 1972.

Latané, B., and D. Nida. "Ten years of research on group size and helping." *Psychological Bulletin,* 89 (1981), 308–324.

Leavitt, H., and R. Mueller. "Some effects of feedback on communication." *Human Relations,* 4 (1951), 401.

Livesley, W. J., and D. B. Bromley. *Person Perception in Childhood and Adolescence.* New York: Wiley, 1973.

Locksley, A., V. Ortiz, and C. Hepburn. "Social categorization and discriminatory behavior: Extinguishing the minimal intergroup discrimination effect." *Journal of Personality and Social Psychology,* 39 (1980), 773–783.

Loomis, J. "Communication, the development of trust and cooperative behavior." *Human Relations,* 12 (1959), 305.

Luft, J. *Of Human Interaction.* Palo Alto, Calif.: Mayfield Publishing Company, 1969.

Maltz, D. N., and R. A. Borker. "A cultural approach to male–female miscommunication." In *Language and Social Identity.* Ed. John J. Gumperz. Cambridge, England: Cambridge University Press (1982), pp. 196–216.

Mamali, C., and G. Paun. "Group size and the genesis of subgroups: Objective restrictions." *Revue Roumaine Des Sciences Sociales—Serie de Psychologie,* 26 (1982), 139–148.

Meulemans, G. "Social interaction and emotional arousal in two training groups." *Bulletin du C.E.R.P.,* 22, No. 3 (1973–1974), 153–160.

Miller, E. J., and A. K. Rice. Systems of organizations. In *Group Relations Reader.* Eds. A. D. Colman and W. H. Bexton. Washington, D.C.: A. K. Rice Institute, 1975.

Mills, T. M. *The Sociology of Small Groups.* Englewood Cliffs, N.J.: Prentice-Hall, 1967.

Morrison, T. L., and D. D. Stein. "Member reaction to male and female leaders in two types of group experience." *Journal of Social Psychology,* 125, No. 1 (February 1985), 7–16.

Mullen, B., J. Chapman, and E. Salas. "Efectos de la composicion del grupo: "Perdido en la multitude," of "centro de atencion." [Effects of group composition: "Lost in the crowd" or "center of attention."] *Revista Latinoamericana de Psicologia,* 21, No. 1 (1989), 43–55.

The New York Times, Article by P. J. Hilts, July 17, 1990.

The New York Times, Section E, (December 8, 1991), page 5.

Nidorf, L. J. "Information seeking strategies in person perception." *Perceptual and Motor Skills,* 26, No. 2 (1968), 355–365.

Nidorf, L. J., and W. H. Crockett. "Some factors affecting the amount of information sought by others." *Journal of Abnormal and Social Psychology,* 69, No. 1 (1964), 98–101.

Nisbett, R. E., and T. D. Wilson. Institute of Social Research, University of Michigan, *Newsletter,* Summer 1978, 4.

NTL Institute of Applied Behavioral Science. *Laboratories in Human Relations Training.* Washington, D.C.: NTL Institute of Applied Behavioral Science, 1969, p. 23.

O'Grady, K. E. "Physical attractiveness, need for approval, social self-esteem, and maladjustment." *Journal of Social and Clinical Psychology,* 8 (1989), 62–69.

Pantin, H., and C. Carver. "Induced competence and the bystander effect." *Journal of Applied Social Psychology,* 12 (1982), 100–111.

Patterson, M. L., S. Mullens, and J. Romano. "Compensatory reactions to spatial intrusion." *Sociometry,* 34, No. 1 (March 1971), 114–121.

Pearson, J. "The effects of setting and gender on self-disclosure." *Group and Organization Studies,* 6 (1981), 334–340.

Pepitone, A., and G. Reichling. "Group cohesiveness and expression of hostility." *Human Relations,* 8 (1955), 327–337.

Piaget, J. *The Origins of Intelligence in Children.* New York: International Universities Press, 1952.

Piaget, J. *The Construction of Reality in the Child.* New York: Basic Books, 1954.

Pratt, L., N. Uhl, and E. Little. "Evaluation of games as a function of personality type." *Simulation and Games,* 11 (1980), 336–346.

Puckett, S. B. "When a worker gets AIDS." *Psychology Today,* 22, No. 1 (January 1988), 26–27.

Quattrone, G., and E. Jones. "The perception of variability within in-groups and out-groups: Implications for the law of small numbers." *Journal of Personality and Social Psychology,* 38 (1980), 141–152.

Reddy, D., A. Baum, R. Fleming, and J. Aiello. "Mediation of social density by coalition formation." *Journal of Applied Social Psychology,* 11 (1981), 529–537.

Reid, D. W., and E. E. Ware. "Affective style and impression formation: Reliability, validity, and some inconsistencies." *Journal of Personality,* 40, No. 3 (1972), 436–450.

Reis, H. T., L. Wheeler, N. Spiegel, M. H. Kernis, J. Nezlek, and M. Perri. Physical attractiveness in social interaction: II. Why does appearance affect social experiences? *Journal of Personality and Social Psychology,* 43 (1982), 979–996.

Rioch, M. "The work of Wilfred Bion on groups." In *Analysis of Groups,* Eds. G. S. Gibbard, J. J. Hartman, and R. D. Mann. San Francisco: Jossey-Bass, 1978.

Rogers, C., and F. J. Roethlisberger. "Barriers and gateways to communication." *Harvard Business Review,* 30, No. 4 (1952), 46.

Rosenthal, R., D. Archer, M. R. DiMatteo, J. H. Koivumaki, and P. L. Rogers. "The language without words." *Psychology Today* (September 1974), 64–68.

Rosenwein, R. E. "Determinants of low verbal activity rates in small groups: A study of the silent person." *Dissertation Abstracts International,* 31, No. 12B (June 1971), 7578–7579.

Schachter, S. "Deviation, rejection and communication." *Journal of Abnormal and Social Psychology,* 46 (1951), 190.

Schellenberg, J. A. "Group size as a factor in success of academic discussion groups." *Journal of Educational Psychology,* 33 (1959), 73–79.

Schriesheim, J. "The social context of leader–subordinate relations: An investigation of the effects of group cohesiveness." *Journal of Applied Psychology,* 65 (1980), 183–194.

Schultz, B. "Communicative correlates of perceived leaders in small groups." *Small Group Behavior,* 17, No. 1 (February 1986), 51–65.

Seaman, D. F. *Working Effectively with Task-Oriented Groups.* New York: McGraw-Hill, 1981, pp. 43–44.

Selman, R. *The Growth of Interpersonal Understanding: Developmental and Clinical Analyses.* New York: Academic Press, 1980.

Shaw, M. "Communication networks." In *Advances in Experimental Social Psychology.* Vol. I. Ed. L. Berkowitz. New York: Academic Press, 1964.

Shaw, M. *Group Dynamics: The Psychology of Small Group Behavior.* 3rd ed. New York: McGraw-Hill, 1981, pp. 134–135.

Slater, P. "Contrasting correlates of group size." *Sociometry,* 211 (1958), 129.

Slater, P. "Role differentiation in small groups." *American Sociological Review,* 20 (1955), 300–310.

Smith, M., R. Reinheimer, and A. Gabbard. "Crowding, task performance, and communicative interaction in youth and old age." *Human Communication Research,* 7 (1981), 259–272.

Snyder, C., and C. Newburg. "The Barnum effect in a group setting." *Journal of Personality Assessment,* 45 (1981), 622–629.

Snyder, M., E. D. Tanke, and E. Berscheid. "Social perception and interpersonal behavior: On the self-fulfilling nature of social stereotypes." *Journal of Personality and Social Psychology,* 35 (1977), 656–666.

Sommer, R. *Personal Space: The Behavioral Basis of Design.* Englewood Cliffs, N.J.: Prentice-Hall, 1969.

Sorensen, G., and J. C. McCroskey, "The prediction of interaction behavior in small groups: Zero history vs. intact groups." *Monographs,* 44, No. 1 (March 1977), 73–80.

Strodtback, F. et al. "Social status in jury deliberations." *American Sociological Review,* 22 (1957), 713–719.

Tannen, Deborah, "You Just Don't Understand: Women and Men in Conversation." New York: Ballantine, 1990.

Turquet, P. M. "Leadership: The individual and the group." In *Analysis of Groups,* edited by G. S. Gibbard, J. J. Hartman, and R. D. Mann. San Francisco: Jossey-Bass, 1978.

Varghese, R. "Ericksonian personality variables and interpersonal behavior in groups." *Small Group Behavior,* 13 (1982), 133–149.

Verplanck, W. "The control of the content of conversation." *Journal of Abnormal and Social Psychology,* 51 (1955), 668–676.

Wandersman, A., and G. Giamartino. "Community and individual difference characteristics as influences on initial participation." *American Journal of Community Psychology,* 8 (1980), 217–228.

Watson, R. I. "Psychology: A prescriptive science." *American Psychologist,* 22 (1967), 435–443.

Watzlawick, P. *How Real Is Real? Confusion, Disinformation, Communication: An Anecdotal Introduction to Communications Theory.* New York: Vintage Books, 1977.

Watzlawick, P. "Reality, reframing, and resistance in therapy." *Family Therapy News,* 13, No. 1 (January 1982), 3–9.

Watzlawick, P., J. H. Beavin, and D. D. Jackson. *Pragmatics of Human Communication: A Study of Interactional Patterns, Pathologies, and Paradoxes.* New York: Norton, 1967.

Wheeler, R., and F. L. Ryan. "Effects of cooperative and competitive classroom environments on the attitudes and achievement of elementary school students engaged in social studies inquiry activities." *Journal of Educational Psychology,* 65, No. 3 (1973), 402–407.

Wimer, S., and V. Derlega. "A test of Kelly's ANOVA model." *Small Group Behavior,* 14 (1983), 50–62.

Winthrop, H. "Focus on the human condition: Interpersonal and interactional processes as extinguishers of structured communication. *Journal of Human Relations,* 19, No. 3 (1971), 418–438.

Wolff, K. H. *The Sociology of Georg Simmel.* Glencoe, Ill.: Free Press, 1950.

Woollams, S., and M. Brown. *Transactional Analysis.* Dexter, Mich.: Huron Valley Institute Press, 1978, pp. 118–120.

Workie, Abaineh. "The relative productivity of cooperation and competition." *Journal of Social Psychology,* 92, No. 2 (1974), 225–230.

Wrench, D. "The perception of two-sided messages." *Human Relations,* 17 (1964), 227.

Yalom, I. D. *The Theory and Practice of Group Psychotherapy.* New York: Basic Books, 1970.

Zimet, C. N., and C. Schneider. "Effects of group size on interaction in small groups." *Journal of Social Psychology,* 77, No. 2 (1969), 177–187.

◆ 2 ◆

Membership

I n *Democracy in America* Alexis de Tocqueville wrote, "Americans of all ages, all stations in life, and all types of disposition are forever forming associations. There are not only commercial and industrial associations in which all take part, but others of a thousand different types: religious, moral, serious, futile, general or limited, enormous or diminutive. . . . As soon as several Americans have conceived a sentiment or an idea that they want to produce before the world, they seek each other out, and when found, they unite."

Researcher McGowan (1987) noted that today de Tocqueville's view still holds true. Tens of thousands of clubs, societies, and coalitions, both personal and professional, exist across the nation. Currently there is an explosion of self-help groups: groups organized to help members deal with grieving, illnesses, divorce, low self-esteem, being a woman, being a man, and numerous other concerns. McGowan believed that in looking at groups he was actually seeing the "American psyche." "We are what we join individually and as a people," he wrote.

Membership is central to our thinking about ourselves. At birth we have our initiation into our first group—our families. This membership in our family of origin teaches us who we are, how to relate to others, how to express emotion, and how to resolve problems. It is so powerful that it remains a part of us and a significant influence even after our parents have died and even after we have moved to another part of the country. Beginning with that first defining membership, most of us hold myriad memberships in the course of our lives.

What gets you into the groups you join? How much does it cost? Do you have a first-class ticket or steerage? Do you even have a ticket? Consider the following situation, in which an individual attempts to become a member of a group.

> Tony grew up as a minimally educated immigrant in a working-class neighborhood. He had worked since he was eleven, he knew, and maybe even before that. One summer he worked at Whitemarsh Country Club, and as he watched the cars, the clothes, the style, and the assuredness of the members, he had a dream. Someday he would be middle class, one of *them*. The dream was always there. Dues were $2,000 per year, and the initiation fee triple that. He saved, he cultivated two members who might sponsor him, he was accepted for membership—and he made it, at last!
>
> The first Sunday he dressed carefully in his expensive, casual-looking sport outfit. He entered, heart pounding. He moved into the card room. Several groups were playing, and as he walked in, a couple of people looked up and then returned to their cards in nonrecognition. He watched some of the players and listened to their talk (he knew none of the people about whom they were talking and nothing about the events they described). He moved to another table and watched. No one came near him, asked him a question, or invited him in. He walked over to the bar, where the bartender was engaged in conversation at the other end. In due time, he came over and asked Tony what he wanted to drink, and said not another word.

Tony looked at his drink, the bar, the card room, the easy ambiance the others had—the kidding, sharing, joking, talking about people they knew and a world he didn't. Suddenly—strange that it should be sudden—Tony realized that he didn't have a ticket to membership. On paper he might "belong" for twenty years, but he still wouldn't really *belong*.

Tony's experience is not unusual. We can move into small towns where families have lived for generations, and thirty years after moving in, still be treated as strangers, newcomers not to be fully trusted.

In a small group, the situation is the same. Each of us enters, not knowing and fearful. How will our appearance measure up? Our status? Our religion, social status, or ethnic origin? Our mode of speaking? What we say? What expectations do those who are already members have of us? And the question we ask internally is "Will I be accepted as a member of this group?" The uncertainty never goes away. Because membership is so important to our sense of ourselves, whenever we enter a new group the old feelings of hopefulness and anxiety return.

◆ Reader Activity

Some tickets to membership are behavior, wealth, appearance, education, religion, and style. What are the tickets of admission in the following groups?

In your classroom _____

In your club _____

Among your social peers _____

In your family _____

Where you work _____

Where don't you feel accepted that you would like to feel accepted? _____

_____

Why? _____

Do you really lack the ticket, or have you simply assumed you wouldn't be accepted? _____

Sometimes we assume we have the ticket, but we may be wrong. Women attending college assume that they are equal and belong. In 1982, Hall and Sandler conducted a study of classroom climate at 120 colleges and universities. They found considerable difference between the classroom climate for men and that for women.

> "Most faculty want to treat all students fairly and as individuals with particular talents and abilities. However, some faculty may

overtly—or, more often, *inadvertently*—treat men and women students differently in the classroom and in related situations. Subtle biases in the way teachers behave towards students may seem so "normal" that the particular behaviors which express them often go unnoticed. Nevertheless, these patterns, by which women students are either *singled out* or *ignored* because of their sex, may leave women students feeling less confident than their male classmates about their abilities and their place in the college community."

A replication of the study (Crawford 1986) was conducted with a random sample of 31 classes and 627 students at a state university. Students were administered a Student Perception Questionnaire that assessed the dynamics of student/professor interaction in the classroom—the "classroom climate." The most important and pervasive finding of the study was a consistently less positive classroom climate for women. Women reported that they received less praise and encouragement and more negative feedback from instructors, that they participated less than men in class discussions in spite of wanting to participate, and that male instructors were not likely to know them by name. ◆

◆ *Reader Activity*

On the basis of the Crawford study, Gershenfeld (1990) developed a number of role plays to help students and faculty become aware of the "classroom climate" and change it.

Is There a Place for Women?

In this role play, a male professor is lecturing on his subject (history or literature). All of the illustrations he cites involve men, and he uses the pronoun *he* generically.

One woman asks whether there were any women novelists or poets in that period (or if women had a role in history).

The professor becomes angry and calls her a "women's libber" or a "radical feminist." He says she is "like the Russians who claim they invented the telephone and every other system. You want us to rewrite history and include women. That's revisionist, and it's hardly the truth."

Imagine that you saw this role play, and consider your replies to the following questions:

1. What did you think of the professor? Was he well prepared? A good teacher? What was his attitude toward students?

2. What did you think of the student who asked the question? Was she angry? Militant?

3. Why did he say, "You must be a women's libber."

4. Should the student have asked the question?

5. The professor raises the issues of scholarship and integrity. Should he deliberately modify his presentation to include women? Would he be justified in feeling foolish (phony) for including women merely to appease female students?

6. What is the effect of using all male illustrations on the level of aspiration and achievement found in women?

7. What do you think will be the effect of what happened in this classroom? What did the look on the student's face, at the end, seem to say?

8. What could the other students in the class do to enlighten the professor? To be supportive of the woman who asked the question?   ◆

Women have thought they had the "ticket of admission," but do they? Is the environment the same for them as for men? Are their opportunities the same? Is communication the same? (Consider the recent Senate hearings on Clarence Thomas's confirmation to the Supreme Court and the charges of sexual harassment by Yale Law School graduate Anita Hill.)

Today, close attention is focused on gender as an issue in work relations and on college campuses.

Relationship of Groups and Membership

We are all members of groups. If we are asked to describe who we are, most of us include information about the groups to which we belong—for example, "I'm a student at Ohio State and a member of the Management Club, Phi Delta Sigma, and hopefully the varsity tennis team" (Tajfel, 1982).

Membership is the relationship between a person and a group of other people. In fact, concepts of membership and groups are so closely related that groups are often defined in terms of members. Here are some properties of groups:

Membership is defined. (It is known who is and who is not a member.)

Members think of themselves as composing a group. (They have a shared identity.)

There is a sense of shared purpose among members. (Members can give common reasons for being in the group.)

Members communicate differently with other members than with nonmembers. (You talk differently to someone with whom you share a common identity and purpose than with a stranger.)

Members have expectations for certain ways of behaving in various situations in which the group finds itself; members will approve or disapprove of another member on the basis of these expectations. (They let you know how you're coming across.) For example, group members always run the risk of group disapproval when they make independent decisions (Carpenter and Hollander, 1982).

There are leadership policies and roles. (Members need to coordinate efforts and maintain conditions for problem solving.)

A status system emerges among members. (There is a hierarchy of worth of the individual to the group; members know how much they are valued and for what.)

No two groups are alike on these dimensions.

Types of Memberships

Formal Membership

When we say membership in a group is clearly defined, we are talking about a boundary condition. Dues-paying, card-carrying people are formally recognized as members of a group and defined as falling within the boundary condition. They perceive themselves as part of the club. They have an image of the group and its purposes that is generally shared by the other members.

Aspiring Membership

Another kind of relationship is that of an *aspiring* member. For years, Tony had been an aspiring member, noting how members dressed and emulating them, trying to talk in their style, practicing golf and tennis as he was "getting ready." Aspiring members are not formally within the boundary of the group. Although they don't have a ticket of admission, they act as though they might get one, and they want to be prepared should the opportunity arise. Consider this example:

> His father had gone to Penn, his mother had gone to Penn, three cousins and an older brother had gone to Penn, and as long as he could remember, he had planned to go to Penn. The family had season tickets to the football games, he always went to Alumni Day, and he followed the news of Penn's progress in sports more avidly than his high school scores. His books had Penn covers, he regularly wore his Penn sweatshirt, and he already knew which were the best dorms on campus. He felt "his" school had made a serious mistake in cutting varsity ice hockey.

If asked, this boy would readily admit that he is a junior in high school, not a member of Penn's student body, but that Penn greatly influences his dress style, his activities, and his aspirations for the future. He frequently feels like a member when he walks around the campus in his sweatshirt with his brother, and psychologically he is a member. In terms of formal membership, however, he is outside the boundary, at least at the present.

Marginal Membership

In contrast, consider the following situation:

> A senior at Penn is being interviewed for jobs for next year. He doesn't attend the football games or get involved in sports scores. He disdains Penn book covers and sweatshirts—for that matter, any Penn emblems. He dashes for the train to New York immediately after his last class on Friday. He belongs, he is a member of the University of Pennsylvania student body, but neither the school nor its members influence him to any noticeable degree. He identifies much more with people making it in New York; college is already in the past. He is defined as a *marginal* member.

Membership might be thought of as falling within a circle. Those who are actively involved and influenced by members can be viewed as being in the center of the circle. Conceptually, they are centrally involved as high-status members. The marginal member may be seen as within the circle (the boundary) but close to the edge (for example, the Penn senior). The aspiring member is outside the circle. Full psychological membership occurs when a person is positively attracted to membership *and* is positively accepted as a member. When this happens, our individual differences are minimized, and we tend to see ourselves and other members as interchangeable (Turner, 1981). In our earlier illustration, Tony was not a full psychological member because he was not positively accepted as a member, despite his positive attraction toward membership. The others he enviously watched were full psychological members.

Being in a group does not influence a person's entire behavior. Membership may involve only a limited investment, such as membership in a country club, a union, a church group, or a neighborhood association. However, the degree to which people are involved affects both the functioning of the group and its significance for them as members.

◆ Reader Activity

Think of the groups with which you are involved.

In which are you a formal member? _____

In which are you a marginal member? _____

In which are you an aspiring member? _____

What do you understand about your "memberships"? _____   ◆

Membership in the Formal or Informal Organization

Within organizations there are often two memberships: membership in the formal organization, in which criteria are usually known, and membership in the informal organization. Criteria for membership in the latter are often unstated, and membership rules may support or contradict the rules of the formal organization.

> According to its organization chart, the director of a state hospital, the two assistant directors, the medical director, and the business manager make up the director's cabinet. The director invites the others to meet with him weekly for staff meetings. The meetings consist of routine reports of actions taken during the week and scheduling or treatment plans for the coming week.
>
> Only the stranger thinks that decisions are made in this group. Real decisions—on strategies for dealing with various inspection boards, on promotions, on personnel problems, on training, on budget—are made by a different group. This group, which cannot be located as an entity on the organization chart, consists of the director, the director of personnel, a psychiatrist, and a physician (internist). The meetings are held in the office of the director of personnel, usually on Tuesdays in the late afternoon. How did this informal group form? How did its members obtain their power? How does the cabinet feel about this "other" group?

In organizations there is usually some overlap between those members who have formal membership in the formal decision-making body and those in the informal group that wields decision-making power. Frequently, political maneuverings, power plays, and other covert actions take place within this informal organization.

Voluntary and Nonvoluntary Membership

In speaking of memberships, we are usually considering participation of a voluntary nature—for example, a consumer's union, a drama club, or a professional organization. But other groups—*nonvoluntary* groups—consist of members who have no choice regarding their affiliation. For example, many individuals who are arrested for driving while under the influence of alcohol are assigned to mandatory group psychotherapy treatment programs in mental health centers. Therapy groups composed of individuals who have voluntarily chosen to attend and nonvoluntary therapy groups for individuals convicted of driving while intoxicated differ sharply.

In the nonvoluntary therapy groups there is a higher level of distrust of the group leader and a lower level of personal self-disclosure and commitment to the group. Nonvoluntary group members usually put the blame for their drinking on their family, friends, or co-workers, so it's hard for them to see any value in being a group member. People who voluntarily join therapy groups, on the other hand, typically think they have a problem and see the group as having real value.

Family-of-origin households are also nonvoluntary groups. Children have no say in who will compose their families; they do not select their parents, siblings, grandparents, cousins, or even boarders. And where divorce and remarriage have occurred, household membership is even further complicated. Children may find themselves living in more than one place with step-parents, step-siblings, and half siblings. They may also have biological parents and siblings with whom they don't live. This illustrates how membership types can overlap; a child may be a formal member of a family household composed of siblings, but if he or she visits them only occasionally, she or he is a marginal member in terms of participation. The child is part of these families as a nonvoluntary member who has no say about the composition of the families.

There are myriad reasons aside from birth for membership in nonvoluntary groups. Examples include age and neighborhood (as in tenth-grade English class at West High), a court order (as in a drug group in a rehabilitation program or a prison group), and political turmoil (as in a group of Americans taking refuge in the American embassy prior to a hasty departure related to a government coup d'etat). Compulsory memberships may be nurturing and supporting, or they may be harsh and punitive, as in some prisons.

Why People Join Groups

There is little we can do about compulsory memberships. The real question is why people join the groups they choose to join.

Some people seem to have a stronger need to belong than others; they are joiners. Some evidence suggests that because women score higher than men on tests of sociability, they are more likely to be joiners. To date, no data have proven this hypothesis absolutely. A more predictable factor in motivating joining might simply be that joining is "good business." For example, some eleventh graders are notorious for hastily joining a broad spectrum of high school groups—a ploy for enhancing their images on college applications. In this context, if one membership is good, six are better, and ten with two presidencies will, applicants hope, gain the screening committees' favor. We see the same flurry of group joining among college seniors who will soon be job hunting.

This self-serving approach to group joining was a significant political issue in a mayoral campaign in a large eastern city. One candidate was a member of over forty organizations. The question was raised whether these memberships were for political show or represented personal interests. In the campaign, the candidate's detractors utilized the memberships to castigate him as a dilettante, and they derisively commented that his running for office was just another passing fancy to which he would not commit the time or priority necessary. His advocates used the same memberships to refer to him as a Renaissance Man, a man of broad interests and knowledge, whose familiarity with such a diversity of groups and organizations especially qualified him for the post.

Some people have more direct reasons for joining groups—for example, to meet people and share interests. Imagine a quiet, middle-aged woman not given to small talk, who used to find herself alone on weekends and holidays—until someone convinced her that collecting stamps was a good hobby, a way to learn and meet people.

Stamps changed her world. To be knowledgeable, she joined stamp groups—first local, then regional, then national, then international. Now there are meetings to go to, friends with whom to talk, conventions and programs on weekends, and international conventions to consider as sites for vacations.

There seem to be three major reasons why people join groups:

1. They like the task or activity of the group. O'Brien and Gross (1981) found that the more connected the individual to the task, the greater the potential for that member's participation in the group.

2. They like the people in the group. Being with people you like is not only a reason for joining social groups but also seems to be the major factor in determining whether a person finds a group experience significant. Stiles found that when a member of a group found a significant other in the group (someone special to him or her), the group experience was a positive one (1973). When we perceive a similarity, such as positive characteristics or attitudes, between us and other members, we are more attracted to that particular group (Compas, 1981; Royal and Golden, 1981).

Keyton (1988) offers further evidence that as we perceive positive characteristics that we value in others, the attraction to become a group member is generated and bonded. Looking for specific characteristics that engender attraction to a group, she questioned (in written responses) 248 college students enrolled in a basic communication course. Prior to the questioning, the students had participated in several acquaintance activities, after which each student signed up to be a member of a particular student group. In this self-selection process, the students' choice of which group to join was based on " . . . an individual's willingness to work, ability to get along with others, openness to communicate, and similarities of interest and personality" (Keyton, 1988). In this instance, the students joined groups that at least promised the completion of a task.

People may join an organization initially because of an interest in the task or activity, and then find they enjoy the people as well. Often, they will maintain their membership long after their task interests have waned in order to continue to participate in the pleasant personal associations. The reverse situation also occurs. A person may originally join an organization only to please a good friend who is already a member, but that person may later become genuinely interested in the project.

3. A third reason for joining a group is that although the group itself does not satisfy the person's needs directly, it is a *means* of satisfying his or her needs. Some early research illuminates the reason for group membership as a means to external satisfactions. Brief observations produce numerous examples. The fledgling lawyer joins an expensive, prestigious luncheon club because it is a good place to meet prospective clients. Funeral directors are well-known for their extensive memberships, because people feel better calling in "one of their own" rather than a stranger at times of sorrow. Other examples include joining a popular activity to make socially desirable contacts and joining the PTA as a newcomer in order to meet others about the same age in the neighborhood.

◆ Reader Activity

How about you? List three groups to which you belong.

1. _____

2. _____

3. _____

For each group, explain why you joined, and why you now continue as a member. What are your main reasons for joining a group?   ◆

◆ Individual Experiment

Choose a group that you belong to, such as a sports team, a club, a political organization, or a fraternity or sorority. Ask several members why they originally joined the group. What were they attracted by? Find out what they like about the group now. You may find that people joined the same group for different reasons, and that their original reasons for joining are not the reasons they continue being members. What did you learn from your interviews that helps you understand these individuals' behavior in the group?   ◆

The Back Experiments

Kurt Back (1951) was intrigued by the following questions: Does *why* a person joins affect the group? Does it make any difference whether the person joins because he or she is interested in the task, because she or he likes the other people, or because the group is a means to meeting his or her needs? If it makes a difference, how? What kind of difference?

Back designed a series of experiments to get answers to these questions. He arbitrarily paired subjects but told them that, on the basis of previous tests of personality and other measures, they had a special relationship to each other. He told some pairs that their personalities were similar and that they would have a great deal in common (the "liking" condition). He told other pairs that they had common goal interests in the project (the "interest in task" condition). In the third grouping, he told each of the partners that the other would be an important person to know and could be influential (the group as a "means to" condition).

The results indicated that why a person joins does make a difference in the functioning of the group. Those primarily attracted as friends interacted at a personal level—they had long conversations, were pleasant to each other, and expected to have an effect on each other. In those groups attracted primarily by the task, members wanted to complete it quickly and efficiently. They discussed only those matters they thought relevant to achieving their goals. In those groups attracted by potential prestige from membership, members acted cautiously, concentrated on their own actions, and in general were careful not to risk their status. When there were none of these bases of attraction, members of a pair acted independently and with little consideration of each other.

The Back experiments lead to the generalization that the nature of group life varies with different sources of attraction (Lang, 1977).

Multiple Memberships

As members, we bring our own interests, values, and personalities to groups. Each membership in a different group creates a unique mix of perceptions, communication patterns, and group values for the individual. Membership involves a give-and-take between the individual and the group, and because we are involved in numerous groups, the impact of multiple memberships is quite complex.

The multiplicity can carry with it a number of assets. There is the acquisition of transferable experiences based on skills obtained in different kinds of groups. For example, sitting on one university committee allows one to learn of the complicated procedures required to arrange for use of a room for a program—procedures that one thereafter finds simpler when making arrangements for another event for another committee. There is the possibility of expediting what one needs to do. For example, knowing someone from one context enables one to make a phone call to check for information or possibilities for action, rather than writing a formal letter. (The often cynical comment "It's not what you know, but whom you know" is based in large part on the access we have to persons in positions of power through knowing them in another context—another example of formal and informal organizations.) A group can often accomplish its objectives more rapidly because of those contacts. There have been a number of studies that point out that memberships on prestigious community boards are held by a small number of citizens of the community (Klein, 1968). When boards are made up of family or friends, the members find it easy to conduct business as personal relationships. Pervasive fears of acceptance have been dealt with previously and have been satisfactorily resolved. Multiple memberships can even be a source of creativity and innovation when a diverse group comes together to search for a mutually agreeable solution to a problem, as in the following example:

> After decades of redevelopment, residents of a large metropolitan area stayed away in droves from a restored neighborhood with housing and quaint shops. Both the business associations and the city were frantic for a gimmick to bring people (and business) to the redeveloped historic area. One idea was to bring together representatives of the mother churches in the area, and have them plan a heritage week or festival. Each church and synagogue had spawned others in the metropolitan area, and the heritage festival might be a method for bringing suburbanites in for the activities. It was hoped that the special events (dancing, cooking, demonstrations) would also induce the nonreligious populations to have a look.
>
> Each of the struggling groups was so delighted by the opportunity for publicity for their special quality, was so encouraged by the funding for a festival, and was so revitalized at the prospect of a heritage festival, which had been beyond their provincial dreams, that they vowed (individually and collectively) to produce a festival that would long be remembered. The first meeting of two representatives of each of the religious organizations began with most of them not knowing each other, but they were committed to the prospect of creating an event. Enthusiasm ran high. Diversity was the key to the excitement. Ideas tumbled over ideas as the initial meeting ran until two in the morning.
>
> The diversity of memberships enhanced what they had to offer, and the heritage festival committee viewed themselves as creating an historic experience.

Multiple memberships coexist in each of us. We may be members of a family, a neighborhood association, a religious organization, a PTA, a tennis group, a professional association, and a faculty journal club. Usually, these memberships coexist peacefully in a person's life. Sometimes, though, conflict arises.

Conflicts of Multiple Membership

Generally, people do not join organizations or groups with conflicting norms or values. A person is not likely to be a member of the National Association of Manufacturers and also a member of the Socialist party, nor of the Catholic church and the Abortion Rights Lobby, nor of the Ku Klux Klan and the Southern Baptist Christian Leadership. But sometimes membership conflicts are unavoidable. A businessperson who believes that survival and eventual success depend on taking advantage of every situation may be uncomfortable on Sundays in church when the minister preaches about ethical behavior. He or she may resolve this discomfort by not going to church, changing business practices, or compartmentalizing memberships—engaging on weekdays in one kind of behavior that is appropriate in the business world and on Sunday in another kind of behavior that is compatible with Christian ethics.

Some multiple memberships result in conflicts that present serious problems, where the dilemmas created cannot be resolved with satisfaction. Adolescence is a time when membership in the peer group often conflicts with membership in the family. Conflict between adolescent peers and the family has become so common that it warrants its own term, the "generation gap." Conflicts of multiple membership can also occur within large organizations in which an individual is often a member of several subgroups. Conflicts can emerge between subgroups, or one subgroup can be in conflict with the larger organization. In college you may be a member of the baseball team, which is planning its victory celebration in the dormitory, as well as a member of the student council, which is accountable to the university for maintaining dormitory policy and rules.

Yet another kind of multiple membership conflict is common when a committee is composed of representatives of subordinate groups. For example, say a new college moves into an old private-school campus in a quiet residential neighborhood. The college wants to add additional parking lots, arrange zoning variances for a new classroom building, and widen roads within the campus. It holds a community meeting to discuss the changes. Present at the meeting are a minister and two members of his congregation from the church across the street, who are eager for the college to have additional parking lots so the church might use them on Sundays. Representatives of the neighbors' association come to build good relations with the new college. They are hoping to sponsor joint community lectures and programs with the college and to convince the college to create and staff a child-care facility. A group of neighbors from across the street arrives *en masse* to oppose parking changes on the street. Other community residents representing various educational and philanthropic organizations come to express support for the new college, which they see as an asset to the community.

This mixed group will argue long and loud. It embodies many conflicting interests and perspectives. The conflicts create intrapersonal dilemmas as individuals vacillate between subordinate groups and the one being forged by the current discussion.

One group of researchers (Schwartz, Eberle, and Moscato, 1973) found that "individuals with high group awareness tended to be less successful in problem solving in an *ad hoc* problem solving environment than groups of individuals with low group awareness." That is, maintaining the links took energy from the present situation.

A group expends energy in activity on the task as well as on interpersonal relations. Devoting increased activity to one aspect (interpersonal relations) means less energy remains for the task. (For further discussion, see Chapter 10 on Bales, IPC.)

The resolution of conflicts generated by multiple membership is often attained at great personal cost and with much anxiety. Often these conflicts are resolved in accordance with the standards of the group that are most salient at the moment. Individuals may struggle to focus on the organization they represent at the meeting, which puts them at odds with the developing opinion. Thus property owners who have come to protect their streets from overparking might hear themselves cast as the "bad guys" as the college representatives marshal support for their plans.

◆ Reader Activity

On a separate sheet of paper, list ten groups in which you have membership. List at least one conflict each membership can produce for another membership.
    How do you resolve these differences?   ◆

◆ Individual Experiment

Talk with an adolescent about his or her group of friends. Find out what behavior, values, and attitudes are held in common by the group. Do they all dress alike? Listen to the same music? Go to the same places? Ask the young person what his or her parents expect of him or her at home. If you don't know any adolescents, write down a list from your own experiences when you were that age. Chances are you will see some disparities between the membership demands of these two important reference groups.   ◆

Reference Groups

Of the many groups to which people belong, which are most important to them? Which influence how they typically feel about things? To which do their attitudes most closely relate? Those groups an individual selects as his or her *reference groups* are the ones whose influence he or she is willing to accept. Consider the following illustration:

A handsome African–American college student, well dressed and with a styled haircut, has pledged for fifteen weeks prior to admission to a prestigious African–American national fraternity. The final ordeal, which determines whether he is serious in desiring membership, requires that he submit to having his head shaved, as a reminder of what slaves endured. There are no exceptions.

Reference groups have been described as serving two distinct functions. An individual uses such a group (1) to compare himself or herself in making judgments and evaluations and (2) to set the norms to which he or she conforms. Both of these functions may be served by the same group. People's reference groups may greatly influence their attitudes toward themselves and may affect their relationships with other groups. If the student in the foregoing example chooses to have his head shaved in order to join the fraternity, he is acknowledging the comparison function of the fraternity as a reference group. If he joins the fraternity and over time conforms to its values and standards of behavior, he is responding to the normative function of the fraternity as a reference group.

Interestingly, studies show that people with strong ties to a reference group often judge their personal situations to be satisfactory but the group's general situation to be *un*satisfactory. That is, when a group is compared to the self (rather than the self to the group), it is the *group* that suffers by comparison with respect to overall well-being. In this way, reference groups have a significant impact on the shaping of social attitudes (Crosby and Clayton, 1986).

The Actual Group

In a given group, only some people function as referents, those whom individuals attempt to influence and who in turn influence them. Each member decides who "makes sense," who seems to be in touch with reality as the member sees it, and with whom he or she can identify. These few—perhaps only eight to ten in a group of thirty (and even their composition may change over time)—represent the effective, or actual, group for that person. It is they who influence him or her, and it is they to whom he or she can relate.

The Group We Represent

There are two levels of reference groups in this concept. At one level are the groups that appoint or elect a member to represent them in another group. A faculty member is appointed by his or her department to represent that department on the university senate; representatives of neighborhoods are elected to sit on the community mental health advisory board; condominium owners select their representatives to the resident council. Here, the group the person represents is thought of as "his" or "her" group, which he or she must speak for, fight for, and defend. In defending his or her group, the representative believes or comes to believe that the group's approach and perspective are his or her own. The representative strives for goals that favor his or her group—these are his or her vested interests. A member relates to the group he or she represents, and it becomes a reference group.

At another level are the groups a member represents when he or she is not officially designated to do so. For example, in a classroom discussion belittling the value of fraternities, a member may feel compelled to enter the discussion in heated terms. Some say that when people defend their vested interests almost blindly, it is because these groups are important reference groups in their lives. Another theory holds that the defense occurs when people are anxious about their membership in that group; they defend the group to assure themselves that they do belong and that belonging is indeed worthwhile.

In both cases, people react to the actual group as well as to the group they represent (formally or subjectively). The group they represent influences their behavior.

Who are those subjective groups that serve as our reference groups beyond those we formally represent? They are all those past and present groups of which we have been a part. We "rubberband" or flash back to them constantly. All the groups we belonged to in our past are present within us. Some are readily identifiable in color, sex, language, and dress, and others are revealed as a discussion or topic collides and triggers one of those other groups. These groups may be classified as abstracted groups, hangover groups, and fantasied groups.

The Abstracted Group

Abstracted groups are the groups that greatly influenced us when we still accepted our parents', teachers', leaders', and employers' words unquestioningly. For example, our experience might have left us with the notions that lenient and materially giving parents are caring and sensitive to their children's needs; that stern, "no-nonsense" teachers accomplish the most in a classroom; that verbal, articulate people tend to be charismatic leaders; and that strict, authoritarian employers are inclined to be very efficient. These are concepts that we have *abstracted* from past experiences and that greatly influence our current behavior in groups.

We run into difficulties, however, when stereotypic truths, as abstracted from our mostly forgotten models, come into conflict with the actual values of a group we are in. For instance, a senior group member may reactivate the notion of the caring and sensitive parent in a younger group member. But when that "parent" figure displays behavior that is obnoxious and callous, the younger member might feel an urgent need to vent emotions that temporarily distract and derail the group's goal. Or a member might have an abstracted sense of leadership that sharply contrasts with the group's true leader, thus generating conflict that could actually destroy the group.

When values abstracted from these forgotten groups come into conflict with the values of the current group, re-examination is necessary: How was the situation then similar to the situation at present? How is the situation now different from that earlier one? What were the objectives then? What are they now? How was the group composed then? Who is in it now?

The Hangover Group

Unresolved membership anxieties and problems in important reference groups may be continuously dealt with in other groups. For example, the child who was the "little brother" or "little sister" in the family—the last to be heard, the most frequently disregarded, the one given almost no responsibility—may in other groups strive continually for leadership as proof of his or her competence. Or, conversely, that person may be very antileadership, rebelling against any authority in retaliation for all the times he or she could not "talk back" as a child.

Some feel that many of the problems of leadership are not legitimate problems of the actual group but are rather *hangovers* from previous groups—for example, unresolved family conflicts. A hangover group can influence the behavior of members consciously or unconsciously.

The Fantasied Group

This is the kind of group that may give a person the emotional support that he or she definitely needs but is not receiving in the present actual group.

A person who has read some legal materials on an issue may fantasize himself or herself presenting the data not as a lay member to fellow members but logically and convincingly to a panel of three judges. Consultants who may know nothing about an organization sometimes come in and fantasize that they are the ultimate authorities on any problems of organization, because they have taught organizational theory in their classes for years. With just a few minutes of background, they handle a serious problem with the aplomb of a professor answering a student question. Other consultants fantasize themselves speaking with graduate students rather than with clients; they theorize or discuss situations in ivory-tower terms rather than coming to grips with the practical realities of the situation.

When people do not accept the actual group and address their behavior to it, they will use some other group or mixture of groups, or even a constructed group, to meet their needs for emotional support. Some people, when gently reminded or prodded, may recognize that they are indeed addressing their behavior to groups other than the actual persons present; to others these groups remain hidden in their subconscious.

In summary, it is evident that there are actual groups that influence us and to which we address our behavior. However, when there is a perplexing situation in the actual group, it is as though we are caught in the web of overlapping memberships. Which membership (real, past, abstracted, fantasied) should guide our behavior? Which one should we use in this instance? Memberships that overlap for us at a particular time are the ones that have special salience for us in that situation. Those cues in the present situation that remind us of another situation and affect our response give us clues about membership roles in which we are anxious.

It even seems that there is a hierarchy of reference groups, because whenever a decision is reached in an overlapping or conflicted membership situation, membership in some groups is enhanced at the expense of membership in others.

Factors Increasing Attractiveness of Membership

The lifeblood of a group is its members; they are the resources through which goals are accomplished. The satisfaction of those members, the degree to which they feel accepted, and the degree to which they want to return are critical to the survival of the group. Accordingly, one of the objectives of a group is to create cohesiveness. Cohesion is the attraction the group holds for its members; the greater the attractiveness, the higher the cohesion.

One variable that increases the members' attraction to a group is a correlation between individual goals and group goals. In a study that examined these factors, Wright and Duncan (1986) found that "attraction to group and group cohesiveness were both related to individual outcome." Thus, the conformity of the group goals with individual members' goals increases the group's attractiveness and cohesiveness.

Excerpts from a graduate student's paper on her experience in a group may serve as an illustration of the growth of cohesiveness in a group.

> My first encounter with the group made me feel uncomfortable. I realized that I was older than most of the group members, and felt that I did not have too much in common with them. Because of my previous life experiences, I felt I had already dealt with conflict, decision making, and not being part of the "in group" more frequently than most of my peers in the class. I kept in mind, first and foremost, my purpose for being in the group—it was to successfully complete the course requirement of being in a group, nothing else. . . .
>
> My relationship with the group grew from one of skepticism in the beginning to total involvement with the group in a very short time. The skepticism was the result of fear of the unknown. Was I going to be accepted by my peers in the group? Quite early in our group relations it became apparent to me that most of the group had the same fears. It also became apparent quite early that the people in the group were warm, friendly people, although initially they didn't look that way. I found some group members more appealing to me than others, but I can say with pride that I know each member and can work with them. I also believe each of us would also say it—not one person in our group was

absent all term, and several times when class ended we were the last to leave. Who would think that I would ever say I love that group? It has been one of the best experiences in my life.

Generally, we know that the attractiveness of a group can be increased if members (or potential members) are aware that they can fulfill their needs by belonging to that group. Because it is difficult to change the members' needs, the more feasible approach is to emphasize the properties that meet members' needs or the gains to be derived from belonging. Let's look at some of the properties that increase group attractiveness.

Prestige

The more prestige a person has within a group, or the more that appears to be obtainable, the more he or she will be attracted to the group (Aronson and Linder, 1965; Kelley, 1951). People who are placed in a position of authority over others are more attracted to the group than those low in authority, and they show more ingroup favoritism (Vleeming, 1983). This is especially true of those in authority who expect to remain in that position. For example, the group or organization will be attractive to a principal who is appointed "for life," to army officers who may be promoted but are rarely demoted, or to chief executives who are appointed and remain in that position until a bigger executive position is available.

However, those in a position of high authority who may be demoted to one of low authority are attracted to a lesser degree. Those of low authority who expect to remain in that position are not attracted to the group. The shipping clerk, the member of the telephone squad, and the "envelope licker" are not attracted. Yet those of low authority who envision being moved up can also find the group attractive—for example, telephone squad members who see themselves as potential officers or committee chairpersons.

Imagine a questionnaire being passed around to a group in which members are asked to rank members on importance to the group. Suppose also that a questionnaire is distributed in which each member is asked how attracted he or she is to the group, on a scale from 0 (not attracted) to 10 (highly attracted). It is likely that when the data are tabulated and analyzed, the results will indicate that those seen as most valued or most important in the group will be those who are most attracted to it. It follows that when we feel our ideas are listened to and acted upon, we are more attracted to the group.

Group Climate

The more group members perceive other members as being committed to the group and compatible with one another, the more attractive the group will be (Piper, 1983; Spears, Lea, and Lee, 1990). A cooperative relationship is more attractive than one that is competitive (Deutsch, 1959, 1967). If a group works together as a team to develop a product (or outcome), and if it will be evaluated on the basis of a team effort, the members will be more friendly toward one another than in a competitive situation. However, when members are rated on the basis of individual performance, there are fewer interpersonal relationships, more withholding of information or failure to volunteer information, and fewer influence attempts.

The Deutsch cooperation studies are classic; more recently, Worchel (Worchel, Andreoli, and Folger, 1977) directly tested the hypothesis that cooperation leads to increased attractiveness of members for the group. The findings were significant for understanding cohesiveness. Among the groups whose members competed with each other, those who were successful found the group more attractive, and those who failed reported decreased attraction to the group. For groups that cooperated, both success and failure increased intergroup attraction. Rosenfield, Stephan, and Lucker (1981) also looked at the attractiveness of cooperative and competitive groups. They found that competent group members are more valued in cooperative situations because they increase the group's chances for success. Incompetent group members fared better in competitive groups where their performance had little effect on others' success.

Degree of Interaction Among Members

Increased interaction among members may increase the attractiveness of the group (Good, 1971; Homans, 1950). Participating in the give-and-take with members, getting to know some of the others, making some good friends—these by-products of membership make the group more attractive. Being a member increases the contact with people who are liked, offers an opportunity to know them better, and allows for real chances for clarification in influencing and being influenced.

Looking at the effectiveness of training psychotherapists in a group setting, Aronson (1990) reported that creative insights into the psychoanalytic process appear more often because of the presence of a leader *plus* the group members. What this means is that the leader alone doesn't effect insights. Rather, members of the group expressing their analysis of the experience promote insights, which generate more understanding. In turn, this more in-depth understanding of the psychoanalytic process raises the level of the interaction between group members and the leader, thus increasing the attraction to the group for its benefits: the fuller understanding of the psychoanalytic process.

Davis (1984) found that the geographic distance a member had to travel to meetings had no significant effect on attraction to the group but that attraction was high toward a similar-attitude group and low toward a dissimilar-attitude group. Further, Brown (1985) found that members were most likely to participate in an organization they considered compatible with themselves. And he stressed that an organization must embody participatory democratic principles if it is to obtain and sustain members' participation.

Although pleasing interaction increases attractiveness of membership, if the interaction is unpleasant (if members disregard each other or bore each other, or if there are members who are considered repulsive), attraction to membership will be decreased (Amir, 1969; Aronson, 1970; Festinger, 1957).

Members' ethnicity also influences people's attraction to a group. Examining relationships between black and white sixth graders in intergroup cooperation, Johnson and Johnson (1985) reported that there was more cross-ethnic social interaction where black and white groups cooperated than in groups where they competed with each other. Further, they found that minority subjects responded more positively to cooperative group experiences and showed more satisfaction in their group's work than did majority subjects.

Size

As most of us have experienced, the size of a group greatly influences our attraction to it. Smaller groups are likely to be more attractive than large ones (Wicker, 1969). In a small group it is easier to get to know the other members, to discover similar interests, to share dedication to the cause, and to have a sense of being a significant participant in the group. As the group increases in membership there is a corresponding heterogeneity of interests. Members' feelings toward each other become less personal, concern with the "cause" is often less intense, and there is a reduction in the degree of individual participation, intimacy, and involvement (Tsouderos, 1955).

Relationship with Other Groups

Relationships with other groups are also a factor in attractiveness. Groups are more attractive if their position is improved with respect to other groups. A group that had been all but disregarded in its efforts to create parent awareness of alienated adolescents suddenly became valued when the governor invited the group to participate with him at a televised news conference. Not only was the group deemed more prestigious, but membership also increased in attractiveness for the individual members.

Success

The maxim that nothing succeeds like success applies to groups also. People are more inclined to join groups or continue as members in groups that are successful.

When a sports team, in competition with other teams, wins more games, membership on that team is more attractive. One need only briefly watch the pandemonium of the winning team after a close game to understand what winning does to enhance membership. And after a big game, the hugging, champagne dousing, embracing, and dancing are all signs of being part of winning teams.

It isn't only sports teams that enjoy winning. A charity group whose fundraising concert was successful and who raised even more money than anticipated has little difficulty inspiring its members to "do even better" next year. They are able to recount how they were a terrific team who pulled it off against great odds. As they congratulate each other on how well they did and on what each contributed to the success, they decide again that they will continue to work for the organization; now the cause is even more important than before.

Because they have been successful, they agree that they are winners. They then become more satisfied with other members and with the task; they know they have the resources in members and the skills to be successful—and consequently they are even more attracted to the group (Meir, Keinan, and Segal, 1986).

Even if, in an experimental condition, members are told that their unit is *potentially* successful, the group takes on new prestige and members are more attracted to it.

It is interesting that if a person desires membership and it is difficult to obtain, he or she will value the membership more than if it were easy (Aronson and Mills, 1959). As if to reduce an internal dissonance, he or she says, "This membership had to be worth it for me to go through such an ordeal—of course it's worth it— it's a great group—I'm lucky to be a member" (Festinger, 1957).

There is no evidence, however, that the same situation prevails if a person does not desire membership. Then the difficulty of the ordeal simply becomes another reason why the membership is unattractive.

Fear and Stress

Under conditions in which subjects (in experimental conditions) were in a situation of fear, they preferred to be with others, and the opportunity to be with others rather than alone increased the attractiveness of the group. When it was appropriate, subjects were more likely to choose to be with the others who were also anxious (or fearful) about the same thing, thus providing an opportunity for "social comparison" of their feelings (Buck and Parke, 1972; Dutton and Aron, 1974; Morris, 1976; Smith, Smythe, and Lien, 1972).

Children in border settlements in Israel report rushing to the bomb shelters at the first sound of attack and being comforted by seeing the familiar faces of adults and other children at the entrance. They already felt less frightened; being with the others felt good. Londoners report similar experiences in the underground during the bombings of World War II.

And it isn't just wars and bombings. The research evidence indicates that subjects aroused by hunger, sexual stimuli, negative evaluations, or danger seek out others to be with.

Sime (1983) had a rare opportunity to investigate the way people affiliate with each other in a crisis. He studied people fleeing a large public building that was on fire. On the basis of his observations, he predicted that in a situation of potential danger, individuals will not only be concerned with their safety but will also be motivated to make contact with group members with whom they have some psychological ties. In the burning building, family members sought each other and tried to adopt an optimal strategy for group survival. This finding contrasts with the panic model, which assumes that individuals in danger are concerned with self-preservation alone and will compete with each other for limited exits.

◆ *Individual Experiment*

Choose a group that you belong to and ask another member the following questions in order to determine his or her level of attraction to the group. Do you find group members cooperative or competitive? Do you feel you have something in common with other group members? Do you feel that you get ample opportunity to say what you think in the group and that others listen to you? Do you feel valued by the group? Are group members generally open and trusting with each other? Is the group successful? These questions cover the general factors that make a group attractive to its members. If you receive positive replies to these questions, you can surmise that the individual likes and is attracted to the group.   ◆

Factors Decreasing Attractiveness of Membership

When does a group become less cohesive? When is membership less attractive so that people prefer to leave? Members will leave when the reasons for their initial attraction no longer exist (the people they joined to be with have left); when their own needs or satisfactions are reduced (a member of the scout parents committee when their child leaves scouts); or when the group becomes less suitable as a means for satisfying existing needs (a young lawyer joins a political party committee and later is appointed to the district attorney's staff; she resigns from the party committee because such membership is frowned on). Members may also leave when the group acquires unpleasant properties, such as a diminished reputation, constant fighting among members, or an activist stand with which they disagree.

Sometimes membership changes brought on by dissatisfaction with the group can actually transform the organization. The American Psychological Association, the professional association for psychologists in the United States, serves as a good example. Until about 1973, the APA was dominated by "academics," those psychologists who taught at universities; practitioners and clinicians were made to feel like second-class members. Many psychologists in clinical practice even wondered why they should bother belonging to the APA, inasmuch as it did not meet their needs. But since 1973, as the number of psychologists grew but the number of university openings diminished, practitioners came to make up the majority of the APA membership. Nowadays, the academics still want the focus of the professional association to be on research and teaching. But the practitioners want the association to deal with their problems: malpractice insurance, state licensing, and building client populations.

Mangan reported in 1987 that academic- and research-oriented psychologists were dropping out of the American Psychological Association in increasing numbers, feeling that the group no longer served their interests. Membership in the APA was then at an all-time high, but old-time members mumbled that they didn't recognize the organization anymore, so drastically had it changed. Much effort has been spent drafting a reorganization proposal to maintain both memberships.

It is possible to be less and less attracted to the group but still to remain in it. A group can retain its members when attraction is at the zero or near-zero level. In such situations, the group is inactive and has little influence over its members; the members in turn provide little internal support for each other or the organization. Members in this category—in conceptual terms, borderline members—are pushed over (and out) when the precarious balance is disturbed, such as when the meeting time is changed or dues are raised even a small amount.

Research findings indicate that groups can lose their attractiveness for several reasons:

1. A group disagrees on how to solve a group problem. Some will walk away from the discussion or not attend the meetings at which such a problem is on the agenda; others withdraw by working on private problems or become "turned off." Members may sense real personal frustration in such instances, and the group is viewed as a source for precipitating feelings of personal inadequacy and impotency.

2. If the group makes unreasonable or excessive demands on people, or if people feel inadequate in the group situation, the group is less attractive and they will leave (Horowitz et al., 1953). If people are assigned a job that is too difficult for them (such as arranging a program) or if people feel inadequate in the group situation (which requires their giving verbal reports at meetings when they feel inadequate as speakers), the group will be less attractive and they will leave, often without stating or being fully aware of their reasons.

3. Groups that have members who are too dominating or who exhibit other unpleasant behaviors reduce the attractiveness of the group.

4. Staff conferences in which there is a high degree of self-oriented behavior are viewed as less attractive to the staff (Fouriezos, Hutt, and Geutzkow, 1950). Members who dominate the discussion, and thus severely limit the opportunities for participation by others, reduce attractiveness.

5. Some memberships may limit the satisfactions a person can receive from activities outside the group. For example, women in some religious groups

are not permitted to drink, dance, wear make-up, or wear short skirts. Membership in such groups clearly limits satisfactions that might be derived from going to dances or being stylish. Police officers on rotating weekly shifts and nurses on night duty are also limited in their outside activities.

6. Negative evaluation of membership in a group by people outside the group (which gives the group low status) also reduces attractiveness of the group. Being a member of the school discipline committee is not a sought-after appointment because of the reactions of peers to members of such committees.

7. Competition among groups also reduces attractiveness unless people have reason to believe they will be with the "winners."

8. People will leave one group to join another if the second is better able to meet their needs or if they have limited time for participation. For example, members may belong to an organization and then move to another part of the same city. They may join a branch of the organization closer to their new home. Or they may instead join a similar, but different, organization because they are moving and planning new relationships.

9. If individuals are "scapegoated" (unjustly blamed for negative events), they come to view those who attribute responsibility for failure to them less favorably. They come to see those members as less competent and less cooperative. They identify less with the group and come to feel like outsiders. This psychological process soon leads to the actual process of separation (Shaw and Breed, 1970).

10. If members in an organization are faced with stringent demands from their superiors, the members have a tendency either to seek or to establish a secondary membership within the organization's underlife. Members retreat to a symbolic "crawlspace" within the group at large (Ingram, 1986). Further, organizations that tend to lump all participants together fail to offer members enough opportunities to establish separate identities within this necessary crawlspace. Thus, both strict leadership and the failure to provide opportunities for members to participate in an institutional underlife reduce group attractiveness.

Attractiveness of Membership and Group Success

What difference does cohesiveness make? How a group functions depends on how attractive it is to its members. This is reflected in the energy members expend on reaching their goal, how easily they attain it, and how satisfying the outcome will be. There is evidence to suggest people who are attracted to membership are more likely to accept the responsibilities of membership (Dion, Miller, and Magnan, 1970). Cohesive groups that value membership status are especially productive if they are also motivated to do the task well (Hall, 1971; Landers and Crum, 1971). However, the cultural context of a group influences the members' view of its tasks. For example, Zander (1983) observed that the "Japanese work for their group's good, while Americans work for their personal good." Thus an American might be drawn to a group that provides help or autonomy for the individual, whereas a Japanese person might be drawn to the group whose purpose is to provide help and autonomy for the group (Zander, 1983). Further, working for a group goal seems to be such a strong driving force in Japanese culture that group members will even deviate from majority behavior when such deviant behavior promotes a desired group outcome (Kouhara, 1990).

If the group is attractive, members are more open to interpersonal influence. It is especially worthy of note that attracted members will change their minds more often to take the view of fellow members.

In conclusion, increased understanding of membership factors can help us be more aware of them in groups and can thereby increase our opportunities and abilities to be more effective. It also enhances the possibilities for success of the groups with which we are concerned.

◆ ◆ EXERCISE 1

An Experience in Building Membership

Objectives

- To build a group beginning with a dyad
- To experience the dynamics of membership building
- To understand that sharing information and our own identities is an effective way to build a group and boost commitment to it

Rationale

Typically we enter groups alone, feeling anxious about being newcomers. Pairing with someone we don't know reduces our sense of isolation and breaks up existing subgroups.

Action

(Time: 30 min.) The facilitator explains that groups will be working to solve some tasks. Then he or she asks each member to "pair with someone you don't know."

The dyads are instructed to discuss with each other the following questions, which are listed on the board:

What is your name?

What is one thing that keeps you busy?

What is one thing you are enjoying about your life?

What is one thing you are proud of in yourself?

What are two groups you identify with (gender, class, race, etc.)?

They begin by focusing on one person. At the end of fifteen minutes, the facilitator announces time, and the other person becomes the focus of attention. At the end of one-half hour, the facilitator

- asks each dyad to join two other pairs to become a group of six.
- asks one member of each pair to introduce his or her partner, adding two points about the person learned during the previous conversation.

After they are introduced in this way, the partners can comment on what was said. Then they in turn introduce their partners, making points they learned in the preceding conversation.

The facilitator asks the entire group, "What do you want from this workshop, or experience?" and allows ten minutes for discussion of objectives.

Discussion

The facilitator asks the dyads,

Why did the exercise begin with the discussion questions?

How do you feel about your group?

After discussing these questions, the dyads report on their answers.

Variation

This exercise can be done in triads as well as dyads.

◆ ◆ EXERCISE 2

Multiple Memberships: Representative Group-Member Role

Objectives

- To experience the conflicts of multiple memberships
- To understand the conflicts of representative memberships in a familiar community situation

Setting

A table with five chairs is placed in the center of the room. The facilitator asks for five volunteers to play various roles in a discussion of whether a high school should teach about AIDS and make condoms available to students in the high school nurse's office. The roles assigned are:

A father, representing the PTA

A mother, representing a church

A middle-aged lawyer, representing a community action group

The principal of the high school, representing the faculty

The executive director, representing the Mental Health Association

Situation

The setting is a suburban community in the Midwest; there are 30,000 inhabitants. The community is conservative and incomes are above the national median. The facilitator describes the situation as follows:

> An anonymous benefactor feels there is a need for education on AIDS and for the protection of the young people in this community. Such education has never been part of the budget, but the benefactor will donate $25,000, which would be sufficient for an excellent program. The community will design the high school program. The donor would like to see such a program instituted this year, but there is a stipulation that we must let him know our decision at the end of the month. If we agree to the program, we can have the funds immediately. If not, the benefactor has made plans to use the funds for a project in another community.
>
> During the past month we have brought the situation to the attention of groups within the community. Opinion has been divided. Your groups are the major ones involved. We must make our decision promptly because today is the last of the month. You have been appointed by your groups to help us arrive at the final decision; the other groups will abide by your wishes.
>
> The following developments have taken place during the month: the PTA has not made a commitment as a result of disagreement within the organization; the church has expressed opposition; the community action group's meeting was unfortunately canceled; the faculty want to represent the wishes of the whole community although they themselves feel it is a desirable project and a special opportunity; the Mental Health Association strongly supports the project and might have been influential in finding the benefactor.

The role players are told to think about their roles and how they will act in the situation as representatives of their organizations. If possible, each player should have a "coach" with whom he or she can practice his or her role. The coach may help the individual to magnify certain aspects or modify others. The coaches should take about five minutes with the role players.

The facilitator announces, "The meeting will begin with the representative of the Mental Health Association as chairperson."

Action

The meeting begins. Nonparticipants watch the role playing, the discussion, and the decision.

Discussion

To the nonparticipants:

> At the beginning, how accurately did the representatives speak for their organizations?
>
> Who deviated from his or her organization's position? How?
>
> What conflicts in membership did you see? For whom were they greater?
>
> Who remained unchanged? How could you interpret this? Observers might be asked to look for egocentric behaviors (such as deflating others, sarcasm, and building up of self), for defensive replies, and for withdrawing or nonparticipating behaviors.

To the role players:

> What conflicts did you feel? When?
>
> What influenced your decision?

◆ ◆ EXERCISE 3

Conflicting Memberships

Multiple memberships are situations in which one person has membership in a number of groups simultaneously. These may or may not be in conflict. In conflicting memberships or conflicting roles, there is conflict within the person as to which membership or role should determine his or her behavior at that moment.

The conflicting memberships can be experienced readily in a number of situations. Take, for example, the family situation wherein a woman plays the dual role of wife and mother.

Setting

The facilitator asks for volunteers to be a family—a mother, father, oldest child, middle child, youngest child. The facilitator assigns each volunteer a role and explains the situation. A number of situations will be presented. For example, one situation might begin with the wife/mother saying: "My husband and children pull at me constantly. My husband wants me to go downtown with him, and my children want me to be at home when they come out of school." (The issue of conflicting memberships—her two roles—is evident.)

The situation is staged with a woman in the center with her arms stretched out at shoulder height. On one side the husband will be pulling her in his direction. On the other side the children will be lined up pulling in their direction. The youngest child might be pulling the mother's knees or the bottom of her skirt. The middle child might be pushing the youngest away and pulling the mother at the waist; the oldest might be pulling the mother's shoulder or arm in his or her direction. Once the members of the family know their roles, the facilitator says, "Act out." The father pulls and entreats, "Come on, honey." The youngest pulls and may say, "I want my mommy." The middle one may pull with determination, silently. The oldest may plead, "Please, listen to me." Each is pulling, and the mother is feeling pulled and swayed and harassed and inadequate. She may simply be moaning, or she may say, "Stop pulling so hard, you're hurting me. Please stop, I feel that no matter what I do I'm being pulled apart. I can't please everyone." (In acting out the situation, participants are encouraged to actually pull and to indicate their feelings nonverbally or with just a few words.) After a few moments of this, the facilitator calls, "Stop." All relax their holds.

Discussion

Then the family is asked several questions. How did it feel? How did you like your role? What were your relationships with the other members of your family?
Some questions are also put to the audience:

> What did you notice?
>
> How did the central person feel?
>
> What behaviors might have helped reduce the conflicts?
>
> What could have been done so that members could be accepted or respected?

There are other possibilities for acting out role conflict in a family situation.

The husband might say, "My wife, my children are strangling me—I can't move, they're clutching me so tightly. I want to get ahead, but how can I if I have to be home every night for dinner at six, if I have to spend every free minute playing with the children?"

One of the children might say, "I'm being pulled in all directions—my parents want me to be one way, my boyfriend wants me to go another way, and my best friend wants me to do other things."

After several possibilities are decided on, the family may act out these new situations and observe the effects. Then both actors and audience discuss the same questions posed the first time.

◆ ◆ *EXERCISE 4*

Reference Groups: "Who Am I?"

Objectives

- ■ To understand reference groups
- ■ To understand priorities within reference groups
- ■ To recognize that we view reference groups subjectively

Materials

"Who Am I?" sheets

Setting

The group is divided into groups of three to five.

Action

"Who Am I?" sheets are distributed to each member. The facilitator asks each person to read and follow the instructions.

"WHO AM I?"

We can all describe ourselves in many ways. How would you describe yourself?
   Write ten different answers to the question "Who Am I?" in the space provided below.[1]

Who Am I?

1.	
2.	
3.	
4.	
5.	
6.	
7.	
8.	
9.	
10.	

1. This exercise is adapted from an exercise in the Life Planning Workshop developed by Herbert Shepard of Yale University.

You may choose to answer, for example, in terms of the roles and responsibilities you have in life or in terms of groups you belong to and beliefs you hold. Try to list those things that are really important to your sense of yourself—things that, if you lost them, would make a radical difference in your identity and the meaning of life for you.

Silent, individual reflection is necessary while you perform this task. Continue by following the instructions in the Identity Review.

Identity Review

Consider each item in your "Who Am I?" list separately. Try to imagine how it would be if that item no longer applied to you. (For example, if "husband" or "wife" is one of the items, what would the end of your marriage mean to you? How would you feel? What would you do? What would your life be like?) After reviewing each item in this way, rank the items in the list by putting a number in the box to the right of each item. Put 1 beside the item that is most essential to your sense of yourself and whose loss would require the greatest adjustment. Put 10 beside the item that is least essential to your sense of yourself. Rank all items in this way; do not give any items a tying rank. Do not rank items in accordance with how much you like them but only in accordance with how great the adjustment would be if you lost them. Some aspects of yourself that you dislike might be very hard to give up!

Sharing

Group members share the experiences in these exercises with the rest of the group. No members should be forced to share their lists, and no one *can* be forced to share all their thoughts and feelings, but participants should be as open as possible. Members who are willing to share their lists can take the initiative, describing their experiences and inviting comments, questions, and comparison.

◆ ◆ *EXERCISE 5*

Increasing Attractiveness of Membership

Objectives

■ To understand that cooperative rather than competitive relationships can increase the attractiveness of the group
■ To understand that increased interaction increases the attractiveness of the group
■ To understand that interdependence can increase the attractiveness of the group

Setting

Participants are divided into tens (approximately) and seated five at a table. Each participant is given a piece of paper. At one table each person is given a crayon. At the other table the entire group is given one crayon. The members at the second table are instructed that they can hold the crayon only twenty seconds and then must pass it to the next person. The groups are instructed to "draw something from your life that is characteristic of you" or "draw something characteristic of you in the group." The facilitator may call out at the end of each twenty-second period or have a timekeeper at the table do it.

Action

The groups draw as instructed. In one group each person works with his or her crayon on the drawing; in the other, members pass a crayon to the next person every twenty seconds.

Discussion

How did you feel about the process?

How do you feel about your product?

How do you feel about your group? Talk about the experience.

Variation

This can be done as a group drawing. Each group is given one piece of paper. In one case each member is given a crayon; in the other group, one crayon is to be rotated. This variation heightens interdependence and cooperative relationships in the passed-crayon group.

The exercise is as described through the action phase. Then, before the discussion, individual evaluation sheets are distributed. These evaluation sheets permit those who worked individually to compare their evaluations with those who worked cooperatively. Some questions in the evaluation sheet might include

1. Did you enjoy working in this way?

1	2	3	4	5
Not at all		Doesn't matter or no opinion		Yes

2. What do you think of your drawing ability?

1	2	3	4	5
Very bad		O.K.		Very good

3. How do you feel about this drawing (product)?

1	2	3	4	5
Very bad		O.K.		Very good

4. Do you feel you helped your group?

1	2	3	4	5
Not at all	A little	Average	Quite a bit	A great deal

Sheets should be identified either by the color of the paper (white to groups who worked individually, colored to cooperative groups) or by a coding designation (I, individual; II, cooperative). Rating sheets are frequently utilized to obtain opinions along a range. Sometimes they are numbered (1–5) and the results tallied with presentation of the lowest, highest, and median scores for each question. Data should be tallied, comparisons made by questions, and results reported.

Discussion

See the objectives as a basis for discussion.

◆ ◆ *EXERCISE 6*

Factors Influencing Attractiveness of Membership

Objectives

- To understand personal sources of attraction in a group
- To become aware of and experience the problems of having new members in a group
- To become aware that changed membership in a group influences not only relationships with new members but also the relationships of older members with one another

■ To understand that changed membership influences sources of attraction to the group
■ To understand that increasing the size of a group has disadvantages
  as well as advantages

Action

The facilitator says, "Select a partner. Get acquainted. Be aware of how you feel
in this pair." Pairs talk for 15 minutes. While they are talking, the facilitator assigns
each pair a number. After 15 minutes he or she tells them to stop talking and
asks, "How do you feel about this dyad? Would you like to continue in this group?
Think about your answer." Then she or he says, "Would groups 2, 5, 8, 11, and
so on [every third group] split? One member go to the group on one side of you;
the other go to the group on the other side of you. There will now be a series of
triads, or three-person groups. Get to know one another."

Discussion

One person comes alone and must develop a whole new set of
  relationships. How does he or she feel? How is he or she treated?

Others were in a pair that was or was not satisfying. How do they
  feel toward one another with the newcomer? How do they respond to the newcomer?

How do members of the triad feel compared to how they felt in the
  dyad?

Variations

Discussion can be within triads rather than with the whole group, or two triads
can be combined.

There can be progressions in the size of groups. Triads 2, 5, 8, 11, and so on
disband. One person goes to the group at the left, the pair goes to the group at
the right. The feelings of one person going into an existing group (newcomer joins
trio) are examined; the same is done with a pair going into an existing group (pair
joins trio).

◆ ◆ EXERCISE 7

Increasing the Attractiveness of a Group:
High Talkers–Low Talkers

Objectives

■ To present an opportunity for "high talkers" and "low talkers" to
  develop empathy for the other

- To recognize the limitations of either behavior
- To give low talkers an opportunity to recognize that their situation is not unique
- To afford an opportunity for high talkers to practice listening and for low talkers to speak
- To experience how group membership can be determined by certain behavioral patterns

Situation

This exercise is appropriate after the groups have been working together for some time and usual behavior patterns are known by the members. The facilitator asks each person to categorize himself or herself as a high talker or a low talker. (This can be written down, and there can be a perception check among the members.)

Action

A fishbowl is set up with the low talkers sitting in the center, and the high talkers standing around the outside observing. The low talkers discuss the problems of being a low talker. (8 minutes)

Then the groups switch. The high talkers go to the center and discuss why they talk a great deal, and what problems spring from this behavior. (8 minutes)

Both groups come together and talk about their feelings and observations.

Variation

Instead of action in a fishbowl setting, action occurs in mixed quartets—that is, two low talkers and two high talkers in a group. In each, there is a discussion of the problems of being a low or high talker. (20 minutes)

The entire group comes together and discusses their feelings and observations.

◆ ◆ EXERCISE 8

Building Group Cohesiveness: Increasing Attractiveness of Membership

Objectives

- To build cohesiveness with a new group through a pleasurable joint activity
- To increase positive interaction through an enjoyable activity
- To increase boundaries of membership and a sense of "us"

Rationale

Group norms are established very early. A group is formed around a task that is exciting and enjoyable and provides opportunities for increased interaction. In this initial experience, members will come to value each other and to look forward to the next session of the group. (One measure of cohesiveness is the degree to which members look forward to returning to the next meeting.)

Materials

Copies of the "Deposit List"

Action

(Time: 30 min.) Small groups are formed and instructed to select names for themselves and then to go on a unique scavenger hunt called Deposit.

One copy of the deposit list is given to each group.

The facilitator explains that everyone is due back in thirty minutes. The team with the greatest number of correct items or correct answers is the winner. (Winners are rewarded with a standing ovation or some other accolade.)

When the groups come back with their materials, the facilitator asks each group whether they have item 1, item 2, item 3, etc. The team with the most items or correct answers wins.

Discussion

Each group is asked to discuss the following questions privately.

> Why do you think you were asked to do this as a first activity?
>
> How do you feel about the members of your group after the scavenger hunt?
>
> How did you like working with your group?
>
> How would you rank your group with the others in your class?
>
> How is this exercise related to building group cohesiveness?

Members are then asked to report out their data to the whole group.

Rules

> Each team will have a leader.
>
> The team must present the deposited item or answer through its leader. Only the leader may give the answer, but the leader may bring another person up to present the item.
>
> The course instructor or a surrogate will settle all disputes.

DEPOSIT LIST
A SPECIAL SCAVENGER LIST

Your job is to find all the items and to answer the questions on the list. Write your answers on a piece of paper. Return to this room in thirty minutes.

1. 6 cents
2. a sneaker
3. something with the name of the instructor or facilitator on it
4. a sock with a hole in it
5. 37×29
6. the number of letters in the name of your school or organization
7. someone who can wink with both eyes, one at a time
8. nail polish
9. a shirt with the word *cotton* on it
10. the fourth largest (in area) state
11. the name of the stadium in which the baseball team the Pirates play
12. a male piggybacking a female
13. mirror
14. breath freshener
15. a twenty dollar bill
16. a gray hair
17. an unattached button
18. the name of Barbie's boyfriend (the doll)
19. a piece of candy
20. a diamond ring (demonstrate)
21. the square root of 289
22. the number of home runs Babe Ruth scored in his career
23. 3 pointer: somebody with his or her shirt on backwards and inside out!

References

Amir, Y. "The effectiveness of the kibbutz-born soldier in the Israel defense forces." *Human Relations,* 22, No. 4 (1969), 333–344.

Aronson, E. "Who likes whom and why," *Psychology Today,* 4, No. 3 (1970), 48–50, 74.

Aronson, E., and D. Linder. "Gain and loss of esteem as determinants of interpersonal attractiveness." *Journal of Experimental and Social Psychology,* 1, No. 2 (1965), 156–171.

Aronson, E., and J. Mills. "The effect of severity of initiation on liking for a group." *Journal of Abnormal and Social Psychology,* 59 (1959), 177–181.

Aronson, M. L. "A group therapist's perspectives on the use of supervisory groups in the training of psychotherapists. Special Issue: The supervision of the psychoanalytic process." *Psychoanalysis and Psychotherapy,* 8, No. 1 (Spring–Summer 1990), 88–94.

Asch, S. E. "Effects of group pressure upon the modification and distortion of judgments." In D. Cartwright and A. Zander, eds., *Group Dynamics.* 2nd ed. Evanston, Ill.: Row, Peterson, 1960, 189–200.

Back, K. "Influence through social communication." *Journal of Abnormal and Social Psychology,* 46 (1951), 9–23.

Berne, Eric. *The Structure and Dynamics of Organizations and Groups.* New York: Grove Press, 1963.

Boszormenyi-Nagy, I., and G. Spark. *Invisible Loyalties: Reciprocity in Intergenerational Family Therapy.* New York: Harper & Row, 1973.

Brown, L. H. *Organization Studies,* 6, No. 4 (1985), 313–334.

Buck, Ross W., and Ross D. Parke. "Behavioral and physiological response to the presence of a friendly or neutral person in two types of stressful situations." *Journal of Personality and Social Psychology,* 24, No. 2 (November 1972), 143–153.

Carpenter, W., and E. Hollander, "Overcoming hurdles to independence in groups." *Journal of Social Psychology,* 117 (1982), 237–241.

Compas, B. "Psychological sense of community among treatment analogue group members." *Journal of Applied Social Psychology,* 11 (1981), 151–165.

Crawford, M. "Classroom climate at Westchester University: A report to the university community." Unpublished report sponsored by the Women's Consortium of SSHE. West Chester, PA (1986).

Crosby, F. "A model of egoistic relative deprivation." *Psychological Review,* 83 (1976), 85–113.

Crosby, F. *Relative deprivation and working women.* New York: Oxford University Press, 1982.

Crosby, F., and S. D. Clayton. "Introduction: The search for connections." *Journal of Social Issues,* 42, No. 2 (1986), 1–9.

Cross, M., and R. Moreland. "Sex differences in group memberships." Paper presented at the 57th annual meeting of the Midwestern Psychological Association, Chicago, May 1985.

Davis, J. M. *Social Behavior and Personality,* 12, No. 1 (1984) 1–5.

Deutsch, M. "Some factors affecting membership motivation and achievement motivation." *Human Relations,* 12 (1959), 81–85.

Deutsch, M., Y. Epstein, D. Canavan, and P. Gumpert. "Strategies of inducing cooperation: An experimental study." *Journal of Conflict Resolution,* 11, No. 3 (1967), 345–360.

Dion, K. L., N. Miller, and M. Magnan. "Cohesiveness and social responsibility as determinants of group risk taking." *Proceedings of the Annual Convention, American Psychological Association,* 5, Part 1 (1970), 335–336.

Dutton, Donald G., and Arthur P. Aron. "Some evidence of heightened sexual attraction under conditions of high anxiety." *Journal of Personality and Social Psychology,* 30, No. 4 (1974), 510–517.

Festinger, L. *A Theory of Cognitive Dissonance.* Evanston, Ill.: Row, Peterson, 1957.

Fouriezos, N., M. Hutt, and H. Geutzkow. "Measurement of self-oriented needs in discussion groups." *Journal of Abnormal and Social Psychology,* 52 (1950), 296–300.

Gershenfeld, Matti K. "Leadership on Community Boards." Report for Federation of Jewish Agencies, Philadelphia, Pa., 1964.

Gershenfeld, M. "A project to improve classroom climate at Westchester University: An intervention." Paper presented at the 4th International Kurt Lewin Conference (1990).

Good, L. R. "Effects of intergroup and intragroup attitude similarity on perceived group attractiveness and cohesiveness." *Dissertation Abstracts,* 1971, 60–3, 3618–B.

Guimond, S., and L. Dubé-Simard. "Relative deprivation theory and the Quebec nationalist movement: The cognitive-emotion distinction and the personal-group deprivation issue." *Journal of Personality and Social Psychology,* 44 (1983), 526–535.

Hall, J. "Decisions, decisions, decisions." *Psychology Today,* 5, No. 6 (1971), 51–54, 86–88.

Hart, J. "An outline of basic postulates of sociometry." *Group Psychotherapy, Psychodrama and Sociometry,* 33 (1980), 63–70.

Hill, A. D. "Administrative-directive versus participatory decision making organizational change: A case study." *Dissertation Abstracts International,* 46, No. 12-A, Pt 1 (June 1986).

Hall, R. M., and B. R. Sandler. "The classroom climate: A chilly one for women?" Project on the Status and Education of Women, Association of American Colleges. Washington, D.C. (1982).

Homans, G. *The Human Group.* New York: Harcourt, Brace, 1950.

Horowitz, M., R. Exline, M. Goldman, and R. Lee. "Motivation effects of alternative decision making process in groups." ONR Tech. Rep. 1953. Urbana, Ill.: University of Illinois, College of Education, Bureau of Educational Research.

Ingram, L. C. "In the crawlspace of the organization." *Human Relations,* 39, No. 5 (1986), 467–486.

Jackson, Jay M. "Reference group processes in a formal organization." *Sociometry,* 22 (1959), 307–327.

Johnson, D. W., and R. T. Johnson. "Relationships between black and white students in intergroup cooperation and competition." *Journal of Social Psychology,* 125, No. 4 (1985), 421–428.

Keyton, J. "Is group self-selection an important organizational variable?" Paper presented at the Annual Meeting of the Southern States Speech Association, Memphis, Tenn., April 7–10, 1988.

Kelley, H. H. "Communication in experimentally created hierarchies." *Human Relations,* 4 (1951), 39–56.

Kelley, H. H. "Two functions of reference groups." In G. E. Swanson, T. M. Newcomb, and E. L. Hartley, eds., *Readings in Social Psychology.* New York: Holt, Rinehart and Winston, 1952, 410–414.

Klein, Donald C. *Community Dynamics and Mental Health.* New York: Wiley, 1968, 47–56.

Kouhara, S. "An experimental study on deviation behavior which promotes group outcome." *Japanese Journal of Experimental Social Psychology,* 30, No. 1 (July 1990), 53–61.

Landers, D. M., and T. F. Crum. "The effects of team success and formal structure on interpersonal relations and spirit of baseball teams." *International Journal of Sport Psychology,* 2, No. 2 (1971), 88–96.

Lang, P. A. "Task group structuring, a technique: Comparison of the performances of groups led by trained versus nontrained facilitators." *Dissertation Abstracts,* 1977, 38 (6–A), 3186–3187.

Larson, C. "Participation in adult groups." Unpublished doctoral dissertation, University of Michigan, 1953.

Lott, A. J., and B. E. Lott. "Liked and disliked persons as reinforcing stimuli." *Journal of Personality and Social Psychology,* 11, No. 2 (1969), 129–137.

Mangan, K. S. "Academic psychologists are dropping out of association in discord with practitioners." *Chronicle of Higher Education,* 33, No. 33 (1987), 12–14.

Martens, R., and J. A. Peterson. "Group cohesiveness as a determinant of success and members' satisfaction in team performance." *International Review of Sport Sociology,* 6 (1971), 49–61.

McGowan, W. "A sense of belonging." *New York Times Magazine* (August 23, 1987), 46–48.

Meir, E. I., G. Keinan, and Z. Segal. "Group importance as a mediator between personality–environment congruence and satisfaction." *Journal of Vocational Behavior,* 28, No. 1 (1986), 60–69.

Mirande, A. M. "Reference group theory and adolescent sexual behavior." *Journal of Marriage and the Family,* 30, No. 4 (1968), 572–577.

Morris, W. N. "Collective coping with stress: Group reactions to fear, anxiety, and ambiguity." *Journal of Personality and Social Psychology,* 33, No. 6 (1976), 674–679.

Nixon, H. I. "Team orientations, interpersonal relations and team success." *Research Quarterly,* 47, No. 3 (October 1976), 429–435.

O'Brien, G., and W. Gross. "Structural indices for potential participation in groups." *Austrian Journal of Psychology,* 33 (1981), 135–148.

Pettigrew, T. "Social evaluation theory." In *Nebraska Symposium on Motivation,* edited by D. Levine, 241–349. Lincoln: University of Nebraska Press, 1967.

Piper, W. "Cohesion as a basic bond in groups." *Human Relations,* 36 (1983), 93–108.

Quey, R. L. "Functions and dynamics of work groups." *American Psychologist,* 26, No. 10 (1971), 1081.

Rasmussen, G., and A. Zander. "Group membership and self-evaluation." *Human Relations,* 7 (1954), 239–251.

Rose, A. *Union Solidarity.* Minneapolis: University of Minnesota Press, 1952.

Rosenfield, D., W. Stephan, and G. Lucker. "Attraction to competent and incompetent members of cooperative and competitive groups." *Journal of Applied Social Psychology,* 11 (1981), 416–433.

Royal, E., and S. Golden. "Attitude similarity and attraction to an employee group." *Psychological Reports,* 48 (1981), 251–254.

Runciman, W. G. *Relative Deprivation and Social Justice: A Study of Attitudes to Social Inequality in Twentieth-Century England.* Berkeley: University of California Press, 1966.

Sagi, P., D. Olmstead, and F. Atlesk. "Predicting maintenance of membership in small groups." *Journal of Abnormal and Social Psychology,* 51 (1955), 308–331.

Schachter, S. "Deviation, rejection, and communication." *Journal of Abnormal and Social Psychology,* 46 (1951), 190–207.

Schachter, S. *The Psychology of Affiliation.* Stanford, Calif.: Stanford University Press, 1959.

Schwartz, T. M., R. A. Eberle, and Donald R. Moscato. "Effects of awareness of individual group membership on group problem-solving under constrained communication." *Psychological Reports,* 33, No. 3 (1973), 823–827.

Seashore, S. *Group Cohesiveness in the Industrial Work Group.* Ann Arbor, Mich.: Institute for Social Research, 1954.

Shaw, M.E., and G. R. Breed. "Effects of attribution of responsibility for negative events on behavior in small groups." *Sociometry,* 33, No. 4 (1970), 382–393.

Shelley, H. P. "Level of aspiration phenomena in small groups." *Journal of Social Psychology,* 40 (1954), 149–164.

Sherif, M. *The Psychology of Social Norms.* New York: Harper & Row, 1936.

Sime, J. D. "Affiliative behaviour during escape to building exits." *Journal of Environmental Psychology,* 3, No. 1 (1983), 21–41.

Smith, R. E., L. Smythe, and D. Lien. "Inhibition of helping behavior by a similar or dissimilar nonreactive fellow bystander." *Journal of Personality and Social Psychology,* 23, No. 3 (1972), 414–419.

Snoek, J. D. "Some effects of rejection upon attraction to the group." Unpublished doctoral dissertation, University of Michigan, 1959.

Snyder, C. R., M. Lassgard, and C. Ford. "Distancing after group success and failure: Basking in reflected glory and cutting off reflected failure." *Journal of Personality and Social Psychology,* 51 (1986), 683–689.

Spears, R., M. Lea, and S. Lee. "Deindividuation and group polarization in computer-mediated communication." *British Journal of Social Psychology,* 29, No. 2 (June 1990), 121–134.

Stiles, D. B. "The significant other as a determinant of positive perceptions of group process experience." Doctoral dissertation abstract from *Dissertations in Education, Guidance and Counseling,* p. 51. University of Miami, 1973.

Tajfel, H. *Social Identity and Intergroup Relations.* Cambridge, England: Cambridge University Press, 1982.

Thelen, H. A. *Dynamics of Groups at Work.* Chicago: University of Chicago Press, 1954.

Tsouderos, J. "Organizational change in terms of a series of selected variables." *American Sociological Review,* 20 (1955), 207–210.

Turnbull, C. M. *The Lonely African.* New York: Anchor Books, 1963.

Turner, J. "Towards a cognitive redefinition of the social group." *Cahiers de Psychologie Cognitive,* 1 (1981), 93–118.

Vleeming, R. "Intergroup relations in a simulated society." *Journal of Psychology,* 113 (1983), 81–87.

Wicker, A. W. "Size of church membership and members' support of church behavior settings." *Journal of Personality and Social Psychology,* 13, No. 3 (1969), 278–288.

Willerman, B., and L. Swanson. "Group prestige in voluntary organizations." *Human Relations,* 6 (1953), 57–77.

Worchel, S., V. V. Andreoli, and R. Folger. "Intergroup cooperation and intergroup attraction: The effect of previous interaction and outcome of combined effort." *Journal of Experimental Social Psychology,* 13, No. 2 (1977), 131–140.

Wright, T. L., and D. Duncan. "Attraction to group, group cohesiveness, and individual outcome: A study of training groups." *Small Group Behavior,* 17, No. 4 (1986), 487–492.

Zander, A. "The value of belonging to a group in Japan." *Small Group Behavior,* 14, No. 1 (1983), 3–14.

DEPOSIT LIST
(ANSWER SHEET)

5. 1,073
10. Montana
11. Three Rivers
18. Ken
21. 17
22. 714

◆ 3 ◆

Norms, Group Pressures, and Deviancy

How does the Supreme Court work? How do nine justices, presumably the most brilliant legal minds in the country, make decisions that can override a president and counter a Congress—and, simply in their decision to take or not take a case, determine which laws stand and which will be changed? How do these nine justices, wedded for life to one another, arrive at their decisions?

Bob Woodward, Pulitzer Prize winning author, and Scott Armstrong went about finding out how the Warren Burger Court functioned between 1969 and 1976. In the course of their investigation, they interviewed more than 200 people, including several Supreme Court justices, more than 170 of their law clerks, numerous employees, and assorted savants. Their object was not to illuminate the problems of the Court or to press for better justices. Their object was to understand and report on the process in a book they called *The Brethren*.[1] (The subject had fascinated them, and they hoped it would also intrigue a curious nation and produce a best seller.)

One after another, reviewers of *The Brethren* expressed incredulity. To quote from John Leonard's review in the *New York Times*,[2]

> The Supreme Court behaves like any other committee with which I've had any acquaintance. Its scruples are relative; its personalities clash; its many pairs of eyes are on the main chance, the good opinion of posterity, the boss, the clock and sometimes the Constitution. One imagines that, even in the Agora, Socrates was hustled. . . .
>
> An associate justice of the supreme court is allowed to be ordinary. . . . We are advised that Chief Justice Warren Burger is most ordinary. He delays voting until he can be in the majority or finagle the assignment of the writing of an opinion; that he is no stranger to tantrums . . . and that he holds a grudge.

The reviews continued, noting that one justice doesn't do his homework and delays decisions because he is ill-prepared; another, on the slightest provocation, launches into one of his favorite ideological sermons as others tune him out and impassively wait for him to finish. One justice was almost blind, and the group had to make special concessions in working with him; another, of high status as a liberal and a favorite with the press, was an "unpleasant man for whom and with whom to work."

One after another of the reviewers expressed shock that these men, esteemed for their fine logical minds and ability to think through enormously complicated legal issues, act like any other committee. It seems impossible that *they* are frustrated with a leader who is not viewed as the most brilliant; that they subtly coerce and

---

1. Bob Woodward and Scott Armstrong, *The Brethren. Inside the Supreme Court* (New York: Simon & Schuster, 1979).
2. John Leonard, *New York Times Book Review,* December 16, 1979, p. 1.

are coerced; that they know what they can and cannot expect of each of the others; and that their way of functioning is quite different from that of the Warren Court, which preceded them.

One of the fundamental properties of groups is that each group has norms. Simply put, norms are the unspoken rules and standards which guide the group and define acceptable and unacceptable behavior by the group's members. Norms emerge from the participants who work together, at a given time, to accomplish a task. These norms emerge whether the groups are in high places or low ones. Norms are probably the most difficult group concept to convey and to understand. We somehow think that when *they* work together, their brilliance and erudition produce an interaction that is of a rarified form, with which we can in no way identify. How can it be that *they* interact like other committees?

This fundamental idea of group norms is a crucial one for understanding what is happening in a group. The main reason why we don't "see" group norms is that we have never looked. We like to think that we act moment by moment, spontaneously and appropriately. We think any problems are somehow related to "difficult" personalities or some kind of unchangeable situation in which personalities as different as oil and water don't and won't mix. We think that we march to our own drummer and are not conformists to a group. Not true. For the most part, we are conformists.

Without acknowledging the impact that group norms have on our behavior and on the interaction of the group as a whole, we have great difficulty exercising individual control over reaching our goals. It is literally the difference between merely looking at a group and actually seeing it. Even highly trained psychologists can miss seeing the group, as in the following example:

> A talented, well-trained Ph.D. clinical psychologist became a member of a university department that had a strong group focus. As part of his familiarization with the departmental group emphasis, he participated in a group led by another member of the faculty. He emerged from the experience shaken. In response to a casual, "How was it?" he raged, "She saw everything, everything. She is a witch; that's the only way anybody can see all that. She saw all these things happening; she predicted what would happen—and it did. It was one of the scariest experiences of my life. There are only two explanations possible. Either I am totally uneducated, and I sure felt that way, or—the more plausible one—she is a witch."

One year later, this shaken individual ran that same group (course). "Today," he boasts, "I am a witch, a seer. After looking and becoming aware of the group in its interactions, understanding its norms and its environment, I can *see*. I can predict, and amaze people who are probably thinking, "How does he do it? Either I am terribly uneducated or he is a witch."

The Concept of Group Norms

Consider this example, reported by C. Haberman in the *New York Times* (1988), of the power of norms:

> All this week, Japan's Parliament was brought to a standstill because an influential member rejected one of this country's most cherished social graces, an apology.
>
> Japanese are expected to say they are sorry when things fly off-kilter, whether they are right or wrong, whether they mean it or not.
>
> They do it because it is expected of them. The apology is an indispensable, all-purpose devise for insuring a social harmony.
>
> Everybody here knows that.
>
> Except, apparently, Koichi Hamada, chairman of the powerful Budget Committee in Parliament's House of Representatives, who uttered public remarks widely judged to be offensive and then refused to retract them. He is a man who means what he says, Mr. Hamada declared.
>
> When Japanese heard that, many of them were dismayed. Where would the country be, they asked, if everyone felt that way?
>
> So serious was Mr. Hamada's breach of decorum that opposition parties refused to attend critical hearings of the Budget Committee, effectively preventing the entire Parliament from doing any work all week. What had begun as a seemingly small episode mushroomed into a major political crisis, the first to strike the three-month-old administration of Prime Minister Noboru Takeshita.
>
> With the pressure upon him intense, Mr. Hamada finally gave in at the end of the week, apologizing publicly and resigning his committee post. Nevertheless, his tale underlined the importance of social imperatives here, and how even the mighty may not escape them. . . .
>
> It was not clear why, but, whatever the reason, he went before television cameras Friday and said, "People of the nation, please forgive me."
>
> He was stone-faced as he spoke. To many Japanese he did not seem the least bit contrite. But that was not important.
>
> The point was that he had come around and behaved the way a proper Japanese should, and that was enough for the Parliament, and the rest of Japan, to feel it could go about its regular business once more.

Apology is a significant national norm in Japan. In this case, the pressure to behave in accordance with this norm galvanized the attention of the entire nation and distracted the population from its routine business. We might even say that one highly visible man's temporary failure to conform to the national norm nearly brought the country to a halt.

Again norms are the *rules of behavior,* the proper ways of acting in a group that have been accepted as legitimate by the members of that group. They are accepted as legitimate procedures of the group as a system, as well as of each member within the system. Group norms regulate the performance of the group as an organized unit.

When individuals first enter a group, their conduct appears to be constrained: their feet shuffle and their hands twitch or become rigid; their eyes flit or are directed at inanimate objects; their conversation is forced and superficial or non-existent; and their laughter is loud and boisterous, tinny, or lacking. When they enter groups, people manifest behaviors that express anxious or uncertain feelings and thoughts about who they are in relation to others, who the others are in relation to themselves, and who the others are in relation to each other.

This confusion is made worse by the absence of a code of conduct, or rules of behavior. Suddenly, out-of-group behavior is inapplicable, and questions arise: "What may others do to me here?" "What may others do to each other here?" and "What may I do to others here?" These and similar thoughts race through a member's mind. As the group functions over time and members come to behave in ways that prove acceptable or unacceptable to individual group members, group agreement is shaped. The initial anxious feelings and thoughts are supplanted by firm, accepted ideas about personal security, safety, and membership status. Members come to feel comfortable in the group. This process of reaching agreement on behavior in the group is called *norming* (Tuckman, 1965).

Norms at the Individual Level

At an individual level, group norms are ideas in the minds of members about what should and should not be done by a specific member under certain specified circumstances. They are learned by members. Usually, norms provide one of the most important mechanisms for social control of individuals' behavior within society.

It is important to understand that norms are not only rules about behavior in the group but also ideas about the patterns of behavior. Rarely can the ideas be inferred directly from behavior; rather, they must be learned. A student in a group project may want to do a considerable amount of reading in preparation for a class presentation. However, he can see from the disapproving looks he receives from the others that it would be wiser to do a project that can be developed on class time so that other group members can do an equal amount of work. The group will now redefine its project to mean one that they can complete in class. Despite instructions from the director of the counseling center that all records must be updated weekly, staff members learn that as long as their records are current at the time of a record review, twice a year, leaving records undone is accepted. A scientific team member learns that attire is of little importance to other members. Dress can be as informal and casual as the individual prefers. However, at monthly report meetings with the divisional managers, members wear business suits and dresses.

Through such experiences, group members learn that the significance of an act lies not in the act itself, but in the meaning the group gives to it. They learn that the meaning may change according to who performs the act and the circumstances under which it is performed. This experience results in what are called *shared ideas* among members about what a specific member should and should not do under certain circumstances. A shared idea means, in the previous examples, that although a class presentation should be well done, it should not occupy personal time; that incomplete records are permissible in that clinic, despite the director's stern speech; and that scientific team members are expected to dress for a more traditional business setting.

When the norms are expectations for the behavior of a particular person, they are called *role expectations.* For example, if someone asks who will take notes at a meeting, and all eyes turn to one member who has unofficially taken notes at several previous meetings, role expectations are readily visible.

◆ Reader Activity

Below are two activities to help you understand the concept of norms.

1. One way to understand norms is to understand the difference between the "green" you and the "veteran" you. Select one of these situations, and using the situation you selected, list five things you found difficult (or were fearful of) as a new member.
   a. Being a first-year student and being a senior.
   b. Being a new employee and being that employee a couple of years later.
   c. Being a member and being an officer in the same group.

   _____

   _____

   _____

   _____

   _____

   _____

2. As you became experienced in the group or organization, you learned what the real rules are. How do you handle these situations now?

   _____

   _____

   _____

   _____

   _____

For example, first-year students are very concerned with what to wear and often read magazines on the current college fashions; they are apprehensive about looking phony or too new and are eager to cultivate the "right" look. Seniors ridicule reading such magazines; they know what to wear.

Consider dealing with registration, meeting people, making friends, having a "crowd," picking the right teachers and the right courses, and, with the college situation, even getting the right hours. Think of yourself then (not knowing the norms) and later (when you knew). The difference is understanding how the system operates; when you know, you can invest much less energy and suffer much less anxiety.   ◆

◆ Individual Experiment

Choose a group of which you are a member, such as a class, club, sports team, committee, work group, or political organization. Make a list of the norms and informal rules of the group. Include such details as

Dress: formal, informal, or uniform

How people are addressed: title, last or first name, or nickname

Language: jargon, intellectual and formal, informal, or street language

Content of the meetings: serious and always work-related, mostly serious but a lot of socializing, mostly socializing and humorous but work gets done, intimate and personal discussions along with more superficial socializing and work

Process of the meetings: Who talks most and who talks least? Do people tend to agree and keep opposing opinions to themselves? Are different opinions debated about openly? Who seems to influence the decisions of the group most often? Are decisions made strictly by the hierarchy of who is in charge or by the group leader? Who informally influences decisions?

Ask two other group members what they think the group's norms are. You will probably have to ask specific questions to help people think about the norms, because they probably have not consciously thought about them or talked about them before. It will be interesting to see what similarities and dissimilarities emerge in your lists.   ◆

Norms at the Group Level

At a group level, norms (or more accurately, the *normative system*) are the organized and largely shared ideas about what members should do and feel, how these norms should be regulated, and what sanctions should be applied when behavior does not coincide with the norms (Mills, 1967). Group norms function to regulate the performance of a group as an organized unit, keeping it on course toward its objectives. They also regulate the functions of individual members of a group.

A culture is, from one perspective, a specific kind of group. Social psychologists have shown that "all of us inhabit numerous local cultures and adopt hundreds of small-scale cultural roles within the large-scale culture" (Hirsch, 1987, p. 97). For example, a variety of cultures exist within a given high school or college.[3] One study (Louis, Blumenthal, Gluck, and Stoto, 1989) revealed that local cultural norms at various research universities had more influence than broad social values in determining whether scientists became involved in entrepreneurship. There are thus subcultures within cultures and norms that exist independently at each level.

Cultural norms can also exist at a broader level. In the Hausa tribe of Northern Nigeria, children are expected to take the role of buying and trading in public while women, who produce the goods for sale, are constrained by other cultural norms to remain in the house (Spradley and McCurdy, 1990, p. 221). In this case, both the roles of children and those of women are influenced by a set of larger cultural norms.

Norms in some cases specify particular behavior, and in other situations merely define the range of behaviors that are acceptable. In some cases, no deviations from expectations are permitted; in others, wide variability may be practiced. This range of acceptable behavior is very often apparent in religious groups. For instance, in the Muslim religion, not all women wear the *hijāb,* the veil and sheath that cover all but a woman's face and hands (Coffman, 1991). Similarly, some groups of Jews do not keep kosher.

◆ Reader Activity

Think of two groups with which you are involved. Consider your role in each. How are you different in each? List as many ways as you can. Among the factors to consider are dress, amount of talking, to whom you talk, seating, responsibilities you take in the group, expectations of you in the group, and your feelings of acceptance in the group.

Group A

_____

_____

_____

_____

3. See case 6 in Chapter 12 for a closer look at cultural norms at an eastern university.

Group B   •

_____

_____

_____

_____

_____   ◆

The Invisibility of Group Norms

Whenever we enter a strange or new group, we are uncomfortable. We need to know how it operates and how we will fit in. Until we know, until we get "the lay of the land," we utilize all of our strategies that have worked in former groups. We are dressed in the way we think they will find acceptable. We scan for clues—who is "in," who is "out"; what the leader is like; who is popular; how people talk; how one gains acceptance. For new members, there is constant strain in scanning, learning, watching, imitating. In order for new members to feel as though they have gained the group's acceptance, they need to know the "rules of the game."

To insiders, the long-term members, the idea that there are rules within the group is viewed as ridiculous. They say they just act naturally and are accepted. They feel acceptance; they are not under any recognizable tension. They can't understand what this talk of tension is about—it must be something that psychologists dreamed up. Insiders are so familiar with group expectations and rules that they don't know these norms exist. This is what social psychologists call cultural relativism, and the phenomena about which James Merrill may have referred when he aptly stated that "life is translation and we are all lost in it" (Geertz, 1983, p. 44).

In real-life groups, then, norms are invisible. They are taken so much for granted that they are given little thought. The invisibility of norms is analogous to the classic figure/ground Gestalts in that norms are often the "undifferentiated ground" rather than the figure that naturally emerges. We see the task, membership, and problem-solving methods, but we don't see the process of interaction, the ways members conform or influence—these are the background.

Too often, when we try to understand the functioning of individuals and groups, we ignore "invisible" norms. Sometimes norms are difficult for us to discuss openly in a group, especially when there are important decisions to make, when membership is changing, or when emotions are running high. Talking about norms at such times may make us feel more vulnerable or fearful about the group accepting us. Thus groups often collude to keep their own norms out of conscious awareness.

This collusion to keep norms invisible is most pronounced in family systems, where some norms or myths literally go unrecognized (and thereby unchallenged) for generations (Boszormenyi-Nagy and Spark, 1973; Ferreira, 1963; Laing, 1972). Every family, after all, is an independent, defined organization with common characteristics within a given culture. Each can be either functional or dysfunctional, often as a result of such invisible norms. For more on the family as a microcosm, see Chapter 10.

According to a study of invisible norms within organizations (Blake and Mouton, 1985), pressure to conform within the group maintains the norm. Once the invisible norms are exposed, however, the group or organization can become involved in changing repressive norms. One requirement for organizational change is the acknowledgment and identification of silent norms.

How Group Norms Develop

In a culture in which independence, equality, and being able to "pull yourself up by your own bootstraps" are highly valued, being influenced by a group does not seem very likely. Yet despite the cultural emphasis on individualism, we are all affected by group norms, even though we may talk of "free will" and "self-determination." How does this happen? There are a number of interpretations.

A Sociologist's View

Sociologist Erving Goffman devoted his life to seeing, cataloguing, and attempting to understand the interaction rituals performed by persons in the immediate physical presence of others. These contacts may be so fleeting and informal as to be unrecognizable as a social function—an elevator ride, a dash for a bus. They also include such major events as weddings and funerals.

"More than to any family or club, more than to any class or sex, more than to any nation, the individual belongs to gatherings, and he had best show that he is a member in good standing. Just as we fill our jails with those who transgress the legal order, so we partly fill our asylums with those who act unsuitably—the first kind of institution being used to protect our lives and property; the second to protect our gatherings and occasions" (Goffman, 1963). Whether behavior occurs in public or private places, the rule of behavior that seems to be common to all such encounters, and exclusive to them, is the rule obliging participants to "fit in."

In his classic *Presentation of Self in Everyday Life* (1959), Goffman views social contact in theatrical terms. Every scene develops as an interaction between the actor and the audience (observers). Goffman is especially interested in "thespian technique": How is it that the actors develop their performances to look real? How do they present their behavior as acceptable to the audience while they are in the "front region" (on stage, before the observers) and act very differently in the "back region" (off stage, not before the observers)? Goffman notes that the audience knows the actors are giving a performance that is not real, but it colludes with the performers to act as though the performance were authentic, spontaneous behavior. Both the actors and the audience seem to desire a good show.

Think of a restaurant with a dining room and kitchen, waiters, and customers. The dining room is softly lit and has immaculate tablecloths and place settings. The waiters move from table to table quietly and slowly, speaking with others in low, well-modulated voices. When waiters go through the doors into the kitchen, however, they yell out orders, dashing around to assemble the necessary glasses and plates, salads or soups—very different from the elegant reserve displayed in the dining room. From a sociological perspective, the dining room is where the waiters are on stage, seeking to create a certain ambience, and the kitchen is off stage, the "back region."

For Goffman, learning the rules of social contact—the rituals and then the more difficult "acts"—is necessary to avoid an asylum. It is a basic condition of social life and social survival that occurs even in the most tenuous contacts. The basic rule in social contact is to fit in. Norms thus develop from an individual's learning to fit in.

A Behavioral Interpretation

Learning theorists have advanced relatively straightforward explanations for what appears to be conformity to group norms. They extend the law of effect; that is, people behave in ways that win them rewards and avoid or suppress behaviors that are punished.

Simply, people learn to identify cues that signal what behaviors will be reinforced and, especially upon entering a new group, are extremely sensitive to cues signaling punishment. For the most part, establishing or retaining membership in a group (itself a reinforcing condition) is a consequence that results only from choosing to conform to these standards—deriving appropriate reinforcements from appropriate behavior. As a pattern of reciprocity appears in this exchange of behavior-for-reinforcement, the phenomena that we call *group norms* take shape.

Because individuals differ in the consequences that they find reinforcing, nonconforming behavior also can be found in groups. Expulsion is the most severe form of punishment. If individuals are to retain membership without conforming, then either they must find a way to change the norms so that deviant behavior becomes redefined as socially appropriate and reinforceable or they must be permitted to formulate a role that permits deviance and reinforces other members' tolerance of that deviance (think of an authority above the law or a lovable class clown).

In fact, in American culture, both conformity and autonomy are considered "desirable qualities in a person . . . one should be autonomous, but one should also conform to the expectations of society" (Hewitt, 1989, pp. 39, 40).

This behavioral interpretation is most frequently applied to the practice of group psychotherapy, where it is hoped that clients will establish socially adaptive norms and that their behavior can be shaped to the desired behavior. In such situations, norms are made explicit and highly visible so that expectations are clear, and coaching is directed to conformity. For example, clear expectations that group members treat each other with respect and share their feelings with one another, rather than talk about other topics, establish norms about self-disclosure and trust (Bandura, 1977; Heckel and Salzberg, 1976; Liberman, 1970; Rose, 1977).

In real life, group norms are often established through a process that is largely outside our conscious awareness. Behavioral research offers evidence for such a subliminal, though potent, social learning process:

1. Stimuli that are outside conscious awareness (such as subliminally presented pictures of popcorn in a movie theatre) can influence behavior (getting up to buy popcorn). Visual perception studies have shown that pornographic pictures presented too quickly to be consciously recognized nonetheless can cause male college students to become sexually aroused.

2. Reinforcement can increase the performance of desired behavior and punishment can discourage undesired behavior, even though the target individual (whose behavior is being modified) remains consciously unaware of the manipulation. Consider two examples.

   a. In many cases, when social teachers apply behavior modification principles to reinforce sitting still and to decrease the incidence of acting inappropriately, such manipulations can be successful without the student even being informed or consciously recognizing the teacher's intervention (Martin and Lauridsen, 1974).

   b. In individual psychotherapy studies, active listening responses such as saying "um hm" and smiling increased the client's tendency to talk about certain subjects or themes, or even show certain emotions, without being aware of or being able to verbalize the therapist's subtle manipulation.

Thus group norms may develop through a process of *subliminal conditioning* as, through trial and error guided by past experience and preconceptions, one learns to identify the criteria by which reinforcements and punishments are meted out in the present group. Social behavior, as the norm to which one conforms, is situation specific; it is based on the features and norms of the specific group.

Communications Theory

Communications theorists build a somewhat different rationale for the formation and acceptance of group norms. The "Palo Alto Group" (Watzlawick, Beavin, and Jackson, 1967) suggest that all behavior is communication. In fact, it is impossible not to communicate, because even the act of choosing not to communicate is conveying a message. The following principles, according to the Palo Alto Group, occur in all communication:

1. The command component implicit in any act of communication is the communicator's proffered definition of the relationship between self and other(s) involved in the act of communication.

2. In response to the first person's act of communication, the second communicates acceptance of the protagonist's definition of the relationship between them—or offers a counterproposal, an alternative definition of the preferred relationship.

3. Successive acts of communication represent a negotiation or bargaining process until, in accordance with social learning principles, a mutually acceptable quid pro quo—a satisfactory exchange of social reinforcements from complementary points of view—is established.

4. If the negotiation process is not successful, the participants will terminate their relationship. That is, the quid pro quo agreed upon will be the end of further communication between them. This bargaining process is largely subliminal, as the participants learn of each other's criteria for social reinforcement and preferred reinforcers as givers and receivers.

Communication itself has inherent in it an aspect that is concerned solely with establishing norms between the communicating individuals. A father talks to his adolescent differently than to his grade school child, and he talks to his wife in a qualitatively different way than to either of his children. In a university some professors teach courses and communicate in a manner that encourages questions, differing opinions, and direct intellectual challenges, whereas other professors communicate to students their dislike of being questioned or challenged. The first type of professor communicates both in what he or she says and in how it is said that "I am the professor and you are the student; part of my job in teaching you is to encourage independent and critical thinking." The second professor communicates "I am the professor and your job in being a student is to learn the material I teach."

Especially in groups that have a history as groups, the give-and-take that leads to the establishment of a quid pro quo is ongoing. The beginning or end of an interaction episode is an arbitrary marker, an act of punctuation that determines how the participants will understand (or misunderstand) what has transpired during the course of their interaction. (Watzlawick gives the example of the experimental rat who "has the experimenter trained to issue food pellets whenever he presses the bar in the cage"—a form of punctuation in their interaction that differs from the experimenter's understanding of the relationship.)

A major controversy in education today is whether language should be made culturally uniform to strengthen the similarity of language between individuals and groups of people. In his speculative book *Cultural Literacy,* Hirsch states that "effective communication requires a shared culture." Therefore, by not providing children with access to the language of the mainstream culture, we are reinforcing the quid pro quo in education (Hirsch, 1987, p. xvii).

Once established, the quid pro quo pattern of the relationship is resistant to change. *It is in the exchange of command components and the subsequent quid pro quo that social reinforcers come.* Information rarely, if ever, has this strong interpersonal impact.

In summary, norms exist in all social contacts. We pick them up in the course of living, even as we go about learning content or information. Norms develop through our communications with others, but not directly and straightforwardly for the most part. Rather, norms develop by subtle, subliminal, beyond-awareness processes of inference; we note raised eyebrows, hear supportive "uh-hums," and watch how others gain approval. They may evolve through an interpersonal process of negotiation as we attempt to follow the rules of fitting in. Within each group there is a history of what is and what is not acceptable behavior. This history has developed over time in that situation, and members learn and understand it well.

Classification of Norms

If it is understood that norms are a set of standards that groups develop for themselves, is there a way to classify these standards? Are there dimensions along which these norms develop? Is there a way to understand a group in terms of its norms, and can this method also be a means to contrast groups? Sociologist Talcott Parsons (Parsons and Shils, 1951) thought so. He thought that norms in any society or group had to provide answers to questions related to at least four dimensions.

1. *Affective relationships.* How personal are the relationships? Are relations among members to be based on the expression of feelings they have toward each other, or are feelings to be suppressed and controlled? Is an expression of emotion considered legitimate and appropriate, or is it understood that any expression of emotion is too personal and will hamper the movement of the group? For example, in a school situation, teachers are not supposed to express their feelings of dislike for a particular student or even another teacher. Hospitals often set aside a separate section in the cafeteria for doctors to ensure their not being too personal with other members of the staff or with patients. In a family, on the other hand, the norm is for eating together, sharing personal experiences, being expressive of feelings, and vocally approving and disapproving of members.

2. *Control, decision-making, authority relationships.* Is the involvement with another to be total and unbounded by time constraints (as with a parent and a child), or is it to be restricted and specific (as with a swimming instructor and a pupil)? Parents have almost total decision-making control over their children, yet the swimming instructor's control over the pupil is limited to the time of the lesson.

3. *Status-acceptance relationships.* Does the relationship with the other person exist because he or she represents a type or a class (a servant, a client, a teacher) or is it due to the personal uniqueness of the relationship with the other (a brother, a cousin, a friend)? In some groups, the norm is to leave the minute

the session is over, without even a goodbye. In others, a personal relationship among colleagues develops as they become friends and regularly "do lunch" together.

4. *Achievement-success relationships.* Is the person valued for his or her personal qualities (intelligent, trustworthy) or for his or her professional skills (as a researcher, as an athlete)? Within the faculty of a college department, some people are respected for their professional contributions, and others are valued because they sit on administrative committees that benefit the whole department. To all, rank is a significant factor.

One way to compare norms across groups might be with regard to answers members give to the foregoing questions. A great variety of combinations is possible. It may prove a simple, meaningful way to contrast groups. It may clarify the difference between members' wishes for norms and the actual existing norms. It may also make it possible to reduce stress for the members or to precipitate action toward changing the norms.

As we noted in Chapter 1, Deborah Tannen has written extensively on the differences between the ways in which men and women communicate. In her book *You Just Don't Understand,* Tannen characterizes conversation between men and women as "cross-cultural communication." In keeping with their normative behavior, "women speak and hear a language of connection and intimacy," one that stresses affective relationships. Men, on the other hand, "speak and hear a language of status and independence," which stresses status-acceptance relationships. By understanding the differing norms that govern women's and men's communication patterns, we may begin to break down the gender barriers.

Kinds of Norms

Understanding norms is not a simple matter; there are many norms, and it is difficult to determine which take precedence over others, which are time specific and which are general, which apply to all members and which to some members, which must be strictly adhered to and which are to be totally ignored.

Written Rules

Some norms are codified, as in bylaws and code books. They may be formal, written statements intended to be taken literally as group rules, and they are enforced by organizational sanctions (that is, actions to ensure compliance). They are stated and presumably available to members who are willing to examine the constitution or corporate policies. But there are complications.

Sometimes statements in code books are not adhered to as stated. For example, it may be stated with regard to procedures for promotion for university faculty that teaching skill, service, and publication will be weighted equally. However, because publication is easier to measure and more prestigious, it in fact takes on greater weight. The norm then is that publication is most important; teaching skill and service become secondary factors.

Sometimes there is a tacit understanding that formal laws can be ignored, much like old statutes that remain on the books but are no longer enforced. A classic example is an old Connecticut statute that makes taking a bath on Sunday unlawful.

People in power can disregard written rules more often than the rest of us. Only recently (1991), Vice President Dan Quayle waived the conflict-of-interest law for a fellow utility owner so that the utility owner might serve on the Council for Competitiveness. The implications of this kind of waiver are enormous. The Council could become dominated by individuals with vested interests in protecting the status quo and the rights of utilities. But the purpose of the Council is to safeguard the public interest especially in protecting the environment. Who will ask the hard questions about the impact of utilities on the environment if the Council itself is directly influenced by members with clear biases? The broken rule and the norm not to question authority can have far-reaching consequences indeed. The problem, of course, is that few people invited to participate on a presidential council will ever confront such an issue and may discuss it as procedural rather than substantive.

The distinction between norms and written documents is an important one, for as some of the formal rules are weighted differently than perceived, as some are adhered to and others are not, a new set of rules is established. Those unfamiliar with this distinction might examine a copy of the group's bylaws and believe these are the procedures by which that group functions, but there may be a world of difference between such official pronouncements and what actually occurs.

Explicitly Stated Norms

Some norms do not appear in the codifications or in formal written form, but may be explicitly stated verbally or may easily be recognized by members. In being hired, an employee may be told, "Everyone gets here by 9:30 (the explicitly stated norm being that you're late if you arrive after 9:30). Although nothing may be said about attire at work, a new employee may notice that all the men he has encountered in the office are wearing suit jackets and ties; there is the easily recognized norm that he will be expected to wear a suit jacket and tie in his work. However, as previously stated, explicitly stated norms may not be the actual norms practiced.

Nonexplicit, Informal Norms

Within each group there may be nonexplicit, informal, or silent norms that influence member behavior. For example, a stated norm may be that all members of a team are expected to be present at weekly hospital rehabilitation staff meetings. However, what happens is that the physician, nominally the team leader, calls just before the meeting stating that she is tied up and asking that they meet without her. The nonexplicit, informal norm that develops is that the entire team is to be present except the physician, who will call to say she won't be there. After weeks of this practice, the team makes assignments to members knowing that they do not have to clear them with the physician. She is informed by reading the weekly staff-meeting minutes. As another illustration, although there may be no assigned seats at committee meetings, the chairperson generally sits at the left end of the room, flanked by the vice-chairpeople.

Sometimes, such norms become known only when they are violated. In Addis Ababa, for instance, many young Ethiopians have a special appreciation of Michael Jackson and other American music stars (Masland, 1987.) In the evenings, the young people exchange dance moves in tiny back-street bars, where they gather to listen to records. They are doing what young people do throughout the world, but here fans go further: they wear special shirts and refer to themselves by a special name: "Michaelites." When too many Michaelites gather at a bar, they can become special targets in military recruitment drives. One report quoted a military spokesman as saying, "Young people should be contributing to Ethiopia's food stocks and bettering themselves through hard work, not 'strutting up and down under a pile of hair.' " Not until the Michaelites began to suffer the consequences did they realize that in adopting Western styles, they had violated national norms—an act punishable by instant conscription.

Another example can be found in the prejudicial norms that develop across cultural groups. According to Sonnenschein (1988), there are countless incidents of criminal behavior resulting from the prejudiced conduct of young people in this country. A seemingly innocuous racial slur or insensitive ethnic joke may become the impetus for racial violence such as that which ended in the death of one youth during the Howard Beach incident in December of 1986. (During the Howard Beach incident a white gang, angered by increasing incursions of blacks into their community, ran down and beat a number of black youths who had stopped for pizza. The brutality of the attack by youths not previously prone to violence shocked and outraged surrounding black and white communities.) Thus, the consequences of these nonexplicit, informal norms can often be devastating.

Norms Beyond Awareness

Some norms are created as if by osmosis, in a gradual, unconscious pattern. We conform without even knowing that we feel these pressures. We automatically raise our hands when we want to be recognized; we say hello to those we know when entering a room; we expect a certain order at a meeting: an opening, the minutes, the treasurer's report, old business, then new business. We expect paid-up members to be notified of meetings.

An illustration of how norms develop, and the confusion that sometimes ensues, may help explain what rationally is unexplainable.

A large, sprawling psychiatric hospital is situated on over a thousand acres, with ten patient buildings. There are over three thousand patients and they are treated by a wide array of professional staff: physicians, nurses, rehabilitation counselors, social workers, psychologists, neurologists, psychiatrists, physical therapists, and occupational therapists. Many of the patients are on medications for chronic illnesses (such as diabetes), as part of psychiatric treatment (antidepressants or tranquilizers), for allergies, or for infections. Medication is a central aspect of patient care. In addition to medications, there are a variety of routine hospital-care items ordered through the pharmacy (for example, thermometers and bandages).

The policy developed by the pharmacy for ordering was simple and easily understood. Pharmacy picked up the list of medications and other items from each unit on set days, twice a week. Staff members who needed to order medications submitted their requirements to the nursing staff, who were responsible for ordering the medications and making up the lists. Although the procedures and the order methods were clear and known, there were indications, in terms of quantities ordered, that some buildings were stockpiling medications. However, because each building had a different kind of patient, admissions fluctuated. And because patients were sometimes transferred from one building to another, the pharmacy orders of each building varied.

When someone from pharmacy questioned a large order, there were a variety of evasive answers, such as "I'm not the head nurse and I didn't compile the list," or "I didn't order it. Maybe the second shift needed it," and "Some of the patients from building 6 are being transferred here next week, and we need their medications." The pharmacy staff was exasperated.

In an organization development program, the chief pharmacist presented his case for study. What emerged was a situation without controls; a method had developed as a way to cope with what had become an impossible system.

Because the nursing staff was sometimes forced to wait a month for certain often-used medications, and serious problems developed for patients who did not have them, a norm developed to increase the order of those medications. In that way, the staff felt they would always have some on hand and would never run out.

When the pharmacy thought an order was excessive, they did not fill it. They would stall by saying they had ordered it and that it would be in soon.

When none of the medications ordered were delivered, requiring a still longer wait, the nursing staff then ordered even more on their next list.

As the order grew, the pharmacy decided to reduce the amount ordered by 80 percent. The informal norm that then developed was that only 20 percent of an order would be delivered.

The pharmacy conjured up an excuse about why the order was short, and the nursing staff repeatedly complained that they needed the medications ordered and that they were always being shortchanged.

Organizational norms were illustrated when the chief pharmacist was out for a week and someone from another institution briefly replaced him. In accordance with the normative system that had evolved, one nurse wrote a high order for a medication rarely used, assuming the usual 80 percent cutback. Instead, the new pharmacist (who was unfamiliar with the system) filled the order as written. The nurse receiving the order was stunned; she now had enough of the medication to last for three years. She was in a real quandary. Should she find storage space for the bonanza, or should she return the excess? Either way there would be problems, but she decided to store the medications.

◆ *Individual Experiment*

Norms are related to a variety of behaviors of group members, one of which is communication within the group. In some groups, strict parliamentary procedures provide rigid norms; in others, communication is informal and more flexible. Choose a group you participate in that has a fair amount of discussion and interaction among members. Discreetly take notes about the interaction of the group, noting such things as how often each individual talks, who seems to talk after whom, which members agree or disagree, who talks about irrelevant and unrelated events, who cracks jokes and when, who talks just about the task or work of the group, and who tries to make decisions in the group. You may notice some patterns in who talks to whom, and so on, or you may not. In about one month, take the same kinds of notes about the group interaction again and compare the two sets of notes. The similarities you discover will represent some of the informal norms about communication in the group.   ◆

Forces That Induce Acceptance of Group Norms

The process by which a group brings pressure on its members to conform to its norms, or by which a member manipulates the behavior of others, is the process of social influence. It is recognized that some groups may legitimately exert pressures for uniformity of behavior and attitudes among members—for example, church groups, political parties, and professional societies. Others exert influence on members without their awareness that it is happening. This occurs among office associates, teachers in a given school, and lunch groups—those who interact frequently, though they have not created any formalized structure. They exert influence through their informal group standards and may have an important effect on members' behavior.

If the norms of the group are compatible with an individual's norms and goals, that person will conform to the norms of the group. However, if an individual finds that his or her behavior deviates from the group norms, he or she has four choices: to conform, to change norms, to remain a deviant, or to leave the group.

Why do people bother to learn the norms of a group so that they can conform? Is it worth the effort? How do members induce other members to conform?

Seeking answers to such questions, Feldman (1984) examined the enforcement and development of group norms. With respect to norm enforcement, he found that "groups are likely to bring under normative control only those behaviors that (1) ensure group survival; (2) increase the predictability of group members' behaviors; (3) prevent embarrassing interpersonal situations; or (4) express the group's central values." Feldman found that group norms develop through "(1) explicit statements by supervisors or co-workers; (2) critical events in the group's history; (3) primacy, and (4) carry-over behaviors from previous situations."

Basically, the forces that induce an individual to conform can be classified in one of two categories: internal forces, those based on intrapersonal conflict, and external forces, in which others attempt to influence the person directly.

Internal Forces Based on Intrapersonal Conflict

One of the major early studies in group dynamics sought to demonstrate how a group influences individuals to conform. In the classic Sherif experiments (Sherif, 1935, 1936, 1961), each subject is placed in a darkened room and asked to judge how far a dot of light moves. (Although the light appears to move, it actually does not. The phenomenon is known as the autokinetic effect.) The subject sees the dot of light and makes a series of individual judgments. Then, the subjects are brought together in twos and threes to again judge how far the light moves. In this situation, their judgments tend to converge to a group standard. Later, when they view the light again as individuals, they retain the group standard and give that answer.

This experiment has been replicated with variations for almost five decades, and the results are so predictable that it is even conducted as a classroom experiment (Hare, 1976; Martin, Williams, and Gray, 1974). The essential finding is that when a situation is ambiguous, and there is no external reality for determining the "right" answer, people are especially influenced by the group. They look at the light and have no objective way of determining how much the light moves; they make a judgment as best they can. When they are in a group, they hear one another's judgments, a clarity develops for them, and they adjust their answers to fall within the range of the others. Generally, the greater the ambiguity of the object, the greater the influence of other group members in determining the judgment of the subject (Keating and Brock, 1974; Luchins, 1963; Mills and Kimble, 1973).

In real life, then, membership in a group influences individuals in many of the things they will see, think about, learn, and do. Given a change in the price of gold or in unemployment statistics, union members will hear a different set of "facts" to clarify that situation than will chamber of commerce members. College students at Berkeley or San Francisco State will understand student involvement quite differently from students at a small midwestern college.

How an event or situation becomes less ambiguous is to a large extent determined by the group memberships of the person. Because of the limited range of events in a group, there evolves a common set of perceptions and convictions among members. Discussion groups, bull sessions, and rap groups all serve this function of helping an individual develop clarity in an ambiguous situation. The process of each member of a group giving his or her own opinion, even without attempting to influence an individual, can be highly influential in developing what the members consequently think.

A second classic and ingenious series of experiments was designed by Asch (1951, 1955, 1956). Asch was interested in understanding when individuals would be independent of the group and when they would conform.

In his experiments, the stimulus materials were two sets of cards. On one set, each card had a single black line (the standard). Each card in the other set had three labeled lines; one of these was the same length as the standard, and the other two were easily recognizable as different from the standard. Individuals from psychology classes who volunteered for the experiment were arranged in groups of seven to nine. They were seated at a table and asked to state in turn, starting at the left, which line was closest to the standard.

◆ Reader Activity

Pretend you are one of the students in the Asch experiment. You are seated in a position to give your opinion sixth in a seven-person group.

TRIAL 6

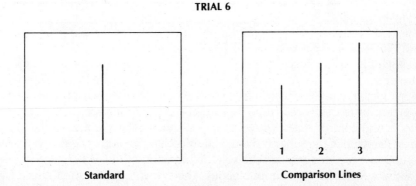

Standard   Comparison Lines

Which of the comparison lines is closest in size to the standard line? Person 1 says line 2, next person says line 2, next person says line 2, next person says line 2, next person says line 2. It is now your turn. What do you say? _____ Person 7 says line 2.

TRIAL 7

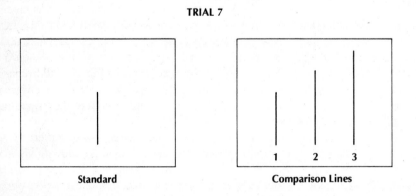

Standard   Comparison Lines

Which of the comparison lines is closest to the standard line? Person 1 says line 2, next person says line 2, next person says line 2, next person says line 2, next person says line 2. It is now your turn to answer. What do you say? _____Person 7 says line 2.

What would you say if you were actually at a table with six others? You look at the lines at the same time they do; they see what you see. How is it that sometimes all of you see the lines the same way and agree, as in trial 6, and at other times they all agree but you see it differently. And this is an issue not of opinion but of perception. It is simple to see which line is closest to the standard. What is happening to you? What would you do?

_____

_____

_____

_____   ◆

What Asch did was to coach six of the seven to give the same incorrect reply on twelve of eighteen trials. In each group, there was 1 naive subject. The experiment was conducted with 123 naive subjects. The findings were overwhelming: nearly 37 percent of the subjects' responses were in error, compared with almost no errors in the control trials. On one trial, less than 50 percent gave the correct answer. Remember, the subjects did not know each other, there was no overt group pressure to conform, each had the solid information of his or her senses to rely on, and the situation was not ambiguous. There was no promise of future favor or advancement, nor was there any threat of ostracism or punishment. How did it happen that so many (over a third) gave the wrong response?

Asch explains the situation as follows: Individuals come to experience a world they share with others; events occur that they and others see simultaneously. They understand that an environment includes them as well as others and that they are in the same relation to the surroundings as others. If it rains, it rains on them as well as on those standing beside them. If an automobile in which they are passengers stops suddenly, they as well as other passengers will be shaken. They know (in the basic internal sense of knowing) that they and others are in a similar experience and that each responds to certain identical properties (they all are wet as a result of the rain, the smoothness of the ride is interrupted for all because of the sudden stop). Because individuals are aware of similarity of experience and similarity of response—which seems to be the inevitable direct response to an identical experience—an intrapersonal conflict arises for them under the experimental conditions Asch set up.

Although a person was likely to give an incorrect answer when responding in a large, unanimous group, especially over time, it should be noted that if even *one* other person gave the correct answer, the person trusted his or her own sensory information and gave the correct answer. No matter what the size of the majority, even one supporter encouraged the subject to trust his or her own senses—an important understanding for anyone attempting to lead or to change norms.

Khoury (1985) tested the Sherif and Asch experiments. He asked how strongly assessments are influenced by the urge toward social conformity. First, he had group members judge the number of coffee beans in a jar and found mild agreement, as in Asch's study. Next, he asked subjects to rate two jokes in terms of humor—a task involving much more ambiguity than guessing the number of coffee beans in a jar.

The results of Khoury's experiment confirmed the hypothesis that the convergence of opinion regarding humorousness would be greater than in the unambiguous, coffee-bean problem—in fact, the convergence of opinion regarding the jokes was *twice* that regarding the beans. Generally, individuals are more likely to conform to group opinion when the object to be judged is ambiguous and the individual must make his or her opinion public. Individuals are highly sensitive to social forces in norm building, and humor is a formidable social force.

Even more recently, in a 1989 study that sought to further verify some of the variables in Asch's experiment, Campbell and Fairey found that the larger the group, the greater the normative versus informational influence of the group. In other words, as the group increases in size, information from individuals becomes redundant and therefore declines in influence. They also found, however, that the normative influence varied as the "norm changed from one that might be correct to one that is clearly wrong" (Campbell and Fairey, 1989, p. 465). Thus the degree to which a group can influence an individual may depend on how extreme the group's responses are. These results have wide implications in terms of social influence. The Asch findings continue to be powerful testimony to how a group influences its members and how members conform (Ross, Bierbrauer, and Hoffman, 1976; Mugny, 1984).

In each of these studies, the group's influence on judgment occurs only when there is internal conflict, not when the judgment is based on personal preference. Here, individuals do not perceive themselves as being in a situation similarly experienced by others; they perceive themselves as having idiosyncratic preferences that are theirs alone. If, for example, they were sitting in a group with others, and a researcher asked for each person's favorite flavor of ice cream, internal conflict would not occur. The first person might answer "chocolate," the next might also say "chocolate," and even if the next three reply "chocolate," the sixth will answer "coffee" or "burnt almond" or whatever his or her favorite flavor is. Personal preference replies are in a different category from judgment replies, in which each person is aware of being in a common situation.

Tendencies to Create a Social Reality

Internal forces can also lead individuals to conform as they seek a social reality. Festinger (1954) proposed that there is a basic drive within each of us to evaluate our own opinions and abilities. It is potentially dangerous, or at the very least embarrassing, to be incorrect or to misperceive how well we can do various things. To avoid that, we constantly seek relevant evidence. For some opinions and abilities, the evidence is directly available to us in our contacts with the physical world. If we are not sure of the time, we can check our watch. If we are not sure whether we can jog two miles, we can go find out. However, for most of our opinions and abilities, there is no objective, nonsocial way to evaluate ourselves. All we can do is turn to other people. If we are not sure how well we speak, we find out by observing how others respond to our talk. If we are not sure how we should relate to the opposite sex (to open doors, light cigarettes, pay for meals), we listen and look for others like us to help us develop a *social reality.*

In addition to other individuals' influences, much of our social reality is constructed through the kinds of institutions we establish. Within our institutions there develops a normative order that enables us to criticize and ultimately transform the existing order (Swidler, 1991, p. 577). In other words, the mere establishment of norms within our various institutions provides us with the mechanism to change our social reality. For example, in a 1989 study of news reporting and its role in the formation of public opinion, Vincent Price points out that the media's depiction of how groups of people are responding to issues actually influences individuals' opinions on those issues. According to Price, "the media perform the key role of linking separate members of the mass to wider trends in public debate" (Price, 1989, p. 221). For better or for worse, a new social reality is created.

In another study (Kahn et al., 1982), individuals were interested in maximizing the social rewards in a situation and in making a positive impression on other group members regardless of their own monetary gain. In fact, situations in which subjects focused on social rewards resulted in their loss of rewards as part of the experiment. In other words, our motivation to join groups, create social realities, and feel accepted by others is a common need we either underestimate or minimize. Therapy groups and self-help groups rely heavily on the process of social comparison and perception of similar experience and feelings in others. In groups this universality of experience and the development of a social reality are primary factors in helping people feel good about themselves and in increasing self-esteem (Brothen and Shovholt, 1981).

In evaluating ourselves, we have a tendency to seek fairly similar others as a comparison group. We seek a similar, attractive reference group and use these individuals as a basis for comparison.

When there are vast changes in social norms, styles, morality, taste, criteria of beauty, child-rearing practices, divorce, and a myriad other aspects of our lives, our reactions to the changes are primarily based on the evaluations of those around us. For that reason, friends or members of our peer group have greater influence than others.

Just as there is pressure to establish the correctness of an opinion, there are pressures to establish the appropriateness of an emotional or bodily state. And because emotion-producing situations are often novel and outside the realm of our past experience, it is not surprising that the emotions are particularly vulnerable to social influence. Consider an example:

> Each weekday morning, year in and year out, there were, with few changes, the same people standing on the suburban station platform waiting for the 7:40 train to take them into the city and to work. As each arrived, they nodded "good morning" or perfunctorily commented on the cold or the rain. For the most part, they got their papers or their coffee and waited in small clusters where they thought the doors would be when the train stopped. There were a few women, and they boarded first; then the older men boarded, and then the others.
>
> On the train they read, worked, or slept. There was almost no conversation. It was just another morning, except on October 15 it wasn't.
>
> In an incredible accident, the 7:40 crashed into a stopped train in front of it with such force that over three hundred people were knocked unconscious and, thought to be dead, were strewn about the cars. Bloody noses and bleeding heads were commonplace as the crash stop hurled passengers into the seats in front of them. Broken glass from the windows spattered all within range. Smoke created a darkness in the cars.
>
> It could have been a stampede for safety through the broken glass windows. It could have been a trampling horde concerned only with reaching a door and getting out. It could have been a caged mob regressed to the basic instinct of personal survival. It was the first commuter accident

in fifty-two years. No one could have been prepared for it or could have known how to act, given the incredible nature of the catastrophe, the early hour of the morning, and the fact that most were half asleep as well.

The norms of the suburban station platform prevailed. The first concern was for the women, as the people next to them helped them with their injuries while they themselves were bleeding. Then passengers shouted for the older men and rushed to their aid; one who was knocked unconscious was picked up by three men who moved him to a bench, covered him with their overcoats, and attempted to revive him. Not one person left; those who were not visibly injured were helping others.

Even when the police arrived, people who had been helping others stayed with them on the trip to the hospital so that they would not be frightened by being injured and alone. People on the train emerged supporting others who were unable to walk and remained at their sides, helping them to phone booths to call their relatives and waiting with them until a family member arrived.

Police, newspaper reporters, and hospital workers alike commented that they had never seen anything like it. No looting or robbing, no pushing or crushing, no abandoning others for the police to care for in due time. Over and over, those injured reported, "I can't believe strangers can be so caring." A woman whose nose had been crushed and whose head was badly lacerated reported, "The man who had been seated next to me, and to whom I had never said more than good morning, held my arm and kept telling me that I would be all right. He would stay with me in the hospital. He would call my husband and daughter. I was so frightened and bloody and hurting, I don't know what I would have done without him. And it was like that throughout the car." One possible explanation is that the daily routine and co-presence had subtly conditioned the riders to each other and that some positive—though subconscious—relationship had developed over time.

◆ Reader Activity

As you read this incident, how do you explain the norms that developed in the train crash? How do you explain people's caring, altruistic response?

_____

_____

_____

_____

Imagine yourself on that train. How do you think it happened that train group members influenced each other and were able to get such conformity?

_____

_____

_____

_____ ◆

External Forces Based on Direct Influence of Others

Coming into a group means interacting, which means influence attempts. From the simplest "Why don't you sit here with us?" to "John is by far the best candidate. How could you consider anyone else?" we influence each other. When we persuade a person to act in a certain way under certain circumstances, we are using direct influence.

There are a number of reasons why people attempt to influence others to comply to certain norms. One is that it will help the group accomplish its goals; another is that it will help the group maintain itself. Both these functions must be developed with strong supporting forces if the group is to succeed.

To Achieve Group Goals   Pressures toward uniformity among members of a group may occur because uniformity is necessary for the group to achieve its goal (Festinger, 1950).

When a group is attempting to raise funds, it develops norms for standardizing pledge cards, assigning members to districts to be solicited, turning in money, and reporting results. All of these procedures develop because they will help the group achieve its objective of successfully raising the money needed. Consider how members will respond to the member who turns in pledges on the corner of a menu or the back of a shopping list. How will they respond to the member who solicits people in someone else's territory? How will they respond if the campaign ends and a member doesn't turn in the money? People exert pressures on others to follow approved procedures that are directed toward achieving the group goal. These are sources of uniformity that are seen as legitimate.

Sororities and fraternities often provide classic examples of how norms develop as part of the process of achieving a group goal. In a 1988 study of binge eating in sororities, Crandall found clear evidence of group norms about appropriate binge eating and its relationship to popularity. Because of the social importance of body size and shape for this group, it is likely that physical attractiveness is one of the group goals that is sought by maintaining these norms (Crandall, 1988).

If a football team is to win, members are expected to learn the plays and execute them. The maverick who disregards the rules (pressures toward uniformity) often will be ridiculed—"So you thought you were the whole team, or better than the whole team?" The norms allow one superstar on the team, but even he must play within the limits set by the group norms.

Members are expected to adhere to the norms viewed as necessary to help the group achieve its goal. Any member who does not adhere will be seen as a threat to that end, and efforts will be made to induce him or her to return to the group procedures—or to leave the group.

For Group Maintenance   Some group standards are sustained to help the group maintain itself. Procedures for paying dues, pressures for attending meetings regularly, and norms of delaying the start of a meeting until enough members are present are all norms that are conducive to maintaining a group or an organization.

Frequently, other norms develop in an effort to sustain the group. For example, members may avoid areas of conflict in discussion for fear that such conflict may evoke anger or loud voices and cause some members to leave as a result of the unpleasant experience. (It is a common norm that outward display of harmony is necessary for group survival.)

One study showed that the norms present in fraternities tend to emphasize a stereotypical concept of masculinity. The behaviors exhibited (such as competition over new members, sports, or women) encouraged a "context in which the use of coercion in sexual relations with women is normative" (Martin and Hummer, 1989, pp. 457, 459). These behaviors seem to reinforce the emphasis on masculinity and therefore help to maintain the group.

On the other hand, norms of announcing honors to the group develop. Whether a member is named in the newspaper, makes the varsity team, or is included in a prestigious representative council, groups brag because doing so boosts their image of being winners and enhances the desirability of membership. These norms will be enforced as members are solicited to report such honors as an invitation to speak, a publication, or a promotion; members may even be reprimanded for not letting others know. The group is thereby maintained by pressures to "let everyone in on" individual achievements.

A Preliminary Theory of Norm Development

A major work on how norms develop emerged from research by Bettenhausen and Murnighan (1985).[4] Initially, these researchers focused on decision making in small groups and were not concerned with norms. However, they noticed that norms developed when their five-member groups came together and that norm development had a major impact on the decision-making process. They, like Feldman (1984), found that in new groups the meanings attached to action were based

---

4. This discussion is based on the work of Bettenhausen and Murnighan (1985).

on the members' prior experiences in what they believed were similar situations. These findings led to the formulation of a preliminary theory of norm development. The accompanying figure illustrates four possible ways members can interpret the situation in a new group.

GROUP MEMBERS' SCRIPTS

	Similar to Each Other's	Different from Each Other's
MEMBER'S DEFINITION OF THE NEW SITUATION — Similar to Each Other's	**I** — Interactions confirm each member's interpretation and are not problematic	**II** — Initial interactions proceed smoothly but latent disagreement may require subsequent development of a group-based understanding
Different from Each Other's	**III** — Initial interactions trigger the development of a group-based understanding of the situation; members must work toward a common definition of the current situation	**IV** — Initial interactions either frustrate the group or trigger the development of a group-based understanding of the situation; elaborate discussions are necessary

The first propositions use this scheme of interpretative possibilities and indicate the directions different groups might pursue.

- *Proposition 1.* In new groups, uncertainty over appropriate behavior leads group members to anchor the current situation to what they perceive as similar, previously experienced situations.
- *Proposition 1a.* If all members use similar scripts and define the situation in the same way, interaction is easy (cell I).
- *Proposition 1b.* If group members use different scripts but respond in similar ways, initial interaction may not be problematic, but latent discord may eventually lead to conflict that is then difficult to resolve (cell III).
- *Proposition 1c.* If group members do not adopt common interpretations of the novel situation, they must develop a group-based understanding of the situation (cells II and IV). If they have different scripts, they must build understanding without the aid of past references.

Initially, one member's action may be incompatible with another member's interpretation of the situation. When this occurs, the group must negotiate (sometimes tacitly) to determine which interpretation is appropriate.

- *Proposition 2.* As group members interact, their shared experiences form the basis for expectations about future interactions.
- *Proposition 2a.* When other members' actions are compatible with the meaning a member has attached to the task, the interpretation is legitimized and confidence in applying the interpretation increases.
- *Proposition 2b.* When some members' actions are incompatible with other members' conceptualizations of the task, the nonacting members may revise their original interpretations, or
- *Proposition 2c.* They may attempt to persuade the group to accept their conceptualization, defining the observed actions as inappropriate.

In trying to persuade the group to accept a point of view, a group member challenges the prevailing interpretation of the situation and what constitutes appropriate action within it.

Although norms can develop without them, threats are crucial to understanding the formation of a norm, because they allow the group to consider its own evolving, taken-for-granted activity publicly.

Threats may be easy or extremely hard to resolve. When a single unsupported group member makes a threat, the situation is often quickly resolved. Just as the conformity pressures of a group break down when nonconformists are supported by other group members (Asch, 1951), so too are *supported* threats expected to provoke discussion and resolution. Successful threats demonstrate that the group's previous behavior may have been due to ignorance (Krech and Crutchfield, 1948) rather than an accurate understanding of appropriate behavior.

- *Proposition 3.* Challenges to the group's evolving pattern of behavior can reveal the subjective meanings the members attached to the group's interaction.
- *Proposition 3a.* Quickly accepted threats indicate general approval of the action expressed in the threat.
- *Proposition 3b.* Quickly dismissed threats indicate general agreement that was expressed only implicitly in the group's actions.
- *Proposition 3c.* Threats not quickly resolved (major threats) indicate that members attached incongruent meanings to the group's actions.
- *Proposition $3c_1$.* Groups that resolve major threats become more immune to subsequent threats.
- *Proposition $3c_2$.* Groups that have not experienced major threats may be particularly vulnerable when one surfaces.

At some point, the group begins to base its actions on the meanings that have developed *within* the group rather than on the meanings the individuals used initially to anchor and understand the task. At that point, we would say that a norm unique to the interacting members exists. Opp (1982) and others proposed that norms are gradual and evolutionary. However, although norms certainly can change over time, the observations of Bettenhauser and Muringham suggest that norm formation is subtle but swift.

The test of any norm is its ability to control behavior. When group members impose sanctions on behavior that violates the group's precedents, a norm can be considered fully operative.

■ *Proposition 4.* Once a norm has formed, any further attempts to alter the behavior it controls will be met with sanctions.

The Power of Groups

What is the power of groups to make people conform? How does it happen that people can be induced under the pressure of a group to commit unusual acts?

Social psychologists, incredulous about what they see about them, have sought to understand and theorize how it happens that people conform, comply, and obey. Kelman (1958) sought to understand how officers had been brainwashed as prisoners during the Korean War. Jahoda (1956) was aroused by the civil liberties issues and loyalty oaths of the fifties and the outrageousness of the McCarthy hearings.

Galenter (1980) has addressed the upsurge of charismatic religious sects in the last several decades and members' abrupt abandonment of earlier social ties. The power of the group to induce people to conform is a continuous source of questions, speculation, and incredulity. Consider the following by-now legendary examples:

Patty Hearst, the abducted heiress daughter of the San Francisco publishing family, was photographed robbing a bank with an ultra-radical group after only two months of being with the group. She testified that she was forced to conform to the group's demands out of fear for her life.

The charismatic Jim Jones brought his followers, the People's Temple, to the jungles of Guyana, where, in a desperate aftermath to the killing of a U.S. Congressman, more than nine hundred men, women, and children committed mass suicide by drinking a fruit punch laced with cyanide.

Cults like the "Moonies," Scientology, Hari Krishna, and others are able to convince typically white, middle-class, college youth to forgo their families, education, career goals, and material possessions.

A tragic example is the experience of a Vietnam veteran[5] who called a Boston radio station on Labor Day, 1972:

---

5. Excerpt from *Time,* "Human beings fused together" in *Time,* October 23, 1972, p. 36. Copyright 1972 Time Inc. Reprinted by permission.

> I am a Vietnam veteran, and I don't think the American people really, really understand war and what's going on. We went into villages after they dropped napalm, and the human beings were fused together like pieces of metal that had been soldered. . . . I was there a year, and I never had the courage to say that was wrong. . . . A lot of guys had the guts. They got sectioned out, and on the discharge, it was put that they were unfit for military duty—unfit because they had the courage. Guys like me were fit because we condoned it, we rationalized it.

In fact, during the Vietnam era, the questioning of authority by youths was transformed into what was perceived as anti-American behavior. During periods of nationalism, norms often became "facts."

Each of these incidents is incredible and almost impossible to understand. How do groups induce people to conform to this extent?

In thinking of how people respond to group pressures, three concepts have been helpful. They are conformity, compliance, and obedience (Baron, Roper, and Baron, 1974).

Conformity

It is hard to resist explaining conformity through an old, old joke. It goes like this: a person is standing on a corner intently looking at the sky. Another person comes by, sees the first person looking at the sky, and also looks up. After a while there is a small crowd clustered around the original person, all looking at the sky. After looking for a while, and waiting, someone finally asks the first person what he is looking for. "Oh," he replies, "I'm not looking for anything. I have a stiff neck and I'm waiting for my friend to pick me up and take me to the doctor." That's conformity! It involves the way we are influenced by others simply on the basis of what they do. Our implicit assumption is that similar behavior will elicit approval and that dissimilar behavior will bring censure.

◆ Reader Activity

When you were in high school, how were you supposed to look?

Hair _____

Clothes _____

Shoes _____

Cosmetics _____

Jewelry _____

Do you remember people who didn't look that way? What happened? How were they treated? _____

_____

_____

Although clothes are readily evident illustrations of conformity, they were not the only example. Which activities were "in"? _____

_____

Which activities were "out"? _____

_____

Why? _____

What did you want to do but chose not to do because it would be "uncool" (or whatever the derisive expression was in your day)? _____

_____

_____

_____   ◆

Conformity occurs because we internally decide to go along with the group. It may be because we are ignorant of the subject, they are more knowledgeable, and we listen to the experts.

A study by Campbell and associates (1986) showed greater conformity where pressure and self-doubt were high and the existing norm was more extreme. Also, conformity increases as the size of the group grows; the larger the number, the larger the group with whom we compare ourselves, and the more likely we are to conform (Gerard, Wilhelmy, and Conolley, 1968).

The more conforming behavior is reinforced, the more likely we are to continue (Endler, 1966). And of course, the more we want others to like us (ingratiating behavior), the more we search for cues to what they want and give it to them (Jones, 1964). In general, the more we like the group, the greater the conformity (Kiesler, 1963; Savell, 1971).

Similarly, the more our values resemble those of some reference group, the more likely we are to conform to that group's norms. Fisher (1988) suggests that "with respect to AIDS, relevant group norms may reject using condoms . . . or promote engaging in other risky sexual practices" because they may fear sanctions for not conforming. One example is that in many cultures, being concerned with AIDS may not be consistent with "machismo" values (Fisher, 1988, pp. 914–915). Thus, conforming to group norms may even take precedence over life-preserving behavior such as AIDS prevention.

Compliance

Although in the *conformity* situation there is no overt pressure on a person to behave as the others do, he or she responds as though there were pressures to comply. In the Asch line experiment, each person responded as he or she saw the line, but when there was unanimous group agreement, it created an internal pressure on the individual to conform. In *compliance* situations, the request is direct. A person asks you to do a favor, to vote for a particular candidate, to contribute to a fund, or to do an unpleasant job.

In conformity, the pressure is invisible; in compliance, it is obvious. Compliance seems to arouse resistence. We are bombarded by requests, from being asked to do a colleague a favor by covering a class for him or her to being solicited to buy tickets to help a cause; from taking minutes at a meeting to being asked to chair a committee.

The request comes, and there is a pause as we think, "Now how can I get out of it and still have them like me?"

For some, a request almost automatically induces compliance. For them, there is now a whole world of literature on assertiveness training (Fensterheim and Baer, 1975) and learning how to say no. Of course, at different times in our lives our need to be accepted by others has a profound effect on our ability to say no. For example, when we're teen-agers it's nearly impossible to say no to friends with whom we strongly identify. Yet when we're older and involved in a career or family, saying no to friends has a different meaning and may be easier to do than before. Ward and Wilson (1980) found that motivational orientation and stage of moral development affect whether an individual will acquiesce to social pressures toward conformity.

Compliance research has focused on how, despite resistance, a person can be induced to comply. One way to get people to comply is to do them a favor so that they are indebted to you. If someone has borrowed your class notes, an unequal relationship exists in terms of costs and rewards. The relationship is no longer equitable. The borrower will feel more comfortable, and equity will be restored, if she or he does something nice for you.

Regan (1971) designed a simple experiment to test the hypothesis that doing someone a favor induces compliance later. In the experiment, presumably on art appreciation, subjects waited in groups of two (however, one of the two was a confederate). In half the situations, the confederate was pleasant and amiable as they chatted, waiting for the "experiment" to begin; in the other half, the confederate was purposely unpleasant. In one condition, the confederate then bought sodas for the two of them; in the other, the two just sat and waited. They looked at more art; then the confederate asked the subject to buy raffle tickets to help the confederate's home town high school build a gym; the person who could sell the most tickets would supposedly win a $50 prize. The results overwhelmingly indicate that whether the confederate was pleasant or unpleasant, the subject was most likely to buy the raffle tickets if the confederate had performed a favor for him or her. Thus compliance is strongly increased when a person feels obligated to the one making the request.

The foot-in-the-door technique is another method to get a person to comply. First, ask the person to comply with a small, innocuous request, then ask for a big one (Freedman and Fraser, 1966). In a fascinating field experiment, they asked subjects to place a large sign on their front lawns that said "drive carefully"; less than 17 percent of the subjects were willing to do so. Another group of subjects were first asked to place a small sign saying "drive carefully" and then at a later time were asked to put the large sign on their lawns. Now, over 76 percent were willing. And interestingly enough, a small initial request seems to be a better technique for inducing compliance than a moderate one (Baron, 1973).

Margaret Singer, whose interest in brainwashing and cults led her to interview every prisoner of war who returned from North Korea and Southeast Asia, developed an understanding of how cults operate. Singer (Freeman, 1979, p. 6) believes that members of religious cults are victims of this foot-in-the-door technique.

> In many cults, when people join they don't realize what it is they are joining, and they are lured a step at a time by very persuasive and deceptive practices. Middle-class Caucasian kids, in particular, are not very street smart. They are trusting and naive and they believe people who approach them with offers (of a dinner, a place to stay, a weekend away, instant companionship) much more than lower-class kids, who are wise to the fact that no one gives you anything without expecting something in return.

What starts as a response to friendship, or an invitation to dinner, insidiously moves with each step of compliance to a greater act of compliance, until after years of being in a cult, leaving is almost unthinkable. The gradual, foot-in-the-door technique escalates to the point where compliance becomes automatic, and decision making as an individual extremely difficult.

Obedience

In compliance, people can say yes or no; there are options and alternatives. They may feel compelled to say yes, but they can be resistant. They don't have to accept the invitation to the group meeting, attend the dinner, or acquiesce to the first request. There will not be severe consequences.

Obedience is different. If one person has power over another person, obedience can be demanded. If the second person fails to obey, power is exercised in the form of negative sanctions such as demerits, demotions, fines, imprisonment, even death. Those who refuse to follow orders are labeled bad, rebellious, uppity, even psychopathic. Here, the social influence is very direct and very explicit. There is a sense of "Do it, or else . . ."

Obedience is instilled in us as children, first when we are expected to obey our parents and later when we hear, "Listen to the teacher. Do what you're told." Enlisted men and women are expected to obey their officers, no matter what the personal consequences or moral concerns, as in the incident that the Vietnam veteran reported.

Whether in Vietnam or Nazi Germany, how is it that otherwise moral, ethical, sympathetic people can be induced to be obedient to commands that inflict great harm on others?

Stanley Milgram (1963, 1964, 1965), at Yale, designed a series of experiments that are among the most important in social psychology. He sought to understand how it could be that people would actually harm one another. This was behavior, not words, called *action conformity*.

The supposed intent of his research design was "to test the effects of punishment on memory." The question Milgram really raised was whether individuals who received a command from a legitimate authority would obey, even though the authority figure had no real power to compel obedience.

In the experiment, subjects were ordered to give a confederate an electric shock whenever he or she got a word wrong. The more words wrong, the greater the intensity of the shock. The confederate was trained to writhe in pain and to pound on the wall. Despite the apparent pain, the intensity of the shocks was to increase whenever he or she was wrong.

When a group of college students was asked to predict how the subjects would respond, the majority guessed that they would refuse to administer extremely strong shocks to an innocent victim. However, most subjects did, in fact, obey the command to continue shocking the victim up to the maximum level. After watching the confederate pound on the wall and refuse to do the next task, only 13 percent of the subjects defied the experimenter and stopped. Even when the intensity of the shock reached the danger level and beyond, well over half the subjects were still administering shocks to the victim.

How did the subjects react as they were carrying out an order to deliver painful shocks to an innocent victim? They were not indifferent or cold-blooded torturers. Rather, they seemed to be very nervous, and the tension appeared to be extreme. Subjects perspired, trembled, stuttered, bit their lips, groaned, and dug their fingernails into their palms. Over a third engaged in nervous laughter. Subjects afterward were embarrassed about the laughter and explained that it was not under their control; it did not indicate that they enjoyed the task.

This experiment puts subjects in a conflict situation—a conflict between their moral values about harming others and their tendency to obey an authoritative command. What is frightening about the results is that, in this case, the authority figure had no real power over the subjects. They would never see the authority figure again. Presumably, obedience would be even higher if the commands came from one who had some control over the subject's life.

Milgram, in a modification of the original experiment, wondered whether subjects could be induced to perform acts that they would not perform individually in response to group pressure (Milgram, 1964). The same general experiment was used, but now the subject administering the shock was joined by two associates (confederates). The level of shock to be administered was suggested on each trial by the subject and his or her two associates; the learner received the lowest of the three suggestions. If he or she wished, the subject could administer the mildest shock simply by naming the lowest (15-volt) level each time. The assistants proposed increased shock levels each time.

As a control condition, to determine how individuals respond without group pressure, some subjects had no assistants and each was told that he or she could select any shock level he or she wished on the various trials.

The group pressure led to much more intense shocks being given than the subject-alone condition. When subjects were by themselves, only 5 percent went past the 150-volt condition in which the learner asked to be released because of a heart condition. Better than two-thirds of the subjects went past this shock level when the confederates urged them on. Once again, it was shown that subjects can rather easily be influenced to inflict pain on an innocent victim.

Although individuals said they would not harm someone and knew it was morally wrong, they did so on command of the experimenter or at the suggestion of the associates in the group condition. If group pressure can induce the subject to continue to give shocks and intensely harm an innocent person, what will encourage the subject to defy the experimenter?

In yet another revision of the Milgram experiments (Milgram, 1965), in the group condition the two confederates went along with the experimenter until the 150-volt shock level. At this point, one of them indicated an unwillingness to participate any further because of the learner's complaints. Despite the experimenter's insistence, the associate got up and went to another part of the room. The experiment was then continued, but after 210 volts the second confederate also decided not to continue, saying, "I'm willing to answer your questions, but I'm not willing to shock that man against his will. I'll have no part of it."

With defiant peers for support, 90 percent of the subjects were able to defy the experimenter and stop shocking the victims. Without such support, only 35 percent did so.

Milgram suggests that in the regular experimental condition, moral pressures probably lead many individuals to come near to defiance, but the moral pressures are not quite enough for them to take the final step. Additional pressure from fellow group members who are defiant is sufficient to push them over the threshold of disobedience. As one subject said, "Well, I was already thinking about quitting when the guy broke off." For others, it was as though the defiant peers had suggested something new. "The thought of stopping didn't enter my mind until it was put there by the other two."

Not surprisingly, most subjects denied that the confederates' behavior had anything to do with their defiance; the data, however, clearly indicate that the confederates exerted a powerful influence.

In real-life situations, if only a few individuals speak out and refuse to engage in acts they consider wrong, their influence can be surprisingly powerful. People have greater freedom to defy immoral standards than they realize, and the defiant behavior of someone else can make that fact obvious.

Collusive Behavior: Maintaining the Status Quo of Norms

Butler (1987) examined the anatomy of another kind of collusion: "cooperating with others consciously or preconsciously to reinforce prevailing attitudes, values, behaviors, or norms." The *effect* of such collusion in a group is the maintaining of the status quo; the *goal* is self-protection.

Conscious collusion is easy to recognize and understand. A consultant, for example, witnesses a meeting in which the boss seeks subordinates' commitment to his proposal. The subordinates suppress their true feelings and say only positive things, believing their boss does not want to hear negative feedback. The consultant senses that the subordinates did not respond honestly and confirms this suspicion in private conversations with them. Nevertheless, he still tells the boss, "You ran a good meeting," fearing that the truth will cause the boss to cancel his contract. The boss wants support for his ideas and uses much rhetoric about team work; he neither sees nor looks for subordinates' reservations.

Everyone at this meeting knows what game is being played. The norms are against telling the truth, and all present act out of socially programmed ignorance (Argyris, 1982). This is a clear example of conscious collusion.

Preconscious collusion occurs when a person does not simply hide his or her feelings but actually remains unaware of them. When people feel threatened, which means they face a loss of power, they may exhibit preconscious collusion. A key motivation for collusion is not losing—and perhaps even winning.

Have you ever become angry at being interrupted while making a point—and then pleasantly denied being upset? Such behavior not only reflects our parents' admonitions against expressing negative feelings but has a self-protective function as well. Admitting to anger gives people important information about you, increasing your vulnerability.

Much collusive behavior is preconscious. Typically, when a supportive observer points it out, people can see their collusion and acknowledge it. Because it is preconscious, however, and likely to stem from deep socialization messages rein-

Messages from Childhood Leading to Collusive Behavior

Message	Alternative internalizations	Possible collusive behaviors
Be nice	I should mask negative feelings	Saying "yes" when you mean "no"
	I am a bad person because I am not nice	Devaluing oneself
You must work harder than white men (a message for women and minority groups)	I am not as good as a white man	Acting in ways fulfilling the "inferior" label
	I will never be appreciated	Feeling bitter and resentful toward white men
Do not question adults	I must defer to those in power and authority	Not saying what one feels
	Those in power and authority may be ignorant, despotic, uncaring, easily embarrassed, or the like	Not threatening or challenging those in power and authority
It is not nice to fight	I must manipulate people to get what I want	Acting passively aggressive
	I must avoid disagreeable situations	Making superficial agreements
Put others first	What I want is not important	Devaluing oneself

forced consistently by past collusion that successfully protected them (see figure), they are likely to continue to behave collusively in similar situations.

Janis's work on "groupthink" (1982) has shown how socialization pressure leads to collusive behavior at high levels and how organizational difficulties arise because people withhold honest feedback. Certainly to live in any society, one must play the collusive game to some degree. But the important phrase here is *to some degree*. More understanding and deeper recognition of our collusive tendencies

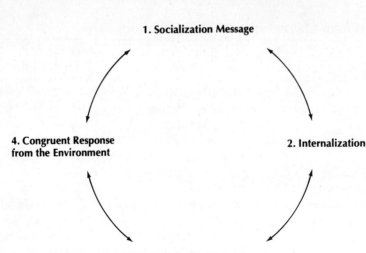

THE CIRCLE OF COLLUSION

may enable us to reduce the frequency with which we harm ourselves through such behavior.

Accepting Group Norms: Under What Conditions?

Under what conditions does a member act like other members and conform to the norms of the group? He or she is most likely to conform when one or more of the following circumstances are a factor.

Continued Membership Is Desired

If membership is desired, people are more likely to be influenced by other members of the group. If the group is a reference group for a person, he or she will be especially influenced by the norms of the group (Buchwald, 1966; Gould, 1969). It is because we want to "fit in" that we look for dress cues on a campus, listen to others and let their opinions mold ours, and withhold our views when they disagree with those of the majority (Singleton, 1979).

Lower Status Is Perceived

In group-pressure conformity experiments, women tend to conform more than men (Cooper, 1979; Eagly, 1978; Eagly and Carli, 1981; Maccoby and Jacklin, 1974). A possible interpretation of this sex difference is that sex functions as a *status cue* in newly formed groups (Berger, Fisek, Norman and Zelditch, 1977; Berger, Rosenholtz, and Zelditch, 1980). According to this interpretation, people who enter groups are identified by others in terms of cues, or attributes, that convey information about their status. Sex is a status cue, because—despite women's efforts to overcome these conditions—men generally have higher status than women in both organizational hierarchies and families. Age, race, and physical attractiveness are other examples of status cues.

Social interaction is affected by these status characteristics, because the cues lead to expectations about performance. In particular, men who manifest higher status characteristics than women are expected to contribute more effectively to the group's task. Consequently, they are usually given more opportunities to participate.

Eagly and Chrvala (1986) found that age carried an even stronger status message than sex and that younger members of both sexes were more likely to conform than older members or female members as measured alone.

Salience of Membership Is Heightened

Imagine a research experiment designed to acquire information on attitudes toward birth control. Let us assume the population to be studied is divided into two groups. One group will be asked their opinion on birth control. For the second group, the design will be changed slightly. One additional question will be asked prior to the central one; each person will be asked his or her religion. How will the responses differ? The question on religion heightens the salience or cues of membership, and the respondent is more likely to remember "how one of us is expected to feel."

When a member receives cues that he or she has been named, for example, a member of the administrative staff of a hospital, a member of a professional organization, a Christian, or a member of Amnesty International, he or she is more likely to accept the pressures toward uniformity for that group than if membership is unconfirmed.

The Group Is Cohesive

A cohesive group is one that members find meets their needs or one in which they desire to remain for some other reason. The more cohesive the group, the greater the likelihood that members will conform to the group norms, and the greater the pressure the members exert on others to conform (Festinger and

Thibaut, 1951; Janis, 1971). It is often said that management or administration should help their lower staffs or employees become cohesive units. A highly cohesive work group might develop group pride and produce at a high level. Worker participation often results in new production innovations and higher-quality output. Several studies indicate the impact of cohesiveness and subsequent norms on group members' behavior. Baird (1982) reports that prior sharing between individuals produces greater cohesion and cooperation in later problem situations. In a study by Norris and Niebuhr (1980), cohesion was significantly correlated with increased performance.

Sanctions Are Expected

Norms exist for specific purposes, and if these purposes are valued by members, those who are deviant can expect to be sanctioned. The sanctions may be fines (for lateness, swearing, and so forth), a negative comment, sarcasm or ridicule, or even exclusion from the group. In some situations the sanctions may be even more severe, such as being dishonorably discharged, being fired, being banished or imprisoned, or even being put to death.

In the book *One Flew over the Cuckoo's Nest,* the cocky hero, McMurphy, arrives at a state mental institution, which is his lazy man's alternative to the chain gang at the state prison. He becomes interested in the patients and involves them in basketball, watching the world series, even reviving their interest in sex and women— all the while defying the rules of the head nurse, which are expressed as the "community norms."

The patients know the system and the obedience expected; group therapy is a farce. Briefly, there is renewed hope that McMurphy will defy the system. As the others marvel at his questioning and noncompliance when it doesn't make sense, they are exhilarated.

It becomes increasingly clear, however, that the system will prevail in the end. It will take away McMurphy's identity (he has defied the rules) and make him and the others dependent on the authorities (who stand futilely by or must punish infractions no matter what). The tragedy unfolds, from electric shock treatments to the ultimate sanction for defying the rules and the authority, a lobotomy.

Sanctions are powerful mechanisms to force members into compliance. When patients, clients, or students are the involuntary members, sanctions can enforce conformity beyond belief. Although the term *sanction* generally has a negative connotation, it is important to note that sanctions can be used for positive reinforcements. Sanctions may also include one's name on the honor roll, the designation "good citizen of the week," a raise, a bonus (to the person with the best safety record in the plant), and a promotion.

Another aspect of sanctions is that they carry two messages, one about present behavior and another about future behavior. For example: "That was quite a mistake (present); that had better not happen again (future)"; or, "You're doing a great job

(present). At the rate you're going, you'll be a vice-president in no time (future)."
Sanctions can be expected to influence both present and future conformity.

Deviance from Norms

What about those who do not conform to norms? An act that violates a shared idea
about what should or should not be done at a particular time (or by a particular
person) is called a deviant act. It is deviant to disagree with Nurse Rachett in *One
Flew over the Cuckoo's Nest,* to sit on the table during a board meeting, or to arrive
at class in a bathing suit. However, not every behavior that departs from the expected
is deviant. The quiet member may become more active; the active member may
take an unpopular position in the course of discussion; one member may change
his or her feeling toward another member. None of these are deviant acts unless
the group has norms that quiet members remain quiet, that no opinions other
than the traditional may be discussed, and that members maintain the same relations
with others. What happens when a person is deviant?

Interaction with the deviant increases when the group first recognizes a member's deviancy. There will be efforts directed toward amplification and clarification
of his or her position, and opposing information will be directed toward him or
her in an effort to lessen the deviancy. If the pressure induces the deviant to return
to the norms of the group, the discussion will continue with the deviant in his or
her usual role. If, however, the deviant continues the behavior, the group may
redefine its boundaries to exclude him or her by ignoring him or her in discussions.
This is most likely to occur in a cohesive group and when the area of deviance is
relevant to the purpose of the group (Schachter, 1951).

However, if the member is respected and valued, the situation may be different.
There is a theory (Hollander, 1960) that prestigious members have "idiosyncrasy
credits"—that is, a kind of credit for helpful behavior in the past that allows them
leeway in following the norms of the present. It is as though their previous work
for the group entitles them to some rewards in the form of increased flexibility
of behavior and immunity from punishment for deviance. A prestigious member
who deviates from the norm may be dealt with in a number of ways. One is that
he or she may be purposely misinterpreted or "not heard." Another is that his or
her behavior may be perceived as idiosyncratic ("You know he has these bad days.
Disregard anything he says; he doesn't mean it"). Or nonconforming acts are now
approved rather than disapproved. (A successful, grant-getting physician and corporation president continues to wear green scrub suits to staff meetings when
other staff members are stylishly dressed in three-piece suits and current women's
fashions. No one comments on the green scrub suit, however.)

Until recently, deviance from norms was regarded only as a negative function,
a behavior requiring reinterpretation and individual or group pressures to return
to accepted norms. But Hanke and Saxberg (1985), who studied isolates and de-

viants in both the American and Japanese workplaces, found evidence that members who are constructively deviant, raising questions while co-workers remain silent, can be productive workers rather than costly troublemakers. Thus deviance can serve a positive function.

Deviance helps members to master norms (it is a demonstration of what should not be done) and helps them to be more articulate about these norms. In addition, it helps them to comprehend what their group is and what their group is not (to feel offended by an act and to see others similarly offended provides information on oneself and on the group that could be gained in no other way). Often, the individual perceives his or her social identity only when it has become problematic (Hewitt, 1989, p. 170). In a sense, the deviant behavior provides a social identity.

A number of studies call attention to the importance of distinguishing true independence (indifference to the normative expectations of other people and groups) from rebellion (direct rejection of the normative expectations of other people and groups). Although both represent nonconforming behavior, it is important to recognize that they are very different in both the attitudes they represent and the resulting behaviors. *Conforming behavior* (to norms) is a consequence of a person's awareness of expectations held for him or her by others or as a member of a group, coupled with a decision to adhere to these expectations. *Rebellion* against norms is a consequence of awareness of the norms, coupled with a decision *not* to adhere to them. True *independence* represents indifference to the norms and expectations of others—personal criteria for behavior, rather than expectations of others, are seen as motivators of behavior.

◆ Individual Experiment

When you broke a rule as a child or adolescent at home, who talked with you and how? By whom and how were you punished? These experiences represent how your family managed deviance. Groups often respond to deviance in less explicit ways, but usually just as predictably. In a group in which you participate, write a list of minor deviant behaviors, such as not raising your hand before you talk, coming late to a meeting or leaving early, talking about completely irrelevant events, or being too adamant in a disagreement. Take your list to the next group meeting and notice how the group responds to the deviant behavior. Does the leader openly scold the group member? Does the leader indicate that he or she would like to talk after the meeting with the deviant member? Does the leader give the deviant a certain look or make a disapproving face? Do other members communicate nonverbally in some way with the deviant? Is a joke made of the behavior? Will a member talk privately to the deviant after the meeting? Will the behavior be tolerated and not commented on? Or will the behavior be tolerated until it occurs too often and then some formal action be taken by the leader, such as a written warning or a failing grade?   ◆

Norms as Inhibiting, Preserving, Institutionalizing, and Stagnating Groups

Group norms themselves can have powerful effects on a group's productivity, goals, and expectations. To illustrate the debilitating functions of norms, John Kenneth Galbraith (1970), in a *Time* magazine article, referred to regulatory bodies, but the phenomenon he described is familiar: "the fat cat syndrome."

> Regulatory bodies, like the people who comprise them, have a marked life cycle. In youth they are vigorous, aggressive, evangelistic and even intolerant. Later they mellow, and in old age—after a matter of ten or fifteen years—they become, with some exceptions, either an arm of the industry they are regulating or senile (p. 88).

After examining the effects of group norms and goal setting on productivity, Lichtman and Lane (1983) suggested that the effects of goal setting are regulated or moderated by the presence of group norms.

Also, group norms tend to preserve the status quo. Procedures that at one time were appropriate and helped the group achieve its purposes may still be in existence long after their appropriateness has diminished.

Yet the resistance to change that promulgates increased difficulties and problems in a differentiated society is one of the group's prime assets. Norms and pressures toward uniformity create security and order in interaction. Members know the rules and procedures for working in that group; they know what is expected, they hope to be rewarded for conforming to group norms.

It is pointless to ask whether group norms are good or bad. But there are fruitful questions to ask: Which norms help the group achieve its purposes, and which are harmful or inhibiting? Which norms are compatible with the goals and values of the group, and under what conditions? How can the norms be changed or reconsidered to permit the group to achieve its purposes under conditions of maximizing its resources? (Bonacich, 1972; Ford, Nemiroff, and Pasmore, 1977; McGregor, 1967).

Changing Group Norms

How many people are giving up smoking or going on a diet? Why is it that every year there is a new fad diet book that enough people buy to produce a best seller for the authors? How many people make New Year's resolutions about how they are going to change—this year, definitely?

If an individual who is convinced of a need to change (he or she reads the diets or throws away the pack of cigarettes) has such difficulty, imagine how hard it is for a group to change—at least ten times as hard. Once norms, which are the group's procedures or expectations for its members, are developed and agreed upon, they are exceedingly difficult to change.

Communication theorists (Watzlawick, Beavin, and Jackson, 1967) describe a homeostatic balance, which any group or organization has, between new change and traditional practices. Communication theory also describes two kinds of change: first- and second-order change. First-order change is just more of the same—when you press down on the gas pedal you go faster. Second-order change is a fundamental rule or norm change, such as when you shift gears in your car in order to go faster. It's something qualitatively different from what you were doing before. It can be an "aha" experience of insight, a significant change in how a group does business and interacts, or a structural change in the roles played by people in a group or organization.

"A chief goal of cultural politics is to change the context and values of the culture," according to Hirsch in the controversial book *Cultural Literacy*. What has been controversial, however, is that what he suggests is *not* a second-order change (Hirsch, 1987, p. 137).

Even a change that promises positive results can cause people to be doubtful and threatened by the unknown that will change group norms. For example, in recent years, when many companies have become computerized, workers have often been reluctant to cooperate, even in the interest of the company. Many groups and organizations involve people in planning new changes, making sure that information is clearly communicated. This diffuses some of the resistance to change that maintains the status quo norms.

The classic illustration of resistance to group norm change is the 1954 *Brown v. School Board* Supreme Court decision, which stated that segregated education was, by definition, unequal education. Thirty-five years later, in a re-examination of integration in the schools, it was evident that the counterforces had prevailed. The primary method for maintaining the status quo (nonintegration of schools) in the South was for whites to send their children to a newly organized system of private schools rather than to the public schools. And in the North, white families moved to suburban areas, where there were almost exclusively other white families. Thirty-five years later there was limited integration, especially in the North. (It had been assumed that the South would be opposed to integration but that there would be no such problems in the "liberal" North.)

Change involves not only increasing the forces in the direction of the desired change but also holding the resistant forces constant or reducing them. How can that be done?

Lewin describes three stages in the change process. First, there must be a *disequilibrium*. People need to re-examine the present system, or feel a tension or dissatisfaction with it, or experience themselves in new ways (for example, to shop for clothes and be shocked at the size that fits). There need to be "ripples," or incidents, or crises in their lives. As a result of that disequilibrium, people experience a sense of urgency, feel off balance, and acquire a different perspective—

all leading to the beginning of a process for change. The women's movements of the late sixties stirred organizations to re-examine their norms toward women. Declining enrollments induced universities to re-examine their admission and recruitment procedures. A deficit in a city budget induces concern about RIFs (reductions in force) and employee morale.

Sometimes heads of organizations say, "We can't change now. Wait until the crisis is over. Then we'll look at what needs to be changed, but not now." However, the greatest inducement for change occurs when there *is* a crisis, an urgency for change.

At the second stage in the change process—behavior changes—people act in a way different from the previous norm, or they come from the disequilibrium (being off balance) to the third stage (behavior) in what is called *freezing*. Some examples of the famous Lewin "action research" during World War II may illustrate these concepts.

Americans are used to eating meat (especially in the 1940s); men especially enjoy red meat. However, there was a war and meat was in short supply. The question became, how could families be induced to try low-priority meats like sweetbreads, kidneys, and liver (Lewin, 1947)? How could their food habits be changed so that they would buy the low-priority meats?

The war effort and the desire to be loyal Americans were the factors that created the disequilibrium; the next step was to produce behavior change. Lewin determined that women were the "gatekeepers"—the major influence on which foods were brought into the house—and he set about changing the behavior of their families through them. Two methods were used to convince them to buy and serve the unfamiliar, unpopular foods. Some women were given lectures on the values of eating the new foods (information); others participated in discussions (which involved information and social comparison).

After discussion, the women reached consensus about what they would do. That consensus was stated and agreed to publicly. Once this public standard existed (for example, "We believe loyal Americans will agree to substitute low-priority meats for high-priority meats once a week"), it was easier to change individual behavior in accordance with this new standard. Lewin found there was greater change among the women who had participated in the group discussion and that more of these women continued in the new behavior. Tjosvold and Field (1983) support the importance of discussion and participation in their study, which states that group decisions meet greater acceptance when they are achieved by consensus rather than majority vote. Falk (1982) similarly found that unanimous decisions created less task conflict in group situations than decisions made by majority rule.

There is extensive research to support the finding that discussion leading to consensus can create a new group norm. In attempting to understand why group discussion seems to be an important element in change, researchers have found evidence pointing to a number of factors. One area of research indicates that breaking down the old value system prior to adopting a new one (creating the disequilibrium stage first) is a crucial element in changing norms (Rokeach, 1971).

Skinner and Cattarello found that in terms of marijuana smoking, once a behavioral commitment was made, group norms had a much greater effect on continuing that behavior than attitudes about marijuana smoking. Thus it may be that in any attempt to alter habitual behavior, examining how the peer group operates in constraining its members' behavior is as valuable as, if not more valuable than, merely attempting to change individual attitudes (Skinner and Catarello, 1989, pp. 1287–1288).

Similarly, what produces the changed behavior is not so much the public decision as the actual group consensus (Bennett, 1955). The pressure for conformity is greater when there is consensus, as in the Asch experiments, in which a person was most likely to conform when there was not a single dissenter.

In the third stage of change, *refreezing* or stabilization of the behavior change occurs. This is often the most difficult aspect of change. Participants can go through a laboratory experience or be in a personal-growth group and learn about themselves in different ways. Under these special circumstances, they can try a variety of new behaviors and be quite proud of how they have changed. Often, they are convinced that when they return they will make major changes in their organizations (Luke, 1972). What a disappointment! They return ready to make sweeping organizational change, only to find that the behaviors that were so appropriate in the laboratory community are discrepant with the norms of the organization. They learn that individual change is very different from organizational change. Although trust and open communication are norms in the laboratory, there are norms of competitiveness, secret information, and distrust in the organization. It is only a matter of weeks before they revert back to the prelaboratory behaviors—often with redoubled frustration: although they were able to make some personal changes, the newly recognized restrictiveness of the organizational norms is even more confining.

Pilot projects are often developed with high hopes, behavior is changed, and then at the end of the project, the system reverts back to where it had been. Initial norms continue. Educators in public schools become wary of innovations; they have become enthusiastic, worked hard, seen projects come and go, and watched the system revert back to where it was before the project began. Some businesses have hired corporate gurus to increase productivity by converting work apathy into worker allegiance. A report in the *Wall Street Journal* (Waldman, 1987) describes a typical effort involving expensive New Age training programs designed to change corporate norms by fostering such feelings as teamwork, company loyalty, and self-esteem.

> Workers, however, have had decidedly mixed reactions to the attitudinal training, creating, in many companies, bitter conflicts between employees who embrace the new concepts and those who don't. Younger employees, especially, are more apt to praise the sessions for addressing productivity problems and for attempting to make jobs more meaningful. But many older employees say the seminars—and management—are simply paying lip service to serious concerns in the workplace.

The article makes clear that while such training may accomplish some transient changes, negative forces increase owing to resistance to the efforts. The training created ripples but failed to change the culture of the organization. Changing organizational norms is extremely difficult.

Perhaps more difficult still is actually playing the role of mover and shaker—effecting change on an individual level. For example, increasing numbers of women have moved into middle- and upper-management positions in many industries, yet most organizations remain predominantly male. Women in these situations often find their options within their work group limited. J. Paaluzzi in *Savvy* magazine (June 1984) shares this revealing anecdote:

> While attending a chamber of commerce luncheon not long ago, I sat next to our city treasurer. Because I was involved in developing a grant application for the city, I took the opportunity to ask her about such issues as tax programs, residential changes, and industrial development.
>
> We had been involved in several minutes of intense conversation when the board member sitting to her other side turned to us, grinned, and said, "Enough of that girl talk. Let's get down to business!" (p. 80)

In any case, a woman's actions are evaluated differently from male group members' actions because she is a woman and, however hard she may try, does not fit into more traditional "male" group norms. Changing norms is not easy. However, there are a number of ways.

Through contagion, as in dress style or patterns of speech.

Through influence on the group from the external environment. Issues here relate to the re-examination of values about the family: sexuality, relationships to children, and the effects of divorce. For example, a mother's asking for time off to attend a conference with her child's teacher would once have been viewed as evidence that she was not committed to a career; it would have been unimaginable that an executive father would ask for such time. Similarly, divorce would have seriously impaired a man's career, and a working wife would have been viewed with suspicion.

Through high-status members, who have earned their *idiosyncrasy credits*. Hollander (1958, 1960, 1964) offers the hypothesis that those who have reputations for demonstrating competence or living up to the expectations of the group have accrued idiosyncrasy credits. These credits are like a bank account of favorable impressions built up over time. They may be exchanged for freedom from criticism or rejection following nonconforming or individualistic acts. A high-status member can attempt to change norms by playing devil's advocate or by offering a "wild idea" or the suggestion "let's try this on for size." However, even high-status members may be viewed as deviant if the changes they are suggesting are too drastic. This hypothesis would indicate that a new member of the group who has not had time to build up idiosyncrasy credits would be accorded less freedom for nonconformity than a senior member who has had ample time to build up good will. In a sense, senior members have "paid their dues" and are rewarded with increased freedom from censure.

By groups diagnosing their own norms and modifying them, so that they are compatible with the group's goals and resources.

By an outside consultant. Outside consultants, who are behavioral scientists and experts in organizations, bring an objective perspective to the organization, and because they are not part of the hierarchy, they can influence changes in norms without the same fear of sanctions. They may offer a variety of alternatives and methods for examining change that may be acceptable to the organization.

By trained internal consultants. In this situation, members of the organization are specifically designated to review procedures in the light of organization goals.

Through group discussion. Norms formed through interaction can be changed by interaction. Group discussion is generally found to result in more change than other forms of persuasion, such as lectures or directives (Lippitt, Watson, and Westley, 1958).

By those with high self-esteem (Constanzo, 1970; Stang, 1972) and who are willing to risk.

In many areas, we have witnessed enormous societal changes, and these have had an impact on norms that would have been difficult to even fantasize.

An order of nuns was founded in the middle of the last century and remained virtually unchanged for 130 years. There were 1,000 women dedicated to treating the poor and the sick.

Women who entered the order knew that they could be sent home for even the simplest disobedience. They wore long black habits made from fifteen yards of material held together with seventy-two tiny buttons that had to be closed with a button hook. They wore immaculate, heavily starched bonnets with attached veils.

Convents housed fifty or more nuns. At the convent, there were no visitors, not even family, and conversation was frowned upon as frivolous or gossip. At dinner, each had her seat at a large table; seating was by longevity in the order. Those who were novices sat at the foot of the table, served, and washed the dishes. No one spoke. Each evening was spent in work or prayer in the chapel. They were not permitted to attend family functions—not even a sister's wedding.

Contrast that description with that of the same order today. Members are still committed to the poor and the sick, but now they may live in a small house in an urban neighborhood where they can be close to those they serve and where they share the lifestyle and community of their people. In small groups of four to six, they become a family for each other. All work, cook, serve on community committees, and can go to the movies or lectures or classes. They are dressed in clothes typical for women their ages. Discussions on how the community should be conducted are essential elements in their planning for the future of the order, and they vote on many issues. They are consulted rather than ordered. Visitors are welcome, and nuns are regularly in touch with their families.

Who would have believed all of this could have occurred in the last ten years?

New members will enter a group confused; the group norms will be unseen or will feel ambiguous. They will feel restrained in their behavior until they can determine what is appropriate behavior and what is expected of them. As they interact with others, the rules become less absolute and more flexible. They appear not only as constraints but also as guides. Newcomers are then better able to see the norms as outer limits within which they are free to operate. When they learn what is allowed, they gain both a sense of confidence and a greater latitude in their behavior—they have options to conform, to deviate, to change, or even to leave.

◆ ◆ *EXERCISE 1*

Awareness of Norms

Objectives
- To develop an awareness of norms by changing the norms
- To develop the understanding that norms function to create an order in the group and regulate the interaction among members
- To note the changes in the group when the normative structure is violated

Setting

The following exercise is illustrated within a classroom setting, but the procedures would be equally applicable in a variety of other situations.

Action

The exercise should not be used until after the group has met for some time; then the teacher (facilitator) examines a number of norms of the class (group) and for one session purposely changes them. This need not continue for more than fifteen minutes of the classroom period.

An example, as the authors have used it, may be helpful. A course in group dynamics is taught to college students. Typically, the chairs are arranged around tables; smoking and drinking coffee in class are accepted; attendance is not taken; observer's reports are returned at the beginning of each class; examinations are not given unless scheduled. The teacher is available for questions or problems that have arisen since the last class; sometimes there are a number of questions and class does not begin promptly. All these norms are purposely broken.

The students enter the class one day and encounter the following:

> Chairs are set in rows.
>
> A pile of examination blue books is on the desk (no examination had been announced).
>
> The teacher (who could be a substitute) sits at the desk and appears to be busy reading; he or she answers no questions and has no discussion.
>
> The class starts promptly.
>
> The teacher announces that the observer's reports are not ready to be returned.
>
> The teacher calls the roll.
>
> The teacher makes a sarcastic comment to someone smoking and to someone drinking coffee.
>
> The teacher answers no questions on her or his strange behavior and appears not to notice the confusion in the class.
>
> Blue books are distributed.
>
> Members of the class are asked to write one or two sentences on how they feel at this moment.
>
> The teacher explains that the norms of the class were purposely violated.

◆ ◆ EXERCISE 2

Survey of Dress Norms

Objectives
- To understand that norms develop uniquely to a particular group
- To develop the understanding that the "character" of a group can be determined from observation of its norms

■ To collect data in order to determine whether there are differences in the norms of groups, and to explore the reasons that might be behind these differences

Situation

It is sometimes thought that norms are not developed by a group itself. Rather, they may exist for a variety of reasons; that is, they may be imposed by exterior forces, they may be common to the environment, they may be typical of all people, and so forth. A simple research project can be another method for seeing that groups do develop their own norms and that these transcend generalized norms for an age group or college population. For example, among the colleges in the Philadelphia area are the University of Pennsylvania, Temple University, LaSalle College, Drexel Institute of Technology, Beaver College, Philadelphia Community College, and Philadelphia College of Textiles and Science. One hypothesis is that college students in the Philadelphia area will dress reasonably alike, because all the students will conform to the dress codes of large Eastern cities. They will wear what college-age students wear at an urban Eastern college, and there will be no difference in dress among the colleges. (A student at Penn will be dressed similarly to a student at Drexel or one at Temple.) Another hypothesis is that each school will have its own norm for dress and that typical dress will be different and recognizable at each school.

Action

The class is divided into work teams of four to six on a team. Teams stand at places on the various school campuses where they can observe the dress style of the students. Each team views a sample of fifty students. Each team visits the various schools at their convenience in no special order over a common two-week period. Team members tally their observations on specific items (see the categories of dress that follow) by a simple categorizing system. Each team tallies its results and describes the attire of a typical male and female at each of the colleges. On a given day, all the teams distribute their reports to the other teams. Data and typical attire for each school are examined for replication in other team reports. The data will indicate the norms that each school develops.

Discussion

How do norms develop? What function do they serve? Are they the result of outside influences? How are they changed? Interviews may also be conducted with some of those being observed and used as a stimulus to further discussion.

Variations

Any number of variations are possible in gathering data on contrasting populations. Examples include dress codes of students or teachers in schools in different parts of a city or the city and suburban areas, the dress of ministers or priests in different orders or denominations, and the dress of members of various civic organizations. Data related to other norms could also be observed after hypotheses are developed for various groups. Dating behavior, conversation patterns in different offices or between classes, and hall behavior in local high schools are a few examples.

CATEGORIES OF DRESS

(Basis for tallies; separate sheets for each institution)

1. Hair length
   a. Females: Short—to nape of neck
                  Average—to shoulders
                  Long–beyond the shoulders
   b. Males: Short—no sideburns, well-trimmed at back and sides
                  Average–sideburns, length not passing the collar in back, sides full but not over the ears
                  Long—that which exceeds the previous description
                  Clean-shaven
                  Facial hair—mustache, beard

2. Slacks
   a. Females: Jeans
                  Designer jeans
                  Other pants
   b. Males: Dungarees
                  Levis
                  Designer jeans
                  Pressed slacks

3. Other attire
   a. Females: Skirts
                  Dresses
                  Suits (skirt and jacket)
   b. Males: Suit pants (tweeds, stripes)
                  Suits (pants and jacket)

4. Shirts
   a. Males: Button-down collar
                  Ivy league
                  White
                  Colored (yellow, blue, and so forth)
                  Patterned
                  T-shirt
                  Turtleneck or other casual shirt

5. Blouses/sweaters
   a. Females: Shirts
                  T-shirts
                  Sweaters
                  Jerseys (turtleneck, jewel neck)
                  Shirt with sweater

6. Shoes
   a. Females: High heels
                    Flats or small heel
                    Loafers
                    Sandals
                    Moccasins
                    Boots
                    Running shoes
                    None
   b. Males: Penny loafers
                    Laced dress shoes
                    Running shoes
                    Sandals
                    Boots
                    None
7. Stockings/socks
   a. Females: Pantyhose
                    Knee socks
                    Colored pantyhose (yellow, green, and so forth)
                    Patterned pantyhose
                    None
   b. Males: Crew
                    Dark
                    Light
                    None
8. Pocketbooks
   a. Females: Shoulder
                    Handbag
                    Bookbag
                    Backpack
                    None

◆ ◆ *EXERCISE 3*

Toward Changing Group Norms

Objectives

- To understand what is meant by group norms
- To recognize the difficulty in changing norms
- To offer an opportunity to examine and change norms at various levels
- To develop insight into how norms can be changed in organizations

When appropriate, this exercise can be used after a group has been working together for some time. It can be a work team, a task group, an organization, a segment of a class group, or a seminar.

Action

Phase 1   The facilitator presents a short lecture on norms—what they are, their influence on a group, and so forth. The material in the first part of the chapter might be the basis for development of such a talk. (Approximately 10 minutes)

Phase 2   The groups are asked to examine their norms. They list on paper as many as possible (dates, times, seating arrangements, order of meeting or work, typical behaviors, and so on). (Approximately 20 minutes)

Phase 3   The group is then asked to change some of its norms. The facilitator says, "Which norms can be changed?" He or she has the group change them and holds a brief session under the new conditions.

   Typically, groups change superficial norms: they will sit on the table instead of sitting in chairs, they will shout rather than talk to one another, or they will attempt to conduct the session nonverbally. This encourages laughter and a reduction in inhibitions—perhaps even a party atmosphere. (Approximately 20 minutes)

   (Usually a break is indicated here.)

Phase 4   The groups are asked to examine which norms they changed and how relevant the changes were in helping accomplish their goals. What impeded changing norms? What norms need to be changed? The group then goes into its work session on this basis. (The ensuing discussion is very different from the party atmosphere of the first change; it raises difficult issues and involves members in high-risk behaviors.) An observer might be assigned to watch for behavior that changes norms.

Phase 5   Later, perhaps the next day, the next week, or at the next group meeting, the group should discuss what norms were changed, which were difficult to change, and why. Who was most influential in changing or proposing changes in norms? Who has the highest status and role in the group? What are the problems involved in changing norms to increase movement toward the group's stated goals?

◆ ◆ EXERCISE 4

Group Influence

Objectives

- To understand the pressure of a group on the individual
- To understand the internal conflict that arises when the group opinion is different from the individual's
- To understand how powerful group influence can be

Action

Invite a former member of a cult or extreme political organization to come to class to describe how he or she became involved in the cult or organization. Have your guest talk about what he or she was like before and after joining. How did he or she come to modify his or her beliefs on family, clothes, education, sex, friends, future? Then, in a question-and-answer period, discuss why he or she left, how it felt to be out of the group, what difficulties he or she continues to have, and how he or she now views the experience.

Variation

Another way to achieve this understanding is to stage the event. The teacher/facilitator contacts a person to enact the role of a former member of a cult or an extreme political organization. There are some vivid first-person accounts of what it was like to be a cult member, as well as books that describe the process of inducing members to accept the cult group norms. The person (who is unknown to the class) can prepare by reading the materials.

The teacher/facilitator announces that there will be a guest who was formerly a cult member who will discuss how cults work and how they pressure members to adhere to group norms above all. This exercise is even more effective if several persons come, and one is assigned to each small group. After the talk and discussion, the teacher/facilitator announces the staging, and the cultists explain who they really are.

Still another method is to have group members design a day (class time) in which they role-play being members of a cult or an extreme political organization, creating a mood so that they can experience the urgency of remaining compliant with group norms.

◆ ◆ EXERCISE 5

Group Pressures on Issues

Objectives

- To understand how group pressure affects an individual
- To illustrate the influence of group decision making
- To learn the distinction between individual responses and individual responses after consensus or discussion

Design

The facilitator distributes the following questionnaire to each of the participants. He or she requests that the participants fill in the answers as honestly as possible; the questionnaires may be answered anonymously. After the questionnaires are collected, the participants are divided into small groups of six to ten. The facilitator distributes additional copies of the questionnaire to each participant as well as an additional one to record the group answer. He or she asks the participants to discuss each question in their group and to arrive at a *single decision* on each of the questions, a decision that represents their group's feelings on the subject. A discussion follows, and the summary sheets are collected. Each group should be named at the top of the sheet. Each person once again answers his or her questionnaire as an individual. (If possible, this should be done after a break or at a later session.) The questionnaire may be responded to anonymously, but the group name appears at the top.

The facilitator tabulates the replies to the first questionnaire (the prediscussion individual replies) and records (on a blackboard or newsprint) the group decisions on each of the questions. He or she then tabulates and records the replies to the individual questionnaires following the group decisions and indicates the individual replies under the group answer.

Discussion

1. How are replies the first time around different from the second individual replies?
2. How do groups influence individuals? What are the implications?
3. Do people act differently in a group from the way they act as individuals? How? What difference does it make?
4. How does group discussion influence individual judgments? Are there implications for social change?

Was there a difference in degree of group replies on the first two questions, as opposed to the third and fourth questions? (The first two are concerned with personal choices, the second two with social issues.) How were the final individual replies influenced by the group on the first two questions? On the last two questions?

QUESTIONNAIRE

The following issues generate a great deal of discussion. How do you feel about each of these issues? Circle the answer you consider most representative of how you feel.

1. Would you marry someone of a different religion?
   Definitely
   Probably
   Undecided
   Probably not
   Definitely not
2. Would you marry someone of a different race?
   Definitely

Probably
Undecided
Probably not
Definitely not
3. Should abortion remain legal?
Definitely
Probably
Undecided
Probably not
Definitely not
4. Should marijuana be legalized?
Definitely
Probably
Undecided
Probably not
Definitely not

◆ ◆ EXERCISE 6

Copernicus and Change[6]

Objectives

■ To use a historical incident to clarify resistance to change
■ To examine bases for maintaining beliefs even when the beliefs are false
■ To explore the likelihood of change in particular conditions

Action

(Time: 15 min.) The facilitator groups participants into clusters of three to five. Each person is given a copy of the "Copernicus" sheet and is asked to respond briefly to each of the questions.

COPERNICUS

Some 400 years ago, a mathematician named Copernicus studied the earth and the heavens and concluded that the conception of the earth as the center of the universe was incorrect. Calculations showed him that it was more reasonable to see the sun as the center and the earth as rotating around it. The German mathematician Johann Kepler confirmed

6. This exercise is adapted from Raths, Harmin, & Simon, 1966.

and refined the findings of Copernicus, but this new idea was too rev-
olutionary to be considered dispassionately on its scientific merits.

"Because man is conservative, a creature of habit, and convinced of
his own importance, the new theory was decidedly unwelcome. Moreover, the vested interests of well-entrenched scholars and religious leaders
caused them to oppose it," wrote Morris Kline in his *Mathematics in
Western Culture.*[7]

Martin Luther called Copernicus an "upstart astrologer" and a "fool
who wishes to reverse the entire science of astronomy." Calvin thundered:
"Who will venture to place the authority of Copernicus above that of the
Holy Spirit? Do not Scriptures say that Joshua commanded the sun and
not the earth to stand still?" The Inquisition condemned the new theory
as "that false Pythagorean doctrine utterly contrary to the Holy Scriptures," and in 1616 the Index of Prohibited Books banned all publications
dealing with the idea.

Galileo was thought to believe the new theory to have some merit and
was called by the Roman Inquisition and compelled under threat of torture
to declare, "The falsity of the Copernican system cannot be doubted,
especially by us Catholics. . . ." Descartes, a nervous and timid individual, on hearing of Galileo's persecution, actually destroyed one of his
own works on astronomy.

Wrote Kline: "Indeed, if the fury and high office of the opposition are
a good indication of the importance of an idea no more valuable one
was ever advanced."

After writing replies, participants discuss their answers to each question. The
goal is to clarify each person's values, *not* to convince people to change.

Variation

There can be an observer for each participant. The observer is to answer the
following questions:

1. Does my participant (the person being observed) attempt to change
   another's view or response. How? Under what conditions?
2. Does my participant change as a result of attempts to influence him
   or her? How?
3. How do participants feel in the end about each other and about the
   group? Are conformity and agreement important? Can the group tolerate differing ideas?

---

7. This material comes from the work of Arnold Rothstein of Hofstra College.

Following group discussion, observers discuss what they saw. Afterwards, participants can comment.

1. Can you understand how people of goodwill might react violently to new ideas they see as threatening to some of their values?
2. Can you recall another situation in history in which partisans resisted the advance of knowledge with similar vigor?
3. Can you imagine something like this happening in the future in the United States if some new idea—say, in sociology or some other discipline—were to seriously challenge the status quo?
4. What methods do you think might be used to fight new ideas?
5. What methods might be used to fight for the right to consider new ideas?
6. How receptive or resistant are you to new ideas? Can you think of conditions under which you would try to repress truth?

◆ ◆ *EXERCISE 7*

Observations and Gender[8]

Objectives

■ To observe gender as a characteristic of communication
■ To determine how, if at all, the speech of men and that of women differ
■ To determine how, if at all, interaction among men and that among women differ

Action

(Time: 30 min.) The exercise can be done in three conditions:

In *condition 1,* four men speak and are observed by others using the "Observing and Gender" sheet.

In *condition 2,* four women are observed, again using the "Observing and Gender" sheet.

In *condition 3,* two men and two women interact. The remaining members observe them, using the "Observing and Gender" sheet.

---

8. The "Observing and Gender" sheet was first presented by Janine Rorberts of the University of Massachusetts at Amherst, at the National Council on Family Relations Annual Conference, Atlanta, 1987.

OBSERVING AND GENDER

Time Observing _____

Place _____

Name	Number of Times Talks (Code with Tallies)	Amount of Talk Time (Code in Minutes)	Talk After Whom (Code in Initials)	Who Responds to Their Talk (Code in Initial & A—Affirmation B—Disqualification C—Neutral)	Body Language Communicates What to Whom (Code with Brief Notes)	Content Is More Socioemotional or Task Related (Code in S or T and Brief Notes)

Observers are instructed to tally behaviors on their sheets and take notes on the interactions that occurred. The facilitator gives each group a topic to discuss. Some suggested topics:

1. What do you consider the state of communication in the United States?
2. How did the October 19, 1987, stock market crash affect people?
3. How do you think the educational system should be changed for greater effectiveness?

Each group speaks for 10 minutes. Round 2 goes on for 10 minutes. Round 3 goes on for 10 more minutes. Observers should use a different sheet for each set of observations. After the three rounds, observers review their notes and report on the following:

1. How did groups 1, 2, and 3 differ?
2. What was the communication pattern?
3. How does gender affect communication?
4. Do you see a relationship between gender and status?
5. What are the implications of this observation?

References

Argyris, C. *Reasoning, Learning and Action.* San Francisco: Jossey-Bass, 1982.

Asch, S. E. "Effects of group pressure upon the modification and distortion of judgments." In H. Guetzkow (ed.), *Groups, Leadership, and Men.* Pittsburgh: Carnegie Press, 1951, pp. 177–190.

Asch, S. E. "Opinions and social pressure." *Scientific American,* 193, No. 5 (1955), 31–35.

Asch, S. E. "Studies of independence and conformity: I. A minority of one against a unanimous majority." *Psychological Monographs,* 70, No. 9 (1956).

Aumann, R. J., and M. Maschler, "The bargaining set for cooperative games." In *Advances in Game Theory,* edited by M. Drescher, L. S. Shapley, and A. W. Tucker (433–476). Princeton, N.J.: Princeton University Press, 1964.

Baird, J. "Conservation of the commons: Effects of group cohesiveness and prior sharing." *Journal of Community Psychology,* 10 (1982), 210–215.

Bandura, A. *Social Learning Theory,* Englewood Cliffs, N.J.: Prentice-Hall, 1977.

Baron, R. A. "The foot-in-the-door phenomenon: Mediating effects of size of the first request and sex of requester." *Bulletin of the Psychonomic Society,* 29 (1973), 113–114.

Baron, R. S., G. Roper, and P. H. Baron, "Group discussion and the stingy shift." *Journal of Personality and Social Psychology,* 30 (1974), 538–545.

Barrett, R. A. *Culture & Conduct.* Belmont, Ca.: Wordsworth, 1984.

Bennett, E. "Discussion, decision, commitment and consensus in 'group decision.'" *Human Relations,* 21 (1955), 251–273.

Berger, J., M. H. Fisek, R. Z. Norman, and M. Zelditch, Jr. *Status Characteristics and Social Interaction: An Expectation States Approach.* New York: American Elsevier, 1977.

Berger, J., S. J. Rosenholtz, and M. Zelditch, Jr. "Status organizing processes." *Annual Review of Sociology,* 6 (1980), 479–508.

Bettenhausen, K., and J. K. Murnigham. "The emergence of norms in competitive decision-making groups." *Administrative Science Quarterly,* 30 (1985), 350–372.

Blake, R. R., and J. S. Mouton. "Don't let group norms stifle creativity." *Personnel,* 62, No. 8 (1985), 28–33.

Bonacich, P. "Norms and cohesion as adaptive responses to potential conflict: An experimental study." *Sociometry,* 35, No. 3 (1972), 357–375.

Bond, G. R. "Positive and negative norm regulation and their relationship to therapy group size." *Group,* 8, No. 2 (1984) 35–44.

Boszormenyi-Nagy, I., and G. M. Spark. *Invisible Loyalties: Reciprocity in Intergenerational Family Therapy.* New York: Harper & Row, 1973.

Brothen, T., and T. Shovholt. "Social comparison theory and the universality of experience." *Psychological Reports,* 48 (1981), 114.

Buchwald, A. "The grown-up problem." In *Son of the Great Society.* New York: G. P. Putnam and Sons, 1966.

Butler, L. "Anatomy of collusive behavior." *NTL Connections,* 4, No. 1 (1987) 1–2.

Campbell, J. D., and P. J. Fairey. "Informational and Normative Routes to Conformity: The Effect of Faction Size as a Function of Norm Extremity and Attention to the Stimulus." *Journal of Personality and Social Psychology,* 57, No. 3 (1989), 457–468.

Campbell, J. D., A. Tesser, and P. J. Fairey. "Conformity and attention to the stimulus: Some temporal and contextual dynamics." *Journal of Personality and Social Psychology,* 51, No. 2 (1986), 315–324.

Codol, Jean-Paul. Du Provence, Lab de Psychologie Sociale, Aix-en-Provence, France. "The phenomenon of superior conformity of one's self to group norms in a situation requiring perceptual estimation of physical stimuli." *Cahiers de Psychologie,* 73, No. 16(1) (1973), 11–23.

Codol, Jean-Paul. Du Provence, Lab de Psychologie Sociale, Aix-en-Provence, France. "Concept of superior conformity of one's own group to accepted norms—Does such a phenomenon exist?" *Cahiers de Psychologie,* 73, No. 16(1) (1973), 25–30.

Coffman, J. "Choosing the Veil." *Mother Jones,* Nov./Dec. 1991, 23–24.

Constanzo, P. R. "Conformity development as a function of self-blame." *Journal of Personality and Social Psychology,* 14 (1970), 366–374.

Cooper, H. M. "Statistically combining independent studies: A meta-analysis of sex differences in conformity research. *Journal of Personality and Social Psychology,* 37 (1979), 131–146.

Crandall, C. S. "Social Contagion of Binge Eating." *Journal of Personality and Social Psychology,* 55, No. 4 (1988), 588–598.

Dentler, R. A., and K. T. Erikson. "The functions of deviance in groups." *Social Problems,* 7 (1959), 98–107.

Dustin, D. S., and H. P. Davis. "Evaluative bias in group and individual competition." *Journal of Social Psychology,* 80 (1970), 103–108.

Eagly, A. H. "Sex differences in influenceability." *Psychological Bulletin,* 85 (1978), 86–116.

Eagly, A. H., and C. Chrvala. "Sex differences in conformity: Status and gender role interpretations." *Psychology of Women Quarterly,* 10 (1986) 203–220.

Eagly, A. H., and L. L. Carli. "Sex of researchers and sex-typed communications as determinants of sex differences in influence-ability: A meta-analysis of social influence studies. *Psychological Bulletin,* 90 (1981), 1–20.

Eagly, A. H., W. Wood, and L. Fishbaugh. "Sex differences in conformity: Surveillance by the group as a determinant of male nonconformity." *Journal of Personality and Social Psychology,* 30 (1981), 384–394.

Eder, D. "Ability grouping and students' academic self-concepts: A case study." *The Elementary School Journal,* 84, No. 2 (1983), 149–161.

Ellsberg, D. *The Theory and Practice of Blackmail.* Santa Monica, Calif.: Rand Corporation, 1959.

Endler, N. S. "Conformity as a function of different reinforcement schedules." *Journal of Personality and Social Psychology,* 4 (1966), 175–180.

Falk, G. "An empirical study measuring conflict in problem-solving groups which are assigned different decision rules." *Human Relations,* 35 (1982), 1123–1138.

Feldman, D. C. "The development and enforcement of group norms." *Academy of Management Review,* 9, No. 1 (1984), 47–53.

Fensterheim, H., and J. Baer. *Don't Say Yes When You Want to Say No.* New York: Dell Publishing, 1975.

Ferreira, A. J. "Family myth and homeostasis." *Archives of General Psychiatry,* 9 (November 1963), 457–463.

Festinger, L. "Informal social communication." *Psychological Review,* 57 (1950), 271–282.

Festinger, L. "A theory of social comparison processes." *Human Relations,* 7 (1954), 117–140.

Festinger, L., and J. Thibaut. "Interpersonal communication in small groups." *Journal of Abnormal and Social Psychology,* 16 (1951), 92–99.

Fisher, J. D. "Possible Effects of Reference Group-Based Social Influence on AIDS-Risk Behavior and AIDS Prevention." *American Psychologist,* November 1988, 914–920.

Ford, D. L., P. M. Nemiroff, and W. A. Pasmore. "Group decision-making performance as influenced by group tradition." *Small Group Behavior,* 8, No. 2 (May 1977).

Freedman, J. L., and S. C. Fraser. "Compliance without pressure: The foot in the door technique." *Journal of Personality and Social Psychology,* 4 (1966); 95–102.

Freeman, M. "A conversation with Margaret Singer." *APA Monitor,* July/August, 1979, 6–7.

Galbraith, J. K. *Time,* March 30, 1970, p. 88.

Galenter, M. "Charismatic religious experience and large group psychology." *American Journal of Psychiatry,* 12 (1980), 1550–1552.

Geertz, C. *Local Knowledge.* New York: Basic Books, 1983.

Gerard, H. B., R. A. Wilhelmy, and E. S. Conolley. "Conformity and group size." *Journal of Personality and Social Psychology,* 8 (1968), 79–82.

Goddard, R. W. "Everything swings off #1." *Manage,* 36, No. 1 (1984), 8–10.

Goffman, E. *The Presentation of Self in Everyday Life,* Garden City, N.Y.: Doubleday Anchor, 1959.

Goffman, E. *Behavior in Public Places.* Glencoe, Ill.: Free Press, 1963.

Gould, L. J. "The two faces of alienation." *Journal of Social Issues,* 25, No. 2 (1969), 39–63.

Grinder, R. E. "Distinctiveness and thrust in the American youth culture." *Journal of Social Issues,* 25, No. 2 (1969), 7–19.

Haberman, C. "Straight talk brings down Japan house." *The New York Times* (February 14, 1988), p. 6.

Hall, J. "Decisions, decisions, decisions." *Psychology Today,* 5, No. 6 (1971), 51–54, 86–88.

Hall, J., and M. Williams. "Group dynamics training and improved decision-making." *Journal of Applied Behavioral Science,* 6, No. 1 (1970), 39–68.

Hanke, J. J., and B. O. Saxberg. "Isolates and deviants in the United States and Japan: Productive nonconformists or costly troublemakers?" *Comparative Social Research,* 8 (1985), 219–243.

Hare, A. P. *Handbook of Small Group Research,* 2nd ed. New York: Free Press, 1976, 19–59.

Heckel, R. V., and H. C. Salzberg. *Group Psychotherapy: A Behavioral Approach.* Columbia: University of South Carolina Press, 1976.

Hewitt, J. P. *Dilemmas of the American Self.* Philadelphia: Temple University Press, 1989.

Hewstone, M., and J. Jaspers. "Explanations for racial discrimination: The effect of group discussion on intergroup attributions." *European Journal of Social Psychology,* 12 (1982), 1–16.

Hirsch, E. D. Jr. *Cultural Literacy.* Boston: Houghton Mifflin, 1987.

Hollander, E. P. "Conformity, status and idiosyncracy credit." *Psychological Review,* 65 (1958), 117–127.

Hollander, E. P. "Competence and conformity in the acceptance of influence." *Journal of Abnormal and Social Psychology,* 61 (1960), 365–370.

Hollander, E. P. *Leaders, Groups, and Influence.* New York: Oxford University Press, 1964.

Homans, G. C. "A conceptual-scheme for the study of social organization." *American Sociological Review,* 12 (1947), 13–26.

Homans, G. C. *The Human Group.* New York: Harcourt, 1950.

Homans, G. C. *Social Behavior, Its Elementary Forms.* New York: Harcourt, 1961.

Ittyerah, M., and M. Modi. "Effect of group pressure on value conformity." *Personality Study and Group Behavior,* 1 (1981), 71–82.

Jahoda, Marie. "Psychological issues in civil liberties." *American Psychologist,* 11 (1956), 234–240.

Janis, I. L. "Groupthink." *Psychology Today,* 5, No. 6 (1971), 43–46, 74–76.

Janis, I. L. *The Anatomy of Power.* Boston: Houghton Mifflin, 1982.

Jenkins, D. H. "Feedback and group self-evaluation." *Journal of Social Issues,* 2 (1949), 50–60.

Jones, E. E. *Ingratiation: A Social Psychological Analysis.* New York: Appleton-Century-Crofts, 1964.

Kahn, A., R. Nelson, W. Gaeddert, and J. Hearn. "The justice process: Deciding upon equity or equality." *Social Psychology Quarterly,* 45 (1982), 3–8.

Keating, J. P., and T. C. Brock. "Acceptance of persuasion and the inhibition of counterargumentation under various distraction tasks." *Journal of Experimental Social Psychology,* 10, No. 4 (July 1974), 301–309.

Kelman, H. C. "Compliance, identification, and internalization: Three processes of attitude change." *Journal of Conflict Resolution,* 2 (1958), 51–60.

Kerr, N., and B. Watts. "After division, before decision: Group faction size and predeliberation thinking." *Social Psychology Quarterly,* 45 (1982), 198–205.

Khoury, R. M. "Norm formation, social conformity, and the confederating function of humor." *Social Behavior and Personality,* 13, No. 2 (1985), 159–165.

Kiesler, C. A. "Attraction to the group and conformity to group norms." *Journal of Personality,* 31 (1963), 559–569.

Kirton, M. J. "Adaptors and innovators: Why new initiatives get blocked." *Long Range Planning* (UK), 17, No. 2 (1984), 137–143.

Kline, Morris. *Mathematics in Western Culture.* New York: Oxford University Press, 1953.

Komorita, S. S., and J. M. Chertkoff. "A bargaining theory of coalition formation." *Psychological Review,* 80 (1974), 149–162.

Krech, D., and R. S. Crutchfield. *Theory and Problems of Social Psychology,* New York: McGraw-Hill, 1948.

Laing, R. D. *The Politics of the Family and Other Essays.* New York: Vintage Books, 1972.

Levine, J. M., K. R. Sroka, and H. N. Snyder. "Group support and reaction to stable and shifting agreement/disagreement." *Sociometry*, 40, No. 3 (1977), 214–224.

Lewin, K. "Frontiers in group dynamics." *Human Relations*, 1 (1947), 5–42.

Liberman, R. "A behavioral approach to group dynamics. I. Reinforcement and prompting of cohesiveness in group therapy." *Behavior Therapy*, 1 (1970), 141–175. "II. Reinforcing and prompting hostility-to-the-therapist in group therapy." *Behavior Therapy*, 1 (1970), 312–327.

Lichtman, R. J., and I. M. Lane. "Effects of group norms and goal setting on productivity." *Group and Organization Studies*, 8, No. 4 (1983), 406–420.

Lippitt, R., J. Watson, and B. Westley. *The Dynamics of Planned Change: A Comparative Study of Principles and Techniques*. New York: Harcourt, 1958.

Lipsitt, P. D., and M. Steinbruner. "An experiment in police–community relations: A small group approach." *Community Mental Health Journal*, 5, No. 2 (1969), 172–179.

Lorenz, K. *On Aggression*. New York: Bantam, 1971.

Louis, K. S., D. Blumenthal, M. E. Gluck, and M. A. Stoto. "Entrepreneurs in academe: An exploration of behaviors among life scientists." *The Administrative Science Quarterly*, 34, Cornell University (1989), 110–131.

Luchins, A. S. "Focusing on the object of judgment in the social situation." *Journal of Social Psychology*, 60 (August 1963), 231–249.

Luke, R. A. "The internal normative structure of sensitivity training groups." *Journal of Applied Behavioral Science*, 8, No. 4 (1972), 421–427.

Maccoby, E. E., and C. N. Jacklin. *The Psychology of Sex Differences*. Palo Alto, Calif.: Stanford University Press, 1974.

Martin, C. L. "A ration measure of sex stereotyping." *Journal of Personality and Social Psychology*, 52, No. 3 (1987), 489–499.

Martin, J. D., J. S. Williams, and L. N. Gray. "Norm formation and subsequent divergence: Prediction and variation." *Journal of Social Psychology*, 93, No. 2 (1974), 261–269.

Martin, P. Y., and R. A. Hummer. "Fraternities and rape on campus." *Gender & Society*, 3, No. 4 (December 1989), 457–473.

Martin, R., and D. Lauridsen. *Developing Student Discipline and Motivation: A Series for Teacher In-service Training*. Champaign, Ill.: Research Press, 1974.

Masland, T. "U.S. Rock stars upstage doctrine in Ethiopia." *Philadelphia Inquirer* (December 31, 1987) p. 3-A.

McDavid, J. W., and H. Harari. *Social Psychology*, New York: Harper & Row, 1968.

McGregor, D. *The Professional Manager*. New York: McGraw-Hill, 1967.

Milgram, S. "Behavior study of obedience." *Journal of Abnormal and Social Psychology*, 67 (1963), 371–378.

Milgram, S. "Group pressure and action against a person." *Journal of Abnormal and Social Psychology*, 69 (1964), 137–143.

Milgram, S. "Liberating effects of group pressure." *Journal of Personality and Social Psychology*, 1 (1965), 127–134.

Mills, J., and C. E. Kimble. "Opinion change as a function of perceived similarity of the communicator and subjectivity of the issue." *Bulletin of the Psychosonomic Society*, 2, No. 1 (July 1973), 35–36.

Mills, T. M. *The Sociology of Small Groups*. Englewood Cliffs, N.J.: Prentice-Hall, 1967.

Mugny, G. "Compliance, conversion and the Asch Paradigm." *European Journal of Social Psychology*, 14, No. 4 (1984), 353–368.

Norris, D., and R. Niebuhr. "Group variables and gaming success." *Stimulation and Games*, 11 (1980), 301–312.

Opp, K.-D. "The evolutionary emergence of norms." *British Journal of Social Psychology*, 21 (1982), 139–149.

Parsons, T., and E. A. Shils, eds. *Toward a General Theory of Action*. Cambridge, Mass.: Harvard University Press, 1951.

Piliavin, J. A., and D. Libby. "Personal norms, perceived social norms, and blood donation." *Humboldt Journal of Social Relations,* 13, Nos. 1–2 (Fall-Summer, 1986), 159–194.

Piper, W. E., "Cohesion as a basic bond in groups." *Human Relations,* 36, No. 2 (1983), 93–108.

Price, V. "Social identification and public opinion: Effects of communicating group conflict." *Public Opinion Quarterly,* 53 (1989), 197–222.

Raths, L. E., M. Harmin, and S. Simon. *Values and Teaching.* Columbus, Ohio: Charles E. Merrill, 1966.

Regan, D. T. "Effects of a favor and liking on compliance." *Journal of Experimental Social Psychology,* 7 (1971), 627–639.

Roberts, Janine. "Observing and Gender." Presentation at the National Council on Family Relations 1987 Annual Conference, Atlanta.

Rokeach, M. "Long-range experimental modification of values, attitudes, and behavior." *American Psychologist,* 26, No. 5 (1971), 453–459.

Rose, S. D. *Group Therapy: A Behavioral Approach.* Englewood Cliffs, N.J. Prentice-Hall, 1977.

Ross, L., G. Bierbrauer, and S. Hoffman. "The role of attribution processes in conformity and dissent, revisiting the Asch situation." *American Psychologist,* February 1976, 148–157.

Savell, J. M. "Prior agreement and conformity: An extension of the generalization phenomenon." *Psychonomic Science,* 25 (1971), 327–328.

Schachter, S. "Deviation, rejection and communication." *Journal of Abnormal and Social Psychology,* 46 (1951), 190.

Schachter, S. *The Psychology of Affiliation.* Palo Alto, Calif.: Stanford University Press, 1959.

Sherif, M. "A study of some social factors in perception." *Archives of Psychology,* 27, No. 187 (1935).

Sherif, M. *The Psychology of Social Norms.* New York: Harper, 1936.

Sherif, M. "Conformity-deviation, norms, and group relations." In I. A. Berg and B. M. Bass, eds., *Conformity and Deviation.* New York: Harper, 1961, 159–181.

Singleton, R. "Another look at the conformity explanation of group-induced shifts in choice." *Human Relations,* 32, No. 1 (1979), 37–56.

Skinner, W. F., and A. M. Cattarello. "Understanding the relationships among attitudes, group norms, and behavior using behavioral commitment: A structural equation analysis of marijuana use." *Journal of Applied Social Psychology,* 19 (1989), 1268–1291.

Sonnenschein, F. M. "Countering prejudiced beliefs and behaviors: The role of the social studies professional." *Social Education,* April/May 1988, 264–266.

Spradley, J. P., and D. W. McCurdy. *Conformity and Conflict.* Glenview, Ill.: Scott, Foresman, 1990.

Stang, D. J. "Conformity, ability, and self-esteem." *Representative Research in Social Psychology,* 3 (1972), 97–103.

Swidler, A. "The Ideal Society." *American Behavioral Scientist,* 34, No. 5 (May/June 1991), 563–580.

Tannen, D. *You Just Don't Understand.* New York: Ballantine Books, 1990.

Tjosvold, D., and R. Field. "Effects of social context on consensus and majority vote decision-making." *Academy of Management Journal,* 26 (1983), 500–506.

Tuckman, B. W. "Developmental sequence in small groups." *Psychological Bulletin,* 63, No. 6 (1965), 384–399.

Wahrman, R. "Status deviance, sanctions, and group discussion." *Small Group Behavior,* 8 (May 1977), 147–168.

Waldman, P. "Motivate or alienate? Firms hire gurus to change their 'cultures,' " *The Wall Street Journal,* Section 2 (July 24, 1987), p. 19.

Ward, L., and J. Wilson. "Motivation and moral development as determinants of behavioral acquiescence and moral action." *Journal of Social Psychology,* 112 (1980), 271–286.

Watson, G., ed. *Change in School Systems.* Washington, D.C.: National Training Laboratories, 1967.

Watzlawick, P., J. H. Beavin, and D. D. Jackson. *Pragmatics of Human Communication: A Study of Interactional Patterns, Pathologies, and Paradoxes.* New York: Norton, 1967.

Willis, R. H., and E. P. Hollander. "An experimental study of three response modes in social influence situations." *Journal of Abnormal and Social Psychology,* 69 (1964), 150–156.

Zander, A. "The value of belonging to a group in Japan." *Small Group Behavior,* 14 (1983), 3–14.

◆ 4 ◆

Goals

Power of a Goal

Distinguishing Between Individual Goals and Group Goals

How Are Individual Goals Formed?

How Are Group Goals Formed?
Individuals Have Goals for the Group: Person-Oriented and Group-Oriented Group Goals
Individual Goals Are Converted to Group Goals

Classification of Goals
Operational Versus Nonoperational Goals

Surface and Hidden Agendas

Relationship Between Group Goals and Group Activities
Content of the Goal Affects the Group

Difficulty of the Goal Affects the Group
Type of Goal Affects the Group
Group Goals Themselves Are Inducing Agents
Groups as Tools for Creating Goals

Group Productivity
Cohesiveness of the Group Affects Productivity
Personalities in the Group Affect Productivity
Productivity Affects the Group

Mission, Goals, and Objectives

The Strategic Plan

The Relationship Between Norms and Goals

Changing Group Goals

Group Goals and the Individual Member

I magine that, at the end of a long search, we finally find the oracle. We ask the ultimate question: What is a happy person? What does a person need for happiness? Here is the simple answer. The things you really need to be happy are

- a dream, to lead you
- a direction, to give you a sense of purpose
- a good friend or a lover to be intimate and comfortable with
- meaningful work that is a source of gratification
- a source of fun, to keep the child in you alive
- a belief in a force beyond yourself, be it truth, justice, or a universal goal

If you analyze this advice, you will see that it is *goal-directed*. Human beings are doers, and happiness comes to those who pursue dreams beyond the day-to-day reality. Dreams give purpose to life, and people who have lost their dreams have lost their energy and youth as well.

Shorter-term goals are important too. They give life meaning on a day-to-day basis. Examples of long-term goals are to buy a house, become a lawyer, and move out of one's parents' house. Short-term goals might be to finish a project, lose five pounds, or pass an exam. Setting up such objectives gives us energy to make use of our time. Without goals, we might drift aimlessly.

Though goals are important to our happiness, life is not about the acquisition of money and material things. Rather, it is about goals *in process*. It is not the ends we strive for but the process of striving itself that is essential to our satisfaction.

As a nation, we are ever willing to acknowledge and work toward short-term goals but unwilling to concern ourselves with process. Thus, we face situations that bring us anger and pain. In an old joke, a passenger asks the driver how far they have to go. The driver replies, "The good news is that we're proceeding at full speed with no obstacles. The bad news is—we're lost." As a nation, we need to understand our goals within the context of their consequences for the overall quality of our lives.

Power of a Goal

Goals have an enormous motivating power, as at least one aspect of the war in Vietnam exemplified. The North Vietnamese had a motivation in the fight that the U.S. forces never had. For decades, they had succumbed to the rule of foreign nations. For them, the war was an effort to reclaim their country. Our service people, on the other hand, were no match in terms of will. In fact, they often understood little about why they were in the jungles of Vietnam or why our country was involved in the fighting. In terms of goals, the North Vietnamese were highly focused, whereas U.S. troops were vaguely and poorly motivated.

Distinguishing Between Individual Goals and Group Goals

As individuals, we are constantly concerned with fulfilling our personal goals, but group goals have a different place in our lives. What is the relationship between individual goals and group goals? What proportion of our goals are individual goals? Group goals?

Actually, early social scientists debated the existence of the group goal. F. H. Allport (1924), an early social psychologist, would have said there is no such thing as a group mind and there could not be a group goal. He argued that

> Alike in crowd excitements, collective uniformities and organized groups, the only psychological elements discoverable are in the behavior and consciousness of the specific persons involved. All theories which partake of the group fallacy have the unfortunate consequence of diverting attention from the true locus of cause and effect, namely the behavioral mechanism of the individual . . . If we take care of the individuals, psychologically speaking, the groups will be found to take care of themselves.

Kurt Lewin (1939) argued to the contrary. He noted that groups were different from individuals and that groups as systems could not be explained solely as aggregates of individuals. For example, person A has the goal of marrying Jane, and person B has the goal of marrying Jane, but it is absurd to say that the group goal is to marry Jane. Clearly, individual goals are distinct from group goals. Although the raging controversy is over; there continues to be confusion in this area (Quey, 1971; Janssens and Nuttin, 1976; Shaw 1981, 57–68).

To arrive at a group goal, we must first conceive of the dyad as a unit or a two-person group and then ask what present or future state of this unit is thought to be desirable to the pair. Clearly, this desirable state cannot be "to win," because the dyad as a unit is not a contestant and has no opponent; the dyad itself can neither win nor lose. Consequently, to refer to the goal of the unit as "to win" is meaningless. What is the goal of the unit?

◆ Reader Activity

Consider the illustration of the two tennis players. Each has an individual goal—to win or, perhaps, not to lose badly. They meet the criterion of a group, which is usually stated as two or more people interacting with a common goal. They will be interacting.

Are they a unit (two or more individuals)? _____ Yes _____ No

Why? _____

Is there a *common* goal? ____ Yes ____ No

Explain. _____

_____

If yes, what is their common goal? _____

_____ ◆

There a number of common goals possible, but in connection with tennis, the goal of the players is to play a high-quality game, where they can land and receive some good shots, and where superior play wins. The group goal, as distinct from any individual goals, is to have a good match.

One needs to understand two levels of goals: an individual goal, which is to win; and a group goal, which is to have a high-quality contest. Of course, the two are interrelated. The individual needs to be motivated to win to help produce a good contest; the rules of play and the process of selecting contestants are designed to stimulate good play.

In another example, let's look at courtship at both an individual and a group level. An individual's goals in courting are primarily to sell himself or herself, to express a romantic impulse, and to convince the other person that the relationship has a future. The group goal of courtship, on the other hand, might be simply to perpetuate the family. Similarly, in marriage the individual's goals may be to transform the partner into the ideal husband or wife, whereas the group goals might be to satisfy expectations for raising a family.

Two points need emphasis. First, the group goal is not the simple sum of individual goals, nor can it be directly inferred from them. It is the desirable state of the group, not just of the individuals. Second, the concept of a group goal is not a mental construct that exists in some mythical group mind. What sets the group goal apart is that, in content and substance, it refers to the group as a unit—specifically, to a desirable state of that unit. The concept resides in the minds of individuals, as they think of themselves as a group or unit. Remember the saying "The whole is greater than the sum of its parts"? The group goal is the interaction of the individual goals, which produces a single goal that is distinctly different from the individual goals.

How Are Individual Goals Formed?

We recognize that we are motivated, and we move with direction, but how is this motivation formulated into a goal? How is it that we keep working in a chosen direction? Some of the most imaginative research was conducted very early in the history of the social sciences by Zeigarnik (1927). According to Zeigarnik's theory, when individuals set goals for themselves, an internal tension system is aroused that is correlated to each goal. That tension system continues to motivate an individual until the goal is actually achieved, or until there is a psychological closure so that a person feels that it has been achieved.

In the experiments on which the theory is based, subjects were given a long series of tasks to do (typical experimental tasks such as putting pegs in holes or crossing out a given letter on a page). On some of the tasks, the subject continued until completion; on others he or she was interrupted prior to completion. A significant finding was that subjects remembered the uncompleted tasks more frequently than those they had completed. This experimental finding showed that there is a tension system connected to a goal and that it continues until the goal is met. This theory has been tested and verified with a wide variety of subjects.

For example, students have a goal to do well in a course, and a subgoal to pass a midterm examination. They review the texts, study their notes, and apprehensively submit themselves to the ordeal of taking the examination. At the end of the test period, is the tension system reduced? Certainly not.

They wait anxiously in the hall and query others on their responses to difficult or ambiguous questions; they enter the next session of class eager to know whether the papers are marked. Someone can be depended upon to ask almost routinely at the beginning or end of each session, "When will the papers be back?"

The tension system subsides when the students have their papers returned and they know more about their progress toward their goal. They then can determine what their next goal will be—with a new tension system modified by the new information.

Zeigarnik found that a tension system was connected to an incomplete task, and Horwitz (1954) wondered if that tension system would also apply to a group. In his variation, he had teams of two go through the series of tasks. In some, he interrupted one person, but the other member was allowed to complete the task. In other tasks, the individual who started the task completed it. A group tension system did emerge. Members feel a closure when a task is completed, whether they perform the final stages of a task or another member of their group actually does.

How Are Group Goals Formed?

How do goals change from individual goals for the person to goals for the group? In the transmittal, what are the problems, the implications?

Cooper and Gustafson (1981) suggest that groups, in a manner analogous to the unconscious planning process of individuals, have the capacity to work collaboratively and plan unconsciously for their collective goal attainment. Goals in groups are sometimes consciously planned and established by the group itself or by the environment in which the group exists; at other times, goals appear to develop naturally from the interaction of the members.

Individuals Have Goals for the Group: Person-Oriented and Group-Oriented Group Goals

Basically, individuals participate in a group because they believe that in doing so, they will derive more satisfaction than if they did not participate or belong.

Individual motives may be characterized as "person-oriented" or "group-oriented." Although the reasons are roughly classified in one category or the other, these motives should be viewed as a mixed bag—a percentage of each will motivate an individual's behavior.

Some people belong to a group for what is termed a group-oriented motive; that is, they accept and conform to the group objective even though accomplishment promises no immediate personal benefit to them individually. They are satisfied by results favorable to the group as a unit. For example, people may be active in their political party although they do not personally know the candidates, are not anticipating a job in government, and do not expect any direct rewards. They are motivated to act because they believe their party represents the better choices in the forthcoming elections; they will be satisfied if their party wins and will be especially pleased if their party "wins big."

Another illustration involves members of a community center board who recognize that facilities at the agency are inadequate and antiquated. They recommend the establishment of a committee to raise funds for a new center. They are fully aware that their children are grown and will not utilize the new center, that spearheading a building campaign will mean they have less time to spend on their businesses, and that it will cut into their already limited free time. It will entail the onerous task of asking people for money, and it will be a thankless job. Yet they vote for the establishment of the fund-raising committee, knowing full well that if it is approved, they will become members.

On the other hand, an individual whose prime concern is the person-oriented motive is likely to consider a suggested group goal in terms of alternatives for himself or herself. Which of the alternatives will be most satisfying? Which offer the greatest benefits at the least personal costs? The individual whose prime concern is the group-oriented motive will consider which goal, if attained, will be most beneficial to the group, even when the consequences may not benefit him or her.

Although the terms we use are *person-oriented* and *group-oriented,* the reader is aware of the similarity of these terms to other more familiar terms. Person-oriented goals are sometimes referred to as "selfish" motivations or "ego orientations," and the person is said to be thinking in terms of "what's best for me." Group-oriented goals are often thought of as "altruistic" motivations or "task orientations." The prime concern of such people is how well the group achieves its goals.

Does it really make a difference for which reasons a person helps a group achieve its goals? Isn't the real issue that he or she be willing to accept the group's goal and move in that direction? Research has indicated that groups with more self-motivated behavior had longer meetings yet covered fewer items on their agendas. Also, they reported being less satisfied with both the decision making and the leadership in their meetings than those groups having more group-oriented members (Rieken and Homans, 1954).

Studying the processes that mediate the relationship between a group goal and group member performance, Weingart and Weldon (1991) report that group members who had a common group goal felt that more satisfaction was gained from the group's process because it was viewed as a personal challenge to work through difficulties to achieve the goal. By contrast, person-oriented group members did not feel satisfaction with the process or resolution of interpersonal difficulties.

The impact of person-oriented and group-oriented motives of the group members has been the subject of recent research. One object of special interest is the goal-setting conditions, or the conditions imposed by outside-the-group sources, such as researchers. For instance, one study examined the effects of four different goal conditions: (1) an individual goal condition, (2) no specific goal condition, (3) a group goal condition, and (4) an individual plus group goal condition. These goal conditions were analyzed in terms of their impact on the group members' performance on an independent task. Performance on that task was worse in the individual goal condition than in any of the other three.

Furthermore, the research indicates that person-oriented group members—that is, people who are working under their own goal condition—tend to be more competitive and less cooperative than those working under the other three conditions. Although the categories of person-oriented and group-oriented denote two separate entities, they really overlap such that individual motives, be they person-oriented or group-oriented, vary over time and therefore fluctuate. Thus goal conditions, or the condition(s) imposed on a group by outside-the-group individuals or group members, do affect group members' performance to achieve goals.

Individual Goals Are Converted to Group Goals

There are certain limitations on the determination of goals. First, there are the limits set in the purposes of the organization. A United Fund Committee does not decide that its goal will be whether to raise money but, rather, how much money to raise. The organizational purposes determine the goal in this case, and it is the subgoal (how much money this year) that is discussed and agreed upon. A second limitation concerns changes in the group or its environment that may necessitate a re-evaluation of its goals. Within these limitations, groups develop goals by applying the criteria of fairness or effectiveness, or some combination of the two.

There seems to be a sustaining myth that groups arrive at goals in a manner reminiscent of a New England town meeting. Each person speaks and makes his or her point of view known. The others listen, consider the information, and arrive at a decision that represents the most effective method for dealing with the situation, or at least the best decision possible. The group decision arrived at is assumed to be compatible with the individual interests of the majority. In reality, the picture is usually quite different. Although ideally each member should have an equal say in the determination of goals, it rarely happens. Some, by their personalities, are more verbal and forceful than others. Some speak eloquently on many subjects, others only in an area in which they disagree. Still others simply do not participate.

On another level, some are excluded from even an opportunity to speak as decisions are made by the executive board or the planning committee. The criterion of fairness—that is, full participation—in setting of goals is not met. Frequently the decision making or setting of goals by a select few or even one person is justified in terms of effectiveness. It is assumed that the head of a company knows best what a group can achieve; the expert is most knowledgeable in setting a goal for the whole group. The argument frequently goes, "If we had unlimited time, we could allow all members to participate, but it becomes such a long and frustrating procedure that it is more effective to have goals set by one person or a few people."

For some, an attempt at fairness means reduced efficiency; they believe time expended in arriving at goals could be better expended in progress toward achieving the goal. However, it is possible that the preceding two criteria may be compatible. That is, it may be possible to widen member participation in setting goals and direction for the group (increasing the fairness criterion) *and,* through this increased participation, arrive at goals that are also most effective. A problem-solving method of arriving at group goals involves discussing alternative choices, examining the resources of members for developing each of the alternatives, considering the time available, and assessing the probability of success.

In terms of the previous discussion of person-oriented and task-oriented motives of participants in setting goals, some differences in behavior may be discernible (Kelley and Thibaut, 1954). If task-oriented motives are dominant, members are more likely to arrive at group goals through problem-solving approaches—that is, through exchange of information, opinions, and evaluations. If person-oriented motives are dominant (Fourezios, Hutt, and Guetzkow, 1950), goals are apt to be determined only after arguments, negotiations, bargaining, and forming of coalitions.

◆ *Reader Activity*

Our membership in groups is not random. We join groups for a number of reasons, and we are committed to the group's goals in different ways. Consider two situations:

1. Think of the group you most want to be associated with.

What do you want from this group? _____

_____

What are you prepared to give to it? _____

_____

What does the group want from you? _____

_____

What does it give to you? _____

_____

2. Think of a group you recently left or are considering leaving.
What do you want from this group? _____

_____

What are you prepared to give to it? _____

_____

What does the group want from you? _____

_____

What does it give to you? _____

_____

3. How do these different situations influence you in working for the group's
goals? _____ ◆

◆ Individual Experiment

Pick a group of which you are a member. It could be the student council, a sports
team, a class project group, or a fraternity or sorority. Interview two group members—one who is centrally involved in the business of the group and one who
is minimally involved. Find out from each what his or her personal goal is in
being a group member, as well as what he or she sees as the goal of the whole
group. Can you identify points of similarity or difference between the group and
individual goals of the two people you interviewed? How do you think similar
or different viewpoints affect how the group works?   ◆

Classification of Goals

In addition to understanding goals from both an individual and a group perspective,
we can also understand goals in terms of a number of classifications. We can classify
goals as formal or informal and as operational or nonoperational. Further, we can
describe the movement on goals as action on a *surface* agenda or a *hidden* agenda
(Bradford, 1961). These concepts are illustrated in a case study of a retreat for
student leaders at a suburban college.

The dean of students at the college was concerned about the lack of involvement, even among heads of campus organizations, in school activities. It is a predominantly commuter school where students come to their classes and then immediately leave for their jobs. In a move to build cohesiveness, college officials decided to subsidize a weekend retreat and encourage campus leaders, as well as those interested in becoming more active at school, to sign up to learn leadership skills.

Following the retreat, the student newspaper reported a very successful, productive weekend had taken place.

So much for the myth! The very next issue of the student newspaper carried a banner headline: "President of student government resigns." The article noted that both the president and the secretary of the student body had resigned their positions before the end of the weekend.

It turned out that under a plan fostered by the dean of students, a coalition was created in which all student organizations would be subsumed under a new head. This plan in effect demoted the student council a layer; now it was just another of the student organizations on campus. Also, it had been determined that there was a need for a student center building and that getting one would be the goal of the new organization.

The president and vice president resigned, ostensibly because they objected to the way the coalition was formed. The president also attributed her resignation to a lack of support: "We've plodded along with no positive or negative feedback. . . . I didn't get support at the weekend retreat, and if you don't get support when everyone is 'up,' when do you get it? Half the student body doesn't know we exist. Why should we even be there?"

At a formal level, the purpose of the retreat was to teach leadership skills to existing and potential leaders and to show them how to have an impact on campus. At an informal, or implicit, level, the group goal was to take power as a group. It was on this level that actions were taken (coalition formed, plan for a student center drawn up, resignations submitted). The formal goals had little meaning in this context, and the actions that took place were hard to interpret in the context of those formal goals. In short, action on goals is understood in terms of the dynamics at the *informal*, not the formal, level.

Operational Versus Nonoperational Goals

Operational goals are goals for which clear, specific steps to achievement are discernible. *Nonoperational goals* are abstract; steps to their accomplishment may be difficult, if not impossible, to discern, and achievement may take a tremendous amount of time—if it occurs at all. The coalition's goal to create a new student center was a nonoperational goal, because the college had its own long-range building plan for the next five to ten years that did not include such a building. The odds were small that students would have sustained interest in a building that, even if constructed, would never benefit them. (Most present students would be long gone before such a center could even be built.) Also, the college, always short of funds, was unlikely to allot several million dollars to a building for student leaders when there was little interest in student activities or student government on campus anyway. One might conclude that the president, despite her *stated* reasons, resigned solely because the other leaders had voted to adopt a nonoperational goal.

Nonoperational goals are broad and vague (for example, supporting motherhood, working for full employment, and favoring a separate building for student activities). There is fundamental agreement among members, and the subject is safe. There are words, but few actions other than vague recommendations and general resolutions.

Operational goals, on the other hand, are specific. They have well-defined targets, action plans, and evaluations set for specific times. A six-month membership campaign to gain additional members for the organization is an operational goal, as are strategies to increase the organization's income. An operational goal in the context of our example might be to hold a series of meetings to decide whether students wanted representation by the student government. The commission would hold hearings on how students wanted to be represented on campus. The hearings and a process for arriving at a conclusion would represent active steps to be taken in the achievement of an operational goal.

Operational goals are specific and carry with them clear direction for movement and recognition of what will constitute a solution or goal attainment.

An analysis of faculty career goals suggests that faculty share a common core of goals specifically geared to their professional advancement (Mann, 1989). In turn, this suggests that common goals breed operational goals that are manifested in decisive action plans, such as clearly delineated targets, professional steps to be taken, and time management to allow for goal evaluation, revision, and resolution. However, operational goals can involve conflicts, as individuals discuss different ideas about steps to be taken and conflicting desired outcomes. Operational goals also entail concepts of success and failure, of time limits and evaluations, and of responsibility and achievement.

Surface and Hidden Agendas

In addition to classifying goals, we can describe movement on goals on two levels: the surface level, or *surface agenda,* and the below-surface level, or *hidden agenda.*

In our weekend-retreat example, the surface agenda was to bring students together to learn leadership skills. Student leaders would get to know each other through extended contact over a weekend—this is a straightforward goal. Though others on campus might have been apathetic, these students were interested in student organizations and had some commitment to the goals of student govern-ment. Their tasks over the weekend were predictable: participants would practice leadership skills, team building, and diagnosis of simulated or real organizational problems.

However, on a hidden level much more would happen. When the dean of students suggested that a coalition structure would help students have a greater impact, what was his goal? Was it simply to establish the coalition, or was it to facilitate his own dealings with student leaders by consolidating them into one group? Or was he perhaps suggesting the coalition in the hope that its head would be a student he favored over the current president of the student association?

When the student president initially accepted his suggestion with enthusiasm, what was her goal? Was it perhaps to simplify the way students were heard through an existing structure? Or was her goal to increase the power of the student gov-ernment association? Or to counter the growing power of the administration over student organizations and ensure that students retained their power?

Perhaps some leaders accepted the dean's suggestion simply because many of their friends would be in the coalition. Perhaps one agreed because he or she saw a chance to be elected head of the new coalition. And dissenters might have opposed the idea merely because they resented the fact that the dean of students could further his ideas without conferring with them.

As we reflect on this situation, it may seem that logical thinking had been foregone and that emotionalism had become the norm. But we need to realize that groups work simultaneously and continuously on two levels. One level is formally labeled. Whether confused or clear, simple or difficult, this is the obvious, advertised purpose for which the group meets. Unlabeled, private, and covered, but deeply felt and very much the concern of the group, is another level (Bradford, 1961). On this level are all the conflicting motives, desires, aspirations, and emotional reactions of the group members, any subgroups, and the group as a whole that cannot be fitted legitimately into the accepted group task. Here are all of the problems that, for a variety of reasons, cannot be explicitly acknowledged. These are called *hidden agendas.*

Hidden agendas are neither better nor worse than surface agendas. Rather, they represent all of the individual and group problems that differ from the group's surface task, and therefore get in the way of the orderly solving of the surface agenda. They may be conscious or unconscious for the member or for the group.

Both groups and individuals can have hidden agendas. In essence, hidden agen-das represent what people want as opposed to what they say they want. Albert Ellis, the founder of rational-emotive therapy, notes that neurotic goals can dom-inate these agendas, but hidden agendas need not be neurotic. They represent a wide variety of "reasons" not to be focused on the present situation. Such goals interfere with our ability to focus on group needs and group goals in the present. Instead, they keep us functioning at the level of our impossible-to-meet needs. Such needs include

- the need to be perfect
- the need to be liked and cherished by every living human being
- the need to appear sure about everything
- the need to have complete control
- the need to appear neutral by concealing feelings
- the need to avoid conflict owing to an inability to confront and work things through
- the need to defend oneself and to resist feedback with defensiveness
- the need to project onto others what one does not want to see in oneself
- the need to judge oneself and others

Remember, leaders as well as members can have hidden agendas.

Each agenda level affects the other. When a group is proceeding successfully on its surface agenda with a sense of accomplishment and group cohesiveness, it is evident that the major hidden agendas have been settled, are being handled concurrently with the surface agenda, or have been temporarily shelved. Let the group reach a crisis on its surface agenda, however, and hidden agendas that have not been resolved may emerge.

Groups can work diligently on either or both agendas. A group often spends endless time getting nowhere on its surface agenda, seemingly running away from its task, and yet, at the end, gives the impression of a successful, hard-working group. Often, group members leave a meeting saying, "Finally we're getting somewhere." When asked what they have accomplished, they might mention some trivial aspect of the surface agenda. What they are really saying is that an important issue on the hidden agenda has been resolved.

A group may have been working vigorously without visible movement on its assigned task. Suddenly, it starts to move efficiently on its task and in a short time completes it. The group had to clear its hidden agendas out of the way before it could work on its assignment.

Let's return to our retreat example. On this college campus, apathy about involvement in student organizations may have prevailed for years, if not decades. However, the retreat changed all that. The first newspaper article, which presented the surface agenda for the retreat, seemed to indicate that the weekend had gone well and that the surface agenda was in fact followed. The second article, however, exploded the myth and brought the hidden agenda to the surface. Real issues—whether students or administration would really run student activities, conflicts between the president of student government and the office of student services, and conflicts between the student president and coalition—all came to light and became the focus of discussion. This sparked more interest in student government than the campus had seen in years.

Hidden agendas can block the progress of a group. If they are not recognized and understood, a great deal of the organization's energy will be wasted in frustration and feelings of powerlessness. Hidden agendas can be dealt with in the following ways:

> Consider that hidden agendas can be present. Recognition of hidden agendas at individual and group levels is the first step in diagnosis of a group difficulty.
>
> Remember that the group is working concurrently on two levels. Recognize that the group may not move so quickly on the surface agenda as the more impatient might wish.
>
> Not all hidden agendas can be brought to the surface; they may hurt group members' feelings if discussed openly, and create an atmosphere of distrust in the group. Other hidden agendas can be talked about and do become easier to handle. It is important to know which can and which cannot be faced by the group.
>
> Don't scold or pressure the group because there are hidden agendas. They are legitimate; each of us is constantly working out individual needs in the group as well as group needs. It is a legitimate part of group life that we see things differently and want different things accomplished.
>
> Help the group work out methods of solving hidden agendas just as they develop methods by handling surface agendas. Methods may vary, but basically they call for opening up the problem, gathering data on it, generating alternatives for a solution, and deciding on one. Data from people and feelings are important.
>
> Help the group evaluate its progress on handling hidden agendas. Each experience should indicate better ways of more openly handling future hidden agendas. There may be short evaluation sessions (ten minutes) at the end to review progress. Are members able to talk more freely in areas that were previously difficult? Is there a greater feeling of comfort?

Groups can deal with hidden agendas via careful planning, perhaps by facilitators or a steering committee. Answering these five questions at the planning stage will help counteract the blocking power of hidden agendas:

1. What are the advertised goals of the program?
2. Do the leaders have any covert or hidden goals?
3. Do the participants have any covert or hidden goals?
4. What do participants expect will be the outcomes of the program?
5. What do participants actually want from the program?

There are several techniques a leader can use within meetings themselves to bring hidden agendas to the surface. Suggesting a quick "go-around," is one. The leader asks each person to express his or her feelings about a proposal before the group votes as a whole. Another technique is to ask directly, "What seems to be blocking us?" Yet another is to separate participants into small groups of three or four and ask them to determine what must happen before the problem at hand can be solved. Small group discussions sometimes yield answers that are blocked from surfacing in the larger group.

◆ *Reader Activity*

Think of a group of which you are a member. What blocks the group's movement toward its objectives; why do things seem to "go off on a tangent"? List as many things as you can think of.

_____

_____

_____

Who has the hidden agenda? (A member? A subgroup? The leader?)

_____

_____

_____

Think about each of these hidden agendas. Given your knowledge of your group, what are some things that could be done about one of the hidden agendas?

_____

_____

_____ ◆

As the group increasingly deals with hidden agendas, it becomes possible to see with greater clarity what the group's goal really is. From the viewpoint of members, goals are sometimes classified as "clear" or "unclear." When clear goals exist, each member, if polled, could respond with a statement of the goal and the steps for attainment of that goal. Clear goals are more likely to be operational goals, they are more likely to be stated formally, and they are more apt to be on the surface agenda. When unclear goals exist, members, if polled, would give a variety of replies depending on their personal interests, and they would have a variety of ideas about how these goals should be attained.

Generally, successful group has clear objectives, not vague ones, and members of the group have personal objectives that are compatible with the group's objectives. The more time a group spends developing agreement on clear objectives, the less time it needs to achieve them, and the more likely the members' contributions are to converge toward a common solution. Lane (1982) demonstrates that making group goals explicit improves the chances of the group to achieve the stated goals.

Relationship Between Group Goals and Group Activities

Goals themselves are powerful inducers of action. What the goal is and what kind of goal it is influence relationships among members (Korten, 1962). Goals also have a powerful impact on the interdependence between goals and resources. When goals are mutually dependent on resources (such as available information given by a computer to aid in a problem-solving task), positive goals promote higher individual achievement and group productivity in problem-solving success (Johnson, Johnson, and Stanne, 1989). When the goal is positive (such as gain in scholastic status) and the resources are readily available, then the group goal encourages group activities that promote success.

Content of the Goal Affects the Group

Let us assume that the goal of a correctional institution is the rehabilitation of prisoners (Zald, 1962). Staff members might be given a great deal of autonomy and might be encouraged to be creative. There would be a large emphasis on programs. There might be a reading program or even a college program on the premises. There might be lectures, plays, and special speakers brought in to keep members informed. There might even be group activities such as an orchestra, chorus, or dramatic group that performs for community groups outside the prison. The goals would be to encourage prisoners to develop their vocational and artistic skills and to become more competent in the outside world while serving time.

Contrast these activities with another correctional institution where the goal is custody of prisoners—holding them so they cannot inflict damage on citizens of the community. In this situation, there would be fewer professional staff and more custodial staff (guards). Authority would be centralized, and rules and penalties would be the basis for relationships.

The difference in content of goals will result in a difference in relationships among staff and prisoners, as well as in a difference in activities.

Difficulty of the Goal Affects the Group

Suppose that in a twelve-game season, a football team won eight games. What will be the team's goals for the next season? Will it set a goal of winning two games? To win only two games would be regarded as a disaster; it would be too easy. Will it set a goal of winning all twelve games? This seems too difficult and would probably doom the team to failure.

Assuming none of the key players graduates or sustains serious injuries, the group would set an aspiration level of perhaps nine or ten games. To win this number would be regarded as a successful season, a fine performance by the team.

This example is meant to illustrate the aspiration level of a group; that is, when a group confronts a set of alternatives ranging from easy to difficult and selects one, this is referred to as the group's *aspiration level.* Performance above this level will be considered successful; performance below this level failure. The level of aspiration will influence members' self-evaluations, group activities, attractiveness of membership, and subsequent group cohesiveness. Groups that are successful tend to be realistic about their aspirations (Atkinson and Feather, 1966).

Failure to reach group goals can undermine the attractiveness and cohesion of the group. Taylor, Doria, and Tyler (1983) conducted a study of an intercollegiate athletic team that experienced repeated failure but was able to maintain a high level of cohesion. Several factors were responsible for maintaining group cohesiveness. First, responsibility for performance was spread over the entire group, rather than being given to specific individuals or subgroups. Also, group members tended to attribute failure more to themselves and less to other group members, yet they did not attribute more than an equal share of success to themselves.

Type of Goal Affects the Group

Whether the goals are competitive or cooperative greatly influences the activities toward the goal and the relationships among members. We are a highly competitive society. We play games in which there are winners and losers; in fact, we speak of people as "winners" or "losers" even outside the context of games. Tennis is an example of a competitive game; baseball is another. If one team wins, the other loses; there is never a tie. However, baseball also has cooperative goals. Each member of the team can attain his or her goal of winning only if the entire group also attains its goal—the team must win as a unit. Members therefore attempt to cooperate with one another, coordinate their efforts, and use their resources jointly. Observers report significant differences between groups working under competitive conditions and under cooperative conditions.

Where there were competitive goals, members would seek to "one up" each other, withholding information and displaying hostile feelings and criticism (Klein, 1956). For example, in schools where grade-point competition is keen and colleges will accept only a limited number from one high school, competition is unbelievable. High-ranking students push to become presidents of obscure clubs, thus gaining one more degree of status to edge out competition. It comes as no surprise that a student will remove the notice of a prospective visit by a prestigious college representative from the bulletin board, or remove information on scholarships to reduce competition. And the competitiveness induces hostility and criticism toward those who figured out the best "angles."

The classic work on the effects of cooperative and competitive conditions in attaining group goals was done by Deutsch (1949). Deutsch explained that in a cooperative situation, group goals are homogeneous—that is, group members hold the same goal for the group. In a competitive situation, group goals are hetero-geneous—that is, group members hold differing goals for the group.

In the competitive situation, when one person reaches the goal, others will, to some degree, be unable to obtain their goals. Each person is out for himself or herself. In the cooperative-goal situation, if one person reaches the goal, all other members are helped in reaching their goals. Whether the situation is cooperative or competitive influences a wide variety of group processes, including attitudes and willingness to work with others as well as the attractiveness, cohesiveness, and effectiveness of the group. Regarding the latter characteristic, Deutsch (1949), in another classic experiment, determined that productivity per time unit was greater in cooperative than in competitive groups and that the quality of both the products and the group discussions were higher in the cooperative groups.

The relationship of cooperation and competition in groups to achievement and productivity is still a much-debated subject. Johnson (1981) compared the effec-tiveness of four types of goal structures in groups: cooperation, cooperation with intergroup competition, interpersonal competition, and individualistic goal ori-entation. He reports that cooperation is considerably more effective than inter-personal competition and individualistic efforts. Cooperation with intergroup competition was also found to be superior to interpersonal competition and individualistic efforts. Kramer and associates (1986) looked at cooperative and noncooperative responses of undergraduates reacting to a simulated resource-conservation crisis. As predicted, cooperatively oriented students responded to the resource depletion with greater self-restraint (that is, greater concern for others) than did the noncooperators.

Cooperative groups, in a task requiring collaborative activity, show more positive responses to each other, are more favorable in their perceptions, are more involved in the task, and have greater satisfaction with the task (Church, 1962; Julian and Perry, 1967; Wheeler and Ryan, 1973). As a result of their cooperative efforts, members are less likely to work at cross-purposes (Gross et al., 1972), are more efficient, and have a better-quality product (Deutsch, 1960; Workie, 1974; Zander and Wolfe, 1964).

Group Goals Themselves Are Inducing Agents

Previously, we discussed the tension systems linked to a goal. It seems that when a group accepts a goal, those who most strongly accept the goal display a strong need to have the group achieve its goals. Acceptance of the goal is for them an inducing agent (Horwitz, 1954).

However, if the group goal is not accepted by a significant section of the group, there is likely to be a high incidence of self-oriented and resistant behavior rather than group-oriented behavior, with activities being coordinated to personal rather than group goals. In a study that examined the motivational effects of feedback and goal setting on group performance, Watson (1983) found that explicit goal setting improved group performance and was a significant factor even where no feedback was given.

In a study of the role of goal setting and its influence on self-efficacy, or the individual's power to produce an effect on group goals, Lee (1989) found that the performance of a female college field hockey team was related to the team's winning percentage. It seems that setting an explicit group goal elicits significant motivation to reach the group's goals: to win.

Further supporting the hypothesis that goal setting is a major factor in inducing better group performance, Harlow (1989) reports that groups with specific goals outperform those who are asked simply to do their best.

Groups as Tools for Creating Goals

Given that goals are important group motivators, it is important to know how groups themselves can set goals. A good model suggested itself in 1985, when a symposium of applied and academic scientists was proposed to improve relations between the two groups. The first symposium was attended by eighteen applied scientists and eighteen academics representing thirty colleges and business firms. Four topics for small group discussion were specified: research and development, education, management of practice, and technical applications. Each group agreed on five goals for improving relations between academics and practitioners. Smith and Culhan (1986) reported that "the high priority recommendations for the four groups agree to a significant degree [and] every group identified faculty internships in industry as a key to improving relationships." This agreement established goals for further action.

Group Productivity

Group goals are meant to be a guide for action. One of the methods by which a group measures its success is to determine whether it accomplished its goals. Were goals clear enough and operational enough to be measured? At what costs? Are members disillusioned and are relationships strained? Are members glad the project is over so they can terminate their associations?

Some might question the validity of raising the question "At what costs?" For them, the productivity question is the most important one. Did they accomplish the goal—raise the money, develop the recommendations, increase membership, or resolve the situation between the executive director and the staff—in the best way?

Nonetheless, it has become standard (Barnard, 1938) to describe the adequacy of group performance in terms of both concepts: *effectiveness* (task orientation), the extent to which the group is successful in attaining its task-related objectives; and *efficiency* (maintenance orientation), the extent to which a group satisfies the needs of its members.

Each factor can be examined independently of the other. It is possible to examine only task accomplishment, and frequently that is the only factor considered. It is also possible to examine only relationships among members and the degree of satisfaction each feels as a member of the group, although this is much less frequently considered by itself. Yet it is important to remember that a group expends energy on both aspects of performance, and the effectiveness and efficiency of a group set upper limits on each other. Some illustrations will clarify this relationship.

Cohesiveness of the Group Affects Productivity

If members spend their time strictly on business—the surface agenda—and ignore interpersonal relationships and hidden agendas, misunderstandings can increase. Communication may be severely limited, subjects to be discussed are highly controlled, and members rely on the "grapevine" and other informal systems to meet their personal needs. In this situation, each individual does his or her job but steadfastly remains uninvolved with other members as people.

On the other hand, if members spend a great deal of their work time getting acquainted, building personal relationships, and developing increased listening skills and influence on each other, there may be high personal satisfaction, at least for some, but no time or energy invested in the task. High personal involvement may mean high morale but little effort on task activity and, consequently, low productivity. The dilemma of whether to sacrifice productivity or member relations is ever present.

However, there is evidence (Thelen, 1954) that if the group spends more time initially on the interpersonal relationships, there will be greater long-run efficiency. If, during the initial phases of the group, members talk to each other, discuss their personal goals, and get to know each other, they build a common frame of reference, a step toward problem solving.

Elias, Johnson, and Fortman, (1989) found that when group members disclosed information about themselves, they later reported a significantly higher "group cohesiveness, commitment to task, and productivity." Furthermore, these researchers suggest that the function of self-disclosure may be to evoke cooperative behavior in task-oriented groups for resolving problems, reducing stressful conflicts, and enhancing positive communication among individuals.

Consider the following example:

> An affluent community was having difficulty coping with drug problems among its youth. To develop strategies, the pastor of the leading church invited heads of six organizations concerned with youth to meet with him: the head of youth services in the township, the head of the juvenile division

of the police force, the executive director of the YMCA, the principal of an elementary school, the principal of a high school, and the executive director of a rehabilitation center. All agreed to serve, but none was really clear about how to proceed, how they should organize, and what they could do to reduce the influence of drugs on young people. Two of the seven members knew each other. The others had met at various public functions but had, at best, a nodding acquaintance. Although each was committed to the goal, all were busy and could commit only two hours per month to this group. Even deciding on a meeting time agreeable to all had been a major accomplishment. Although members were willing and committed, they were frustrated by the first two meetings and questioned why they had agreed to serve. Very, very little was happening.

Because the meetings occurred from 8:00 to 10:00 A.M. (to reduce the amount of time taken from work), the group decided to meet at 7:00, have breakfast together, and then proceed. That should have produced horror at getting up and to a central location at such an early hour. Instead, the group, in its first enthusiastic decision, agreed.

The effectiveness of the committee markedly changed after that first breakfast meeting. While eating their eggs, the members socialized and developed a knowledge of one another that greatly enhanced their ability to make decisions on how they would proceed with their task. Members came to like each other in the process and became committed to becoming a "terrific" task force. One member jokingly said that he enjoys the breakfast meetings so much that he eats breakfast at the restaurant *every* Thursday morning so that he won't miss the meetings (the group met the second Thursday of the month).

Members learn over time that some issues are to be avoided whereas others can be readily discussed. They learn which subjects are special favorites of particular members and in what areas members agree. Members develop a clearer view of their roles and where they fit into the group.

Frequently, more cohesive groups are more productive than less cohesive groups (Norris and Niebuhr, 1980). The more attractive the group is to members, the more membership is valued, and the more members can influence each other. There seems to be a general circular relationship between group solidarity and efficiency. Group solidarity, satisfaction, quality of interaction, and goal attainment have all been shown to be positively correlated (Wheeless, Wheeless, and Dickson-Markman, 1982). As members work together and come to see one another as competent, they are drawn even closer together, and this relationship increases the likelihood of successful performance.

However, increased cohesiveness does not always mean increased productivity. Increased cohesiveness means that members are able to influence one another more. If they decide to use this influence for increased productivity, they could be very effective. However, low productivity may have several related causes within a group or organization, in which case simply increasing the cohesiveness of the group will not solve the productivity problem.

When groups seem bogged down in movement on their goals, one way of understanding the difficulty is to examine the relationships between time spent on task and time spent on interpersonal relations (task and maintenance behaviors). Or, to put it differently, study the relationship between effectiveness and efficiency.

Personalities in the Group Affect Productivity

How is productivity related to personality? Which is better, people who are all task-oriented—who want to get the job done and leave—or members who want warm, intimate personal relationships? Which will be more productive? Or is it better to have a mix, so that they can complement each other?

The prime consideration is the nature of the task. If the group has a purpose that emphasizes problems of expressing emotions in relationships (an alcoholics recovery program), members should not have difficulty being close or expressing emotions. On the other hand, a project that emphasizes problems of control (procedures for conducting a census) should not be composed of members who have difficulty following directions or working on an ordered task.

If the task involves the major steps in problem solving, persons who have high individual scores on intelligence tests or problem-solving ability reflected in higher levels of education usually form a more productive group than those who are less able (Tuckman, 1967; Turney, 1970).

"Interdisciplinary research teams are faced with special coordination and productivity problems different from those faced by individual scientists in organizational settings," reported Fennell and Sandefur (1983). The Laboratory for Social Science Research at Stanford University studied several such research teams from 1975 to 1978. The data indicated that individual scientists seemed to be hampered by formal organization but still required structure for effective communication and interaction. In fact, they suggested that where a clear, formal structure was lacking, team members were likely to spend extra time and energy constructing a workable informal structure. Further, clear authority and evaluation processes were necessary for the smooth functioning of a team.

Findings in general indicate that groups composed of those who prefer more formal relationships when working on a task were most productive (Berkowitz, 1954), but groups composed of members who prefer closer and more intimate personal relationships were also productive (Schutz, 1958). That is, groups made up of similar types, either task-oriented or relationship-oriented, were more productive than groups made up of some who preferred closer relations and others who wanted more distant interpersonal relations. This last group was characterized by recurring personality clashes and lower productivity (Reddy and Byrnes, 1972) Roethlisberger and Dickson, 1939).

According to Jungian personality theory, two personality factors related to the way people gain information affect group productivity. Some gain information by what Jung called sensing; others are intuitive. Sensing types acquire data through their senses—by seeing, hearing, smelling, reading, and touching. "Intuitives" acquire data from their inner sense of what is happening. Jaffe (1985) found that sensing types focus on regulations, step-by-step explanations, and facts, whereas intuitive types focus on outwitting regulations, supplying theoretical explanations, and ignoring details. Conflict between these two types can account for decreases in group productivity.

The compatible groups were found to be more productive, presumably because they were able to agree in the social-emotional areas and, in so doing, freed themselves to work on the task.

For the same reasons, groups tend to be more productive when they are made up of members of the same sex (Gurnee, 1962), and groups of friends are usually more productive than groups of strangers (Weinstein and Holzbach, 1972).

These are only a few of the personality factors that affect productivity. Stress, lack of interest, and self-oriented behaviors might also influence productivity. It is important to recognize that productivity can be understood only by examining both the nature of the task and social-emotional factors.

Productivity Affects the Group

What happens to a group in the process of achieving a goal? How are members influenced as they work together to determine their goals, to integrate personal goals into a group goal, to synchronize a series of activities with specialized roles for members, to evaluate the outcomes, and perhaps to modify or change their goals? How is the group different after this process?

First, groups have real, practical knowledge of their resources. After a group has worked together, the members know one another and what can be expected of each.

Second, they have increased experience in working together as a group. They now know how to determine a goal, how to get information they may need, and what skills are required to complete a task.

Especially if they were successful at the first task, members have increased confidence in the resources of the group. The first time is the hardest and the most uncomfortable. The initial floundering lessens, the reluctance to make a decision diminishes, and the early inexperience is replaced by growing experience and confidence. Members may begin to feel more comfortable and express themselves more freely and clearly.

Third, there may be an emergence of new group procedures and norms. Working together, members may realize that they could be more effective if they revised some of the procedures. They may even have changed some of the patterns of working relationships. Based on experience, they may decide to modify their methods of arriving at goals; they may modify the aspiration level that was based on their previous experience; they may even develop different criteria for success and failure.

Also, the emotional level of the group changes. The initial surface politeness is gone. Members get to know one another, and friendships develop. There may be greater flexibility in role behaviors; people who were too shy or fearful to volunteer for certain roles may now feel free to volunteer. Members may feel more comfortable in the group and so may say what they are thinking more spontaneously.

Then again, it might mean just the opposite. There may be a small status group, and others may feel less acceptance. The high-status members may speak only to each other, and most may feel outside the ruling clique. There can be increased hostility among members (as each may blame the others for failure) and a reduced willingness to accept group goals or to work together.

Most successful groups, when compared with less successful ones, seem to make a fuller commitment to the group goal, communicate more openly, coordinate activities aimed more specifically toward the goal, and achieve better personal rapport. And the effect is a spiral one. Work on one task influences the next, and there is a greater likelihood of success in pursuing goals in each subsequent task.

Mission, Goals, and Objectives

A set of terms that are goal-related but vague have become popular in current organization parlance. These terms are *mission, goal,* and *objective.* Too often in planning a course of action, organizations misuse these terms, and their semantic confusion reflects a more fundamental confusion about how to execute the plan. For clarity, we define these terms here.

The *mission* is the organization's vision of its fundamental work. It should express the *heart,* not the mind, of the system. It is the mission that gives the organization its energy to move. The mission statement is the wide-ranging goal that reflects the values and direction of the organization.

Goals are the means of achieving the mission. They are measurable, outcome-oriented, relatively short-term products.

Objectives, or subgoals, are steps to achieving the goals.

As an example, the *mission* of a business organization might be to become the central identifiable firm in the field, one perceived as having quality and integrity. The *goal* of the organization may be to acquire a 50-percent share of the market by 1995. *Objectives* might include placing the product in a particular chain of supermarkets, doubling the number of salespeople in the western region of the United States, and creating production plants in the South, in the Chicago area, and in the West.

The Strategic Plan

Businesses frequently work on their goals through a strategic plan. The word *strategy* is from the Greek *strategos* and has its roots in military parlance. Literally it means "the art of the general," and the term was originally used to describe the grand plan behind a war or battle.

Business has adopted the term and applied its concepts to long-range plans and management of the resources needed to achieve the goals and objectives of such plans. Often short-term decisions that may have long-term effects are described as strategies.

Of course, goals need to be more specific than general, long-range plans expressed in nonoperational terms. But the opposite mode—crisis, "seat of the pants" decision making—is also recognized as insufficient. Nor can organizations achieve their goals on "automatic pilot" by following an inflexible set of rules. A meaningful plan needs both overarching goals and specific strategies to achieve them.

The traditional definition of *strategy,* adapted by business leaders and academicians from its military roots, is "the broad plan for operating in a competitive environment to achieve organizational goals." The strategic plan provides for implementing a successful campaign to realize goals, and it serves as the backdrop for tactical decisions that are made in pursuit of an ultimate goal. Tactical decisions, in contrast, are the short-term actions designed to implement strategy, the plays that drive the game plan to success (Carnevale, Gainer, and Villet, 1990, pp. 159–160).

For most organizations there are at least two levels of strategies. Umbrella or organization-wide strategies are the long-term plans the business has for achieving success in the marketplace; functional or divisional strategies are the operating plans that concern the day-to-day activities performed to implement the overarching strategy.

To create a strategic plan, an organization defines its objectives and then sets about developing a broad game plan to pursue its goals. From this plan flow operational, strategic, and tactical decisions that move the organization toward those goals. The overarching plan provides the organization with a well-thought-out and clear picture of its basic approach to gain the competitive edge. It also gives the organization the flexibility to modify its tactical approaches without losing sight of the overarching plan.

The marks of a strategic decision are that it is future-oriented and that its implementation affects the long-term prosperity of the organization. It involves the allocation of large amounts of company resources and influences many or all of the organization's divisions or departments. It hinges on the involvement of top management in the planning processes and considers both the multiple (and frequently inconsistent) goals of the organization's various components, as well as the impact of such external factors as the state of the economy and the labor market (Pearce and Robinson, 1985, pp. 7–8).

A successful strategic plan can be built only on a broad base of knowledge about the organization and its capabilities. It draws on the insights and creativity of people throughout the organization. Its centerpiece must be the collective input of employees, supervisors, and managers at varying levels of the organization.

Small groups from the organization are usually assigned to develop parts of the strategic plan. An executive board, heads of departments, or other management groups will work to ask the following key questions.

1. Where is the corporation now?
2. If no changes are made, where will the corporation be in one year, two years, five years, ten years? Are the answers acceptable?
3. If the answers are not acceptable, what specific actions should the corporation undertake? What are the risks and payoffs involved? (Wheelan and Unger, 1986).

The Relationship Between Norms and Goals

Norms, understandings about the roles we are expected to play in groups, are intimately related to group goals, sometimes directly and sometimes unconsciously. When norms are incompatible with a group goal, the group is unlikely to achieve the goal. For example, if a chairperson of a meeting indicates that he would like to hear ideas about how the company can expand its markets but the norm of the organization is to take cues from the chair, no ideas will be forthcoming. The normative structure or creative environment that would foster the expression of ideas does not exist.

Thus norms may affect the attainability of goals. But goals may also influence norms, which in turn will influence future goals. Consider a situation in which there is great pressure to achieve certain difficult goals. These goals may engender norms that are competitive and that reduce the organization's ability to achieve successes in the future.

Consider this example. A computer organization has been struggling with declining sales and the possibility that it may be closed. In a last-ditch effort to spur sales, the company offers an extraordinary bonus to the salesperson who can produce delivered sales of $3 million within the next six months. Suddenly, salespeople begin taking leads from newspaper ads and even from each other's desks. Salespeople begin bribing the secretary to send future leads to them, rather than waiting their turns as policy dictates. They solicit in each other's territories and stop sharing tips and strategies on how to close with particular clients. In short, war erupts in the sales force. Each seller is now out for number one, and the norms of the organization have changed dramatically. Even after the six-months cutoff date, the norms of the work group are still competitive and secretive.

High school teenagers offer a clear illustration of the relationship of norms and goals. They have strict dress norms—the goal is to be attractive and to be noticed.

Clothes are not simply a means of appearing attractive but become the end. The goal becomes to always have the latest styles. Having the new look guarantees being noticed. The need to have new things leads to a norm of dressing in "outrageous" current fashion. In this way a norm becomes a goal that reinforces the norm.

To use another example, consider partners in a marriage who fear divorce and set a goal of remaining married at all costs. Within that context, conflict comes to mean "bad marriage." Therefore, the partners establish a norm of suppressing conflict and eschewing arguments. This leads in turn to a norm of speaking only about noncontroversial subjects. Alienation and boredom result and spur a new goal: to have an affair for the excitement and closeness missing from the marriage. Thus norms shape goals that may then affect the norms and influence the outcome of the original goal.

The reciprocal influences between norms and goals reveal the fact that norms, our unstated rules, evolve. We need some drive or consensus to adhere to them. If we look closely enough, we see that norms are really subtle goal behavior. Individual goals are more frequently expressed overtly, but group goals often remain unstated norms. Sometimes these normative goals are eventually stated outright, but often they remain the unidentified motivators of a group.

Changing Group Goals

Goals in the broadest sense include a future-oriented perspective. Sometimes group goals are inappropriate and should be re-examined and changed, but goals, like norms, are difficult to change. However, it is more likely that new goals will be supported, with concomitant implementation, if there is active discussion in creation of the new goals. If those to be involved at a later date in carrying out the new policies or procedures are also involved in setting them, it is more likely that they will integrate the new goals into their personal goal structures. Where behavior change is desired, setting goals through group discussion is more effective than separate instruction of individual members, external requests, or imposition of new practices by a superior.

Erez, Earley, and Hulin (1985) tested the hypothesis that the level of group acceptance increases as the level of participation increases and, further, that increased participation in goal acceptance increases performance. In one study, they asked college students to work on a simulated scheduling task under four conditions. In another study, they used animal caretakers to determine whether involvement in goal setting would increase goal acceptance. Findings in both studies supported the hypothesis: "Participative and representative goal setting significantly increased individual goal acceptance, and individual goal acceptance significantly contributed to performance."

The paradox, however, is that because of the very support members receive from one another, it is difficult to change the group's goals. A number of steps have been suggested (Lippitt, 1961) to help a group be more productive.

1. The group must have a clear understanding of its purposes.

2. The group should become conscious of its own process. By improving the process, the group can improve its problem-solving ability.

3. The group should become aware of the skills, talents, and other resources within its membership and should remain flexible in using them.

4. The group should develop group methods of evaluation, so that the group can have methods of improving its process.

5. The group should create new jobs and committees as needed and terminate others when they are no longer compatible with the goals.

Group Goals and the Individual Member

Initially, members act in a new group as they acted in others (Mills, 1967); there is for them an undifferentiated membership role. They scan others for guides to norms and expected behaviors. As they become familiar with the processes of the new group, they learn which behaviors are rewarded and which are deviant. They widen their understanding of what is acceptable behavior in this group. Their personal goals are no longer the only considerations.

They begin to operate at a higher level. They come to understand the group's goals and accept them. They commit their personal resources to accomplishing the goals, and give them higher priority than their own goals. They eventually come to evaluate their performances and the performances of others in terms of accomplishment of the group's goals. They even modify their behavior to help the group become more effective.

Goals are such a central concept of groups that the most common definition of a group is "two or more people interacting with a common goal." Social scientists agree that group goals influence all aspects of group behavior.

◆ ◆ *EXERCISE 1*

A Series of Skill Exercises

Objective

■   To increase skills in goal areas

Rationale

Goal setting seems obvious; participants often feel they have no difficulty setting goals or agreeing on them. Frequently, any difficulties that arise are seen as "personality conflicts," which is another way of saying that nothing can be done. These exercises give participants an opportunity to check out their perceptions on goals and movement toward goals. They also enable members to build skills in goal setting or in stating the problem. These exercises focus on the group problem rather than on inducing individual defensive behaviors. They should be used individually as appropriate.

1. Setting Up the Problem

Usually, when defining a problem, we do so in a way that implicitly suggests a solution. This may cause some people to become defensive and work on their private or personal goals rather than the group goals. This exercise attempts to help participants overcome that difficulty.

Action

Participants are divided into groups of six to ten. The facilitator introduces the exercise by saying, "Though all of us publicly state that we want the group to make a decision, we behaviorally don't mean it even when we think we do. For example, we say the office secretaries use the phone too much and ask what we can do about it. But this question does not allow the group to make a decision based on determination of the situation. Rather, it puts the secretaries on the defensive. We do this all the time. How can we state the problem in such a way that some people do not begin to feel guilty and in which there is no implied solution? This will be an exercise to practice these skills."

The facilitator may state one or several problems that have occurred in the life of the group (one is preferable). In each case, the facilitator asks each participant to assume the appropriate position for asking the question (in the illustration cited, he or she could be the office manager). Each person writes the problem so as not to make anyone feel guilty and not to imply a solution. Then each member reads his or her statement, and the others critique it for meeting the criteria. The group suggests improvements, and the next person is heard. As the analysis goes on, some general principles of stating the problem emerge. Each group reports its best statement of the problem and the general principles. As additional skill building, groups make up a problem and submit it to the next group. The same procedure is used, and there is a testing of the general principles. This exercise is cognitive, but members find the experience interesting in that they come to appreciate the difficulties of avoiding predetermined solutions as they refine their skills. Here are some problems for restatement, if the group does not create its own:

1. A bus driver reports that children in the buses are destroying property, using abusive language, and picking on younger children. The high school buses especially have this problem on the morning run at 7:00 A.M.

2. Shortly, we will be electing class officers. I believe that they should be truly representative of the class. In the past, this has not been so.

3. Ms. Brown, from the American Federation of Teachers, came to visit me yesterday, and she urges us to affiliate. Last year Bill and John led the opposition, and we did not join.

2. Clarity of Goal Setting

Here the objective is to increase observer skills in goal setting and to increase awareness of various aspects of goal setting. The facilitator introduces a role-playing situation (the hidden-agenda example in this chapter is appropriate, or another that involves a current group issue). Depending on the facilitator's objectives, he or she may have one group role play and all others observe, or he or she may divide the total membership into a number of role plays with two observers for each role-playing group. The first method builds common skills in observation and goal setting; the second develops an understanding of personal and group goals via observation.

Observers are instructed to note whether behaviors are person-oriented or group-oriented, which behaviors helped to clarify the problem, and which impeded movement on the problem. The facilitator cuts the role playing when a decision is reached or if it becomes evident that a decision will not be reached. Role players report how they feel, especially with regard to movement toward a goal. How did their private agendas help them? Or did they impede them? What would have helped them become involved in the group goal? Was there a group goal? The observers also report. In the hidden-agenda role play, there are usually so many more individual behaviors that it becomes obvious that a decision cannot be reached until these factors are dealt with. Some might be brought out into the open, some consciously ignored.

After the exercise, members begin to understand both the problems and pervasiveness of work at several levels on goals. They also develop increased awareness of the behaviors needed to help the group focus on group issues rather than personal goals.

3. Diagnosis of Goal Clarity and Goal Movement

If groups are to work efficiently at goals, at both task and maintenance levels, it is essential that they become aware of their own processes. It is important to gather data on the current state of the group and use this information to help the group set its goals, clarify them, and learn the degree of involvement.

Simple Reporting   One method is to stop each session 10 minutes before the end. The members of the group then discuss their answers to these two questions: How much progress do you feel we made on our goals today? What would help us?

This can be done in a workshop at the end of each session; it can be used effectively in ongoing work groups. Initially there is resistance to the concept as well as the process. If it is begun at a routine session or becomes part of an ongoing process, it loses much of its threat and becomes a simple, effective device for helping the group get feedback on its movement toward goals.

Individual–Group Reaction, Reporting   The design is similar to the one above. It is used about 20 minutes before the end of the session. Sheets with the following questions are distributed to each group member.

    1. What did you think the explicit goals of the group were?
    2. What do you think the group was really working on (implicit goals)?
    3. What was helpful?
    4. What hindered movement?

Each person replies to these questions privately and individually. Members then share their replies and consider actions based on the data collected.

This method is also initially threatening to members, but if it becomes routine, it develops increased skills in diagnosing group problems and allows for greater group productivity.

Feedback on Goals, Instrumented   Another method for achieving clarity of goals, as well as movement on the goal, is to use a chart that is distributed and scored and the results fed back to the members. Because it has a more objective, statistical format, it sometimes encourages members to be more open to the findings and less defensive. It takes more time, and perhaps a half-hour should be allowed. The group is rated on the following three dimensions.

GOALS

1	2	3	4	5
Poor (e.g., goals are confusing or conflicting)			Good (e.g., goals are clear or shared)	

PARTICIPATION

1	2	3	4	5
Poor (e.g., a few members dominate or are passive)			Good (e.g., all members participate or are listened to)	

FEELINGS

1	2	3	4	5

Poor (e.g., members may   Good (e.g., members
not express feelings)   express responses honestly)

The sheets are collected. One member tabulates the data. A check is scored at its numerical value on the scale (a check between 3 and 4 is scored 3.5). The numbers are totaled for each question. The findings on each dimension are reported in terms of highest and lowest scores as well as average. The higher the score, the closer the group is to the objectives of goal clarity, group participation, and openness in response. Members then discuss the findings.

Although these techniques may meet with some initial resistance (this is why the simple, open-ended discussion is the first recommended), each helps the group diagnose its own situation and modify its behaviors toward increased productivity.

◆ ◆ *EXERCISE 2*

Setting Individual Goals and Reassessing Them

Objectives

- To increase understanding of what is meant by setting goals as an individual
- To develop skill in stating goals clearly and specifically
- To recognize that goal setting is an ongoing process
- To periodically re-evaluate goals and determine whether any changes or modifications are needed
- To increase understanding and skill in giving and receiving help

Rationale

We participate in many group experiences with only a vague idea of what we expect to derive. This exercise is designed to help the participant formulate his or her goals specifically and realistically, and then re-evaluate them at regular intervals. It is hoped not only that he or she will develop skill in formulating goals in the course of the experience, but also that once this has been brought into consciousness, he or she will be motivated to pursue these goals in his or her activities. As we move toward a goal, we encounter new insights, new obstacles, new understandings. Thus, as a result of increased understanding at time A, we can make revisions of goals and move into time B. At this time we again reassess goals for time C, and so on.

Timing

Phase I of the design should take place early in the program. It might be used after an initial "microlab" or "getting to know each other" opening session. It is appropriate for a workshop or course that will continue over a period of time. Phase II should occur about the middle of the program, Phase III at the end. Each phase takes approximately one hour.

Action

The facilitator announces the exercise and may informally state some of the objectives. The group is divided into trios. These trios become a support system for each individual, helping to redefine his or her goals as well as analyze the forces that help or hinder him or her. Each helps and receives help from the others. The facilitator reads and explains Phase I, Steps 1 and 2, and when these are completed, suggests the group continue with Step 3. Discussion questions may be considered at this point.

Phase II is scheduled midway through the learning experience. The groups form into their original trios. The facilitator reads and explains Phase II. The trios work. If there is time, a discussion similar to the one after Phase I occurs; however, the exchange will be very different from the first one. Trio members will be much more comfortable with one another; there will be much less anxiety and more willingness to share and to help. More time should be allowed.

Phase III should be scheduled at the end of the learning experience. It will be conducted similarly to Phase II, but there will be a marked change in atmosphere. Trio members will feel closer and will honestly discuss their feelings and reactions to the workshop. The prospect of continuing in a home setting produces mixed responses. There are those who "can't wait" to continue on the goals, and others who are apprehensive about whether their situations will permit even tentative movements in the directions they would like to go. However, Phase III cannot be eliminated. It must be continued in "real life" if developing skills in individual goals is to have any permanent value. A discussion following Phase III might enable participants to discuss the aids and hindrances they expect to encounter, and to show how they may find alternatives for dealing with these factors.

Goal-Setting Procedure

PHASE I INITIAL GOAL SETTING

Step 1   Take five minutes to write one to three responses to the following question: *What do I want to learn most from this workshop* (or course or laboratory experience)?

Step 2   Take turns going through the following procedure: One person starts by reading one of his or her responses from Step 1. All discuss the response (goal). The following guideline questions may be helpful to clarify and amplify the goal under discussion.

> Is the goal specific enough to permit direct planning and action, or is it too general or abstract?
>
> Does the goal involve you personally—that is, something you must change about yourself?
>
> Is the goal realistic? Can it be accomplished (or at least progress made) during the period of this program?
>
> Can others help you work on this goal?
>
> Is this the real goal, or is it a "front" for a subtle or hidden goal?

During or following the discussion, the person whose goal is being discussed revises his or her goal so that it is specific and realistic. This procedure is used for each goal listed. Allow about 20 minutes per person.

Step 3   Discuss in turn the barriers you anticipate in reaching your goal(s). Write them down as specifically as you can. Take a few minutes to list ways in which you individually, or with the help of others, can overcome these barriers. Discuss your lists with your trio.

PHASE II REASSESSMENT

Earlier this week (day, month, session) you prepared your initial assessment of goals for this workshop. One purpose in this session is to re-examine your goals in light of your experience so far. Refer to your earlier responses. Look at the goals stated there. Also look at the helping and hindering factors you listed earlier.

Step 1—Goal Reassessment   Within your trios, take turns reassessing and discussing your goals. As you discuss them, one of the other members should enter your modified or reconfirmed goal on the list of goals. These statements should be checked out to your satisfaction.

Step 2—Analysis of Helping and Hindering Factors   After your goals have been reformulated or reconfirmed, discuss in turn your perception of the present helping and hindering forces—in yourself, in others, in the setting—and make a list.

PHASE III REASSESSMENT

We are now in the concluding period of this workshop. Within your trios, re-examine your goals as modified and the helping and hindering forces you listed. How much progress did you make? What still needs to be done?

Step 1—Evaluation of Progress on Goal   In turn, discuss how much you feel you accomplished on your goals. What helped you most? What hindered you?

Step 2—Goal setting for the Home   Discuss how you could continue on your set goals at home. What forces will help? What will hinder? As you discuss these questions, another member of the trio should enter the new goals on the lists.

Discussion

For some people, revealing personal goals and inadequacies is extremely difficult. Attempting to verbalize expectations is a formidable task for others because they lack practice in doing it. Giving help and accepting help may also be new and difficult experiences. Some of the following questions give participants an opportunity to discuss their feelings in these areas and thus reduce anxiety.

> What problems did you encounter in first stating your goals? Why?
>
> How did your goals change after discussion?
>
> How do you feel about help on your goals?
>
> Are these your real goals? How honest do you feel you were in stating them?
>
> What is the relationship between your goals and the goals of this workshop?
>
> Are they compatible? Where is there conflict?

◆ ◆ EXERCISE 3

Skills in Goal Setting

Objective

- To demonstrate how individual behaviors affect action on goals
- To demonstrate how characteristics of group goals affect group behavior
- To build skills in goal setting through observations of behavior in two conditions

Setting Up the Situation

The facilitator discusses the general nature of group goals ("a place the group members want to reach in order to reduce some tension or difficulty they all feel") and how these goals are made explicit through the coordination of individual motives and needs.

The class is divided into subgroups of five or six persons. The facilitator explains that each of us has our own way of dealing with problems related to goals.

Action

PHASE I

Members receive sheets listing three problems of goal setting:

1. When I am a member of a group that does not seem to have a clear awareness of its goals or how they are to be achieved, I usually . . .

2. When I am a member of a group that has a clear understanding of its goals but seems to have little commitment to accomplishing them, I usually . . .
3. When I am a member of a group that has conflicting opinions on what its goals should be, or that has members with conflicting needs and motives, I usually . . .

Members fill out the sheets and then discuss problems with goals and their individual solutions. (Allow 15 minutes.)

Groups are asked to report their conclusions about how to deal with certain group problems. The facilitator then reviews the conclusions as indicators of proper procedures in goal setting.

The facilitator briefly reviews proper procedures in goal setting.

PHASE II

The facilitator asks a volunteer from each group to be an observer. The observers are briefed (by the facilitator, outside) to pay attention to (1) the number of times members attempt to clarify the goal, (2) disruptive, ineffective behavior by members, and (3) general productivity.

Observers return and the facilitator gives the groups a short time to accomplish a vague, abstract, complex task.

Task 1 (time: 7 to 8 min.): Reach agreement on this statement: "What are the most appropriate goals for maximizing social development in a democratic society?"

After the time is up, the facilitator gives the groups a concrete, clear, simple task.

Task 2 (time: 7 to 8 min.): "What are your goals in taking this course and how will they be met?"

Analysis

Observers report to the total group on what they have noticed (for example, "The first task evoked long silences, considerable angry feeling, many calls for clarification, and long, vague, intellectual comments. The second task produced an initial burst of laughter and very rapid discussion, and nearly everyone took part, which was very different from the first task").

The class members generalize about characteristics of effective types of goals (for example, "attainable, clear, challenging") and examine the reasons for the negative, disruptive behaviors appearing in the first task (which involved an ineffective goal).

◆ ◆ *EXERCISE 4*

Hidden-Agenda Role Play

Objectives

■ To increase the understanding that groups work simultaneously at an explicit as well as an implicit or hidden level
■ To increase awareness of "hidden agendas"

Rationale

Each of us has all of the personal, private needs that motivate our behavior in addition to the publicly stated reasons for our being present in a group. We all operate from these hidden agendas to some extent; they are part of us. The object is not to label them bad or to ignore them, but to be aware of them in our efforts to understand what is happening in a group. The role play presented allows members to understand the hidden agendas and to become aware that these implicit goals greatly influence movement on the group goals.

Design

The facilitator asks for four volunteers to participate in a role play. The volunteers are selected, and each gets a piece of paper with the role he or she is to play. The role players are given a few minutes to study their roles and be sure they understand them. The roles on the pieces of paper are as follows:

1. Not only are you very eager to be elected to this committee, but you seriously believe that unless you are the one elected, it might not be successful. You like your fellow faculty members, but you feel that they tend to be authoritarian, and you are afraid that if anyone else is elected, the students will be allowed to make decisions in name but will not be allowed to really influence the decisions. You feel very strongly that young people should learn autonomy and responsibility.

2. You are eager to be elected. You are taking courses for your doctorate. You want to become a principal. The activity will look good on your record. It might even develop into a vice-principalship in this school.

3. Not only are you very eager to be elected to the committee, but you seriously believe that unless you are the one elected, the committee might not be successful. You like and respect your fellow faculty members as teachers, but you seriously believe that they do not understand the sort of guidance that students (who are really still children) need in order to learn how to behave responsibly on committees. You feel that if you are elected to this committee, you can guide these students to success, and this will then make a student–faculty disciplinary committee a permanent thing. You are afraid that if the other faculty members get the job, the whole thing will result in chaos and the whole movement will be dropped.

4. You are in a hurry to leave the meeting, but the principal has asked that you be on the committee, and you want to stay on his or her good side. You had a fight last night with the person you are considering marrying. You are eager for the meeting to end so that you can meet that person.

Aside from the four role players, the others are asked to be observers for the role play. They are asked to note:

How clear is the goal?

Is it understandable?

Is it attainable?

Are the steps to goal accomplishment known?

How productive is the group?

What impedes the members?

At this point the role players are asked to be seated at a table.

Action

The committee is told that they are members of a high school faculty. The students have asked for more responsibility in resolving matters of discipline. The principal has agreed to the establishment of a committee to handle such matters. The membership will be made up of students and one faculty adviser.

The principal feels that each of the members invited would be a suitable faculty adviser and hopes the faculty committee will determine among themselves whom they would like to represent them. The committee is meeting after school. The members will decide who the faculty adviser will be and submit his or her name to the principal so it can be announced at the assembly in the morning.

The committee meets. The facilitator should break in after about 5 to 7 minutes if no decision is made, and the role play should be cut so that interest does not wane.

Discussion

Observers are asked to report what they saw.

If the group goal was clear, why was progress so slow? In many groups this role play is not resolved; no decision is made. If all the members understand the goal, if it is attainable, and if the members know the steps to attain it, why is the group not more productive? What prevented the group from arriving at a simple decision? Consider the roles. Who wanted the job? Why?

What were the members' hidden agendas? That is, what seemed to be motivating them? How do private goals influence group goals and productivity? What are the implications for other groups?

◆ ◆ *EXERCISE 5*

Cooperative Versus Competitive Goals

Objectives

- To observe differences between cooperative and competitive goals
- To experience cooperative or competitive goals
- To recognize that group goals influence individual behavior

Materials

A roll of wide, white shelf paper

Masking tape

A large number of felt-tipped pens (broad) or other, similar pens

Preparation

Hang a large segment of shelf paper on the wall as the basis for creating a mural. Hang other segments of the same size on other walls. There should be a minimum of two, a maximum of any even number. There should be a batch of pens (and other materials, if desired) for each group. Divide the groups into the same number of units as there are murals. (Groups might be created randomly by having members count off.)

Action

Give each group written instructions. For half the groups, the instructions should read, "This is a contest to create a mural. A prize will be given to the person who makes the greatest contribution to the mural."

The other half of the groups should receive instructions that read, "This is a contest. Your group is to create a mural; the group with the best mural will receive a prize."

There should be one observer for each group who observes the behavior of the group in creating the mural. The facilitator gives the signal to start and announces how long the group has to complete the mural. He or she stops the groups at the end of the time allotted.

Discussion

Ask members of each group, by groups, to discuss how they felt in the project and ask observers to report. Then lead a general discussion of how being in a cooperative group is different from being in a competitive group.

In some way, have groups decide which mural is best and who contributed the most—individual votes, observer's opinion, outsider's opinion—and have small prizes available. Then discuss how it feels to receive (or not receive) a prize as an individual and as a member of a group.

◆ ◆ EXERCISE 6

Implementing Goals

Objectives

- To illustrate goals that initially seem clear but are in fact not clear
- To demonstrate how goals change in implementation

Setting Up the Situation

The facilitator assigns participants to groups of four to six.

Action

(Time: 15 min.) The facilitator instructs the groups to choose themes for pictures that each will draw on paper.

He or she gives each group a large piece of newsprint or shelf paper and a colored magic marker of a distinct color.

The facilitator then instructs the groups that at the word *begin* they are to draw the picture they decided on. However, there are two restrictions: (1) as of the signal to begin, no one is to speak or influence each other in any way, and (2) members will work on the drawing one by one until everyone has had a turn. The finished pictures are to be hung on the wall.

Discussion

The groups then discuss the following three questions for about 10 minutes.

1. What helped you come up with a theme? Which approaches or behaviors were helpful?
2. How did you feel when you heard that the project was nonverbal and that you could draw only once? How did you feel when someone added to what you did? How did you feel about your group before drawing? How do you feel about your group now? If your feelings have changed, what produced the changes?
3. Do you think your group solved the problem adequately? Are you satisfied with the result?

One person is to do a presentation for each group, explaining the group's theme, how members feel about it, and how their feelings about the group changed. This person should address these questions:

1. What could group members have done differently in arriving at their theme to make their drawing successful?
2. What are the implications of this exercise for goal setting and goal implementation?

◆ ◆ EXERCISE 7

Communicating Goals[1]

Objectives

■ To demonstrate goal transmission under three conditions

---

1. This exercise was first used by John D'Angelo and his group in a graduate class in Psychoeducational Processes, Introduction to Group Dynamics, at Temple University.

Rationale

Often an individual has a clear idea of the goal he or she would like to accomplish but has difficulty communicating that goal to others. This exercise demonstrates these difficulties.

Setting Up the Situation

The facilitator must provide

Moveable chairs

Copies of the diagram for half the participants

Three sheets of blank 8½ × 11 paper for half the participants

Members will be working in pairs. Pairing can be accomplished by drawing numbers—for example, in an 18-person group, the pairing might be

1	18
2	17
3	16
4	15
5	14
6	13
7	12
8	11
9	10

Action

Participants are grouped in pairs, and pairs are instructed to sit in their chairs back-to-back so the individuals cannot see each other's faces and can only respond to verbal instructions.

Odd-numbered people are called the instructors. The facilitator distributes a copy of the diagram to each instructor and three sheets of blank paper to the second member in each pair, the learner.

STAGE ONE (TIME: 5 MIN.)

The facilitator then explains to the learners, "Listen carefully to the instructor. He or she is your guide. Do not ask questions and or respond in any way. Simply follow instructions."

The instructors, using the diagram, give verbal instructions on folding the paper. The learner follows the instructions and labels his or her attempt "Stage 1." Under no circumstances should the learner see the diagram.

STAGE TWO (TIME: 5 MIN.)

Again, the pair members are seated back-to-back. The facilitator explains, "In this condition, the learners can ask the instructors for more information when the instructions are not clear. They can ask the instructors to go back and review instructions."

The pair continues. The instructor gives instructions; when necessary, the learner asks questions. The learner, however, may not see the diagram.

At the end of five minutes, they stop and the attempt is labeled "Stage 2."

THE DIAGRAM

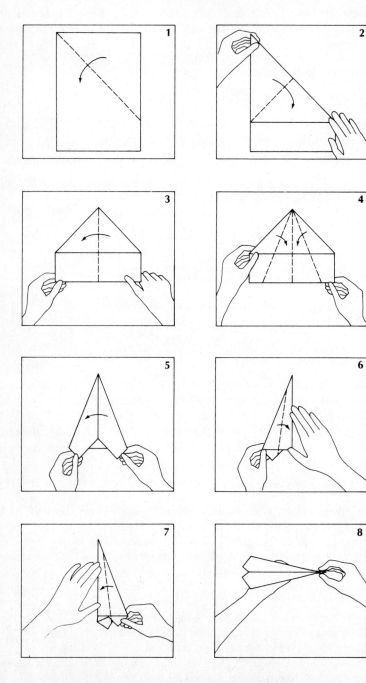

STAGE THREE (TIME: 5 MIN.)

Now the members of the pair face each other. In this condition, anything goes short of sharing the diagram. The learner can ask questions, and the instructor can demonstrate moves.

At the end of five minutes, they stop. The attempt is labeled "Stage 3."

Discussion

The facilitator asks the pairs to discuss how they felt about following the instructions in each set of conditions. The participants consider these questions:

1. How did the learner feel about the instructor?
2. How did the instructor feel about the learner?
3. What is important about transmitting a goal that one clearly understands?
4. What would happen when ideas that are not as graphic as the one presented here are to be transmitted to a group of ten people?

Following the pairs' discussions, the group as a whole discusses the exercise.

References

Allport, F. Social Psychology. Boston: Houghton Mifflin, 1924.

Atkinson, J. W., and N. Feather. A Theory of Achievement Motivation. New York: John Wiley and Sons, 1966.

Barnard, C. I. The Functions of the Executive. Cambridge, Mass.: Harvard University Press, 1938.

Benne, K. D., and P. Sheats. "Functional roles of group members." Journal of Social Issues, 4, No. 2 (1948), 41–49.

Bennis, W. G., K. D. Benne, and R. Chin. The Planning of Change. 2nd ed. New York: Holt, Rinehart and Winston, 1969.

Berkowitz, L. "Group standards, cohesiveness, and productivity." Human Relations, 7 (1954), 509–519.

Bradford, L. "Hidden agenda." In Group Development. Ed. L. Bradford. Washington, D.C.: National Training Laboratories, 1961, pp. 60–72.

Carnevale, A. P., L. J. Gainer, and J. Villet. Training in America. San Francisco: Jossey-Bass, 1990, pp. 159–163.

Cartwright, D., and A. Zander. Group Dynamics: Research and Theory. 3rd ed. New York: Harper & Row, 1968, pp. 403–405.

Church, Russell M. "The effects of competition on reaction time and palmar skin conductance." Journal of Abnormal and Social Psychology, 65, No. 1 (1962), 32–40.

Cooper, L., and J. Gustafson. "Family-group development: Planning in organizations." Human Relations, 34 (1981), 705–730.

Deutsch, K. The Nerves of Government. Glencoe, Ill.: Free Press, 1963.

Deutsch, M. "An experimental study of the effects of cooperation and competition upon group process." Human Relations, 2 (1949), 199–231, pp. 129–152. Reprinted in Group Dynamics. 2nd ed. Ed. Cartwright and A. Zander. New York: Harper & Row, 1960, pp. 348–352.

Elias, F. G., M. E. Johnson, and J. B. Fortman. "Task-focused self-disclosure: Effects on group cohesiveness, commitment to task, and productivity." Small Group Behavior, 20, No. 1 (February 1989), 87–96.

Erez, M., P. C. Earley, and C. L. Hulin. "The impact of participation on goal acceptance and performance: A two-step model." Academy of Management Journal, 28, No. 1 (1985), 50–66.

Fennell, M. L., and G. D. Sandefur. "Structural clarity of interdisciplinary teams: A research note." Journal of Applied Behavioral Science, 19, No. 2 (1983), 193–202.

Fourezios, N. T., M. L. Hutt, and H. Guetzkow. "Measurement of self-oriented needs in discussion groups." *Journal of Abnormal and Social Psychology,* 45 (1950), 682–690.

Gross, D. E., H. H. Kelley, A. W. Kruglanski, and M. E. Patch. "Contingency of consequences and type of incentive in interdependent escape." *Journal of Experimental Social Psychology,* 8, No. 4 (July 1972), 360–377.

Gurnee, H. "Group learning." *Psychological Monographs,* 76, No. 13 (1962).

Hansler, D. F., and C. Cooper. "Focus groups: New dimension in feasibility study. *Fund Raising Management,* 17, No. 5 (1986), 78–82.

Hare, P. *Handbook of Small Group Research.* New York: Free Press, 1976.

Harlow, K. C. *Psychology Reports,* 65, No. 3, Pt. 1 (December 1989), 861–862.

Horwitz, M. "The recall of interrupted group tasks: An experimental study of individual motivation in relation to social groups." *Human Relations,* 7 (1954), 3–38.

Jaffe, J. M. "Of different minds." *Association Management,* 37, No. 10 (1985), 120–124.

Janssens, L., and J. R. Nuttin. "Frequency perception of individual and group successes as a function of competition, coaction, and isolation." *Journal of Personality and Social Psychology,* 34 (1976), 830–836.

Johnson, D. "Effects of cooperative, competitive, and individualistic goal structures on achievement: A meta-analysis." *Psychological Bulletin,* 89 (1981), 47–62.

Johnson, D. W., R. T. Johnson, and M. B. Stanne. "Impact of goal and resource interdependence on problem-solving success." *Journal of Social Psychology,* 129 (October 1989), 621–629.

Julian, James W., and Franklyn A. Perry. "Cooperation contrasted with intragroup competition." *Sociometry,* 30, No. 1 (March 1967), 79–90.

Kelley, H., and J. Thibaut. "Experimental studies of group problem-solving and process." In *Handbook of Social Psychology,* Vol. II. Ed. G. Lindzey. Reading, Mass.: Addison-Wesley, 1954, pp. 735–785.

Klein, J. *The Study of Groups.* London: Routledge, 1956.

Korten, D. C. "Situational determinants of leadership structure." *Journal of Conflict Resolution,* 6 (1962), 222–235.

Kramer, R. M., C. G. McClintock, and D. M. Messick. "Social values and cooperative response to a simulated resource conservation crisis." *Journal of Personality,* 54, No. 3 (1986), 576–592.

Lane, I. "Making the goals of acceptance and quality explicit: Effects on group decisions." *Small Group Behavior,* 13 (1982), 542–554.

Lee, C. "The relationship between goal setting, self-efficacy, and female field hockey team performance." *International Journal of Sport Psychology,* 20, No. 2 (April–June 1989), 147–161.

Lewin, K. "Field theory and experiment in social psychology: Concepts and methods." *American Journal of Sociology,* 44 (1939), 868–897.

Lewis, H. B. "An experimental study of the role of the ego in work. I. The role of the ego in cooperative work." *Journal of Experimental Psychology,* 34 (1944), 113–116.

Lewis, H. B., and M. Franklin. "An experimental study of the role of ego in work. II. The significance of task orientation in work." *Journal of Experimental Psychology,* 34 (1944), 195–215.

Lippitt, G. "How to get results from a group." In *Group Development.* Ed. L. Bradford. Washington, D.C.: National Training Laboratories, 1961, p. 34.

Mann, M. P. "An Analysis of Faculty Goals: Personal, Disciplinary, and Career Development Decisions." Presentation at Annual Meeting of the American Educational Research Association, San Francisco, March 27–31, 1989.

Mills, T. M. *The Sociology of Small Groups.* Englewood Cliffs, N.J.: Prentice-Hall, 1967, pp. 81–82.

Morrow, A. J. "Goal tension and recall. I and II." *Journal of General Psychology,* 19 (1938), 3–35, 37–64.

National Geographic Society (April World) 1986.

Nichols, M., and V. Day. "A comparison of moral reasoning of groups and individuals on the 'defining issues test.'" *Academy of Management Journal,* 25 (1982), 201–208.

Norris, D., and R. Niebuhr. "Group variables and gaming success." *Simulation and Games,* 11 (1980), 301–312.

Parsons, T., and E. A. Shils, eds. *Working Papers in the Theory of Action.* Cambridge, Mass.: Harvard University Press, 1951.

Pearce, J. A., II, and R. B. Robinson, Jr. *Strategic Management: Strategic Formulation and Implementation.* 2nd ed. Homewood, Ill.: Irwin, 1985, p. 15.

Quey, R. L. "Functions and dynamics of work groups." *American Psychologist,* 26, No. 10 (1971), 1077–1082.

Rabow, J., F. J. Fowler, D. L. Braadford, M. A. Hoefeller, and Y. Shibuya. "The role of social norms and leadership in risk-taking." *Sociometry,* 29, No. 1 (1966), 16–27.

Reddy, W. B., and A. Byrnes. "Effects of interpersonal group composition on the problem-solving behavior of middle managers." *Journal of Applied Psychology,* 56, No. 6 (1972), 516–517.

Rieken, H. W., and G. C. Homans. "Psychological aspects of social structure." In *Handbook of Social Psychology,* Vol. II. Ed. G. Lindzey. Reading, Mass.: Addison-Wesley, 1954, p. 810.

Roethlisberger, F. J., and W. J. Dickson. *Management and the Worker: Technical vs. Social Organization in an Industrial Plan.* Cambridge, Mass.: Harvard University Press, 1939.

Schutz, W. C. *FIRO: A Three-Dimensional Theory of Interpersonal Behavior.* New York: Holt, Rinehart and Winston, 1958.

Shaw, M. E. *Group Dynamics, The Psychology of Small Group Behavior.* New York: McGraw-Hill, 1981.

Smith, R. D., and R. H. Culhan. "MS/OR Academic and practitioner interactions: A promising new approach. *Interfaces,* 16, No. 5 (Sept./Oct. 1986), 27–33.

Stoner, J. A. F. "Risky and cautious shifts in group decisions: The influence of widely held values." *Journal of Experimental Social Psychology,* 4, No. 4 (October 1968), 442–459.

Stoner, J. A. F. "A comparison of individual and group decisions including risk." Master's thesis, 1961, School of Industrial Management, Massachusetts Institute of Technology, Cambridge, Mass.

Taylor, D., J. Doria, and J. Tyler. "Group performance and cohesiveness: An attribution analysis." *Journal of Social Psychology,* 119 (1983), 187–198.

Thelen, H. *Dynamics of Groups at Work.* Chicago, Ill.: University of Chicago Press, 1954.

Tuckman, B. W. "Group composition and group performance of structured and unstructured tasks." *Journal of Experimental Social Psychology,* 3 (January 1967), 25–40.

Turney, J. R. "The cognitive complexity of group members, group structure, and group effectiveness." *Cornell Journal of Social Relations,* 5, No. 2 (Fall 1970), 152–165.

Watson, C. "Motivational effects of feedback and goal-setting on group performance." Paper presented at the 91st annual Convention of the American Psychological Association, Anaheim, Calif., August 1983.

Weingart, L. R., and E. Weldon, "Processes that mediate the relationship between a group goal and group member performance. *Human Performance,* 4, No. 1 (1991), 33–54.

Weinstein, A. G., and R. L. Holzbach. "Effects of financial inducement on performance under two task structures." Proceedings of the 80th Annual Convention of the American Psychological Association, Part 1, 7 (1972), 217–218.

Wheelan, T. L., and J. D. Unger. *Strategic Management and Business Policy.* 2nd ed. Reading, Mass.: Addison-Wesley, 1986, 4–5.

Wheeler, R., and R. L. Ryan. "Effects of cooperative and competitive classroom environments on the attitudes and achievement of elementary school students engaged in social studies inquiry activities." *Journal of Educational Psychology,* 65, No. 3 (1973), 402–407.

Wheeless, L., V. Wheeless, and F. Dickson-Markman. "A research note: The relations among social and task perceptions in small groups." *Small Group Behavior,* 13 (1982), 373–384.

Workie, A. "The relative productivity of cooperation and competition." *Journal of Social Psychology,* 92, No. 2 (1974), 225–230.

Zald, M. "Organization control structures in five correctional institutions." *American Journal of Sociology,* 38 (1962), 305–345.

Zander, A., and D. Wolfe. "Administrative rewards and coordination among committee members." *Administrative Science Quarterly,* 9, No. 1 (June 1964), 50–69.

Zeigarnik, B. "Uber das behalten von erledigten und unerledigten handlunger." *Psychologische Forschung,* 9 (1927), 1–85.

Ziller, R. C. "Four techniques of group decision making under uncertainty." *Journal of Applied Psychology,* 41 (1957), 384–388.

◆ 5 ◆

Leadership

A few years ago, a young army captain in one of Africa's newly emerging nations became disenchanted with the progress of social and economic reform in his country. At that time, his nation was plagued by a failing economy, public disillusionment, and a poorly paid military. Working within a seedbed of discontent with the support of other young officers, and making full use of his considerable personal charm, idealism, and chárisma, the captain led a coup and took over the reins of power. His immediate popularity was tremendous, and the future of the country suddenly seemed bright.

Now, only a few short years later, the country is on the brink of financial ruin, the new leader's popularity is declining, and he is scrambling to maintain his precarious base of power and influence. One thing he recognizes is that the leadership skills that enabled him to take control are not what he needs currently to maintain his position and move the country ahead. That flamboyant, dictatorial, and very personal leadership style was well received at first, but it rapidly lost appeal as promises were left unfulfilled and hopes evaporated into the parched African air. Meanwhile, the young leader's style and approach changed—he is now more subdued, more eager to listen, and more willing to reach out to his own constituents for help. Further, he seeks more dialogue with those who must respond to his decisions, and he realizes that the success of change depends on the acceptance of those who must live with it. This leader has become acutely conscious of the fact that power can be a short-lived illusion if hope, expectations, and realism are not carefully balanced.

Gone suddenly are this leader's brashness, irreverence, and distaste for politics and bureaucrats. Today, he knows that both politics and bureaucrats are part of his reality and essential to his success. Charisma and promises are not enough. He recognizes the tenuousness of his situation and realizes that in all likelihood another young, disillusioned officer somewhere is plotting his demise.

Six Theoretical Views of Leadership

This chapter looks at the evolving nature of leadership theory and practice and its implications for small groups and organizations. Leadership is a concept that has a chameleon's ability to take on a new appearance with every new occasion. Even the definition of leadership varies with the circumstances. One study (Kraus and Gemmill, 1990) found that the subjects' own definitions of leadership greatly influenced how responsible they believed the leader was for the outcome of the group. How we define our leaders, therefore, may be related to how well they lead. It has been estimated that this word *leader,* not even coined until the middle of the nineteenth century, has more than 100 definitions.

Robert Terry of the Center for Advanced Leadership at the Hubert H. Humphrey Institute of Public Affairs, has attempted to bring clarity to the muddle by identifying six theoretical views of leadership: (1) leadership as power, (2) organizational leadership, (3) trait theory, (4) situational theory, (5) vision theory, and (6) ethical assessment. In the following sections, we explore the notion of leadership from each of these theoretical perspectives in turn.

Leadership as Power

Where leadership is viewed as power, the term is actually synonymous with *action*. Here, *leadership* means getting things done or making things happen that, without the intervention of the leader, would not occur. Whatever the style, position, or behavior utilized, in this context the leader acts as a central catalyst that moves the group toward action.

In some cases, the leader may attempt to lead by creating the desire for action within the followers themselves. The focus is still on making something happen, but there is a shift toward *empowering,* or enabling, followers to take responsibility for the resulting action. A good example of such empowerment occurs in a typical community action program in which a leader mobilizes support to address critical problems that influence the lives of his or her constituents.

In this context then, where leadership is power, *leadership* can be defined as the frequency with which an individual influences or directs the behaviors of others within a group. The crucial questions here are these: What allows *power* to occur in the first place? Why does a group do what a particular person suggests? Why do group members listen carefully to, and consider the suggestions of, one person while they dismiss those of others even before the speakers finish talking? How does the person whose suggestions are frequently accepted achieve this influence? And why do members do what he or she advocates? Simply put, when one person does what another wants him or her to do, we say that the influencer has *power* over the other. Leadership clearly involves power—that is, the ability to influence other people by whatever means necessary (McDavid and Harari, 1968).

Fairhurst and Chandler (1989) revealed that people identified as leaders speak differently to subordinates than they do to other identified leaders. From our earlier study of norms, it is easy to understand how a consistent and quite clear expectation of these rather obvious language patterns can influence the existing relationships. Predictable, patronizing, and condescending behavior can subtly reinforce old stereotypes and attitudes.

A person may be very influential and have a great deal of power in one group, and he or she is considered the leader because the group frequently accepts his or her direction. In another group, he or she may have little power; his or her suggestions are infrequently accepted by the group, and he or she would not be identified as one of the leaders. It is not unusual for a person who is a clerk in a business to be a powerful board member in a Boy Scout council. The reverse also occurs, though less often. The chairperson of a university department—high power in the department—may only be window-dressing (low power) in a community association. *Power is not a universal: it is limited by the person being influenced.*

A powerful person has power over only those whom he or she can influence in the areas and within the limits defined by the person being influenced. In other words, you have only the power those being influenced let you have.

Discussions of leadership sooner or later evolve into a discussion of power. The word itself evokes visions of manipulation, the omnipotent "big brother," and personal feelings of powerlessness. We think of Machiavelli's *The Prince* and his strategies of power; we recall the dictum of Lord Acton, "Power corrupts, and absolute power tends to corrupt absolutely," in relation to the centralization of power; and politics is defined as the ultimate power game.

According to Clemens and Mayer, Machiavellian politics can easily be translated to encompass modern concerns. Machiavelli was, of course, the "first management thinker to actually bring power out of the closet" (Clemens and Mayer, 1987, p. 105). Even so, power is rarely addressed and remains a kind of taboo in management. What do we personally think of power? Would we rather be powerful or powerless?

◆ *Reader Activity*

In what situations do you perceive yourself as having power and influence?

_____

_____

_____

What are the behaviors you use when you are being powerful and influential? _

_____

_____

What do people whom you consider powerful do to convey that image?

_____

_____

_____

Can you imagine exercising power with others in that way? _____

_____

_____

_____ ◆

Perhaps it is the influence of American history, with its ideal of egalitarianism, that is the basis for our ambivalence about power. Perhaps we are fearful of being thought deranged—to need power is definitely viewed as "sick." We want power—

to be decision makers, to be controllers, to have things go our ways—yet we are ashamed to admit, even to ourselves, that we desire power. According to John W. Gardner, former Secretary of Health, Education and Welfare and author of extensive leadership papers, most of us want leaders who are not hungry for power, but (ironically enough) we have created a system in which only the power-hungry will stay the course (Gardner, 1989, p. 43).

And why wouldn't we want to be powerful (except for our confusions on the subject)? The more powerful members of a group tend to be more popular than low-powered members. They speak to, and are addressed by, the other higher-powered members more than are lower-powered members (Stogdill, 1974). They participate more, they exert more influence attempts, and their influence is more accepted (Gray, Richardson, and Mayhew, 1968; Hoffman, Burke, and Maier, 1965; Mulder, 1971; Rubin et al., 1971; Rubin and Lewicki, 1973). Groups tend to be better satisfied when more powerful members occupy leadership positions (Stogdill, 1974), and those in positions of power enjoy being in the group more (Kipnis, 1972).

Further, being in a position of power correlates with positive self-concepts. In an experiment with groups of Harvard undergraduates, Archer (1974) found that those with high power over the experimental period changed in the direction of more positive self-concepts and that those with low power changed in the direction of more negative self-concepts.

What determines who has power? One conceptual scheme (French and Raven, 1960) distinguishes five different kinds of power:

Referent Power First, there is the kind of influence we do not even think of as power. We may emulate the clothes of someone we consider fashionable, we may espouse an argument we first heard from a brilliant intellectual with whom we identify, we may buy a book because someone whose opinion we value commented favorably on it. These people have *referent power* over us; we identify with them in certain areas, and they influence us without our feeling manipulated.

In smaller groups, we hear the suggestions of those whom we perceive as having good ideas quite differently from those whose thinking we categorize as pedestrian. We hear the member who speaks for us, who represents our point of view, who sounds as though he or she understands our position, and we are much more influenced to act in accordance with his or her suggestions. We may be influenced by those of higher status, a position we regard as important, a personal style, or charisma. In each situation, the powerful person has power because we accept his or her influence and do it voluntarily. Obviously, this power exists only as long as that person is a referent for us. Parents are powerful referents for children until they are teen-agers and then perhaps become powerful negative referents for a while; later their referent power usually becomes less direct.

Legitimate Power A second kind of power is *legitimate power*. This is an authority relationship, in which one person through his or her position is given the right to make certain decisions for others. It is the congressperson who represents our voting preferences, the department chairperson who represents us at the faculty executive committee, the foreman who supervises our work. It may also be the person we elect president of an organization, the members of the committee we agree will make arrangements for a banquet, the observer we ask to process our behavior at today's session.

The legitimacy may be derived from a number of sources. It may be from a higher level of the organization, it may be by law, it may emerge from the group. However, the recipients of influence see it as legitimate that the powerful person has a right to make decisions for them (Goldman and Fraas, 1965; Julian, Hollander, and Regula, 1969). Additionally, leaders with legitimate power get more support from the group when there are other group members with personal power (Spillane, 1983).

Expert Power   Frequently allied with legitimate power is *expert power*. Over time a person may become expert in an area; for example, a congressperson may point out to a citizens' group a strategy that will be carefully considered, because he or she is seen both as an ally through his or her legitimate power and as an expert familiar with the machinations of Congress. Expert power may also exist independent of position. It is based on the person's specialized knowledge, information, or skills.

In a group, it is easy to understand that those with expert power are asked more questions, they participate more, and they are more likely to attain power in ongoing groups than in spontaneous groups (Richardson et al., 1973). As with all classes of power, we determine who the experts are, for how long we will be influenced by them, and the area of their expertise.

In each of these first three types of power, we are voluntarily influenced. Somehow, because they are voluntary actions, we hesitate to think of these influence situations as power. We are more likely to conceive of power in the emotional "kid glove" or "iron fist" dimension; we normally think of power as reward or coercion.

Reward Power   In the *reward* situation, the powerful person gives carrots, promotions, gold stars, or *A*'s to the recipients for complying. It may be the "bribery" of a parent, as he or she entreats a child to finish dinner with a reminder of ice cream for dessert, or the parent who tells his or her teen-ager that if he or she makes the honor roll, he or she can have the car on weekends. Usually, reward power is situational—that is, determined by position. The parent rewards obedience in children, the boss gives rewards to workers.

Often the recipients of the reward feel controlled. It means compliance, running the rat race, playing the "company game," or carefully following the rules. We do, however, tend to accept reward power when the reward is more pleasant than the task or the other alternative is unpleasant; we perform the task in anticipation of the reward. However, when the reward is not one that we perceive as more favorable than the other alternatives, the person who can administer the rewards has no power over us. If the child does not like ice cream, the inducement to finish dinner is clearly lacking. The student who does not care about grades may consider the rewards of being with his or her friends and other alternatives more important. Reward power can be exerted only when the recipient values the rewards offered.

Coercive Power   If the reward does not bring compliance, those in authority frequently resort to *coercion.* Children who do not finish dinner are told they cannot leave the table until they finish or are sent to their rooms. Teen-agers who do not bring up their grades are threatened with having their allowances cut off or rights to the family car revoked (Kahn and Katz, 1966). The student who continues to create a disturbance is coerced with threats of detention, the employee with dismissal; the committee member who does not perform on a high-status committee with the threat of not being reappointed. Coercive power, however, is not just the opposite of reward power. Whereas with reward the individual does what the powerful person desires in hopes of attaining the reward, in a coercive situation the individual usually first attempts to escape the punishment. Coercive power invokes not only coercion but also no possibility of escaping the powerful person's influence.

These are the types of power. Acts of leadership, if they are to be effective, must rely on some basis of power. Referent power, in which the person identifies with the other and respects him or her, often has the broadest range of influence. With reward power, there is increased attraction because of the promise of reward and low resistance. Coercive power is likely to produce increased resistance, although the more legitimate the power, the less the resistance. At the right time, when it is functional, each type may be very powerful. In many situations the leader's influence is based on a combination of sources of power, as we see in this example:

> Students mechanically attend the first session of class in a required course. They carefully scrutinize the teacher for clues as to how much reading will be required, how much work they will have to do, how often examinations will be given, and how interesting the lecturer sounds. They also look for clues on attendance requirements and the possibilities for getting a good grade. Simultaneously, they acquire data on how expert the instructor seems to be and, over time, determine how they feel about the instructor as a teacher, as a scholar, and as a human being.
>
> The university gives the instructor legitimate power to teach the course and to administer rewards or coercions in the form of grades. The students also perceive the legitimacy of this power. The students, however, determine the degree of expertness they attribute to the instructor; that is, the students determine the extent of their being influenced by the instructor as someone to emulate or relate to. How much influence the course will have on the students will depend to a large degree on how much power

the students attribute to the instructor. It may be only coercive power, and in a hostile environment the students "get by." Or the course may have a profound influence; the students may relate to the instructor as a personal model, consider him or her genuinely knowledgeable, and find the course personally rewarding in adding to their insights or skills. Although legitimate power is the basis for influence of an instructor, and some students may even question this and drop the course, other bases for power develop and determine the extent of influence.

For some, legitimate power is enough. The right to be in a position to make decisions that affect others is everything. Wielding power gives them enormous satisfaction and a sense of prominence. There is something about being able to control others that is overwhelming. Consider an example:

> The lobby corridor was wall-to-wall with about 20 elevators. As the woman came around the corner, she noted one with the door open and the "up" light on; she immediately darted in, pleased that she didn't have to wait. Then, she "caught it." From someplace down the hall she heard, "Hey, where do you think you're going? I'll tell you which elevator is going up; I'll tell you where you stand to get the elevator. You want to stand there? Fine. But it isn't going up—not 'til I say so." It was incredible; in just seconds the woman felt like a bad child. She meekly got out, waited until he told her which one was going up, and got on feeling intimidated (he might not have liked her and then she would never get to the thirty-second floor). All the while the woman was thinking, "Can you believe it? I got into a power hassle over getting into an elevator! His bit of legitimate power is determining who gets into which elevator, and he's power mad."

For some, wielding power in the form of rewards or sanctions is everything. Being liked is unimportant or, at best, secondary to having power. Being in a position of legitimate power, of being able to influence decisions and the "lives of others," is the insatiable quest. This can lead to corruption, manipulation, and the loss of a sense of purpose and vision.

◆ Individual Experiment

Think of two separate groups of which you are a member. Identify one or two individuals in each group whom you think of as powerful. Make a list of the specific behaviors that he or she uses in exercising that power. What type of power is he or she using? Compare the types of power used in each of the two groups. Is one type of power more effective than others?   ◆

Organizational Theory

In organizational theory, one's power is defined by one's *position influence* and one's role within a bureaucratic/hierarchical structure. In other words, a person's influence stems from his or her role, clearly defined in terms of function and position, within the hierarchy. Complex organizations require control, order, and discipline to ensure some degree of efficiency and predictability in what might otherwise be chaos. Thus, clear paths of authority and an understanding of where one must go for help, information, or direction emerge. Except where revolution or internal reorganization take place, leaders are those who wear the cloak of authority at each level in the organization; it is position alone that gives the occupant power to influence (Abrahamson and Smith, 1970).

Where, for example, a new superintendent of schools is elected, the school staffs experience apprehension, wondering how the new superintendent will act. What decisions will he or she make? What programs will be cut? Such apprehension is directly related to the degree of power inherent in the position of superintendent. One source of tension in particular is concern about how the new person will use his or her authority in relating to employees in lower-status positions.

In all bureaucracies, be they in the military, business, or educational world, the roles and functions of members are clearly defined, so in theory at least, no questions need arise regarding authority and responsibility. Unlike theories of power in which need, timing, and personal charisma all contribute to a person's influence without regard to formal structure, here the structure itself affords the legitimacy of authority. Thus an assistant principal responsible for discipline in a large urban school has a clearly defined role and unquestioned authority. Similarly, a captain in the military and a vice president of marketing are guided by clearly defined roles. Subordinates may provide information and ideas, but each knows his or her place in the organization and thinks twice before challenging the authority of those in higher positions in the hierarchy.

Clearly, the values of such an approach to leadership are the order, predictability, and consistency created in complex systems wherein it is necessary to minimize confusion and inefficiency. But the price paid is often the creation of dependency and an attitude of unquestioning obedience to superiors in those waiting docilely for the opportunity to move up the ladder. Such groups can demoralize personnel and reduce efficiency within the organization. Because "bosses" wield preordained influence over the lives of subordinates, real openness, the free expression of feelings, and other truths are often limited to the safety haven of the informal system and are conspicuously lacking in the formal structure where they might be most useful. Superficial concerns—looking good, keeping a clean record, and *apparent* loyalty—often replace honesty, creativity, and risk taking as employees' values with respect to their work. Consider the following example:

A few years ago, a colonel in the United States Army Corps of Engineers was faced with deteriorating morale and efficiency at the large military base he ran in Germany. This man was scheduled to retire the following year without having been promoted to the grade of general. His personal goal was to leave his post in the best condition possible and to end a distinguished career with pride and honor.

His key staff was composed of both military and civil service officers, both German and American, who were responsible for maintaining the base. These top aides had, like the colonel himself, been rotated into their positions from other bases for two- or three-year tours of duty; staying anywhere much longer was a sign that one's career advancement was in trouble. Given that time frame, it was clear to all personnel that identifying problems was useless, because there would never be enough time to solve them. Furthermore, problems, as everyone knew, stuck to one's name like honey sticks to fingers, so trying to solve them was considered "making waves" and was therefore avoided. The abiding norm, then, was to look good at all times, to maintain the status quo, and *never* to have any problems.

At this base, years of such avoidance had resulted in a facade of normalcy covering a caldron of inefficiency, low morale, and corruption. The colonel, who had no more steps to climb on the organizational ladder and who nurtured a desire to end his career with a flourish, had the "nerve" to hire a management consultant to look under the lid into this long-brewing organizational stew.

It took the consultant only two days to discover the problem. The pattern had existed for years and was obvious to anyone who cared to observe.

What the consultant found horrified the colonel. As a result of the short-term orientation of the top-level supervisors, many of whom could not even speak German, the civilian work crews and their first-line German supervisors had developed a routine of "work" that included

1. the addition of unnecessary men on almost all work crews
2. extensive travel times to and from the work sites that were often double and triple what was actually required
3. up to an hour of prework briefings of crews that required only a few minutes
4. the general practice of quitting early several times a week with regular beer drinking and card parties at the equipment barn

Top-line staff and supervisors knew about the rampant inefficiency but chose not to take action that might call blame down on themselves. They simply bided their time, waiting to be transferred to their next tour of duty. The lower-level supervisors, not wishing to incur the wrath of the German workers, colluded with the perpetrators and became part of the problem.

The colonel submitted a report. Instead of exploring a potential solution, the colonel's boss—a highly respected lieutenant general—threw a banquet to celebrate the good work of the consultant, thanking him for his effort and sending him on the next plane home. He then sent the colonel to headquarters to take a soft desk job pending his retirement. He shelved the report to avoid embarrassment and the possibility that similar conditions were rampant at other bases. The final results were these: the colonel retired with honor, the workers remained happy, the general's record remained unblemished, and the consultant left frustrated.

Although many hierarchical bureaucratic organizations are efficient, well managed, and high in morale, their rigid system of promotion by position often results in the tendency among personnel to deny problems, develop norms of self-protection, and avoid conflict with ongoing attempts to please the leader. Over time, this tendency can result in inefficiency, mistrust, and dishonesty among even the best-intentioned participants in the organization.

Bailey and Adams (1990) suggest a strategy for nonbureaucratic leadership whereby the concerns within the organization become, for example, innovation versus stability, efficacy versus accountability, and empowerment versus control. This would help minimize the formation of powerful, informal subgroups that often develop within troubled organizations and in which frustrations are vented.

The foregoing example raises a logical question: Can we say that a high-status position automatically implies leadership in the person holding that position? History is replete with actions of kings of very limited intelligence who had tremendous influence and whose whims were law. Does the organizational theory of leadership suggest that such behaviors are appropriate? We all know from experience that there have been position leaders whom we saw as excellent or outstanding and others who were failures and about whom we raised questions about their qualifications.

It is necessary to draw a distinction between leaders and leadership (Holloman, 1968). A leader may be a person in a position of authority; he or she is given the right to make decisions for others—as a teacher is given the right to teach the class, or the foreman the authority to assign work for his or her unit. From that position, the leader may influence others who look to him or her for clues or seek to emulate him or her.

From another perspective, it might be said that whoever influences the group is the leader—that is, any person who influences the group (whether in a formal position of leadership or not) exhibits leadership behavior. Leadership behavior is distinguished from the leader position; leadership behavior has to do with influence on the group regardless of the position.

One study of emergent leadership (Myers, Slavin, and Southern, 1990) found that leaders emerge according to the needs of the group. These results imply that we may be able to foster environments wherein different leaders emerge once we decide what kind of leadership is lacking.

Finally, there is the problem of the "power behind the throne." We are all aware of persons who occupy this position. Well-documented accounts of boss rule in politics are generous in their details of mayors or governors who were handsome, mellifluous-voiced errand boys for the "boss," who himself held no official position. Each of us knows of occupants of positions who are given the name-on-the-door trappings of office but who in reality must check almost everything with someone who may be in a higher position, or with someone who has retired from office but who still must be consulted prior to any move. Study limited to the occupants of positions obscures who influences the decision making, the processes in that group, how they develop, and with what consequences.

Trait Theory

Perhaps the oldest and, over the years, the most popular theory of leadership has to do with the belief that leaders are born, not made—that is, that they are genetically determined. The words "she is a natural leader" convey the sense that a particular individual's rise to power and glory is inevitable and that no amount of education and training will enable "nonleaders" to experience such a rise. Thus trait theory views leadership as part of one's personality, a characteristic that differentiates those who have it from the pack. As might be expected, this view is controversial, given the evidence that training *can* be beneficial in developing leaders.

Leadership became a prime subject of social science research at about the time of World War I. With our increased knowledge of testing and new statistical tools, there was a strong impetus to accumulate data and determine what traits leaders shared. If these could be identified, perhaps those who exhibit them could also be identified, and leaders could be selected quickly and efficiently. The usual procedure in studies on leadership has been to select certain personality attributes and relate them to success or lack of success in certain leaders.

◆ Reader Activity

Think of people you know who are leaders of groups. What traits do they possess?

_____

_____

_____

Do you think those traits apply to leaders generally?

_____

_____

_____   ◆

Implicit in much of the research on personality traits and leadership is the belief that the qualitative components that make for effective leadership are consistent. In other words, you have it or you don't. The leader might have been born with these traits (one theory) or might have acquired them (another theory), but in either case, the person possesses the traits of leadership. The only problem, it would seem, is that personality traits are still poorly conceived and unreliably measured. It is thought that as we refine our methods of measuring personality traits, we will be able to determine what traits we need to find or teach. In this theory, the ability to create leadership effectiveness is just around the corner.

Results of this approach, however, have been disappointing. The sorting out of leaders with various leadership traits from those without them has been notoriously ineffective. One early study (Bird, 1940) extensively reviewed the relevant research and compiled a list of traits that seemed to differentiate leaders from nonleaders in one or more studies. However, only five percent of the traits listed appeared in four or more studies; many of the other traits listed appeared in only a single study. Mann (1959) reviewed 125 leadership studies searching for a relationship between personality and performance in small groups. His search yielded 750 findings about personality traits, but no traits as conclusions. He found a lack of consistency among traits described as significant for leaders and, further, found that some traits listed as significant were diametrically opposed to significant traits listed in other studies. Researchers continue to search for the behavioral scientists' (if not the alchemists') gold, and with similar results. In studying discussion leaders, Guyer (1978) found no statistically significant relationships among traits of discussion leaders, student evaluations of them, and the grades received by students of discussion leaders. His conclusion: "Attention to personality traits . . . would have been of limited value in the selection of discussion leaders" (p. 697).

There is some evidence that leaders tend to be a bit taller, more intelligent, and more enthusiastic and to have greater self-confidence and social participation than nonleaders (Berleson and Steiner, 1964; Smith and Cook, 1973; Sorrentino, 1973; Zigon and Cannon, 1974). However, it is impossible to predict and to use this information in selecting and training leaders. For example, it has been repeatedly demonstrated that the person who does most of the talking (greater social participation) becomes the leader, *unless* he or she talks so much that he or she antagonizes other group members (Stang, 1973). An intelligent student may be a leader, unless he or she gets all A's and is viewed as a "curve wrecker" (scores so high that other students get a lower grade by comparison); then he or she becomes an outcast (Davie and Hare, 1956).

After extensive surveys of the literature seeking to identify leadership traits, researchers are increasingly coming to the weary conclusion that leadership does not emerge from some combination of traits (Stogdill, 1948, 1974). Rather, "in every instance, the relation of the trait to the leadership role is more meaningful if consideration is given to the detailed nature of the role" (Gibb, 1954, p. 878). Since traits of an effective leader are so closely related to the functions that that person will perform, the most general rule would be to focus on what task needs to be performed and to select those who are willing to perform that task and have the skills to do so.

Yet the search goes on to somehow find the magical attributes that will transform us into esteemed leaders (Hall and Williams, 1971). There are a variety of theories about why the romantic conception of the leader with magic attributes persists. Many find security in that idea. Because each of us continues to need security, perhaps we carry with us from childhood an oversized image of the leader. Such an assumption makes it more readily understandable that the leader, or the person we conceptualize as the leader, should be larger, more intelligent, more cultured, more impressive than we. The leader represents the symbol, the ink blots onto which people project their desires for security, dependence, glamour, and power. It perhaps makes more understandable the persistent search for leaders who will arrive full-blown, without an abracadabra or seven-league boots, but who by their presence can remove difficulties, overcome obstacles, and attain the goal. And yet most of us realize that this is fantasy.

An interesting new line of inquiry has begun during the past five years. It suggests that although a small degree of a leader's success can be predicted from a trait analysis, and even more can be predicted by considering past performance (grades, test scores of achievement and aptitude), new variables that support the views of Peter Senge and others are gaining prominence. These variables have to do with the degree to which leaders (in this case, business leaders) appear open to learning from the ideas of others or from personal feedback about their own performance. The more open they are to such information, the greater their success as leaders. Initial research by McCauley, Lombardo, and Morrison (1988) reflected in their book *The Lessons of Experience* support this thesis. Additional research appears to lend credence to this view (McCauley, Lombard and Usher, 1989).

Furthermore, in what appears to be a healthy new direction, there is increasing emphasis on helping leaders assess their own effectiveness and compare their behavior patterns to those of leaders identified by their own peers as particularly effective. Such an approach is bound to make leaders more conscious of their impact on individuals and their own organizations (McCauley et al., 1989).

Styles of Leadership

Because social scientists have been unable to find consistent evidence that particular traits are related to leadership, they have shifted the focus in recent years to leadership "styles." Plato was perhaps the first to deal with the idea of leadership style. In *The Republic* he provides an analysis of leadership powered by "self-serving individualists," "benevolent tyrants," and of course the dialectic style of leadership. (Clemens and Mayer, 1982, p. 39). The term *dialectic style* suggests an open dialogue among individuals seeking positive change though a rational discussion of opposing arguments. It was the seedbed of a more open and "democratic" approach.

In this subsection, we digress temporarily from our consideration of Terry's theoretical categories to explore the consequences of this point of view.

Style is simply another word for a collection of *behaviors* in a particular situation. Many contend that people with the broadest range of leadership-related behaviors are the most effective leaders—as long as they have the ability to choose the right behavior for the situation. Conversely, in this view, individuals with a limited range of leadership behavior (styles) have a limited ability to influence. People who are inclined to be nice, gentle, and solicitous and cannot confront or deal openly with conflict are seen as handicapped in their ability to lead. Likewise, those who are overly serious, directive, and in need of control may have difficulty in such areas as delegating, motivating, or being playful—all useful leadership behaviors. In this way, leadership becomes a function of particular modes of behavior.

Today, it is generally acknowledged that leadership qualities are intimately linked to our personalities—which in turn are the products of our upbringing plus our inherited traits. At the same time, social scientists widely believe that training and education *can* have an impact and that, with experience and practice, people are capable of altering their behaviors and developing effective leadership styles.

Conceptions of Other People   A leader's conception of human beings has implications for his or her leadership style (Maslow, 1954; McGregor, 1960; Schein, 1969). There are two images or theories of how to lead. In the first (Theory X according to McGregor; rational-economic man according to Schein), people are seen as having little ambition, a reluctance to work, and a desire to avoid responsibility. People are motivated by economic competition, and conflict is inevitable. Without managerial effort, men and women do virtually nothing. The leader operating under these assumptions must motivate, organize, control, and coerce. He or she directs; people under him or her accept and even prefer it, because they have little ambition or desire for responsibility. The leader bears the responsibility and burden of his or her subordinates' or followers' performance. This represents the traditional theory of management, especially business management. Another theory (Theory Y for McGregor, self-actualizing man for Schein) holds that people are motivated by a hierarchy of needs. The assumption in this theory is that as basic needs are met, new emergent needs become motivating forces. Each of us has a desire to use our potential, to have responsibility, to *actualize* ourselves. The theory assumes that men and women enjoy work as well as play or rest. Thus individuals will exercise self-direction and self-control toward the accomplishment of objectives they value. Furthermore, they can be creative and innovative. They will not only accept responsibility but also seek it. That potential for imagination, ingenuity, and resourcefulness is widely distributed within the population but poorly utilized in modern society. In this theory, the leader creates challenge and an opportunity for subordinates to use their abilities to a greater extent. There is no need to control or motivate; the motivation is waiting to be unleashed. A leader's conception of men and women greatly affects his or her style of supervision and the bases of power he or she will implement. The first theory is more likely to use money as a motivating reward and coercion to compel compliance. The second theory is likely to promote intrinsic rewards of self-satisfaction and pride in achievement; coercion is used infrequently.

Does Leadership Style Make a Difference?   Classic research by Lewin, Lippitt, and White (Lewin, Lippitt, and White, 1939; White and Lippitt, 1968) investigated the following questions: What effect does style of leadership have on the group? Is the group more productive if the leader is autocratic, democratic, or laissez-faire? Does it make a difference in how members relate to one another? Is there a difference in the social climate?

In each experimental situation, three leadership types were established: the autocratic leader, the democratic leader, and the laissez-faire leader. Each leader had legitimate power as he worked with ten-year-old boys on basically similar craft projects. The findings were dramatic. The results indicated that demonstrably different group atmospheres developed. And further, in each experimental group, there were readily perceived differences in relations among members and their ability to handle stress, as well as in their relations with the leader. The findings convincingly demonstrated that in that particular situation, the best leader was the democratic leader.

One review of the literature dealing with gender and leadership style revealed that women tend to lead in a more democratic or participative style, whereas men's style is more autocratic (Eagly and Johnson, 1990). In many cases, however, women are not viewed as capable leaders, as in Butler and Geis's 1990 study which found that female leaders were given more negative and less positive indications than men offering the same suggestions and arguments. Goktepe and Schneier (1989) found that regardless of the person's sex, a group member who exhibited male gender role characteristics emerged as a leader more often than those with female, androgynous, or undifferentiated role characteristics. As research of this type becomes more readily available, perhaps we will be able to determine a leadership style that is not associated with gender or traditional role characteristics. This potentially fruitful area for continued research should be of vital interest to organizations concerned with developing the most effective leadership regardless of gender.

Choosing a Leadership Style   Which leader is "best" depends on how we perceive that label. Describing a person as an *autocratic leader* conjures up an image in which he or she is allied with demagogues, dictators, and coercive administrative processes. Yet the term *autocratic* can also describe a person who is directive, who stands firm in his or her convictions, who accepts the responsibilities of supervision and ultimate responsibility for his or her decisions—in short, one who has the necessary attributes of leadership.

To be labeled a *laissez-faire leader* is to be viewed as in a fog, incompetent, fearful of making a decision, and shirking responsibilities. This is clearly an offensive label. Yet on the other hand, "Creativity must be given free rein" and "He who rules least, rules best." Shall the leader supervise closely, or "trust his or her people"?

To be labeled a *democratic leader* usually suggests that the person is well liked. As for his or her behavior, does it mean that he or she shares all decisions with others regardless of the consequences? Does it mean that the staff members are one big happy family, that they talk in terms of *we* rather than *I,* and that all relationships are collaborative rather than competitive? Do all decisions have to be group decisions? Is giving up power the price of popularity? Is the "big happy family" the goal to strive for no matter what? Is any aspect of competition to be avoided at all costs?

At one time this labeling was important, as we sought to understand the continuum that went from the laissez-faire leader, who was minimally involved, to the autocratic leader, who arbitrarily made decisions based solely on his or her own style. At that time, the democratic leader stood for a middle-of-the-road view, neither the "abdicrat" who avoided being decisive or assertive, nor the autocrat, who demanded adherence to personal dictates, and there was a desire to reinforce our conviction that democracy is "best." The entire concept of experimentally inducing three different leadership styles, analogous perhaps to governments, was powerful. The results generated increased understanding of the problem and of the limitations of each style.

The studies have been so effective that they continue to be replicated (Bernstein, 1971; Koch, 1978; Sargent and Miller, 1971; Scontrino, 1972; Sudolsky and Nathan, 1971); researchers find the early hypotheses continue to be valid. In fact, there has been quite a bit of research on style of leadership. Sanders and Malkis (1982) found that leaders who were categorized as Type A (coronary-prone who work hard, rest little, and are impatient) did not do so well with problem solutions as Type B people (who pace themselves, relax at regular intervals, and manage stress better). Drory and Gluskinos (1980) studied personality styles they characterized as either high or low "Machiavellian," named after the Italian prince who wrote about power. They found that "high Machs" tended to give more orders and were less supportive when in group leadership positions than "low Machs."

Yet today, the question of whether one is democratic or autocratic, or whether a high-pressure personality makes a better leader than a low-pressure personality, is less meaningful. We have come to look at effective leadership as the relationship between the individual leader and the rest of the group. We no longer view leaders as being in a box that can be labeled, whether by their detractors, their friends, or even their own dilemmas, yet their style does affect how the group members communicate (Barlow et al., 1982).

Effective Leadership   For more than 20 years, Fred Fiedler and his associates have been exploring the influence of people's behaviors on group effectiveness

(1967, 1969, 1973). Recent information reported by Adams (1985) focuses on how individuals with a task or product orientation to a work group differ from those more concerned with the process or people dimension of group life. Fiedler is interested in how such differences in an individual's orientation to the group may influence effectiveness.

◆ Reader Activity

What follows is a well-known instrument, the Leader Preferred Co-worker Scale (LPC), used by Fiedler (1967) in his early research on leadership style.[1] Taking this test will help you understand your own style and will allow you to relate more personally to the research discussed in this chapter.   ◆

THE LEAST PREFERRED CO-WORKER SCALE

Think of the person with whom you can work *least well*. This person may be someone you work with now or someone you knew in the past. This person need not be the person you *like* least well but should be the person with whom you had the most difficulty working to get a job done.

Please describe this person by putting an X in the appropriate space on the following scales:

Pleasant	☐☐☐☐☐☐☐☐	Unpleasant
Friendly	☐☐☐☐☐☐☐☐	Unfriendly
Accepting	☐☐☐☐☐☐☐☐	Rejecting
Helpful	☐☐☐☐☐☐☐☐	Frustrating
Enthusiastic	☐☐☐☐☐☐☐☐	Unenthusiastic
Relaxed	☐☐☐☐☐☐☐☐	Tense
Close	☐☐☐☐☐☐☐☐	Distant
Warm	☐☐☐☐☐☐☐☐	Cold
Cooperative	☐☐☐☐☐☐☐☐	Uncooperative
Supportive	☐☐☐☐☐☐☐☐	Hostile
Interesting	☐☐☐☐☐☐☐☐	Boring
Harmonious	☐☐☐☐☐☐☐☐	Quarrelsome

1. *Theory of Leader Effectiveness* (p. 41) by F. E. Fiedler. New York: McGraw Hill (1967) Copyright 1967 by McGraw Hill Publishers. Reprinted by permission of the author.

Self-assured									Hesitant
Efficient									Inefficient
Cheerful									Gloomy
Open									Guarded

To score yourself on this exercise, identify the favorable pole for each item—for example, *relaxed* versus tense; *cooperative* versus uncooperative; *supportive* versus hostile; *cheerful* versus gloomy, the italicized words being the favorable poles in these pairs. An *X* closest to the favorable pole is an 8, in the next space is a 7, in the next a 6, and so forth to 1 in the least favorable spot. Total your marks to get your score. There are 16 items, so the highest score you could receive would be 128. This would mean that you would have scored 8 points for each of the items. Similarly, your lowest possible score would be 16; for this you would have placed a 1 in the least favorable place for each item. Your score, then, will fall somewhere between 16 and 128. The higher your LPC score, the more "relationship-oriented" you are. A very low score would indicate that you are a "task-oriented" individual.

Situational Theory

A far cry from the rigidly traditional trait theory is the theory of *situational leadership*. This notion rests on the assumption that human beings are ultimately able to learn the techniques of leadership and that virtually anyone can become a more effective leader by mastering certain skills and knowledge.

This point of view was espoused by Reddin (1970), Blake and Mouton (1969), and others in the late 1960s and was popularized by Hersey and Blanchard as their life-psycholeadership theory (1969, 1975, 1977). The latter created a framework that attempts to explain why the results of leadership training have been mixed and why efforts to produce effective leaders have been limited, even though training can be effective in teaching new behaviors. The essential point is knowing *which* behaviors to use *when*.

According to a noted author and professor of business administration at the University of Southern California, "managers are people who do things right, leaders are people who do the right thing" (Berons, 1989).

Task and Relationship Dimensions As scoring for the LPC scale suggests, there appear to be two central dimensions of any leadership situation—that involving a *task* (a goal or project) and that involving a *relationship* (social-emotional issues, consideration for others, and interpersonal relations). See the accompanying figure.[2]

2. From Hersey, P., and Blanchard, K. H. "Life-cycle theory of leadership." Copyright 1969, *Training and Development Journal*, American Society for Training and Development. Reprinted with permission. All rights reserved.

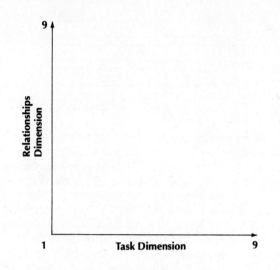

In this formulation, task behavior is illustrated on the horizontal axis. Task (production) becomes more important to the leader as his or her rating advances on the horizontal scale. A leader with a rating of 9 has a maximum concern for production.

Concern for people is illustrated on the vertical axis. People become more important to the leader as his or her rating progresses up the vertical axis. A leader who has a rating of 9 on the vertical axis has a maximum concern for people.

In one study of situational variables and gender, Petzel, Johnson, and Bresolin (1990) found that male participants spoke more and were selected as leaders more frequently than female participants in a situation where an impersonal task was presented. In a "personal" group, however, women spoke more and were also chosen as leaders more often.

As shown in the figure on page 247, the four quadrants produced by the grid describe leader behavior (five in the Blake-Mouton formulation, the fifth being at the cross of all four quadrants). Quadrant I represents a leadership style that is high on task and low on people; quadrant II represents a style high on both task and people; quadrant III is high on people with little concern for the task; quadrant IV is a style low on both task and people.

After identifying task and relationships as the two central dimensions, some management writers have suggested a "best" style. Most of these writers have supported an integrated leader behavior style (high task and high relationships) or a people-centered, human relations approach (high relationships). However, some of the most convincing evidence that dispels the idea of a single "best" style was gathered and published by Korman (1966). Korman reviewed more than 25 studies that examined the relationship between dimensions of "task" and "consideration" (people) and various measures of effectiveness, including group produc-

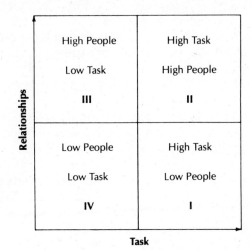

tivity, salary, performance under stress, administrative reputation, work group grievances, absenteeism, and turnover. He came to the conclusion that "very little is now known as to how these variables may predict work group performance and the conditions which affect such predictions. At the current time, we cannot even say whether they have any predictive significance at all" (p. 360).

Korman saw no predictive value in terms of effectiveness, as situations changed. This would suggest that because situations differ, so must leader style. In his studies of leadership over fifteen years, Fiedler (1967) came to similar conclusions. He found that both directive, task-oriented leaders and nondirective, human relations–oriented leaders are successful under some conditions. Other investigators have also found that different leadership situations require different leader styles.

One hypothesis that could be proposed on the basis of this dimensional analysis is that the best leaders would be androgynous, because woman have been traditionally associated with relationship and men with task. Uhlir (1989) believes that an androgynous person would possess varying combinations of attributes and would be able to represent a full range of desirable behaviors that suited each particular circumstance. This reinforces a study by Kenny, Zaccaro, and Stephen (1983, pp. 678–685) suggesting the strong possibility that differences in leadership effectiveness that were once attributed to a traditional personality trait may instead involve the ability to perceive the needs and goals of a group and then to adjust one's personal approach to meet them. Thus the ability to move between the task and relationship dimensions as called for by the changing situation would be essential. Such a suggestion adds credence to the work of Fiedler (1967, 1973) discussed previously.

The Effectiveness Dimension   To measure more accurately how well a leader operates within a given situation, Hersey and Blanchard added a third dimension—

effectiveness—to the two-dimensional model. The effectiveness dimension cuts across the two-dimensional task/relationship factors and builds in the concept of a leader's style, integrated with the demands of a specific environment. When the leader's style is appropriate to a given environment measured by results, it is termed *effective;* when her or his style is inappropriate to a given environment, it is termed *ineffective.*

If a leader's effectiveness is determined by the interaction of his or her style and environment (followers and other situational variables), then any of the four styles defined by the grid quadrants may be effective or ineffective, depending on the environment. Therefore, there is no single ideal leader behavior style that is appropriate in all situations. In an organization that is essentially crisis-oriented, such as the police or military, there is evidence that the most appropriate style is high-task orientation; under riot or combat conditions success may depend on immediate response to orders. Studies of scientific and research-oriented personnel show that they desire or need only a limited amount of social-emotional support. They know what they are doing and "want to get on with it." They view meetings as "wasting time." Under these conditions, a low-task and low-relationship style (leave them alone for the most part) may be the most appropriate.

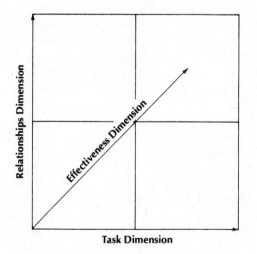

Task Dimension

In summary, an effective leader must be able to *diagnose* the demands of the environment and then either adapt his or her leadership style to fit these demands or develop the means to change some or all of the variables.

The Maturity Factor   In their situational leadership theory, Hersey and Blanchard have, in response to the vague concept of *situational determinants,* sought to conceptualize the possible situational determinants and how they are related to leadership behavior (task and relationships). The primary element in the theory is that an effective leadership style is related to *the level of maturity of followers.* Followers are vital not only individually as they accept or reject leaders, but also as a group, because they determine what power the leader may have.

According to what Hersey and Blanchard call their life-cycle theory, as the level of maturity of one's followers increases, appropriate leader behavior requires not only less structure (task) but also less social-emotional support (relationships).

Maturity, in life-cycle theory, consists of several components. First, mature people have the capacity to set high but obtainable goals and a desire for task-relevant feedback (how well am I doing?) rather than task-irrelevant feedback (how well do you like me?). Second, they are willing to take responsibility, which involves willingness (motivation) and ability (competence); the highest level of responsibility would be taken by those high on ability and competence. Third, maturity can be thought of as involving two factors: (1) job maturity, the ability and technical knowledge to do the task; and (2) psychological maturity, a feeling of self-confidence and self-respect as an individual. These two factors seem to be related; high task competence leads to feelings of self-respect, and the converse also seems to be true.

Finally, although the maturity concept is useful, we must remember that diagnostic judgments may be influenced by other situational variables such as a crisis, a time bind, or one's superior's style.

According to the theory, as the level of maturity of followers continues to increase in terms of accomplishing a specific task, leaders should begin to reduce their task behavior and increase their relationship behavior (beginning at quadrant I with immature, inexperienced followers, moving to quadrant II and then III as the individual or group moves to an average level of maturity). As the individual or group reaches an above-average level of maturity, it becomes appropriate for leaders to decrease not only task behavior but also relationship behavior (moving now to quadrant IV). Now, members are not only task mature but also psychologically mature and so can provide their own psychological reinforcement and need much less supervision. An individual at this level of maturity sees a reduction of close supervision and a delegation of responsibility by the leader as an indication of positive trust and confidence. This theory, then, focuses on the appropriateness or effectiveness of leadership styles according to the task-relevant maturity of the followers.

This cycle can be illustrated by a bell-shaped curve going through the four leadership quadrants. See the figure below.

Determining Appropriate Leadership Style   What does the bell-shaped curve mean to a leader with a specific task to accomplish with a given organization or group? It means that the maturity level of one's followers develops along the continuum from immature to mature—and that the appropriate style of leadership moves accordingly.

To determine what leadership style is appropriate in a given situation, a leader must first determine the maturity level of the individual or group in relation to a

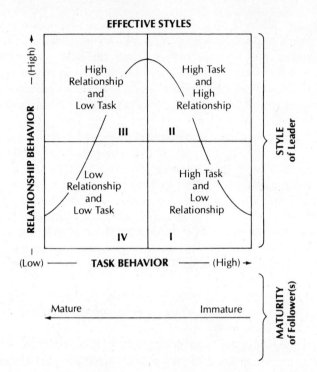

EFFECTIVE STYLES

specific task that the leader is attempting to accomplish through their efforts. Once a leader identifies this maturity level, he or she can determine the appropriate leadership style. If the followers are of low maturity, the leadership style of quadrant I would be most effective, the style of quadrant II second most effective, quadrant III next, and quadrant IV least effective.

The theory has broad applicability not only to leadership in organizations but also to leadership in other groups, even families.

An Organizational Example

Let's look at a detailed example of leadership operating in a business context. Combining the two medium-sized printing companies representing two different regional markets seemed to be a logical move that would ultimately reduce overall business expenses. Both companies were profitable, and the two presidents had been friends for many years. The president of the northern company was a quiet, warm, personable former political science professor whose leadership style centered on client satisfaction and harmonious human relations both within and outside the company. Walking into the company's offices, one found large, open spaces with few visible barriers to separate the different organizational levels. Shirt-sleeve informality was the rule, and office relationships spilled easily into the social realm.

The other company, equally successful, was run by a dynamic, hard-driving, charismatic individual who, while engaging and personable in nature, was a stern taskmaster with little tolerance for incompetence. Stepping into the southern company's office, one found executives in the latest Brooks Brothers suits sitting in plush, paneled offices. Unlike the family feeling in the northern company, here there was an air of tough competition marked by locker-room humor, sarcasm, and liberal use of four-letter words balanced by pride, efficiency, and a certain rugged confidence.

As one might expect, the management styles in these organizations differed markedly. The northern president prided himself on involving his co-workers in the decisions that affected them and on delegating as much responsibility as possible. He saw himself mainly as an agent of public relations and support. In contrast, the southern president was clearly a hands-on boss involved directly in most of the activities in his firm. Personnel went to him for advice and counsel before making critical decisions.

As a result of the merger, the popular, easy-going northern president became the CEO responsible for the daily operations of the now combined company. The southern president moved up to become chairman of the board and took responsibility for long-range planning and development.

Trouble began almost immediately. One of the leaders from the northern division depicted his southern counterparts as aggressive sharks interested only in the bottom line and caring little about relationships or concepts of modern participative management. He characterized them as abrasive, quick to act, and often insensitive to those around them. In contrast, disgruntled leaders in the southern division complained that the northern division was inefficient and unprofessional. They saw the new CEO as only barely competent and as relying more on his own personality than on hard-nosed business practices.

During the year following the merger, antagonism between the two organizations became so profound that meetings often had to be held in a neutral setting. Threats of quitting and retaliation were commonplace, and although dollar profits remained reasonable, employees constantly evaluated and criticized the new CEO. The problem was further exacerbated because the new CEO continued to delegate authority and therefore did not meet the southern group's needs for counsel, feedback, and direction. The response of the latter was to turn to their former boss, who, in spite of his new role, still made himself available to hear questions and complaints. The outcome appeared to be a stalemate, with each group setting up roadblocks for the other and blaming the other for any failures that occurred.

The situation seemed hopeless, and in fact there was talk of ending the merger. However, at a critical time one of the most powerful executives in the southern division resigned, leaving a vacuum in the company but creating the opportunity to hire someone with a philosophy more consistent with that of the northern division. In addition, the CEO finally recognized the fact that he had to become more directive during what was to be a long transition period. He suddenly "took charge," which allayed some of the fears of the southern group.

In this example, even though both organizations showed bottom-line success, the different management styles resulted in very different levels of organizational maturity. The new CEO had failed to recognize that the southern division's dependency, created by the hands-on management style of the former president, required a slow weaning process. Without such a transition, the leaders of the southern group felt abandoned, left to flounder, and they became resentful as well, because their tough, businesslike attitudes would not let them admit their need for support and direction. Their immature organization was matched with a new CEO who proved inflexible in adjusting his own style to their needs, and this in turn almost resulted in the CEO's overthrow. In the end, he had to reach beyond his "natural style" and adopt new behaviors—ones he had intentionally discarded years before. In sum, his short-term inflexibility and inability to see the quadrant 1 needs of his southern counterparts almost proved disastrous for the entire organization.

◆ *Individual Experiment*

Identify a group in which you participate that is not working very well. Write down a list of adjectives that describe the style of the group leader. Write down your description of the group members' ability to set reasonable goals, degree of motivation, and willingness to take responsibility to make sure the work of the group gets done. Does the leadership style match the group members' maturity? If not, how should the group leader change? How should the group members change?   ◆

Vision Theory and Ethical Assessment

Vision theory and ethical assessment are the last two of the six theoretical positions presented by Terry (1987) in his effort to explain leadership in small groups or organizations. *Visionary leadership* involves purposefully exploring societal needs and drawing public attention to the future. Unlike situational leadership, which focuses more on current concerns and daily operations (and is seen by some, such as Bennis and Nanus [1985], as "management rather than leadership"), visionary leadership focuses on identifying future needs and mobilizing resources to reach projected goals. By capturing the imagination of followers around the issue of "what could be," the leader mobilizes idealism and hope. Obviously, turning such a vision into action requires other aspects of leadership discussed previously, but the visionary must be able to ignite the flame and set the direction. Such leaders attempt to find effective managers to handle the problems of day-to-day operations and focus on the bigger picture, including the strategies and planning necessary to drive the organization toward realizing the vision.

Most organizations start with a dream that becomes translated into a vision and then into a specific, obtainable goal. Landing a person on the moon and garnering support for the civil rights movement were goals set by visionary leaders who also helped provide the energy and focus needed to mobilize people into action. On another level, but equally visionary, is the factory supervisor's goal of fostering cooperation and efficiency in his plant or the coach's dream of building team spirit that goes well beyond the winning of any single game. According to Rouche, Baker, and Rose in their 1989 book *Shared Vision,* historical visionary leaders such as Thomas Jefferson and Martin Luther King, Jr. shared dedication to achieving a goal, but even more significantly, they influenced others to share their vision with them. In short, "a vision is more than any one individual's perspective" . . . it is the cultivation of followership (p. 111).

Burns (1978, p. 19) defines *ethical assessment,* the final view of leadership identified by Terry:

> Some define leadership as leaders making followers do what the follow-ers would not otherwise do, or as leaders making the followers do what they want them to do; I define leadership as leaders inducing followers to act for certain goals that represent the values and motivation—the wants and needs, the aspirations and expectations—*of both leaders and followers.*

Such leaders are driven by a conscious awareness of the public good and a desire to serve the interests of their constituencies. Both Burns and Terry agree that, in tapping the followers' will and interests and mobilizing them to serve those interests, this form of leadership transcends many of the others in importance. For leaders of this sort, a keen sensitivity to moral and ethical considerations is essential, and often their first task in leading a group is raising the group's consciousness. Calabrese (1988) states the guidelines for ethical leadership as including "respect for all members of society, tolerance for divergent opinions and cultures," among other things (p. 1).

To clarify, the quality of the ethical vision and its relationship to the public good set it apart from the dream of the visionary leader. Both kinds of leaders are conscious of needs, trends, and the future. Both focus on increasing their followers' awareness. But the leaders who set goals with respect to their *ethical* assessments raise both their followers and themselves to higher levels of performance and achievement.

Functional Leadership

Our understanding of leadership has changed dramatically over the last half-century (Golembiewski, 1962; Stogdill, 1974; Vacc, 1975). It is changing and will continue to change as research and practical experience modify our present understanding of leadership.

Above all, we have learned to view leadership from a group perspective. What actions are required under varying conditions to achieve the group's goals, and how do members take part in these various group actions? From this perspective, we define leadership as those acts that help the group achieve its goals. In his book *The Tao of Leadership,* John Heider puts it concisely when he states that "the wise leader is not collecting a string of successes" but rather is helping others to find, in themselves, his or her "own successor" (p. 161). Finding the right leader for the moment is the key. Thus, when the question is recast, leadership can, in principle at least, be performed by any member. Leadership acts are those that help the group set goals, that aid in movement toward the achievement of goals, that improve the quality of interpersonal relationships among members, or that make needed resources available to the group. When the leadership question is reframed in terms of behavior that furthers the goals of the group, it is difficult to distinguish leadership from followership. Chris Lee argues that because we tend to view leaders in isolation, the followers are often viewed as "empty vessels waiting to be filled" (Lee, 1991, pp. 27, 28). Effective organization needs to alter these conceptions, for "effective followers are partners in creating the vision in the first place."

There are some who feel that the word *leadership* impedes understanding of group processes and that the term would be better eliminated. Regardless of the term, many agree that the functional approach to both leadership and membership permits increased understanding of the processes and dynamics of groups. This approach recognizes the uniqueness of each group. Actions required by one group may be quite different from those of another, so the nature and traits of the persons having influence differ in each group. In addition, a variety of factors affect leadership: the goals of the group, its structure, the attitudes or needs of the members, and expectations placed upon the group by an external environment (Bass, 1960; O'Brien, 1969). Leadership, then, depends on the interplay between the group members and the leader; there is no absolute quality of leadership because each group has its unique set of needs.

For example, a pilot may be the acknowledged leader of his or her group while in the air. He or she may have the skills of coordinating the crew, knowledge of the mission, and ability to cope with the difficulties with which the crew is faced. But what if the plane crashes and the crew is faced with the goal of surviving in the wilderness and finding its way back to safety? The skills needed are now very different. Who knows the terrain on the ground? Who knows about "survival training"? Who knows what plants are edible? Who can calm the members and reduce squabbling? Who can organize the group for utilizing their resources? The person who will be the crew leader on the ground may be very different from the leader in the air. The functional approach recognizes that a variety of behaviors by any member may be helpful in the achievement of the group's purposes. It stresses behaviors that influence the group. If a group is threatened by conflicting subgroups, members who engage heavily in mediating functions may be expected to be influential. If, however, a group is faced with low prestige in the community and members are leaving, quite different behaviors will be required to be influential.

Types of Functional Roles

Leadership is basically the execution of a particular kind of role within an organized group, and this role is defined essentially in terms of power or the ability to influence others. Conceived of as a role, leadership may be more or less specific to the particular structure of a particular group (McDavid and Harari, 1968). A leader in one group does not automatically emerge as the leader in another group. As membership changes, the leader may change; or if the purpose or activities change, the leader may change then too. Leadership implies followership. One person exerts influence or social power, and others are influenced. Leadership is defined as the frequency with which an individual in a group may be identified as one who influences or directs the behaviors of others within the group. Murphy (1988, p. 658) states that very often, however, "leaders can . . . achieve results by acting like followers and depending on followers to act like leaders."

Early studies by Bales (Bales, 1950, 1970) and others (Benne and Sheats, 1948; Rieken and Homans, 1954) have identified three types of leader–member behaviors (hereafter referred to as member roles, because they can be performed by any member). Each is worth examining closely.

Group Task Roles   Roles of members here are to help the group select and define the common goals and work toward attainment of those goals.

Suppose representatives of school and community groups decide to work together to "do something about the drug problem." Members whose actions would be categorized in the task realm may *initiate* discussion of what could be done or how the problem might be approached, or they may suggest different methods for getting teen-agers involved. Someone else may offer *information* on what other groups in the city are doing and what official agencies are available for further help.

Another may offer *opinions* on the subject. Others may *elaborate* from their experience or reading. With this variety of opinions and suggestions, some can *coordinate* or clarify the various suggestions in terms of which are appropriate for this group to work on and which more appropriately fall within the province of other groups. One person may summarize what has happened, perhaps point out departures from the original goals, and question whether the group can proceed as suggested or whether it lacks the resources it needs. (That person would be *orienting* the group.) There may be *critics* or *evaluators* who question the facts as presented, or the effectiveness of such a volunteer group. An *energizer* may prod the group to reconsider its potential and stimulate members to greater activity. There may be a *procedural technician,* who knows where materials on drugs can be obtained inexpensively. That person may have access to means of distributing leaflets or to a speaker who could help clarify some of the technical questions being raised.

These are functions that members undertake to help the group accomplish its task. The group member who acts in some of the above ways is exercising leadership by moving the group toward its goal. He or she is not necessarily the designated leader, yet he or she displays leadership behavior by influencing the group.

Group Maintenance Roles   Although task roles focus on the rational problem-solving aspects of achieving movement toward a goal, equally important but at a different level are the roles that focus on the personal relationships among members in a group. These are known as group maintenance roles.

Just as task roles help a group to achieve its explicit goals, maintenance roles help a group to work together. These behaviors help the group maintain itself so that members will contribute ideas and be willing to continue making progress on the group task. Both kinds of roles are needed, and each complements the other. The chapter on problem solving (Chapter 6) examines these relationships in greater detail, but it can be briefly noted here that the relationship is not only complementary but also spiraling—successful work on the goal increases members' sense of the attractiveness of the group and liking each other. Liking each other and having worked out interpersonal relationships free energy to put into the task and its accomplishment.

Let's return to the illustration of the group studying the drug problem. As opinions are given, the *encourager* may ask for additional examples or inquire whether others have similar opinions. The *supporter* may agree with suggestions of others and offer commendations. The *harmonizer* may attempt to mediate differences between members or points of view or may relieve tension with a joke. Someone who previously felt that public health agencies and not citizens' groups should work on the drug problem may, after hearing the discussion, come around and agree to a compromise, whereby the coordinating group sponsors a series of meetings in which public health officials describe their efforts. Someone, a *gatekeeper,* may notice that the representatives from one community group have not spoken and may ask if they have any ideas on the subject. These roles help a group maintain itself so that work on its task can proceed without becoming immobilized by inappropriate social behaviors and so that individuals are brought effectively into the emotional sphere of the group's life.

Individual Roles   Another set of behaviors has been identified in which members act to meet individual needs that are irrelevant to the group task and are not conducive to helping the group work as a unit. In fact, this individual-centered behavior frequently induces like responses from others. An attack on one person leads to a response of personal defense; a joke may escalate to an hour of "I-can-top-that" jokes; and blocking by one member may lead to retaliatory blocking. The goal and the group are forgotten; the individual acts primarily to satisfy his or her personal needs.

In our representative citizens' group, the *aggressor* may question, with thinly veiled sarcasm, the competence and veracity of the person giving his or her opinion. The aggressor may imply that the speaker does not have the foggiest notion of what he or she is talking about. Or the aggressor may sneer that this "half-baked" committee hasn't the competence to solve a serious problem; why not sponsor a day for the kids at the ball park and accomplish something? It might have been agreed that drug addicts would be referred to the local community mental health center; however, the *blocker* persists in stating that unless a center is opened especially for addicts, the committee is useless. The blocker may turn every request for suggestions into a renewed attack on present plans or a renewal of advocacy for a treatment center. The *self-confessor* may use the audience to express personal problems and gain sympathy through catharsis. The self-confessor may reveal the problems he or she is having with a son who is disrespectful, shocks the neighbors with his late hours, and is a disgrace in general—to a parent who has worked hard all his or her life in order that the children may lead better lives than the parents did. In an emotional voice, the self-confessor despairs that family relations and respect are not what they once were. The *recognition-seeker* may respond with his or her own personal advice and describe in glowing detail how it was successful in numerous other instances; or he or she may remind the group of the paper he or she has just delivered at the convention or of other important committees on which he or she has served. The *dominator* attempts to take over with an assortment of strategies such as interrupting others, flattery, and asserting superior status.

Integrating the Six Dimensions of Leadership

There is a growing case for the argument that while we can identify the six distinct types of leadership described here (power, organizational, trait, situational, visionary, and ethical assessment) in our daily lives, the most powerful and effective leadership involves the integration of most or all these types. Terry (1987, p. 22) sees leadership on a continuum from transactional, or means-oriented, to transformational, or ends-oriented, leadership. Put simply, *transactional leadership* focuses on the business of getting things done. Here, reciprocal negotiations result in an ever-changing relationship between leaders and followers ("I'll vote for you if you give me a job"). Such leadership is basically rooted in the here and now, where reaction, conflict, and crisis drive us more than thoughts of ethics, responsibility, and morale.

As everyone knows, however, life consists of more than reacting to crises and fulfilling basic needs. Satisfaction and effectiveness are partly related to issues beyond our own self-interest; they depend on our accomplishing tasks in a way that improves or contributes to the world. In this context, leadership is perceived as a *transformational* process focusing on the mutual needs, aspirations, and values that produce positive social change. Howell and Higgins (1990) examined transformational leadership behaviors in champions of technological innovations and found that these behaviors were used to a larger extent by such champions than by others. More specifically, the champions' abilities to stimulate a shared vision, as well as to display and motivate others to display innovative actions, were what enabled them to achieve their goals.

Bennis and Nanus (1985) studied 90 of the most successful leaders from both the public and private sectors of society and found that all were truly *transformative* leaders who created changes within themselves, those around them, and society in general in order to achieve their goals. These leaders differed dramatically in appearance, education, background, and personality styles, but they all had most of the qualities described below—all qualities that can be acquired or developed through training or experience. These qualities characterize the transformational leader.

A *Clear Sense of Purpose*   All 90 people studied were driven by a clear purpose, and all had a long-term picture of what success would be for them. The specific outcomes they identified brought focus and challenge to their lives.

Persistence*   Though some if not all of these individuals showed impatience at one time or another, almost all realized that they were in the game for the long haul and were committed to doing what was necessary to accomplish their goals. Few in the sample started out in large organizations, and those who did persisted in carving out their own particular areas of success.

Self-Knowledge*   The leaders were keenly aware of their own strengths and abilities and knew how to maximize them. Many turned down early routes to quick success in order to take jobs that provided them new experiences, skills, or practice and allowed them to capitalize on their particular strengths.

A *Perpetual Desire for Learning*   In every case, these successful leaders had the insatiable desire to continue their own professional development and learning. They were driven to learn everything they could about their own organizations, to inform themselves constantly on all changes, and to develop the skills necessary to their organizations' continued success. Most perceived life as an adventure in discovery and seemed to share humility at the amount always left to be learned.

Love of Work*   By normal standards, this group probably worked harder and longer than most others, but few of the subjects seemed to have regrets. Whereas the workaholic is often driven by a need to escape other aspects of life, most of these successful leaders had a true love of and belief in the work they were doing and apparently found joy in it without feeling obsessed or controlled by it. (This does not mean that those around them might not see them differently, however.)

The Ability to Attract Others   Where transactional leadership is operating, people are motivated by exchanging one commodity or product for another, whether the exchange be in time, physical strength, services, money, benefits, or recognition. For this group of transformational leaders, however, motivation tended to be related to the sharing of a vision that became integrated with the followers' sense of self. Rewards such as money were still important, but commitment, loyalty, and dedication in this group of 90 were almost always generated by a set of higher ideals.

Emotional Maturity   These leaders seemed to have an awareness of the importance of people to the success of an endeavor. In this regard, many of those interviewed

- made a great effort to accept people as they were.
- had the ability to acknowledge the importance of individuals in their presence to themselves and to the current enterprise.
- never took people for granted but appreciated them for the parts they played in the overall process.
- trusted people as much as possible to do what had to be done and to take responsibility and be accountable for the work delegated to them.
- showed little apparent need for constant approval from those around them and thus had little need to constantly please others and seek their attention.

Risk Taking   Virtually all those in the study, regardless of the size or type of their organizations, were risk takers who were willing to put money, time, and their own security on the line to meet their goals. They appeared to focus on what they stood to gain from the risk rather than on what might be lost.

An Unwillingness to Believe in Failure   For many it appeared that life was a journey of opportunity where mistakes were simply steps in the learning process. Seeing mistakes as necessary for growth freed them to explore consequences and minimized the need to "walk on eggshells."

A Sense of the Public Need   Most seemed to attribute their success partly to their ability to identify and satisfy the needs of a particular group or population.

Each of the 90 successful transformational leaders undoubtedly had other personal qualities that distinguished them from their more ordinary peers. But these 10 qualities alone and in combination most certainly set them apart from average individuals.

Contemporary Leadership

Bennis and Nanus (1985) helped focus our understanding of how leaders and followers interact in our highly technological, fast-paced society. Their central notion involved *translating* power—turning energy and intention into reality and empowerment. Increasingly since the 1940s, social scientists have realized that people are more receptive to change when they *care* to change, when they feel involved in the changing process, and when leaders do not take them for granted but appreciate them for their contributions.

Not until after World War II did most people even feel they had the *right* to question authority. Unions, of course, had long been questioning the country's leaders, but the civil rights movement represented the first challenge of traditional authority by an unorganized people—in this case, blacks and idealistic youths—who until then had always "stayed in their place." The Vietnam War also became an issue around which the traditional values of loyalty, patriotism, and service espoused by politicians, the military, and parents met new resistance. Suddenly, leaders found tradition unraveling: they were confronted with the demands of an increasingly alienated youth culture demanding truth, fairness, and a voice in decisions that affected them.

With the maturing of the radicalized youth of the seventies into the citizen leaders of the eighties, the questioning of authority gained legitimacy, and followers came to expect honesty and accountability in their leaders. Such scandals as Watergate, Iran-Contra, and the Noriega-CIA affair reinforced a sense of disillusionment and mistrust of leadership that simply had not existed a mere 30 years before. Put simply, the question is no longer *whether* leaders will share authority with their followers, but to what degree they will do so.

Many of the leaders still in positions of responsibility today were trained and educated under the "old rules," which ensured compliance and obedience. However, people in all walks of life are now demanding to be heard on the issues that influence their lives. The process will take decades, but it is clear that there is no turning back and that techniques of collaborative and shared problem solving will eventually be integrated into every aspect of society. Bennis and Nanus (1985, p. 27) developed a set of leadership strategies that they believe provide the keys to maximizing what we have termed transformational leadership through the "empowerment" of others.

Establishing the Vision

Power is ignited by stimulating a vision or an abiding purpose that drives the leader toward his or her compelling view of success. The vision serves as a platform upon which the required kinds of participation are built. A meaningful vision can inspire others, challenge them, focus their attention, and generate purposeful direction.

Crucial to establishing such a vision—be it a practical goal or one on a higher plane of thinking involving ethical assessments and moral evaluations—is lively dialogue with those being asked to follow. Burns (1978, p. 4) expresses this need well:

> The transforming leader recognizes and exploits an existing need or demand of a potential follower. But, beyond that, the transforming leader looks for potential motives and followers, seeks to satisfy higher needs, and engages the full person of the follower. The result of transforming leadership is the relationship of mutual stimulation and elevation that converts followers into leaders and may convert leaders into moral agents.

Burns's description might sound a bit lofty for the average group, but its essence applies in all group endeavors. If followers' personal needs go unrecognized, and if followers cannot see true benefits for themselves and others in the leader's vision, then the leadership will ultimately fail.

Some have said that Jimmy Carter was able to win the presidency of the United States because he had an attainable vision to which, in a complex world of half-truths and suspect leaders, people could actually relate. These same analysts suggest that Carter was a weak president not because he lacked a vision or communicated it poorly but because he lacked the skill to translate his vision into practice.

Peter M. Senge, of the MIT Sloan School of Management, calls this process of moving toward the vision creative tension. Creative tension requires a gap between where a group is (current reality) and where it is going (the vision). According to Senge, it differs from problem solving in that the motivation for change comes from the vision rather than the problem (Senge, 1990, pp. 9, 10). This supports the strong belief that change is motivated more positively if it is positioned as moving toward a "desired" state rather than becoming bogged down in the current reality and its attendant problems. Psychologically, it appears easier to create a new future than to pick away at the current problems or limitations of a situation.[3]

Communicating the Vision

The ability to marshal the support of followers depends on the leader's ability to communicate the vision. Being articulate is not necessarily the whole answer; neither is high intensity, personal charisma, or humor. As Bennis and Nanus put it,

> all organizations depend on the existence of shared meanings and inter-
> pretations of reality, which facilitate coordinated actions. The actions and

---

3. The seminal work in this way of thinking was first pioneered by Lewin (*Principles of Topological Psychology,* New York: McGraw-Hill, 1936) nearly sixty years ago and followed by his applied theory of change fifteen years later (*Field Theory in Social Sciences,* New York: Harper & Row, 1951).

symbols of leadership frame and mobilize meaning. Leaders articulate and define what has previously remained implicit or unsaid, then invent images, metaphors and models that provide a focus for new attention (p. 39).

The research of these investigators showed that successful leaders develop a creative method for communicating their message in a unique and personal way. The objective is to engage listeners or followers intellectually and psychologically and to motivate them to hear and do more. Again, whether the leader is a teacher engaging students in a lesson, a sales manager stimulating interest in a new product, or a group leader facilitating the solving of a problem, the critical factor is that the communicated vision is necessary to the empowerment of participants.

Senge likens this combination of individual and organizational visions to a hologram: "If you divide a hologram, each part, no matter how small, shows the whole image intact. Likewise, when a group of people come to share a vision for an organization, each person sees an individual picture of the organization at its best. Each shares responsibility for the whole, not just for one piece" (p. 13).

◆ *Reader Activity*

Take a moment to consider your own life. Are you personally the initiator of any visionary activities? How are you communicating your vision to others? Is it working? Alternatively, are you involved in the visions of others? If so, how did they gain your support?   ◆

Trust Through Positioning

The next task is the arduous one of making something happen so that participants gain hope and trust in the endeavor. Dedication and persistence in realizing the vision are crucial to maintaining belief in both the process and the dream itself. In this context, then, *positioning* refers to actions or strategies necessary to implement the vision of the leader and, by this time, of the participants as well. How this process occurs—how participants become engaged and involved in living out the vision, how they gain their stake in the action—is a subject of interest that took hold only recently. The strategy of creating that change is the subject of Mintzberg's study of creative strategies in business organizations. His analogy is one of a potter who serendipitously creates opportunities from mistakes. Accordingly, he calls his thesis a "crafting" strategy as opposed to a "planning" one (Mintzberg, 1976, p. 26).

Organizational trust, which is at the heart of positioning as Bennis and Nanus describe it, rests both on the constancy of purpose modeled by the leader and others in the organization and on the constancy of the "process," which comprises problem solving, decision making, and implementation styles. A breakdown in these areas could spell failure. Thus the leader must embody the vision itself through purposeful action, and the recognition that those who will "live the vision" must be involved in that vision's pursuit.

In the days when patriotism and loyalty in war were unquestioned standards and our enemies were clearly defined, our leaders had a relatively easy job of mobilizing public support for World War II. But developments in Korea, Vietnam, and later Cambodia presented new problems to those intent on convincing young people to serve their country. In this effort, with respect to the first three requirements of effective leadership presented here—vision, communication, and positioning—miserable failure was the result. In the case of the Vietnam War, the vision—the purpose of the engagement—was unclear from the start and grew increasingly muddied as more and more lives were lost. Obviously, this lack of clarity made communication, the second requirement, difficult. Schools, businesses, and small groups face similar stresses when visions and the communication of them conflict dramatically with implementation plans.

Self-Management

The fourth crucial element of effective leadership falls into the arena of human relations. Of their research, Bennis and Nanus wrote, "Our top executives spent roughly 90% of their time with others and virtually the same percentage of their time concerned with the messiness of people problems. Our study of effective leaders strongly suggested that a key factor was the creative deployment of self" (Bennis and Nanus, 1985, p. 56). This finding suggests that the well-intentioned visionary can "spoil the stew" with too much intensity, motivation, or anxiety. The key to success is the leader's recognition of his or her personal strength and the ability to compensate for personal weaknesses. This recognition is possible only if he or she receives a constant flow of feedback from those involved. Too often, commitment to the task and desire for personal success can shut down openness, reason, and the ability to hear. Stifled by the leader's energy and commitment, and thus unable to share critical information, participants fail to become empowered. Research showed that leaders have to have a high degree of "self-regard" to allow the necessary feedback and openness of communication. Further, they have to be able to make personal changes when required. These requirements not only facilitate implementation but enhance the ability of participants observing such flexibility in their leaders to acknowledge their own mistakes and to be flexible in their turn. An open process of this kind has a direct impact on positioning and fosters confidence, self-esteem, and trust in participants.

The research went on to identify five skills most often used by the 90 leaders in their attempts to improve human relations through effective self-management:

- the ability to accept people as they are, not as one would like them to be
- the capacity to approach relationships and problems in terms of the present rather than the past
- the ability to treat intimates with the same courteous attention extended to strangers and casual acquaintances (not taking people for granted and showing appreciation for their efforts was crucial in this regard)
- the ability to trust others, even if the risk seemed great
- the ability to work without constant approval and recognition from others and to make tough decisions that could displease but still be correct, while providing support and nurturing where necessary in the organization or group

What Transformative Leadership Is Not

An organization's values, philosophy, and image are easily discernible in how the leader and key associates communicate and position their vision. Conversely, these same factors can reveal insensitivity to or ignorance of the organization's principles, which in turn can lead to failure. The following story reveals the latter: here arrogance and insensitivity overrode a firm's vision and spelled disaster.

Ten years ago, few had ever heard of this tiny midwestern advertising agency. But the bold, creative, and even brash challenge it made to the New York goliaths was soon to be reckoned with. Always willing to push to the edge of propriety, this audacious little firm adopted trendy and often assertive views of the world and blended humor, sarcasm, sex, and outrage in a way that titillated the buying public and created an increasing demand for its services. Clients and revenues multiplied, and million-dollar accounts became commonplace. The firm's leaders were in demand, the future was bright, and opportunity continued to knock.

At a statewide annual conference on the marketing for representation of higher education services, this company was represented by one of its top designers, who provided the audience with a taste of the agency's upbeat, unconventional, and irreverent attitudes and practices. One woman in the audience, a Ph.D. who had represented her university at the conference for 10 years, took offense at the sexist language and the general tenor of the presentation. After the conference, she sent what she felt was a reasonable letter to the presenter, indicating that she had been impressed by the creative level and quality of the work but had been annoyed and offended by the negative stereotypes of women in the presentation. "I appreciate the personal apologies you made at the time for the tone of that material," she wrote, "but they didn't make up for those negative stereotypes or for your company's obvious interest in perpetuating what I can't help thinking of as a macho style of doing business." She concluded by expressing disappointment that a company on the cutting edge had to resort to such shopworn ideas to convince people of its creativity.

Although such criticism is not easy to take, there are certainly many ways of responding to it and of acknowledging its usefulness as feedback. But the firm's presenter took a different route. He sent the woman a letter thanking her for her "deeply thoughtful and perceptive letter." That done, he suggested she might find it interesting to visit the East African home of the Dinka tribe to study a custom used in tribal initiations that appeared explicitly lewd and distasteful and left the professor shocked and dismayed.

Her response to this offensive and bizarre form of male humor was to send her letter and his response to a woman's consortium that acted as a clearing house for 170 women's groups. Two staff members of the consortium sent a letter to the president of the company asking whether the reply of the presenter represented company policy. The letter from the consortium stimulated two replies from the company, neither sent to the consortium itself—both were sent to the writer of the first letter. The letters of the CEO and the chairman both included profuse thanks for interest and then both continued the "joke." One offered her a one-way ticket to Dinka land for the opportunity to study the ritual first hand. The other sent her a mosquito net and pith helmet for the trip.

The monumental arrogance, rudeness, and bad taste that somehow eluded the men resulted in the members of the consortium sending copies of all the transactions, without comment, directly to selected clients of the agency, to several potential clients, and to local newspapers and a number of trade journals. The company was deluged with letters of outrage, criticism, and some support. A week after the materials were made public, the company sent a conciliatory letter to the professor. By then, however, the company had experienced $10 million in canceled accounts and was threatened with the loss of an estimated $20 million in new accounts.

Though the leaders of this firm had created a monster, similar mistakes, perhaps on a smaller scale, happen every day. Therefore, it's worth studying the reasons for these leaders' enormous gaffe.

1. While conscious of the changing norms of society that allowed them to push the boundaries of propriety, they failed to realize how sharply their attitudes conflicted with that very society's changing views of women.
2. Perhaps because of their success and the rewards they had received for their brazen advertising style, the leaders had allowed themselves

to become isolated from external feedback—a critical error, because many of their clients, as well as many of their own staff members, were women (Davies and Kuypers, 1985).

3. Complacency, fear, and ignorance kept internal feedback from reaching the leaders. Even the women within the organization were either unaware of changing views or unable to express their own outrage at the course of events. This would suggest that other information was inaccessible to the leaders as well.

4. Arrogance and old-boyism created nonfunctional individual goals and roles (protecting egos, getting even, using scapegoating and humor at other people's expense).

5. The leader's response was cause for particular concern, because it represented a studied response to a small problem. The punitive and hostile attitudes expressed there could only be symptoms of how other issues would strike these leaders personally and how they would be handled within the agency.

Summary

Because this chapter has covered a great deal of complex material on leadership, we conclude with a summary of the key points.

- Leadership is not a rare commodity, nor is it an inborn gift. Almost everyone can be trained as a leader at any level of society.
- Leadership originates in people's willingness to organize and commit themselves to goals and visions to which they have applied themselves. Though leadership skills can be learned through training and practice, the success of the leaders studied in this chapter resulted largely from their goals and attitudes toward themselves.
- Leaders attempting to effect change must be conscious of the need to work *with* those who are to live with the impact of that change. Often, creating and communicating a vision will succeed only insofar as others are able to internalize and pursue the vision with the leader.
- Collaborative problem solving and the development of creative design strategies (see Chapters 6 and 8) can enhance the leader's ability to lead while involving others in action (Terry's term) or positioning (Bennis and Nanus's term).
- At the simplest level, leadership is a *transaction* between a leader and an individual or a group of people. The transaction is based on each receiving something of importance from the other, such as a vote for a political promise or money for a job.
- Leadership can also be a more complex phenomenon, extending into the domains of power, visionary thinking, and ethics. In its most in-

tegrated form, leadership is *transformative*. In this process, individuals and groups are drawn into action by a clearly communicated vision that fulfills specific needs. When the followers internalize that vision, its values, and the process of change, and in turn become leaders and inspirers of further change, the transformational process has been completed.

■ Finally, regardless of how clearly a goal or vision is communicated or how well organized a plan of action is, ineffective or insensitive behavior on the part of leaders can result in failure. Thus open channels of communication, feedback, and leader flexibility are all critical. Furthermore, initial success can breed arrogance, distance, and limited access to critical information, which in turn can result in a deterioration of morale and performance within the group or organization.

◆ ◆ *EXERCISE 1*

A Series of Nonverbal Experiences in Leading and Being Led

The following exercises focus on our feelings of leading and being led and provide data to examine both our behavior and our attitudes in being a follower and being a leader. The exercises are appropriate as a beginning microlab in a longer workshop. They are also useful to members as a means of examining their typical roles and understanding areas in which modification or reevaluation may be needed.

The exercises lead to nonintellectualized discussions of leadership in terms of personal satisfactions or conflicts, areas of skill and ineptness, and enjoyment of authority or fear of responsibility. They also allow participants to see the complementary nature of leader–member relationships in trust, openness, spontaneity, communication, and dependence–independence.

The exercises are of varying lengths and, depending on the purposes, can be expanded or reduced. They involve varying degrees of risk and should be used with an understanding of both the purpose of the exercise and the type of group involved. For some groups, any touching is beyond the bounds of propriety, so certain exercises should be eliminated. Because touching is counter to the norms of the group, much tension is generated and effectiveness in examining leader–follower relationships is severely curtailed. Some groups who consider themselves serious and work-oriented may frown upon games that call for a childlike spontaneity; they may consider games contrived and not regard them as a legitimate basis for learning. The values and resistances of the group should be taken into account so that the exercises used will help members achieve their purposes.

The procedure is as follows: the exercise is named, as illustrated below, and the facilitator gives instructions so that the reader has a feel for the exercise and how it is to be carried out.

1. Connectedness by Rubber Bands

The facilitator begins by saying, "Pick someone. Put your hands out in front of you. Almost touch the hands of your partner. Pretend now that your hands and his or hers are connected by rubber bands. Move—feel what happens" (5 min.). "Pretend your feet are also connected by rubber bands" (5 min.). "Talk about what happened" (10 min.).

The objectives of the exercise are to increase awareness among participant pairs of their own boundaries and those of others and to increase body awareness, control of self, and control of another person. It also presents a leadership–followership situation. Did one person lead all the time? Did the participants reverse roles? When? At what signals? Which role was more comfortable, leading or following? Did one partner see the other as being more comfortable leading or following? Did it make a difference whether it was hands or feet that were connected?

Not all of these questions are asked. A few may be suggested, depending on what clues the facilitator observes. He or she may mention a few as a basis for discussion, but it is important not to spend too much time in discussion. Rather, participants should express their response to this experience and let their impressions build with subsequent exercises.

2. Communication by Clapping

With this approach the facilitator gives the following instructions: "Pick someone who has not been your partner previously. Clap a message. Then let the other person respond." (The facilitator should select a member of the audience and demonstrate. The two stand facing each other, and the facilitator claps the phrase "How are you?" The other person claps back, "fine," or "angry," or whatever.) "You see how it is done. Remember that it involves restructuring meaning from familiar sounds. Now try having a conversation through clapping" (10 min.). "Between you, discuss what happened. What was expressed?" (5 min.). Then the entire group discusses what they experienced (5 min.).

At one level, this exercise allows participants to experience expression through tactile and auditory sense, to create and hear rhythm and sound as expressive of emotion and sequence. At another level, communication is seen as a process requiring a sender and a receiver; one side is insufficient for communication. At yet another level, it is essential to recognize who initiated the "conversation," who "talked" more, who led, who followed, who was frustrated and withdrew. The exercise can also be used to examine functional roles of members.

3. Leader–Follower Trust Walk

The facilitator begins: "This exercise focuses on being a leader or a follower. Half of you will be blindfolded. Those who are not blindfolded will select a partner. This is a nonverbal exercise, so you may not speak to your partner to tell him or her who you are. Let's begin by counting off in twos." (Participants count off "1, 2, 1, 2," etc.) "Will all of the ones come to this side of the room? Here are handkerchiefs to use as blindfolds. Put them on and adjust them so that you cannot see." (The ones arrange their blindfolds and wait.)

Now, the facilitator talks to the twos quietly so that the others cannot hear. "Each of you will select a partner from the group of ones. Stand beside the partner you choose so that we can determine who still needs a partner. Remember, you and your partner may not speak, but by all means try to develop a nonverbal language between you. You will be the leader. How can you help your partner experience his or her world? Can you enlarge his or her world? Be aware of how you see your role. Is it to protect him or her, to get him or her through safely? Is it to be with a minimum of effort on your part? Is it to be serious; is it to be fun? (Pause) Now select your partner."

"Explore your world, nonverbally, of course. I will see you back here in 15 minutes." (If this occurs in a building, 15 minutes is adequate time. If it is outdoors and time permits, allow up to an hour. It is frequently a moving experience to see the partners develop their own signals, an increased sensitivity to each other, a trusting relationship.)

The facilitator alerts the group two minutes before time is up. If the setting is outdoors, he or she simply hopes that they will straggle back reasonably on time.

When they return, the facilitator has the "blind" remove their eye covers to see who their partner is. (This produces tension, anxiety, even fumbling, as the "leader" wonders whether his or her follower will be disappointed when identities are revealed. There is also the anxiety of returning to the "real world," which does not encourage the closeness and trust some of the partners felt. Now the mood changes; the "uncovering" produces laughter and squeals of recognition or surprise.)

The facilitator proceeds: "Would you share your feelings in the experience? What did you find out about yourself that was new? What did you find typical of yourself? How did you feel about your role as a leader or a follower?" (15 min.).

"I am sure each of you wants to experience the other role. Will all of the twos come to this side of the room? Now, it is your turn for the blindfolds. You know what to do."

He or she then talks to the ones as previously to the other group. Although they have been through the experience and know what they want their partner to experience, nevertheless it seems helpful to remind them, through the questions, of a variety of possible relationships they may have with their partner in the leader role. Once more, those not blindfolded select a partner and stand beside him or her. Frequently, the choosing partner will select his or her former partner in order to "repay" his or her felt interest. For a variety of reasons, a person may prefer to select a new partner. After selections are made, the exercise continues as in the first pairing. The groups return, see each other, and share their feelings.

Sometimes the participants feel their reactions are significant and relatively private; they may want to share only with their partners. Sometimes participants are quite eager to share their new understanding of themselves with the whole group. If there is a group sharing, one of the questions the facilitator should ask is how it felt to be a leader and how it felt to be a follower. What was learned?

This exercise has usually been considered primarily an experience of trust; however, it is striking how often members report on their relationship with authority. Students frequently note that it helps them understand their parents or gives them insight into what kind of parent they would like to be. Men and women discuss their societal sex roles, in which a man is expected to be the leader, and their feelings when those roles are reversed. Some who usually see themselves as leaders are surprised at their reactions to being followers and gain a different perspective on the relationship; those who are usually followers give similar reports. Participants also talk about clues they pick up from each other—being tired, bored, excited—which greatly influence the other person and the relationship; new insights are reported on complementary relationships.

As an aside, if a supply of handkerchiefs is difficult to obtain, paper towels as they come from a dispenser and masking tape are equally effective as blindfolds.

4. Follow the Leader—A Musical Variation on the Children's Game

Select an instrumental record with a diversity of moods, tempos, and sounds (Vivaldi's *Four Seasons,* for example). Participants are divided into groups of eight to ten and stand in a circle facing each other; in some groups, participants take off their shoes to enhance a feeling of movement.

Then the facilitator says, "I'm going to play a record. Listen to it, get a feel for the mood. If it reminds you of something, or if you want to express what you feel, come into the center of the circle and do it. Those of us who can feel it with you will follow you in our places. When the mood of the music changes, return to your place. Someone else, who is feeling something he or she would like to share, will go into the center. O.K.?" (10–15 min.).

"How was it? How did you feel about what happened?" (10 min.).

One of the questions to be raised is "Who initiates leadership?" It is someone who knows what is needed, feels he or she has the skills or resources to do it, and feels it is safe to try. Discussion encompasses all these issues. Some will say they could not even think in terms of what music could mean in a public place; their minds went blank immediately. Others had a mental image of what the music evoked but did not seem to have the skill or resources to transfer that image into body movement. Still others hesitated to come into the center for fear of appearing clumsy, childish, or not very original. Another area for brief discussion is how the situation changed. When did you start to feel comfortable, or enjoy it? What happened?

5. Building a Group by Music

This exercise is done with an instrumental record that has an easily discerned tempo, rhythm, and mood; ethnic folk dances are especially suitable (African dances and Irish or Israeli folk dance records work well).

1. *Pair.* The facilitator gives the following instructions: "Select a partner. When the music starts, one of you move to the music, as you feel it. The other person will be your mirror image; he or she will do what you do. If it helps to be more realistic, pretend each of you is touching a mirror with the palms of your hands. The person who is the mirror will try to follow facial expressions as well as body movements. Change who is mirroring when you want to." The record begins. (About 3 min.).

2. *Quartet.* "Add a pair to your group. Continue to move to the music but do it as a group." (About 3 min.).

3. *Octet.* "Add a quartet to your group. Continue to move to the music as a group of eight." (About 3 min.).

4. *One more time (a group of sixteen).* "You're right. Add an octet to your group. Stay with the music. Move to the music as a group." (About 3 min., preferably to the end of the record so that there is a natural feeling of closure.) This produces exhilaration but also a good supply of creaking joints, and a surge of business for the water fountain. There should be no discussion for at least 15 minutes.

The objectives of this exercise are to examine leader–member relationships in varying group sizes. Who follows, who leads? Is it easier to lead in a small group than a large one? Do some leadership patterns remain? Why? How is leadership determined? What role do members play? Do they have inputs that are listened to? Who was the leader (or leaders) at the end? How did he or she get influence? On what was it based? The facilitator asks how some of the members felt in this experience. He or she expands on some of the answers given to the foregoing questions or raises a few new ones. Once more, the discussion should be brief and informal.

Conclusion

The facilitator might close by reminding the group that they have been through a battery of nonverbal experiences that explore leader–member relationships. They may consider what new understanding they have about themselves—for example, how they acted when they were asked to pick a partner. Did they choose or wait to be chosen? Why? What new insight do they have on the subject of leaders, members, and followers?

Participants may be asked to write a log, or self-report, verbalizing what they have learned. They can be divided into small groups to discuss some of their experiences. A large group discussion leaves too many as listeners without an opportunity to participate; at best, it might be used briefly to begin the discussion.

The facilitator should be particularly sensitive to norms of the group with whom he or she is working. These exercises should be used only where appropriate. As noted earlier, they should not be used with groups who consider touching inappropriate, nor should they be used unless they will enhance the goals of the training.

◆ ◆ *EXERCISE 2*

What Is My Role in a Group?

Objectives

- To learn who is perceived as leader of the group
- To understand the many roles in a group
- To develop data on what contributes to being the leader in a particular group
- To increase data to participants on their perceived roles
- To increase data to participants on the relationship between their perceptions of their roles and others' perceptions of their roles

Materials

Copies of the Behavioral Description Questionnaire (included with this exercise) are needed; also newsprint to record the data. If it is a large group that has been working in smaller units, data can be recorded within each unit. If there are ten members, each person requires ten questionnaires.

Rationale

This exercise is appropriate after members of a group have been working together and know one another. It provides information to members on their roles as others perceive them and as they themselves perceive their roles. This information may be congruent, or it may be at great variance. It is valuable feedback to the member on his or her influence in the group. It also permits data on who is seen as the leader and with what dimension leadership in this group is allied. Data are also available on the degree of commonly shared perceptions. Do many see the same person as the leader, or are several people seen as leaders?

Action

A questionnaire is distributed listing 15 statements. Under each is a five-point scale. Each member is given enough questionnaires to fill one in for every member of the group. The facilitator may begin by briefly stating that each group develops in a unique manner depending on the composition of the group, its task and its situation. He or she continues: "Each of us takes on a unique role within a group. Sometimes it is our typical role, sometimes a blend of roles from many experiences. Sometimes we see ourselves taking one role, and others see us quite differently. Perhaps by developing and sharing this information, we can learn more about ourselves and our group." It is important that the facilitator explain this rather seriously. Sometimes groups are apprehensive about getting or giving feedback and need support from the leader that such data are both legitimate and helpful.

Each person lists the name of the person he or she is describing at the top and then proceeds to indicate how typical that behavior is of that person (30 min.).

An easy way to collect data is to give one person all the sheets for another person (not his or her own). He or she then charts the data on a blank questionnaire and totals points on each question (a rating of 3 is 3 points) (15 min.).

The facilitator asks for a report from each person on the behaviors seen as most typical for the person tallied or asks for the highest points on each question. The person who scores the highest points on question 9—the true leader of the group— is the leader. In what other areas did the people who score highest on that question also score high? What are the behaviors required for leadership in this group?

Following the discussion, all the papers are given to the person whose name is on top. The person then has all the reported data on himself or herself and can examine its congruence with or variance from his or her own perceptions. (15 min.)

BEHAVIORAL DESCRIPTION QUESTIONNAIRE[4]

Indicate how well each statement describes each group member (including yourself) on a five-point scale running from "very true of him or her" (5) to "not true of him or her" (1).

4. Morris, C. G., and J. R. Hackman. "Behavioral correlates of perceived leadership." *Journal of Personality and Social Psychology,* 1969, 13, 350–361. Copyright 1969 by the American Psychological Association. Reprinted by permission of the author.

1. He[5] prodded the group to complete the task.

```
┌──────────────┬──────────────┬──────────────┬──────────────┐
1              2              3              4              5
Not true of him                               Very true of him
```

2. He was the real "idea man" in the group, suggesting new ways of handling the group's problems.

```
┌──────────────┬──────────────┬──────────────┬──────────────┐
1              2              3              4              5
Not true of him                               Very true of him
```

3. He is a creative person.

```
┌──────────────┬──────────────┬──────────────┬──────────────┐
1              2              3              4              5
Not true of him                               Very true of him
```

4. He was concerned only with his own ideas and viewpoint.

```
┌──────────────┬──────────────┬──────────────┬──────────────┐
1              2              3              4              5
Not true of him                               Very true of him
```

5. He influenced the opinions of others.

```
┌──────────────┬──────────────┬──────────────┬──────────────┐
1              2              3              4              5
Not true of him                               Very true of him
```

6. He interrupted others when they were speaking.

```
┌──────────────┬──────────────┬──────────────┬──────────────┐
1              2              3              4              5
Not true of him                               Very true of him
```

7. He criticized those with whom he disagreed.

```
┌──────────────┬──────────────┬──────────────┬──────────────┐
1              2              3              4              5
Not true of him                               Very true of him
```

8. He was an aloof sort of person.

```
┌──────────────┬──────────────┬──────────────┬──────────────┐
1              2              3              4              5
Not true of him                               Very true of him
```

5. The generic male pronoun is used for convenience here, but the spirit of the questionnaire is, of course, "he or she."

9. He was the real leader of the group.

1	2	3	4	5
Not true of him				Very true of him

10. He worked well with others in the group.

1	2	3	4	5
Not true of him				Very true of him

11. He was disruptive to the group.

1	2	3	4	5
Not true of him				Very true of him

12. He was in the forefront of the group's discussion.

1	2	3	4	5
Not true of him				Very true of him

13. He kept the group from straying too far from the topic.

1	2	3	4	5
Not true of him				Very true of him

14. His attitudes hurt the group's chances of success.

1	2	3	4	5
Not true of him				Very true of him

15. He seemed to be a tense, nervous person.

1	2	3	4	5
Not true of him				Very true of him

Scoring   The scores participants gave themselves and those they received from other members are summed to provide an overall indication of how characteristic each of the 15 statements was of their behavior.

Discussion

The data gathered and presented are the basis for discussion. Any issues considered appropriate should be developed.

Who are the most influential members of this group? Why? What behaviors are valued?

What behavioral roles seem to be missing? How does this affect your group?

What difference was there between your perceptions of your role and how others see you? How do you feel about that?

◆ ◆ EXERCISE 3

A Task-Maintenance Exercise

Objectives

- To increase understanding of task-maintenance roles
- To increase skills in observing a group; to learn to categorize by functional roles of members
- To increase learning about the difference between intended behavior and perceived behavior

Rationale

This exercise permits participants and observers to understand that intent is not enough. Attempting certain behaviors does not mean that a person will be perceived in the role he or she intends. In addition, intending to behave in a certain way does not indicate a person's skill in this role, factors that may interfere with his or her intentions, or the fact that more conscious behaviors are called into play. Participants come to understand some of the complexities in the interpersonal and group processes that go on in meetings.

This exercise is not appropriate unless the members have become familiar with the task-maintenance concept and functional roles and are willing to consider the implications of what they have learned. It can be followed by skill sessions in practicing each of the task and maintenance roles. The role play may be repeated after discussion or skill session, with members attempting to be more congruent or skillful in their roles and observers attempting to focus more clearly on behaviors.

Materials

The following materials are needed: two copies of the role-play situation described below and six role-play names; six copies of the Explanation Sheet of Task and Maintenance Roles, to be given to role players only; newsprint, felt-tip markers, and tape; and a table and six chairs for the role play.

Design

The facilitator introduces the design as a role play. He or she explains that in a role play, a situation is concocted that is not real but could be. Participants enact not their usual roles but rather the roles they are instructed to play. The role play permits an examination of behavior without embarrassing anyone and helps develop increased skills in the situation.

The facilitator asks for six volunteers to participate in the role play, selects six people and briefs them in private, and then distributes six pieces of paper (usually holding them face down and having the role players select one of the papers). The papers should read as follows:

> Association President—assume number 1 task role and number 1 maintenance role.
>
> Teacher Representative—assume number 2 task role and number 2 maintenance behavior.
>
> Association Negotiator—assume number 3 task role and number 3 maintenance role.
>
> Superintendent of Schools—assume number 4 task role and number 4 maintenance role.
>
> School Board Representative—assume number 5 task role and number 5 maintenance role.
>
> School Board President—assume number 6 task role and number 6 maintenance role. You are somewhat hostile to the teachers and their position on the salary increase.

The association negotiators, the board, and the superintendent are given a few minutes to discuss as individual groups what they plan to do. While they are doing this, observer sheets are distributed to others in the group.

The facilitator instructs observers to tally every time any of the role players' behavior falls under either Task or Maintenance, as described on the Explanation Sheet. He or she asks them to record words or acts that will help recall and support their observations and also to write the names of the role players at the top of the sheets. The facilitator answers any questions observers may have. Then he or she calls the role players back into the room, seats them at the conference table, and reads the role play to the entire group. He or she gives one copy to the role players to keep before them.

The Role-Play Situation

A negotiations impasse over salaries between the Teachers Association and the school board is imminent. The association's original proposal called for a beginning salary of $19,000, with a $2,000-per-year increment for 12 years. This would have given the association the highest beginning and ending salary in the country.

The first counterproposal by the board maintains the existing salary of $19,000, but with $1,000-per-year increments for 12 years. This was refused by the association. A second counterproposal by the board maintains the existing salary increment of $2,000 per year for 20 years but begins at $12,600. This would give the association the lowest starting salary in the country but the highest maximum salary. A special levy has already been called for, and the amount, which includes no salary adjustment, has been earmarked. As the scene opens, the board members say that they cannot change the earmarking of the special levy funds and that no other funds are available. The teachers say that they cannot accept the last proposal, maintaining that it will decimate the professional staff of the district. The association negotiators have agreed that if they cannot get the board to utilize the reserve funds (7½ percent of the total budget), they will declare an impasse at the present meeting.

The facilitator continues the role-play situation for 10–15 minutes. He or she cuts it when it appears that there will be no further movement, before interest lags. Then he or she asks observers to meet in trios and compare their perceptions and tallying. The trios do this and arrive at a joint report indicating what role each player was primarily playing (about 10 minutes). The facilitator returns to the general session and places the names of the role players on newsprint. He or she asks for reports from trios, and next to each name he or she writes the role the trio thought each person was taking. Then he or she asks each role player to reveal the role assigned to him or her and what he or she was attempting. That information is written next to his or her name on the newsprint. The prediction is that there will be a discrepancy between the way the role player understood his or her role and the way he or she actually acted it out. Also, it is predictable that the observers will vary in their reports of how the role players were acting.

EXPLANATION SHEET OF TASK AND MAINTENANCE ROLES[6]

(To be given to role players only)

Task roles

1. *Initiating:* Proposing tasks or goals: defining a group problem; suggesting a procedure or ideas for solving a problem.

2. *Information or opinion seeking:* Requesting facts; seeking relevant information about a group concern; asking for suggestions and ideas.

Maintenance roles

1. *Encouraging:* Being friendly, warm, and responsive to others; accepting others and their contributions; rewarding others by giving them an opportunity or recognition.

2. *Expressing group feelings:* Sensing feelings, mood, relationships within the group; sharing own feelings with other members.

6. Based on Benne and Sheats, 1948.

Task roles (cont.)

3. *Information or opinion giving:* Offering facts; providing relevant information about a group concern; stating a belief; giving suggestions or ideas.

4. *Clarifying or elaborating:* Interpreting or reflecting ideas and suggestions; clearing up confusion; indicating alternatives and issues before the group; giving examples.

5. *Summarizing:* Pulling together related ideas; restating suggestions after the group has discussed them; offering a decision or conclusion for the group to accept or reject.

6. *Consensus testing:* Sending up trial balloons to see if the group is nearing a conclusion; checking with the group to see how much agreement has been reached.

Maintenance roles (cont.)

3. *Harmonizing:* Attempting to reconcile disagreements; reducing tension through "pouring oil on troubled waters"; getting people to explore their differences.

4. *Compromising:* When own idea or status is involved in a conflict, offering to compromise own position; admitting error, disciplining self to maintain group cohesion.

5. *Gate-keeping:* Attempting to keep communication channels open; facilitating the participation of others; suggesting procedures of others; suggesting procedures for sharing opportunity to discuss group problems.

6. *Setting standards:* Expressing standards for the group to achieve; applying standards in evaluating group functioning and production.

Discussion

Role players are asked how comfortable they were in their roles. Was it like their usual roles? Which players enacted their roles most faithfully—were they perceived by others as being in their assigned roles? Which players had the greatest discrepancies? Why? Which behaviors caused difficulties in attempting to attain observer agreement? Are there generalizations that can be made about our observations?

The facilitator might briefly dwell on the several factors that influence the interpersonal and group processes going on at meetings. At least two factors appear prominent as a result of this role play:

   1. *A perceptual factor*   Not all of us perceive the same thing when we are watching the behavior of another person. Some perceive a person giving feelings, while others hear him or her giving information or expressing opinions.

   2. *Our intentions are different from our behavior*   Participants might have intended to play a given role but might have given out mixed messages. Their words said one thing, but their nonverbal behavior in body or tone emitted another message.

Sometimes we intend to play roles at which we are not skilled; we mean to behave in a certain way but get "off the track." Sometimes cues from another person evoke responses we had not intended. We sense that the person does not like us, and we become defensive or see the person as an opponent rather than, as previously assumed, a friend. How we feel about others personally affects our behavior.

◆ ◆ EXERCISE 4

Functional Roles of Membership

Objectives

- To increase the understanding of functional roles of membership
- To see leadership emerge
- To practice observing types of behavior
- To develop an increased understanding of leadership requiring followership

Materials

The materials needed are the same as for the role play above. Also needed are copies of Group Building and Maintenance Roles and Group Task Roles (included with this exercise).

Rationale

Any of the role-play exercises in this book or the problem-solving exercises in this chapter are appropriate as a situation to examine functional roles of members. The goal is to develop skills in observing types of behavior and increasing awareness of the functional roles.

Design

The facilitator establishes the role play included with this exercise or uses tinker toys and asks each group to create a symbol of its group. Or he or she can use newsprint, crayons, and other materials and ask each group to create a collage. Two observers are assigned to tally for functional roles. Each time someone behaves in a role, a tally is made. One person can tally for task roles, the other for maintenance roles. A better procedure is to have two observers for task roles and two for maintenance roles so as to check reliability. Following the activity, the observers feed back their findings in the emerging roles.

Sometimes a questionnaire can be distributed to participants immediately following the situation, in which each person is asked to state who he or she felt was the leader of the group, who was most influential, and with whom he or she would like to work again. These results are determined. There is discussion about the amount of agreement or variety of responses. This discussion gets at the various bases of power. Following the administering of questionnaires, the observers feed back their findings. The group examines how these results support or are different from their ratings on the questionnaires.

GROUP BUILDING AND MAINTENANCE ROLES

Categories describing the types of member behavior required for building and maintaining the group as a working unit.

Usually helpful	Usually destructive
1. *Encouraging:* Is friendly, warm, and responsive to others; accepts others and their contributions; is giving to others.	Is cold, unresponsive, unfriendly; rejects others' contributions; ignores them.
2. *Expressing feelings:* Expresses feelings present in the group; calls attention of the group to its reactions to ideas and suggestions; expresses own feelings or reactions in the group.	Ignores reactions of the group as a whole; refuses to express own feelings when needed.
3. *Harmonizing:* Attempts to reconcile disagreements; reduces tension through joking, relaxing comments; gets people to explore their differences.	Irritates or "needles" others; encourages disagreement for its own sake; uses emotion-laden words.
4. *Compromising:* When own idea or status is involved in a conflict, offers compromise, yields status, admits error; disciplines self to maintain group cohesion.	Becomes defensive, haughty; withdraws or walks out; demands subservience or submission from others.
5. *Facilitating communication:* Attempts to keep communication channels open; facilitates participation of others; suggests procedures for discussing group problems.	Ignores miscommunications; fails to listen to others; ignores the group needs that are expressed.
6. *Setting standards or goals:* Expresses standards or goals for group to achieve; helps the group become aware of direction and progress.	Goes own way; is irrelevant; ignores group standards or goals and direction.
7. *Testing agreement:* Asks for opinions to find out if the group is nearing a decision; sends up a trial balloon to see how near agreement the group is; rewards progress.	Attends to own needs; does not note group condition or direction; complains about slow progress.
8. *Following:* Goes along with movement of the group; accepts ideas of others; listens to and serves as an interested audience for others in the group.	Participates on own ideas but does not actively listen to others; looks for loopholes in ideas; is carping.

GROUP TASK ROLES

Categories describing the types of member behavior required for accomplishing the task or work of the group.

Usually helpful	Usually destructive
1. *Initiating:* Proposes tasks or goals; defines a group problem; suggests a procedure or ideas for solving a problem.	Waits for others to initiate; withholds ideas or suggestions.
2. *Seeking information:* Requests facts; seeks relevant information about a group problem or concern; is aware of need for information.	Is unaware of need for facts or of what is relevant to the problem or task at hand.
3. *Giving information:* Offers facts; provides relevant information about a group concern.	Avoids facts; prefers to state personal opinions or prejudices.
4. *Seeking opinions:* Asks for expression of feeling; requests statements of estimate, expressions of value; seeks suggestions and ideas.	Does not ask what others wish or think; considers other opinions irrelevant.
5. *Giving opinion:* States belief about a matter before the group gives suggestions and ideas.	States own opinion whether relevant or not; withholds opinions or ideas when needed by the group.
6. *Clarifying:* Interprets ideas or suggestions; clears up confusion; defines needed terms; indicates alternatives and issues confronting the group.	Is unaware of or irritated by confusion or ambiguities; ignores confusion of others.
7. *Elaborating:* Gives examples, develops meanings; makes generalizations; indicates how a proposal might work out, if adopted.	Is inconsiderate of those who do not understand; refuses to explain or show new meaning.
8. *Summarizing:* Pulls together related ideas; restates suggestions after the group has discussed them; offers decision or conclusion for the group to accept or reject.	Moves ahead without checking for relationship or integration of ideas; lets people make their own integrations or relationships.

ROLE PLAY TO PRACTICE OBSERVING FUNCTIONAL ROLES

Second Observation—Role Play—Preliminary Negotiations between Union and Management

 1. *Mediator from Chamber of Commerce.* You want both sides to be happy. Your goal is to arrive at a solution that satisfies both sides. It would look bad for business in town if there were a strike; on the other hand, if the word goes around that labor gets everything it wants, business will not be attracted to this city.

 2. *Union Representative.* The workers must have a raise: too many are beginning to question why they pay dues. If you can't get a raise, get an equivalent. The president

of the company is a nice guy if you treat him with respect (he goes for that), but you don't like to kowtow. You will if things get bad; the most important part is to come out with something.

3. *Shop Steward.* You want a raise for the workers. It makes you feel important to sit down with the president of the company and feel that you are his equal. You want to be sure he treats you as his equal. You are easily hurt by any slight; your voice must be heard. Remind them you can cause a strike, make trouble for them, and so forth. You want to show the workers in your plant how important you are and to get them a big "package."

4. *Company President.* You are head of a large company. You are in the midst of modernizing your equipment, which will mean more automation and laying off workers. Possibly workers can be shifted to other places in the plant but not at the same level. A small raise wouldn't be bad (profits have been substantial), but how about the layoffs next year and the possibility of a strike then? Perhaps something can be worked out, but you want them to understand that you are considering such alternatives. You are a leader in the community; you are not the equal of the working person in intelligence, education, or standard of living—you are superior.

5. *Independent Businessperson.* You are a small businessperson. An increase in this industry means an increase for every worker. You are just barely making ends meet; you can't afford a raise; you would be faced with going out of business. You like being on a par with the president of the large company, a prominent person in town. You certainly see his point of view better than that of the workers, who care only about their earnings; they are unconcerned with yours.

Discussion

What did you learn about your behavior in a group? Which roles do you usually play? Which do you wish you could take on more frequently? These questions can be listed in a short questionnaire and fed back as data to participants. There could then be sessions allowing participants to build skills in the roles with which they have difficulty.

What kind of leadership is helpful to the group? What blocks movement? These questions usually lead into a discussion of clarity—or lack of clarity—of goals. It becomes obvious that we are open to the influence of only some members. Frequently, we have difficulty in putting out needed behavior for fear of its not being accepted.

◆ ◆ *EXERCISE 5*

Increasing Understanding of Leadership and Power

The exercises that follow focus on various aspects of leadership and power. They are quite simple and appropriate when a group is working on some aspect of leadership and when acquiring data on the group would be useful. These exercises may be used in a variety of contexts: as a warm-up for further discussion or a theory session, as a "quickie" to help the group understand its own processes at a given moment, or as a beginning for thinking about aspects of leadership.

How Many Leaders?

Generally two leaders emerge in a group: the task leader concerned with goal accomplishment and the social–emotional leader whose prime behavior is in maintaining working conditions within the group. Either of these or another may have the most influence in the group. A simple sociogram will provide data for determining who the leaders are. Each person is asked to respond to the following questions: Who has the best ideas in the group? Who is best liked? Who is most influential?

The data are gathered, they are tallied visibly before the group, and results are determined. The group discusses findings. Is the same person the leader in all three areas, or are there three different people with highest scores? What are the implications for the group? What generalizations can be derived regarding leadership?

Power—In a Line

When people seem concerned about their relative influence in the group, or about who is listened to and who is not listened to in terms of influencing action, this is an appropriate exercise. The facilitator simply asks the group whether it would be willing to try something. If members reply yes, he or she proceeds. The facilitator asks that all members arrange themselves in a line, with the person who sees himself or herself as the most influential at the head of the line and the person who sees himself or herself of lesser influence farther down the line, according to the degree of influence he or she feels he or she has in the group. The facilitator asks that members who believe someone is misplaced move that person to where they think he or she should be. Then the members look at the ranking and discuss how they feel about it. If they discuss how they feel about their influence, it elicits data on how they feel about the group, its task, and their relationships with others. It can also lead to a discussion of how influence by some members could be increased (for example, the silent member who ranks at the tail because he or she rarely speaks or attempts to influence).

Higher and Lower Status

This exercise is a variation on the preceding one. In everyday conversation, we may refer to someone as "the big cheese" or "a prestige member." We say of others, "Oh, her," or "It doesn't matter that Bill isn't here; we can start without him." We often imply in these expressions, as well as by our nonverbal cues, that some have higher status than others (even in a so-called nondifferentiated group). High status means greater ability to influence; low status means limited ability to influence, although low status may produce negative influence.

The following questions are then asked: Who has the highest status in the group? Who is next? Who has least? Members are now instructed to arrange themselves so that the person of highest status stands on a table and those of lower status stand on chairs farther out from the center. Those of still lower status stand on the floor and farther from the center. Those lower yet crouch or lie down, even farther from the center. Once more, members may rearrange one another if they feel someone is misplaced. Members complete their hierarchy and then discuss it. How many are in the center? What are the problems? How "far out" and how "small" do low-status persons feel? What problems in the group could be reduced if this were changed? How could it be done?

A variation involves not only the height and distance relations but also pairing and cluster relations. The exercise is the same as before, but people now also group themselves in terms of whose influence they are most open to and cluster around their status people.

Who Are You in a Group?

Frequently we categorize ourselves and others in dichotomies: good–bad, leader–follower, talkative–quiet. We rarely seem to see the variety of behaviors required in a group or our own roles in them. This exercise helps participants begin to see their own roles and the roles of others. The facilitator asks members to write down on a piece of paper their typical behavior in a group. He or she asks that they fold the sheets and lay them aside and then divides the group in half, naming the halves group 1 and group 2. Each member from group 2 is asked to select a partner from the other group. The first group is assigned a task, such as building a creation from tinker toys or making a collage of the world as it may be in 1999. The members of the second group observe their partners' behavior specifically. They can be given the functional roles listing as a basis for observing. At the end of the task, the observer feeds back all the various behaviors of his or her partner. Then members look at the earlier statement on their typical behavior and discuss it among themselves. Next the procedure is reversed. The second group performs a task; each member is observed by his or her partner. Descriptions of behavior are fed back again; they examine earlier sheets and discuss them. Finally, a group discussion is held on the variety of group behaviors observed and the range of behaviors exhibited.

Who Would I Like to Be?

Most of us wish we could be more effective in a group. Some roles come easily, and we are skillful; others we rarely use. Each member is given a copy of the functional roles and is asked to list the roles he or she uses most frequently plus those he or she uses infrequently or rarely. The facilitator divides the group into triads. One person interviews another on which roles he or she rarely uses and asks why. The third person takes notes. The interviewer asks which he or she would like to be able to use more, what stops him or her, and what he or she might do to change. The interviewer asks only clarifying questions; responses come from the person being interviewed. The triads reverse and continue until all members have discussed the roles they take, those they rarely take, and those they wish they could become more skillful in. They are given the notes on their interviews as a basis for future planning or skill sessions.

◆ ◆ *EXERCISE 6*

Decision Making Along a Continuum— Problems

Objectives

- To experience some of the roles people play in decision making
- To experience ambiguity with a leader and note how it affects both the process and the product
- To understand the choice-of-leadership continuum and its implications for members
- To increase understanding that a leader–member relationship is a dynamic one, each previous relationship affecting the present one
- To increase observational skills of a dyad in change

Rationale

This exercise yields very dramatic learnings. It becomes obvious that the leader–member relationship is a fundamental one in understanding group process and organizational functioning. The leader and member roles are defined much as they frequently are, and the leaders have more direct access to instructions from the top than the members. The information members receive is based on how the leader decides to transmit it—whether limited, ambiguous, or honest. Although the leader becomes more member-oriented in his or her decisions, the member may not perceive himself or herself as having a more significant role. He or she may be reacting to previous behaviors of the leader and may have developed a lack of trust and an apathetic response. Participants become aware of the dynamic relationships in a group. That is, they recognize that members' trust of the leader influences the degree of work in decision making and that clarity in decision making is an important factor in leader–member relationships. It also permits members to understand the effectiveness of multilateral versus unilateral decision making.

Materials

There should be three lists of innocuous items to be rank-ordered. (The lists are not important in themselves; they are simply a basis for discussion and decision making.) Some examples: What are the most important qualities of a good teacher? Ten qualities are listed, with a dash as a place for ranking before each item. The qualities listed might be education, initiative, creativity, persistence, fairness, a sense of humor, diligence, love of teaching, interest in travel, and experience. Other similar questions: Rank these 10 presidents in order of their importance in history. Then the names of ten presidents are listed. Another example: Rank these people in order of the importance of their contribution to mankind: Charlemagne, Julius Caesar, Socrates, Martin Luther, Galileo, Darwin, Shakespeare, Queen Victoria, Karl Marx, and Adam Smith.

Three different lists are required, and there should be two copies of each list, preferably on different-colored paper. One color (let us say green) should always be given to the leader; the other color (white) should always be given to the member. There should be enough lists for two-thirds of the participants. There should also be sheets printed for observers. The sheet is headed Observer's Sheet and should list questions to direct the observer's attention to the data to be gathered (see the sample Observer's Sheet included with this exercise). These sheets are needed for one-third of the group.

Action

The group is divided into trios. One person is the leader, one the member, and one the observer. Each trio will be asked to perform three ranking tasks and to turn in their decision on each, according to specific instructions. Following the third exercise, observers report their findings, and leaders and members respond with their feelings on the situations. This is followed by a general discussion.

The group is again divided into triads and told that they will be asked to perform three tasks, each of which involves reaching a decision. In the tasks, the participants are to maintain the same roles throughout; that is, the person who is the leader will continue in his or her role as leader in all three tasks, the person who is the member will occupy that role for all three tasks, and the observer will maintain that role throughout.

Instructions are given at the beginning of each task, but the members are asked to leave the room first. Only the leaders receive instructions, as frequently happens in many groups and organizations. Instructions are then transmitted from the leader to his or her member or subordinate. It is important that the members leave prior to instructions so as to avoid the psychological effect of feeling left out, and because they should not know the changed rules for each task.

TASK I

Instructions are given to leaders; members are not in the room. The leaders are instructed that they and their paired member will each be given a list of items to rank-order. (The leader is given the green sheet, the member the white sheet.) Each person will rank the items individually. Then the leader and member will discuss the lists between them. No attention is to be given to the member's list. At the completion of this task, the leader will turn in only the list he or she made. No mention is made of the member's list. Members are not told about the special instructions. The leader may discuss his or her list with the member in any way he or she likes, but only his or her list represents the final selection. Observers will not participate. They will be concerned with gathering observational data. Members are called back in. The leaders and members take their sheets and rank the items individually. The facilitator announces that the group has 20 minutes to work before each group is asked to submit a list. The groups work on the task; at the end of 20 minutes, the leaders turn in their sheets.

OBSERVER'S SHEET

Pay particular attention to the following:

> How does the leader act toward the member (friendly, cordial, patronizing, and so forth)? Attempt to note specific behaviors—verbal or nonverbal.
>
> How does the member act toward the leader?
>
> How open are they to each other's influence in this situation?
>
> How is this situation different from the previous one for the leader? For the member?
>
> *Task I:*
>
> *Task II:*
>
> *Task III:*

Discussion

The facilitator should be aware of how members feel when they are asked to leave the room and how they feel about only the leaders receiving instructions. They feel left out, apprehensive. They feel that "this is how it always is"; the members are given the information secondhand and only to the extent that the leader wants to relay information to them. They also feel "used" because the leader paid no attention to their suggestions and submitted only his or her own ranking. Leaders often feel that they should discuss issues with members, frequently leaving members with expectations of influence. It is a disillusioning experience to find that members' suggestions were not considered. This discussion is not brought before the group. It is outlined here so that the facilitator may understand some of the dynamics developing in the relationship.

TASK II

Members are asked to leave the room; instructions are given to the leaders. The leaders are instructed that they and their paired member will each be given another list of items to rank-order. However, this time they are to use a fair and equitable decision-making process. They are told to consider the member's list adequately so that a collaborative ranking is developed. They are told not to mention their special instructions to the members. The members are called back in. The leaders and members take their sheets (a new listing but maintaining the same colors for leaders and members) and again rank the items individually. The facilitator announces that the groups have 20 minutes to work before each group is asked to submit a list. The groups work on the task; at the end of 20 minutes, joint sheets are submitted.

Discussion

The member once more feels left out but feels it more acutely following the unilateral decision making just experienced. This person's feelings about the leader may range from strong anger at being manipulated to "you can fool some of the people some of the time, but you won't fool me again." This member will be more guarded and less willing to be involved in the task and may feel the leader is pressuring him or her. This person may be verbally antagonistic to the leader, may see the leader turn in a joint list, or may still feel the leader is turning in his or her own list. It is important to note that the member's subjective reality greatly influences the climate of the group as well as his or her relationship to the leader.

TASK III

The members are again asked to leave the room; as previously, instructions are given only to the leaders. The leaders are again instructed that they will be given a list of items to rank, as will the members. Once more the new lists are distributed on the same colored and white paper. The instructions to the leaders now are, "The list you turn in really does not matter, because we will throw it away. Let the members turn in whatever they want; their list will be the one representing the group. Once more, do not tell the members of these instructions."

Members are asked to return. The members and leaders take their lists and rank them. The facilitator announces that each group will work on its task and will be asked to submit a list for the group. Usually this takes about 10 minutes. The members submit their lists.

Discussion

The members become even more annoyed at being left out of the instructions. Attitudes toward the leader are mixed. In some groups they are beginning to reconsider their relationship, partially and somewhat grudgingly. In other groups, the relationships are strained and viewed as a "personality clash." However, now the leader either acts apathetically or seems to be pressuring the member in order to influence his or her list. The relationship is ambiguous. The level of involvement is low, effort on the task is greatly reduced, and the climate is characterized by minimal communication and maximal suspicion. The member has more influence in making the Task III decision, but neither he or she knows nor is involved at this point. The actions of the leader leave this person confused and increasingly less sure of his or her own role.

General Discussion

Following the three tasks, the group observers report on the behaviors they have seen. Leaders and members respond with their feelings on each of the situations. There can be a discussion with the entire group related to their reactions in each of the situations, the level of involvement, and their feelings about the group as a whole. Discussion can be in terms of how participants felt after each task, and perhaps they can generalize some of the learnings.

The following questions might be the basis for general discussion: How do people feel about multilateral versus unilateral decision making? Both the leader and the member experienced a task in which each made decisions irrespective of the other; they also experienced a time when they shared the decision making. How does it affect both the process (the degree of involvement) and the product (how good the participants think their list was)?

How did the members feel when they were asked to leave? Why? (Allow time here; feelings are generally quite strong.) How did members feel about the leader? Why? What are the implications for working with ongoing groups? What are the implications of this exercise for decision making in a group? What behaviors are helpful? Which hinder progress?

References

Abrahamson, M., and J. Smith. "Norms, deviance, and spatial location." *Journal of Social Psychology,* 80, No. 1 (1970), 95–101.

Adams, J. *Effective Leadership for Men and Women.* New York: Alex Publishing Company, 1985.

Archer, D. "Power in groups: Self-concept changes of powerful and powerless group members." *Journal of Applied Behavioral Science,* 10 (1974), 208–220.

Bailey, Gerald D., and William F. Adams. "Leadership strategies for nonbureaucratic leadership." *NASSP Bulletin,* March 1990, 21–28.

Bales, R. *Interaction Process Analysis.* Reading, Mass.: Addison-Wesley, 1950.

Bales, R. *Personality and Interpersonal Behavior.* New York: Holt, Rinehart and Winston, 1970.

Barlow, S., W. Hansen, A. Fuhriman, and R. Finley. "Leader communication style: Effects of members of small groups." *Small Group Behavior,* 13 (1982), 518–531.

Bass, B. *Leadership, Psychology, and Organizational Behavior.* New York: Harper & Row, 1960.

Benne, K. D., and P. Sheats. "Functional roles of group members." *Journal of Social Issues,* 2 (1948), 42–47.

Bennis, W., and B. Nanus. *Leaders: The Strategies for Taking Charge.* New York: Harper & Row, 1985.

Bennis, W., and B. Nanus. *Leaders: The Strategies for Taking Charge,* Audio-cassette study guide (Nos. 1 and 2), *Sybervision.* Neward, Calif.: CML Company, 1985.

Berelson, B., and G. A. Steiner. *Human Behavior.* New York: Harcourt, 1964.

Bernstein, M. D. "Autocratic and democratic leadership in an experimental group setting: A modified replication of the experiments of Lewin, Lippitt, and White, with systematic observer variation." *Dissertation Abstracts International,* 31, No. 12A (1971), 6712.

Bird, C. *Social Psychology.* New York: Appleton-Century, 1940.

Blake, R., and J. S. Mouton. *Building a Dynamic Corporation Through Grid Organization Development.* Reading, Mass.: Addison-Wesley, 1969.

Burns, J. M. *Leadership*. New York: Harper & Row, 1978.

Calabrese, Raymond L. "Ethical leadership: A prerequisite for effective schools." *NASSP Bulletin,* Dec. 1988, 1–4.

Clemens, John K., and Douglas F. Mayer. *The Classic Touch: Lessons in Leadership from Homer to Hemingway.* Homewood, Ill.: Dow Jones-Irwin, 1987.

Davies, D., and B. C. Kuypers. "Group development and interpersonal feedback." *Group and Organizational Studies,* 10, No. 2 (June 1985), 184–205.

Dore, B. and Florence L. Geis. "Nonverbal affect responses to male and female leaders: Implications for leadership evaluations." *Journal of Personality and Social Psychology,* 58, No. 1 (1990), 48–59.

Drory, A., and U. Gluskinos. "Machiavellianism and leadership." *Journal of Applied Psychology,* 65 (1980), 81–86.

Fairhurst, Gail T., and Teresa A. Chandler. "Social structure in leader–member interaction." *Communication Monographs,* 56, (Sept. 1989).

Fiedler, F. E. *A Theory of Leadership Effectiveness.* New York: McGraw-Hill, 1967.

Fiedler, F. E. "The trouble with leadership training is that it doesn't train leaders." *Psychology Today* (February 1973), 23–26, 29–30, 92–93.

Fink, L. "Ad agency is target of angry women's groups." *City Business,* (December 28, 1987), 1, 17.

French, J. R. P., Jr., and B. Raven. "The bases of social power." In *Group Dynamics,* 2nd ed. Ed. D. Cartwright and A. Zander. Evanston, Ill.: Row, Peterson, 1960, pp. 607–623.

Gardner, John W. "The moral aspects of leadership." *NASSP Bulletin,* Jan. 1989, 43.

Gardner, John W. "Leader–Constituent Interaction." *NASSP Bulletin,* Nov. 1988, 61.

Gibb, C. A. "Leadership." *Handbook of Social Psychology,* 2 (1954), 877–920.

Goldman, M., and L. A. Fraas. "The effects of leader selection on group performance." *Sociometry,* 28, No. 1 (1965), 82–88.

Golembiewski, R. T. *The Small Group.* Chicago, Ill.: University of Chicago Press, 1962.

Goktepe, J. R. and C. E. Schneier. "Role of sex, gender roles, and attraction in predicting emergent leaders." *Journal of Applied Psychology,* 74, No. 1 (1989) 165–167.

Gray, L. N., J. T. Richardson, and R. H. Mayhew, Jr. "Influence attempts and effective power: A re-examination of an unsubstantiated hypothesis." *Sociometry,* 31, No. 1 (1968), 245–258.

Guyer, B. P. "The relationship among selected variables and the effectiveness of discussion leaders." *Dissertation Abstracts International,* 39, No. 2A (1978), 697–698.

Hall, J., and M. S. Williams. "Personality and group encounter style: A multivariate analysis of traits and preference." *Journal of Personality and Social Psychology,* 18 (1971), 163–172.

Harragan, B. L., "The $10 million blunder." *Working Women,* (May 1988), 94–98.

Heider, John. *The Tao of Leadership: Leadership Strategies for a New Age.* New York: Bantam Books, 1985.

Hersey, P., and K. H. Blanchard. "Life-cycle theory of leadership." *Training and Development Journal,* 23, No. 5 (1969), 26–34.

Hersey, P., and K. H. Blanchard. "A situational framework for determining appropriate leader behavior." In *Leadership Development: Theory and Practice.* Ed. R. N. Cassel and R. L. Heichberger. North Quincy, Mass.: The Christopher Publishing House, 1975, pp. 126–155.

Hersey, P., and K. H. Blanchard. *Management of Organizational Behavior: Utilizing Human Resources.* Englewood Cliffs, N.J.: Prentice-Hall, 1977, pp. 106–107, 162–183, 307–324.

Hoffman, L. R., R. J. Burke, and N. R. F. Maier. "Participation, influence, and satisfaction among members of problem-solving groups." *Psychological Reports,* 16 (1965), 661–667.

Holloman, C. R. "Leadership and headship: There is a difference." *Personnel Administration,* 31, No. 4 (1968), 38–44.

Howell, Jane M., and Christopher A. Higgins. "Champions of technological innovation." *Administrative Science Quarterly,* 35 (1990), 317–341.

Julian, J. W., E. P. Hollander, and C. R. Regula. "Endorsement of the group spokesman as a function of his source of authority, competence, and success." *Journal of Personality and Social Psychology,* 11, No. 1 (1969), 42–49.

Kahn, R., and D. Katz. *The Social Psychology of Organizations.* New York: John Wiley and Sons, 1966.

Kanter, R. M. *The Changemasters.* New York: Simon and Schuster, 1983.

Kellerman, B. *Leadership: Multidisciplinary Perspectives.* Englewood Cliffs, N.J.: Prentice Hall, 1984.

Kenny, D., A. L. Zaccaro, and J. Stephen. "An estimate of variance due to traits in leadership." *Journal of Applied Psychology,* 68, No. 4 (Nov. 1983), 678–685.

Kipnis, I. "Does power corrupt?" *Journal of Personality and Social Psychology,* 24 (1972), 33–41.

Koch, J. L. "Managerial succession in a factory and changes in supervisory leadership patterns: A field study." *Human Relations,* 31 (1978), 49–58.

Korman, A. K. "Consideration," "Initiating structure," and "Organizational criteria—A review." *Personnel Psychology: A Journal of Applied Research,* No. 4 (Winter 1966), 349–361.

Kotter, J. *The Leadership Factor.* Glenview, Ill.: Free Press, 1988.

Kraus, George, and Gary Gemmill. "Idiosyncratic effects of implicit theories of leadership." *Psychological Reports,* 66 (1990), 247–257.

Lee, Chris. "Followship—The essence of leadership." *Training,* Jan. 1991, 27–35.

Lewin, K., R. Lippitt, and R. K. White. "Patterns of aggressive behavior in experimentally created social climates." *Journal of Social Psychology,* 10 (1939), 271–299.

Lippitt, R., N. A. Polansky, and S. Rosen. "The dynamics of power: A field study of social influence in groups of children." *Human Relations,* 5 (1952), 37–64.

Mann, R. D. "A review of the relationships between personality and performance in small groups." *Psychological Bulletin,* 56 (1959), 241–270.

Maslow, A. H. *Motivation and Personality.* New York: Harper & Row, 1954.

McCauley, Cynthia D., Michael M. Lombardo, and Claire J. Usher. "Diagnosing management development needs: An instrument based on how managers develop." *Journal of Management,* 15, No. 3 (1989), 389–401.

McDavid, J. W., and H. Harari. *Social Psychology.* New York: Harper & Row, 1968.

McGregor, D. *The Human Side of Enterprise.* New York: McGraw-Hill, 1960.

Miller, A. "A Donnybrook in the Ad World" *Newsweek,* 111 (January 18, 1988), 55.

Mintzberg, Henry. "Crafting strategy." In *On Management.* Cambridge, Mass.: Harvard Business School, 1976, pp. 25–42.

Mulder, M. "Power equalization through participation." *Administrative Science Quarterly,* 16 (1971), 31–38.

Murphy, Jerome T. "The unheroic side of leadership: Notes from the swamp." *Phi Delta Kappan,* 1988, 654–659.

Myers, Marvin R., Michael J. Slavin, and W. Thomas Southern. "Emergence and maintenance of leadership among gifted students in group problem solving." *Roeper Review,* 12, No. 4, 256–260.

Naisbitt, J. *Megatrends.* New York: Warner, 1982.

O'Brien, G. "Effects of organizational structure, leadership style, and members' compatibility upon small group creativity." *Proceedings of 76th Annual Convention.* Washington, D.C.: American Psychological Association, 1969.

Ouchi, W. J. *Theory Z.* Reading, Mass.: Addison-Wesley, 1981.

Peters, T. J., and R. H. Waterman, Jr. *In Search of Excellence.* New York: Harper & Row, 1982.

Polansky, N. A., R. Lippitt, and F. Redl. "The use of near-sociometric data in research on group treatment processes." *Sociometry,* 13 (1950), 39–62.

Petzel, Thomas P., James E. Johnson, and Linda Bresolin. "Peer nominations of leadership and likability in problem-solving groups as a function of gender and task." *The Journal of Social Psychology,* 130, No. 5 (1990), 641–648.

Prigogine, I. *Order Out of Chaos.* New York: Bantam, 1984.

Reddin, W. *Managerial Effectiveness.* New York: McGraw-Hill, Inc., 1970.

Richardson, J. T., J. R. Dugan, L. N. Gray and B. H. Mayher. "Expert power: A behavioral interpretation." *Sociometry,* 36 (1973), 302–324.

Rieken, H. W., and G. C. Homans. "Psychological aspects of social structure." In *Handbook of Social Psychology,* Vol. II. Ed. G. Lindzey. Reading, Mass.: Addison-Wesley, 1954, pp. 786–832.

Rouche, John E., George A. Baker, III, and Robert R. Rose. *Shared Vision (Transformational Leadership in American Community Colleges)* Washington, D.C.: Community College Press, 1989.

Rubin, J. Z., and R. J. Lewicki. "A three-factor experimental analysis of promises and threats." *Journal of Applied Social Psychology,* 3 (1973), 240–257.

Rubin, J. Z., C. T. Mowbray, L. Collette, and R. J. Lewicki. "Perception of attempts at interpersonal influence." *Proceedings of the 79th Annual Convention of the AOA,* 6 (1971), 391–392.

Sanders, G., and F. Malkis. "Type A behavior, need for control, and reactions to group participation." *Organizational Behavior and Human Performance,* 30 (1982), 71–86.

Sargent, J. F., and G. R. Miller. "Some differences in certain communication behaviors of autocratic and democratic group leaders." *Journal of Communication,* 21 (1971), 233–252.

Schein, E. H. *Process Consultation.* Reading, Mass.: Addison-Wesley, 1969.

Scontrino, M. P. "The effects of fulfilling and violating group members' expectations about leadership style." *Organizational Behavior and Human Performance,* 8 (1972), 118–138.

Senge, Peter M. "The Leader's New Work: Building Learning Organizations." *Sloan Management Review,* Fall 1990, 7–23.

Senge, Peter M. *The Fifth Discipline. The Art and Practice of the Learning Organization.* Garden City, N.Y.: Doubleday, 1990.

Smith, R. J., and P. E. Cook. "Leadership dyadic groups as a function of dominance and incentives." *Sociometry,* 36, No. 4 (1973).

Sorrentino, Richard M. "An extension of achievement motivation theory to the study of emergent leadership." *Journal of Personality and Social Psychology,* 26 (June 1973), 356–368.

Spillane, R. "Authority in small groups: A laboratory test of a Machiavellian observation." *British Journal of Social Psychology,* 22 (1983), 51–59.

Spooner, P. "Telling managers some home truths." *Chief Executive* (U. K.), (Feb. 1984), 25–26.

Stang, D. J. "The effect of interaction rate on ratings of leadership and liking." *Journal of Personality and Social Psychology,* 27 (1973), 405–408.

Stogdill, R. M. *Handbook of Leadership: A Survey of Theory and Research.* New York: Free Press, 1974.

Sudolsky, M., and R. Nathan. "A replication in questionnaire form of an experiment by Lippitt, Lewin, and White concerning conditions of leadership and social climates in groups." *Cornell Journal of Social Relations,* 6 (1971), 188–196.

Terry, R. "The leading edge." *Minnesota,* (Jan.–Feb. 1987), 17–22.

Thomas, Alan Berkeley. "Does leadership make a difference to organizational performance? The leadership–performance debate." *Administrative Science Quarterly,* 33 (1988), 388–400.

Toffler, A. *Future Shock.* New York: Random House, 1970.

Townsend, R. *Up the Organization.* New York: Fawcett, 1970.

Uhlir, Ann G. "Leadership and gender." *Academe,* Jan.–Feb. 1989, 29–32.

Vacc, N. A. "Cognitive complexity: A dimension of leadership behavior." In *Leadership Development.* Ed. R. N. Cassel and R. L. Heichberger. North Quincy, Mass.: The Christopher Publishing House, 1975, pp. 278–288.

Vecchio, Robert P. "Theoretical and empirical examination of cognitive resource theory." *Journal of Applied Psychology,* 75, No. 2 (1990), 141–147.

White, R., and R. Lippitt. "Leader behavior and member reaction in three social climates." In *Group Dynamics.* 3rd ed. Ed. D. Cartwright and A. Zander. New York: Harper & Row, 1968.

Zigon, F. J., and J. R. Cannon. "Process and outcomes of group discussions as related to leader behaviors." *Journal of Educational Research,* 67 (1974), 199–201.

◆ 6 ◆

A Systems View of Small Group Behavior

G roups, like people, are fascinating because of their diversity, their lack of predictability, and the variations they play on so many themes. Despite these variations, though, people seem naturally to seek order and simple, understandable interpretations of complex phenomena. We feel more comfortable with the familiar and easily recognizable. As a result, we are forever creating theories to make sense of our experience.

To Friesen (1985), a theory is a mental model or map to help us perceive reality. Theories provide structure that helps us bring order to the information we take in. Most often, especially in the social sciences, a theory evolves gradually and is based on values, experience, goals, empirical research, and, of course, other theories. A theory is not necessarily "true" but is taken as a well-intentioned effort to explain events. Two theories may explain the same phenomenon in two entirely different ways and may exist side by side for years until one is finally accepted over the other. The origin of the universe, for instance, has given rise to many diverse theories, as has the movement of land masses and the causes of depression in human beings.

To be useful, a theory must relate the basic concepts, assumptions, and hypotheses associated with the phenomenon it addresses in a manner that is both logical and consistent. As Friesen notes, a theory must be applicable to many situations while still maintaining internal consistency. And a theory must be testable in accordance with the scientific method. It must help make sense of the phenomenon—an event or behavior we have observed—by helping us sort out and categorize our observations and come to some conclusion.

General systems theory provides a structure and vocabulary that illuminate much that happens in small groups. It is useful in helping us comprehend the nature of certain events at the national, organizational, and individual levels.

General Systems Theory and Behavior in Organized Settings

Cause-and-effect relationships have preoccupied Western scientists since the beginning of the scientific age. The result of this dominant view has been a rather "mechanistic" approach to science that has had a powerful influence on our understanding of both the physiology and the psychology of human beings. In medicine, for instance, this approach would lead a doctor to treat a particular symptom (such as pain or nausea) by removing it in the simplest, most direct manner possible. The removal of the symptom would signify the cure of the patient. Nowadays, with cause-and-effect giving way somewhat to more holistic perspectives on illness, we consider such a view simplistic and sometimes even counterproductive to determining the real problem. We know that a tumor in one part of the body can create stress or pain in another, chemical imbalances, or sleep disturbances.

Further, we have learned that physical and emotional stress can induce a wide range of physical ailments, and that eliminating a symptom in such a case in no way addresses the cause.

Not until the 1940s was any attempt to change our purely mechanistic thinking taken seriously. It has not been easy to wean ourselves from our simplistic causal mentality and to adopt a more holistic approach. After all, viewing the whole and acknowledging the possibility of multiple causes of phenomena render human behavior much more complex. At the same time, however, focusing on interrelatedness makes life much more understandable.

Ludwig von Bertalanffy (1968), a biologist, was the first to create a theory that enabled us to see the significance of interrelationships in the functioning of the total organism or system. He summarized his remarkable approach this way:

> The basic assumptions of our traditions and the persistent implications of the language we use almost compel us to approach everything we study as composed of separate, discrete parts or factors which we must try to isolate and identify as potential causes. Hence, we derive our preoccupation with the study of the relation of two variables. (p. 16)

He went on:

> While in the past, science tried to explain observable phenomena by reducing them to an interplay of elementary units investigated independently of each other, conceptions appear in contemporary science that are concerned with what is somewhat vaguely termed with "wholeness," i.e. problems of organization, phenomena not dissolvable into local events, dynamic interactions manifested in the difference of behavior of parts. (pp. 36, 37)

Von Bertalanffy opened gates in all the sciences, but in the social sciences he triggered a revolution in thinking that continues today. The mode of thinking he described was called *systems theory*.

For our purposes, we will define a *system* as a set of interrelated elements or units that respond in a predictable manner and where the nature of the interaction is consistent over time. Thus, a change at any one point will eventually have an impact on the total system and upon its various subparts.

Applying "Systemthink"

One of the authors recounts the following story to demonstrate the impact of systems theory:

> Some years ago, while attending a training program, I met Jim, a likable, articulate professor from a major western university who, like myself, had

come to learn more about the nature of group dynamics. As members of an intense support group, Jim and I and the other participants were encouraged to learn as much as possible about each other, our family backgrounds, and our personal ambitions, goals, strengths, and weaknesses. Once we gained knowledge and began to trust each other, the stories that each member told were touching, humorous, sad, and joyous. The fact that barriers began to slip away and we each allowed ourselves to be "known" gave the group great energy and a sense of significance.

One evening, Jim took a deep breath and said, "The truth is that even after all we've shared and been through together, you don't know me at all, and it's important that you do if this process is not going to be a farce and a lie for me and you." To say that we were shocked and curious is an understatement, since by this time we had all shared an enormous amount of information. Jim went on to tell us about his loving childhood on a Pennsylvania Dutch farm, where his mother had devoted her life to nurturing, supporting, and feeding her family. Eating her luscious homemade breads, cakes, and pies was one way people had of expressing their thanks and appreciation for her devoted love. And feed them she did with joy and abundance. By the time the six-foot-tall Jim left home for college, he weighed more than 350 pounds.

We gasped, since before us was an athletically fit 175-pounder. Jim went on to say that barely six months ago he had weighed 320 pounds even though he had dieted for years. Part of the problem, he told us, was that whenever he began to lose weight and returned home, his mother would shriek that her poor boy was wasting away without her home cooking, and she would feed him "back to normal." Jim also discovered that he used food as a source of personal affirmation when he doubted himself or felt lonely.

Though he had not been able to lose weight, Jim had become quite successful as a professor and research fellow and had a satisfying professional life. He was also happily married and had a thriving social life. In fact, many of his most endearing qualities were those of the stereotype— the jovial, good-natured, compliant fat man, a well-liked encourager who was always there when needed.

Still, Jim knew that his obesity was a threat to his physical health. It kept him tired and played havoc with his own self-concept, especially since he knew he suffered not from a physical problem but rather from a lack of discipline and will power.

Finally, Jim met a health specialist who guaranteed him weight loss if he changed his "eating-for-affection lifestyle" and combined a normal diet with regular daily exercise for six months. The Jim we saw was the product of this agreement. We in the group were awed and filled with questions when he passed around a picture of his "old self," showing some embarrassment at the uncomfortable laughter with which each person responded. How did he like his new self? What did his wife and friends think? Were there consequences for his work and social life? He tackled each question patiently as if carefully protecting a still-tender wound.

To our surprise, the results of his effort had been nearly catastrophic. It was only the valiant support of his wife and his personal desire for physical health that kept him from returning to his old fat-and-happy self. In fact, he had just resigned his position at the university and was about to begin a new job several thousand miles from his old home. Somehow he had lost the support of his colleagues and many of his friends, and at this point he wasn't even sure whether he liked himself or not.

The information did not match our expectations at all. We thought he would report joy and affirmation at his obvious success and were aghast that this thoroughly witty, energetic, intelligent, and supportive person could have experienced such devastating consequences just by losing weight.

◆ Reader Activity

Consider major changes you have experienced at various times in your life. What unanticipated consequences resulted that influenced your family or work "systems"?   ◆

The Complex Consequences of System Change

Jim's need to alter *his own* system (his body) resulted in a variety of unanticipated consequences. First, his "soft," compliant image was replaced by the image of a handsome, athletic man who was attractive to many and had become a threat to some. Second, Jim suddenly had considerably more energy and drive than before; he needed less sleep, was able to work longer, and as a result could produce more. He responded more efficiently to challenges and generally felt more motivated and enthusiastic about his work. His increased desire to publish altered the delicate balance between competitiveness and personal achievement in his department, and some of his colleagues became annoyed and even jealous of his newfound confidence. He became aware of a constant stream of such statements as, "I just don't know who you are anymore," or "You're so driven lately, it's almost as though you've become a workaholic," or "What happened to the old happy-go-lucky Jim?" Quite simply, Jim had disrupted the balance in his work group system (of which he was a part, or subsystem). He was generating unwanted competition and resentment while reducing the amount of humor, goodwill, and support available to the group. The emergence of his new, slimmer self was like the sudden appearance of a new and unwanted rival on the scene. Everyone had to adjust whether they liked it or not—and many did not.

The work system was in turmoil, and many individuals within it made strong efforts to return it to the old levels of comfort and expectation by somehow attempting to sabotage the new Jim. But this was difficult, because Jim was less compliant now and less easily manipulated. He had spent years "feeding his colleagues" by supporting them and complying with their wishes in order to gain their acceptance; it was the style he had learned in his family. His mother would feed the family in order to gain appreciation, and Jim would obediently eat whether he was hungry or not. In his work system, he himself would feed the group—with humor, service, and support—for which he was given love and acceptance in return. But his tolerance for this behavior vanished along with his excess weight. Needless to say, his new impatience—with his old ways and those of the group— left him increasingly alienated and isolated within the group itself.

Jim felt himself being rejected from the group almost as though he were a transplanted heart being rejected by a body. What appeared to be a rather simple and positive isolated event (the loss of 145 pounds) had created disruption not in one system alone but in a multitude of systems: his body, his work group, his social community, his nuclear family, and his extended family.

At the new university—where he was hired for his energy, assertiveness, and leadership, the very qualities that were threatening to his former peers—he was accepted easily and he adjusted without problems. In this case, the old system was not thrown out of balance (*equilibrium* in systems terminology) by his arrival, because his presence filled a critical gap in the organization that had prevented its effective functioning and had created a certain imbalance (disequilibrium). Jim's troubles and his eventual resolution of them might seem mystifying from the single cause–single effect viewpoint, but a systems approach accounts for all the consequences he related.

General-systems-theory thinking—the mode of thinking that involves viewing a particular problem not in isolation, but as the problem is connected to, and therefore interrelated with, other problems—is new and complex. When Jim recounted his successful weight loss, the group members' expectations were shattered. Jim's weight loss, instead of resulting in joy and self-satisfaction, led to his resigning from his job, moving far away from his home, losing his colleagues' support, and doubting himself. While viewing causes as a whole, systems theory specifically necessitates thinking about the individual as a part of many systems and thinking about the emotional–cognitive process as a system. General systems theory can greatly enhance our understanding of the diversity that people and groups exhibit. It encourages the explanation, description, and clarification of individual and group dynamics. Thus the systems theory approach may represent the expansion of our concept of group dynamics to include complex social interactions, such as meetings of political heads of state (Konigwieser and Pelikan, 1990).

Developing a Systems Perspective

There is nothing difficult about thinking and observing from a systems point of view, but systems thinking does demand that we ask questions of consequence about the impact of a given event on the parts of any group. It is common knowledge that people who are able to predict the consequences of an action make the best problem solvers and that this skill, in turn, can increase their effectiveness as leaders.

In a group, a keen awareness in both members and leaders of the predictable consequences of a particular action will yield an array of alternatives from which an effective response can be chosen. For example, when Michelle is depressed or sullen, her group's natural response is to try to cheer her up with upbeat talk and positive conversation about the weather or life in general. If over time the members had realized, however, that this particular system response seemed to generate in Michelle a feeling of inadequacy ("If everything is so great, why do I feel so miserable? I must really be a mess.") and actually *reinforced* the downward emotional spiral, they might have chosen a response that had a more positive system impact.

Though it would not be difficult to notice the impact of Michelle's depression on herself and the group, it would take discipline for the group to avoid making the one-cause/one-effect response and to choose one based on a full awareness of the system. Systems thinking demands that groups sharpen their observations and quite often become more creative and sensitive.

The Invisible Group

If you have ever attempted to build a house of cards, you know that no matter how patient you are, how careful your effort, or how stable the house may appear, it could collapse at any moment for a wide variety of reasons. The more complex the house, the more possible causes of collapse. Many such reasons will not be observable to the naked eye—a sudden draft or breeze, for instance, or an unanticipated vibration, a misplaced card, a slight imbalance, even a loud noise. In a similar fashion, what appears to the untrained eye to be going on in groups may have nothing to do with the actual success or failure of the group.

For years, small groups were seen as nothing more than a collection of individuals, and a group's success or failure was viewed as related to the impact of certain individuals on the group. If a problem existed, the usual mode of operation was to find the "problem individual" and "fix" him or her. This approach is still used in classrooms, office groups, families, and on sports teams. The group ignores the impact of individual behavior on the *system,* because the participants and leaders are simply not trained to observe in that manner. Thus, in the case of Jim, his weight loss was not perceived as a problem, even though it was the inability of the group to deal effectively with the consequences of his weight loss on many of its established norms, goals, and membership issues that was generating the difficulties.

Agazarian and Peters (1981), in their fascinating publication *The Visible and*

Invisible Group, explore in depth group phenomena that occur commonly in any group and that are lost to observers who focus exclusively on individuals. Their work reinforces the idea that the system of a small group is much more than individual behaviors coming together at one point. By understanding systems, one is much better able to understand the impact of norms, membership, goals, communication patterns, and leadership (authority and influence) on the behavior and expectations of the group. Sorting through the activity that goes on in this "invisible group" yields clues to what is really happening at any given time. It also gives us some understanding of what must occur for the group to mature.

Kurt Lewin (1951) developed a goal-oriented systems view of a group in which he literally "mapped out" a group's progress toward a particular goal, showing the barriers that had to be overcome for success to be possible. To Lewin, there were many paths to the same goal, some where the resistances or barriers to success were increased and some where they were minimized. As Lewin saw it, the job for any group is to discover the most efficient and productive route to the goal, which in the language of Agazarian and Peters's "invisible group" requires some understanding of such potential barriers as

- individual goals versus group goals
- norms blocking effectiveness
- individuals feeling lack of membership
- ineffective communication patterns

Because solving one problem could create others, Lewin showed that it is necessary to perceive the group in the context of the *whole,* one of the underlying principles of Gestalt psychology.

Lewin's point of view fits nicely with von Bertalanffy's general systems theory, which stresses the interrelationship of all parts to the total system and the impact of any act on all of those parts. In Lewin's terms (Agazarian and Peters, 1981, p. 36), an observer must grasp the total *life space* of a group to understand fully the events that occur in that group.

The implications of the developments in general systems theory and its relationship to group dynamics, psychiatry, and family therapy have recently gained in importance. Specifically, the focus of psychoanalytic thinking is the difference between the group dynamics approach, or viewing the group as a whole, and the systems theory approach. In Lewin's terms, this is the total *life space* of the group. For instance, Wimmer (1990) views recent developments in systems theory as beneficial because they " . . . add to an understanding of group dynamics as a social and historical phenomenon." An innovative way to describe the relationship between group dynamics and systems theory is captured in the title of Krainz's (1990) journal article "Alter Wein in Neuen Schlauchen? . . ." ("Old wine in new flasks?") The old wine symbolizes group dynamics sheathed in a new, larger container: systems theory. Use of the general systems theory approach seems to be whittling away at the boundaries of "old" group dynamics.

◆ *Reader Activity*

Identify a life goal you currently have. Explore the "barriers" in your life space that could keep you from achieving your goal. Pay particular attention to how the barriers are related to each other and how addressing one barrier could affect the others.   ◆

The Case of the Misplaced Nightcaps

Lewin's view of life space can be applied to a maturing individual or a small group or even a nation attempting to move toward some set goals. A story drawn from the history of China's early contact with the West offers a good example of how the systems approach can clarify understanding. In 1840, shortly after the British presence was first felt in China, a British merchant became convinced that there was a potentially huge market for nightcaps among the Chinese. Even if he convinced only a small percentage of China's 200 million men of the merits of sleeping with a nightcap, he believed, he could easily become very wealthy. As a good entrepreneur, he saw a scarce supply of a proven product as the key to his fortune. Thus he sold his personal assets, borrowed from friends and relatives, and shipped a large supply of nightcaps to his waiting population. The poor man's dream crumbled when he sold nary a one. He had failed to identify the barriers within his own life space to his goal of wealth and good fortune. These included

1. the lack of words to even explain the concept of *nightcap* in Chinese
2. no easily explainable benefits for people who had slept capless for thousands of years
3. no established network for selling nightcaps (or, for that matter, anything else) in China

Had this man understood the system and the barriers to reaching his goal, it is likely that he would have arrived at a different goal.

Organizational Systems and Issues of Culture[1]

Not long ago, an executive came to us with a problem. He had been hired by a unique board to help develop a new manufacturing organization that was to create several high-tech products and introduce them into competitive world markets.

---

1. "Here the term *culture* refers to the behavior patterns of an organization in which newly adopted corporate values are instilled by senior management who are involved in the structuring and managing of that organization." (Deal and Kennedy, 1982; Peters and Waterman, 1982).

The board was creating this small entrepreneurial company of perhaps a hundred people by drawing on some of the best product developers and researchers working at two huge high-tech conglomerates that considered the new products potentially beneficial to themselves. The anticipated reduction in the lag time between concept and production was considerable, given the energy, talent, and simplicity of the small new organization.

The president and his key managers sincerely wanted to incorporate the best that was known about "new management" so that productivity (task efficiency and quality) and the morale of the workers (the maintenance or process dimension) would reflect the latest information on effective management. They also appeared to have a realistic understanding of the amount of time and the depth of commitment such an ambitious goal would require from them.

For us, this was a rare opportunity to bring together, at the very beginning of an organization's life, much of what we had spent years learning. It was agreed that our first step would be to gather information from those already in the organization concerning their view of their new organization and to discover from them what their ideal might be like. Accordingly, we gathered information from the 100 or so individuals who had come together at a common work site (50 from one parent organization, 30 from the other, and 20 hired from the outside). The views of these individuals were quite consistent with those of the key leaders. Their areas of agreement included the following:

Areas of Agreement

1. *"Open" communication*   They desired "open" communication. This encompassed an interest in having important information, data, and events available to members of the organization and not held in secret, as was often the case in the large bureaucracies from which many had come. Furthermore, they expressed a desire for two-way communication, which suggested that they hoped their ideas, feelings, and concerns would be actively solicited by those in positions of authority and that management would make timely responses to them.
2. *Nonhierarchical organization*   They hoped to maintain a rather flat, or nonhierarchical, organization in which people would be respected for their contributions and treated as equals. Further, they wanted few titles or other means of making "class" distinctions within the system.
3. *Problem solving with participation*   Many expressed the hope that problems influencing their lives in the organization would be solved with their participation—at least their input, but ideally their active involvement. They suggested that whenever possible, problems should be solved at the point in the organization where those having to live with the consequences would be the most highly involved.

4. *Desire for real "community"*   There was a desire for a sense of real "community" and for the development of teams around projects in the work setting, wherever possible.

5. *Balance between work and family*   Finally, the employees hoped that a balance could be found between work and family time.

Although those interviewed mentioned other conditions, this handful of desires stood out. Management agreed that such goals were certainly in its best interest and promised to promote them actively during the coming year.

From the Lewinian point of view, the life space of the organization was to be framed by these fairly specific goals, and steps would be taken to help make them a reality. However, a life space involves much more than goals; it also encompasses the potential barriers to reaching them. It took several months of our consultancy for us to realize that the new organization was *already* a complex system and that efforts to reach one of the goals created new barriers to the achievement of others. What appeared to be simple, straightforward, and ultimately reachable goals turned out to be a mine field of norms, personal goals, issues of authority, and habits of communication that posed huge problems on the road to solution. The following is a list of some of the barriers we identified within the life space of the new organization:

Barriers

1. *Tension resulting from divergent leadership styles*   It became readily apparent that the two cultures from which most of the members of the organization had come were very different and clashed in many ways. Though both firms were successful in their own fields, one had democratic/participative management, and the other was run as a conglomeration of project-based benevolent autocracies, where responsibility, control, and leadership were held tightly by specified leaders. It is not surprising that these two divergent views of leadership created tensions from the outset.

2. *Differing personal motives and ambitions*   The idealistic view that everyone was there as part of a team to develop a new community was shattered almost immediately. People came from the two parent organizations for an array of different reasons. Some came simply to escape the complex bureaucracies. Feeling "lost in the line" was common to many, and they were drawn by the opportunity to identify with a small, community-based organization. Others came in rebellion at the authority of the large system and were dedicated to the idea that decision making and problem solving would be shared. A good number simply wanted to be left alone to work in peace, not burdened by the responsibilities and expectations of a more complex system. A few

simply couldn't get along with their bosses or had somehow dug a hole in the organization that was difficult to climb out of and found it easier to start afresh somewhere else. Finally, some saw the small organization as a source of real opportunity for advancement and creativity. Common to all these individuals was the fact that they had volunteered for their new positions and had been competitively selected. The result was a highly heterogeneous organization driven by the energies of individuals who had quite different personal motives and ambitions as well as different views of what the organization should be.

3. *Predictable burnout*   By the time the organization was six months old, a view of its place in the world of work had already been established. Within the firm, success seemed to be defined as everyone pitching in and solving one crisis situation after another. Loyalty and recognition were both seen as the measures of people's willingness to put themselves out for the organization. Because one of the norms was not to complain—certainly never about the time spent in fulfilling work responsibilities—the predictable burnout of talented and well-motivated people was already clearly etched on the horizon.

4. *Failure to achieve desired balance between work and family*   Because no boundaries were placed on people's time, and success was partly measured by the degree to which people were willing to give time, the desired balance between family and work life was never achieved. Obviously, a gap existed between people's expressed values and the behavior the organization rewarded.

5. *Nonhierarchical organization only an ideal*   People professed a desire for a nonhierarchical organization, but developing rules were already differentiating people on the bases of type of job, amount of pay, special privileges, the distribution of profit sharing, and other rewards. Equality in concept but not fact was fast becoming the reality.

6. *Despite Promises, Arbitrary Decisions*   The fast pace of the developing organization had already shut down lines of communication and had resulted in what appeared to be arbitrary decisions made by the very people who professed a desire for collaboration and participation. This set poorly with those who had left their parent organizations because they sought involvement in the issues that affected their lives. Signs of open hostility toward some of the leadership were already surfacing.

7. *Norm against formal supervision reexamined*   A strong norm in the organization existed from the beginning against specific and formal supervision. Somehow the expectation arose that employees (many of whom were engineers or specialists) hired for their technical competence and maturity could be expected to accomplish their work without much "hands on" supervision. This compelling argument clashed with the considerable differences in the quality of performance and

failed to acknowledge such indirect aspects of supervision as performance standards, career development, education, and training.

8. *Negative attitude towards training* The two parent organizations
had spent enormous amounts of time and money on leader and management training over the years, but the concepts espoused in the
training were not often modeled in the organization itself. As a result,
participants came away with a negative attitude toward almost any kind
of training at all. In the new firm, an assumption prevailed that people
had the requisite skills because at one time they had taken the training.
But the fact was that few had had the opportunity to practice or internalize the skills they had learned, and their expertise existed more in
name than in substance. Thus the organization tended to act as though
it were humane, collaborative, and open as a result of good leadership
training—when in fact it modeled a limited amount of these behaviors.

9. *"Communities" versus time spent on production* Finally, "communities" evolve through participants' hard work and willingness to
devote time and effort to both the task/product and the process/main-
tenance dimensions. In this organization, time was spent on production
only, and as a result any sense of community was a long way from
reality.

These were but a few of the barriers in the life space of this newly formed
system. Addressing any one proved to have consequences for the others. In such
a system, solutions are possible, but a naive belief that intelligent people, good
intentions, and clear goals will eventually lead to success spells certain failure. The
complex and interrelated issues in such a system must be choreographed as carefully as any complex dance. Planners must anticipate these realities and map out
resistances and barriers. Leaders must educate themselves in the complexity of
their own system and the need for integrated strategies. As in any successful therapy,
taking possession of the problem is the first big step required; next comes forging
a clear understanding of the implications of the problem for all parts of the system.
Only then can effective problem solving begin.

Background of Organizational Culture as a Concept

The idea of an organizational culture is fairly new. In fact, it has been largely
ignored in psychoanalytic literature; roles, norms, and values in the social psychology of organizations have received much more attention. In the 1950s and
1960s, the study of organizational psychology began to distinguish itself from industrial psychology by focusing on groups instead of individuals (Bass, 1965; Schein,
1965). As the focus shifted from individuals to groups, whole organizations emerged.

Now the focus was on groups and entire organizations, which were viewed as a system. This system was understood to encompass the total social unit: individuals, individuals in groups, and individuals in groups within organizations. Katz and Kahn (1966) developed their analysis of organizations around systems theory, and the new term *systems dynamics* was coined. This provided the important theoretical foundation for thinking about organizational culture.

Definition of Organizational Culture

The concept of an organizational culture rests on the assumption that people, living together, have had time to form common traditions, rites, and history. Out of these commonalities, a culture has emerged. That culture is binding in the sense that it determines how people learn to survive, learn to live together, and learn to solve problems in such a way that their culture is upgraded (in their minds) and maintained. This learning is continually occurring, whether consciously or unconsciously, and regardless of the quality of the problem-solving decisions being made to uphold the culture. And, of course, the machinations it takes to form and preserve a culture may or may not be viewed as right or just by other people. The term *organizational culture* denotes whatever ideations are dominant and operating in any given group or nation, for it is these ideations that continuously feed and sustain the ever-emerging organism called culture.

The Vocabulary of General Systems Theory[2]

As stated earlier, our goal in this chapter is to present a new way of thinking about groups by reducing the dependence on cause-and-effect relationships and emphasizing the relationship of the parts to the whole. To help in this effort, we introduce a number of concepts here that enable us to describe systems with some consistency. To bring concrete references to these terms and concepts, we use them to explore a real-life small group as it attempts to define itself within the context of a larger group system.

Most systems, in addition to existing as a collection of interdependent parts, are also parts of larger systems in which they are necessary units or subsystems. Thus any individual in a system is also usually part of a number of group systems, which in turn are parts of large organizations, and so on. The interrelationships among

2. This section represents an effort to integrate the views of many contributors to the field of systems theory, including Agazarian, Alderfer, Friesen, Goldenberg, Prochaska, von Bertalanffy, and Wilden.

multiple system organizations can be complex indeed. One primary purpose of management is to create a workable and utilitarian structure in which various systems can operate smoothly, harmoniously, and efficiently.

The Case of "No Way, New Way"

The large parent system in this case is an insurance company directed by a distant group of senior officers whose primary concerns are bottom-line profits and who maintain a corporate image of beneficent paternalism. At the time described, the company was in a period of high growth related to both sales and fiscal belt tightening, and every dollar spent had to be justified by more than a dollar earned. As in many organizations of this type, support services never quite caught up to the increase in growth, so those in the trenches (such as underwriters, clerks, and secretaries) seemed to be forever overworked, underpaid, and unappreciated. At the same time, those generating sales and direct service to the client were paid well and recognized as the heroes of the organization.

One primary goal of those directing any large system is finding ways to make the subsystems more cost-effective. In this particular organization underwriters had to handle, rate, and bill for every policy sold, so they, along with ancillary, secretarial, and clerical staff, represented a constant-cost factor. The underwriters worked in a "Dickensian" pool of more than 100 desks where they pushed paper in a work environment that permitted their supervisors to oversee and control them easily. They had no privacy within the confines of their huge work "bin" and received little affirmation or support; rather, they were under constant pressure to complete the never-ending flow of paperwork generated by sales. As one might expect, the morale of the underwriters was low, and this was reflected in less than satisfactory productivity, considerable absenteeism, and rapid turnover.

The director of the underwriters had been asked to cut costs in the recent cash flow crunch and had attended a training program exploring the benefits of "autonomous work groups." These were simply small, interdependent teams of individuals who had related responsibilities for certain product goals. The idea was to give them specific goals and responsibilities and to allow them to direct themselves in most areas of their work lives as long as specified standards regarding both quality and productivity were maintained. Quite often, groups of this type are more productive, have a greater sense of purpose, and show lower rates of turnover, absenteeism, and down time than individuals working in isolation.

As in the case of the Chinese nightcap merchant, the director rushed home from his training with visions of the extraordinary benefits his department would reap from the new organizational structure. With little to lose, he immediately established an experimental group to test the concept. From a pool of volunteers, he selected a group of six underwriters, three clerks, and a secretary. He also matched them with a supervisor and assigned two days for team building. The supervisor had no formal instruction in autonomous work groups, team building, or group dynamics, but the manager arranged for her to have a brief orientation and a private screening of a film on the subject. The team, which was to be called the New Group, was given a separate work space marked off by portable 6-foot separators. This 30- × -30-foot alcove was about 100 feet from the other 90 or so underwriters, who remained in their "bin."

During their orientation, the New Group spent considerable time defining their own goals, ways to use each other, and ways to create a work flow process that would maintain productivity and ensure that they met the quality standards established for them. Management believed that if the New Group maintained the same standards as the larger group and if the experiment resulted in higher morale (and, as a result, in less turnover and absenteeism), then the program would be a success. Any increased efficiency would be considered a bonus.

The team members discovered immediately that they liked each other's company and that work was becoming "fun" again. The supervisor recognized this and gave the team plenty of free rein while providing support, minimal direction, and the clarification of policies, standards, and work expectations. Other than that, the group created its own roles, relationships, policies on the use of space, and work schedule.

Systems Note: In relation to general systems theory, the new autonomous work group fulfilled the definition of a *system,* because it remained associated with but independent of the other underwriters. It was a subsystem of the total organization, but its internal roles and functions were clear and interdependent, with each of its own subunits having a clear relationship to the whole. This meant it could operate with relative independence.

The New Group fulfilled the definition of an *open system.* Although it was predictable and consistent in how it managed its work and how it functioned with respect to the total organization, it remained responsive to the larger environment. It maintained a constant flow of information and kept its production free-flowing and functional with a clear goal-directed emphasis.

The members of the New Group were highly motivated and had an increasing desire to be effective for their own sakes. But they also realized they were a test case for the organization and wanted to prove that the small group atmosphere, with its focus on *team,* was a much better means of operating than the old bin system. Thus they were highly conscious of their own efforts. They monitored their own performance in daily meetings and constantly adjusted their work flow to increase their efficiency. In any such dynamic and open system, new influxes of energy, increasingly differentiated roles resulting in higher levels of performance, and a tendency toward increasing complexity and specialization may all be apparent. One might liken the group to a basketball team that over the years develops intricate patterns of play that the team members could not have even conceived during their initial work together. The New Group, with its growing abilities to communicate, give mutual support, and accept each other, showed increasing productivity even though its members were working at their own pace during hours they themselves chose. The group found itself with ever more free time while it still maintained high levels of productivity and quality.

Systems Note: Compare the New Group with a *closed system,* which tends to exhibit low levels of energy and to be static, lacking in innovation, and highly resistant to change. In theory, closed systems eventually shut down and die, because the ability to adapt—which they lack—is crucial whether in nature, business, or social systems. The concept of *adaptability* is useful. We know that non-adaptive human organizations become restrictive, inflexible, and resistant and that trouble inevitably ensues. Symptoms of such groups or organizations are often reflected in decreasing productivity and low morale. In our example, the 90 remaining underwriters in the bin had many symptoms of low morale. New ideas were virtually nonexistent, energy was low, conformity rather than innovation was the norm, and individual roles were much more isolated than in the New Group, where interdependence was the norm. Also, caution was much more the rule in the bin, where there was always more work than time available and little recognition for effort. Still, the larger system—the parent organization—was more open than some; it sought new ideas (for example, the autonomous work group) in order to increase efficiency and allow differentiation (as occurred in the New Group).

It is clear that it was the open communication channels and feedback mechanisms that enabled the New Group to achieve its high level of organization and sophistication. These, in turn, created a natural state of awareness, which enabled members to view adaptability as positive. Such a natural and highly productive mode is referred to as a *steady state* in systems terminology. It suggests the presence of a dynamic tension that allows for a healthy *disequilibrium* so that positive input and change beneficial to the system can occur with minimal disruption.

As the New Group became increasingly efficient, it allowed itself to take larger than "normal" breaks, to hold small celebrations, to meet to discuss members' problems and work relationships, and to take exercise breaks to maintain their physical health and high energy during the work day. Simultaneously, the supervisor, careful to keep too much of a good thing from ruining the group, distributed increasing amounts of work to the New Group—far surpassing the normal expectations of the underwriters performing laboriously in the bin. Group members received this additional work without complaint because it was clear to everyone that the New Group was thoroughly enjoying its autonomy and would never voluntarily return to the bin.

Systems Note: When a system is *closed,* there is a tendency for a certain degree of chaos or disorder to occur. In human systems, this results in the breakdown of communication, the loss of information, role confusion, and a general increase in organization. One might assume that an old, habituated system would exhibit fewer such conditions, but without new energy and ideas and healthy adaptations, this state of *entropy,* as it is called, tends to increase naturally. In organizations where tenure is prevalent and personnel turnover rare, intellectual stagnation is common and individuals tend to isolate themselves and pay increasingly less attention to the needs of the whole system. In such a context, *entropy* becomes a sort of "noise" that reduces the system's ability to function efficiently with optimal morale.

There was little entropy in the New Group. More characteristic, owing to the continued influence of new ideas and energy, was the state of *negentropy* typified by growth and development. In a state of negentropy, people are rewarded for new ideas and for the sharing of information, which in turn reinforces the healthy steady state of the system.

Systems Note: In theory, most groups and organizations show some signs of entropy and move over time toward some level of disorganization. In human organizations this process can be arrested, thanks to the human capacity to use new information and ideas and to respond to *feedback*. Removing *all* "noise" is difficult, but efforts to reorganize, sensitize, and integrate can have positive benefits, and ongoing sources of feedback can keep the system in a healthy balance. Quite simply, giving feedback is the process of providing specific information concerning the consequences of a particular action. Such information allows reaction to a particular event to return to the system to be studied and acted on. The physical body is full of feedback mechanisms—for example, too much heat triggers the onset of perspiration, which cools down the system.

In human groups, giving feedback sensitively is a challenge. Too often, the task is undertaken without sensitivity or skill; as a result, group members feel blamed or judged negatively, which can trigger defensiveness or denial rather than openness and acceptance. Still, feedback is our primary source of information on "how we're doing" (see Chapter 1). In theoretical terms, feedback is the information that permits the adjustments necessary to bring the system into *homeostasis*—that is, balance. All systems periodically get out of adjustment, and feedback is the built-in cycle or loop of information that allows for continual realignment. In organizational life, a lack of useful, descriptive feedback inhibits the ability to solve problems effectively and, if necessary, to reorganize.

For a time the New Group prospered. In systems terms, it was a healthy, open system, existing in a dynamic steady state with an overall homeostatic balance. The presence of negentropy proved that the system was responsive to its internal and external environments. The group received and appeared to be using feedback when necessary. In fact, the New Group seemed to be succeeding beyond anyone's wildest expectations, and two more autonomous groups were planned for the near future. Then disaster struck.

Systems Note: A system such as the New Group may run smoothly within its own sphere of influence, but if it creates conflict or stress in the life of the larger system, its own life may be threatened. In systems terms, if it throws the parent system out of equilibrium (out of homeostasis), that larger system will do anything necessary to return to its state of balance or comfort, including getting rid of the problematical subsystem.

One winter morning at 10:00 A.M., a vice president far out of his territory was making his way toward the underwriter bin. As he passed the New Group area, he nonchalantly peeked over the six-foot barrier and was astonished at what he saw. There six people performed some kind of aerobic dance to music while two others casually read magazines and another put the finishing touches on a small model airplane. The executive's initial astonishment turned to outrage, and he burst onto the New Group scene demanding an explanation of what he deemed totally inappropriate behavior. Before receiving a response, he launched into a lecture on professional behavior within the organization. The more he talked, the more angry he became. It was clear to the group members that they had broken a basic if unstated law of the organization against having fun, "wasting" time, exercising on work time, or simply taking a break from desk work on the job. Intuitively, the members knew their efficiency and productivity would mean nothing to the executive and would not assuage his anger at their "inappropriate" behavior. To the uneducated vice president they had sinned, and he would make them pay. As he left, he let it be known that they would be hearing from him again.

It did not take long for him to make good on his promise. Both their supervisor's supervisor and their own supervisor quickly read them the riot act. Productivity, efficiency, and morale suddenly weighed little against their having broken a basic rule. Although no one threatened the New Group with dissolution or firings, it was clear that members were to shape up and straighten out. In pursuing their fitness break on the job, they had clearly gone too far.

Systems Note: The vice president who reacted so strongly was concerned about the well-being of the entire system. In his eyes, the group's behavior threatened all parts of the organization. Also, the New Group had, in their isolation, lost touch with some of the basic organizational realities. Though it had been meeting organizational goals, the group was fast becoming an uncontrolled maverick. As the accompanying table shows, the New Group, without being conscious of it, had developed a work ethic that conflicted with many traditions and expec-

Table 6.1 A Conflict in Values

	The Large System View	The New Group View
Norms	■ Time on the job is for work, not play.	■ Work is to be distributed over job time to maximize effort and efficiency and to maintain morale.
	■ Play is frivolous.	■ Play keeps people fresh and invigorated and able to do more work.
	■ Task and product, not maintenance or process, are of concern to the organization.	■ Maintenance is critical to a healthy working environment.
Goals	■ Treat everybody the same, and expect the same behavior in return.	■ Treat groups and individuals in unique ways as long as they remain productive.
	■ Keep busy all the time.	■ Maintain a balance of work and relaxation to maximize both productivity and morale.
	■ Produce as much as you can in the time available.	■ Produce what is consistent with a healthy work environment.
Membership	■ Full membership means putting in a fair day's work for a fair day's pay.	■ The well-rounded, whole person who contributes fully to the New Group through support, sharing, efficiency, and enjoyment will have the fullest membership.
	■ One gains acceptance by obeying the spoken and unspoken rules of the organization.	■ As long as it follows organizational policies and meets expected goals, the autonomous group has the right to develop its own rules of operation within some proper limits.

	The Large System View	The New Group View
	■ People can gain membership by participating fully in the numerous "extra-curricular" activities available after work.	■ We spend the greater part of our lives at work, so fun should be incorporated into the workday.
Leadership	■ Keep on the troops, stay attentive to their performance, and maintain control.	■ Individuals work more effectively when they have the opportunity to govern themselves and establish their own work rules and responsibilities within production guidelines.
	■ As much as possible, treat everyone the same or you will be seen as playing favorites; this pertains both to individuals and to separate work groups.	■ Individuals work differently because they have different needs and styles. These differences should be encouraged as long as productivity is maintained and the group functions effectively.
	■ Too much autonomy is by definition threatening to any large system. It encourages the expectation of exceptions to the rules and values individual differences.	■ Group autonomy leads to teamwork and a sense of ownership and responsibility in the work process. As long as people's individual styles do not impede group effectiveness, diversity should be encouraged; it will increase individual morale.
	■ All efforts should focus on creating as much product of the highest quality as possible.	■ Work and productivity must be seen in a long-range context in which maintaining high performance over time is always a delicate balance between task and process.

tations of the large system. Such words as *fun, sharing, the whole person, participative management,* and *autonomy* were seldom heard in the benevolent autocracy of the company at large. Thus when the vice president glanced over the room divider, he knew it was his responsibility to stop such behavior immediately before the "disease" spread and endangered the organization.

In most large, hierarchical bureaucracies, a powerful reprimand from a powerful vice president would have put the matter to rest. But because of the group members' camaraderie and ability to talk through problems, they called a meeting to discuss the situation. They concluded that they were being treated unfairly and decided to draft a letter to their supervisor on stationery sporting their own "new way" logo. It should be noted that they had been explicitly told ten days earlier that such individualized logos were unacceptable, because they ran counter to the feeling of "community" in the organization. The New Group had been irritated at this affront to their individuality but had accepted it as a small price to pay. Now, however, things had changed, and they considered it necessary to take a stand for what to them seemed right and just. The letter addressed a variety of concerns that the group had previously been unwilling to put on the line but were ready to deal with now because of the vice president's insensitivity. The issues included the possibility, under discussion, that one of their senior underwriters would have to be shared with another autonomous team that was being created. Another plan also bothered them. Jan, the manager, would be expected to manage both their team and another. And management's habit of increasing their workload fueled disillusionment. Here is the letter they sent:

Dear Management:

WAIT A MINUTE!!!!!
Whatever happened to job satisfaction?
We've really worked hard at making this team work—what is the limit? We've really slugged our guts out to satisfy your expectations with very little feedback from management, except Jan! Now you expect even more from us. We're only human . . . slow down!!
Our Concerns Are:

1. Bruce being senior underwriter for both our team and the proposed new team:
   • We expect the majority of his time will be spent with the other team.
   • What happens to us?
   • We need him for his knowledge, training, leadership qualities, positive personality, and the work he does as part of our workload.
   • Will he be able to divide his loyalty between the two groups?
2. There is going to have to be too much of an adjustment made when we lose Jan's "hands-on manager" influence.
   • She's our support and a large factor in our morale.
   • Will the other team resent her "favoritism" to the New Group?
   • We expect morale will suffer—even when she's just there physically, we feel her support and it aids in our production.

- Out of all of management, she's the only one who knows what we're going through and cares about our feelings and concerns—<u>we're scared</u>!!
- We're concerned not only about the pressures on us, but also those on Bruce and Jan themselves. <u>We can see it—can you</u>???

3. Workload: we're overworked compared to others doing our same job.
   - Our volume is considerably more than that of people doing the same type of work.
   - There is a proposal to take away 1.5 people—strong people—from our team because we're being so productive. Isn't that punitive?
   - What about self-administration? It takes time and planning, which for some reason is not legitimate in the organization.
   - Group dynamics: we're not willing to give up our sessions, which help us work together as an effective team.
   - Our fitness break is an important factor in keeping up morale, energy, and even productivity.
   - Where do we find time for all of these??

4. Recognition:
   - There is none.
   - We do more work and assume more responsibility, and keep getting better—all without appreciation.
   - We're trying all of these new ideas—we were the <u>test team</u>—but who uses our ideas?? Anybody?? Does management really know what it takes to create the team we've so successfully managed to do?

5. Productivity:
   - Quality and production are suffering because of all the extras being put on us.
   - Management always looks at statistics and always wants more rather than trying to understand why we've been successful in increasing our output.
   - <u>We can't do more</u>—that is, produce more and take on all the extras management would have us do.

Because of all these things, you are really asking a lot of us, and we really feel the pressure. We've put a lot of personal effort into our work, but we do have our own personal lives— not everybody will do this. We are extremely frustrated and are starting to revert to our old ways, which we know are the "pits." <u>Morale is dropping</u>

We came into the team trusting management to make things better. What are you doing to us? We feel used!

We're willing to continue to make an honest effort to make it work. We need time and support. At the present we feel pushed against the wall.

<u>You're</u> asking too much . . . too soon!

Signed: _____ _____

_____ _____

_____ _____

The letter was personally signed by all the members of the New Group, and copies were sent to their supervisor and her supervisor in the expectation that one would find its way to the vice president who originally criticized them. Though the language was not in formal "corporate" style, it was quite specific, and the expression of real feeling was clear. If the larger system really was "open," as it defined itself, it would take the information as an indication of problems that needed prompt solutions—in short, as a feedback loop.

However, management read the letter as an attack on its own integrity and as an expression of the New Group's desire to step out of its subordinate role and influence the management process through intimidation. One executive described its tone as "childish petulance." Even though the larger system professed to support the idea of independently thinking work groups, because of its inexperience with them it failed to anticipate the consequences of loosening its firm grip on its employees.

The letter served only to outrage management as much as the exercise break had angered the vice president. With this letter, the New Group had broken three organization norms that were never discussed but were always adhered to:

1. No employees would join together to increase their influence.
2. No group would question management's decisions or process. These were traditionally management functions, not to be interfered with by "line" workers in the organization.
3. No one would, with emotion and feeling, complain about their treatment in the organization, because management prided itself on "fairness" and taking care of its own. The very idea that people were treated unfairly was simply unacceptable.

Systems Note: For years, management had discouraged real collaboration among subordinates in the organization, believing that meetings of concerned individuals would give people a sense of power in numbers. Several years previously, a local union had attempted to organize workers in the firm. This so frightened management that it came to see any organized disagreement on the part of the workers as a hostile act. The New Group's expression of opinions and feelings was seen not as a natural outcome of the more creative and independent group process but as a veiled threat to organize.

By its nature, the autonomous group rewarded independent thinking, collaboration, shared decision making, and a sense of equality among workers. As a result, members' loyalty to the team was greater than to the total organization. Paradoxically, the group's higher-level steady state and its own homeostatic equilibrium had triggered the need for a new relationship with the larger system, and this need itself had resulted in a struggle with the organization. The larger system, mixed in entropy, immediately came down hard on the New Group and attempted to influence it in every area, including its *goals* (focus on product, not process), *membership* (team loyalty and commitment are always subordinate to those to the total organization), *communication* (problem identification, the sharing of information, and the seeking of solutions are management functions and of little concern to subordinates), and *leadership/authority* (control, dependency, and the resulting passivity are the true promotable qualities). These underlying truths were woven into the very fabric of this company's life, and the challenge to them in one angry confrontation was felt at every level within the New Group system. The consequences of that encounter, given its fundamental nature, had the potential to affect the entire large system as well. Note that viewing this incident from the point of view of simple cause and effect would have failed to acknowledge the complexity of the relationships involved.

As a result of the letter, the "autonomous work group experiment" was put on hold for six months until management could gain a "greater understanding" of its impact and could form a comprehensive set of expectations and training plans that would be consistent with the philosophy and values of its system.

◆ Reader Activity

Taking your own family as an example of a system, describe it by using the system terminology introduced in the "No Way, New Way" case. The following guidelines may prove useful:

1. Is your family an open or a closed system? Explain.

2. Provide examples of entropy or negentropy in your family system.

3. Feedback is essential to the development of an open system. Does your family provide opportunities for regular feedback? Give specific examples of recent feedback you have given or received—in your family or other groups to which you belong.   ◆

Summary

A healthy system is one that has the ability to remain in a state of *dynamic equilibrium.* The two words may seem antithetical, but they clearly reflect the facts that most systems are alive with activity and that the question is not *whether* change is occurring but rather *how* it is occurring and what the consequences will be.

Stopping the free flow of communication and blocking the paths of necessary feedback will result in the breakdown of information, role and goal confusion, and/or the setting of unattainable objectives. Such a state has characteristics of entropy rather than the more dynamic, creative, and progressive condition of negentropy.

In small groups and human systems, entropy—system breakdown—is not inevitable. Both members and leaders can inhibit it by identifying the nature of the complex relationships in their system and acting with an awareness of consequences. By asking hard questions and using the language of group dynamics, participants can gain a true understanding of the complex system in which they are involved and learn to intervene in a positive manner.

References

Agazarian, Y., and R. Peters. *The Visible and Invisible Group.* Boston, Mass.: Routledge & Kegan Paul, Ltd., 1981.

Alderfer, C. P. "An intergroup perspective on group dynamics." In J. Lorsch, ed., *Handbook of Organizational Behavior.* Englewood Cliffs, N.J.: Prentice-Hall, 1986.

Bass, B. M. *Organizational Psychology.* Boston, Mass.: Allyn and Bacon, 1965.

Beishon, J., and G. Peters, eds. *Systems Behavior.* London: Harper & Row, 1972.

Deal, T. W., and A. A. Kennedy. *Corporate Cultures.* Reading, Mass.: Addison-Wesley, 1982.

Friesen, J. D. *Structural-Strategic Marriage and Family Therapy.* New York: Gardner Press, 1985, pp. 3, 5.

Goldenberg, I., and H. Goldenberg. *Family Therapy: An Overview.* Belmont, Calif.: Wadsworth, 1980.

Katz, D., and R. L. Kahn, *The Social Psychology of Organizations.* New York: Wiley, 1966.

Konigwieser, R., and J. Pelikan. "Anders—gleich—beides zugleich: Unterschiede und Gemeinsamkeiten in Gruppendynamik und Systemansatz ("Different, the same, or both? Differences and similarities in group-dynamic and systems approaches"). *Gruppendynamik,* 21 (February 1990), 69–94.

Krainz, E. E. "Alter Wein in neuen Schlauchen? Zum Verhaltnis von Gruppendynamik und Systemtheorie ("Old wine in new flasks? On the relationship between group dynamics and systems theory"). *Gruppendynamik,* 21, No. 2 (1990), 29–43.

Lewin, K. *Field Theory in the Social Sciences.* New York: Harper & Row, 1951.

McLeod, R., Jr. *Management Information Systems.* (Casebook) Chicago: Science Research Associates, 1987.

Peters, T. J., and R. H. Waterman, Jr. *In Search of Excellence.* New York: Harper & Row, 1982.

Prochaska, J. O. *Systems of Psychotherapy.* Homewood, Ill.: The Dorsey Press, 1984.

Schein, E. H. *Organizational Psychology.* Englewood Cliffs, N.J.: Prentice-Hall, 1965.

Schein, E. H. "Organizational culture." *American Psychologist,* 45, No. 7 (February 1990), 109.

von Bertalanffy, L. *General Systems Theory.* New York: George Braziller, 1968, pp. 16, 36, 37.

von Bertalanffy, L. *Perspectives on General System Theory.* New York: George Braziller, 1975.

Whitner, P. A. *Gestalt Therapy and General Systems Theory.* 1985.

Wiener, N. *Cybernetics.* Cambridge, Mass.: The M.I.T. Press, 1962.

Wilden, A. *Systems and Structure: Essays in Communication and Exchange,* 2nd ed. London: Tavistock, 1980.

Wimmer, R. "Wozu noch Gruppendynamik? Eine Systemtheoretische Reflexion gruppendynamischer Arbeit ("Why continue studying group dynamics? A systems-theory perspective on group-dynamic work"). *Gruppendynamik,* 21, No. 1 (February 1990), 5–28.

◆ 7 ◆

Group Problem Solving and Decision Making

D ecision making is at the center of our very being. A thousand times each day we make decisions, sometimes casually, almost without thought, responding to long-established routine. Who we are as decision makers is no more or less complex than who we are as people. The web of factors influencing us can be incredibly complex: our cultural backgrounds, parents, schooling, feelings of attractiveness, social status, religion, and general level of achieved success. Add to this mix our willingness to risk, our dreams, goals, fears, biases, and a hundred other variables, and you begin to have some idea of how complex even our most casual or spontaneous decisions might really be.

Now place five or six, or ten or twenty such complex individuals together, attempt to develop an agreed-upon decision, and the potential differences seem almost beyond comprehension.

◆ Reader Activity

Take a sheet of paper and make two columns. On the left-hand side, list the qualities and characteristics of the last group you attended in which members successfully solved a significant problem together. In the right-hand column, list the characteristics of the last group-solving session you attended that ended unsuccessfully. Extend this list to include specific behaviors or events that worked against success. Thinking in this manner should bring perspective to the following pages and help you relate to the common patterns that exist in many groups.   ◆

Human Beings and the Decision-Making Process

Sources of Tension and Conflict

For every potential decision there are two potential sources of tension and conflict. First, whenever the decision involves a choice between alternatives, the loss-and-gain factor must be weighed. To eat roast beef means no chicken, to have another drink means feeling less alive in the morning, to buy six shares of IBM means foregoing making a down payment on a piece of property, to offer a suggestion means possible rejection.

Similarly, merely being in a group poses tension and decisions for an individual. What must I do to be accepted here? Should I relax and just be myself? They say they want my opinion, but should I risk having it rejected? I really don't like the way things are going. I wonder whether things will be any better if I say something?

These and hundreds of other personal decisions add enormous tension to any group even before its task has begun. When the group does begin its own process of decision making, further conflict may result from disagreement among individual participants, as well as from the implications any decision will have for the group as a whole (Adams and Adams, 1967; Lewin, 1948, 1951; Jacobs, 1983).

A second source of natural tension and conflict is created after the individual or group makes a decision. This stems from the need to live with the decision that has just been made and thus the need to continually justify it to the group and others (Festinger, 1957).

It appears natural, therefore, that tension and points of conflict should exist within decision-making groups. The question becomes whether the sources of tension are clearly recognized and dealt with constructively. All too often the greatest sources of tension and conflict are completely avoided (denied or ignored). If the actual sources of tension are not uncovered and dealt with, it is likely that they will be diffused into other areas of the group's experience. Here is a case in point:

> There had been a long, divisive teachers strike in a large metropolitan city. The situation was particularly nasty at one high school. Teachers on strike had picketed and gone without paychecks for nine weeks. Other teachers, saying they could not "punish the students," crossed the picket lines and continued to teach: they taught combined classes and subjects with which they were unfamiliar, and they were prepared to face jeers and flat tires when they left. The strike ended before Thanksgiving, and all teachers received a substantial raise that had been negotiated as a result of the strike.
>
> In June, at the end of the school year, that school hired a consultant to plan, with the faculty, how to deal with some serious school problems: drugs, an increased drop-out rate, three close "suicide scares," and gangs from another neighborhood roaming the halls and "shoving" students.
>
> When the consultant arrived, the faculty were seated in a large lunchroom in clusters—reading the paper, playing cards, chatting. The consultant indicated that she was ready to start. The group continued as though nothing had been said, pretending to be absorbed in their papers, cards, or conversation. As the consultant tried to start again and again, they would not even begin to participate.
>
> What was the problem? The consultant knew it could not be related to some previous run-in; she had never worked with this school before. Pointing to five people who looked as though they were influencing others, she asked them to come up to the microphone and say whatever they wanted to the teachers. They came up and vented seven months of fury.
>
> First, they had come to this meeting only because they were 3 days short of the required 180 days. They had been told they could come to the 3-day training program or be docked 3 days' pay. They had opted to present

their bodies. Second, they were furious that the "scabs" had gotten pay-checks and raises. They refused to be associated with them.

It was clear to the consultant that in the face of such tension and conflict, any discussion of even serious school problems would be viewed as minor. Instead, she established the following ground rules to apply for the next 8 hours: the consultant would recognize anyone who wanted the micro-phone. The person recognized could then speak for up to 5 minutes. There would be no physical violence.

It was frightening to hear such venom, such accusations, such yelling and counter-accusations, but the next day started off with coffee and dough-nuts. The problems were addressed and task forces formed to work all summer creating plans that would be implemented in the first week of the fall term. Ultimately, major changes were made in faculty/administration relations with students, and there were very positive outcomes.

Who knows how long the divisiveness and withdrawal from school concerns would have continued? Those 8 hours of yelling and accusations brought the tension and conflict to everyone's attention and made it clear that healing had to occur among them before they could even think of the problems they were supposed to solve.

Often the issues causing conflict are personal and emotional, whereas those to be dealt with are intellectual. By asking himself or herself what is causing the group to avoid the possible alternative and what are the real underlying issues of tension, a person standing apart may be able to move the group to another stage in its problem solving. Thus, if a person is really concerned with understanding why a group is functioning as it is, it may help to know the stated goals and by-laws of the group. Of even more value would be observing the group objectively, sorting out various behaviors in relation to possible causal factors. Most important would be developing an awareness of how the individual members personally feel about the group itself, their role in it, and the issue being discussed. Too often, we remain at a technical level when the sources of conflict are emotional (Lewin, 1936).

In an interesting experiment, Forgas (1990) induced positive, neutral, and neg-ative moods by using audiovisual presentations. He found that subjects made more positive judgments when happy than when in the neutral mood and more negative judgments when sad. Group discussion resulted in further polarization of positive judgments and the attenuation of negative judgments. Findings support the role that affect plays in mediating individual cognitive processes and interactive social behavior.

Sources of Resistance

Much of the frustration that often accompanies working with a decision-making group results from an inability to understand and accept as perfectly natural many of the resistances that develop during the problem-solving process. Acknowledging them can in itself reduce some of the strain.

Most of us organize our lives in a manner that reduces the amount of stress we must face. We do this by building a pattern of existence that is familiar and comfortable—a pattern in which habit, ritual, and precedent play a relatively large part. We attempt to bring our lives into a state of equilibrium in which we are able to predict events and reduce conflict. Changing this relatively stable, steady state means changing accustomed patterns of behavior and creating (at least temporarily) discomfort and tension. Problem solving and eventual decision making often lead to innovation, alternative courses of action, and a disruption of a group's or individual's state of equilibrium. This is one reason we resist new ideas. It is why we sit in the same seats, tell the same tried-and-true jokes, harbor the same prejudices, and continue the same work habits. A particular solution, even though it appears acceptable and useful, may nevertheless be met with the most subtle and resourceful resistances. Just as even positive changes in our lives, such as a job promotion, school graduation, or marriage, are stressful, productive changes in a group create stress and resistance.

When we work with the familiar and within a framework of accustomed behavior, the relationship we have with others in positions of authority is clear; we know what is expected of us and what we expect from others. When people change their relationship to powerful authorities, when they take on new responsibilities, they immediately become more vulnerable and less sure of their own position. Thus relationships in which we depend on others are altered, and personal security is lessened. When decisions alter such relationships, one may anticipate conflicts and tension, which are likely to be expressed in overt or covert resistance to the proposal being considered.

People fear being perceived as inadequate or impotent. It is one thing to *feel* inadequate and impotent; it is more difficult to accept public affirmation of our most private fears of failure. It is often an illusion of impotence that reduces the desire to risk, to try a new approach. This is a primary force behind the "Oh, what's the use?" or the "That's been tried before" syndrome. It is based on experience, unfulfilled dreams, and real feelings of inability to alter one's conditions.

Research shows that individuals who have a medium level of self-esteem do better in group decision-making situations than do individuals with either high or low self-esteem (Schwartz, Wullwick, and Shapiro, 1980). The attitude a group has toward its role as decision maker is greatly influenced by the combined measure of its own potency and sense of adequacy to carry out decisions. (Later, we will discuss ways of reducing this and other resistances that may hinder the problem-solving process.)

Groups build security, as do individuals, by establishing standards and rules of behavior. They tend to value the traditional. They withdraw from tests of their own potency and rebel against outside intrusions that may throw their own stable and tranquil world into disequilibrium. These and other resistances are generated from the emotional dimension of group life and may have little to do with the actual "goodness of fit" of the intellectual idea being considered. It is by looking within the labyrinth of emotions upon which any group is built that one finds the keys to real movement and progress. The first step is to discover what state prevails within the group at a given time and to attempt to seek validation of these perceptions. This requires looking beyond the rational scope of the problem and into the rational and irrational perspectives of both the individual participants and the group as a whole (Heider, 1958). Armelius (1980) suggests that the state of the group, or the group culture, is definitely related to the individual members of the group.

It is evident that unless individuals feel personally secure and relatively unthreatened within the problem-solving group, they will tend to respond with their own characteristic patterns of defense. These behaviors can themselves be important sources of diagnostic information. The obvious withdrawal of individuals from participation, signs of passive or active aggression, subgrouping, or an excessive amount of dependency or resistance to authority often suggests emotional issues that reduce effectiveness. The conflicts and resulting tensions synonymous with these behaviors can usually be traced back to one of four areas of concern. First, there are conflicts arising from *personal goals and needs* that are at variance with those of the group. Second, there are problems of *personal identity and acceptance* (membership issues). Third, there are problems generated from the *distribution of power and influence*. And finally, there is the question of *intimacy,* which encompasses issues of trust and personal openness.

As long as such issues remain unresolved, much of the group's energy will be directed toward self-oriented behaviors, and the accomplishment of the task will be disrupted. Research shows that groups who were able to delay expression of emotions were also capable of high-quality decisions and that members experienced the group as effective and energetic (Guzzo and Waters, 1982). Naturally, it is impossible to remove all sources of personal tension, nor would it be desirable. But the more such problems can be raised and dealt with, the more attention can be given to the substantive issues.

Cognitive Dissonance

Decisions by their very nature suggest alternatives, argument, and conflict. Basically, a decision represents the termination of a controversy with a particular course of action. However, the conflict and tension do not end with the decision. How the individual or group copes with the doubts, suspicions, and skepticism generated during the discussion has important implications (Festinger, 1957; Festinger and Aronson, 1968). The longer and stronger the discussion, the more ambivalence will be created (whether it is overtly recognized is another question), leading to a state of *cognitive dissonance.* This dissonance is a continuous source of tension, and the individual or group attempts to reduce it in a number of ways. For example, once the decision is made, there is a tendency to begin valuing it even more than before (Brehm, 1956). As with a religious convert, many of the old questions and doubts are forgotten and the decision is constantly reinforced. If it took so long to reach a decision, it must be the "best."

The trouble is that the decision may become overvalued, and an intransigent attitude may develop that closes the door on future discussion of alternatives or even a fair evaluation of the decision at a later date. A subtle process of rationalization and justification may evolve. This is particularly true if the decision turns sour and must still be lived with (a leader is chosen who proves inept, a tax is imposed to curtail inflation and unemployment increases, a surplus is guaranteed and a deficit is incurred).

Similarly, people are inclined to make the best of a bad thing when the decision is out of their control. Thus, even though it can be proved that most school grades lack objectivity and validity, students and parents alike still defend them. Outwardly they may go through a long and involved defense of the system, noting the value of the grading process, whereas inwardly their desire to perpetuate the system lies in the more clouded area of "I've suffered and so should you." This rationalization has nothing to do with the questions surrounding the legitimacy of grades. Still, such internal justifications tend to reduce dissonance and constitute the major source of support for maintaining the status quo. Therefore, one needs to justify one's expenditure of time, energy, and hope in a decision that is a matter more of image than of principle and will shape future behaviors and accompanying decisions (Festinger and Aronson, 1968; Festinger and Carlsmith, 1959).

By this time, it's clear that any problem solving implies the possibility of change and the exploration of alternatives to the status quo. Because of this point of potential discomfort, using a group can compound the difficulties of problem solving beyond those resulting from the volatility created by a roomful of different personalities with all of their individual needs, biases, and personal agendas.

Let's look at the disadvantages of group decision making as well as its advantages and benefits.

Disadvantages Group decision making does have its "downside."

1. The results of group decision making are often dismissed by those in positions of influence who are unwilling to give credence to a process few of them have experienced positively.

2. All too often, participants learn that what appears to be a fair, democratic process is really a charade in which decisions have already been made and group participation is provided as a means of placating those who have to live with the ultimate decision.

3. Unless well designed, a group effort at problem solving can be a colossal waste of time, money, and effort.

4. Few group leaders are trained in the effective utilization of group members, which can result in a deterioration of both the process and task dimensions of group life.

5. As a result, instead of morale and team spirit improving because of a group approach, it may degenerate.

6. If the selection of group members is not related carefully to the task at hand, the technical and experiential components simply will not be available when needed.

7. It is common for members of a problem-solving group either to be briefed inadequately prior to the meeting or to fail to do the premeeting work that enables the group to begin with clearly defined goals.

8. A few individuals may take over a group and dominate its process or inhibit the participation of members whose contribution represents the reason for the group in the first place.

Advantages   With so many possible pitfalls for groups, there appears to be justification for questioning their use. Assuming that groups are not always the best vehicle for problem solving, why and when should a group be utilized?

1. A group solving problems together will provide those participating with a baseline of common understanding and information that cannot be replicated in a memo or less personal means. Such involvement inevitably results in a greater sympathy toward the complexities of the problem and lays the groundwork for the group's acceptance of the eventual solution. Increasingly, we are understanding how critical to any solution is its acceptance by those who must live with it. Thus effective communication, understanding, and the eventual accepting of the solution are tied closely together.

2. As we have indicated, it is only natural that individuals enter into a problem-solving situation with personal biases, needs, and perspectives. A group setting offers an environment that legitimizes a variety of viewpoints. Usually, provided that good information is translated in an intelligent manner and a climate exists in which individuals are not compelled to defend their positions, a group, like any individual, will move toward the best ideas.

3. Given even a minimal level of trust and good will, a group is capable of producing a greater quantity and variety of ideas than the average individual.

4. A good experience in a group can generate enthusiasm and can be contagious. The commitment toward eventual action can be born out of the teamwork, arguing, building of alternatives, and movement toward choice. Individuals can feel good about their contribution to the group and their relationship to it.

5. The give-and-take of open and free discussion in a group can bring new ideas into play that might have never been considered by an individual. Different from the formal presentation of new ideas in a group setting, open discussion enables group members to be irreverent, to question even the unquestionable, and to challenge old absolutes. This process can tap the group's natural creativity.

6. Problem solving is a multidimensional process. It is quite possible to involve large numbers of people (fifty, one hundred, five hundred, or more) during

the problem identification, diagnostic (clarification), and ideational (generating alternatives) phases. As suggested earlier, people feel better about the solution they have to live with if they have been given a fair opportunity to participate and are aware of all the factors underlying an issue.

It is true that many problems can be solved more easily and efficiently and with less conflict and stress individually. On occasion, such individual problem solving can be justified because of the special expertise of the problem solver, because of limited time, or because of the nature of a crisis that might exist. However, when we realize that the decision itself is in many ways only half the battle, group participation makes increasing sense. In a society that cultivates the idea of participative democracy, the sensitive leader will encourage it. Individuals simply want to be heard and to have a sense that their organization reflects their ideas. The knowledge that their ideas are considered is more important to them than the demand that they be used, although many innovations in the structure of an organization or how a particular job is completed have emerged from groups of employees who were encouraged to be innovative. Increased participation and empowerment in decision making can also boost the group's productivity and morale, and reduce absenteeism.

A study done in one factory clearly demonstrates how participation in decisions raises morale and increases production (Fox, 1987). In one group, changes affecting members were imposed by management; three other groups were allowed to participate in the decision-making process that led to changes. In the first group, members resisted the decision, production and morale dropped, and a few group members even quit. In the other groups, which all decided to make the changes imposed on group 1, work enthusiasm and production rose.

Group problem solving and employee involvement in decision making have tended to be viewed as a luxury in which corporations indulged when times were good. In a surprising turnaround, there has recently evolved a trend toward utilizing employees in group decision making when times are bad.

According to an article published in *Time* magazine, "Is Mr. Nice Guy Back?" (January 27, 1992, 42–44), some companies realize that worker morale has been shredded by layoffs with the elimination of some six million jobs since 1983. There is a further recognition that restoring competitiveness to American industry will require serious collaboration between workers and management. There is a resulting acknowledgment that people need to be empowered.

One manager who is emblematic of this shift in approach is GE chairman John Welch. Known in the '80s as "Neutron Jack" for zapping 100,000 employees—25% of the company's work force—Welch now stresses the importance of teamwork. Says he: "To get every worker to have a new idea every day is the route to winning in the '90s."

To help bring good ideas to life, GE holds "work-out" sessions in which groups of workers and managers spend three days in shirt-sleeve meetings on anything from gripes to pitches for new products. The high point comes on the third day, when employees pepper their bosses with scores of suggestions that the brow-mopping managers must accept or reject on the spot. Most turn out to be keepers. In a session at an aircraft-engine plant last September, one team pitched a plan that cut the time needed to produce a jet-combustion part nearly 90%. And an electrician proposed a design for an aluminum reflector that has cut the plant's light bill in half. Over two years, the grueling workouts have spawned dozens of innovations, ranging from improved light-bulb packaging to the elimination of reams of paperwork.*

The Continuing Controversy Surrounding "Groupthink"

Irving Janis (1982), in the most recent edition of his book *Groupthink,* raised an important concern related to the use of groups as vehicles for problem solving and decision making. He asked what norms formed in a group where unanimity and conformity were valued and where disagreement, argument, discord, and dissent were equated with disloyalty and even infidelity to the group. The pressure on the members, he argued, was to agree not to disagree—especially regarding the ideas of the leadership. He called this insidious process *groupthink*.

There is increasing evidence that such was the mentality in the White House during the days of the Watergate cover-up (Cline, 1983). All the classic signs of groupthink were present: President Nixon and his staff were isolated and defensive and found strength in strategies that built a sense of cohesion—for example, "stonewalling." They increasingly isolated themselves from the criticism of the press and even from colleagues, and they excluded dissent—along with impartiality and objectivity—from the decision-making process. They stopped critically discussing and carefully considering the particular consequences of immediate decisions, and as each of their decisions in turn created controversy and intensified their need to justify their actions, their exclusivity as a group increased.

Perhaps the most extreme example of such social conformity in our time was the mass suicide that took place in "Jonestown," Guyana, at the instigation of Reverend Jim Jones (Ulman, 1983). It might seem easy to attribute this and the Watergate example to a "siege mentality" resulting from unusually great stress. But the pressure to conform can be overwhelming in groups where loyalty to the group is so strong that members censor their own doubts and blindly follow the leader.

The implications of groupthink are serious not only for prestigious, high-level presidential advisors but also for more mundane committees. It might be useful to examine the conditions that spawn groupthink and therefore to understand when groups are most vulnerable to it. Janis (1977) emphasizes that high cohesiveness (here defined as attractiveness of belonging) and a directive leader who makes known early what course he or she favors are the two most significant

*From *Time,* "Is Mr. Nice Guy Back?" by John Greenwald, January 27, 1992, p. 42–44. Copyright 1992 Time Inc. Reprinted by permission.

preconditions, but for full-blown groupthink there need to be others: the group should be under stress, facing a crisis situation, and should not have established procedures for considering a variety of viewpoints. Janis's analysis of groupthink by policy-making groups has helped clarify the antecedent conditions, the symptoms of groupthink, and those of the defective decision making that results (see Table 7.1).

It is frightening to think that committees can make vital decisions that affect all our lives while they are victims of groupthink. But it also helps us to recognize that mundane committees who could develop better decisions might be mired in groupthink.

How can groupthink be reduced? Janis (1982) suggests a number of approaches:

1. The leader can assign the role of critical evaluator to each member, making clear that it is critical examination, not agreement, that is valued.
2. The leader should avoid stating his or her personal preference among the alternatives being considered.
3. At intervals the group should break into subgroups, each studying the

Table 7.1 Analysis of Groupthink by Policy-Making Groups

Antecedent Conditions		Symptoms of Groupthink	Symptoms of Defective Decision Making
1. High cohesiveness 2. Insulation of the group 3. Lack of methodical procedures for search and appraisal 4. Directive leadership 5. High stress with a low degree of hope for finding a better solution than the one favored by the leader or other influential persons	CONCURRENCE-SEEKING →TENDENCY→	1. Illusion of invulnerability 2. Collective rationalization 3. Belief in inherent morality of the group 4. Stereotypes of out-groups 5. Direct pressure on dissenters 6. Self-censorship → → 7. Illusion of unanimity 8. Self-appointed mind guards	1. Incomplete survey of alternatives 2. Incomplete survey of objectives 3. Failure to examine risks of preferred choice 4. Poor information search 5. Selective bias in processing information at hand 6. Failure to reappraise alternatives 7. Failure to work out contingency plans

Analysis based on comparisons of high- and low-quality decisions made by policy groups.
Source: Reprinted with permission of The Free Press, a Division of Macmillan, Inc. from *Decision Making: A Psychological Analysis of Conflict, Choice, and Commitment* by Irving L. Janis and Leon Mann. Copyright © 1977 by The Free Press.

same problem. They should then reconvene, report their recommendations, and negotiate a resolution to their difficulties.
4. As appropriate, outside experts (including those who disagree with the plan) should be brought in and heard.
5. And finally, once a plan (decision) has emerged, there should be a "second chance" review of the alternatives.

Just as some committees have a well-earned reputation for creating abysmal decisions, there are also committees that work productively—even extraordinarily well. Groups can harness the efforts of individuals to greatly enhance individual performance, or they can fall very short of it. Which it will be depends on how effectively the group's organization and norms exploit members' skills and apply them to the task. The more we understand fundamental group processes, the better we can design groups to work at their full potential.

Constructive Controversy and Conflict

In recent years, conflict has been allowed out of the proverbial closet. Perhaps because our society has always equated conflict with pain, dissonance, and destructive behavior, until recently most groups have avoided it at all costs (Wall, 1986). Alternatively, it may have been a lack of experience in turning conflicts in group settings into something more positive that inhibited most of us from allowing them to surface. Whatever the reason, nowadays conflict is increasingly seen as useful and sometimes even necessary to effective group problem solving (Goddard, 1986; Jacobus, 1983; Tjosvold, 1985). Research now indicates that groups with dissenters as members can accomplish more than those whose desire for agreement is high. Where dissent is supported, teamwork comes to be valued over competition, individual participation is encouraged, and the diversity of ideas is actually promoted (Goddard, 1986). Mutual goal setting, along with a clear understanding of problem-solving and decision-making strategies, results in increased trust and cohesion, not negativity or a critical attitude, and the decisions reached are more easily implemented and with less resistance than in a no-conflict group.

When an effective design makes it possible to define expectations clearly and to understand safe avenues of participation, conflict can be viewed as a means of expression. Dissent and controversy become assets to creative problem solving rather than blocks and sources of tension. This is not to say that inappropriate, hostile, or insensitive personal behavior will not pose problems. But in groups such behaviors often reflect frustration and disillusionment at the problem-solving process itself and, being symptoms, actually disappear when the problem—repressed conflict—is solved.

Open-Ended Versus Closed-Ended Problems

Before taking an in-depth look at a structured, rational problem-solving method-ology, we shall explore a major reason why problem solving often fails. The issue is one of attitude and perceived opportunity. Many of us, as individuals or as part of a group, enter a problem-solving situation with a predisposition toward the problem itself and the range of solutions open to us. Quite often we establish what might be called premature boundary conditions for the problems that by their very nature restrict our ability to see creative alternatives. Traditional education does not encourage active, creative thinking but instead emphasizes learning rote answers. Too often, well-intentioned teachers turn out students who know the "right" answers but do not even know how to begin to use creative reasoning to solve an unfamiliar problem. Of course, children have more limited cognitive capacities than adults, so learning universal "shoulds" is a reasonable place to begin. However, as adults we know that most problems have more than one solution and that answers become more relative.

In addition to becoming dependent on what Rickards (1974, p. 10) calls the "defining authorities" for the boundaries of solutions and on the accompanying reluctance to challenge those boundaries, many people feel impotent within their institutions and, lacking real power, feel it does little good to look for creative alternatives. More likely than not, the individual suspects that additional effort will result in embarrassment or rejection. Thus there is little perceived payoff for extending oneself.

The fact is that there are few problems that are closed and not open to a variety of creative solutions. It is the job of problem solving to draw out the best alternatives and to break down artificial barriers, including those that psychologically bind the problem.

Groups themselves, when composed of a variety of individuals, often provide the different perspectives necessary to push boundaries away. Most of us have experienced situations in which our own close proximity to a problem reduced our ability to see the logical or creative solution. Marriages are particularly prone to this, as predictable patterns of behavior come to establish a very limited vision of what is possible. One purpose of therapy is to reduce boundaries and help us reframe problems (Watzlawick, 1978, p. 117).

Many problems, except for such things as math equations, puzzles, and controlled scientific problems, are open-ended. Even complex mathematical problems often resist predictable solutions. The great majority of problems, however, are not so restricted or governed by theoretical tests. Rather, they tend to be more variable in scope, with relatively fluid boundaries imposed only by our own habits, inflex-ibility, limited experience, and personal agendas or vested interests. Productivity on a production line, a communications problem, the need for a new invention, marketing strategies, selling, public relations, and interpersonal conflicts are often approached from a limited perspective that limits the range of solutions. Again, effective problem solving, whether structured and quite rational or more intuitive, depends largely on our ability to open ourselves to all the possibilities.

The Right/Left Hemisphere View of the World[1]

In current scientific language, many of the behaviors conceived as successful in problem solving would be classified as originating in the left hemisphere of the mind—that part of the brain where most logical and rational thought takes place. It is here that intellectual ideas are translated in a linear fashion into words and are eventually articulated through speech. But in recent years scientists have discovered that the right hemisphere of the brain is responsible for another type of thinking that is crucial to problem solving, although less valued for its own sake. Here, the brain processes emotional cues, nonverbal behaviors, and visual clues that add significantly to our knowledge and understanding of a problem. We are talking about the intuitive domain, the area of the irrational, illogical, and often spontaneous reactions to an event that often move us to act without much apparent thought. The question is not whether we use right-hemisphere thinking but how much and in what ways it interfaces with that of the left? Some believe that, like anything else that has not been valued, rewarded, or nurtured, it remains an area of tremendous unutilized potential. One school of thought holds that although we spend much of our time acting as if we are rational, objective, and in control of our problem-solving faculties, we are in fact driven to solutions all too often by subtle influences of the right hemisphere—by feelings, emotions, and nonverbal information we pick up and translate. We then justify the eventual decision on the basis of rational, scientific arguments, giving no credence to the often critical right-hemisphere influences. It is not uncommon for some groups to make an intuitive decision and then scurry around finding the logical reasons to support it.

> The art department of an advertising agency is assigned a new project to work on. On the first day of the project, the department is given a description of the product—what it does, who might use it, and how long it lasts—and is told what other similar products are already being sold. A meeting later in the week draws the group together in one room, and they toss out ideas that might sell the product—everything from slogans to vignettes for commercials and logos for sportswear. To an observer, the meeting is chaos: people all talk at the same time, there are excited interruptions as one person uses what someone else has just said to generate another idea, and someone across the room says, "Yes! What about . . ."
>
> Two weeks later the bare bones of the advertising campaign are sketched

---

1. This discussion is drawn in part from the thoughtful studies and application of research by such writers as Richard Bandler and John Grinder, Henry Mintzberg, Robert Ornstein, Paul Watzlawick, and Benjamin Young. They are exploring previously uncharted territory in the related areas of thinking, problem solving, and change.

out and the planning to clarify, coordinate, and expand the design is begun. It is only after this point that all that "necessary" information given to the team on the first day is dug out from under the drafting table. Group members can now look at their product and begin to figure out how it fits in with the budget, what the client expected, and the market the product is aimed at. It is only near the end of the process that the art department finds rational reasons to substantiate the creative work it has already completed.

There appears to be a growing recognition that any complex decision goes far beyond rational data, far beyond what can be formally organized and tabulated, and that the underlying, nonquantifiable issues such as morale, relationships, individual egos, power, competition, and what is generally called "politics" are of equal importance. These are the areas translated by the right hemisphere and incorporated, along with rationality and the scientific method, into the decision-making process.

◆ *Individual Experiment*

Choose a problem that you have thought about recently. It may be a problem concerning other people in a group setting; it may be a question concerning career direction, job choice, or living arrangements. Sit in a comfortable position in a quiet place where you will not be disturbed. Relax for a few minutes by letting your mind wander or concentrating on your breathing. Imagine a picture of yourself once your problem has been solved. What will you be like? How will you be different? Fill in your picture with as much detail as you can, such as how you will be feeling, what you will be doing, saying, wearing, and so on. Your picture can be one snapshot or several frames, as in a movie. In this process your right brain has been working, projecting you into the future. It has gone through an intuitive problem-solving process that tends to go on unnoticed. Now evaluate your picture. Are there any surprises? Is the picture realistic? If you took a more logical, planned route, do you think you would have arrived at the same solution?   ◆

Rational Problem Solving: A Left-Hemisphere Focus

The study of problem solving by social scientists has shown the process to be not the straightforward one dictated by the scientific method, but rather a nightmare of complexity—something so tortuous to use that few people have the time, energy, compulsion, or know-how to do it right. The reason is that people initiate the process and are affected by many other factors, including the organizational environment and their own personal needs. The fact is that no one model can account for all the complexity and richness of the human spirit and behavior.

Our purpose here is to provide a general overview of rational problem solving, integrating insights drawn from systems theory, communications theory, group dynamics, and organizational development. We will then provide a more comprehensive model that elaborates the more general perspective and its potential for use in a group setting.

The Six Stages of Rational Problem Solving

For the most part, the steps one moves through in solving a problem are quite simple. First come the identification and clarification of the issue. There follow the developing of alternatives, a selection of one or more of these, implementation phase and, finally, evaluation of the outcomes. It is a wonder that a process so straightforward and so lacking in complexity can result in so many problems and pitfalls. See the exercises at the end of this chapter for examples of how to implement these six stages of problem solving.

Stage 1: Problem Identification   One can recognize that a problem exists either by chance or as a result of systematic inquiry. More often than not, it seems that problems arise naturally and announce their presence through increasing tension and conflict or, perhaps, inefficiency. Conditions worsen if the presence of such tensions is not confronted or if they are denied or covered over so that accompanying frustrations become a breeding ground for other problems. This is too often the case in groups in which a little internal festering is somehow preferred to dealing directly with the issues as they arise.

In some cases, there is simply no mechanism available to help bring the problems into the open. Something as simple as a suggestion box (if there is evidence that it is being used) can be a direct line to sources of individual, group, or organizational problems. Once these problems are recognized, it is important to discover the degree to which they are shared by others as well as the level of urgency. Occasional questionnaires or small group discussions can be helpful in drawing problems into the open before they become destructive. Such problem sensing of both task and emotional issues can help keep communication channels open. Other problems will arise, however, if the group or individuals are encouraged to identify specific problems, and those problems are then avoided or minimized by those in positions of influence. Problem identification is just the first step of a process, not an end unto itself.

Stage 2: The Diagnostic Phase   Once the symptoms have been recognized and brought to the attention of others, several steps seem to follow quite naturally. First, the problem must be clarified and relationships identified. Too often the symptoms are little more than a generalized recognition of discomfort or stress and reveal little about the underlying factors creating the disturbance. At this point it must be discovered how much the problem is shared by others as well as its degree of urgency. A second step in the diagnostic process is to gather supporting evidence on the nature of the problem. Third, with this new information, the problem should be restated in terms of a condition that exists and that, to some extent, needs to be changed.

Quite often, problems are stated simplistically in relation to an "either-or" situation or in terms of "good" or "bad," which immediately polarizes the potential problem solvers into win-or-lose camps. If a condition can be shown to exist that is less than optimal, then the problem of the eventual decision-making group becomes one of identifying the factors that keep the condition from being optimal. Energy can then be directed toward isolating specific causal factors, such as a single person dominating the discussion, lack of time, or the need for clear goals. Thus arguments become limited to the relative strength of such factors, not to whether they exist. This approach encourages compromise and multiple solutions.

Finally, having gathered as much data as possible concerning the problem, stated it as a condition to be changed, and isolated the various causal factors, the group must make a determination regarding its own ability to solve the problem. This involves looking squarely at the group's own power to influence the prevailing condition, what kinds of resources are going to be necessary, and how much impact their efforts will have on others. Nothing is more frustrating and deflating than for a group to design a clever scheme for solving a problem, only to realize that it lacks the resources to carry out the plan. Therefore, before developing solutions, the group must test its own situation. The most important finding may be that because of certain limits (time, money, personnel, access to power), the problem should be stated more realistically, others should be drawn into the problem-solving process, or the issue should be directed to another group that does have the resources to solve the problem.

For change to occur, those involved must see the problem as "their own." It cannot be imposed on them. Thus the diagnostic process is vital for involving those who will eventually be responsible for implementing the solutions. This principle has important implications for who takes part in the diagnostic process and which people are kept closely informed about what is happening. Developing solutions proves to be nothing more than an academic exercise if those who will be affected have not even admitted that a problem exists.

Stage 3: Generation of Alternatives Groups and individuals seek quick and easy solutions. This is one reason why the problem-solving process so often breaks down. As we fasten onto what we perceive as a logical and resourceful solution, we automatically screen out numerous other possibilities, some of which (difficult as it is for us to believe) may be more appropriate. We commit ourselves to one idea and are then compelled to defend it. This may be particularly true in a group in which some of us have a need to convince others of our wisdom and skill.

Formulating solutions before ideas have been thoroughly explored not only reduces the potential quality of the eventual solution but also inhibits open communication. It has the same effect as stating a problem in either–or terms. It forces individuals into a premature position of evaluation and places all members in defensive postures. Thus it is a major pitfall to evaluate solutions at a time when the intent should be merely to explore every potential solution. Done effectively, this process can reduce the tendency for groups to polarize around answers that are comfortable, and it may also help them look toward new approaches.

After the ideas have been generated and explored in relation to specific causal factors (isolated during the diagnostic stage), then there should be a general screening process to integrate and synthesize the solutions into a smaller number. Again, the goal here is not to select a "best" solution, because the problem is likely to be multifaceted, with a number of possible alternatives. Before any final decision is reached, a period of weighing and testing of the alternatives should be initiated. If time and resources allow, an effort should be made to gather data about the various solutions reached up to that point. This could range from establishing a pilot study to seeking the opinions of other individuals, such as experts.

Stage 4: Selecting Solutions   Along with gathering new data and taking time to think about the alternatives, it is ideal to consider the consequences of each alternative in relation to the problem condition. Many times a group, anxious to get under way, fails to explore the unanticipated consequences and focuses only on the obvious benefits to be gained. Thus, it is at this stage that each potential solution should be carefully evaluated in terms of its possible limitations as well as its strengths. The discussion should lead to decision by consensus, in which all members are willing to support a particular plan. Although this does not assume complete agreement on the part of all participants involved, it suggests at least a temporary accord during a period when the decision can be fairly evaluated. There are, of course, times when decision by consensus is impossible, but when effective implementation of the decision is based partly on support of those involved, consensus has important advantages.

Stage 5: Implementation   Many participants of decision-making groups, after being successful in developing a useful decision, have watched helplessly as the ideas so carefully designed and agreed on are never implemented. Part of the problem often can be traced to the early stage of the process and the failure to involve, or at least to keep informed, those with the power to kill the idea and those who will be influenced by the final decision. Equally damaging is the failure to build accountability into the action or implementation phase. Too often, interest is not developed in the decision-making group. Accountability must be carefully cultivated so that individuals feel responsible for the outcome and are answerable to the others involved.

Stage 6: Evaluation and Adjustment   One reason why people are resistant to new ideas is that they believe that once change occurs, the new status quo will be just as impervious to change as was the previous idea. Building in a mechanism of evaluation as well as the flexibility to make adjustments once the data are analyzed can keep the entire problem-solving process flexible and open to new alternatives. Most important, it gives those who are being influenced by the decision the recourse to alternative procedures and a feeling of some potency in the process. Also, the notion of accountability is tied directly into the evaluation and adjustment. Thus evaluation becomes more than a superficial exercise and tends to be used as an integral part of an ongoing problem-solving process.

The basic approach to problem solving outlined here is very reasonable. Rational problem solving is designed to keep us making sense, to manage productively irrational biases and limiting customs and habits, to expand our vision, to look at the consequences of our choices, and to make sure that ultimate decisions result in constructive action. Whether we work in the context of a group or as individuals, the same principles prevail. For those of us who spend our lives attempting to facilitate the problem-solving process, the key is asking the tough questions and not allowing our tendency to avoid pressures of reality (for example, limited time, habit, bias, limited experience) to take over and corrupt our positive efforts. Good intentions in problem solving don't count; a satisfactory outcome is the only measure. The orderly, stepwise process that follows is designed to draw the participant(s) along in a systematic manner. It takes time and should not be done in a hurry. Quick-and-dirty problem solving inevitably leads to quick-and-dirty solutions that simply mirror preconceived notions we wish to sell. In fact, Hirokawa (1980) found that groups who spent more time on procedural matters were better able to reach agreement and make effective decisions. Similarly, in our haste we fail to assess all the viable alternatives or the consequences of those alternatives. Rarely do we allow ourselves the time to do the job right.

Problem solving is a circular process that continues in an ongoing fashion (see the accompanying diagram). Individuals and groups are self-adjusting and self-maintaining organisms in which the evaluation and adjustment stage feeds back into the initial problem-identification stage. In fact, Koberg and Bagnall (1981) suggest that the stages occur simultaneously as well as progressively. We gain constant feedback by checking the previous steps as we proceed in solving a problem.

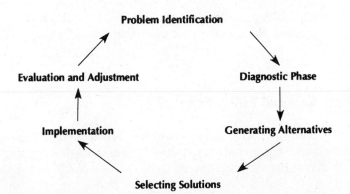

It should be noted, as an aside, that one reason why we fail to invest enough time and energy in problem solving is that problem solving forces us to admit that there is a problem in the first place, that we are less than perfect, and that change is likely to be called for. These are difficult pills to swallow. Change is usually uncomfortable at best and painful at worst. Who needs it? With that in mind, let's take an excursion into rational problem solving.

◆ *Reader Activity*

The goal here is to consider thoroughly a problem you have and then generate as many alternatives as you can discover. Whether you decide that change is not worth the price or choose a conservative or even radical alternative is up to you.

Identify three problems that play important parts in your life—problems that have been with you for a while and that you would like to resolve. In this instance, a problem is defined as a state or condition in your life that you believe probably requires changing. Now, think of a friend you respect and trust and who knows you rather well. Ask this person to take an evening with you to problem-solve one of the conditions you have indicated. Promise to do the same for that individual if he or she believes the process is worthwhile. The purpose of the friend's involvement is to provide you with a different perspective, to help turn over stones that you might not see, to push you further, and to ask tough questions you might not be willing to ask. The friend will represent another side of reality.

You can also perform this activity with a small group. Because a group represents more ideas, concerns, and points of view, a bit more time is required to do justice to the problem-solving process.

Follow the problem-solving process outlined in the following section a step at a time. Don't hurry. Probe each explicit question and then ask yourself other questions that naturally come to mind. Your goal is to find a better way. But be warned that problem solving is serious business, because it should influence you and your life. One reason we fail to take such activities seriously is that many of us have spent time doing just this with inconsequential problems. If there is nothing important you wish to explore in order to enjoy the stimulation of the search, then move on and read through the process with the thought that it may prove valuable later.   ◆

A Model for Rational Problem Solving

Step 1. Make a general description of the problem condition as you see it. What seems to be the crux of the problem? How does it influence you? Where's the rub? Talk the problem over in general terms, trying to outline the parameters.

Step 2. Describe what the defined condition would be like in an ideal but reachable state.   Here we are trying to establish a sense of the changes that would have to occur by looking hypothetically at, for example, how production operations in a factory might differ, how the attitudes of people might change in certain working relationships, how discipline in a classroom might change, how a group might solve problems differently. Again, it is important to talk over the ideal condition and obtain a feel for it. This in itself will often help sharpen the focus on the real problem. The concern is *what* could be rather than *how* to achieve it.

Step 3. Identify the specific discrepancies that exist between the present view of reality (step 1) and the ideal state (step 2).   The problem(s) should begin to take on a different shape as a result of this analysis.

Step 4. Analyze the nature of the condition more thoroughly.   Do this by asking a series of critical questions:

1. Does there appear to be more than one problem, each of which warrants individual attention? Although the relationships between certain problems must be recognized, the more concretely a problem can be defined, the less difficult will be the task of problem resolution.

2. What benefits does the present condition hold for the individual, group, or organization that is defining it as a problem? One reason why problems don't just disappear is that very real satisfactions have to be given up to solve them. Consider for a moment the benefits that the smoker who "wants" to quit must give up, the benefits that the obese individual will have to sacrifice, the benefits that accrue to the person with the volatile temper who would "really like to stop blowing up all the time," the benefits realized by the "talker" even though the individual knows his or her talking alienates some people, and the benefits to a group that constantly complains about starting a meeting late or about members arriving late. Until a group or an individual is willing to look such benefits squarely in the face, the chance of significant change occurring will be slight. If we are not somehow compensated for these lost benefits, it might be crazy to change, even though we'd be the last to admit it.

3. What are the blockages that have been thrown up in the face of previous attempts at change? Underlying a blockage may be a hidden benefit that subtly supports the existence of the status quo.

4. Finally, what solutions are currently being attempted unsuccessfully? By taking a hard look at our unsuccessful efforts, we often gain a clearer understanding of the problem itself. For example, one supervisor would procrastinate in getting corrected work reviews back to her subordinate, who often needed the information but would "simply make do." The subordinate hated conflict and couldn't confront his boss. Not only that, but he couldn't stand the feeling of being a nag. Thus, instead of mentioning his need, the subordinate withdrew from the problem and never faced up to the difficulties being created. The boss, on the other hand, was being subtly reinforced (not being accountable meant not having

to do the work). Thus, part of the problem was the subordinate's attitude toward the problem.

Step 5. Now, in light of all the new information about the problem condition, redefine it as clearly and succinctly as possible.   It is not uncommon to discover that there are several problems. But in order to ensure that the time invested will be put to good use, it is necessary to isolate the one problem that is most important to solve and whose solution might have the greatest impact on other existing conditions. Several examples of clear, succinct problem conditions follow. Note that a problem condition simply describes a state that needs changing; there is no implication of good or bad and no implied solution.

1. The present level of shared participation in our meetings.
2. My ability to state my personal opinions in a group.
3. The present level of productivity by team A.
4. The present level of absenteeism in this department.
5. My ability to assert myself in conflict situations in which I wish to make my point.

Step 6. Without considering the implications of a particular solution, generate as many alternatives as possible.   Potential solutions might result from reflection on any of the previous steps. The key in this stage is not to worry about implementation or consequences but simply to develop real, concrete choices that presently are not available to you.

Step 7. Screen the various alternatives by changing them into specific objectives that by their nature suggest direction and quantity and where and when they will occur.   Also make an effort to determine which of the resulting objectives will have the greatest impact at the least cost to you or the organization and which objectives, for whatever reason, seem impractical. This is a preliminary screening step; more will occur later. Taking the first condition used as an example in step 5—the present level of shared participation in meetings—possible objectives might include

1. To provide each participant with ten chips at the beginning of each meeting. They must give up a chip each time they speak. Once a person's chips are gone, she or he has no opportunity to speak again unless more chips are negotiated from other members.
2. To establish the rule that during periods of discussion an individual can make a second point only after each other person in the group has been given the opportunity to speak.
3. To have a person appointed prior to each meeting to the role of "participant observer." This person is responsible for pointing out, through various means (for example, a chart of how often each person speaks), how effectively the group is communicating.

4. To identify the leader as primarily responsible for gaining the input of all members.

An objective for the fourth condition—the present level of absenteeism—might perhaps be to use the last six months as a baseline for absenteeism and to provide a paid day off every two weeks when team members have, as a group, averaged 30 percent below that baseline for a month. Recipients of the paid day off would be rotated throughout the team over time.

The most effective objectives are those that are specific enough to be measured in some manner. At this point we are less concerned with practicality than we are with clarity and specificity. Once clarity has been insured, other considerations related to the value of a particular objective can be discussed.

Although you may not necessarily agree with the objective for attacking absenteeism, it is clear, is specific in intent, and provides information about what would occur, when, to whom, and under what conditions—and that is our aim during step 7.

Step 8. Consider the consequences, the price to be paid, the impact on the individual or the organization or group if each of the selected objectives were implemented.   Then decide whether to alter the objective, either to improve its effectiveness or to reduce the negative consequences that will result. This hard-nosed step of anticipating consequences is often overlooked because of the enthusiasm and blush of success that often surround the generation of solutions. As we showed previously, there are numerous attempts at change and many reasons for their failure. Thus the surrendering of chips as individuals talked might initially be seen as fun but later be resented as a game and tossed off as impractical. Assigning a process observer the legitimate role of keeping participation high and communication open seems not only appropriate but feasible. Even this idea has its limitations, however, because most observers must be trained, given time in the group, and supported.

Thus, this step is down-to-earth and ultimately practical. Its purpose is to make an objective workable or to discard it. Questions need to be raised about such issues as

- motivating people to accept a particular idea
- ensuring the group has the necessary skills to facilitate success
- overcoming cost factors
- educating people to the value of a new idea
- exploring issues of timing and the pace of implementation of a new idea
- overcoming previous failures as well as the "we've-done-it-before" syndrome.

These and any number of other factors could render a potentially good idea, as translated into an objective, ineffective. This step, then, explores not only consequences but also the strategies necessary to overcome potential resistances and to polish the objective into something that will work.

Step 9. Monitor and develop appropriate support systems to insure the stabilizing of most change efforts.   Actually, generating alternatives is the easiest part of problem solving! Getting those alternatives into action often proves impossible. Looking at consequences and building support strategies in step 8 are helpful. But equally important is establishing the means of effective accountability. The reason why New Year's resolutions are seldom kept is that there is no accountability built into the process, not to mention the problem of consequences that we aren't about to consider at the time we commit ourselves. Increasingly, we find that for change to work, groups and individuals need to know that some time in the future, the results of their promise to act will be assessed. Viewed in this light, monitoring can be utilized as a means of support and development rather than as a means of punishment and control. Monitoring suggests adjusting and adapting a process to insure success. Thus it should occur early enough to be motivating and helpful, before mistakes are made that cannot be corrected and prior to the setting in of guilt.

Support systems are vital to most monitoring processes. For example, legitimizing all the talk about the process of change with people who have been through it before (AA, Weight Watchers, new students, ex-convicts) or with people who are undergoing similar experiences in the present can be gratifying, reassuring, and profitable. It is always helpful to learn from others' experience. In addition, making public one's own objectives tends to have a positive impact; one's commitment is supported by others who now expect action to occur and will reinforce it.

Step 10. Evaluate problem-solving efforts to decide what steps should be taken next.   There are several ways in which a relatively simple evaluation can occur. First, at a designated time in the future, assess the degree to which the discrepancies between the present situation and the ideal have increased or decreased from the period of original assessment. A second approach is to take the objectives established in step 7 and compare them to specific outcomes.

Further problem solving can occur at this point. It is ill-advised to consider problem solving, as many do, a one-shot operation. Most problem solving is a jerky, inconsistent process that results in success and failure and, one hopes, an overall sense of accomplishment. But as long as all are willing to continue looking at the process of change, there is a good chance that the natural mistakes that inevitably occur and the natural resistance that accompanies virtually any efforts at change will disappear.

Some of you may be wondering how a simple problem became so complicated. It is we who are complex, along with the multitude of factors that impinge on us and make simple decisions difficult. The problem-solving process in which you have been wandering about is, in fact, rather simple compared to some (Easton, 1976; Kepner and Tregoe, 1968). The problem is that it is rare for individuals to have the time, patience, endurance, or courage to expend the kind of energy required to tackle some of these creative and technically sound approaches to problem solving and decision making. Furthermore, the issue is complicated by the question of who should be present during the problem solving. Sound and highly structured problem solving can take literally thousands of hours of time; and with many problems, it is difficult to measure whether a complex or a simplified process is preferable. Perhaps it is most important to help people adopt a tough-minded view of problem solving that they can bring to bear without requiring a cumbersome and time-consuming procedure except in special situations.[2]

Pareto Analysis

Another form of "left-brain" analysis is the Pareto analysis and diagram, which is being used increasingly in organization management and with organizational work groups.

Pareto Analysis and Diagram

Much advice on decision making appears in management literature, but only rarely does one find any reference to the Pareto system (also known as the 80/20 rule and the ABC method). Nevertheless, the Pareto principle can be a significant decision-making aid.

The Pareto diagram takes its name from the Italian economist Vilfredo Frederico Damaso Pareto (1848–1923). In the course of his studies on the unequal distribution of income, Pareto found that 80 percent of the wealth was controlled by only 20 percent of the population. The essence of the Pareto method of inspection and analysis, then, is identifying that vital few to which corrective action can be applied where it will do the most good, the most quickly.

Steps in Developing a Pareto Diagram:

1. List the condition(s) or cause(s) you wish to monitor—for example, absenteeism. (In the list, discussion, and illustrations that follow, we draw on an example suggested by Dr. Gloria Bader, president of the Bader Group, San Diego, CA.)
2. Collect the raw data (names, numbers of days absent, and so on.)
3. Rank the various conditions or causes from highest to lowest (most absent to least absent). See Table 7.2.

---

2. For an alternative strategy for individual or group problem solving, refer to Exercise 3 at the end of the chapter (Lewin, 1948, p. 51).

4. Under a horizontal axis, write these causes in descending order (the most important cause to the left and the least important to the right). Thus in Figure 7.1 we find John on the left with 9 absences and Don on the right with only 1 absence.
5. On the left-hand vertical axis, note the measurement scale (total number of days absent).
6. On the right-hand vertical axis, note the percentage scale (the total number of absences must equal 100 percent).
7. Plot the data and then the cumulative frequencies.

In a hypothetical example, consider a group of 15 workers. Table 7.2 gives data for the employees who missed at least one day of work in October.

This table shows that John, Alice, and Bob are the worst offenders. One could have anticipated that these three would be somewhere near the top. However, one would not have guessed that between them, they would account for nearly 75 percent of all absences. Confronted by these results, the organization may feel that it has been too tolerant—especially in the case of John.

Advantages and a Disadvantage

A Pareto diagram is an extension of the cause-and-effect-diagram in that the causes are not only identified but also listed in order of their occurrence. The possible applications of a Pareto diagram are almost infinite. Because cost, quantity, and quality are the three main concerns of management, the Pareto diagram is a powerful tool that should be familiar to every decision maker or group of decision makers. It can be used as a motivator, and it is easy to implement and understand.

Table 7.2 Absenteeism

Name	Days Absent	Percent of Total Days Absent
John	9	30.0
Alice	7	23.3
Bob	6	20.0
Mark	3	10.0
Kim	2	6.7
Diane	2	6.7
Don	1	3.3
Totals	30	100.00

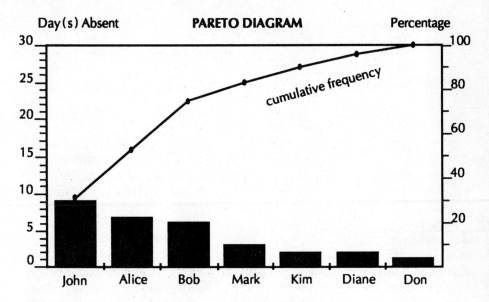

Figure 7.1 Comparison of Day(s) Absent from Work Per Person

The main disadvantage of a Pareto diagram is that only quantifiable data can be used in constructing it.

Intuitive Problem Solving: A Right-Hemisphere Focus

The only problem with an orderly, systematic, linear approach to problem solving is that it overlooks the important intuitive aspect of problem solving. Many of us would like to believe that the product of a rational approach will be the most reasonable, appropriate, and qualitatively best response possible. But anyone who has experienced serious problem solving realizes that many of the most creative decisions result from some unexpected thought, from an aside tossed off in jest, from a moment when defenses were down, or at a point of exhaustion, frustration, or exasperation that could never have been programmed or anticipated.

Thus, a key to effective problem solving is not just providing order and a tough-minded approach to viewing causes and consequences. It also involves bringing to the surface as many of the existing solutions as possible. This means overcoming our personal predispositions, defenses, and habits in order to give ourselves as many choices as possible. So it is that serious problem solvers are forever looking for ways of becoming "unstuck," of taking a new and different look, of redefining the problem in a manner that may provide a new perspective and freedom to consider alternatives not yet accessible to them.

Becoming "Unstuck"

Opening the floodgate to new ideas may occur in many ways, some of which are created by rephrasing a question or by posing one that gives permission to look outside the psychological boundaries we often impose subtly on a problem. One approach is simply to step back and take the time to redefine the problem in a number of ways, using totally different words. Legitimizing new words and pushing ourselves to other definitions often uncover a useful approach to the solution, because many answers fall too neatly out of the problem statement itself.

Another approach to uprooting one's mind-set is to discuss the problem via analogies, thus forcing ourselves to think about a problem in terms of its similarity to other, unrelated situations or objects. This approach is based on the assumption that if two things are similar in some respects, it is very likely that they are similar in others. A stubborn person standing in the way of progress, seemingly intransigent, may be likened to a boulder or a rooted tree stump. Pausing to consider ways of removing the boulder or uprooting the stump may open up the discussion. Pushing the boulder in the direction opposite to forward progress may free it and then allow rapid forward movement. Similarly, an individual may be insisting on a point of view simply because others have refused to recognize its legitimacy. Giving due credit is often difficult in arguments, but it may be the key to inducing the individual to give up a cherished—though impractical—position. Saving face seems a long way from the pushing of a boulder, but they may be similar indeed.

Another related approach is to have problem solvers think metaphorically. Talking about old age and retirement conjures up fear and resistance in many individuals. For some it suggests the end, giving up, relinquishing one's sense of potency, and becoming dependent. But if a discussion by people about to retire is framed in terms of how to enjoy the "freedom years," then resistances might be reduced.

A route that is a bit more unusual is to have individuals take apparently very different situations and ideas and probe for similarities. Such an exercise forces another look at the givens, at the reality of a problem, which in turn opens up the possibility of new insight.

Stopping a discussion and injecting one of the following open-ended statements may be all that is needed to discover new entrances into the problem:

> This situation or problem is just like . . .
>
> A different way to describe this is . . .
>
> The only time anything like this happened before was . . .
>
> This feels like a . . .
>
> This situation reminds me of . . .

◆ Reader Activity

Consider any recent open-ended problem you or your group have had or still are concerned about. Now take at least two of the methods suggested here and reconsider the problem. Try to use different words to describe it, perhaps developing several definitions of the same problem. Utilize a metaphor or develop an analogy and try to uncover every possible similarity between the problem and that to which you are making the comparison. You will be surprised at the number of insights that result from being forced to stretch your thinking in this simple approach to problem assessment.   ◆

Brainstorming

The first real break away from strictly rational, linear, and highly controlled approaches to problem solving came nearly half a century ago when Alex Osborn (1953) introduced the concept of brainstorming. He discovered that by establishing a few simple rules and utilizing a limited amount of time in a different manner, he could dramatically alter the atmosphere in a problem-solving session and, in his estimation, create more and often better ideas than might otherwise occur. Needless to say, such innovation is always a source of controversy, and the real value and significance of brainstorming have been a subject of heated debate for years. Whether, for example, brainstorming groups are actually more productive than individuals working alone is a question that needs discussion. There is no question, however, that this procedure opened the gate to more creative approaches to problem solving.

Brainstorming is a technique designed to do two separate things:

1. To make sure that the creativity of each individual is not limited by various influence processes that occur in groups, such as fear of social embarrassment, pressures for conformity, and status systems that discourage low-status members from participating.

2. At the same time, to take maximum advantage of whatever creativity-enhancing forces exist in groups: social support, reinforcement for contributing, cross stimulation, and the positive norms of working together.

For many people, brainstorming is a strange sort of experience, and it can create an initial sense of discomfort (Collaros and Anderson, 1969; Hammond and Goldman, 1961; Vroom, Grant, and Cotton, 1969). Butler (1981) argues that brainstorming is an important group process that can help us understand how creative innovations and strategies for change happen in groups.

To a relaxed group familiar with the process, brainstorming may be a stimulating and useful approach to generating ideas. To a restricted, self-conscious group, however, it could actually prove a hindrance, because it forces members into new patterns of behavior and violates certain norms that usually protect the participants (Bergum and Lehr, 1963; Bouchard, 1969). Conversely, if it is used at the right time, brainstorming can break open a stuffy and inhibited group. Research has shown that even when group members anticipate some sort of evaluation, brainstorming remains a productive process for the group (Maginn and Harris, 1980). Much depends on the facilitator's ability to read effectively the behavioral cues of the group and on the group's familiarity with the following ground rules of brainstorming:

1. There is usually a preliminary practice to make sure the rules are understood. The subject will be a basis for having fun and getting the creative juices flowing. Men's canes have gone out of style. What could you do to repopularize them? In what ways might graduation exercises be improved?
2. One person agrees to serve as "secretary" and record each idea.
3. A time limit is set—anywhere from 1 minute to perhaps 15.
4. Ideas are presented and placed before the group as rapidly as possible with no discussion, clarification, or comment.
5. <u>Criticism or evaluation of ideas is not permitted.</u>
6. Quantity is very important. Each individual should not screen his or her ideas. Each person can piggyback on ideas he or she has heard in order to generate more ideas.
7. When moving around the group, it is often helpful to limit members to one idea at a time to encourage less vocal members to get their ideas out.

After a list of ideas has been generated, those most obviously impracticable or ridiculous are eliminated from the list. The substantial number of ideas that remain are then subjected to serious scrutiny.

It is important to follow the rules of brainstorming. Otherwise, participants often criticize ideas and dominant individuals exert too much influence. Recent research reveals that this damages the essential rationale for brainstorming and gives creative problem solving a bad name (VanGundy, 1984, p. 16).

What is the real value of brainstorming? Are there ways in which it might benefit a group beyond simply generating a large quantity of ideas for solving problems? The fact is that we are living in a time when people are demanding to be heard and involved. People are using group decision-making procedures for an ever-widening variety of problems. How is it possible to facilitate the work of these groups? Brainstorming, given the proper exposure and a relatively nonjudgmental climate, has much to offer a decision-making group, particularly during the diagnostic stage and the generating of alternatives in problem solving. For example, brainstorming

■ reduces dependency on a single authority figure
■ encourages the open sharing of ideas

- stimulates greater participation within the group
- increases individual safety in a highly competitive group
- provides for a maximum of output in a short period of time
- helps to insure a nonevaluative climate, at least in the ideation phase of the meeting
- provides the participants with immediate visibility for the ideas that are generated
- develops some degree of accountability for the ideas among the group because they have been generated internally and not imposed from outside
- tends to be enjoyable and stimulating

Thus the process is self-reinforcing; it draws the participants into new avenues of thought and into a new pattern of communication. How efficient the method is—and it can be efficient—is secondary in importance to its potential for facilitating shared problem solving.

◆ Reader Activity

After all the discussion of brainstorming, you probably want to try it on for size. What follows might be used as a warm-up activity for a group involved in serious problem solving. Like anything else, brainstorming requires the participants to be in the right mood if the benefits of the process are to be gained. Thus, the following could be used with a group of fifty or with as few as two or three people. It helps if a large sheet of newsprint is available to write down the ideas as they are generated.

We live in a highly critical society in which competition and a win–lose atmosphere are often the rule. It is not uncommon to see people getting ahead by putting someone else down. Brainstorming is a means of reducing this inclination. Still, it requires practice to overcome the inclination to be negative and overly evaluative. With this in mind, get ready to brainstorm. Read the following brief story:

> A small wholesaler in the hinterlands of Mexico had called his buyer in Vera Cruz and asked him to obtain an order of pipe cleaners from the United States. Señor Gonzales, the buyer, agreed. He also agreed to advance Señor Gomez (the wholesaler) a substantial sum to finance the deal. A month later, just as the ship was arriving in Vera Cruz, Señor Gonzales received a frantic phone call from Señor Gomez. Apparently the warehouse and outlet store had burned down and there simply was no more business. Gonzales was suddenly faced with somehow selling 200,000 pipe cleaners.

You and your group have exactly three minutes to generate as many creative alternatives as possible. Don't think, don't hold back, anything goes.

After three minutes, your list may include as many as 20, 30, or even 40 items. Depending on how far you wish to go, the next step would be to take the five or six best ideas and spend time creatively developing them further. Usually the screening process is based on criteria that are developed by the group and that incorporate parameters important to the problem solvers. ◆

Other Methods of Generating Ideas

Brainstorming is meant to reduce inhibitions, to encourage new ideas, to legitimize the unthinkable, and to push the participants past the bounds of their normally restrictive thinking. Over the years, a variety of methods related to brainstorming have been developed that can be used with small groups (Gordon, 1961; Phillips, 1948; Prince, 1970; Rickards, 1974).

Nominal Group Technique It has been noted that groups that use conventional interactive techniques tend to pursue a limited train of thought (Dunnette, Campbell, and Jaastad, 1963; Taylor, Berry, and Block, 1958); confer undue influence on high-status persons (Dalkley and Helmer, 1963; Hare, 1976; Torrance, 1955; and Tuckman and Lorge, 1962); and generate group pressure for conformity (Dalkley and Helmer, 1963; Hoffman, 1962). There also arise dysfunctional "hidden agenda" effects (Collaros and Anderson, 1969) and an amount of time required for the group to maintain itself (Maier and Hoffman, 1962).

The nominal group technique (NGT) (Dalbecq, Van de Ven and Gustafson 1975) was developed to gain the benefits of group participation and to improve group participation while minimizing competition, domination by a few individuals, and the pressure of time constraints. The nominal group technique is most frequently used in generating goals and in choosing among alternative goals or policies.

In an impressive series of 8 studies—involving 228 groups—that compared NGT with conventional interactive techniques, NGT was found to be superior in every instance (Carr, 1975; Chung and Ferris, 1971; Frederick, 1976; Gustafson, Skukla, Delbecq, and Walster, 1973; Nemiroff, Pasmore, and Ford, 1976; Van de Ven and Delbecq, 1974; and White, Blythe, and Corrigan, 1977).

NGT involves a two stage process. Individuals work separately in the first or elicitation stage, then work as an interacting group on the evaluation (choosing) stage. The first stage involves generating alternative means, generating alternative goals, or deciding on the best answer. The second stage involves the group collectively listing and then evaluating the plans, ideas, or judgments that were generated in the first stage (McGrath, 1984).

The nominal group technique is being used with increasing frequency. Recently Fox (1989) has introduced some modifications for an improved nominal group technique (INGT) by communicating the purpose of the meeting in advance to participants and inviting them to submit on 3 × 5 cards any ideas they have. The cards are duplicated and sent to each participant in advance. The participants are then invited to bring the full list, and their suggested changes or combinations, to the meeting. To reduce further the power of personality or status at the evaluation stage, Fox recommends that each participant use a 3 × 5 card to state his or her concern, suggestion, or modification. The facilitator picks these cards up and reads them.

The improved nominal group technique is appropriate for identifying and evaluating options, positions, or problems; solving a problem when no standard is available; and reviewing and refining written proposals or other documents. Typically, an INGT is designed to address one purpose in a 1½-to-3-hour session. For example, a meeting might be devoted to identifying and ordering the most pressing problems confronting a group. Then a second meeting is used to solve one of the top-priority problems identified.

The nominal group technique can be especially powerful because it allows individuals to generate ideas independently (the creativity of brainstorming) and then brings them together to evaluate those ideas. Some feel it offers the best of both worlds.

Brainwriting   VanGundy (1984) discussed the benefits of brainstorming versus brain*writing*. In brainwriting, as in nominal groups, individuals write down their ideas on sheets of paper. The papers are then exchanged and other members of the group make modifications and suggestions in writing. Research shows that brainstorming rated high on "accommodation of social interaction" and "contribution to group cohesiveness," whereas brainwriting was low in these areas. However, brainwriting ranked high in idea quantity and quality, whereas brainstorming ranked medium in these areas. Given that most methods have advantages and disadvantages, one must continually ask, "Which method best addresses the needs of the particular group at hand?" (VanGundy 1984, pp. 17–19).

Trigger Groups   An attempt to build on the strength of nominal groups (no fear of group competition, domination of a few individuals, or the constraints of time as in traditional brainstorming), this approach has each member read his or her individually developed ideas to the whole group. The group gives its full attention to each person. Thus each member of a group may be asked to consider the 10 best or 10 wildest ideas in relation to a particular problem. The group's task in a series of 5- or 10-minute periods is to take each idea and clarify, expand, or build on it or in some manner trigger new ideas that will further develop the thought. Each individual has his or her ideas exposed to the constructive assistance of the group, and during the first round, no attempt is made to criticize. Members feel that they are heard and that their ideas are received positively, and a real effort is made to see where each idea may have value. After enough of the ideas have been explored in this manner, the group develops criteria to determine which ideas have the greatest value. Then there ensues a discussion that ultimately reduces the suggestions to a single one or perhaps two or three.

One can easily imagine a number of creative variations on this theme. For example, a group of seven or eight people is asked to develop perhaps 10 ideas around a particular theme in a brainstorming fashion. The ideas are then discussed openly in terms of the strengths of various items. A second group, which has been watching the activity quietly from outside the group, is then asked after 10 or 15 minutes of discussion to switch places with the first group. They are requested to develop 10 new ideas, considering the strengths discussed by the first group. They then discuss their ideas, again focusing on strengths. Finally, after 15 minutes or so of discussion, clusters of four are formed by two members from each group. These clusters (approximately four or five) are then asked to develop two or three of the best ideas that seem to incorporate as many as possible of the strengths suggested in both of the large groups. These finely tuned ideas are then presented to the entire group perhaps an hour later. A group that is representative of the whole then determines which idea or combination of ideas best suit their requirements. The advantages of such a design include

> the generating of ideas in a nonthreatening atmosphere
>
> a relatively nonjudgmental screening process
>
> the opportunity to build on one set of ideas after listening to benefits, thus reaching beyond ordinary limits or boundaries
>
> the development of competition in the best sense of the word as individuals in the second group of eight try to generate new and even better ideas, and the groups of four attempt to develop the best idea or combination of ideas knowing that three or four other groups are doing the same thing
>
> full participation by a large number of individuals
>
> the utilization of individual resources, both in the development of ideas and in the important critiquing and selecting phase
>
> the efficient utilization of time itself

Round Robin Groups   Another creative means of generating ideas involves a small group of perhaps five individuals (simultaneous groups of five can be working on the same problem at the same time). Five problems that need solving and are recognized as open-ended are selected by the group. Generally, these are operational problems—those that influence people who work together, are hindering a particular task, or are seen as within the purview of the group working on them. They should be problems that do not depend on some outside authority for determination. Each individual writes the problem he or she has been given on the top of three 5-by-8-inch cards and then proceeds to write a different idea or solution on each card. After perhaps five minutes, each individual passes his or her three cards to the next individual, who then writes a new solution or idea on each of the three cards. Ideas can be original or can simply be constructive additions to what is already there. After each individual has had the opportunity to respond to all the problems, each original problem is summarized by one person, integrating the ideas from each of the three cards onto newsprint. These are then returned to the whole group of five, whose job is to discuss the pros and cons of the various ideas and determine whether a creative and operationally viable idea emerges. Obviously, such an approach assumes that the group has the necessary time (from one to two days) to work effectively on the various ideas. If less time is available, a variation of the design would be to develop only one or two ideas with a slightly different manner of passing the various cards through the group.

The Wildest Idea   Strange as it seems, one reason why creativity is minimized in a group of creative individuals is that permission is not given to be "wild and crazy." Telling individuals in either a brainstorming group or a nominal group to generate the wildest ideas they can imagine in relation to a particular problem elicits thoughts that never would be considered in the normal course of events, when most people are usually worried about their image or what is appropriate. Thus when a group is bogged down, ideas are not coming, and frustration is mounting in a problem-solving effort, the simple request to drop all pretense and let go for five minutes with the most outrageous ideas possible will inject fun, energy, and new interest into the group. In addition, it is very likely that among the "wild and crazy" ideas lie the seeds to some creative new approaches to a solution.

Synectics

William Gordon (1961) worked for years with methods for expanding the vision and creativity of people in problem-solving situations. Dissatisfied with the constructive and yet limiting approaches of brainstorming and nominal groups, he experimented with a variety of methods that would release some of the restricted capacity we have for creative problem solving. Gordon saw our ability to speculate as the key to removing normal resistances and the stereotypical and predictable traps we often fall into while solving problems. From this assumption, Gordon developed his *synectics* theory:

> The word *synectics,* from the Greek, means the joining together of different and apparently irrelevant elements. Synectics theory applies to the integration of diverse individuals into a problem-stating, problem-solving group. It is an operational theory for the conscious use of preconscious psychological mechanisms present in man's creative activity (Gordon, 1961, p. 1).

Prerequisites of a Successful Synectics Group   In their study of problem solving with groups, Gordon and Prince and their colleagues discovered a number of elements that must be present. Just as a synectics excursion must evolve out of the needs of a group and cannot be "canned," although we can provide some productive guidelines, there are no easy formulas for helping a group work more effectively together. Following are some critical areas that merit attention in any problem-solving approach but are of particular importance to those using synectics in a group context.[3]

1. It is necessary to maximize participation and convince individuals that their ideas are valued, which will increase feelings of trust, openness, and willingness to risk. Destructive competition and the developing of win–lose attitudes are the aspects of traditional problem solving that must go. Thus, a prerequisite to any synectics group is paying attention to the need to develop effective group process, with members aware of their impact on the group, and a willingness of the group to monitor its own behavior.

2. A critical factor in any problem-solving group is the willingness and ability of group members to listen. People are so busy selling their own ideas, proving themselves, and reacting to personality rather than words that it is a wonder we hear as much as we do. There are so many intrusions into our listening that something needs to be done that legitimizes "hearing" others and that protects us from our own inclinations to "yell and sell." Active listening (see Chapter 1) is one of the central themes of synectics. Basically, it means being aware of both the verbal and the nonverbal messages being communicated, as well as of the feelings that often carry the real information. By rephrasing, paraphrasing, or in some manner feeding back what we hear another saying, we can make speakers less defensive because they realize they have been heard. Individuals who know they have been heard are less inclined to say it one more time. Thus, if active listening can be built into the problem-solving process and individuals know that it is part of the game, an immediate change in climate can be detected. When we feel understood, it matters less whether the idea itself is eventually adopted because we personally feel accepted.

3. A rather simple pattern that occurs in many groups is created out of our desire to protect ourselves and to put responsibility or, on occasion, blame onto another individual. The pattern is one of asking questions. You might respond to this "wondrous" revelation by shouting back at the page, "Of course, problem solving is all asking questions, probing reality, testing the value of an idea." True, but the trap is that behind nearly every question that an individuals asks is a statement—often an implied answer. The question, then, often incorporates a message we are trying to give with minimal risk, putting the individual who responds on the spot and absolving us from responsibility for the implied statement. Thus, by asking questions, we often shift attention and a sense of blame or guilt onto the person being asked. Questions tend to corner the individual, leaving him

3. See Rickard's discussion (1974, pp. 71–73).

or her feeling trapped and vulnerable—and likely to justify or rationalize his or her response with much more vigor than might otherwise be necessary.

Individuals using synectics attempt to reduce the number of questions being asked and instead encourage participants to make statements that provide new meaning or clarification to a problem or to another idea. In addition, statements provide information about one's own point of view, indicate alternatives, or request additional information. Statements are direct, and they tend to establish ownership immediately. This leads to a sense of integrity in the group itself and again helps to build a climate of trust.

4. One of the crucial differences between a synectics-type meeting and others is that individuals with special influence or power are requested not to run the meeting. It is assumed that their ideas are crucial but their influence is not. All too often the leader is also the boss, with his or her own agenda, whose style and status can create a sense of intimidation, resistance, fear, dependency, or even anger that can corrupt the open problem-solving approach that is being attempted. How often is the boss's idea somehow magically accepted with surprisingly little discussion? Such leaders are so often biased toward predetermined outcomes that people begin to acquiesce at a mere whiff of his or her idea. Participants will take great pains not to place themselves in a win–lose situation with their boss. Selecting a group leader who can lead the problem solving from a position of neutrality and take an objective view of the process boosts the group's chance of success. Of course, such a leader should be acceptable to the group, should not be easily manipulated, and should have skills in active listening, goal setting, and group maintenance.

5. Perhaps one of the most insidious factors that undermine productive group problem solving stems from the natural inclination of group members to be overly critical of each other. Most of us have cut our teeth on a view of group participation that encourages criticism. The problem is that such criticism is often born out of a desire to minimize someone else's success and has little to do with a desire for group success. If we can make someone's ideas appear inadequate, perhaps our own will grow in stature. A simple rule developed in synectics meetings—focusing at first on the strengths of an idea—is validating of the giver and reduces the inclination to defend. In addition, focusing on the positive aspects of an idea often reveals that part of a solution can be used. Even when the idea is clearly inadequate, the first effort is directed at finding ways of improving the idea so that it may be workable. This method reflects the conviction that the more good choices a group has, the better will be the quality of the final product.

6. A synectics viewpoint encourages effective group process. Many of the suggestions would be useful even in more traditional, well-ordered, rational approaches to problem solving. But they are absolutely critical for synectics participants, because at the center of their approach is the *excursion*. There are many ways for an excursion to occur, but all have the common theme of pulling the problem solver away from premature solutions, from patterned, expected, or pre-

dictable thought. The excursion is designed to relax the group, to build a sense of purpose with the added dimension of fun so that participants will be inclined to move beyond the tried and true, away from any preconception of "the right way." The excursion is a trip away from reality and the constraints of expected thought into a realm where unrelated, untested, and creative ideas are valued. Clearly, for participants to allow themselves the freedom to try on totally different, often outrageous, and absurd ideas requires a climate of trust and openness in which there is no fear of being judged and there are no recriminations.

Though ample evidence attests to the effectiveness of synectics, the method is used relatively rarely. Perhaps the benefits are not great enough to warrant the cost in time, the expense of an outside facilitator (few organizational trainers have the necessary skills), and the trust required to complete the process successfully. A recent study by Thamis and Woods (1984) reviewed a longitudinal study within the research-and-development arm of a large multinational organization where synectics are used along with other creative problem-solving techniques aimed at stimulating innovation and creative thinking. To the investigators' surprise, even though synectics was fairly effective, it apparently lost ground to a less successful technique and was eventually phased out of use. In searching for reasons why a problem-oriented group would voluntarily choose mediocrity over a more successful method, Thamis and Woods discovered that the managers using synectics did not like what they deemed its lack of consequence and logic. In a sense, their linear, left-brain attitudes and habits found the creative excursions into nonlinear thinking too uncomfortable, and they opted for the more traditional but less effective approach.

Who Should Decide—The Leader or the Group?

The bulk of this chapter has been involved with how groups and individuals can become more effective problem solvers. Problem solving is nothing more than the process used for developing alternative forms of action that resolve a source of tension, an uncertainty, or a difficulty. Without giving some thought to *how* we solve problems, we have seen our inclination to fool ourselves, narrow our vision, not look at relevant consequences, and sabotage ourselves without even knowing it. Although we have alluded to the actual selection of various choices after certain creative deliberations, we have not talked about the implications of decision making itself.

The Leader's Role

As we have suggested before, many decisions result naturally from a thorough problem analysis in which clear goals have been established, alternatives developed and systematically weighed, and potential consequences measured. Yet there is a way of thinking about decision making that is essential for both the leader and the participant. The critical question that forever plays on the mind of the leader is "Should I make this decision? Can I risk leaving it to the group?" Leaders get themselves into trouble when they are not willing to define the boundaries of their power—when they refuse to let their constituencies know the limits of their influence. By not defining their range of authority, they are capable of arbitrarily making any decision they wish, or they can benevolently turn authority over to the group if so inclined. Their failure to give real definition to how decisions will be made creates a climate of uncertainty, suspicion, and dependency. Many leaders are fearful that by defining their real areas of decision-making power they will leave themselves vulnerable to the irrationality and perhaps irresponsibility of the group, for which they will ultimately be accountable. They don't realize that groups tend to be thoughtful and rational (often too much so) and, if provided with the necessary time and effective problem-solving procedures, will often contribute significantly and make the best decision.

Effective leaders, then, are willing to look carefully at their areas of influence and let their subordinates know categorically what decisions they themselves will always make and what decisions other groups or individuals will be responsible for. At the beginning of any problem-solving activity, the group should reach an understanding about how any decision will be made. If the group's ideas are advisory, the group's advisory status and the reason for it should be made very clear. If the decision for eventual action is to be in the hands of the group, then the particular decision-making method should be understood and discussed. All too often, the dominant players in a group focus on the norms that yield the greatest advantage to themselves (Murnighan, 1985). Leaders should take care when possible to legitimize *all* members by establishing a decision-making process in which everyone participates.

This decision on making a decision occurs prior to the problem solving, because people often lose their rationality as vested interests are threatened. Thus people naturally protect themselves regardless of their goodwill toward the group. A group is usually more willing to commit itself to a fair decision-making method (such as a two-thirds majority) prior to problem solving, before they experience the fear that they may actually have to give up their own idea and go along with one that is less acceptable to them. The integrity of the problem solving is often salvaged by applying this insight and laying the ground rules early. Let's briefly discuss a few simple approaches to making decisions.

Simple Majority Rule

A group should be willing to accept this approach only when the decision is of relatively little consequence and they need a rather quick response. We all know that there are many ways to block a decision so that implementation never occurs. In theory, decisions are made to be implemented. But if 45 percent of a group disagrees with a decision that has significance for them and the life of the group or organization, then the quick-and-dirty majority rule will be perceived as a means of control and manipulation by the majority. Even if the decision is implemented, the large minority may spend its time deviously attempting to disrupt the decision or seeking the means to overthrow it. Finally, invoking majority rule is an easy way of shutting off discussion and the thoughtful views of the minority. This can leave the group wounded and result in future insensitivity and psychological "paybacks." Thus the consequences of how a decision is made may have important repercussions later. However, Falk and Falk (1981) found that a majority rule reduces power inequalities in groups that have a wide range of members who vary in status and power. Campbell (1981) found that a rule by majority can be more useful than that of a plurality because the subgroup coalitions that form can respond to and reflect individual preferences.

Two-Thirds Majority Rule

"Plurality rule" should be used for decisions of greater consequence. If individuals have had the opportunity to discuss various alternatives thoroughly and agree prior to the discussion that a two-thirds vote is "fair," members find it easier to accept the eventual decision. Somehow, the feelings of manipulation that often accompany simple majority rule occur less frequently when members know that it takes 68 percent of the group to influence the total group.

Consensus

This is a terribly misused and abused approach to problem solving and decision making. When using it, one must make a number of assumptions that are rarely justified in working groups.

- A level of trust exists in the group that allows honesty, directness, and candor.
- The group is aware of its own process and can deal with its own behavior openly so that individuals cannot dominate or manipulate the group, so that ideas are actively solicited, and so that members listen and support each other as individuals even when disagreeing with each other's ideas.
- The group is not leader-dominated.
- There is time available to consider opinions, alternatives, and consequences so that time itself does not become a coercive element in the process.
- Members of the group are privy to all necessary information prior to the meeting so that they are familiar with critical issues and can respond intelligently.

Groups that enter a decision-making situation under these conditions find consensus an invigorating and often efficient approach. Those that do not will often find the process painful, aggravating, and nonproductive. The major reason why consensus fails is that people do not understand it. It is not a method that demands agreement by the total group. It simply requires that individuals be willing to go along with the group's predominant view and carry out the implications of the decision in good faith. People may disagree with the view of the great majority. In fact, they are encouraged to hold onto their position until they are willing to live positively with the decision being recommended. It takes trust to argue for one's position in the face of group pressure and just as much trust to back off one's own position and go with the group.

A group that wants to use a consensual approach to decision making must be willing to develop the skills and discipline and take the time necessary to make it work. Without these, the group becomes highly vulnerable to domination or intimidation by a few and to psychological game playing by individuals unwilling to "let go" as the group moves toward a well-conceived decision—and toward inefficiency. Most people are not well trained in the consensus process, so under normal conditions groups are likely to find it neither efficient nor pleasurable. This is because good consensus building induces the need to acknowledge and resolve conflict that is minimized in the nominal group and trigger group methods. Furthermore, because most people are rarely trained in conflict resolution, the consensus process, with its emphasis on grappling with conflict, can alienate members of the group who do not perceive it as a legitimate or welcome part of the problem-solving process.

But even when groups are not particularly well trained in the consensus-building process, once agreement is reached, group satisfaction and the willingness to support the decision are usually high. Furthermore, group members who complete a consensus process tend to be positive about their participation in the group (Schweiger, 1986; Tjosvold and Field, 1983). One study (DeStephen, 1983) showed that the more feedback and discussion were encouraged during the decision-making process, the higher was the group's satisfaction with the decision, and this was consistently the case in groups rated high in consensus.

Thus, if people are willing to pay the price in time and training, to see conflict as a natural and healthy part of decision making, and to let go of their personal agendas in favor of what appears to be good for the group, then consensus may work and will certainly provide many benefits. Satisfaction and commitment to the eventual decision will be the primary outcomes. And because successful consensus building requires effective listening and analysis, the result is often a more skilled and cohesive group prepared to solve problems and make decisions even more effectively in the future.

Delegated Decisions

The more that decisions can be delegated to representative bodies or even to individuals, the more efficient most groups will be, especially those composed of more than seven or eight individuals. Delegated decisions hinge on parties being willing to "take the pulse" of the group, testing ideas thoroughly before moving ahead with a particular idea. Again, this depends on the members' trusting that decisions made for the group are not based on the vested interests of individuals. Clearly, decisions of a controversial nature should be accorded a problem-solving forum that allows maximum participation. Essential to delegated decisions is the presence of procedures for critical review and accountability so that members of any delegated task force realize how the effectiveness of their efforts is to be measured.

Double Vote

Many organizations would like to involve relatively large numbers of people in decision making on a wide range of issues that influence their lives. This rarely occurs, however, because leaders believe that these individuals will not be as rational as they themselves would be or because they hear that an emotional speech or bandwagon effect might influence the outcome in some irrational and undesirable manner. The following method, although imperfect, has proved highly successful in minimizing these legitimate concerns.

Let's imagine that as a result of a thoughtful problem-solving process, a large number of alternatives are being considered for a department of 100 people. The ideas have been drawn from committee and task-force recommendations that have involved a large number of the people at one time or another. Being considered are ideas ranging from alternatives for using the parking lot to methods for participative management, and recommendations, some of which require choosing between two alternatives. The management has agreed that all the ideas are acceptable if the group desires them. Ideas not selected may be explored further at a later date, but present policy will continue if a new idea is not selected. The method for decision making is as follows:

1. Each alternative that is proposed is written as a brief paragraph stating as specifically as possible what changes will occur, when and how they are to be accomplished, and how they will be monitored.

2. The task force or committee responsible for the recommendation is noted so that clarification and discussion can continue during the coming week.

3. The following week a ballot is distributed. Ideally, this would occur at a large meeting where time would be provided for further clarification but not debate, because it is assumed that controversial issues have been discussed at length during the preceding week. Because the voting process is based on 100 percent of the distributed ballots, a meeting at which those who are present vote is often preferred.

4. Individuals are requested to vote for each alternative they find acceptable.

5. Any alternative that receives a two-thirds vote is placed on a second ballot. A report containing all of the results is distributed the next day. The following

week, members are encouraged to lobby and discuss their views prior to a second vote. We find that the first vote serves as a reality test and energizes the participants to new levels of interest.

6. The second vote, held a week after the first, relates only to those items that received at least two-thirds of the vote on the first ballot. Those alternatives receiving a two-thirds vote on the second ballot are then accepted to be implemented. A representative group is selected from the total population to help in the implementation phase and to monitor the progress of each recommendation for several months.

The benefits of such a complex and time-consuming process are many. First, participation, discussion, and influence on the system are being exercised by individuals who must live with their own decisions. Second, knowing that ideas not accepted in the voting can be raised at a later date encourages members of the organization to seek constructive change and support for their ideas. As a result, they feel potent and interested in the life of the organization. The major drawback is that the leader of such an organization must have a clear view of which areas of influence are shared, and this must be communicated specifically so that false expectations are not raised. Finally, the leader must be willing to accept the group's recommendations even though he or she does not necessarily agree totally with them. Limits on policy issues and on the expenditure of funds can be explored before alternatives reach the ballot.

Questions Frequently Asked

In many ways, effective decision making requires as much creativity and judgment as the formal problem-solving process. There is no question that decision making should not be taken for granted and that it can be designed in a variety of ways depending on the realities of each situation and the goals of the leader. Issues of participation, acceptance, and overall morale are all influenced by how the leader decides to decide. For participants, it is important always to understand what is happening, and why, and whether the process seems equitable. Often, leaders have never considered the implications of their own decision-making behavior and would be open to alternatives once educated to the consequences of their own actions.

The following questions are frequently asked in relation to the use of groups in problem solving and decision making.

Do groups appear more effective in problem solving than individuals, especially considering the number of hours invested? Over the past twenty years there has been little evidence to refute the idea that there are good reasons for using groups in some problem-solving endeavors. However, few of these reasons involve efficiency. Increasingly, research suggests that individuals and nominal groups are equal to or more effective than natural groups (assuming no training) when undertaking problem-solving activities (Campbell, 1968; Rotter and Portergal, 1969; Principle and Neeley, 1983). (A nominal group, as defined earlier, is one in which ideas are generated by members working independently and then pooled; a *natural group* is one in which members work cooperatively at the same task.) Some working groups are slowed down and reduced to a level of performance equal to the slowest member (McCurdy and Lambert, 1952); others become polarized as a result of the group discussions (Moscovici and Zavalloni, 1969). Furthermore, even in groups designed to facilitate the open sharing of ideas, differences in status and perceived authority can inhibit productivity (Collaros and Anderson, 1969; Voytas, 1967; Vroom, Grant, and Cotton, 1969). Yet it is true that in a number of specific instances, a group effort can be justified over that of nominal groups or individuals. For example, when a task involves the integrating of a number of perceptual and intellectual skills, it has been found that group members tend to supplement one another as resources (Napier, 1967). Also, when a major goal of the group is to create commitment to certain goals or to influence opinions, the involvement of individuals appears essential (Kelley and Thibaut, 1969; Lewin, 1948). However, when it comes to simply producing ideas in quantity or even quality, the evidence (though in some cases it is mixed) does not support the enthusiasm shown in recent years for working in groups (Moore, 1987).

Does training enhance the problem-solving capabilities of a group?

Work groups have existed as long as there have been problems, and there seems to be a casual assumption that the process is natural and even simple. But as previously shown, using group resources effectively requires great skill on the part of the facilitator as well as skill and understanding on the part of the members. One reason why problem-solving groups' efforts tend to fare poorly when compared with the work output of individuals or nominal groups is that they are invariably untrained and, to make matters worse, they are usually "stranger" groups. The result is that the group members not only have to coordinate their work efforts but are also caught in the midst of tensions common to any developing group (see "The Stages of Group Development," Chapter 9). There is still little research comparing the quantitative and qualitative products of trained and well-practiced groups with those of individuals or nominal groups. However, the early evidence that laboratory training sessions, in which individuals are given the opportunity to learn group skills through the systematic observation of their own performance on a variety of tasks, have impressive transfer value to other group situations (Hall and Williams, 1970; Stuls, 1969; Tolela, 1967) still holds today.

In one interesting experiment, requiring the solution of a specific task-oriented problem, groups were involved in an interdependent, multistage problem-solving process. Trained groups revealed greater improvement, had higher-quality products, and used the knowledge of members more effectively than untrained groups. In fact, it was shown that groups of institutionalized, neuropsychiatric patients scored significantly better than untrained managerial groups that were assumed to have greater knowledge of procedures and problem-solving operations (Hall and Williams, 1970). Although such research is limited because of the type of training undertaken and the problems involved, the implications are clear. Effective training can maximize the benefits possible within the framework of problem-solving groups. It is important to remember that a general decision-making model does not *always* apply to all groups (Poole, 1981). A group's membership structure, task, and stage of development all affect how it makes decisions.

What are the strengths and limitations of the democratic approach to decision making in groups?   For most working groups, it seems that the key to decision making is a rather loose concept of the democratic process and the rule of the majority. It provides governing "by the people," reduces the threat of tyranny from within the group, and insures that at least half the members will support a particular issue. Nevertheless, this approach to decision making has a number of severe limitations when applied to a group that must live by its own decisions. For example:

1. Under pressure of a vote, individual decisions are often made for the wrong reasons. This is partly the result of different levels of knowledge and understanding present in the group and partly because of extraneous pressures (friendships, propaganda, payment of past favors, and so forth). Thus the group often loses sight of issues in favor of other variables, such as voting "for the person."

2. During the discussions leading to a vote, it is assumed that people will have an opportunity to express their opinions and to influence the group, but this is seldom the case. Many individuals simply do not have the skills to influence their own destinies in groups. It is the rare group in which silence is not taken as consent, the shy person is drawn into the discussion, and everyone's intent is to consider all ideas, not just to project one's own. Therefore, the basis on which a vote is taken is often faulty or at least premature.

3. The will of the majority can be used effectively as a means of reducing tension (strong differences of opinion) and the time needed to discuss a problem. A vote can be a means of getting on to other business. This, of course, fails to take into consideration whether the support for the decision is enough to insure effective implementation.

4. There is also the problem of power and despotism in a democratically run group. How often is the dissenting minority perceived as a disrupting influence? How often is the minority opinion seen as a threat to the cohesion of the group? And how often are such pressures used to coerce the dissenters back into line? If the vote is used to override the opinion of this minority faction, the vote itself stands to further polarize the group and magnify the divisive lines upon which the vote is taken.

5. Similarly, rather than providing a solution, the vote may actually create more problems. Instead of resolving differences, the minority may

spend its time proving the vote wrong and reasserting itself in the eyes of the group. Or, labeled as radicals or malcontents, it may try to live up to the image and really become a disruptive force.

6. Finally, by encouraging a move toward quick decisions, the democratic approach may foster a tendency to simplify problems in terms of either–or dichotomies, and failure to explore all the issues influencing the problem may result. A quick vote based on an inadequate exploration of issues will inevitably create difficulties. Members may have second thoughts and fail to support the vote or rationalize their vote and become intransigent.

Given that these kinds of problems are often linked with a simplistic notion of the democratic process, it might seem worthwhile to study other alternatives. The fact is that the operation of a truly democratic group requires enormous patience, understanding, and cooperation. It also is very time-consuming. Few groups are willing to face these realities, so they reduce the process to one of convenience rather than effectiveness. Gaenslen (1980) concluded that a group decision-making process that combines trust, the desire of unanimity, and advocacy may yield both efficiency and a sense of democracy.

How useful is **Robert's Rules of Order** *as a procedure within which to make decisions?* *Robert's Rules of Order* is based on the notion of debate (Robert, 1943). It is a complicated procedural method keyed to the majority vote and the democratic process. It can probably be stated fairly that nearly everyone who has worked in groups has at one time or another been frustrated by the limitations of this system. Those who understand the complexities of the process can easily control the meeting, but few people know the rules of a quorum, tabling a motion, adjourning, or even amending a motion.

On the one hand, the moderator of a meeting can wield considerable power. On the other hand, because chairpeople are not necessarily chosen for their understanding of *Robert's Rules,* it is fairly easy for them to lose control of the meeting to a few individuals who know the finer points. Another problem is that because the system is based on debate, there is a constant tendency toward polarization. True, the amending process allows compromises, but usually these are political compromises, and the real issue can be pulled to pieces as factions based on broader ideological issues use the problem at hand to solidify their political positions rather than seek the best solution. Furthermore, it is relatively easy for the majority to stifle discussion by pushing for an early vote or using some other defensive measure to shift the focus of discussion. Finally, because the system is not based on a cooperative and interdependent approach to problem solving, there tends to be a great deal of politicking, bargaining, and bidding for power outside the meeting itself. In relatively small groups (under 25 or 30), the method reduces open communication and the amount of participation. In larger groups, if the participants understand the system, it can prove useful in organizing discussion and stabilizing work procedures. Again, large numbers of participants present a limiting factor in the decision-making process, so accepting *Robert's Rules* entails gaining order at the expense of interdependence and, to some degree, cooperation.

Is decision by consensus a viable method for small-group decision making? Reaching a decision through consensus represents the ideal in terms of group participation, but it is by no means the most efficient or least tension-producing approach to decision making. It assumes that a decision will not be made without the approval of every member, but that does not mean each member must agree totally with what is going to happen. It simply indicates that each member is willing to go along with the decision, at least for the time being. The process provides for full group participation and a willingness to compromise. Immature groups that lack skill in processing their own interpersonal behavior may find this a painful approach to problem solving. Unlike a system based on majority vote (basically a tension-reducing system), decision by consensus seeks out alternative viewpoints and then struggles to find a solution at the expense of no particular group or person. The value in using this sometimes slow and belabored process is that by the time a decision is reached, it does represent a group decision, and therein lies an important component of support. Schweiger, Sandberg, and Ragan (1986) found that satisfaction with groups, acceptance of group decisions, and willingness to continue working with decisions were all higher with the consensus approach to decision making than with other approaches tested.

At times, a provisional straw vote is used to test sources of differing opinion so that the full dimension of the problem can be explored. If it becomes coercive, the process breaks down. Usually it requires time, familiarity within the group, and trust in the process before consensus becomes effective. Once this occurs, however, decisions can be made rapidly, because there is a willingness to get to the core of the issue quickly, analyze the alternatives, and then compromise in finding the solution.

Why do institutional committees become so ineffective? Most committees are part of an inefficient hierarchical system that has developed over time with little built-in flexibility for change. Procedures become routine and more complex, and the interest of those participating wanes. Within the committees themselves, there are other barriers—for example:

1. Decision-making procedures are usually imposed and based on tradition rather than on what is most useful.
2. People are often appointed to committees, and even if they volunteer, they may be there for a variety of reasons (from interest in meeting important people to helping out a friend who is chairperson).
3. Often committees lack the power to implement the decisions they make; thus they feel their own impotence.
4. Committees seldom see processing their own interpersonal behaviors as part of the job, especially if the group meets only once every three or four weeks.

5. The committee is not necessarily composed of the people best equipped to discuss the issues confronting the group.

These obstacles do not mean that most committees are not designed with a functional purpose in mind or that their participants are not well-intentioned. They merely suggest that such groups often become self-defeating because of their membership, their decision-making procedures, and their lack of potency within the larger organization.

Are there useful alternatives to the committee system?   One possible alternative is the use of a task force. Ideally, when a special problem arises within an organization, instead of pushing it off to an already overburdened committee, management appoints or elects a task force. This group is composed of representative individuals (or, in some cases, individuals with special skills) who are given the job of solving the problem. It is assumed that their recommendations will be taken most seriously, and, in essence, they are given the power of the large group. Task forces are unlike committees in several ways:

- They often have more power.
- Appointments are for a short term.
- A definite, measurable outcome will be the result.
- The members may develop working procedures that best fit the nature of the task and are not limited by tradition or precedent groups.
- They must work through all phases of the problem-solving process, including the diagnosis, actual implementation, and follow-up.
- Because of the immediacy of the problem, there should be high motivation and involvement, especially because the product will be its own reward.

One potential problem with a task force is that given support and some feeling of potency, these groups generate recommendations that are much less conservative than might have been expected and that are much more thoroughly documented than usual. Unhappy is the executive who turns an issue over to a task force and then, instead of the problem losing importance and momentum, which often happens when problems are referred to committees, the task force provides the organization with clear methods for altering the situation. These methods may unveil other problems.

It is often true that task forces are also used for political purposes. The aim is to look as though something is being done, but the real objective is to mark time. An example of this situation occurs when prestigious people are appointed to the task force and, because of other commitments, find it impossible to do the kind of job necessary. The final product is a watered-down and poorly conceived attempt to look competent with a minimum commitment to action.

What influence does an individual who talks excessively or in a dominating manner tend to have on the group?   There are most certainly talkers who are not heard and who wield little influence on the life of a group. But for the most part, socially verbal talkers tend to have a high degree of influence over other members regardless of the chatterers' knowledge or ability (Hoffman, 1979, p. 378). The simple fact of talking more than others may be all that is necessary to increase one's impact on the group. It has even been shown that known talkers, when not dominating the conversation, often influence the problem-solving effort through their support of someone else's ideas. Thus, regardless of the intent of the talker (whether devious, out of personal need, or out of interest), talking garners influence. This is a major reason why many problem-solving designs have built-in mechanisms for ensuring greater freedom of participation and access of other members to the ideas of more retiring members. Brainstorming techniques and synectics excursions are but two approaches that support this view.

Some time ago, Bottger (1984) resolved the conflict in the small group literature regarding the hypothesis that member influence is determined by the quantity rather than the quality of one's contribution. In a study of 33 problem-solving groups, Bottger did find that members attributed influence to the leaders who commanded the most time. However, the actual *movement* in the group resulted more often from those individuals who were perceived as having the most *expertise*.

It is interesting to note that groups in high-pressure conditions shared time less equitably than did groups that were not under pressure (Isenberg, 1981). In other words, group members experiencing more stress did a poorer job of sharing the opportunity to speak in the group. It helps to remember that individuals and groups work in settings that place a variety of demands on them.

Do women as leaders in small groups garner the same respect and influence as men?   Research suggests that the gender of a group's leader clearly influences the group. Even though male and female leaders may act the same, there is a tendency for women to be perceived more negatively or to have to act differently to gain leadership.

Also, in traditional groups composed primarily of men who have had little experience with a woman as leader, there is a degree of confusion. The confusion is related to how the men should relate to a woman who is not acting in a supportive (often secretarial) position. It is also confusing to the woman, who may have had little experience leading a primarily male group. In such a group, power and leadership issues remain unresolved longer. These results reflect more on the gender issue itself than on the actual behavior of the leader (Israeli, 1984; Owen, 1986; Staley, 1984). Thus competent female leaders are often handicapped by the unresolved gender issues or negative attitudes of those they are attempting to lead.

If a group is interested in exploring issues of gender, a good way to stimulate such learning is to create a group with a woman leader and allow ample time to "process" the issues that inevitably rise to the surface. No clever initiatives, games, or simulations need be developed. All that is necessary is a "real" task group with a real purpose and one real female leader. Issues of role, membership, expectations, influence, and authority will appear like magic (Reed, 1983).

Effective Problem Solving: A Summary

Strange as it may seem in light of the many studies we have discussed, group dynamics is still a novel idea in problem-solving theory. Nevertheless, research continues to point in the direction of common sense, confirming the importance of our knowledge of groups in problem-solving and decision-making situations. The following statements summarize many points in this chapter and stand as generally accepted principles.

- Leaders must be trained in the way groups work so they can exploit the group process to advantage, not simply react to unanticipated consequences (Hunsaker, 1983).
- Attention to the development of trust and openness is necessary to successful problem solving and must be encouraged and rewarded in groups. Without these qualities, groups can be seduced into groupthink, which will lead to compliance, dependency, and ineffective results (Brightman and Verhoeven, 1986).
- An effective group creates a natural synergism (the situation in which people working alone are not capable of achieving what the group can accomplish together). Over time, this will increase members' appreciation of the group, which in turn will increase their listening skills, their willingness to take risks, their ability to deal with conflict, and their openness to new ideas—all essential in effective problem solving (Berry, 1983).
- A smoothly functioning problem-solving group has the ability and desire to deal with its own process so that it does not become blocked by, for example, the violation of its own procedural norms, the wielding of undue influence by dominant members, the majority's insensitivity to the needs or ideas of the few, and the tendency to deal from bias and stereotypes rather than objective information (Fox, 1987; Phillips et al., 1986).
- Successful problem-solving groups tend to develop a systematic problem-solving procedure that helps them analyze the problem in a stepwise fashion and reduces the tendency to leap to premature solutions (Hirokawa, 1983a,b).
- The quality of problem solutions is often linked to a group's ability to generate diverse solutions, then to discuss them, and finally to choose from them the best possible alternative. Implicit in this process is a participant diversity that maximizes the potential of the ideation process (Wanous and Youtz, 1986).
- There is increasing evidence that the quality of a group's performance in problem-solving tasks is related to its cohesion. In a cost-conscious world, this suggests that we ought to invest in problem solving by

directing our resources toward increased training and team-building activities (Missing and Preble, 1985).

■ The dominance of the problem-solving process by a few zealous individuals can be minimized by the use of effective strategies [trigger groups, nominal groups, round-robin groups, and the like] determined by the nature of the task (Brightman and Verhoeven, 1986).

■ Whenever possible, those influenced by an eventual solution should be represented in the problem-solving process itself.

◆ ◆ EXERCISE 1

Brainstorming: Useful in Conducting an Effective Large-Group Needs Assessment

Action

Brainstorming can be used as a central activity in a design for assessing the needs of a group where active participation is desired on the part of the group members. In this example, the directions are to be given to a group of 24 participants. Many alternative formats could easily be designed, but the following one has proved successful.

After the problem has been stated clearly (one hopes it is an issue of relevance and concern to members), three large sheets of newsprint are placed next to each other in front of the group. Three participants are chosen as recorders, given markers, and asked to stand in front of one of the newsprints. The group is instructed that it will have between three and five minutes to list all the possible causes for this particular problem (on another occasion they might brainstorm solutions). The first recorder posts the first response, the second recorder the second, and so on. After approximately three minutes, the result should be three sheets with an equal number of responses.

The large group of 24 is then broken down into three groups of eight, each taking a sheet with causes for the particular problem. Their task, to be completed in about 30 minutes, is

1. to clarify and expand any of the statements.
2. to integrate similar statements and to delete any that are irrelevant.
3. to develop from the items a list of causes that are most important to deal with immediately and that are within the power of the group (basic priorities).
4. to present this high-priority list of perhaps three causes to the total group of 24. In all, nine high-priority causal factors will have been identified. Some of these will be very nearly the same, so the real list will contain about five items.

If the group agrees that something must be done with these five causal factors, it may prove useful to halve the groups of eight and have each group of four design specific action solutions to two of the problems. It is suggested that within 45 minutes or an hour the groups of four reconvene within their original group of eight and present their ideas to each other for a critique. This will take another 20 to 30 minutes. Again, if integrating the ideas (solutions) is possible, it should be done.

Finally, the crystallized ideas of the three groups are presented to the entire group. There should be about nine separate ideas presented. It is very important that the facilitator stress the need to minimize the time of the various presentations (no more than five minutes). The main purpose of this session is to give visibility to the various ideas and to bring some closure to the problem-solving process. The total time for this session will be between 2.5 and 3 hours. It is an exhausting process and may not result in final decisions. What often helps is to have a representative of each of the groups of four act as a steering committee and, at a later time, report on specific recommendations that incorporate the various solutions offered.

Discussion of the Problem-solving Sequence

There seem to be a number of practices in this sequence that could be used under a variety of circumstances and with different kinds of problems.

1. It is important that the ideas being explored are the result of the group's effort. This is the first step in building accountability for the eventual solutions.

2. If the ideas are developed in a nonevaluative atmosphere, there will be less of the vested interests that tend to be present in any group and that surround any important problem.

3. The process forces a look at a variety of alternative approaches *after* important causal factors have been isolated. This builds a norm into the group for exploring new ideas and stimulates interest and involvement in the process itself.

4. The participants must honor strict time limits during their various work sessions. Their being held accountable to other groups at the end of the brief work periods insures a continuous flow of ideas, and withdrawal because of boredom is almost impossible. It seems to be very true that people will use the time made available to them.

5. Each product is a product of a number of people's ideas, and this reduces the possibility of one or two vociferous individuals taking over the group. Even in the presentation, it is important that the presenting groups not try to sell their ideas, but simply reveal them.

6. Having a representative body make recommendations to the entire group based on *all* the members' efforts makes consensus much easier to use as a final decision-making device. By this time the group should be ready to stand

accountable for its own product. And, of course, the decision is only as good as the group's willingness to implement it.

◆ ◆ ## *EXERCISE 2*

Phillips 66: Discussion and Decisions in a Large Group

Objectives

- To involve large numbers of people in discussion of topics relevant to them
- To maximize the use of time as a factor in reducing argument
- To insure greater accountability in large groups, which often tend to be impersonal

General Description

D. J. Phillips (1948) at first saw this method as a means of involving large numbers of people in the discussion of a particular issue. For example, after a presentation, debate, or panel, he would have the large group break into groups of six and develop, in about six minutes, a question that the group could agree was important to them. The relatively small groups would have their interest focused, many individuals would have an opportunity to interact, and they could have some impact on the total group's discussion. It was impossible for a few people to dominate their discussion, and the technique guaranteed a high rate of interest.

More recently, the method has been adapted to meet the needs of many groups. Members are given six minutes (it could just as easily be 10 or 15) to develop an agenda for the meeting. With all groups reporting, certain items are immediately perceived as having interest to many in the group. Or, in other sessions, members are asked to offer a solution for a particular issue. Usually six minutes is long enough to define and clarify the issue, and it has been shown that an enormous number of good ideas can be generated in a relatively short period of time and then refined later. Brief reports on these findings can be an important stimulating factor in the large group.

Others, including Maier (1963), have used adaptations of this method for larger groups with as many as two or three hundred people. Groups of six are given a problem to solve or an issue to discuss, and then these groups are polled by the facilitator in terms of certain logical categories. Immediately the group gains a picture of how others feel and the range of ideas that exist in the group.

Of great importance in using this method is to make sure that the topics used for discussion are specific enough to allow an almost immediate discussion to get under way. Questions that are moralistic in tone only frustrate people because there is no hope for any kind of resolution in a limited period of time. Similarly, when looking at a particular problem, the participants should not be limited to an either–or type of response. The enjoyment lies in the opportunity to be creative and to look beyond the commonplace response. The great value of having many people together doing the same thing is that one is assured of wide-ranging responses that may not develop in the more traditional committee work group, which is partly controlled by past experience and behavior.

◆ ◆ EXERCISE 3

Utilizing Traditional Force Field Analysis:[4] From Diagnosis to Action

Objectives

- To provide participants in the decision-making process a means of thoroughly diagnosing the factors causing the particular problem
- To help those involved to look beyond the obvious and into new responses to the problem condition
- To focus on the possible repercussions of any decisions

Rationale

It is assumed that in most of the decisions we make, we fail to have access to or (if it is available) to use all the information related to a particular problem.

Basically, we fail on three counts in the problem-solving process. First, we often enter problem situations with some preconceived notion of what we would like the outcome to be. Thus we fail to do a very thorough diagnosis of all the causal factors that created the tensions, and it is seldom that all the relevant data reach us. (That would take time and energy and might lead to conclusions not desired.) Second, for similar reasons, we often limit our perception of all the possible alternatives for changing the existing condition. Finally, when making particular decisions, it is seldom that we look beyond immediate reactions and explore all the possible repercussions.

The primary aim of this exercise is to give the participant access to more data and alternatives and a greater awareness of their possible implications in terms of later consequences.

4. This design is drawn from Lewin, 1948, 1951. Lewin attempted to view a problem as a "field of counterveiling forces which represented restraints toward solution." A force field analysis attempted to assess all of the various forces in the field and then alter the balance by using new strategies and removing other blocks to resolution.

Setting

Groups of about six or seven are ideal for this exercise, but the method can be effectively used by individuals or large groups in general problem-solving sessions. Often the method is quickly presented and the group fails to understand the reason behind the approach. Superficially, it may appear to be nothing more than listing positive and negative forces that influence a decision. However, it represents a way of thinking about a problem and the changes (intentional or unintentional) that any decisions resulting from the problem analysis will create. Enough time must be allowed for the process to develop, although it is difficult to suggest how long; it depends on the nature of the problem, the motivation of the group, and the actual time available. Some designs have allowed two days for the analysis and development of specific solutions. Less than two or three hours on organizational problems or those of a small group may prove to be sufficient. Newsprint, markers, and tape should be available so that the ideas developed can be easily seen and recorded as the group moves through various phases of the exercise toward solution.

Action

A group using force field analysis should be involved in a brief theory and practice session. For example, the facilitator may point out that groups, when looking at a problem that needs to be solved, tend to (a) move too rapidly toward a solution, (b) begin to argue and polarize, and (c) fail to look at all the causal factors behind the problem.

The following method helps to get out the data and explore them in a rational, nonjudgmental fashion. The first step is to view the problem as a condition that needs to be changed, and success will be determined by just how much this condition is altered. For example, smoking is a condition that exists to a certain degree in some people. If a person smokes a pack of cigarettes a day and thinks he or she should stop, then the problem becomes altering the particular condition (one pack a day). One reason why individuals who attempt to stop smoking find it so difficult is that they make it an all-or-nothing proposition, and it becomes a test of personal will. As in many other problem conditions, the person fails to look at the multitude of factors that are causing him or her to smoke. The self-will issue is only one and by no means the most important. Unless all the restraining forces inducing him or her to smoke are understood, a strategy for altering the condition will tend to be limited in its impact. The strategy must attack many of these factors, some of which are depicted in the accompanying figure.

In the mind of the individual, each of these factors has a different weight and importance in restraining him or her from reducing the amount of cigarettes. Furthermore, these restraining forces may change in weight and in character. For example, a parent-in-law visiting the house may add another source of tension, another force that may actually increase the number of cigarettes smoked. Thus,

RESTRAINING FORCES (TO INDUCE SMOKING)

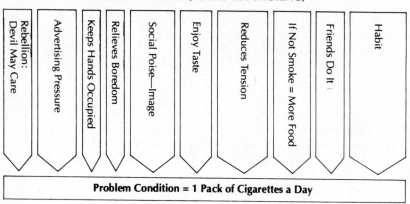

Problem Condition = 1 Pack of Cigarettes a Day

with more weight pushing downward, the problem condition changes, and more cigarettes are smoked.

However, we have looked at only half the picture. There also exist in this individual's life a multitude of forces driving or pushing him or her to give up smoking: health advertisements, family pressure, sore throat, his or her own test of will, cost, and so forth. Each of these forces also has its own weight and is pushing against the restraining forces. They too can change in their importance (weight), as, for example, when the individual is visited by a relative who has had a lung removed because of lung cancer and it is discovered that he or she smoked two packs a day before the operation. This revelation may add enough of a push to actually reduce his or her smoking for a few days. It is at the point at which the restraining forces and the driving forces impose the same theoretical amount of pressure that the level of smoking is determined. With more pressure from below (cancer reports, sick relative, and so on) the problem condition will change to less smoking. More tension at work, a visiting parent-in-law, or fear of weight gain may alter the balance of forces and increase the amount of smoking. See the second figure where the "driving forces" have been added.

In one sense, the one-pack-a-day level represents a point of temporary equilibrium between the two competing forces. If a person is really interested in altering this level, or problem condition, then he or she may work at reducing the number of restraining forces, or he or she may work at increasing the number of driving forces that will then push the point of equilibrium (amount of smoking) to a new level representing fewer cigarettes a day. (*Note:* During the process of this brief theory session, it is helpful to have the participants add the forces in this example while the facilitator sketches them on newsprint or a blackboard. It is important that they grasp the feeling of weight or forces that are acting on the person.)

At this point, the facilitator may wish to ask which (if there is to be a choice) appears more useful: trying to remove the restraining forces or trying to add driving forces in order to reduce the level of smoking. The majority of individuals will tend to feel that adding to the driving forces would be easiest and most appropriate. Given more time to think and discuss the question, there will be a movement to a position of removing the restraining forces. The fact is that for most people change is the result of force or coercion. The problem is that it seems to hold true in the social sciences almost as much as in the physical sciences: for every action there is a reaction. People, whether individually or in groups, react to force or pressure. They build defenses to offset such driving forces. For example, "If you keep smoking, you're going to cut five years off your life" (coercion, threat). A frequent response may be, "Well, I would rather die sooner and be happy than cut out all the little pleasures of life" (rationalization, compensation). The response by cigarette companies to the Surgeon General's famous cancer report was to increase cigarette advertising to a point where six months later total consumption had actually risen (however, significant declines have since taken place). The

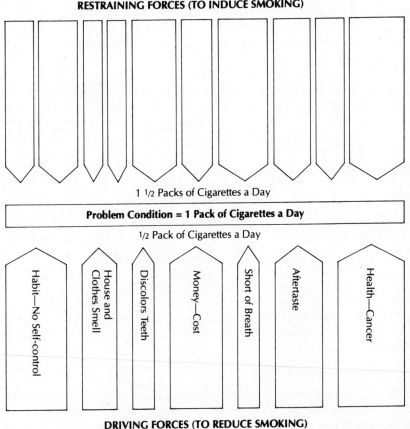

RESTRAINING FORCES (TO INDUCE SMOKING)

1 1/2 Packs of Cigarettes a Day

Problem Condition = 1 Pack of Cigarettes a Day

1/2 Pack of Cigarettes a Day

Habit—No Self-control

House and Clothes Smell

Discolors Teeth

Money—Cost

Short of Breath

Aftertaste

Health—Cancer

DRIVING FORCES (TO REDUCE SMOKING)

point is that none of these compensating reactions occurs when effort is directed at reducing the restraining forces, particularly those with the greatest force.

The use of driving forces can be an important factor in any movement toward change. The problems arise when unanticipated reactions create more problems than the newly introduced driving force is worth. It is from the driving forces, however, that creative new ideas tend to be generated. Thus the arrival of a new manager is likely to bring many problems as people adjust to his or her new style and expectations, but it is possible to anticipate these and offset them with orientation sessions, social hours, personal discussions, and employee involvement in some of the accompanying changes.

Problem-Solving Sequence Using Force Field Analysis

Having introduced the group briefly to some of the theoretical notions (it may be useful to take a few minutes to help the group work through an issue more relevant to them from a group perspective, the facilitator then gives the group an opportunity to use the approach systematically in exploring a problem and developing specific solutions. Taking three hours as an example in this case, a possible problem-solving sequence might look like this:

STEP 1 (10 MIN.)

The problem is defined as a condition that exists with forces impinging on it. The issue must be specific and one that the group has an interest in and some power to change. (Again, how the problem is arrived at is a very important step for the facilitator to consider.)

STEP 2 (20 TO 30 MIN.)

The driving and restraining forces impinging on this particular condition are brainstormed. It is best not to qualify or evaluate any responses during this phase but simply to list them on a large sheet of newsprint (the restraining forces are placed on the left of the sheet going down the paper and the driving forces on the right.)

STEP 3 (30 TO 40 MIN.)

The groups now concentrate their efforts on the restraining forces (particularly if time is limited). They do this by ordering the list they have brainstormed into priorities. Thus they are, in a sense, weighting the forces and can more easily see those with which the group must come to grips. This process of establishing priorities is also a diagnostic process for the working group. It is best if the priorities can be agreed on through consensus and if individuals try to be relatively flexible, because a variety of solutions will probably be forthcoming.

STEP 4 (10 TO 15 MIN.)

Having arrived at agreement on priorities and having defined the restraining forces more clearly, it should be possible for the group to eliminate some because they simply do not have the time, money, resources, or power to do anything about them. This important period of reality testing enables the group to focus its energies on those restraining forces that they do have the power to change.

STEP 5 (40 TO 60 min.)

Having established those restraining forces that the group can work with, the participants attempt to establish specific ways of reducing those restraining forces in a manner that will minimize possible offsetting reactions. It might be best to have subgroups of two or three people focus on particular forces and, after they have developed a number of concrete solutions, report them to the larger group. If time permits, suggestions for new driving forces may also be developed.

STEP 6 (20 MIN.)

Specific proposals, including methods for implementation and group accountability, are developed.

STEP 7 (30 MIN.)

The total group is presented with the specific proposals, and a discussion follows (the group will probably not be able to handle more than 30 or 40 minutes after working for three hours). At this time, suggestions should be entertained for making sure that the various proposals are integrated into a strategy for action. This step is of utmost importance; it insures follow-up and commitment of further involvement by the very people who have developed the proposals. A cross-group steering committee may be a useful mechanism.

STEP 8

An evaluation takes place at some agreed-upon date in the future. It gives the large group the opportunity to appraise what impact the various suggestions actually had.

Obviously, there is no magic in these eight steps or in this particular time frame. They simply provide a structure in which to implement the force field as a tool in the problem-solving process. It focuses on the building of constructive alternatives for action and attempts to draw out as many factors as possible that may inhibit potential solutions.

◆ ◆ *EXERCISE 4*

The Acid Floor Test

Objectives

- To analyze decision making and problem solving under extreme time pressure
- To develop supportive roles within a group

■ To observe individual behavior under stress—both facilitative and inhibiting

Setting

This task is more effective when it is done competitively. If there are enough materials available, as many as three or four teams of from six to ten players can participate at the same time. If materials are limited, competitiveness can be achieved by placing a time restriction on the exercise (each team works in isolation). For each group that participates, it is necessary to have available eight empty number-10 cans. It is also helpful to have observers assigned to each group to watch carefully the nature of the problem solving that takes place, how resources in the group are maximized, and how leadership develops within the context of the activity.

Action

The facilitator gives the following directions to the team(s).

You are members of a gang that has taken a short-cut across another gang's territory. You have been spotted by one of their lookouts and are aware that they are mobilizing a group of some 30 kids to come after your small group. You have decided to cut through an alley that leads to your own territory. Halfway down the alley you see that the other gang has spread acid across the alley. It stretches at least 30 feet or more ahead of you. You realize that it is too late to go back the way you came. Near the point where the acid begins, the group sees a number of large cans that might offer a way over the acid. But how? Can they figure out how to get all of their gang over the acid before the other gang arrives?

There are some specific rules. No part of a person's body may touch the acid floor. If it does, he or she must return to the starting point and bring his or her cans with him or her. No person may sacrifice himself or herself and run through the acid setting up cans. When the last person crosses, he or she must bring the cans to the far side with him or her so that the pursuing gang cannot follow over the acid.

This event is timed.

Discussion

By teams, the observers describe how they saw the decision-making process develop. The group may be asked to comment on these observations and discuss what might have been done better. Why were (or why were not) other alternatives developed? Was there dependence in the group on one or two people? Why? Was there consideration for all the members of the team? Was their performance (going across on the cans) ridiculed, or was there a supportive, all-for-one attitude?

◆ ◆ EXERCISE 5

Developing Feedback: An Important Step in Open Communication

Rationale

Any system, whether it be an individual human being, a small group, or an organization, must have some source of information about itself (we are notoriously poor judges of our own performance). This process of receiving information about oneself is referred to as *feedback*. An examination is one source of feedback for a student, even though more and more it is merely used as a means of classifying individuals and often loses its value as a meaningful feedback instrument. In the course of a group meeting, thousands of verbal and nonverbal communications take place, thousands of internal responses occur within individuals, and a great deal occurs that is never recorded in the minutes. Yet the next meeting of the same individuals may be dramatically influenced by just these events. Unless a feedback system is established within any working group, an enormous amount of time and energy may be poorly used as individuals attempt to cope with the many procedural and human problems that can hinder a group. The diagnostic process described in the previous exercise is, in fact, a form of feedback. However, if it is really to benefit the group over time, it must be legitimized as an important part of the work process. Feedback ideally is a welcome source of information for the group as a whole or for individual members. If misused, it can be a destructive, inhibiting, and degenerative force; if skillfully integrated into the group, it can facilitate more effective communication and better working relationships. The following exercise represents one means of introducing the concept of feedback to a group so that the group can explore whether it is ready to use feedback more systematically.

Setting

There are many ways in which information can be developed to provide a group with insights on its operating procedures and the consequences of its behaviors. Such information, however, will not be useful if it is imposed or if there is no opportunity for the group to do anything about it. The group, like the individual, must be ready to hear about itself and must desire to act on what it hears. If the facilitator has evidence that the group is ready to deal more directly with its own process, the following exercise may be useful. One means of discovering readiness is simply to raise as a point of discussion whether the group would like to take time to explore how it operates (that it will take too much time is an easy defensive response and suggests a rather low priority for the process efforts).

Action

The group is divided into subgroups of about three people, and each is asked to develop a set of rules that might be discussed and applied to any feedback efforts. For example, how can the group learn about its operation? How effective or ineffective is it? How does it facilitate or hinder the working process? Perhaps there are rules the group can agree on that will make the feedback more easily received and thus more easily given.

After 15 or 20 minutes, the facilitator posts the results on newsprint, asking each group to give the most important recommendations first. The posted list represents a loosely grouped statement of rules and recommendations that have some priority to the various subgroups. To this list the facilitator may wish to add a few suggestions and integrate those already listed into a brief theory session. The key is that if people are going to hear about themselves, it must be done in a manner that creates the fewest possible defenses and insures a climate of acceptance. Some of the suggestions that may be forthcoming from the session follow.

1. The information about the group should be descriptive and not colored by value-laden adjectives of a good–bad nature.
2. The examples of group behavior being discussed should be specific and clarified through examples.
3. Whenever possible, the information should be given sooner rather than later. The longer the time between the behavior and its discussion, the less value.
4. The information must be confined to matters that it is within the power of the group to do something about.
5. The group must seek the feedback. If it is not solicited, it will be met with resistance and will probably have little positive impact.
6. A person and a group can internalize only a certain amount of information at any one time. It is important not to overload the. system with more than it can handle.
7. When a person presents his or her perception of how the group behaved in a certain instance, it is important to discover whether others share his or her view.

Following this, it may be useful to focus on the areas of group activity about which information might be collected in a somewhat objective manner. A five-minute brainstorming session might result in some of the following:

- communication patterns in the group (who talks and how much)
- problems that seem to keep the group from moving

- how problems are actually solved and decisions made
- the goals of the group (implicit and explicit)
- the level of involvement and interest among the participants
- whether there is shared leadership in the group
- the physical structure of the group
- the roles taken by group members (constructive and destructive)
- the degree to which the group is open or closed

Thus, in a matter of about 40 minutes, the group can establish some suggestions that it feels necessary for the presentation of feedback to be effective as well as useful. Now, following these guidelines, the final 20 minutes are designed so that the original groups of three reconvene and agree on one piece of feedback that should be presented to the larger group in a manner that will benefit the whole group in its future work together. This feedback may be in the form of a comment on the group behavior that indicates the need for new behavior. However, it should be left for the large group to interpret the feedback and decide on any relevant action. The idea, at this particular point, is to get the group practicing the process they have been discussing. This gives them a good starting point for the next session.

Follow-up

If the group has been able to accept the notion of feedback with some equanimity, the way will be open for the facilitator to suggest (or, if there is time, to have the group develop) a number of ways that feedback within a group may be carried out. Here are some examples:

1. Appoint an observer of the group's process who reports his or her systematic observations at the end of a meeting. A discussion of the implications should follow (it may take no more than 15 minutes).
2. Have the group fill out reaction forms at the end of a session. These may focus upon various aspects of the group process.
3. Tape the meeting. Then replay a portion of the tape and briefly discuss its implications.
4. After building confidence in the feedback process and trust in one another, members look at the roles and specific behaviors of individual members to see how they influence the group. This level of feedback may take a long time to evolve, and it is best for it to develop naturally out of a deeper concern and involvement on the part of the members. In other words, no group suddenly becomes ready for individual feedback. It is simply a natural extension of the slowly developing willingness of the group to process its own behaviors.

◆ ◆ *EXERCISE 6*

Post-Session Feedback

Rationale

Most task groups hardly have time to complete their business commitments, let alone spend much time exploring the process of the group. The comment is often heard, "If we get into that subject, we'll be here all night." This fear of personal overinvolvement outside the actual working agenda can shut down all efforts to develop more effective working relationships. It is not necessary for a group to spend an inordinate amount of time in its process efforts, nor need members become overly personal. However, time must be allowed for the group to improve its own working relationship, or tensions and problems will subtly build up and eventually reduce the group's effectiveness. Following are two simple suggestions for helping to keep the process level of group work legitimized.

1. After the working session, 10 minutes is set aside for a discussion, in pairs, of this question: "What are one or two ways in which this group could improve its working procedures or relationships the next time it meets?" It is important that the participants focus on specific, constructive suggestions. If, for example, one member dominated the discussion and created hostility among many of the other participants, it might be helpful to establish a temporary mechanism for insuring that more individuals have an opportunity to share their views and also to help move the group past individual roadblocks. In a group with a high level of trust and acceptance, it would not be inappropriate to share with an individual the problems created by his or her particular behavior. But as suggested previously, the climate must be such that the individual desires the information and those giving it are skillful enough not to appear punitive or judgmental.

The group may also find the postmeeting session an avenue for suggesting a change in the structural format in the meeting—for example, the role of the chairperson. Similarly, the way the agenda is being formed may influence the feeling of individuals about participating, and a change in how this is accomplished may affect other aspects of the meeting.

The issues briefly raised by the individuals in the paired groups are then shared briefly with the total group. They are first shared without discussion in order to establish how much agreement there is among the members. Then suggestions are taken to remedy the situation in time for the next meeting. The total process should take no more than 20 or 30 minutes. After the group has developed acceptance of the feedback idea, the first step of breaking into twos or threes will be unnecessary, and observations can be shared by the whole group. This would cut the process time down to 10 or 15 minutes, although as groups become more open and communicative, there is a tendency to broaden the scope of the feedback process. It is possible that this can become a problem because many members may find sharing feedback a fascinating and personally satisfying experience. Groups have been known to spend more time discussing their process than the task. Obviously, it is a sign of a mature group if it is able to use feedback in a constructive fashion rather than a means of meeting individual emotional needs that extend far beyond the purpose of the group.

  2. If certain members of the work group are involved in establishing the format of a particular meeting (often this is a rotating responsibility in which responsibilities for agenda building and building procedures for a meeting change hands regularly), the following feedback procedure may prove useful. At the end of a meeting, a reaction sheet is passed out to participants, who answer explicit questions on the operation of the meeting and on possible improvements. The group responsible for the next meeting analyzes these responses (thus it takes only about five minutes of the group's time), and they make plans to incorporate various changes in the format of the next meeting that they feel respond to the concerns and suggestions given. These new procedures or innovations are then evaluated in the reaction sheet developed for that meeting. In this way, there is a constant willingness to look at how the group is working together and an opportunity to develop new ideas. Theoretically, each person eventually has a chance to improve the meeting. It may be that a certain format develops that is basically satisfactory to the members; this too will be found through the regular use of reaction sheets.

References

Adams, J. K., and P. A. Adams, "Realism of confidence judgments." *Psychological Review,* 68 (1967), 33–45.

Armelius, K. "The task as a determinant of group culture." *UMEA Psychological Reports,* 156 (1980).

Bader, Gloria, "Pareto analysis and diagram." Bader Group, San Diego.

Bandler, R., and J. Grinder, *Frogs into Princes, Neuro-Linguistics Programming.* Moab, Utah: Real People Press, 1979.

Bergum, B. O., and D. J. Lehr. "The effects of authoritarianism on vigilance performance." *Journal of Applied Psychology,* 47 (1963), 75–77.

Berry, W. "Group problem solving. How to be an effective participant." *Supervisory Management,* 28, No. 26 (June 1983), 13–19.

Bottger, P. C. "Expertise and air time as bases of actual and perceived influence in problem-solving groups." *Journal of Applied Psychology,* 69, No. 2 (May 1984), 214–221.

Bouchard, T. J., Jr. "Personality, problem-solving procedure, and performance in small groups." *Journal of Applied Psychology,* 53, No. 1, Part 2 (1969), 1–29.

Brehm, J. "Postdecision changes in desirability of alternatives." *Journal of Abnormal and Social Psychology,* 52 (1956), 384–389.

Brightman, H. J., and P. Verhoeven. "Running successful problem-solving groups." Part 2. *Business* 36, No. 2, (June 1986), 15–23.

Butler, R. "Innovations in organizations: Appropriateness of perspectives from small group studies for strategy formulation." *Human Relations,* 34 (1981), 763–788.

Callaway, M. R. "Effects of dominance on group decision making. Toward a stress-reduction explanation of groupthink." *Journal of Personality and Social Psychology* 49, No. 4 (October 1985), 949–952.

Campbell, D. "Some strategic properties of plurality and majority voting." *Theory and Decision*, 13 (1981), 93–107.

Campbell, J. P., "Individual versus group problem solving in an industrial sample." *Journal of Applied Psychology*, 52 (1968), 205–210.

Carr, D. F. "A comparative study of nominal interacting and brainstorming groups and pooled individual work in ideation phases of the reflective thinking process." Unpublished Master's thesis, Auburn University, 1975.

Cline, R. J., "Small group dynamics and the Watergate coverup. A case study of groupthink." Paper presented at the annual meeting of the Communication Association, Ocean City, Md (April 1983), 27–30.

Collaros, R. A., and L. Anderson. "Effects of perceived expertness upon creativity of members of brainstorming groups." *Journal of Applied Psychology*, 53, No. 2, Part 1 (1969).

Chung, K. H., and M. J. Ferris. "An inquiry of the nominal group process." *Academy of Management Journal*, 14 (1971), 520–524.

Delbecq, A. L. and A. H. Van de Ven, D. H. Gustafson. *Group Techniques for Program Planning*. Glenview, Ill: Scott Foresman, 1975.

DeStephen, R. S. "High- and low-consensus groups: A content and relational interaction analysis." *Small Group Behavior*, 14, No. 2 (1983), 143–162.

Dunnette, M. D., J. P. Campbell, and K. Jaastad. "The effect of group participation on brainstorming effectiveness for two industrial samples." *Journal of Applied Psychology*, 47 (1963), 30–37.

Easton, A. *Decision Making: A Short Course in Problem Solving*. New York: Wiley, 1976.

Falk, G., and S. Falk. "The impact of decision rules on the distribution of power in problem-solving teams with unequal power." *Group and Organization Studies*, 6 (1981), 211–223.

Festinger, L. *Theory of Cognitive Dissonance*. Evanston, Ill: Row, Peterson, 1957.

Festinger, L., and E. Aronson. "Arousal and reduction of dissonance in a social context." In *Group Dynamics Research and Theory*, ed. D. Cartwright and A. Zander. New York: Harper & Row 1968, p. 125.

Festinger, L., and J. Carlsmith. "Cognitive consequences of forced choice alternatives as a function of their number and qualitative similarity." *Journal of Abnormal and Social Psychology*, 58 (1959), 203–210.

Forgas, Joseph P. "Positive influences on individual and group judgments." *European Journal of Social Psychology*, 20, No. 5 (September–October 1990), 441–453.

Fox, W. M. *Effective Problem Solving*, San Francisco: Jossey-Bass, 1987, pp. 3–6.

Fox, William M. "The improved nominal group technique (INGT)." *Journal of Management Development*, 8 (1989), 20–27.

Frederick, L. F. "A comparison of performance, personality characteristics, and perceived satisfaction in nominal and interacting groups in the problem-analysis stage of the problem-solving process." Ph.D. thesis, Mississippi State University, 1976. *Dissertation Abstracts International* (1976) 37, 1486B, University Microfilms No. 76–20, 756.

Gaenslen, F. "Democracy vs. efficiency: Some arguments from the small group." *Political Psychology*, 2 (1980), 15–29.

Goddard, R. W. "The healthy side of conflict." *Management World*, 15, No. 5 (June 1986), 8–12.

Gordon, W. J. *Synectics*. New York: Collier Books, 1961.

Gouran, D. S. *Discussions: The Process of Group Decision Making*. New York: Harper & Row, 1972.

Gustafson, D. H., R. K. Skukla, A. L. Delbecq, and G. W. Walster. "A comparative study of differences in subjective likely estimates made by individuals, interacting groups, delphi groups, and nominal groups." *Organizational Behavior and Human Performance*, 9 (1973), 280–291.

Guzzo, R., and J. Waters. "The expression of affect and performance of decision-making groups." *Journal of Applied Psychology*, 67 (1982), 67–74.

Hall, J., and M. S. Williams. "Group dynamics training and improved decision making." *Journal of Applied Behavioral Science*, 6 (1970), 39–68.

Hammond, L., and M. Goldman. "Competition and non-competition and its relationship to individuals' non-productivity." *Sociometry,* 24 (1961), 46–60.

Hare, A. P., *Handbook of Small Group Research,* 2nd ed. New York: Free Press, 1976, p. 207.

Heider, F. *The Psychology of Interpersonal Relations.* New York: Wiley, 1958, pp. 75–82.

Hirokawa, R. "A comparative analysis of communication patterns within effective and ineffective decision-making groups." *Communication Monographs,* 47 (1980), 312–321.

Hirokawa, R. Y. "Group communication and problem-solving effectiveness I: An investigation of group phases." *Human Communication Research,* 9, No. 4 (1983), 291–305.

Hirokawa, R. Y. "Group communication and problem solving effectiveness II: An exploratory investigation of procedural functions." *Western Journal of Speech Communication,* 47, No. 1 (1983), 59–74.

Hoffman, L. R. "Applying experimental research on group problem solving to organizations." *Journal of Applied Behavioral Science,* 1593 (1979), 375–391.

Hunsaker, P. L. "Using group dynamics to improve decision-making meetings." *Industrial Management,* 25, No. 4 (1983), 19–23.

Isenberg, D. "Some effects of time-pressure on vertical structure and decision-making accuracy in small groups." *Organizational Behavior and Human Performance,* 27 (1981), 119–134.

Israeli, D. N. "The Attitudinal Effects of Gender Mix in Union Committees." *Industrial and Labor Relations Review,* 37, No. 2 (January 1984), 212–221.

Jacobs, S. "Managing departments in conflict." *Computerworld,* 17, No. 10 (March 7, 1983), 25–33.

Janis, I. L. *Groupthink: Psychological Study of Policy Decisions and Fiascos.* 2nd ed. Boston: Houghton Mifflin, 1982.

Janis, I. L. "Groupthink and group dynamics: A social psychological analysis of defective policy decisions." *Policy Studies Journal,* 2, No. 1 (Autumn 1973), 19–25.

Kelley, H. H., and J. Thibaut. "Group problem solving." In *The Handbook of Social Psychology.* 2nd ed. vol. 4. *Group Psychology and Phenomena of Interaction.* Ed. G. Lindzey and E. Aronson. Reading, Mass.: Addison-Wesley, 1969, p. 1.

Kepner, H., and B. Tregoe. *The Rational Manager.* New York: McGraw-Hill, 1968.

Koberg, D., and J. Bagnall. *The Universal Traveler.* Los Altos, Calif.: Kaufman, 1981, p. 21.

Leana, C. R. "A partial test of Janis' groupthink model: Effects of group cohesiveness and leader behavior on defective decision making." *Journal of Management,* 11, No. 1 (1985), 5–17.

Lewin, K. *Principles of Topological Psychology:* New York: McGraw-Hill, 1936, p. 25.

Lewin, K. *Resolving Social Conflicts.* New York: Harper & Row, 1948.

Lewin, K. *Field Theory in Social Sciences.* New York: Harper & Row, 1951.

Maginn, B., and R. Harris. "Effects of anticipated evaluation on individual brainstorming performance." *Journal of Applied Psychology,* 65 (1980):219–225.

Maier, N. R. F. *Problem-Solving Discussions and Conferences.* New York: McGraw-Hill, 1963, pp. 193–195.

Maier, N. R. F., and L. Hoffman. "Group decision in England and the United States." *Personnel Psychology,* 15 (1962), 75–87.

McCurdy, H. G., and W. E. Lambert. "The efficiency of small human groups in the solution of problems requiring genuine cooperation." *Journal of Personality,* 20 (1952), 478–494.

McGrath, Joseph E. *"Groups, Interaction, and Performance."* Englewood Cliffs, N.J.: Prentice-Hall, 1984, p. 128.

McWhirter, William. "Is Mr. Nice Guy Back?" *Time,* January 27, 1992. pp. 42–44.

Mintzberg, H. "Planning on the left side and managing on the right." *Harvard Business Review* (July–August 1976), 49–58.

Missing, P., and J. F. Preble. "Group processes and performance in a complex business simulation." *Small Group Behavior,* 16, No. 3 (1985), 325–338.

Moore, C. M. *Group Techniques for Idea Building,* Beverly Hills, Calif.: Sage, 1987.

Moorehead, G. and J. R. Montanari. "An empirical investigation of the groupthink phenomenon." *Human Relations,* 39, No. 5 (May 1986), 399–410.

Moscovici, S., and M. Zavalloni. "The group as a polarizer of attitudes." *Journal of Abnormal and Social Psychology,* 12 (1969), 125–135.

Murnighan, J. K. "Coalitions in decision-making groups: Organizational analogs." *Champaign Organizational Behavior and Human Decision Process,* 35, No. 1 (February 1985), 1–26.

Napier, H. "Individual versus group learning: Note on task variables." *Psychological Reports,* 23 (1967), 757–758.

Nemiroff, P. M., W. A. Pasmora, and D. L. Ford. "The effects of two normative structural interventions on established ad hoc groups: Implications for improving decision-making effectiveness." *Decision Sciences,* 7 (1976), 841–855.

Ornstein, R. *The Psychology of Consciousness.* San Francisco: W. H. Freeman, 1975.

Osborn, A. F. *Applied Imagination.* New York: Charles Schribner's Sons, 1953.

Owen, W. F. "Rhetorical themes of emergent women leaders." *Small Group Behavior,* 17, No. 4 (November 1986), 475–486.

Phillips, D. J. "Report on discussion 66." *Adult Education Journal,* 7 (1948), 81.

Phillips, G., J. T. Wood, and D. T. Pedersen. *Group Discussion: A Practical Guide to Participation and Leadership.* New York: Harper & Row, 1986.

Poole, M. "Decision development in small groups: A comparison of two models." *Communication Monographs,* 48 (1981), 1–24.

Principle, C. D., and S. E Neeley. "Nominal versus interactive groups: Further evidence." *Mid-Atlantic Journal of Business,* 21, No. 2 (Summer 1983), 25–34.

Reed, B. G. "Women leaders in small groups: Social psychological strategies and perspectives." *Social Work with Groups,* 6, Nos. 3 and 4 (Fall/Winter 1983), 35–42.

Rickards, T. *Problem Solving Through Creative Analysis.* London: Halsted Press, 1974.

Robert, H. M. *Robert's Rules of Order.* Chicago: Scott, Foresman, 1943.

Rohrbaugh, J. "Improving the quality of group judgment: Social judgment analysis and nominal group technique." *Organizational Behavior and Human Performance,* 28 (1981), 272–288.

Rotter, G. S., and S. M. Portergal. "Group and individual effects in problem solving." *Journal of Applied Psychology,* 53 (1969), 338–342.

Schwartz, T., V. Wullwick, and H. Shapiro. "Self-esteem and group decision making: An empirical study." *Psychological Reports,* 46 (1980), 951–956.

Schweiger, P. M., W. R. Sandberg, and J. W. Ragan. "Group approaches for improving strategic decision making: A comparative analysis of dialectical inquiry, devil's advocacy, and consensus." *Academy of Management Journal,* 29 (1986), 51–71.

Staley, C. C. "Managerial women in mixed groups: Implications of recent research." *Group and Organizational Studies,* 9, No. 3 (September 1984), 316–332.

Stuls, M. H. "Experience and prior probability in a complex decision task." *Journal of Applied Psychology,* 53, No. 2, Part 1 (1969), 112–118.

Taylor, D. W., P. C. Berry, and C. H. Block. "Does group participation when using brainstorming facilitate or inhibit creative thinking?" *Administrative Science Quarterly,* 3 (1958), 23–47.

Thamis, S., and M. Woods. "A systematic small group approach to creativity and innovation: A case study." *Research and Development Management,* 14, No. 1 (January 1984), 25–35.

Tjosvold, D. "Implications of controversy research for management." *Journal of Management,* 11, No. 3 (Fall/Winter 1985), 21–37.

Tjosvold, D., and R. Field, "Effects of social context on consensus and majority vote decision making." *Academy of Management Journal,* 26, No. 3 (1983), 500–506.

Tolela, M. *Effects of T-group Training and Cognitive Learning of Small Group Effectiveness.* Unpublished doctoral dissertation, University of Denver, 1967.

Torrance, E. "Some consequences of power differences on decision making in permanent and temporary three-man groups." In Hare, A., E. Borgatta, and R. Bales (eds.), *Small Groups.* New York: Knopf, 1955.

Tuckman, J., and I. Lorge. "Individual ability as a determinant of group superiority." *Human Relations,* 15 (1962), 45–52.

Ulman, R. B., and D. W. Abse. "The group psychology of mass madness: Jonestown." *Political Psychology,* 4, No. 4 (December 1983), 637–661.

Van de Ven, A. H., and A. L. Delbecq. "The effectiveness of nominal, delphi, and interacting group decision-making processes." *Academy of Management Journal,* 17 (1974), 605–621.

VanGundy, A. B. *Managing Group Creativity.* New York: American Management Association, 1984, pp. 16–23.

Voytas, R. M. *Some Effects of Various Combinations of Group and Individual Participation in Creative Productivity.* Unpublished doctoral dissertation, University of Maryland, 1967.

Vroom, V. H., L. D. Grant, and T. S. Cotton. "The consequences of social interaction in group problem solving." *Journal of Organizational Behavior and Human Performance,* 4 (1969), 79–95.

Wall, V. D., and L. L. Nolan. "Perceptions of inequity, satisfaction, and conflict in task-oriented groups." *Human Relations,* 39, No. 11 (November 1986), 1033–1051.

Wanous, J. P., and M. A. Youtz. "Solution diversity and the quality of group decision." *Academy of Management Journal,* 29, No. 1 (1986), 149–159.

Watzlawick, P. *The Language of Change.* New York: Basic Books, 1978.

White, D. D., S. E. Blythe, and D. R. Corrigan. "A comparative analysis of three group decision-making techniques applied to organizations in varying phases of physical expansion." in Ray, D., and T. Green (eds.), *Management in an Age of Complexity and Change.* Proceedings of the Southern Management Association, 1977. Mississippi State University, Central Duplicating (1977), 90–95.

Young, B. L., Jr. "A whole-brain approach to training and development." *Training and Development Journal* (October 1979), 44–50.

◆ 8 ◆

The Use of Humor in Groups

How serious we are! Observers note that our era is the most humorless in history. The deterioration of our stable social institutions, critical health and environmental problems, and a changing morality all tug at our national psyche, leaving many with a deep sense of pessimism and futility. For some, the solution seems to be the seeking of an elixir—something that goes down easily that they can take to minimize the pain. Thus increasing numbers of people allow themselves to be drugged by sedentary activities, television, and substance abuse. They are unable to draw pleasure from each moment and humor from life itself.

Still, humor and attempts at humor are all around us. Advertisers of personal computers use it to make their products seem more "friendly." Teachers and lecturers throw in a joke or two to keep students' attention and interest. Star athletes sport humorous nicknames that endear them to us. There's been a resurgence in nightclub comedy for local humorists. Newspapers, magazines, and news programs all include a column or news spot devoted to a humorous look at the world.

It is surprising then, that humor, which seems to be a basic way for people to communicate, has hardly been examined as an important variable in groups. Although we spend much of our lives in groups—in our family, school, and workplace, with friends, playing sports, listening to music, and in a myriad of other settings—there are very few references to the impact that humor has on how groups function or on membership or problem solving. Perhaps the reason for the lack of "serious" study of humor as an important group dynamic is that we tend to think humor is too playful, not work-related, and a diversion rather than what it actually is—an integral part of a group's identity.

What Is Humor?

In some way, we seem to know exactly what humor is. Yet if asked to define *humor,* we offer definitions as varied as the theories on humor themselves, and we remain unsure of the true dimensions of this concept (Keith-Spiegel, 1971). For a sampling of the diverse opinions on the status and nature of humor, let's look at what some noted thinkers, writers, and comics have said. These samples are derived from *Laughing Matters,* a quarterly journal on humor in business, education, and health care (Goodman, 1985).

- "He deserves paradise who makes his companions laugh." (Koran)
- "People who laugh at death feel superior to those who are dead." (Fred Allen)
- "The art of medicine consists of amazing the patient while nature cures the disease." (Voltaire)
- "A joke's a very serious thing." (Winston Churchill)
- "The most acutely suffering animal on earth invents laughter." (Frederick Nietzche)

- "Laughter is the most inexpensive and effective wonder drug. Laughter is the universal medicine." (Bertrand Russell)
- "Comedy is allied to justice." (Aristophanes)
- "A fun working environment is much more productive than a routine environment. People who enjoy their work will come up with more ideas. The fun is contagious." (Roger Van Dean)

Despite these different perspectives on humor, there is a commonality to all, and that is humor's ability to erase, cleanse, or change what, until the transformation, was embarrassing, oppressive, sorrowful, or painful. Humor, like a feather in the wind, will sail gently earthward. Just when we think its life is exhausted, it will float lightly up and away, propelled by an unexpected breath of air, changing everything. Unpredictable humor can ease our embarrassment, calm our anger, and relax our tensions. Most of all, it can free us from pedantic, ritualized, thoroughly predictable behaviors or events.

In a group, humor is often a scarce natural resource whose presence can literally change the life of the group. It can make what was merely tolerable both interesting and exciting and what was boring bearable, while keeping reality in perspective. Although it may be planned and carefully staged, humor is more often generated spontaneously from unpredictable turns in events that flow from the natural development of the group itself, from the success and crises its members experience together.

Most of us seek order, comfort, predictability, and stability in our lives, and if we succeed we may well drive away what is the essence of most humor, which often springs from uncertainty, discomfort, and disorder. All of us have experienced dull, predictable, boring relationships, committees, and organizations where there is little room for new and exciting ideas, for play or outrageous spontaneity, or for release from the challenge of shared risk taking. Too often we are lulled into familiar, patterned, humorless responses that we help to create by the norms we allow to dominate the groups in which we participate.

In reality, a marvelous source of humor that is readily available to any group member is the group itself. Group members share basic human characteristics, such as

Power and impotence

Anger, joy, and sadness

Security and insecurity

Likes and dislikes

Interest and boredom

Success and failure

These, and more, are the heart of any group. People attempt to maintain their personal sense of integrity, to look "good" rather than "foolish," to walk away wanting to return and knowing they are wanted. The constant struggle within any group of individuals attempting to meet their own needs as well as those of the group creates marvelous dynamics and is a never-ending source of humor. Whether the humor is recognized or used as a constructive part of the life of the group is another question.

Sometimes people take others so seriously that they fail to recognize the humor in a situation even when it has reached absurd proportions. For example, Allen Funt, founder of the television show *Candid Camera,* related the following caper: "We set up a roadblock on a narrow road between New Jersey and Delaware. A sign said, 'Delaware is Closed Today.' Motorists asked why, and they were told that Delaware was overcrowded and under repair, and it was suggested that they try tomorrow. Just about everybody obeyed. One lady asked meekly if New Jersey was open." (Goodman, 1985). Funt's observations have led him to believe that people are gullible, easily led by strong suggestion, and often blind obeyers.

For those who know how to observe, there is a bottomless reservoir of rich anecdotes, or vignettes, that can provide as much humor as any theater. By actively developing and utilizing in a positive manner the humor that exists in any group, both leaders and participants may have an important influence on attitudes, performance, and membership—not to mention norms, goals, and communication patterns.

Situational humor drawn from shared experience may reduce defenses and increase enjoyment, the willingness to risk cohesiveness, and open communication. As a result, it increases individual feelings of membership. Humor is no panacea for creating harmony or group success. But as will be shown, not to cultivate the humor that is present will certainly influence how a group develops, the attitude of members, and how the group functions. Humor can become a natural and constructive part of a group's life. Furthermore, if it is true that many groups move into patterns of defensiveness, noncreativity, and even hostility, the utilization of humor in an increasingly supportive atmosphere may be an important ingredient in reversing such a nonconstructive pattern or in reducing the opportunity for its initial development.

An example of how humor can be used positively in a work situation was submitted by a reader to a periodical that requested tips on just that subject (Goodman, 1985): "I use humor with my colleagues to help us lighten up our working relationships. We enjoy writing spoof memos and notices to help us know wits end is up. Here's an example:

NOTICE
This department requires
no physical fitness program!
Everyone gets enough exercise
Jumping to conclusions,
Flying off the handle.
Carrying things too far,
Dodging responsibilities,
And pushing his luck."

Jim Pelley, president of *Laughter Works* Seminars in Sacramento, was recently interviewed in *Principal* magazine. Pelley, whose organization is dedicated to "bringing more laughter to the job," suggests adding laughter to the workplace by creating an office humor file or a personal "humor first-aid kit" to be used at any time to reduce tension or bolster the spirits of you or your co-workers. Pelley also suggests that if complaints are a "chronic" problem, require that they be "put to music and sung" (Durdick, 1990).

Humor is simply the response to discovering something that is laughable. Most of us relate it closely to outcomes such as being entertained or amused. For our purposes, we are attempting to explore what it is in a group that allows humor to occur—humor that is constructive to the development of the group and the individual members. Clearly, we are after much more than ways of tickling a group's psychic funny bone. Optimistically, we wish to increase your awareness, your understanding of humor in groups, and ultimately your ability to capitalize on its use so you will be increasingly willing to risk using it.

Strange as it seems, participants in groups, without being born comics or particularly humorous themselves, have the capability of generating humor within the group—everything from warm internal smiles to belly laughs. The explanation lies in the ability to design certain events that allow humor to take shape and emerge from the ongoing life of the group—its activity and purpose. If a group has developed a certain amount of trust, humor will be easier to exploit because individuals will feel less embarrassed, will find it easier to show feelings, and will be less competitive and therefore able to support a shared positive experience. Without the development of a certain initial trust, it might be impossible to tap one of the greatest sources of humor available to a group—the members themselves. Their frailties, failures, successes, idiosyncrasies, and personal styles are what make each of them unique. Laughing with each other rather than at one another can be enormously freeing, even exhilarating. It can turn into positive support and a sort of stroking rather than being used at anyone's expense. It appears that humor and trust are reciprocal, each less likely to evolve without the other and each building on the other. The same seems to be true of openness in a group, the ability to risk, and even the ability to provide descriptive feedback to members. All seem to be enhanced in a group capable of laughing "with itself."

Barriers to Humor

It seems paradoxical, then, that although most people love having fun and enjoy humor, they are often resistant to its use, and some groups are just as humorless as some individuals we know. Actually, the reasons are not too complex. Many groups equate humor with being silly or wasting time. After all, people can't be working if they're busy having fun. In one large corporation, whenever the boss travels, people emerge from their offices, talk, smile, and walk around joking a bit, resembling groundhogs coming out of hibernation. They are not aware of their changed behavior, but it is quite evident that the boss's absence gives them an opportunity to relax and allow natural humor out to play. The people are quite professional and they don't take advantage of the situation. They simply allow themselves to be natural and to enjoy the pleasure derived from well-intentioned humor. If supervisors and bosses encouraged humor in their presence instead of inadvertently allowing it in their absence, perhaps much of the growing disillusionment and apathy that exist in the workplace today would be diminished. In addition, research has shown that humor is associated with health, creativity, and efficiency. These findings imply that in the workplace, laughter can ease tensions, create bonds among workers, and make bosses seem more "human" (Krohe, 1987).

Perhaps the greatest example of resistance to the use of humor is the ingrained sense that school is school and work is work and play is play. Our Puritan ethic subscribes to the idea that work should be hard, serious, important, direct, and efficient. Humor and fun suggest lack of focus, failure to have correct priorities, a misuse of time, and a lack of attention to what is really important and is to be rewarded.

Not only is humor related to silliness, wasting time, and laziness, but it is often seen as a measure of immaturity. Because work is such an important part of our lives, many individuals will avoid discrediting themselves and being labeled "jokesters." Historically, the jester was often likened to the fool. Similarly, an individual who thoroughly enjoys humor will be labeled as not being serious or tough-minded, and it is not uncommon to find a career path blocked by stereotyped views such as these. Of course, certain types of humor are genuinely offensive— for instance, those that have a competitive or cruel edge or are indulged in at the expense of others. Many comics, and even scholars, concerned about the perils of humor agree that the safest form of humor is that directed at oneself (Machan, 1987). A group, in fact, can be viewed as a kind of collective self, wherein humor directed inward, or generated from within, can prove not only to be safe, but to be constructive as well.

The Role of Humor in Groups

Quantifying humor is extremely difficult—a bit like describing the light emitted by a firefly. We see it and know it exists, but how it's created is baffling. In this exploration of humor, we are attempting to develop theory based on our own experiences. We know humor plays many roles in any group, but there is little empirical evidence of the exact degree to which humor can influence a group.

According to Freud's psychoanalytic theory of humor, humor actually helps us to "mask aggression . . . and escape from the control of our conscience" by camouflaging hostility (Berger, 1987). This can have a net positive or negative effect on a group.

For example, we know from personal experience that humor can be used effectively in disorienting individuals, redirecting them from potentially hostile, aggressive, or tense situations, and diffusing negative events. It may also be used as a means of avoiding much-needed conflict or confrontation in a group. Conversely, humor can be used by members to hurt or injure others or to minimize the value of their contributions. Rossel (1981) proposes that humor can become hostility unless it periodically comes under negotiation and is thus regulated by the group's leader and the members themselves.

Group leaders who are diagnostically aware of problems within their own group would ideally intervene in the life of the group in a positive manner to facilitate the group's development. Thus, if the group were using humor to avoid needed conflict, the source of humor would have to be identified and in some constructive manner pointed out, and possibly extinguished, so the group could be responsible to itself. If, as many believe, humor introduced into a group that is defensive will reduce tension and provide a climate that is more positive and constructive, then it only makes sense for leaders to try to inject some levity into such a situation. Many groups tell the same humorous stories time and again, yet individuals still laugh together. Just as when old friends reminisce, the group's litany of old stories and jokes becomes part of the history and tradition of the group. As new members join, stories are retold, and the storytelling and laughter serve to welcome the new member and strengthen the bonds of the group.

Allen (1986) suggested that in the workplace leaders schedule meetings in which employees share success stories. This, he said, would motivate employees to use fun and laughter. He further suggested creating work-related contests and companywide celebrations to lighten the atmosphere. A study by Isen, Daubmar, and Norwicki (1987) suggested that creativity, or innovative problem solving in the workplace, could be promoted by inducing a "happy feeling state" perhaps brought on through the use of humor.

Scogin and Pollio (1980) found that "enduring" groups—that is, groups with a history—made more frequent and longer use of humor than did groups just beginning to form.

In recent years, interest in humor has increased markedly. One expression of this interest is an annual "humor conference," The Positive Power of Humor and Creativity Conference, where researchers present current information on humor related to business, health care, education, and personal living. What was conceived as a scholarly conference—with a less serious side for "gluttons for funishment"—has in recent years enticed thousands of people to a small town in upstate New York.

An early and now famous example is Norman Cousins's theory, detailed in his book *Anatomy of an Illness,* that laughter eliminates pain. This worked so well for Cousins in his own illness that 10 minutes of belly laughs resulted in one pain-free hour. At first Cousins was ridiculed for this theory, but later became a member of the faculty of the UCLA School of Medicine and lectured widely on the subject.

Cousins sparked the growth of what some called "ho-ho-holistic health." Science is now showing increasing interest in the biochemistry of emotions, especially the relationship between pain and laughter.

In a related phenomenon, patient support groups, which encourage people to make jokes and learn how to see the humorous side of a critical health situation, are proliferating. And the idea of increasing the use of humor in education as an alternative to standard means of classroom control is also gaining support. Research has indicated that college students consider a teacher's use of humor in the classroom one of the significant positive traits of an effective teacher (Check, 1986). In short, an explosion in the use of humor has occurred during the past decade.

More researchers are studying the role of humor in task-oriented groups in the workplace. For example, one study examined the role of humor among managers versus nonmanagerial employees. One outcome, which contradicted the stereotype that managers don't have time for humor, was that managers were in fact more likely than nonmanagers to be involved in humor networks. Further, "humorous" managers tended to be overchosen (selected more frequently than would be expected by probability) as one criterion of social interaction, and they tended to be overchosen on other criteria also (Duncan, 1985).

A survey in *Forbes* magazine (Machan, 1987) found that 98 percent of chief executives reportedly would hire a candidate with a good sense of humor. Similarly, Duncan (1989) suggests that because joking improves the cohesiveness of a group, it's likely that it indirectly affects the group's productivity. According to Duncan, "the single most important reason that joking behavior is a universal part of work is that joking . . . makes people feel that they belong" (Duncan, 1989, p. 29).

Although having a sense of humor involves finding the absurd in everyday life, joke telling can involve making fun of others, and ignoring the distinction between humor and jokes can be perilous. The superiority theory of humor holds that the basis of humor represents the triumph, or sense of superiority, of one person over another. According to one superiority theorist, the famed English philosopher Thomas Hobbes, "the passion of laughter is nothing else but sudden glory arising from a sudden conception of some eminence in ourselves by comparison with the infirmity of others, or with our own formerly."[1]

Duncan (1985) tested the superiority theory by studying small, task-oriented groups in three business firms and three health care organizations to determine whether humor in the workplace actually fell into the category of "superiority" humor. In the study, members of the groups were asked to complete a structured questionnaire designed to assess the relationship between social interaction and perceived joking relationships.

Results indicated that with highly trained and professional health groups, humor was not predicted by "superiority theory." Humor was not high-level staff making jokes about lower-level staff. Jokes could go from the top down, and just as fre-

---

1. This is also the characteristic that allows one to laugh at oneself, having "become 'superior' to what we once were" (Berger, 1987, p. 7).

quently from the bottom up, or could move about at the same level among colleagues. This contrasted with the result in business groups, where persons low in the organizational hierarchy were more often the butt of jokes than those higher in the organization. In business groups, there was support for the superiority theory of humor (also referred to as "scapegoat" humor.)[2]

Another similar but contrasting study by Pogrebin and Poole (1988) examined the strategic use of humor by a police department. The researchers found that in "observations of jocular aggression . . . There were numerous occasions on which officers directly ridiculed their supervisors." These results are contrary to many studies of this kind, because according to Pogrebin and Poole, not only does the effectiveness of the superior's position depend on the cooperation of the officers, but the very "relations between sergeants and patrol officers reflect a structured ambiguity" (Pogrebin and Poole, 1988, pp. 206--207). The variety of ways in which different groups use humor within the organizational hierarchy indicated that the nature of the group itself, rather than the level in the hierarchy, may better determine how humor is used among its members.

In the personal arena, one question that arises is this: Does liking the same humor influence interpersonal attraction? Murstein and Brust (1985) administered a humor test composed of cartoons, comic strips, and jokes to 30 college couples (26 single, 4 married) who rated them for humor. Students also indicated how much they loved or liked their partners and recorded the likelihood of their marrying. Results confirmed the prediction that couples who rated degree of humor and degree of loving and liking each other similarly would have an increased predisposition to marry. The data suggested that shared humor reflects similar values and needs and that humor is indeed associated with attraction. It is presumed that humor is not only significantly associated with attraction but actually precedes it. This study suggests that it is important for members of a couple to have similar humor preferences.

Having similar preferences for humor may not prove as easy as once thought. Krohe (1987) asserts that men and women tend to enjoy different kinds of humor. Similarly, the wide range of humor styles apparent in different ethnic groups demonstrates that such preferences may be culturally based as well. Finally, research by Smeltzer and Leap (1988) found that new group members (inexperienced employees) rated mutual jokes as less appropriate than did experienced employees. Thus, apart from gender and cultural affiliations, there are actual circumstances that may affect our humor styles.

In one of the few studies of its kind, Baron (1974) found that of two groups of individuals who were subjected separately to anger-inducing situations, the group that was shown a series of humorous cartoons later exhibited markedly less aggressive, less hostile behavior to the object of anger. Given the opportunity to shock the individual who had angered or provoked them previously, the group

---

2. Superiority theory should attract increasing attention in the coming years as humor at the expense of others—especially minorities—will become the subject of new research.

tempered by humor had apparently diffused some of their anger, whereas those not provided a means of diffusing their anger were significantly more punitive in their responses. There is little doubt that the intervention of humorous material reduced the anger and distracted the focus of tension in an indirect manner. As in Freud's psychoanalytic theory of humor, it may be in this case that existing anger was hidden by the presence of humor, resulting in a positive outcome. The humor distracted the students enough to allow them to develop increased tolerance for their hostility and a parallel reduction in their need to act out their feelings as strongly as they would otherwise have done (Berger, 1987).

In essence, the study suggests that not acting positively toward the group (providing humor) promotes certain negative outcomes. Thus group members have real power to redirect the emotions of the group in a positive manner. In this case, to do nothing can be perceived as a negative intervention. Because most of us are leaders in groups at one time or another, it is interesting to note that the leader is often caught between a rock and a hard place. He or she is in the unenviable position of manipulating the group by acting *or* not acting.

From our point of view, it is no more manipulative to facilitate a group in an active, intervening manner than to omit from an agenda an item that has known consequences for the group. If humor can be used to move a group constructively toward its task and maintenance goals, then the leader has the obligation to do everything possible to help. Because leadership is situational and is shared among group members, the remainder of this chapter views the group member as an active interventionist, a person capable of using humor to influence the life of a group and, in many cases, the attitudes of other members. As in everything else, the value of an individual's contribution can be measured in relation to need, intent, honesty toward the group, skill of the intervention, and outcome in relation to how the group was helped and how much it valued the help. Accordingly, we are going to look at what actively creates humor in a group and at the critical interface between the leader and other group members.

◆ Individual Experiment

In a group in which you participate, observe very closely a humorous story, joke, or situation. Think about what impact the humor had on the group. What occurred just before and right after the humorous incident? Was it a way of avoiding a conflict? Was it an expression of individual anxiety? Was the joke made maliciously at someone's expense? Or was it good-natured? Was it sharing a common experience? Was it an attempt to improve the morale and energy level of the group? Did it appear to have a positive or a negative influence on the group? The role humor plays in groups is difficult to determine. Looking closely at what occurs before and after a humorous incident sometimes provides a clue. Trace how it happened. What was the initial humorous moment? What happened then? What was the incongruity or unpredictable incident that stimulated laughter?

Sometimes it is necessary to analyze the norms set up through humor. Norms can be set up that encourage trust and openness or that encourage caution and defensiveness.   ◆

Sources of Humor

Every time we are made to laugh by a play, film, song, or picture, we trace it predictably back to the unpredictable. Catching us off- guard is the essence of humor, which is created by presenting us with a paradox, a discrepancy between words and action, a startling event, a slight twist of perspective, or a sudden truth or personal insight; all have a common thread. But there are other sources of humor that we will find valuable to consider in our understanding of group be- havior. Shared success or failure, the absurd or outrageous, something very familiar and personal, or a strong memory may evoke humor. Even the experience of being faced with great fear and defeating it can generate both relief and humor.

Of course, every situation is different. What we are interested in is the part of any intervention or experience in a group that can be applied in some manner to another rather similar event. It is this ability to generalize that is the foundation of all work in the social sciences. So for each type of humor and for each example, we will attempt to generalize as much as our own limited experience will allow.

◆ Reader Activity

There are many ways to react to humor—a belly laugh, a smile, an internal grin that only you know occurs, the giggle of embarrassment, a shriek of delight, or the helpless laughter when everything has failed and all you have left is your sense of humor. Think of the last few times you laughed in a group. Can you remember how it felt and what caused the humor? Was it strictly situational or could you generalize what happened to other situations? In other words, would such humor be predictable? Could it be created intentionally?   ◆

Let's take a look at two jokes, both capable of generating humor. The quality and quantity of humor drawn from each will depend first on where you, the reader, are in your life, on your previous experience, and on your personal needs. How humorous you find each joke will depend on the degree to which you personalize the experience of each of the two stories, whether the style of the joke is appealing, whether you are dealing with any of life's universal questions, whether you antic-ipate the catch, and whether either provides you with something more than a laugh. A laugh attached to a personal insight obviously has much more significance.

The first story concerns two American tourists traveling through the English countryside. Stopping at an old monastery, they decide to have lunch. The brother who greets and waits on them brings each a huge and quite delicious plate of fish and chips. Appreciating the hospitality and the tasty meal, one of the Americans asks the brother whom he might thank for the meal. He nonchalantly points to the kitchen and suggests that the two chefs would be happy to hear the compliment in person. First, there would be the fish friar, and after him there would be the chip monk.

The twist, the catch, the play on words all make the situation believable so you can be slipped the unbelievable. Even though the joke represents a prepackaged effort at humor, it incorporates much of what must be present in a spontaneous situation that might create humor in a small group.

The second story involves a fifty-year-old businessman. After years of work-ing at break-neck speed without vacations and without enjoying either himself or his family, he began to ask the question, "What's life all about, anyway?" The question represented the beginning of a personal odyssey. He took a leave of absence for a year, read all of the great philosophers, talked to as many great thinkers as he could, took special courses, and became a scholar in his own right, all in answer to the pursuit of the question "What is the meaning of life?" After nine months, the man had exhausted nearly all of his financial resources in his search, and his leave of absence was coming to an end. Still he had no satisfactory answer. One day, he heard of a famous wise man, a guru, who lived on the top of a mountain in a distant European retreat and was reputed to have found the meaning of life. Worn down, doubtful, he set out to find the famous man and make a final attempt to understand. The journey was a most arduous one, but finally, at sunset one evening, he trudged the last mile to the ancient retreat. Seeing an old man sitting by himself, the searcher urgently asked, "Sir, are you the wise man reputed to have discovered the meaning of life?" "Well, my son, I have certainly given it thought and, yes, some say I have come close to the answer."

His anticipation mounting, the searcher begged, "Please, then tell me. I have looked for so long." Putting a hand on his shoulder, the guru told the businessman, "My journey, my own personal search tells me that the meaning of life is . . ." The man was virtually beside himself as the old man's words " . . . it's a waterfall" came from his lips. The man stood amazed, confused, feeling helpless. "You mean to tell me that I've come all this way and exhausted all my personal resources for you to tell me that the meaning of life is a waterfall? You have the nerve to tell me this?" The wise man suddenly looked terribly pained. He held his head for a moment in thought and then, looking the man in the face, asked in a puzzled tone, "You mean it isn't?"

Who among us has not taken the journey, struggled with the question, felt disillusioned by our life on this earth, prayed for time to think about the bigger questions? Who has not felt the doubt or hoped that there is an answer? Who has not hoped that the work of defining the answer could be done by some guru? And who could not at least smile at the trap into which we have fallen and at the renewed insight—that we are the answer. Again, the packaged joke personalized, related to our own experience and to a question of ultimate significance and providing a zinging insight snapped our head around and made us laugh as much at our own foolishness as anything.

The two jokes, although different in level of seriousness and intensity, had aspects in common and "set us up" in a predictable manner so that, again, the unpredictable could work on us. With this in mind, we are ready to explore various ways of generating humor in groups.

The Paradox

Years ago, an American tourist drove his car up a steep European mountainside terraced with level after level of small, stone huts, each looking the same and equally impoverished. Each sat on a tiny parcel of land and gave the impression that a strong wind would topple it off its precarious perch. The small plot of tilled soil next to each could hardly sustain the occupants, and the walk to the valley below and back would take several hours a day. The middle-class American tourist sympathized with the peasants and was puzzled by the smiles and good humor that greeted him at every turn. The road was overrun with men, women, children, donkeys, cows, and goats. Suddenly the road took a sharp turn to the right at the top of a sharply rising precipice. What he saw took his breath away. Unbelievable beauty! Azure blue sky, emerald green mountainside, all framed by the crystal blue hues of the Mediterranean. The laugh was on the tourist. Each of these "poor" people had a piece of this jewel, bathed in clean air and sun, and a simple lifestyle that seemed to put things in perspective.

According to William F. Fry, in his essay "Humor and Paradox" (1987), "the word 'paradox' designates a breakdown in our logical system . . . and humor is a veritable thicket and maze of paradox." Fry suggests that because many of the paradoxes inherent in much of our humor are unsolvable, restricted by our own logical limitations, if these were suddenly to become "resolvable, a massive shift of humor style would take place" (p. 42). This difference between what might normally be expected and what occurs, or between what we might normally do and what should be done to make a difference can be seen clearly in the following story of a paradox.

A group of recently divorced men and women had come together in a workshop setting to talk about mutual problems and concerns generated from their recent traumas and to seek commiseration from others who might understand. Such groups are increasingly common and can be tremendously beneficial or, on occasion, terribly dissatisfying, depending on the skill of the leader. If the experience is used as an opportunity to blame the other fallen spouse who is not there to defend himself or herself (which is the immediate inclination of almost everyone), it can be self-destructive, although momentarily satisfying.

Realizing that blame and self-pity are the food for depression, the leader decided to take the proverbial bull by the horns. She asked the participants to form small clusters and talk about all the reasons why the divorce was the fault of the other spouse. Predictably, the group needed little encouragement. Off they went into the corruption of their own marriages and what their partners had done to shatter the marital bliss they had so desired. After perhaps 20 minutes of catharsis, the leader suggested that they not leave out any bloody details, to make sure the other participants had a clear picture and that it was all right to exaggerate a bit to help make a point. Well, the room was in an absolute uproar of self-justification and blame. As the stories became more exaggerated, laughter began to well up from the various small groups. Cautious levity turned to hilarity as exaggerated truths and one-sided stories of anger, pain, and absurdity filled the air.

Then the leader challenged the group to look at itself, asking the members to consider how much power they had somehow, in all of this exaggerated blaming and storytelling, given away to their partners. The paradox was suddenly all too clear. How little responsibility each was willing to take, how dependent and helpless they sounded, how utterly out of control. The humor drawn from exaggeration surely made many of the participants gasp as much as when the tourist turned not to see the beauty of the Mediterranean but the degree to which his initial sympathy had been narrow, self-serving, and distorted. Therefore, the real humor in the workshop did not lie in the initial bursts of energy and laughter but in the later deep and probing humor of self-realization and insight.

In the workshop for these divorced individuals, the humor generated from the exaggerated storytelling and then from the paradox would fit into the personal experience of each individual. Certainly the leader was not a comic, a joke teller. Rather, she was a skilled facilitator of social interaction who allowed humor to be woven into the fabric of a productive educational experience by those who must live with their own learnings. The revelations (and laughter) that often result from these learnings are evidence of the enrichment that can occur when an individual or group manages to step out of the common experience and acknowledge the inconsistency.

Irony

Some of the most generally accepted theories of humor, according to Berger (1987), are the incongruity theories. Included in this perspective that humor involves "some kind of difference between what one expects and what one gets" is ironic humor. Ironic humor evolves from the discrepancy between what is real and what is perceived. Human beings are capable of great distortions of reality. That we see what we need to see is obvious to anyone willing to take a hard look at himself or herself. Obviously, we become masters of self-deception because we somehow are not ready or do not wish to face that which is real. For most of us it is merely the way we protect ourselves from a very difficult world. Taken with a grain of salt and kept in perspective, the discovery of our own self-deceptions can provide us with useful insights about ourselves and our world.

◆ Reader Activity

When was the last time you remember fooling yourself? A time when suddenly you were struck with a new reality—perhaps an idea you had previously denied, only to discover it was absolutely true. And there you were—caught with your face hanging out and only a smile to cover it! Sometimes we are so wrong it almost feels good to admit loudly that "yes, I can be wrong, dead wrong."

◆

Groups, like individuals, have marvelous ways of deceiving themselves about those things they do not wish to "own." Just as an individual is capable of denying that a problem exists, so can a group persuade itself that information has meaning other than that which is most obvious. The fact that a teen-ager goes out with others who take drugs, has declining grades, and returns home with eyes occasionally dilated may mean little to her or his parents, because it is quite possible for many parents to read these symptoms and attach totally different meaning to them. For these parents it would be out of the question that their child, a product of their home, could possibly be involved in drugs.

The faculty of the elite eastern girls' prep school had somehow denied all the signals that "their girls" were involved in the use of drugs. The symptoms were all there. But somehow, their own fears and fantasies made denial easier than facing the problem. Even though interviews suggested that the problem existed, the outside consultant knew he could not simply tell the faculty that drug use was at a rather severe level in the school. After all, they could easily use the age-old justification, "What could he possibly know about our school—he didn't even go to boarding school himself." (So much for consultant expertise.) Instead, a group of faculty had gathered to help develop questions that needed to be asked about the school to help improve the social and academic climates. As good academics, the faculty did not avoid the hard questions. Among them was one framed about drug use. They asked parents, faculty, and students the question "What percentage of students use alcoholic beverages or drugs (marijuana or pills) as regularly as every week or two?" They then asked parents and faculty what they thought the students would say and asked the students what they thought the faculty would say. Without quite realizing it, they had set up the possibility for major discrepancies to occur. In the theory of change, one of the major stimuli for change is a dramatic difference in our perception of reality from other believable data.

Several weeks later, the entire faculty was gathered together to listen to a report on the data. The data feedback session was turned into a workshop exploring each question in depth, with the faculty predicting responses prior to the data being revealed, interpreting the results, and then discussing the resulting information. Later it was announced that there would be a two-day problem-solving program with both faculty and students to attack major issues cooperatively.

Throughout the feedback session, considerable humor had been generated as predictions were confirmed or denied by the data. Inevitably, the greatest laughter would result at points of greatest discrepancy. Finally, the question relating to drug use in the school was approached. The data were presented on individual sheets of newsprint paper, one at a time.

Faculty perception of students using drugs regularly—32 percent

Parent perception of students using drugs regularly—22 percent

Having digested these two pieces of information, the faculty were asked to write down their prediction of the student response on a small piece of paper and to move into groups of four for discussion. Now the student data were shown:

Student perception of students using drugs regularly—71 percent

Nervous laughter, groans of disbelief. Asked to discuss the implications of the data, many immediately tried to explain away the data. The students exaggerated, they were trying to be smart, they saw others do it and assumed even more took part, and on and on. Finally, the other data were shared.

Faculty perception of what students would say—48 percent

Parent perception of what students would say—33 percent

Student perception of what the faculty would say—36 percent

Asked to summarize the significance of all the data relating to the question and provide their summary to all the faculty, the various small working groups huddled and almost whispered as they shared their points of view. When reporting the data, virtually every group agreed in a variety of humorous, self-effacing, and generally nondefensive ways that they as a faculty had been short-sighted, that a problem did exist, that they had resembled ostriches more than intelligent faculty, and that "in all of their wisdom they needed to be educated" before they could be expected to grasp all the significance of the data. The humor in response to the discrepancies may have been the result of not being able to fool themselves any longer.

Although one assumes the faculty could have been angry—perhaps experiencing a sense of being duped and feeling foolish—our experience in many similar situations is that once reality is grasped, the group is more likely to perceive itself as rational and less willing to deny the true significance of the information. In this instance, humor acted as an almost predictable vehicle for admitting imperfection and beginning to deal with the new reality. By working in small, intimate clusters, the faculty could first defuse their own discomfort and possible embarrassment with the data and begin putting it into perspective with humor and candor. They could begin to see they were not alone in their failure to predict successfully. The weight of judgments was lessened and the possibility of guilt diminished, thus freeing the group.

The Unanticipated

Twelve male seminary students had been meeting for more than a week readying themselves to move to new posts as the heads of inner-city parishes. Although some had previously worked in poor communities, they saw their new role as a challenge and were somewhat awed by the problems they were anticipating. Part of the training was directed at helping each of the students gain better self-understanding in relation to his own behavior and the impact his own leadership might have on his new parish.

Four days into the program, a climate of work had evolved that was supportive and trusting and allowed no room for the usual game playing that occurs in many meetings of professional peers. On one occasion, Jim was discussing a particular point in his usual forceful and colorful manner. It was his style, as a member of an inner-city parish for many years, to use what might be called the "local vernacular," complete with a wide variety of colorful four-letter words. Every time he spoke, Vic and several other members of the group would grimace. Finally, it became too much for Vic, who shouted, "Do you always have to express everything with such a filthy mouth? Aren't you creative enough to talk as a civilized adult?" For what seemed like an eternity, no one spoke. Then, in the understatement of the year, the group facilitator quietly said, "It appears that some of us have some strong feelings about the type of language Jim has been using." For about ten minutes, chaos prevailed as sides were drawn over the use of profanity, especially by representatives of the church.

Seeing that the argument was going nowhere in a hurry and that members were becoming increasingly polarized, the facilitator suggested, "Because we all have strong feelings over this issue, I would like to have each of us think of the most filthy, disgusting statement we have ever actually heard. I would like us all to share these." Several of the students almost fainted away at the thought, others thought it was a wonderful idea, and still others actually blushed as they half-whispered a patently common four-letter word. Eventually, the group reached a consensus on the word that was most vulgar to them. The facilitator then told the twelve students in a most serious voice, "I would like us all to say this word three times as a group, a bit like a cheer, saying it louder each time." The group was absolutely befuddled and disoriented, not knowing whether to follow the directions, to be serious, or to take it all as a joke. Up to this point, although there had been a few snickers, the tone had been quite serious. "On the count of three," the leader said. "One, two"—it was like the moment before a balloon bursts—"three!" As a result of all the pent-up emotion, the group only whispered the word. They looked at each other sheepishly. "Come on, fellas, we can do better than that. Now, once again." This time there was real gusto and a bit of pleasure as the word was shouted and most everyone either smiled or laughed. "O.K., one last time. Let's really give it a go. Let's hear it!" At that point, out came a roar, and the group was beside itself, laughing at the absurdity of it all—discovering together how little it all meant and how foolishly and judgmentally they had acted. Not that it was necessary or desirable to swear, but they realized that a word of no real importance beyond how they themselves interpreted it had made them so uptight and embarrassed.

Here the humor—the punch line—had once again been created out of the feelings and emotions of the group itself. Thrown into a totally new and unanticipated situation in which there was no prescribed role, being totally disoriented in relation to each other and the previous norms of the group, the individuals gained a new and different perspective. Chafe (1987) proposes that "the basic, evolutionary, adaptive function of humor is a disabling one." Because humor "diverts attention," it allows people to focus on something besides the state they were in, where they might have had to act or take something seriously. In short, Chafe says that "while in the humor state you can't act effectively, and you like it" (Chafe, 1987, pp. 21, 24). It was that new vantage point, totally unexpected, that allowed many to see that their own narrow biases surely would pose problems for them in their new parishes, where such words were part of the culture and certainly could not be passed off as filthy. The facilitator knew the humor was there, thought the group would find it, and then simply designed the particular intervention to tap it. Without the predictable humor, the group would have been left in the win–lose battle, leading to further polarization.

◆ Reader Activity

Take a break and ask someone close to you (both in proximity and personally if possible) whether he or she can remember a situation or two in which something happened that was so unanticipated, perhaps so paradoxical, that humor was the last thing he or she would expect but exploded in laughter anyway. Why was it so funny? Was it emotion? Fatigue? Surprise? Frustration? Or was there nothing left to do? Again, can you generalize this? Relate it to other situations. Does it have any implications for you as a group member?   ◆

Sudden Awareness

The parents of students at a junior high school were outraged at what they perceived as a total breakdown in discipline in the school and blamed it mainly on the teachers. The teachers felt that they had been blamed unfairly and had been made scapegoats and that the real problem lay in permissive parents who could not care less what happened to their children once they left home. The students felt totally alienated from both the faculty and parents, who they felt simply didn't understand them. All three groups were feeling unappreciated and didn't trust the others.

A day had been planned to bring together about one hundred parents, children, and faculty to look at problems that could be solved collaboratively and to begin developing workable solutions. But the participants were expected to be defensive and unable to listen. Because beginnings are so crucial, it seemed important for everyone to stop nursing their own hurt and anger, to put things into perspective, and to begin working in a cooperative manner. If humor could not be injected into the situation, one could predict a quick departure of the various groups into stereotyped role behavior, kids acting as parents expected, parents acting as kids expected, and teachers acting as everyone expected, even the teachers. Humor was needed as an equalizer. But how?

The fact is that most adults are so busy acting adultlike around adolescents that adolescents seldom see their fun, childlike side. And similarly, adolescents are so busy acting like adolescents for themselves and adults that they seldom have the opportunity to be more adult. If each group could be placed in a situation that showed the other group a new side, then the chances for understanding and trust to develop would be greatly increased.

Everybody met in the gym feeling totally strange and uncomfortable. Mixed groups of between six and eight were formed, with three or four boys and girls and the rest teachers and parents. The intention was to provide more support for the students than for the teachers or parents, because youth can be an inhibiting factor. After several warm-up activities designed to get people talking, each individual was provided a piece of drawing paper and access to coloring materials. The task was for each person to draw two pictures representing school—one thing he or she disliked about school when he or she had been a teen-ager and one thing he or she really liked (other than gym, lunch, and recess). They were to draw these impressions as best they could and share them with the group. Immediately, the discomfort level in the room rose, but there was no way to withdraw from the task easily. Teen-agers and adults began an equalizing experience in which almost all would fail a bit (the drawing) and all would succeed a bit (sharing experiences). When the individuals reconvened into their small groups to share their drawings, a profound awareness took hold of most groups. They realized that virtually everyone could appreciate each other's likes and dislikes, regardless of age, and that teachers held some of the same fears and apprehensions that resulted in their disliking school as did the kids in the group. Not only that, but they also felt a little embarrassed to share not only their inadequate drawings but their past feelings. The awareness that we are all in the same boat provided a common point of discussion and understanding. The relief at no longer feeling so uncomfortable with each other and at having their discomfort channeled into a common task created a release of tension so great that most groups were laughing with each other—over drawings, personal experiences, or the simple satisfaction that they were surviving a terribly uncomfortable experience.

Finally, each group was asked to design a skit from either their original discussion or the later exploration. These would represent a common problem that existed today in the school that would require the cooperation of students, teachers, and perhaps parents to solve. The skits were performed for the entire workshop. Common problem themes were then identified, and a structure was developed to begin generating potential solutions.

Without the use of a humor-producing format designed to reduce the members' tensions and resistance, without "equalizers" and a climate in which laughter was legitimate, it is doubtful whether the productive outcomes of this situation could have occurred. The awareness the group gained of common roots, insights, and feelings freed them to listen, to take themselves less seriously, and to be less reactive and more proactive with each other. This illumination liberated the latent humor and good feelings in the group. Also, within the situation of the workshop and the climate of humor and goodwill that prevailed, new perceptions could be established as both student and adult stereotypes came crashing down. As equal partners in the task, working toward a common goal, no one was tempted to preach or talk about good communications. The positive common experience created by focusing on similarities, not differences, had a profound impact.

Shared Risk Taking

Mutual risk taking is one of the surest ways of increasing cohesion and a sense of membership in a group. An initiation is in fact a ceremony of introduction to membership. In this country it often is associated with hazing or activities incorporating fear, the unknown, or adventure, so that an individual has to earn the privilege of membership. People who have gone through initiation rites as part of a group know that the sharing of the common experience draws the group together and creates a bond that is seldom experienced under less stressful conditions. Within the initiation rite, whether it be that of a fraternity or sorority, military boot camp, or a social club, the common goal and performance anxiety of the group provides a natural and expected role for humor as a "safety valve." If team building is a group goal, it will be enhanced if some of the characteristics of the initiation rite can be incorporated into the program. Here is a case in point:

> A group of counselors, teachers, and administrators came together to learn to be more effective leaders. So that they could learn from each other, their facilitators believed it necessary to help them become a team as rapidly as possible. Thus, on each of five days, the group was faced with a task that required individual ingenuity and courage but that would be easier if assistance could be had from the group. On day one, small groups were taken deep into unfamiliar woods and given brief orientation lessons and the directions to their next meal (whenever they arrived). Although people did not fear being abandoned, the situation provoked enough anxiety that humor became a common tool for coping. Because the humor was generated by the situation and not directed toward any individual, the group established an implicit norm of supportive humor rather than humor at someone's expense. On the second day, each individual was required to climb a sheer cliff, supported by the goodwill of the group and a rope tied to another member. As each person successfully completed the ordeal, gales of laughter were heard. People laughed about their fears, the overcoming of potential failure, and the good feelings of success. Similarly, a third day saw small groups taken to a river with boards, rope, inner tubes, and a bit of canvas and told that camp was five miles down the river. They were to construct a raft and meet the rest of the group there. Swimmers and nonswimmers alike were drawn together by the challenge, excitement, fear, and fun of the task, with some people playing counselor to the nonswimmers, some acting as architects, and others playing less-defined support roles. The laughter and merriment as each raft was launched and

stayed afloat (some did not) was like a glue drawing the group together. In all of these experiences, humor not only reduced anxiety but also became a sign of the group members' support for each other and confidence in overcoming the odds they faced.

Another example involves a group of university students who agreed that each would do something in front of the group that he or she had always wanted to do but had been too afraid to do in the past. Although the group knew each other and thought doing this would provide a good evening's entertainment, they had no understanding of the degree to which it would unite the group in a bond of experience that would never be forgotten. One of the first members stood before the group and asked them not to laugh at his effort to read part of *Don Quixote,* because he had wanted to do it most of his life in front of an audience. He proceeded to render a rather ineffective reading. There wasn't a smile, not the glimmer of a laugh until he was done. When he finished, the group cheered and laughed with him at overcoming his own great fear. The laughter was in the spirit of caring and having made it through the rite. Another person, who had always wanted to be a famous athlete, had the group cheer his mock heroics, which allowed him to act out a fantasy and put away a dream by admitting his own limitation. Again, the scene produced tremendous laughter and humor, but at what? Not at the scene, but at the never-to-be-reached dream in all of us that we may yearn for until we die. Here he was putting it to rest. It was the laughter at themselves that spilled over into goodwill for him. Finally, one woman had each individual in the group promise to say something about her they felt she could improve, because she perceived that she had spent her life being "nice" and avoiding conflict or arguments. The group did—and then laughed at how inconsequential it all was in light of other things they felt. But the initiation rite of it all was real and the experience of shared anxiety and success was also real.

The two examples here were both extreme, one on an emotional level and the other combining the physical and the emotional. At a less intense level, some of the same feelings and team-building benefits can be gained by taking a group of people who work in the same department away for a day and, after anonymously identifying problems that block their effective work together, providing a structure for working several of the issues through to solution. Five small groups working on the same problem that people were previously afraid even to mention can have a releasing effect and provide a sense of trust not experienced before. Of course, the problem solving will be for naught if the group does not make a commitment to follow-through and action. However, if people believe that they are being heard and that solutions are possible, the outcome in terms of the life of the group will generate an enormous outpouring of humor and goodwill as people risk revealing their view of common problems and try to develop mutually satisfying solutions together.

◆ *Reader Activity*

Have you ever been in a group that is caught in the grip of fear? Most of us have. It seems that there is always someone who, even in the worst possible situation, can find something humorous. At times the humor just creates a ripple through the group, but on other occasions it bursts through the group, removing a heavy burden. What is it that draws this type of humor from deep inside? Is it simply a raw, primal response to uncontrolled anxiety, or are there other ingredients? What is your experience? Can you recount an incident when such humor changed the entire complexion of a situation? How? What did you experience personally?

◆

Generating Personal Truths

The most important person to each of us is ourselves. We do an amazing job of building defenses against an insensitive world. Any time a group leader wishes to gain a group's attention and increase interest and motivation, he or she has simply to develop an activity around the sharing of each person's personal ideas on the subject or, better yet, the sharing of something personal and meaningful from each individual's life experience. The interest others show in us will increase our ability to show interest in someone else. The fact is that in each of us is a never-ending stream of enjoyment, because out of our personal pain of growing older emerges the secret to our growth, understanding, development, and (above all) humor. Consider an example:

> A group of thirty professionals in the social sciences and related fields spent ten days attempting to understand themselves and others better. The group had been together about five days, and the leader knew about half the group well, although some he didn't know at all. The room was darkened and the group was asked to lie on the floor with their heads toward the center like the spokes on a wheel (admittedly not a common activity for a social get-together). The members were then asked to shut their eyes and try to remember the things that happened in their lives that they really didn't like but couldn't do anything about. They were especially encouraged to consider events from their families, the way they were treated as kids that they resented, or people who created special pain for them. When they felt like it, they were to describe the situation in a word or a sentence or more in a way that would help each of the others understand it.

They didn't move for two hours. After five minutes, the group was one. The laughter was intense; each readily recognize his or her own pain in virtually everyone there. An uncle, a grandmother, a sister, a neighbor, teachers—the commonality of it all brought a sense of ecstasy; along with the pain of bad memories and the joy of having overcome most of them like everyone else. It was like the combination of delicious memories and sadness when a vacation is over. But the realization important to us here is that within each of us are a thousand stones that we have merely to turn over to discover huge quantities of humor and shared experiences with other very tough, very fragile survivors. Lying on one's back in a darkened room is obviously not the everyday method of unlocking this type of humor. But people are forever ready to talk about themselves, their successes and failures, their joy and sadness in ways that will inevitably enable them to laugh through the sharing of it. As long as people feel protected from ridicule or contempt, they will share, especially in small clusters of people in which they don't feel too vulnerable. It is for us as group leaders and members to create events that can spring free some of this humor. The activity is much more than traipsing back over the clutter of time or rummaging through nostalgia for its own sake. It is reconnecting ourselves to important parts of the past and present with others who share elements of history and who have other unique dimensions from which we can learn.

How well the stage had been set by the leader. How easily each member received permission to share and to enjoy the experiences of others. The situation did not just occur. It was carefully developed with predictable results.

◆ *Reader Activity*

What would you have thought to say had you been lying on the floor that night? Is there any pain or sadness in your past that tickles you now or that would both bring relief and make others laugh? Think for a moment of the rituals, the expectations, the defeats and later victories, the demands, and personal embarrassments suffered that were later triumphs or, at the very least, were put in less traumatic perspective. How do they look now? Can you recapture the feeling of both the pain and the pleasure?   ◆

Similarly, one might ask a small group of businesspeople to share a significant insight from a major success that might help someone or to identify a mistake that influenced the course of their careers and that they wouldn't want others to experience. The responses would both enrich the listeners and help them get to know the other individual better than would normally be possible. It is the personal connection made through one's own experiences and the new insights gained through others that will set humor into motion. However, by always conforming to the impersonal norms of the organizational mentality, people risk losing their sense of humor. The well of humor will dry up, leaving little but one-upmanship, sarcasm, and put-downs.

Using Humor in Groups

Our effort in this chapter has been to explore the concept of humor in small groups, to understand it, and to use it in a manner that is constructive to the life of the group itself. Although the chapter is not meant to be prescriptive, some rather broad generalizations can be made that will prove helpful as individuals consider their roles in the group, either as supports or leaders.

First, although much humor will flow naturally from a group as it evolves, it has been shown that humor can actually be built systematically into the life of the group. By being sensitive to the needs of the group, individuals in positions of responsibility can take active, interventionist roles and exploit the fact that within almost any situation there is an underlying well of humor that can be tapped.

Second, people have an enormous capacity to feel joy as well as sadness. Groups are always complex and sometimes difficult to understand, so it is not surprising that group members take the group seriously and recognize that it warrants nurturing attention. This is all to the good and in no way conflicts with the constructive use of humor. By looking closely at the process of the group, we can always find opportunities to cultivate humor. By taking advantage of

paradoxes within the group

discrepancies

the unpredictable

the unanticipated

universal truths

the absurd

the familiar and the memorable

it is always possible to capitalize on a never-ending source of humor.

Finally, it appears that a healthy group is a humorous group. Groups able to laugh at their failures will be able to take risks together, will tend to communicate openly and without fear, will be sensitive to the membership needs of the participants, and will be open to change. Humor appears to play an integral part in these and other aspects of a well-functioning group.

◆ ◆ *EXERCISE 1*

Understanding Humor

Objectives

■ To involve group members in the development of humorous situations
■ To develop an understanding of various types of humor
■ To explore the positive and negative aspects of various attempts to inject humor into a group situation

Rationale

Most of us take humor for granted. Because most humor is spontaneous, we tend to be reactive, seldom if ever considering the underlying causes in a particular situation that helped set the stage for what developed. Was it an accident springing from an unpredictable situation? Was it carefully choreographed? Was success or failure in the style of a key individual? If we wish to use humor to our advantage in group settings, we must take careful aim at such questions and begin to determine what types of humor can intentionally be developed among a group of individuals through the implementation of planned activities.

Action

Ideally, twenty to thirty-five people are present, although the design can be easily adapted for larger or smaller numbers. The facilitator should divide the large group into random clusters of from three to five. Then he or she instructs the clusters to do the following:

> Develop one or possibly two activities that will involve every member of the large group in a humorous experience. Each activity should be self-contained and can last anywhere from 1 to 5 minutes. You will have 15 minutes to design your activity and prepare yourselves. Other than what I have said, there are no rules, so be as creative as possible within the bounds of some social propriety.

At the end of 15 minutes, the facilitator draws from a hat the number of one group at a time. The small cluster then involves the rest of the large group in their activity. At the end of the allotted 5 minutes and before the next cluster has been drawn from the hat, the facilitator should lead a large-group discussion stimulated by such questions as

1. What were the planned sources of humor designed into the activity?
2. If you felt the situation that developed actually evoked humor, describe why. Was it in the event, in the behavior of the facilitator, or both?

3. If the situation or activity failed to generate a humorous response, why do you believe it failed?
4. In retrospect, what could have been done to increase the effectiveness of the design and gain the humorous outcome that was intended?

Follow-up Discussion

After each of the clusters has had the opportunity to present an activity, a brief summary session of perhaps 10 minutes should occur. The purpose of this large-group discussion is to draw from those present a series of concise statements that reflect the principles of developing humor in groups and that might be generalized from one group to another. It might prove useful to let individuals meet in informal clusters of three or four for perhaps 5 minutes to help formulate the statements they present to the large group. Our experience is that a rather insightful and sophisticated list results that covers many of the points raised in the chapter. For this reason, the activity is best utilized before the chapter is presented. The combination of design and the development of theory and its application seem to make this an appropriate introductory activity.

◆ ◆ EXERCISE 2

Moderating Tension-Producing Issues with Humor

Objective

■ To provide practice in designing activities for dealing with stressful issues without polarizing a group or antagonizing the participants

Rationale

There are always issues among groups that by their very nature are going to create tension and stress. It is not uncommon for us to avoid such issues until a crisis occurs and dealing with them becomes a necessity. One reason why avoidance is not unusual is that individuals simply are not familiar with methods for minimizing the conflict and maximizing the positive attributes of a situation. Humor is one means of reducing stress and allowing individuals to maintain perspective.

Action

The facilitator should survey the participants and discover a number of issues of social and personal significance to the group members. These could include topics such as women's rights, marital infidelity, sexism, the problems with a two-party system, grading, organizational racism, or many others. From a group of, say 24, the facilitator divides the group into four groups of six. Two of the groups should be instructed to select one high-stress issue, and the other two groups should take a second issue. At this time, the facilitator assigns each group to work independently to design a process for exploring the issue they have selected in accordance with the following principles:

1. in a manner that raises points of view but not defenses
2. in a manner that is direct and open
3. so that humor is allowed to develop and is utilized as a means of maintaining member perspective

After 15 minutes of planning, each group is allowed 15 minutes to involve the other eighteen (or more if desired) members of the large group in a structured process for looking at their particular issue. Thus, if groups A and B both are designing around the issue of organizational racism, group A would present their activity followed immediately by group B's presentation around the same issue and involving the total group. At this point, there should be a 15-minute open discussion that compares the designs of the two groups and the ways that each helped or hindered the promotion of an open climate for discussion and learning. The discussion might focus on

1. identifying the role of humor in each design and how it did or did not create some perspective
2. comparing and contrasting the two designs in terms of their strengths and benefits, again focusing on planned or unplanned humor
3. ways of improving each design, given the goals of opening communication and reducing antagonism

After this set of presentations and the period of discussion, the final two groups (which have a different issue) are given 5 minutes to caucus and revise their designs, if necessary, on the basis of what they have just learned. The process is then repeated for the final two groups, and similar comparisons are made.

This activity focuses on the participants' "doing" so that they develop the belief that humor can be facilitated by their planning and structured designing.

◆ ◆ EXERCISE 3

A Series of Strategies for Building Humor-Using Skills

Objective

■ To improve the ability to see humor and introduce it into a situation

Rationale

What is the key to perceiving the world as funny? How can a person learn to transcend the usual ways of reacting or responding? Can humor, in fact, be learned?

People trained to work with groups are rarely taught how to inject humor into their interactions. This exercise contains a series of strategies for improving our ability to see and express humor. If we understand that humor is beneficial and sharpen our skills at perceiving it, humorous incidents and moments will emerge naturally in the groups we participate in.

BUILDING SKILLS

The following ideas for sharpening our humor-perception skills are drawn from the "Grin & Share It" section of *Laughing Matters* (Goodman, 1985).

- At work, I will open any page in the dictionary and will then use the words on that page to discuss the day with my staff. This is a challenging—and fun—pop that invites creativity and laughter.
- I keep a joke-a-day calendar on my desk as a conversation piece. It usually turns into a laughter piece too.
- When our staff gets too serious on a subject, I break out in "Row, row, row your boat." It's become a byword for us to lighten up.
- I cut funny pictures out of magazines. Sometimes my staff and colleagues will have fun making up captions for these pictures.
- As a physical therapist, I have used tapes of comedy routines with patients while they are relaxing during treatment applications ("Who's on First?", a comedy routine developed by Lou Abbot and Bud Costello, is my favorite).
- I have begun asking others what makes them laugh. When they answer, we both usually end up laughing.
- I have been trying to spend more time with people who I think have a good sense of humor and who make me laugh—I seek the positive contagion of laughter. I've also been trying to let go of seeing things too seriously—to acknowledge the absurd and to value inconsistency.
- I have used the humor skill of reversal and find it to be quite effective. When I'm having a bad day, I completely stop whatever I'm doing, pause for a moment, and reflect on some of the things that make me happy and the reasons why I should be smiling. It's amazing how quickly this can turn my mood around.
- I pun on a daily basis at work and at home. Word play fascinates me, and there are lots of ways to use it in the health field. For example, when a patient doesn't need a cane anymore, you can say there was a cane mutiny.
- When our office is in the midst of a crisis, we keep perspective by using humorous quotes—"There is no such thing as failure—only successes we don't like very much."
- I Xerox cartoons or jokes on company letterhead stationery to be used as office memos.

- When in the middle (or muddle) of a stressful situation, I imagine how I will see this situation 20 years from now. Then I really see the humor in it.
- I help people see the humor in their situations by telling funny stories about things that have happened to me.
- I put jokes and cartoons in my exams to help the students decrease their anxiety and increase their performance. It works!
- Set up an office bulletin board where workers gather. Encourage employees to contribute work-related cartoons, funny signs, anecdotes, sayings, and other funny items.
- Practice predicting stressful situations you might encounter and prepare alternative humorous responses you might use. By practicing these responses, you will more likely be able to use humor to defuse the heat of the moment.
- Experiment with jokes. Take one, adapt it to yourself and your work situation, and try it out with several co-workers.
- We have a running gag in our office that enables us to laugh at ourselves. Whenever one of us makes a ridiculous or obvious statement ("In order to have any energy, I have to eat"), we all say in unison, "A Statement!" and hold up an index finger. This has helped us to put a finger on our own humor.
- When things are tough at work, we ask each other, "Are we having fun yet?" It really breaks the tension. We then take a "happy minute" (as opposed to a "happy hour") to get a humorous perspective on the situation.
- I send "wanted posters" in advance of my sales or training meetings. These posters look authentic, and the text explains in a humorous way the agenda for the upcoming meeting.
- Instead of using verbal abuse, I overdramatize and exaggerate petty arguments or fights. It helps us to get perspective and laugh.
- I use cartoons (especially from *The New Yorker*) in management-training materials. I also stick them inside correspondence to colleagues and friends.
- Riddle time in my classroom is a great tension-reliever and very relaxing for me as well as for the students.
- Whenever a stressful situation occurs in our office, we have a quote we repeat with enthusiasm: "Oh! What an opportunity for growth and learning!"
- We have a favorite saying in our office: "Never wrestle with a pig—you both get dirty and the pig likes it." We use this saying in the midst of conflict, and it helps to break the tension.
- In setting agendas for potentially boring committee meetings, I make each agenda item a familiar song title, with "chorus" for group discussion. It's fun to see if people can "name that tune" as the meeting progresses.
- I enjoy adding levity to faculty meetings by contributing "lay" perspectives on educational jargon. ("We need to interface with the community." "You want me to do what? I only do that with my husband!")

HUMOR-INDUCING EXERCISES

1. Playing either/or games is an entertaining way to stretch your imagination. You can do this by yourself or with others. Other people's thinking is often tellingly revealed when they respond to such questions as

- Which travels faster, a lead weight dropped off a cliff—or a rumor?
- Which takes up more room, an elephant—or a laugh?
- Which is more dangerous, a hungry mosquito—or a constipated hippo?

2. Finding metaphors for yourself can also be mind stretching and fun. Ask yourself, for example,

- Are you more like a bing, a bang, or a bong?
- Are you more like a backbone, a funny bone, a jawbone, or a trombone?
- Are you more like a calm lake, a bubbling brook, a flood, or a swamp?
- Are you more like New York City, Carson City, or Paris?

The object of these questions is to encourage divergent thinking and unusual association.

3. Another strategy is to keep a log of amusing perceptions. This helps you develop the habit of looking for humor. Divide your log into sections—for example, work, family, interactions with colleagues, friends, and so on.

Here are some entries from a teacher's journal of classroom oddities:

- An action verb shows action.
- A passive verb shows passion.
- Chicago is nearly at the bottom of Lake Michigan.

4. Consider creating a bogus self-improvement workshop, such as

- Creative Suffering
- Overcoming Peace of Mind
- How to Overcome Self-Doubt Through Pretense and Ostentation
- Using Burn-out to Get Sympathy

5. Some of the classic exercises to prepare people for a brainstorming session can stimulate humorous thinking. Here are two examples:

- You are a farmer in Nebraska. You just received C.O.D., and paid for, two huge cartons containing 10,000 magnetic coat hooks. There is no return address on the cartons; the post office refuses to get involved and tells you that the cartons are yours. Divide the class into small groups. Ask each group, "If you were the farmer, what would you do with 10,000 magnetic coat hooks?" One person records ideas. At the end of a specified time, the groups stop and read their lists aloud. The group with the longest list wins.
- Imagine the same scenario but with one million toothpicks in the cartons instead of the coat hooks. What could the farmer do?

6. Create a jargon dictionary. Make a list of the common words and phrases used in your organization, and give humorous definitions for them. Here are some samples:

- "Where are you at?" = "You look like I feel."
- *Negotiate* = substitute for *argue*.

- "I'm comfortable with that" = "I agree with you," "I'm tired," or "I trust you to do the work."
- Brainstorm = "No one knows the answer, but if we all talk at once. . . ."
- "It's under consideration" = "The issue is dead."
- "I'll have to think about it" = "I'll have to figure out how to make you agree with me."

7. The following is an interview schedule designed to encourage people to think about humor and to increase its use.

Interviewers ask the questions on the interview schedule and record the answers. Everyone takes a turn at both being interviewed and interviewing. Participants can be divided into groups of six; they report some of their answers to the whole group. These questions are designed to stimulate discussion, but the answers themselves are often hilarious.

THE GRINNING OF AMERICA[3]

- Humor is . . .
- Humor could be . . .
- When do you feel most humorous?
- With whom do you laugh the most? What is it about that person that "invites" you to laugh?
- How are you humorous? How would an observer describe you when you are your most humorous self?
- What is your favorite kind of humor, and what is it that you like about it?
- What is your least favorite kind of humor, and what is it that you don't like about it?
- Who is the best comedian/comedienne you know? What makes him/her effective?
- Can you recall a childhood memory related to humor?
- What blocks or gets in the way of you being able to tap your own sense of humor?
- What advice would you give to someone who wanted to develop more of a sense of humor?
- What thoughts do you have about "put-down" humor?
- Do you have any ideas about how humor could be used in solving social or societal problems?

References

Allen, S. B. "Laughing matters—Particularly for financial managers." *Financial Managers' Statement*, 8, No. 5 (Sept. 1986), 40–42.

Baron, R. A. "The aggression-inhibiting influence of nonhostile humor." *Journal of Experimental Social Psychology*, 10 (1974), 23–33.

3. This is reprinted from the *Laughing Matters* magazine edited by Joel Goodman and published quarterly by The HUMOR Project. For more information on this publication and for a free information packet on the positive power of humor, contact The HUMOR Project, 110 Spring St., Saratoga Springs, N.Y. 12866 (518–587–8770).

Berger, A. A. "Humor, an introduction." *American Behavioral Scientist,* 30, No. 1 (1987), 16–25.

Chafe, W. "Humor as a Disabling Mechanism." *American Behavioral Scientist,* 30, No. 1 (1987), 16–25.

Check, J. F. "Positive Traits of the Effective Teacher—Negative Traits of the Ineffective One." *Education,* 106, No. 3 (1986), 324–334.

Cousins, N. *The Anatomy of an Illness as Perceived by the Patient: Reflections on Healing and Regeneration.* Boston: G.K. Hall, 1979.

Duncan, W. J. "Perceived humor and social network patterns in a sample of task-oriented groups: A re-examination of prior research." *Human Relations,* 37, No. 11 (Nov. 1984), 895–907.

Duncan, W. J. "The superiority theory of humor at work: Joking relationships as indicators of formal and informal status patterns in small, task-oriented groups." *Small Group Behavior,* 16, No. 4 (Nov. 1985), 556–564.

Duncan, W. J., and J. P. Feisal. "No laughing matter: Patterns of humor in the workplace." *Organizational Dynamics,* 17 (1989), 18–30.

Durdick, G. "Learning to Laugh on the Job," *Principal,* 69, No. 5 (1990), 32–34.

Fry, W., Jr. "Humor and Paradox." *American Behavioral Scientist,* 30, No. 1 (1987), 42–71.

Goodman, J., ed. "Grin and Share It." *Laughing Matters,* 7, No. 3 (1991), p. 86; 5, No. 1 (1988), p. 6; 3, No. 1 (1984), p. 29; 7, No. 4 (1991), p. 126; 5, No. 2 (1988), p. 46; 5, No. 4 (1989), p. 126; 5, No. 3 (1989), p. 86; 5, No. 3 (1989), p. 86.

Isen, A. M., K. A. Daubman, and G. P. Nowicki. "Positive affect facilitates creative problem solving." *Journal of Personality and Social Psychology,* 52, No. 6 (1987), 22–113.

Krohe, J., Jr. "Take my boss—please." *Across the Board,* 24, No. 2 (Feb. 1987), 31–35.

Keith-Spiegal, P., D. Spiegal, J. Gonska. "Cartoon appreciation in suicidal and control groups." *Journal of Psychiatric Research,* 8, No. 2 (June 1971), 161–165.

Murstein, B. I., and R. G. Brust. "Humor and interpersonal attraction." *Journal of Personality Assessment,* 49, No. 6 (Dec. 1985), 637–640.

Pogrebin, M. R., and E. D. Poole. "Humor in the briefing room: A study of strategic uses of humor among police." *Journal of Contemporary Ethnography,* 17, No. 2 (July 1988), 183–210.

Rossel, R. D. "Chaos and Control: Attempts to regulate the use of humor in self-analytic and therapy groups." *Small Group Behavior,* 12, No. 2 (May 1981), 195–219.

Scogin, F., and H. Pollio. "Targeting and the humorous episode in group process." *Human Relations,* 33 (1980), 831–852.

Smeltzer, L. R., and T. L. Leap. "An analysis of individual reactions to potentially offensive jokes in work settings." *Human Relations,* 41, No. 4 (1988), 301.

◆ *9* ◆

The Incredible Meeting Trap

A t any given hour during virtually any working day there are a million meetings going on throughout the United States. We are a society of meetings. There are meetings to plan, to solve problems, to dream, to organize, to resolve crises and to create them, to explain things, to make us feel better, to punish, to reward, to build and to dissolve, and to give hope. There are meetings to plan meetings to plan meetings. The cost is staggering—perhaps a billion dollars worth of people time each day. Often the value is hardly worth the cost or effort.

It has been estimated that professionals spend a minimum of 20 percent to 40% of their time at work in meetings, and the higher they are in the organization, the more meetings they attend (Mosvick and Nelson, 1987). There is also a growing pressure associated with meetings as participation from all levels of an organization becomes more and more of a necessity. The problem is that most lower-level employees lack the general experience needed to plan and participate in successful meetings (Tobia and Becker, 1990).

Meetings are meant to be sources of stimulation, support, and solutions, and they should fulfill any number of personal and organizational needs. For some of us, though, meetings are an annoyance and a waste of time. Exploring why meetings fail, why they become traps, and what we can do to improve them is the thrust of this chapter (Antony, 1976; Bradford, 1976; Miller, 1972; Mosvick and Nelson, 1987; Schindler-Rainman and Lippitt, 1977; Tobia and Becker, 1990).

◆ Reader Activity

The first step in becoming either an effective leader or a valuable participant in a meeting is to become keenly aware of what is occurring that either facilitates or hinders progress. Utilizing a number of the concepts discussed in the text to this point, diagnose the effectiveness of the last meeting you attended.

1. What individual and group goals influenced the group?
2. What type of communication patterns occurred?
3. Did any norms act to block the group?
4. Were the roles of individual members clear?
5. Was real membership accessible to those present?
6. How was leadership gained? Was it effective?
7. To what degree did members of the meeting seem interested and involved, and does it appear that they would be motivated to attend another? (This is an informal measure of group cohesion.)   ◆

As you know by this time, much of what occurs in a meeting that affects the life of the group passes unnoticed by the participants. Often they are too busy reacting to the task at hand or simply do not know the questions to ask in order to get a comprehensive picture of the group process.

If there is so much potential value in meetings and they can be so beneficial, then why are they sometimes disastrous? On one side of the ledger we can blame the fact that many leaders simply are not trained in the art of conducting stimulating and productive meetings. On the other side is the less optimistic view that many leaders are quite satisfied with the meetings as they are, whether those attending like it or not. Many meetings are held for a variety of reasons, and it is not uncommon for the reasons stated to have little to do with the real purposes.

In many organizations, people are "meetinged" to death. Individuals literally become burned out from meetings. Thus, when groups are regularly called together out of courtesy, habit, or formality and little of constructive value occurs, individuals tend to become passive and a sort of group lethargy takes over. Passive resistance can become more overt when participants are feeling overburdened with other work and have no recourse but to attend. Other sources of frustration result when a meeting is billed as participative but those present sense quite early that the meeting is really designed to elicit support for a decision already made and that the leader's goal is to appear democratic without having to relinquish any real control.

Many leaders do not know how to make meetings creative, stimulating, and participative, so their behavior, as well as that of other participants, becomes repetitive. This is true even though there are a wide variety of meetings, each of which demands a different type of structure and format—a different design. The failure to utilize different designs for meetings with different purposes results in a high degree of failure and, ultimately, in frustration on the part of many of the participants.

Types of Meetings

The great majority of organizational meetings probably fall under one of the following categories:

Information Sharing—Communication Meetings   Such meetings are usually directed at providing information across diverse sections of an organization. They are motivated by a desire to keep people informed of changes. One of the major sources of alienation within organizations is the sense of isolation or impotence that many people feel, and informational meetings provide a channel of formal communication.

Diagnostic or Fact-finding Meetings   Effective organizations spend considerable amounts of time identifying problems, establishing priorities, and generally attempting to take the pulse of the organization. Such meetings may be focused on a particular topic or may have a more general thrust, but the primary purpose is to generate information to provide a better understanding of existing problems or conditions. Meetings that provide a forum for feedback also fall into this category.

Brainstorming Meetings   Increasingly, problem solvers agree that idea building and actual decision making should be separated in time and place. Having people consider a wide range of alternatives can best be done when decision making can be delayed while those ultimately accountable consider the cost and benefits of the various ideas developed. Brainstorming meetings can also serve as problem-solving meetings in that within such meetings, ideas can be generated about the plan of attack for a given problem.

Decision-Making Meetings   In these meetings, participants consider the variety of alternatives and decide which they should take. In each individual case, the consequences of such action deserve special attention.

Planning Meetings   In this instance, we identify planning as a particular function whose primary purpose is to establish the means of implementation for decisions made.

Coordination and Monitoring Meetings   Because delegation and accountability are two of the critical foundation stones upon which effective management is built, managers need to conduct well-organized and well-executed periodic meetings of those involved in the implementation phase to insure that all aspects of the program are being covered accurately.

Ongoing Business Meetings   Many organizations rely on committees that meet regularly to work with issues of what could be called system maintenance, including selection of new members, discipline problems, promotions, employee grievances, marketing, and many others (DeLuca, 1983).

Each type of meeting warrants careful planning and design and has its own peculiar problems that deserve special attention. Thus, if an organization is considering new policies and if the process is to be thoughtful and intellectually honest, then a number of meetings should probably occur, each building on the goals and progress of the last. Meetings can provide the foundation for rationality, as long as each has a purpose or theme that is clearly understood and a framework that will facilitate its execution. Even meetings with more general purposes that are less structured (for example, an operations meeting held every day in a plant for participants to review problems and procedures) can be looked at in light of the various categories established previously. Later we will talk more specifically about the concept of design, which is the keystone to the success of any meeting for which particular goals or purposes have been defined.

The Interpersonal–Personal Dimension

Meetings are group vehicles for accomplishing various tasks. As group settings, they represent a developing social environment that can provide a constructive and positive experience for the individuals involved or, as often happens, can result in frustrating and dissatisfying interpersonal relationships. The point is that the group—the committee, team, or staff—can also be a vehicle for improving the overall life of the organization and can help meet the kinds of individual needs that people have whenever they get together in a group context. When meetings fail, that failure is often due to poorly addressed interpersonal relationships rather than inattention to the product or task concerns. Conversely, there is a definite correlation between the success of a meeting and whether interpersonal–personal needs of the group are satisfied.

Potential Benefits of Meetings

The following are a number of personal and interpersonal needs that can be satisfied in a well-functioning meeting. In meeting these needs, it may be possible to justify the occasional use of a group even when delegating a task to individuals might be more time-efficient and cost-effective.

> Meetings give individuals the opportunity to belong or have membership in a number of groups that support the organization. Belonging gives individuals further identity beyond a single job role. This is true at any organizational level but is of particular importance when job roles tend to be monotonous.

> Meetings make individuals feel that their ideas are being sought and that there is a mutual building from these ideas to new procedures, policies, or programs.

> Beyond the creation of the ideas, a meeting gives group members the psychological satisfaction of being able to identify with visible outcomes that have value for the organization.

> People are psychologically committed to ideas that they help generate in meetings, which goes beyond the product itself.

> Those involved in meetings have a chance to experience the full cycle of opposition, conflict, and positive resolution. The level of trust within the group may increase and be transferred to the organization because mutually agreed-upon solutions require the sacrificing of personal self-interest or gain. The giving up of one's personal vested interest often increases one's stake in the organization itself.

> Accountability within a group is often clearly defined in meetings. A commitment of the group or other individuals to action and the monitoring

of areas of responsibility within the group can provide important sources of the success, reinforcement, and support necessary in any healthy organization.

The meeting allows the differentiation of roles according to skill and provides a healthy source of status.

People learn from each other by working together in meetings and enhance their interpersonal or technical skills by observing other people's performance.

Meetings help build an overall sense of mutual accomplishment in having achieved a mutual goal, having risked certain new ideas or innovations, and having experienced success and overcome failure.

Meetings build personal relationships through the legitimate work process. Individuals begin to know each other within the organization on a different and more meaningful level because of shared goals, shared points of view, and the satisfactory resolution of conflict. Put simply, people get to know each other by acting together.

Meetings provide the opportunity for fun and social rewards that can occur spontaneously only when people work together with a common purpose and are under some obligation to each other (Bradford, 1976; Burke and Beckard, 1976; Marrow, Bowers, and Seashore, 1967).

Obviously, the list of characteristics suggested here could be expanded or reduced. It is meant only as a guide to some of the personal and interpersonal needs that can be met by effective work in organizational meetings. We can easily describe the organizational benefits of meetings that go hand in hand with individual benefits. Effective meetings are an integral way for information to be communicated throughout the whole organization, both from the top down and from the bottom up. Any organization is better able to use its resources of people, money, and material when there is a coordinated effort among groups or departments that happens, in part, through meetings. In addition, having opportunities for input increases morale and productivity and creates a climate in which the work gets done and people are respected. In other words, many of the things that characterize the benefits of a meeting also contribute to the meeting's success.

Insuring the Success of Meetings

If a meeting represents a one-time gathering of individuals, it can be treated somewhat differently from a meeting that is part of an ongoing series of events among the same group of people. Nevertheless, any leader should consider the following general guidelines. The extent to which any one of the following points warrants attention will depend on the particular goals of the meeting, but success can be enhanced if

> Participants in the meeting are, to some degree, stimulated through a variety of activities and experience, their minds and spirits kept active.

> Each goal is considered separately in terms of the kinds of activities that will best insure the appropriate outcome. Creative designing by its nature does not allow for pat, routine, or stereotypic approaches to either problem solving or discussion. Meetings can be simple, straightforward, complicated, or sophisticated, depending on what is demanded by a particular group and its goals.

> Participants feel utilized in a meaningful manner during the meeting itself. All too often, meetings consist of intelligent people sitting and consuming information that can be shared in other ways or listening to the opinions of others while their own ideas lie dormant within themselves.

> The individuals in the meeting experience some feeling of success, with outcomes that are visible to themselves and others and suggest that the meeting has been purposeful and worthwhile.

> Participants feel as though they have some personal responsibility for the success of the meeting (Forsyth, Berger, and Mitchell, 1981).

> Individuals have the opportunity to learn something new and interesting during the meeting, either from other participants and the experience itself or from a structured learning activity provided by the leader.

> Participants feel not only that the group is worth being in but also that the cause is one that merits their time and effort (Kieffer, 1988).

> The participants feel challenged by what they are doing so that they have to draw on their own resources and extend themselves beyond what might be called "the routine."

> The members of the group enjoy themselves. The fact is that fun can be designed into a meeting just as can a serious discussion, a debate, or a problem-solving activity. The norms of seriousness and appropriateness that govern the nature of many meetings can be broken through effective designing, and they will not be jeopardized by the simple desire of a few individuals to lighten the flavor of the meeting.

> People feel that they are members of the group and that they are accepted by each other as equals, even though they may not be equal as resources to the group.

> When the group is more than a one-time group, an effort is made to create a sense of a team so that members feel interdependent and supportive of each other and the task at hand.

If the leader is not skilled in the issues of group process and design, the chance that he or she will utilize the resources of individual members and maximize the potential of the group as a whole is minimal. In subsequent pages, we will address the problems and processes involved in the proper design of meetings. However, first we must examine some difficulties that can impede the group process and undermine the effectiveness of meetings.

◆ Reader Activity

Use the eleven criteria in either of the previous sections to measure the value of the last important meeting you attended. Simply imagine a 1-to-10 scale for each item, with 1 representing that the particular criterion was not reached at all and 10 indicating total accomplishment. If you haven't been to a meeting of consequence lately, use the criteria to measure several classes you attend or your department at work. Clearly, we are talking about some rather universal qualities of effective organizations that are directed at meeting participants' needs as well as organizational goals.   ◆

Blocks to the Effectiveness of Meetings

One primary reason why committees fail is that leaders and members alike refuse to see the meeting as a social system and often as a microcosm of the larger organization itself. Thus leader and participant style, member interest, the degree of interaction, the amount of interdependence or dependence that exists, and the norms, membership criteria, and communication patterns all tend to reflect the kinds of messages being given by the parent organization. If those in the meeting are not asking serious questions relating to both task and process, much of what is occurring that blocks the group from being productive and enjoyable will simply not come to light. A group not aware of its own functioning will inevitably run into trouble, lose its sense of direction, and tend to flounder. This may be revealed by fights with each other, by avoidance of the task at hand, or in a variety of ways that undermine the purpose of the group with or without the participants even knowing it. In one study, a number of managers and professionals were polled as to what they thought the specific problems of meetings were. Out of the 1,305 problems cited, 16 of them were mentioned so many times that they accounted for 90 percent of the list. Included in these 16 problems were ineffective leadership, individuals dominating the discussion, the meeting being steered away from the objective, or the lack of a goal to begin with (Mosvick and Nelson, 1987). Following are five examples of ways in which success is blocked in meetings. In every case, had the group stopped to take stock, to look at its own process, the course of the meeting could have been changed and the outcome might have been more productive.

The Domination of Single Members

A committee of ten—six faculty and four students—had the task of establishing a new discipline policy for their high school. Asked to observe the group for a period of an hour and then to comment in a way that might be helpful to its development, an outsider simply commented on the unequal distribution of "air time" that was occurring in the group. At the end of an hour, four of the members had talked 80 percent of the time about a subject that everyone in the school lived and breathed. Not only that, but three of these four people were faculty.

By the end of its first hour as a group, the committee was beginning to show telltale signs of participant withdrawal, passivity, and disinterest in a topic that was vital to them all. The four who were involved simply assumed that anyone who wanted to get into the conversation would do so. There didn't appear to be any overt power struggle, just simply insensitivity to the degree to which all members felt able or welcome to participate. Not only were good ideas being lost to the group, but energy was being drained away and passive hostility and disillusionment were slowly getting a foothold. A two-minute commentary on the observed data, along with five minutes of talk about its implications, got the committee back on the right track. The members immediately developed certain procedures for involving everyone's ideas, and by the end of two hours, a lively debate was ensuing in which people were listening and participating with vigor.

Critical Norms

A group was meeting to generate new ideas in marketing for a rapidly expanding market. The session was designed to develop new ideas in a positive manner and not to come to decisions. During the first 15 minutes, discussion was lively, ideas were batted about, there was considerable laughter, and nearly everybody was participating. By the end of 45 minutes, the meeting had obviously become hard work for everybody. Instead of all 8 members participating in a rather restrained manner, the flow of ideas almost came to a halt.

On this particular occasion, not only did the observer watch which individuals talked, but he also noted the number of positive, neutral, and negative statements made by people as they were throwing out ideas. During the initial 15 minutes, positive ideas outnumbered the negative ones by 4 to 1, with neutral responses making up 15 percent of the conversation. By the end of 30 minutes, the negative comments, or "yes, but" statements, and divisive critical remarks had increased to almost an equal share. Finally, by the end of 45 minutes, the group found itself wallowing in a myriad of negative statements. Virtually every idea that was raised was met by two or three statements that negated or questioned its validity. The better the idea, the more the resistance. Much of the tension was generated by a group of young, aggressive, competitive participants who seemed bent on making others appear to be losers.

The group was not even aware of its own pattern. If asked, members would have found it difficult to explain how almost every meeting had degenerated into debates and haggling. As strange as it may seem, the group had created a norm that, although destructive to the group itself, was perceived as protective of individuals by deterring the success of others.

Vested Interest

A group was composed of seven executives of a representative organization that bought and sold fuel. During the period of initial fuel shortage in the United States, the company found itself in a position of having less fuel to sell than it had commitments to buyers. For the first time in its history, the company's sales force was told to reduce the volume it sold. This meeting was established on an ad hoc basis to explore how this was to be done. Appropriately, the first hour and a half of the three-hour meeting was a review of the present situation from both the group and individual perspectives. The leader then directed the group to discuss overall corporate goals in relation to fuel allocations. Again, there were no problems and many creative ideas.

After about 80 minutes, the topic changed to focus on short-term realities and the sacrifice individual sales personnel would have to make if the company was not going to be embarrassed by not being able to meet its fuel commitments. Almost instantly, the tone of the meeting changed. From an atmosphere of listening, support, and goodwill, the air became charged, defensive, and resistant. People stopped listening and began to defend their own postures. One hour later when the meeting ended, the high morale of the group was gone and any optimism with which the meeting began had disappeared. Decisions had to be made and the group appeared ready to make them, up until the time when each individual's vested interests were attacked. Salespeople who had always been highly regarded for selling suddenly found themselves in a position of letting down clients and appearing ineffective. Because the decision-making process had not been established prior to this point of the meeting, it suddenly became impossible to make any decisions to which the group would commit itself. Any attempt to establish a fair decision-making process would simply be perceived as an attempt of one individual to maintain control over others.

The Dilemma of New Members

An eight-person committee was one of the three ongoing committees of a hospital. Its purpose was to establish and review policies that cover all hospital employees. For the sake of continuity, two new members were rotated into the committee every year and two others left. The committee had the reputation of being amicable and businesslike, and it was somehow run without the petty problems of many committees that bog down and are unable to work effectively because of hidden agendas, authority problems, or some of the other "sticky wickets" of group life. This year, however, shortly after two new members were elected and rotated into the committee, the committee began to experience a wide variety of problems and tensions that had not existed before. It wasn't even possible to link the problems to the behavior of the two new members, who were generally well liked and respected. Nevertheless, things went from bad to worse as individuals began to listen less and talk more, to resist each other's ideas, and in many ways to act like a committee of adversaries rather than colleagues.

The problem, of course, was that the loss and addition of members simply created a new group. Suddenly, who had membership and on what basis was up for grabs; norms that somehow had been a stable part of the committee were opened to question and to the pressure of new behavior from the entering members. In addition, roles and goals and expectations of people's behavior in the group changed, and individuals began to vie for both authority and attention in a manner that would not have been acceptable several weeks before. Only by taking time to assess the changes in roles and expectations, goals and norms, and membership criteria would the group begin to deal with the blockages that were being created. The interesting part is that in this particular group the resolution of these new tensions would probably not be very difficult because most of the participants enjoyed their place on the committee, worked in a spirit of good will with each other, and saw their participation as a real opportunity. It was very likely that just raising the issues in such a supportive group would be enough to reestablish some of the previous behavior patterns as well as some of the good will that still remained.

Problems of Physical Structure and Space

Virtually everything one does as leader of a group—in this case a committee—can influence the life of the group. Most of us have been at committee meetings as the members of the group sit scattered around an auditorium in rows, looking at the necks of their colleagues, with little opportunity to share ideas or collaborate within the meeting itself. The size of the room and the lighting, acoustics, and seating arrangements all have a subtle impact on the climate of the group. If interaction among group members is desired, it is best to arrange seating in a face-to-face fashion rather than around a long, narrow table or in rows.

Most of us have attended committee meetings at which we sat around a long wooden table with some 15 or 20 people, with all eyes directed at the primary source of influence at the table or at those few individuals who share the wealth of influence through either structural proximity around the table or status gained through other sources of power and control. One committee observed recently was an almost "textbook" version of a group governed by how its members were positioned around the table. The two individuals who were most antagonistic toward one another sat on opposite sides of the table. Individuals closest to the leader in authority and trust tended to be on the same side of the table, and those with less influence and involvement tended to fade off toward the ends and corners and were physically far from the appointed leader. The committee, which met once a month, virtually always moved into these positions and thus immediately reinforced each other as to interest, power, influence, and general involvement. The patterned routine of the group made certain antagonisms almost inevitable.

These five brief examples are by no means the exception. In every instance the meetings were meant to be purposeful and effective. None was a case of people being forced together to do things they didn't want to do. Even though the apparent causes may have differed drastically in each situation, the results were similar: morale, productivity, and interest declined in each situation. Each represented a misuse of people's time and energy, in which participants inevitably left the committee meeting less satisfied than when they entered. Individuals avoided taking responsibility for themselves and for the group by not actively requesting more positive input from all members. The troubling part is that each of the committees would predictably become worse or less effective as time went on, simply because the members and leaders were not aware of the causes undermining their effectiveness. Nor are the solutions necessary to change the situations terribly demanding or complex. In most instances, a simple awareness of the problem would make the solution rather self-evident. The problem, of course, is that there can be no solution without an awareness that the problem exists. It's because the leaders and members fail to ask the right questions or are unwilling to stop and look that the problems in groups tend to persist over time, causing increasing frustration and tension among those involved (Auger, 1972; Maier, 1963; Prince, 1972; Schindler-Rainman and Lippitt, 1977).

◆ Reader Activity

Most of us are involved in organizations (school, work, social groups) that conduct meetings, and often more meetings. Pick a meeting of several hours' duration that you will be in a position to observe. Select two of the five brief topical vignettes you have just read and observe the meeting with those in mind. For example, you might select *the domination of single members,* and *critical norms.* Then, first analyze the meeting in light of whether one or two individuals tend to dominate the meeting and the impact of their behavior on the group, the product, and the overall atmosphere of the meeting. At the same time, try to determine whether certain norms exist that are helpful and whether there are others that seem detrimental to the goals of the meeting. If you were the leader, what might you do to solve the problems you observed? What type of norm would you attempt to instill in the group? What might you say? If you were a group member, what might you do and say to improve the group situation? As members become more aware of the factors that influence the outcome of a meeting, they find that there are things they can do to change the situation.   ◆

Designing and Running an Effective Meeting

Assessing the Needs of the Group

We learn to run meetings from our previous experience in meetings. Just as few parents are trained to be parents, few leaders are trained to chair groups. For the most part we learn by observation, filtering into our repertoire of behavior those models or approaches that seem somehow appropriate in our society. Rarely are these approaches questioned, because we usually focus on the task or issue at hand, not on the functioning of the group. As a result, those running the meetings seldom receive necessary feedback and are rarely stimulated to do anything differently. In most instances, even if the feedback were available, the norms or patterns are so habitual and ingrained that it would take a terribly dedicated leader to change the way it's always been done.

Even in the five brief examples we discussed, it is clear that these are only five of thousands of situations that one might expect to occur. Each new group takes on a life of its own, which in turn creates a multitude of new and interesting problems. We can provide people with the ability to be aware of the problems that do exist and the ability to develop the skills to design what might be called "nonprescriptive" solutions for the problems that are identified. One cannot carry around a bag of guaranteed solutions to be dealt out in any particular meeting; rather, solutions must be "custom made" for the particular situation. Still, we can provide a way to think about potential group problems and about designing a group meeting to best resolve problems. And we can also give some basic guidelines for making meetings more productive.

Following are some rather simple and direct but tough questions that leaders should ask prior to virtually any meeting. Although these are not absolute or all-inclusive, they represent the essence of how we believe a leader should psychologically approach a meeting.

Knowledge of the Participants   Although it seems obvious to ask, "Who's coming?" to a particular meeting, here we are interested in knowing everything we possibly can about the participants, not simply their professional affiliations or status. Thus, we ask the following questions:

1. Whom does each of the participants represent within or outside of the organization?

2. Why have these individuals been chosen and not someone else?

3. What are each individual's organizational interests and needs? What does each of them want from the meeting? What hidden agendas might be influencing the life of the group?

4. What is known about each individual's personal goals and needs? Is his or her ego on the line? Do any members have a stake in certain outcomes in addition to the organizational needs they represent?

5. Do the participants come with individual biases toward the leader, other members, the task at hand, or the general format of the meeting?

6. What are the personal skills and strengths available in the group that can be utilized if necessary?

7. What are the personal limitations and idiosyncrasies present in the group that might block the task at hand?

History of the Group   It is essential in planning any meeting that the leader be keenly aware of "unfinished business" left in the group. This unfinished business can relate to task issues or psychological interpersonal ones. The questions to be asked include

1. How did the participants leave the last meeting? Were they pleased? Did they experience success or failure?
2. As a result, what are the expectations of this meeting?
3. What were the sources of pleasure experienced at the last meeting, of accomplishment for other rewards?
4. What were the sources of tension, frustration, or conflict?

Realistic Goals   A crucial aspect of planning an effective meeting is goal setting. Planners must have an idea of the realistic goals that can be reached by the group, given the limitations of time and human resources. To set such goals, planners might ask

1. What are the real task priorities of the members?
2. How is it possible to best utilize the resources available in meeting these priorities?
3. What needs to be done to ready the group to work on the task so members can hear each other and focus on the job to be done?
4. What do the individuals know when coming to the group?
5. What information do they not know but need to have in order to work effectively on the priorities at hand?

It is not uncommon for planners to pass informally through these kinds of questions prior to entering a meeting. The problem is that the answers are rarely reflected in the design of the meeting. Meetings tend to be very similar because even when we have diagnostic information, we fail to apply it in a creative manner to meet the needs of the group. We are also quite capable of fooling ourselves by seeing what we want to see from impressionistic information, rather than seeking out more descriptive data from which to build a plan for the meeting.

In one interesting study (Amidon and Blumberg, 1967), the views that school principals had toward the meetings they ran tended to differ significantly from the impressions of teachers at those same meetings. Principals liked to believe that their teachers felt free to say anything they wished, but teachers saw themselves as cautious and rather careful. Similarly, although the principals said they felt open and free to say anything, teachers saw the principals as cautious in what they said and in how they conducted themselves at meetings.

It becomes apparent from this information that leaders and group members may carry distorted views of how others feel about meetings. Although in this particular study the differences were not dramatic, there were enough differences to suggest that in the eyes of the teachers, the meetings were not nearly so open and honest and effective as they might be. In one sense, the principals as a group may have been deluding themselves into believing that the meetings were not in need of improvement. Because they did not seek more objective data than their own impressions, there is little reason why many would be motivated to change. But by maintaining an observant stance, leaders who conduct meetings can remain aware of the changing needs of the participants as they enter a meeting, what leftover feelings or business remains at the end of the meeting, and how the process of the meeting itself was helpful in achieving the goals of the particular session (Burke and Beckhard, 1976; Marrow, Bowers, and Seashore, 1967; Schindler-Rainman and Lippitt, 1977; This, 1972).

The Concept of Design

Once leaders take into account members' needs, feelings, and interpersonal relationships, they are ready to design the meeting itself. It is not unusual for a leader to spend as little as ten minutes pulling together an agenda at the last minute before a particular meeting, and this kind of preparation may serve to get the leader through another mediocre session. Because few people have ever experienced well-designed meetings, the standard of expectation is low indeed.

For our purposes, *design* means the building of a series of activities or events that move the group in an integrated manner toward the accomplishment of certain goals. Effective designing is a learned skill that assumes that the leader has a thorough understanding of group process and at least minimal diagnostic skills, as well as a clear understanding of group problem-solving and decision-making practices. It is our assumption that unless leaders set aside the appropriate amounts of time to design meetings, an ineffective meeting is virtually guaranteed. This assumption is well supported by research.

A Typical Meeting

The meeting was scheduled to last the usual 2½ hours. The group met regularly (every two weeks) to discuss its department goals and problems. The 20 members of the department usually straggled into the meeting somewhere between 4:15 and 4:30 P.M., even though first arrivals began appearing at 3:55 for the 4:00 P.M. starting time. The same ones were always there on time, and the same ones were always late. The sidelong glances of annoyance among the early arrivals as the stragglers arrived were all too apparent, and humorous digs floated out occasionally to greet them.

Once the meeting began at 4:18, the leader handed out the agenda, which had been prepared minutes before the meeting and looked much like every other agenda during the past five years. People glanced at it dutifully and put it aside. The agenda read as follows:

1. Review of the minutes
2. Old business
   a. Report of the committee on filling the departmental vacancy
   b. Report of the Christmas party committee
   c. The issue of preferential parking places for senior members of the department
   d. Review of budgetary cuts discussed at meeting of November 1
3. New business
   a. Yearly review of departmental programs
   b. Organization of the department basketball team
   c. The condition of the lunchroom facility
   d. Report of the financial department on new guidelines for expense reimbursement
   e. Cost-of-living increases versus organizational pay schedule
   f. Other business from department members

Five minutes were spent reviewing the minutes of the previous meeting. Nitpicking comments were made by several of the early arrivals while most of those present ignored this ritual and either carried on conversations or conducted activities of their own, including reading the organizational newsletter or the help-wanted section of the daily newspaper, knitting, and doodling.

There was no discussion of the agenda, and the leader simply began with the first item on the agenda under "Old business." The first two reports took a total of ten minutes, with a few questions of clarification from the participants. At this point, the leader casually opened the topic of preferential parking places for senior members, which had been raised at the last meeting but not discussed. To put it mildly, "all hell broke loose." It seemed that everyone had an opinion, and issues of equality, tenure, loyalty, service, and favoritism sailed around the room. Somehow, what had appeared to be an inconsequential issue devoured 40 minutes of the meeting, and the exasperated leader in frustration decided to table the problem pending further study prior to the next meeting. A committee was appointed to review the issues that had been raised.

At this point, feeling the meeting getting away, the leader requested to move to item *d* under "New business" because a representative of the financial department was present and it would be polite to utilize him at this time. The new guidelines for expense reimbursement were explained, and because it was a mandated decision, the individual simply asked for questions of clarification. Warmed up by the previous discussion and frustrated by it, the members of the department attacked. How was the decision made? Why were they not represented? Did they realize the hardship the new guidelines created? Twenty minutes of harassment, defensiveness, and rationalizing left the group further antagonized with nowhere to go. The financial representative thanked the group and assured them their ideas would be shared with the appropriate individuals. Murmurs of discontent followed him out of the room.

Sensing that the review of budgetary cuts (item *d* under "Old business") would not be well received in the present climate, the leader moved directly into "New business," explaining that the present issue would demand more attention than the time remaining allowed. The few weak protests from the members fell on deaf ears. The next 30 minutes were spent on the review of five departmental programs (five minutes each). The goal was to keep everyone informed of what was happening in different areas of the department. But it was clear that the previous discussion had not resulted in a climate conducive to listening, and most of the group faded into daydreaming or related activities as each presenter hurried through his or her report.

At this point, someone in the group requested that it might be of interest to the group to move to item *e,* dealing with pay schedules and the cost of living, rather than the organization of the basketball team. The leader, in a kindly and understanding manner, agreed except that the beginning of the interdepartmental league demanded at least some attention be given to the issue of team selection and practice so they wouldn't be embarrassed. Besides, there was less than 30 minutes left and perhaps it would be better to deal with the lunchroom issue and wait until there was more time to really get into the salary issue.

The meeting ended on time with several proposals being passed in relation to both the basketball team and the lunchroom, with surprisingly little discussion or involvement on the part of the staff. Adjournment came at 6:26 P.M.

For the most part, the failures of this meeting were unintentional and the result of poor planning or lack of know-how. The result was a staff divided, frustrated, angry, and feeling its own impotence. Worse than that was the fact that most meetings of this group resulted in similar feelings even if the circumstances were somewhat different. There had been virtually no design. An agenda is not a design, because in theory each item on the agenda deserves to be viewed separately and developed in a manner that reflects the realities of time, interest, need, and probability of success. This meeting resembles thousands of others. It is not a fabrication but one that occurred and was attended by real people of goodwill and talent, including the leader. The problems it exemplified are many:

1. The participants were not involved in establishing the goals of the meeting.

2. The very format of dealing first with old business results in passing over critical issues in favor of less important ones.

3. People need successes to feel their ability to influence their environment. At this meeting there was almost no possibility for success, given how the issues were arranged.

4. Priorities according to the agenda seemed arbitrary or based on the hidden agenda of the leader.

5. Meetings at the end of a workday are often self-defeating. In this instance the first 40 minutes of a 150-minute meeting resulted only in frustration and hostility. The leader had lost control before the meeting even began.

6. The history of the group and personal antagonisms were working against the success of the meeting, and there was no mechanism for altering the process to take care of such tensions.

7. The meeting was predictable, boring, and in most instances unproductive. There was little excitement (except around vested interests or scapegoating) and almost no humor.

8. Participation was almost totally reactive and not constructive.

9. The resources of the group were poorly utilized.

10. Any decision making was not defined, and every detail was left to the leader's arbitrary whim.

11. At least half the agenda items could have been dealt with outside the meeting itself with greater efficiency.

12. The parking place issue would never have gotten out of hand if the leader had taken the pulse of the group, known the importance of the issue, and designed a means of problem solving that would not have opened old wounds.

◆ Reader Activity

Before reading the next section, think of yourself as a consultant or leader who is in a position to revise the meeting just described. Select five factors from the list of twelve presented above. Think about how you would manipulate these factors to redesign the meeting and make it succeed. How would you restructure the meeting? What have you built to make the outcomes different? If you were the leader of this meeting, would you actually be able to make these changes? Do you think the participants would accept them? What do you think would be the overall effect of your new design on participants?   ◆

◆ *Reader Activity*

Consider an important meeting that you attended in recent weeks. Make two separate lists. First note four or five aspects of the design or execution of the meeting that could have been improved. Make a second list of specific things you believed "worked" to make the meeting successful.

Now, having completed the two lists, join with four or five others and compare your lists. It is not unusual for the list of improvements to be longer and easier to generate than the list of positive factors. Are there problems that appear in all or most of the lists? Are they easily correctable?

You may wish to compare the areas of needed improvement identified by your group with those identified in the meeting analyzed in the preceding pages. ◆

A Meeting Revisited

Let's look again at the typical departmental meeting. In making reference to the general guidelines discussed up to this point, we should be able to gain some ground that is much firmer to walk on than that created by the leader's agenda and overall format.

Twenty people sitting around a table are bound to be self-defeating unless a variety of activities are designed to draw them into participation. Usually in a group of this size, a majority will feel "out of it" unless a special effort is made. Ideal planning for such a meeting should include one or two members from the group plus the leader. These individuals must have the respect of the other participants. In this case, it would have been easy to list all of the potential agenda items and have the participants interviewed prior to the meeting to determine which issues were of greatest importance to them and whether there were other issues they felt deserved attention. Undoubtedly, a pattern of priorities would have evolved, and issues of less significance might have been delegated to committee action prior to the meeting itself. The fact is that the agenda was so long, so unfamiliar to participants prior to the meeting, and so potentially complex that there was little hope that the leader would escape with his hide given the limited time and the intensity of feelings underlying many of the issues.

Once it is understood that only a limited amount of work can be accomplished in the time available, then specific activities must be designed to deal with each, all within a time-limited framework. It is the leader's responsibility to communicate with participants in advance to let them know the agenda, how it was decided, why the meeting is important, what they will need to prepare prior to coming, and that the meeting will begin promptly. Starting with an issue that is important to the group will inevitably encourage people to arrive on time. It is up to the leader then to start on time. If meetings are important and people feel their presence is important, they will be there.

Parking was an issue of importance (emotional if not substantive) to the participants. Clearly it was symptomatic of other issues of favoritism, seniority, and privilege that created adversary positions among the members. In the actual meeting, 40 minutes were spent raising feelings and hostility, and then the issue was tabled unresolved. At the outset, the leader should have made it clear that after appropriate discussion and deliberation, the decision would be made. Second, it should be made clear that several viable alternatives, along with a rationale for each, would be developed. Here is one possible design for this process:

> State the problem and a history of the issue to this point in time. Next, reach agreement that at the following departmental meeting a decision will be made that will be tried for six months and then reopened for discussion. Define the condition that a 60 percent vote will be required to change the present system. Randomly create some groups of three or four and give each group 20 minutes to develop two alternatives to the present situation. After 20 minutes, combine the six groups into three groups of six and ask each to negotiate a single best solution in 30 minutes. Then ask a member of each group to present the idea of his or her group to the total group. Ask the members to discuss these ideas during the period between meetings (one assumes considerable discussion will ensue) and take a vote at the beginning of the next meeting. If the group cannot reach a 60 percent majority at that time, discuss the two favorites for a limited amount of time. If a 60 percent vote cannot be attained, then use the system presently in vogue for a period of six months.

This design encourages a movement toward consensus and an exploration of a variety of issues. It insures participation and involvement in an issue that influences nearly everybody. It utilizes time outside the meeting for preparation and discussion. The process tends to minimize the chances of failure. One of the leader's goals is to provide the group with success experiences. Creating what appears to be a temporary solution mitigates the resistance to any change and minimizes a win–lose mentality. The initial move from groups of three to six forces a consensus process on the group with the assumption that any idea that six people could agree to would probably be acceptable to most people in the group. The opportunity for wide-open discussion enhances the exchange of information, ensures interaction among people of varying persuasions, and initiates the beginning of a proactive rather than a reactive approach to problem solving. Another reason why this design is successful is that it pays attention to important issues of membership, task, time frame, and goals of the group. These can be thought of as group boundaries: who is in, what are we doing, how will we do it, and for how long? The clearer these boundaries are and the more explicitly they are stated at the outset, the better able the group will be to accomplish its task (Bader, 1982).

After a period of approximately the same amount of time as the original meeting, the design for the hypothetical meeting would have allowed the groups to have experienced several small successes and to have seen the light at the end of the tunnel in a more controlled and rational process.

To accomplish an effective design, the leader must always be conscious of both the task and the process domains of a group. If the leader is not aware of both individual and group needs, of interpersonal relationships, of the efficiency of various task activities, and of a wide range of other variables, it will be impossible to develop a coherent design. Similarly, if the individual leader is concerned with the symptoms and not the causes that are blocking group effectiveness, the design cannot reflect the changes that need to occur to move the group forward. Finally, what blocks the successful implementation of a design often has nothing to do with the design itself and more to do with the "plumbing" of the meeting. So often it is the little things that need to be taken care of before they destroy the environment of the meeting or make it less effective than it might be. Information about the meeting, the language in the invitation, seating arrangements, the availability of necessary visual aids and materials, the presence of refreshments, right down to the nuts and bolts of name tags or some other means of identifying the members of the group—all are important considerations. The ability to anticipate obstacles that can influence the psychological atmosphere and remove them before they pose a problem is critical. Who is invited and how they are notified can affect the attitudes of participants before they even walk in the door. One need not be a nervous wreck or become overly compulsive prior to a meeting, but it seems crucial to try to step into the shoes of the participants and ask questions about their needs, expectations, and concerns. The following section describes an effectively designed meeting.

An Effectively Designed Meeting

It had been building up for weeks. Tension, hostility, and frustration from a group of 30 African-American parents were being directed at the faculty and principal of the small neighborhood elementary school. Communication had broken down, and the parents felt the primarily white faculty was not being sensitive to the needs of their children. Several outspoken critics of the city school system had been drawn into the battle and it appeared that a classic confrontation was about to occur.

Finally, it was agreed that a meeting would be held between the parents and the faculty. Predictably, the community group was suspicious because the school system had avoided every effort at previous meetings and the local press had labeled the parents "radical." The consultant who was asked to help design the meeting knew there was little chance that either group would hear the other initially. Thus, something had to be done to keep each group off balance and to minimize the tendency to accelerate the tension by increasing the adversarial climate. Somehow the meeting had to reduce the fears and threatened feelings of the faculty without appearing to the black participants as avoiding the issues that concerned them.

White and black, parent and teacher, educated and unschooled were drawn into the gym for the three-hour meeting beginning at 6:00 P.M. It seemed that nearly everyone had their arms stiffly folded, watching, occasionally laughing among friends as if to deny the tremendous discomfort. The principal thanked everyone for attending and threw the ball to the consultant, who immediately divided the group of 60 into ten groups of six. An effort had been made to invite equal numbers of faculty and community members. The ten groups included:

> two all-parent groups
>
> two all-faculty groups
>
> two groups, each composed of three faculty members and three individuals
>   representing the community

Each of these groups was asked to develop a list of statements reflecting *what they as a group agreed* the school should be providing the children of the community in the way of educational services. Each of the groups began their tasks; this format allowed concerns to be aired but minimized a polarizing, win–lose climate.

At the end of 40 minutes, the groups were asked to write their lists on large sheets of newsprint so that all 60 participants could review them together. The groups were asked not to identify themselves on their paper. By 7 o'clock, all six sheets had been posted, and faculty and parents were asked to note similarities and differences among the various groups. As individuals scrutinized the sheets, there was a release of nervous energy, laughter, talking. It seemed impossible. There were almost no major differences among the sheets. It became obvious to everyone that there was tremendous overlap—that people regardless of background seemed to want the same things for the children. Even the "radical" parent groups were not so different and could not readily be distinguished from the other groups. The barriers of stereotypes, past experience, fear, suspicion, and racism had to yield to the positive tone that filled the room.

Clearly, the issues were less educational than personal. The parents felt unheard, impotent, and misunderstood and believed they lacked access to the principal and the faculty. The faculty felt they should be left to do their job and were insulted at the accusations and recriminations being made. The children were a vehicle for the community to gain the access it needed.

The design allowed people to vent their concerns, helped individuals gain some much-needed perspective, and increased levels of trust in the two groups. Each could find the other group credible, because both parties had some obvious good sense and had showed their wisdom by agreeing with the other. Instead of a confrontation and a series of predictable justifications by the two groups, each now had the opportunity to look at the real issues.

Perhaps the most important aspect of design is the diagnostic phase, in which one is able to focus clearly on where the group is and what needs to be done. From this reality, many useful and creative designs will literally fall out quite naturally. Thus a group that needs success must be given an opportunity to succeed. A group needing information must be provided information. A group needing to problem-solve, requiring information, or needing to relax and have fun must have access to fulfilling these needs or the meeting itself will stand a good chance of failing. The monsters of most meetings are created from inadequate planning, lack of an effective diagnosis, and a poor design.

Guidelines for Effective Meetings

Theoretical and Practical Guidelines for Design Improvement

Managers, executives, and other supervisory personnel are the keys to effective meetings, because they are responsible for preparing, planning, and executing the meeting's design. The following steps can serve as guidelines for creating productive meetings:

1. Establish a specific, measurable objective for each meeting.
2. Make sure participants know the purpose of the meeting ahead of time so they can prepare.
3. Set specific time limits for the meeting.
4. Set rules for decision making, select a recorder, and record all decisions.
5. Make sure people affected by the problems under discussion attend the meeting.
6. Build a means of evaluation into the meeting itself.
7. Select a type of format and a leadership style.
8. Treat all questions at meetings as legitimate and answer them honestly (Brewer, 1984; Leigh, 1984; Klumph, 1984; Selinger, 1985; Mosvick and Nelson, 1987; Kieffer, 1988).

From a theoretical perspective, meeting effectiveness depends strongly on the design established by the leader. But even a well-mapped-out design does not guarantee effectiveness. Besides creating a design, leaders must simultaneously monitor the meeting for activities and events that jeopardize its effectiveness. These observations will also be useful in the planning of future meetings.

Certain practical considerations have an impact on meeting effectiveness. Even the physical location of tables, chairs, windows, and doors, as well as room size, decor, and appearance, can greatly affect a meeting's outcome (Swan, 1984). In the British House of Commons, because only about two-thirds of the members show up on a regular basis, the room does not seat the entire group. This actually adds to the "sense of urgency" in the event of an actual crisis session (Doyle and Strauss, 1984, p. 187).

The seating pattern of the leader and participants seém to be especially important in promoting participation. Studies show that when a person is set apart by sitting at a table's head, he or she tends to exert more power than those in peripheral places, reducing the freedom of other members to participate. In a seating arrangement where the leader is not set apart, conversation flows better, participants are more satisfied with their contributions, and participants think and talk more freely without feeling pushed to premature conclusions. Maximum participant involvement seems best achieved by a circular seating arrangement (Henderson, 1985).

Other practical considerations include the increased use of technological devices to augment design and meeting effectiveness. Meloche (1985) suggests that audiovisual aids be used to present dull data. Meyer and Bulyk (1986) recommend using a microcomputer attached to a video projector to allow participants to see the meeting on a screen. This enables the participants actually to see how they relate to ideas and to alter the course of the meeting in response to this visual feedback. But researchers warn that when technological aids are incorporated into a meeting, leaders need adequate time to learn how to use them efficiently and effectively.

In running a meeting, it is important for the leader to maintain a balance between task issues and interpersonal issues. If too much emphasis is placed on the task, there is a risk of losing the interest and participation of individuals, yet an overemphasis on feelings may interfere with work on the task. Conducting an effective meeting entails structuring the meeting to insure both accomplishment of the task and constructive participation by the group members. The following guidelines, compiled from several sources, including Januz and Jones (1981), Mackenzie (1972), and Yalom (1970), provide specific steps leaders can take to increase the effectiveness and productivity of meetings and the satisfaction of participants.

Before the Meeting

Choose an appropriate time and place for the meeting. It has been argued that people are most creative before 9:00 A.M. However, to make sure a meeting ends on time, Mosvick and Nelson (1987) suggest that it be scheduled for 10:30 A.M. or 3:30 P.M. so that participants will be thinking of lunch or dinner in an hour and a half. If possible, limit the participants to those directly involved with the task. The number of participants can influence the group as well. For example, voting deadlocks can be prevented by inviting an odd number of people (Mosvick and Nelson, 1987). Select participants who will contribute to or benefit from the meeting— carefully selected participants are more likely to be motivated. Notify participants well before the meeting about the time, place, and purpose of the meeting, and specify any resources or materials needed from the participants for the meeting. Prior to the meeting, distribute a clear agenda that allows participants to prepare for the meeting.

Planning and preparing an agenda is an essential step. First, reread minutes or reports from the last meeting to see if you have completed any assigned tasks. In developing an agenda, clearly list the goals and objectives of the meeting and select items in terms of relevance, possibility of success, and expectations about how the group will respond to them. Order the items on the agenda as they relate to your particular group or goals. It may be that the group typically needs a warm-up exercise or does better when it talks about a trivial issue before getting to the important ones. Other groups may spend too much time on the front end and never get to the important items. Whatever the case, each agenda must be planned with the meeting's design in mind. Identify the time allowed for each item, who will be responsible for presenting the item, and what the procedure will be for addressing each item (Whitehead, 1984). By doubling the preparation time, you can, in theory, cut the meeting time in half (Hobbs, 1987).

During the Meeting

Start on time. If necessary, start without people who are not on time (Sullivan, 1988). Starting a meeting late actually punishes those who were there on time. Begin by summarizing the last meeting, clarifying who will be responsible for recording the minutes, and introducing any new members. It is important to state the purpose of the meeting and the existing agenda, indicating whether these items are for discussion, decision, or information sharing only. If appropriate, request and encourage additional agenda items and prioritize new agenda items with the group. It may also be helpful to ask group members to state their own expectations for the meeting (Reeves, 1988, p. 15) or for each person to come to the meeting with an objective of their own (Kieffer, 1988). Try to stick to allocated agenda time whenever possible, but do not overlook the emotional and interpersonal needs of the participants. The group leader should ask for progress reports from task groups or individuals, allow adequate time for discussion, and call for decisions when appropriate. Keep agenda items in full view during the meeting on a large piece of newsprint or on a chalkboard. This helps everyone focus on the problems or objectives instead of on the participants (Doyle and Strauss, 1984, p. 41). Visual aids of any kind can be an important addition to any meeting, because pictures can often be comprehended instantly (Frank, 1989). Observe yourself. In facilitating the meeting, did you

Create a positive atmosphere?

Support and encourage participation?

Listen and respond to varying opinions?

Clarify statements or ask clarifying questions?

Share opinions, feelings, ideas, and suggestions honestly and clearly?

Help others stay on agenda topics?

Identify and utilize resources within the group?

Observe the group process and evaluate progress?

Comment on interpersonal process issues when helpful?

Encourage others in taking group-building and maintenance roles?

Before ending the meeting, it is important to summarize what happened in the meeting and to check to make sure all the participants concur. Include in your summary decisions made, issues raised, unfinished business, next steps agreed upon, and follow-up arrangements made. The leader can identify agenda items for the next meeting and evaluate group progress. Be sure to allow time for feedback from group members concerning the progress and process of the meeting. Listen and acknowledge feedback. Thank group members for their participation, and conclude the meeting on a positive note by underlining the successes of the group. End the meeting on time.

Periodically it is helpful to evaluate meetings that occur on a regular basis more fully. A brief meeting evaluation questionnaire can be filled out by participants just before a meeting is over. Potential questions include

Was the purpose of the meeting clear?

Was the agenda received in advance, along with any materials necessary for preparation?

Did the meeting start on time?

Were the necessary individuals present?

Were the group's resources adequately used?

Did the meeting stay sufficiently on task?

Did the leader display too much or too little flexibility?

Was "air time" fairly distributed?

Were your opinions listened to?

Was the purpose of the meeting achieved?

Were assignments, deadlines, and responsibilities clearly and appropriately established?

What parts of the meeting did you find most effective? What parts least effective?

What might you do differently?

After the Meeting

Concise minutes should be completed and distributed within a day or two after the meeting. Minutes can be used as a reminder and to identify follow-up mechanisms. Follow through and make sure that others get information from the meeting as needed.

Ratteray (1984) suggests what he calls an "executive summary." With this written tool, leaders emphasize important meeting content, which can lead to greater productivity for the participants. Here are strategies for creating and using an executive summary:

1. Select a summarizer to record proceedings.
2. Tape the meetings.
3. Save charts or handouts.
4. Question attendees for specific information.
5. Transcribe only critical data.
6. Synthesize information clearly.
7. Assess and summarize feedback from post-meeting evaluation forms.
8. Publish summaries in company newsletters.
9. Index and file meeting summaries.
10. Use expertise collected in summaries as useful information for the future.

Initially, implementing even some of these strategies may not be time- and cost-efficient. However, in the long run, executive summaries may well reduce the mystique of meeting ineffectiveness and justify the investment of time and money.

Although it may be difficult, refrain from complaining about decisions agreed upon in the group and from appeals and expressions of dissatisfaction outside the meeting. If you are unhappy with a decision or if others have voiced concerns and complaints, you should plan to discuss them in the next meeting. Tobia and Becker (1990) suggest that feedback be limited to observable behavior and how that behavior affects the group.

One good way to find out what participants think of a meeting is the most direct: simply ask them. It can be particularly effective to distribute a simple evaluation form, sometimes called a postmeeting reaction (PMR) sheet. Typically, a PMR sheet contains fewer then eight questions or statements and asks participants to check or circle a response from a given range. Respondents remain anonymous. The questions relate to the goals, objectives, and concerns of those conducting the meeting. See the two accompanying examples of PMRs. It is important to note that there is no set form. The questions relate directly to the objectives of the particular meeting.

Date _____

Meeting _____

POSTMEETING REACTION

Use the following form to evaluate this meeting by placing an X on the line at the place that best describes how you feel.

1	2	3	4	5
Unproductive				Productive

1	2	3	4	5
Fragmented				Cohesive

1	2	3	4	5
Frustrating				Satisfying

1	2	3	4	5
Tense				Relaxed

1	2	3	4	5
Solidarity-oriented				Task-oriented

1	2	3	4	5
Distant				Close

I think I learned

1	2	3	4	5
Very little				Quite a lot

I think in general group members learned

1	2	3	4	5
Very little				Quite a lot

POSTMEETING RESPONSE

1. How clear was the problem of _____ to the group?

1	2	3	4	5
Quite unclear		Some confusion		Completely clear

2. How well did the group use its resources?

1	2	3	4	5
Very poorly		Somewhat		Very well

3. Were members encouraged to participate in the discussion?

1	2	3	4	5
Not at all	A few were encouraged		Most were encouraged	All were encouraged

4. How much attention was given to differences in feelings among members?

1	2	3	4	5
None		Considerable		Too much attention

5. With the decision we have made, I am

1	2	3	4	5
In complete disagreement		Dissatisfied but will accept		In complete agreement

6. With the decision we have made, I believe others in the group to be

1	2	3	4	5
In complete disagreement		Dissatisfied but will accept		In complete agreement

Members quickly fill in PMR sheets at the end of a meeting, and designated people analyze the responses. PMR data are used in various ways. The leader may review the responses and then, alone or with several others, design the next meeting with reference to them. Sometimes two rotating members are assigned to report at the new meeting on the PMRs as feedback on the current state of the group. Presumably, the sharing of the data will result in changes in subsequent meetings. And sometimes, the PMR data are used by a planning committee but are not formally fed back to the group. In any event, these postevaluation forms serve as a simple and direct means of obtaining individual participant responses immediately after the meeting.

Meetings: An International Perspective

The International Society for Intercultural Education, Training and Research (SIETAR International) is working toward its goal of world peace by stimulating a greater awareness of our common humanity and a wider understanding of the diverse cultures of the world. Recent SIETAR conferences have seen considerable ferment, however, as intercultural specialists have argued about how to integrate the differing meeting and decision-making styles of the cultures represented. The following discussion is derived from a monograph on a number of ideas and approaches discussed at SIETAR conferences and on others drawn from Micael Olsson's knowledge and experience.

Olsson (1985), an Australian at the University of Papua New Guinea, worked with small groups in various parts of the world and reported having seen too often a Western meeting style imposed on groups of other cultures. Is it possible, he asked, to devise a meeting style that bridges the modes of thinking of different cultures— one in which various styles are synthesized and no one style is allowed to dominate?

Olsson noted a tremendous variety of meeting elements and meeting styles in the cultures of different countries. His first step in developing a "universal" style was to identify various aspects of meetings that could be manipulated. He arrived at nine flexible aspects of meetings—that is, aspects that could be altered:

- Participant roles
- Sequence of participation
- Topic control
- Decision-making process
- Pace
- Space orientation
- Punctuality
- Language choice
- Amenities

Participant Roles

Leader/Audience	Leader/Participant	Facilitator/Participant	Participant only

First, in designing a meeting, consider the participant roles. Should the meeting have a leader and, if so, what type? As illustrated here, this relationship varies along a continuum from strong leadership to no defined leadership at all. (This model is similar to one developed by Tannenbaum and Schmidt, 1960.)

The "leader/audience" end of the continuum involves a primary speaker who presents a point of view to an audience in lecture format. "Limited audience participation" may consist of a question-and-answer period largely controlled by the speaker. The "leader/participant" structure allows more give and take between the leader and other participants, but the leader still has significantly greater influence; this format may occur as the leader asks for input or a brainstorming session. The "facilitator/participant" option decreases the role of the leader. The facilitator's role is primarily one of encouraging discussion and coordinating the training design; his or her influence is only slightly greater than that of other participants. Finally, at the other end of the continuum there is no leader. Members of the group work together within the rules that govern their assigned responsibility.

Sequence of Participation

Ordered	Monitored	Open

Another flexible aspect involves the sequence of participation by various speakers. The three types of participation are placed along a continuum indicating the degree to which acceptable sequencing is prescribed by convention or authority. In "ordered" sequences the order of speakers is strictly prescribed. In some traditional cultures, the newest members speak first and then the more senior members, until finally the chiefs speak. A "monitored" sequence occurs when one person recognizes speakers according to some predetermined criterion, such as equal time for opposing opinions, equal opportunity to speak, or discussion limited to a specific length of time. "Open" sequencing, as its name implies, places no restrictions on sequence or duration of participation.

Topic Control

Fixed	Flexible	Open

The topic of discussion may be fixed in advance and closed to modification or change. In "fixed" topic control, each speaker is expected to address the main topic and only that topic. Another option is to begin with a specific topic but to handle it with greater flexibility. References to sub-topics are allowed as long as they are relevant. With "open" topic control, the meeting begins with a broad general topic and then progresses spontaneously without any topic-related guidelines.

Decision-making Process

Vote	Vocal Assessment	Consensus

The voting process involves one part of the group agreeing to accept another part's point of view. "Winning" a decision can be based on voting systems ranging from simple majority rule to a completely unanimous vote. Another option, different from formal voting, is to have a leader assess opinion on the basis of vocal participation within the group, as in listening for *yeas* and *nays*. Group consensus involves an effort for all to come to a common agreement. Discussion continues until common agreement is reached.

Pace

Efficient	Tolerant	Patient

Pace concerns the amount of work accomplished in a given amount of time. An efficient pace is one where verbal participation moves through a lot of material in a relatively short amount of time. Such a pace is heavily task-oriented and little concerned with the development and maintenance of relationships among group members.

The other end of this continuum is "patience"—which allows each member the time needed for self-expression without concern for lost time. Stating the objective at the beginning of the meeting should effect the pace. For example, the leader's stating that a decision must be reached by the end of the meeting will set a different pace from the leader's allowing discussion over three consecutive meetings.

Space Orientation

Formal Rows	Layered Circle	Loose Circle	Unstructured

Space orientation is probably the easiest of the variables to control. "Formal rows" arrange participants so that all are facing in the same direction but at varying distances from the focal point.

The "layered circle" is a circle or semi-circle in which a distinction is purposefully drawn between those at the heart of the circle and those at its outer periphery. Olsson notes that this arrangement characterizes meetings of the Barai of Papua New Guinea, who have four identifiable layers in their circle. The inner core is reserved for key speakers; next are the more interested men; then the more interested women; and finally there is an outer layer of younger people and observers.

The "loose circle" or semi-circle makes no distinction among members within the group. This structure is significant because it maximizes the potential for participants to face one another. Still another possibility is *not* to create any set pattern and allow members to form their own physical shape.

Punctuality

Fixed	Flexible	Loose

Punctuality is one of the more difficult variables both to manipulate and to recognize in intercultural groups. That is because familiar patterns in traditional and Western circles are often diametrically opposed.

A "fixed" time orientation, the Western approach, involves the expectation that the meeting will begin when it is scheduled to begin and will conclude again as stated. A "flexible" time frame anticipates a moderate variation between the set times and the actual times. This flexible time has considerable variation within it, from a meeting beginning one-half hour after stated to even one or two hours late. Many traditional societies have a "loose" time orientation. It is not uncommon to wait for a meeting to take place up to a full day after the appointed time.

Language Choice

Prestige	Common	Multi-lingual

The choice of a language is obviously a concern in intercultural meetings. It is especially important to remember that the choice of language is critical to effective dialogue. There is not only the issue of clear expression but also the problem of communicating among the varied subgroups.

The options on the language choice continuum range from "prestige," whereby only one language is used, to the "multilingual" approach where every member speaks in his or her native language and interpreters are employed to insure clear communication. The "common language" approach falls in between the two. One common language (the language of the majority) is used, and again interpreters participate where needed.

Amenities

Minimal	Moderate	Extensive

The issue of amenities concerns the extent of social activity accompanying the discussion and decision-making processes.

In some situations ("minimal"), brief introductions, greetings, and acknowledgements may be the only social activities. In some societies ("moderate"), there may be a period of small talk or an exchange of tobacco, betel nuts, or some other refreshment. In still other situations ("extensive"), the amenities are so important that they are built into the design and outweigh the discussion process.

Lorenz Aggens (1985), in his discussion of the Samoan Circle, notes that several days of feasting and drinking together may be expected before the discussion begins and that the meeting may be closed with yet another drink. For many of the world's cultures, it is simply unacceptable to sit down to discuss business without some level of social interaction first.

Reconstructed Meeting Styles

By manipulating these nine variables, then, it is possible to design a meeting to meet specific goals. A few examples from Olsson will convey the range of possibilities. For example, he describes a meeting style developed by Chicago's Regional Planning Agency to cope with difficulties in dealing with controversial issues. The main problem was that even though the chairperson did everything possible to be equitable and fair, the participants still feared that the chairperson was controlling the meeting. The group adopted the Samoan Circle model, whose central feature is that it is leaderless. Two flexible aspects are manipulated to create a Samoan Circle: space orientation and sequence of participation.

Seating is in concentric circles; an inner circle of five chairs is arranged around a small, round table. All verbal interaction takes place only at the table, and everyone has access to the central five chairs. If all five chairs are filled and someone outside the center wants to speak, that person stands and waits until another person gives up a seat at the table and moves to another row. If some table seats are vacant, the person who wishes to speak sits in the empty chair. The key element in this meeting styles is the participants' proximity to each other around the table. This proximity both increases their personal relatedness and reduces the kind of verbal abuse that is often hurled around the room when members remain distanced from each other.

Sequence of participation is open in the Samoan Circle, and the spatial orientation is the layered circle. These characteristics influence participant roles: the format becomes participant only, unusual for large meetings in the West.

Another meeting style, known as the Park Bench, was developed to encourage meeting participants to express their feelings to one another. In this structure, whoever wishes to express his or her feelings sits down on a small park bench (or substitute) and asks the person or people being addressed to sit there too. The size of the bench forces the two or three people seated there into close proximity, allowing personal conversation to take place while the other participants watch. Those on the bench may express support for one another, make peace, or express particular feelings about the meeting topic or even about each other.

The Park Bench is related less to accomplishing the goals of the meeting than to the airing of the members feelings about each other. It stresses personal relationships and social dynamics, and it may actually be used to close a meeting. In terms of the variables discussed earlier, the sequence of participation is monitored, topic control is open, space orientation is the layered circle, and participant roles are limited to participant only.

The Quaker business meeting is another interesting meeting style. Here there is no chairperson, only a clerk who introduces the topic to be discussed and records the discussion. All members have the power to guide the course and outcome of the meeting, and participants speak when they are moved to do so. No decision can be reached without the unanimous consent of the participants, and this consensus has to be reached through the involvement of all. At intervals, the clerk reads back the recorded discussion to the participants. Discussion continues until an extended period of silence signals consensus. The entire assembly works cooperatively at a pace that deemphasizes concern for the efficient use of time. In terms of the variables, then, participant roles are facilitator/participant, sequence of participation is open, decision-making process is by consensus, and pace is patient.

These three examples suggest the range of possibilities for matching meeting styles to particular settings. The objective in each case is to promote full participation and free information flow. Although Olsson developed his mode of thinking in an intercultural context, his model has great potential in all kinds of meetings.

◆ Reader Activity

Consider a problem you would like to see solved in a meeting. Describe it in writing. Now, making reference to the nine flexible variables of meetings, design a meeting to achieve the stated objective. Choose an option from the continua for all the aspects we have discussed.   ◆

◆ ◆ EXERCISE 1

The Newspaper Interview: A Means of Discovering the "Real" Issues in a New Group

Increasingly it is being recognized that if a group is not responsive to the emotional needs of its members as they work together, its task may never be completed.

Thus it is necessary for groups that work together for any length of time to spend some of that time taking care of the problems that are bound to arise because of their own insensitivity to each other or simply because of their own lack of interpersonal skills. The problem is that people may willingly talk for hours about problems involving technical, task-related skills but will avoid looking, even for a few minutes, at how the group operated on the human level. Were individuals in the group shut out of participation? Did certain individuals dominate? Was hostility suppressed? Was problem solving shared? Were the real issues raised? These and many other questions reveal how closely personal feelings are related to overall objectives. The aim is not to have the group solve all the personal problems of its members. Rather, it is to come to grips with procedures, fears, or behaviors that reduce the effectiveness of that group.

Following are a few exercises that can help a group begin to work with process skills at both a personal and a group level.

Objectives

■ To bring into the open issues that may influence how a group operates from the beginning
■ To establish an immediate climate of honesty and leveling among the participants

Setting

Very often when a group of people comes together for the first time, the members bring with them an assortment of feelings, concerns, and expectations that may influence their participation for some time. It is very important to help clear the air from the beginning and to give people an opportunity to express themselves. This particular exercise is effective with a group of more than 10 (ideally 20 or more) and as many as 100. From the large group, the facilitator selects a random group of "reporters"—enough for one reporter in every group of seven or eight. These individuals should be brought together while the larger group is still milling around waiting for the beginning of the program (allow 10 minutes). The facilitator gives the following directions to reporters.

Each of you represents a different newspaper. It is your task to interview a group of about seven or eight of these people and find out as much as you can about them—as a group and as individuals. Names are not important, but you may wish to find out:

Why are they here? What do they expect to get out of the meetings?

Did they have any reservations about coming?

Outside of the stated reasons for the group being together, do different members have any particular hidden goals that they would like to share?

Do they have any doubts, suspicions, or special concerns about the meetings and how they are going to be conducted?

If they could wish for one thing during this period of time together, what would it be?

You should feel free to pursue any line of questioning you like and to use these questions as guidelines. After about 20 minutes of interviewing, you will be asked to synthesize your findings and report to the larger group. It is doubtful that there will be time to hear a full report, so please give only information that is not presented by other reporters and is particularly important for your group.

Action

After a general introduction, the facilitator suggests that one way the members can become acquainted rapidly is by taking part in a brief exercise that will clarify the purposes and focus on the expectations of the group. He or she then quickly organizes the group into sets of about seven or eight (so as to break up any cliques). Once in groups, the participants are told that they are to be interviewed by the local press and that it will be important for them to give the reporters the cooperation they need. They will not be quoted by name, so they should feel free to express any of their concerns or feelings about this meeting. The interview will last about 20 minutes; then each reporter will share his or her findings with the large group.

It is important that the facilitator not allow one or two reporters to dominate the reporting session. A reporter gives a piece of information on a point, and then the next reporter speaks on that point. It is helpful to have the points being made recorded on newsprint. Most of the information will be obtained in about 15 or 20 minutes. Then those in charge should develop a general overview of the program. Considerable effort should be made to link this presentation to the expressed concerns of the group. It is possible that a brief discussion about an issue or two may prove necessary. The major reason for this activity is to help express a norm of openness and allow the participants to express their feelings and expectations. Once expressed, they can be related to the actual plans and may be used by the organizers to alter some of those plans.

◆ ◆ EXERCISE 2

The Process Diagnosis: A Means of Altering Group Behavioral Patterns

Rationale

Most groups are suspicious about being observed or looking at their own patterns of operation. This exercise will help group members diagnose the factors that both facilitate and inhibit problem solving within the group.

Objectives

■ To help establish a desire in the group to process its own behaviors and procedures; to look at what happened, how people felt, and what helped or hindered movement toward goals.
■ To present explicit information about how the group is operating without becoming personal and focusing on any single individual
■ To help the group look at alternative operating procedures, thus introducing a degree of organizational flexibility that might not have been present

Setting

This exercise is directed primarily at relatively small working groups (five to eighteen members) who need and desire to maximize the use of time and available resource personnel. This type of experience should not be imposed on a group by the well-intentioned facilitator. The diagnosis format and reviewing of data should be explained in detail before it is attempted. Usually, if the group is concerned about maximizing its working efficiency and if there is the assurance that the diagnosis looks at group behavior rather than individual behavior, there will be enough curiosity for members to proceed. Although most people fear looking at their own or their group's behavior, it also has a fascination for them, and they will be willing to experiment if the risks are not too high. If possible, this exercise should be conducted after a period of work. The collection and analysis of the data and the report back to the group take between 45 minutes and 1 hour. Time must also be left for discussion. In all, the facilitator should figure on 1½ hours (in this example six questions are used, but three might be enough). The keys to success in this exercise appear to be

1. Making certain that the questions are not too threatening.
2. Presenting the data in an objective fashion and letting the group sort out the implications.
3. Leaving the group with the feeling that an expert is not necessary to carry out this type of process analysis.

Action

Having agreed that they would like to participate in the diagnosis, members are given a brief questionnaire or asked the questions directly from newsprint charts on the board. The latter approach seems to promote a feeling of less secrecy and allows data to be transferred directly to the board. However, if trust is a real problem in the group, the questionnaire tends to give a greater feeling of security and confidentiality (the facilitator should state as casually as possible that the responses will be completely anonymous). The diagnosis is aimed at painting a more descriptive picture of the group, which is not often available in a discussion. It usually takes about 15 minutes to answer the questions. Then, while the data are being tabulated and posted for presentation and discussion, a number of options are open to the facilitator. He or she may suggest that the group break into triads and discuss a particular question on how the group operates and what implications there may be in the various responses. Or he or she could have the members (again in subgroups) discuss the kinds of behaviors in this group and other groups they have noticed that reduce participation and increase defensiveness in themselves and others. The posting takes about 20 minutes, and the task during that period should be process-oriented and directed in a manner that will lead to more rather than less openness in the subsequent discussion. Following are six questions that exemplify a wide range of possible questions that could develop important data. All of the data derived from them can be tabulated easily and presented visually to the members for their own interpretation.

Question 1

Indicate which of the diagrams best represents the relationships that exist among the members of this group. Place the letter *A* beside the figure that *you* feel best represents the group. Place the letter *B* beside the figure you believe most group members will choose.

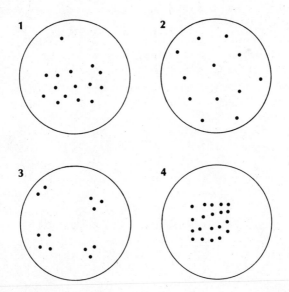

Rationale for Question 1

Most people have a definite feeling about their group and how its members relate to one another and to the group as a whole. It is also true that in many groups, members feel that others see the group differently than they do. If, as it is assumed, the group wishes to maximize its working relationships and it is discovered that most of the members choose the diagram that reflects subgrouping (diagram 3), then the group must face the implications of this in its decision-making efforts. If some members of the group see it as a group of individuals (diagram 2), it is likely that there is considerable blocking and that active or passive hostility is being generated as members attempt to win points for themselves, while failing to work for the benefit of the group. Further, a group that sees itself as dominated by a single personality may well wish to explore means of reducing such dependency-building relationships (diagram 1). Finally, a discrepancy between what individual members think and what they feel others think about the existing pattern of relationships can provide an important reality test for a group.

Question 2

In this question, a person who feels that he or she has the greatest possible influence and respect in the decision-making process would place himself or herself at 1 in the circle. A person who feels he or she has no influence at all in this group would place himself or herself at 7 in the circle. Place an *A* at the point in the circle where you feel that you belong. Place a *B* where you believe most members of the group will tend to respond to the question.

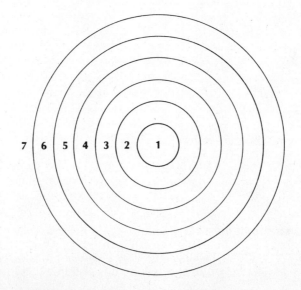

Rationale for Question 2

People need to have influence; to feel impotent and remain in the group is seldom tenable. Thus individuals often rank themselves higher in this particular question than they see others. It is an important discrepancy, for example, if all twelve members of a group see themselves in the first four circles while six of the members see the group as tending to have very little influence (points 5, 6, and 7). Also, the second question supplements the first question. For example, in the first question, if members see the group as dominated by a single person, or if they see a sharply divided series of subgroups, they would have to explain the discrepancy if most of the group felt influential. Also, if four or five members of the group feel they have considerable influence and another four or five (or even one or two) feel they have virtually none, then there is almost inevitably going to be tension and nonproductive behavior (withdrawal, defensiveness, dispute) as those who feel controlled try to cope with their own feelings of impotency. Again, it is for the group to interpret the data and for the facilitator to make them aware of the evidence so that they can raise the most helpful questions.

Question 3

In a perfect group, a person is able to say almost anything he or she thinks or feels as long as it is not totally irrelevant or destructive. Mark an A on the diagram at a point that represents how free you feel in communicating with the group. Place a B at the point you feel most members of the group will mark in response to this question.

1	2	3	4	5
No openness—group closed; no freedom to speak		Some openness, moderate freedom to speak		Completely open and free to speak

Rationale for Question 3

When the data are presented in graphical form, it is difficult to avoid certain implications. For example, a wide difference in perceptions of the openness that exists immediately suggests that certain members are more open than others, which in turn implies an issue of control and raises some of the questions suggested previously. As in the other questions, it is important to explore the difference between how individuals perceive themselves in the group and how they perceive the group responding to the question. It is possible to compare individual and group averages in this and the previous question and, if desired, to compare deviations from the mean. However, most of the implications will be quite visible when charted.

Question 4

Suggest two reasons why this group is not as productive as it might be when working together.

Rationale for Question 4

All groups have problems working together, and those unable to recognize some specific conditions that need to be improved are probably not very involved (a problem in itself) or are not being honest. Human relations problems are part of the game and are to be expected. The only real problem occurs when the group does not face them and try to remedy them. This question is strictly designed to get some of the issues out on the table so the group can begin to deal openly with them. Resolution probably will not come in this session, although the mere mention of some problems will go a long way toward solving them. The responses to this question should be integrated to some degree so that members can see which areas seem to be of most concern. Thus, instead of recording all twenty-four responses of a group of twelve, there may be six or eight that can be identified in terms of importance (that is, the number of members who made those responses) and noted next to the statement. Of course, a point mentioned only once may represent an important issue that others were afraid to mention and therefore should be given equal time for exploration.

Note: If the participants have numbered their questionnaires or responses, there can be some interesting comparisons between responses made to the first three questions and those made to this question. However, one must also be careful not to overwhelm the group with data. There is just so much that can be digested at one time.

Question 5

What are two of the best qualities of this group?

Rationale for Question 5

A person or group grows not only by eliminating its weaknesses but also by maximizing its good qualities. Seldom do we take time to focus on these characteristics. The simple expression of its strengths can give a group the lift needed to deal effectively with its limitations. It may also be a first step in legitimizing praise, which is crucial in any effort to describe clearly the nature of the working group.

Question 6

What behaviors do you feel occur in groups with which you work (not necessarily this one) that you personally find annoying and disturbing to the progress of the group?

Rationale for Question 6

It is quite possible that group members are not able to face some of the issues hindering progress. By focusing on other groups, members may indirectly raise problems that have direct implications and can be used as a source of diagnostic questions at a later time. Most important, the group may wish to build some preventive measures into its own operations to make certain that some of these problems do not occur.

Conclusions

The questions are diagnostic in nature, and although some of the statements imply solutions, the data should be used mainly to establish a desire to look toward solutions. If steps are not taken to resolve some of the problems raised, and if the new awareness and facing up by the group are not matched by an effort to develop more effective problem-solving and communication patterns, the exercise may introduce a period of disenchantment and increased tension. Thus, again, the group and those in a position of influence must desire not only to *look* but also to *do*. As in any problem-solving situation, this will take time and energy away from other issues. But in the long run, it should be worth it.

◆ ◆ EXERCISE 3

The Open Chair: A Means of Ensuring Greater Group Participation*

Objective

■ To interject new ideas and opinions into a group meeting without losing the advantage of a small number of participants

Rationale

Quite often a large group (perhaps 10 to 25 members in this case) is faced with an issue that requires the involvement of all its members, but the facilitator is

*This "design" is similar to the Samoan Circle described by Olsson on pp. 460–461.

aware that an open discussion probably would only polarize positions and cloud the important aspects of the problem. Thus, although it is important for members to feel that their ideas are being represented in the discussion, they must feel some identification with and responsibility to the group as a whole. If those involved in the discussion can make this responsibility to the group a higher priority than the need to defend their own positions, the chance for compromise and eventual consensus is greatly enhanced.

Setting

The large group selects a representative group of individuals to discuss the topic that is posing a problem. The smaller group of perhaps six or seven takes seats in a small circle, and an extra chair is placed there. Those not directly involved take chairs on the outside of this inner circle.

Action

As the discussion develops, individuals on the outside of the circle may move to the empty chair. They may make an observation or express an opinion either on the issue (task level) or on how the discussion is being conducted (process level). Unless asked to remain for a few minutes by the inner group, the contributor then leaves the circle, and the chair is open to another interested person. This structure ensures the outside members that their concerns are being represented, and as observers, they also have a better opportunity to note any personal factors that may be reducing the effectiveness of the group. This particular problem-solving structure assumes that the group is at a point in its development where it can delegate authority in a reasonable manner. It also assumes that participants would like those in the middle to resolve the problem being discussed. If this is not so, it is possible for disruptive persons on the outside to destroy the intent by dominating the inner group with personal biases or irrelevant points of view.

◆ ◆ EXERCISE 4

Role Reversal: A Means of Unblocking a Polarized Group

Objectives

- To help group members gain a broader problem-solving perspective
- To help a polarized group with a particular issue on which certain members are especially intransigent

Setting

If, regardless of the facilitating methods used, a group is making little progress in reaching a joint decision because of strong differences of opinion, it is often helpful to pull individuals away from their defensive positions. This can be done by introducing a role-play situation in which the participants are asked either to argue from the point of view of the opposition or to design a solution that is as far as they can go in satisfying the opposing position.

Action

A group that has moved from a format of open discussion and the presentation of ideas to one of defensive debate is doomed to failure, frustration, or both. The facilitator may wish to give the group members a short break (often merely changing the physical scene can help) so that they have a chance to move away from the positions they have taken. Sometimes members may wish to come to a compromise, but the vigor of their argument has boxed them into an all-or-nothing position. It is for the facilitator (or a skilled member of the group) to help remove this barrier. Thus, on returning from the brief break, members of the group are asked to think for a few minutes about the opposing positions being expressed. The discussion begins, and it is evident that many of the arguments on both sides have not been heard as the members argue those issues that are most difficult for them to accept.

At the end of about 10 minutes, the total group is asked to consider the role reversal and what implications it has for the group. Stepping into the other person's shoes and having to argue his or her side often makes it easier to understand diverse points of view and may give those desiring to break the deadlock an opportunity to do so honorably.

People usually argue from extreme positions. There is generally (except on issues of morality) a wide range of acceptable compromise, but intensive debate and argument lead to a condition in which personal image more than personal belief or idea is being defended. Not to lose assumes greatest importance. Asking members to think of a solution that they might not like, but which would incorporate as much of the opposing position as possible, forces them to do something constructive rather than merely argue and defend. Just getting the group to move in the direction of being constructive may induce the compromise and resolution that are needed. Once the group is willing to make a few concessions, the process becomes easier, and it is no longer a problem of saving face.

There are many ways of going about helping groups move off what appear to be irreconcilable positions. One way is simply to get them thinking about the other person's position and not just their own; another is to encourage them to build a workable solution instead of just arguing intellectually. Most action programs represent compromise merely because many people must be satisfied.

References

Aggens, L. "The Samoan Circle: A small group process for discussing controversial subjects." Unpublished manuscript, 1985.

Amidon, E., and A. Blumberg. *Understanding and Improving Faculty Meetings.* Minneapolis: Paul Amidon & Associates, 1967, pp. 30–35.

Antony, J. "How to run a meeting." *Harvard Business Review,* No. 72604 (March–April 1976), 43–58.

"Are today's executives meeting with success?" *Journal of Management Development,* V, No. 10 (Winter 1991), 14.

Auger, B. Y. *How to Run a Better Business Meeting.* St. Paul: Minnesota Mining and Manufacturing Company, 1972.

Bader, L. "Guidelines for designing workshops." Unpublished paper, 1982.

Bradford, L. *Making Meetings Work.* La Jolla, Calif.: University Associates, 1976.

Brewer, J. D. "How to have effective meetings." *Supervision,* 46, No. 6 (1984) 6–8.

Bunning, R. L., "Smooth steps to transition meetings." *H/R Magazine,* August 1991, 59–64.

Burke, W. W., and R. Beckard, eds. *Conference Planning.* 2nd ed. La Jolla, Calif.: University Associates, 1976.

Caernarven-Smith, P. "You don't really have to be at this meeting." *Technical Communications,* April 1991, 270–271.

DeLuca, N. "Meetings: With effective leadership, they can work." *NASSP Bulletin,* 67, No. 464 (1983), 114–117.

Doyle, M., and D. Strauss. *How to Make Meetings Work.* New York: Jove Books, 1984.

"Enemies of efficiency: Meetings and memos." *The Wall Street Journal,* December 27, 1990.

Forsyth, D., R. Berger, and T. Mitchell. "The effects of self-serving vs. other-serving claims of responsibility on attraction and attribution in groups." *Social Psychology Quarterly,* 44 (1981), 59–64.

Frank, M. O. *How to Run a Successful Meeting in Half the Time.* New York: Simon and Schuster, 1989.

"Helping a team find all the answers." *Training and Development Journal,* December 27, 1990, 15.

Henderson, C. E. "Meeting seating." *Association and Society Manager,* 17, No. 3 (1985), 42–43.

Hobbs, C. *Time Power.* New York: Harper & Row, 1987.

Horlock, C. "Breathing new life into faculty meetings." *Thrust for Educational Leadership,* 16, No. 5 (1987), 36–37.

"How to keep meetings from turning into marathons." *Business Week,* November 26, 1990, 126.

Januz, L., and S. Jones. *Time Management for Executives.* New York: Charles Scribner's Sons, 1981.

Kieffer, G. D. *The Strategy of Meetings.* New York: Warner Books, 1988.

Klumph, N. "Effective meetings—A management must." *Supervisory Management,* 29, No. 12 (1984), 28–32.

Leigh, A. "Wringing some benefits from those dreaded meetings." *International Management,* 39, No. 5 (1984), 18.

Mackenzie, R. *The Time Trap.* New York: American Management Association, 1972.

Maier, N. R. F. *Problem-Solving Discussions and Conferences.* New York: McGraw-Hill, 1963.

Marrow, A., D. G. Bowers, and S. E. Seashore. *Management by Participation.* New York: Harper & Row, 1967.

Meloche, W. J. "Eliminate the flop factors when planning meetings, conferences." *Canadian Insurance,* 90, No. 10 (1985), 32, 48.

Meyer, N. Dean, and J. C. Bulyk. "Augmented meeting support: Increasing executive effectiveness." *Information Strategy: The Executive's Journal,* 2, No. 2 (1986), 24–29.

Miller, E. C., ed. *Conference Leadership.* New York: American Management Association, 1972.

Mosvick, R. K., and R. B. Nelson. *We've Got to Start Meeting Like This.* Glenview, Ill.: Scott, Foresman, 1987.

Olsson, M. "Meeting styles for intercultural groups." *AFS International/Intercultural Programs, Inc.,* 7 (1985), 1–19.

Prince, G. M. "Creative meetings through power sharing." *Harvard Business Review,* No. 72410 (July–August 1972), 47–55.

Ratteray, O. M. T. "After the meeting, then what?" *Successful Meetings,* 33, No. 2 (1984), 76–77.

Reeves, C. *Managing Meetings.* New York: DeLoayza Associates, Altamont, 1988.

Schabacker, K. "A short snappy guide to meaningful meetings." *Working Woman,* V, No. 16 (June 1991), 70.

Schindler-Rainman, E., and R. Lippitt. *Taking Your Meetings Out of the Doldrums.* La Jolla, Calif.: University Associates, 1977.

Schwartz, A. E. "How to get the most from the meetings you manage." *Supervisory Management,* March 1991, 10–11.

Selinger, O. "Corporate meetings can be more productive." *National Underwriter (Life/Health),* 89, No. 2 (1985), 12, 26–27.

Stella, P. "Running the next staff meeting . . . Now what do I do?" *Audio-Visual Communications,* V, No. 25 (April 1991), 20.

Strauss, B., and F. Strauss. *New Ways to Better Meetings.* New York: Viking Press, 1951.

Sullivan, G. *Work Smart, Not Hard.* New York: Facts on File, 1987.

Swan, P. "The conference change." *Management Today,* (April 1984), 85–100.

Tannenbaum, R., and W. H. Schmidt. "How to choose a leadership pattern." *Harvard Business Review,* 36, (1960), 95–101.

This, L. *The Small Meeting Planner.* Houston: Gulf, 1972.

Tobia, P. M., and M. C. Becker. "Making the most of meeting time." *Training & Development Journal,* August 1990, 24–28.

Waller, L. "Making meetings work." *Black Enterprise,* V, No. 21 (September 1990), 92.

Whitehead, J. L., Jr. "Improving Meeting Productivity." In *Professional Communication in the Modern World: Proceedings of the 31st Southeast Convention of the American Business Communication Association,* Hammond, (April 1984), 185–191.

Yalom, I. *The Theory and Practice of Group Psychotherapy.* New York: Basic Books, 1970.

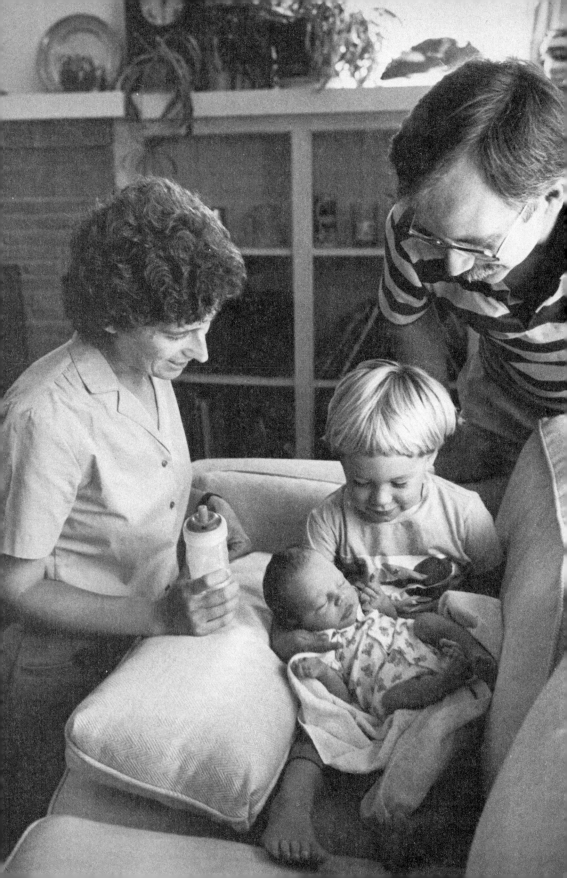

◆ *10* ◆

The Evolution of Groups

The young assistant professor, not yet used to the letters Ph.D. following his name, had been hired by the large urban university to teach courses in the behavioral sciences. He arrived on campus both excited about sharing his new wisdom and terrified that he was ill-equipped to deal with his students.

Before classes began, one of his colleagues asked if he had ever had a course in group dynamics. Nonchalantly, he told her he had had several experiences with it, though in truth he had no idea what she was talking about. She invited him to join her group dynamics class as a student to help orient him, and out of courtesy he accepted, wondering how much more there was to learn after nearly seven years of graduate school in psychology.

The course was like nothing he had ever experienced. The group members sat around in a circle attempting to learn about group behavior simply by becoming a group. There was no other agenda, no text on which to lean, no rules, no predetermined roles or goals. The instructor sat quietly, observing the students as they struggled to define their goals and determine whether they were succeeding or failing. The void filled with the students' identity, influence, purpose, and control. Occasionally she made an observation on the group's process, but she kept her contributions to a minimum. The lack of structure resulted in an explosion of feelings.

The young man was amazed at what he saw. In the fertile ambiguity of this unstructured environment, every kind of behavior he had ever studied began to surface; the group became a true laboratory of human behavior. Three-hour meetings took place once a week for thirteen weeks, and at every one the group faced a new crisis as it came to grips with issues of identity, trust, frustration, and power.

What amazed him most of all was his colleague's behavior. Each week, she calmly threw out one or two brilliant, pointed observations that propelled the group to new levels of understanding. He was both grateful for her wisdom and angered by his own inability to see and understand what seemed obvious to her. She seemed to see deeply not only into the present but also into future events, while he floundered along with everyone else, struggling with whatever was blocking the group's purpose at any given moment. Long after the course ended, he confided to her that at times he had seen her as a cross between a witch and a magician— serene, all powerful, and one who somehow knew what would happen in the group, perhaps in all groups, before it even occurred.

This woman's power and the source of her influence on the group was her ability to understand the predictable developmental patterns of virtually any group— but particularly one so ill defined as this one. Her "crystal ball" consisted of her experience with the issues all groups face and the predictable consequences of dealing with or failing to deal with them. This chapter probes the phenomenon of group development and explores those identifiable stages.

The Task and Emotional Aspects of Groups

Society, institutions, and small groups are often established with the goal of being democratic and egalitarian and maintaining lines of communication, yet tensions are often created by contradictory forces. The forces are real, and one must grasp their nature if one is to understand the sources of many stresses that derive from human interaction. An example will help describe the nature of these forces (Cooley, 1909; Parsons, 1951).

> The young religious novice enters the convent in an order that specializes in medical services. Her goal is to be a missionary and to work as a hospital administrator in one of the developing countries. Her personal training focuses on two areas: the technicalities of hospital administration (accounting, deployment of services, supervision) and her own personal growth as a sister dedicated to such virtues as love, charity, and faith. Her relationships with the other novices and sisters are warm and affectionate, and she finds it difficult to leave for her first assignment in a small Ghanaian hospital. The transition proves to be overwhelming. From the nurturing atmosphere of the convent where acceptance was immediate and unqualified, where gentleness and consideration for others were rewarded, she enters her new environment. Here, there is never enough time, every day is a new crisis, decisions are immediate and based less on human feelings than on expediency and efficiency. Her value to the hospital has little to do with Christian virtues. It depends on how effectively she can keep the hospital out of the red, how efficiently she can keep the illiterate workers working, and how well she is able to marshal the limited resources available. Failure means transfer, perhaps into an even less desirable situation or into another area of work.

In this example there was a large discrepancy between expectations and reality, between what was desirable and the conditions that prevailed. What stands out is the constant struggle between work efficiency and personal needs, between success measured in terms of task roles and success in terms of emotions. The dichotomy, of course, is less apparent in the absence of such a dual set of expectations. In the army, the rules, regulations, and codes of behavior are clearly detailed. A career soldier is fully cognizant of these and can accept the depersonalized nature of many of the relationships that exist. Similarly, a young person applying for a job with a Wall Street bank finds a complex set of rules (both explicit and implicit) that governs his or her behavior, clothes, hair style, language, accepted level of feelings to be displayed, and relations with other workers in the bank. When individuals accept these rules and know full well what is expected of them, they usually experience little tension, because the personal-emotional factor has been largely screened from their work involvement.

In most groups and organizations, however, no such clear distinction exists, and this is exactly where the stress often originates. For example, in some groups, people wish to be accepted for themselves and not because of academic degrees, superficial knowledge, or other artificial standards; but some groups tend to define success in terms of some visible achievement. Material wealth (how much do you earn?), status (executive assistant to whom?), power (how many people under you?), or tenure (you have 25 years with this department?) are much easier to grasp than the hazy variables that form the basis of most personal relationships. Thus, most groups and organizations are established in such a manner that personal acceptance is conditional and based on some implicit or explicit achievement criteria.

Work-oriented task groups tend to be high in control, to depend on material rewards for motivation, to stress accuracy, to organize their use of time, and to minimize the range of free expression and autonomy allowed. Similarly, such conditions encourage individual competition rather than interdependence, conformity rather than individuality. Management becomes uncomfortable when informality creeps in, when personal relations begin to get in the way of efficiency, and when regulations are altered to meet the peculiar needs of particular individuals. The fabric of army life would break down if exceptions were made to the rule. The same could be said for big business, the organized church, and large school systems.

For example, it is difficult to imagine the following situations occurring:

> On the day of a major battle, a young private remarks to his field sergeant, "I hope you won't mind, but I probably won't be going to the front today. This headache is killing me." The sergeant looks on with great sympathy and says, "That's all right, Joe, we all have days like that. Why don't you just rest and take it easy today and save yourself for tomorrow?"

> "Miss Jones, you mean you didn't get that rush report out that I asked you to do?" "No, I'm sorry," she replied, "but Johnny surprised me last night, and we went out for the most heavenly lobster thermidor you can imagine." "Well," he said, "I know how you feel about John, and there will be other contracts. After all, we're only young once."

> "Well, Mr. Gibbs, how are you today, and did you like my sermon?" The minister waited expectantly for the usual monitored reply. "To tell the truth, I really felt you were talking down to us, and if there is one thing I don't appreciate, it's being lectured to in a condescending fashion. Also, you tended to stray from the point by bringing in humorous asides which, although interesting, tended to distract me from the issue."

Sympathy from a field sergeant, acceptance of gross inefficiency from one's boss and criticism of a minister are difficult to imagine within the context of expected role behaviors and institutional demands. But multiplied a thousand times, these expectations condition our behavior in nearly all groups in which people are involved. They are tied to a Puritan ethic and to years of involvement in schools, businesses, and churches, where acceptance is linked to one's output, dependability, efficiency, and conformity.

Implications for Small Groups

When entering a group, we look for familiar hooks on which to hang our hats, signs that make the unpredictable predictable, sure ways of being accepted. Even in a social group, we often begin by sharing credentials, strengths, or skills in order to establish a tone of respectability. When working on a task, meeting a deadline, or in some way remaining highly task-oriented, there tends to be an order and safety in working relations; but if the curtain of formality is drawn away, one can almost feel the strain of another set of forces pushing for greater intimacy and the personalizing of behavior, as well as greater authenticity. Informality implies increasing one's vulnerability and willingness to take risks in a group in which trust is typically built around performance. Indeed, it is the rare group that can effectively combine social–emotional interests with those necessary for getting the job done. It is not so much that they cannot be combined, but that the combination necessarily increases the complexity of the existing relationships and the risks for the participants. It simply may not be worth the trouble, and, in fact, efficiency may decline and overall problems increase.

◆ *Reader Activity*

We seldom take the time to sit back and consider the subtle, rarely discussed sources of stress and tension that we experience within an organization simply because the values and priorities of the organization differ from our personal needs, self-interests, and values. These differences are natural and, to some degree, we must accommodate them. Take a moment and respond to the following questions in relation to an organization (and group) in which you are a participant. This could be a church, social or professional club, school, place of work, or even your family.

1. What gives members status? Are there certain attitudes, behaviors, or accomplishments that are particularly important to the group that seem much less important to you as an individual?

2. If a new person were to join your group, what would the individual have to do to gain the most immediate acceptance? How do you feel about this? Are there behaviors that you believe are important but that are given almost no weight by the group or by the organization of which it is a part.

3. In a typical day, what are the kinds of emotions people tend to show? Are there emotions or feelings you wish would be acceptable but are not?

4. Are there certain rules (stated or unstated) within the group or organization that are absolutes and that you feel are too inflexible or that tend to dehumanize its members? In what areas is there no room for individual differences where there should be?   ◆

In many cases the nature of the group or organization simply will not allow the legitimate expression of basic social–emotional needs. If the resulting pressures and frustrations do not find release outside the group, or if informal avenues are not created within, it is likely that tensions will be released indirectly. Usually this occurs by creating interpersonal conflicts around the task issue at hand. Thus the task itself becomes the avenue for non-task-related expression of tension. Strange as it may seem, the very presence of restrictions designed to prevent extraneous issues from undermining the group's work creates new areas of stress that may be even more insidious and difficult to deal with. A group goes through predictable stages in development that affect how these interpersonal forces influence the group.

The Stages of Group Development

Groups, like individuals, develop through predictable stages of growth over time. In work groups, social or political groups, sports teams, and classroom groups, a predictable pattern of group evolution emerges in which each stage has certain definite characteristics. A child matures through the toddler years into the school years and eventually becomes an adolescent. We can expect that the behavior of the child will be markedly different through each developmental era. And because every child is different, each child will pass through the stages in his or her own individual manner. Despite these individual differences, however, certain general similarities characterize children who are in the same stage. For example, a child in the "terrible twos" can be expected to say "No!" much of the time and have temper tantrums when things do not go his or her way. Groups also come in a wide variety and have individual differences, and they also progress through stages that have characteristics that are common from one group to another.

The following description of the events that may occur as a group develops, and the accompanying driving forces, is a composite of many views.[1] It is presented not as a model for all groups but as an example of events that may take place and needs that may exist. By becoming more keenly aware of the changes in group behavior and raising appropriate questions in relation to them, the leader should be in a better position to respond effectively to the group's present needs. The case that follows assumes an ongoing group with a reason for being, wherein members have relatively little personal information about fellow members, differing perceptions of the task, and different methods in mind for reaching the goals. Finally, it assumes a group that is starting out, although much that is suggested is relevant to groups at various stages of development.

The Beginning

People have expectations of what will occur in a group even before they attend. They flavor their first perceptions with these expectations and their personal needs. They bring with them their individual histories and experiences in previous groups. It is these factors that provide the lenses through which the group is perceived. First, it is necessary to become included in the group and then to attempt to be relatively secure in an unknown situation. For most, it appears to be a time for waiting, anticipating what lies ahead, sorting out potential dangers, and acting with discretion. Thus there is a period of gathering data and processing them through the filter of our own previous experiences, biases, and stereotypes. Like children on the first day of school, we tend to

> keep our feelings to ourselves until we know the situation
>
> look more secure in our surroundings than we might feel
>
> be watchful
>
> lack a feeling of potency or sense of control over our environment
>
> act superficially and reveal only what is appropriate
>
> scan the environment for clues to what is proper: clothes, tone of voice, vocabulary, who speaks to whom
>
> be nice, certainly not hostile
>
> try to place other participants in pigeonholes so that we can feel comfortable with them
>
> be confused about what is expected of us
>
> desire structure and order to reduce our own pressure to perform

1. The composite was drawn from the views of many people working with a wide range of experiences and types of groups. They include W. Bennis, W. Bion, R. B. Cattell, V. Cernius, A. M. Cohen, E. Erikson, J. Gibb, R. Handfinger, G. C. Homans, B. C. Kuypers (et al.), R. Lacoursiere, D. C. Lundgran, E. A. Mabry, R. D. Mann, T. Mills, F. Redl, W. Schutz, H. Thelen, C. Theodorsen, B. W. Tuckman, and J. P. Wanous (et al.).

wonder what price we must pay to be "in" and whether the rewards are
worth the effort

find our own immediate needs to be of primary importance

wait for the leader to establish goals, roles, and who has responsibility
(even if we resent its being done)

Therefore, the beginning is a time for testing, a time of inhibition guided by the
rules of other places and experiences. Our task in the beginning is to include
ourselves and become oriented to the norms and expectations of the group. It is
a time not for heroics but for first impressions. Often, it is an environment based
more on suspicion than on trust, partly because of our initial discomfort and partly
because we simply do not know. However, because people always want something
better and seek to reduce tensions, more often than not they will risk involvement
and at least a minimal sharing. Our needs to be liked and accepted tend to light
the way, and though we are seldom satisfied, there usually are indications of better
things to come. On either side of this position there are, of course, the groups
that from the first minute are so tightly controlled that one's very breath and
individuality are lost and those equally rare groups in which a sense of openness
and security prevails immediately. However, most groups are a mix of hope and
trepidation, in which our own needs and the views of others provide the ingredients
for an initial climate of doubt and hesitation.

Movement Toward Confrontation

It is not until the initial probing into the boundaries of appropriate behaviors has
taken place that façades are dropped and individuals establish personal roles and
reveal more characteristic behaviors. Much of the new movement in the group
relates to the patterns of power and leadership that are being established. The
initial period of unfamiliarity often leads to increased dependency, an acquiescence
to authority, and a seeking of structure that allows members to move with a certain
ease in the strange environment. For many, however, this soon results in a desire
for more influence in what is happening and focuses attention on those with power.

How to be liked and accepted by those with influence becomes of central
importance to some, and others begin to seek personal recognition and their own
spheres of influence. Suddenly the leader becomes not only a source of dependency
and admiration but also an object of criticism whose inadequacies become a regular
topic of discussion. How things are to be done, how decisions are made and by
whom, and issues of freedom and control all become preeminent. Whether there
is a leader focus or a member focus, influence and so-called territoriality among
the participants become central. It is the assertive seeking of one's place in the
group that promotes behavior formerly hidden, and thus it is a period of new
behavioral dimensions for various members and a period in which stereotypes are
often revealed as invalid. This springing forth of new behaviors creates suspicion

and mistrust in some and forms the basis for new alliances within the group. It is bound to cause tensions and conflict. Not uncommon are such statements as "I wouldn't have suspected that of John"; "I knew there was more to her than that soft voice and smile"; and "I didn't know he was capable of being so angry."

Within this more assertive environment, members begin to take more definite stands, and issues become polarized. Instead of an argument being looked at in terms of data and facts, it also becomes a testing ground for personal influence and prestige. Tenacity may be as important as rationality in winning, and for some it is winning or losing and not the issue itself that is important. The tentativeness is gone, hostility is legitimized, and in many ways the group is much more real than it was in the beginning. Alliances within the group are redrawn more on the basis of experience and behavior than expectations and wishful thinking. Along with the increased amounts of anger being shown there is probably more laughter and a generally wider range of affective behaviors.

In this phase, we as group members may feel dissatisfied, angry, frustrated, and sad because we perceive the discrepancy between our initial hopes and expectations and the reality of group life, between the task and our ability to accomplish the task. During the first phase it is often difficult to concentrate one's energies on task issues as long as one's own role and secure position in the group have not been established. Now, however, the task becomes a means of exercising other spheres of influence and expertise. Underlying issues facing the group may involve such things as status, prestige, and power. Amid increased signs of rigidity among the participants and an unwillingness to compromise, less assertive members tend to withdraw as others in the group now bring personality issues into what previously had been content or task issues. If the group is able to face its own natural destructive tendencies, there is very likely to be a confrontation followed by resolution and an effort to get people together and back on the track.

Compromise and Harmony

A confrontation over work and personal issues will usually occur when individuals who are more willing to compromise recognize how self-defeating the present course of events seems to be. Acting as intermediaries, they reopen issues and help to get individuals talking again. Such a confrontation may also result when some of the more aggressive members realize that their own personal aims are not being met as a result of the present course of action. They begin to see a more amicable climate as essential to any further movement or growth on the part of the group.

The result is a countermovement to shut off the growing hostility, to reopen communication, and to draw the group together into a more smoothly working body. This effort often ushers in a period of good will and harmony during which there is a reassessment of how people have or have not been working together and how conditions for work might be facilitated. The dissensions are eased, deviations in member behaviors appear to be more readily accepted, and self-expression is encouraged. Greater familiarity with each other and the experience of some success result in a willingness to accept people as people in light of both strengths and limitations. Compromise is no longer seen as equivalent to losing face. Collaboration is more readily sought and competitiveness is played down, if not rejected, by the members. The group tends to exude a new confidence and begins actually to see itself as an integrated unit that can be facilitative when it wishes to be. There is a genuine effort to look at issues, discover appropriate resources, and avoid the personalizing of issues that occurred earlier.

After the nearly destructive series of events and the mistrust previously generated, members are careful not to step on one another's toes, to avoid signs of hostility, and to make sure everyone is heard. Real honesty and openness are encouraged on the one hand, but on the other hand, there is a subtle pressure not to raise any problems that might break down the harmony that has been so difficult to obtain. Thus everyone is given "air time" and encouraged to voice his or her opinions. There is a tendency to let people talk (even extraneously) rather than cut them off. Joking and laughter are common, and personal irritations, unless couched in veiled sarcasm, tend to go unnoticed. An increasing discrepancy develops between feelings and behavior, but even so, the group may increasingly talk of its openness and ability to work together. Yet the denial of personal issues tends to increase tensions that remain unexpressed. With this submergence of issues there is less participant involvement, stimulation, and overall interest.

Thus, although fences have been repaired and wounds covered, it has been done at a cost of some of the group's integrity and efficiency. Instead of the anger and overt blocking that occurred previously, issues are overdiscussed, and it is very difficult to make decisions. Resistance appears to be more covert. Instead of leading to greater productivity, this harmony often spells even less efficiency. Eventually the realization dawns that the behaviors within the group are actually inhibiting authenticity and directness. One reason it takes so long to reach decisions is that covert resistance and passivity block progress. The initial elation shared during the beginning of the period gives way to disillusionment and increasing tension. The group's efforts toward harmony simply have not succeeded.

Reassessment

Having worked under a period of relative structure and under conditions of less control, with neither resulting in a satisfactory climate for work, the group seeks a new alternative. One obvious solution is to impose greater operational restrictions to insure a more rational approach to decision making. Such a thrust would streamline work procedures and redirect the group toward the task with greater efficiency. It would not, however, confront the source of many of the problems created within the group. As with many life problems, this approach only attacks the symptoms and eases the pain of the current situation, but it may be enough to insure a smoother decision-making process.

If, however, the group decides to delve more deeply into the problems at hand—into causal factors—then considerably more time, energy, and involvement will be the cost. It requires a sizable risk on the part of the members because many issues that have long been submerged will be forced to the surface. Member roles, decision-making procedures, and leadership and communication patterns are likely to come under close scrutiny, as are the personal behaviors that facilitated or inhibited the group. Thus, this becomes a period of reflection on goals and performance, means and ends. There is usually a recognition of how vulnerable the group is to the personal needs, suspicions, and fears that can determine how successful the group is in reaching these goals.

If the group chooses this latter course of action, it must build a mechanism that allows it to appraise its own ongoing operations and to alter its pattern of working behaviors when it is obvious that current methods are not proving effective. The group must face the question of how honest it can be and just what level of personal intimacy must be reached before it can accomplish its goals in the most effective manner. Thus the period of harmony and compromise, although not raising all the issues that needed to emerge, did prove of great importance in the development of the group. Because it was a period of reduced competition, greater informality, and increased familiarity among members, it provided a needed foundation upon which to build. What had been missing was a means of legitimizing the feelings that were not positive and the communication of feelings and ideas that might create conflict or force the group to consider alternative approaches. The negative feelings of the previous stage are more realistically resolved, and group members feel more capable of completing the task.

Often there is a simultaneous realization that as the functions of the group become increasingly complex and there is a need for more resources, greater interdependence is necessary. Greater participation through the division of labor becomes essential, and with it accountability and personal responsibility are spread throughout the group. With greater freedom to communicate and methods of feedback built into the group's operations, necessary tasks are increasingly undertaken by those with particular skills and interests, leadership is shared, and participant involvement is generally increased. The notion of accountability is crucial here, and it suggests that individuals know what is expected of them, that their expectations are shared by the group, and that their progress toward meeting these expectations is to some degree measurable.

There is, of course, the possibility that a temporary period of intense conflict will result as tensions and stresses previously withheld are brought out. If the group can overcome the fear of such conflict and realize that conflict can be put to effective use without being destructive to individuals, then there will be less reluctance to deal more openly with such issues in the future. Thus, during this period the group realizes that if it is to survive, it must increase shared responsibility as well as personal accountability. This in turn will increase trust and insure more individual risk taking as well as a willingness to devote the necessary time to resolve working issues of both a substantive and personal nature.

Resolution and Recycling

Effective working groups are not necessarily harmonious and free of tensions and conflict. There seem to be periods of conflict resolution and harmony and even times when the group tends to regress into a pattern of indecisiveness and floundering. As a group matures, it should find itself resolving conflicts more quickly and with a minimal expenditure of energy. The group at this stage is quite productive, and positive feelings are often generated by succeeding in the task and being part of the group. And, like any mature person, the group should be increasingly able to recognize its own limitations and strengths and build effectively around them. It has been found, however, that if the group is suddenly faced with a crisis, a series of critical deadlines, a number of new participants, or even a controversial new idea, that event may usher in a period of readjustment and a reappearance of old and not necessarily helpful behaviors.

For example, let us take the South Pointe School in Miami Beach, Florida. As in most schools, the teachers and the principal had worked together for a long time, even decades. They all knew how the principal "operated" the school and how teachers related to him.

Suddenly, there was a major change. In response to complaints that children were neither learning nor being stimulated, South Pointe was selected as the first public school in the country to be managed by a private company. South Pointe became a very public trial of educational reform.

How would the teachers and principal fare in a very different form of education? In a report in *The New York Times,* we learn a little about the pilot school:

> The school has no traditional classrooms in the sense of having desks arranged in a row and teacher up front. In fact, it is often difficult to locate the front, since desks are arranged in geometric patterns of scattered groups.
>
> The 720 students are divided into four mini schools or communities, each made up of one class from each grade, pre-kindergarten through sixth. Each community gathers at the start of each day to sing together, play and mingle.

Not only has the faculty in this pilot school, the Educational Alternative, built a very different pattern for working together in communities, in small groups, and with flexible boundaries to become a "mature" group, but think of the impact it has on other schools. The entire system is being disrupted—if children in the pilot school benefit from being part of a mini-community and it enhances their sense of being part of a larger system, then teachers in other schools should be thinking about how they can provide the same for their students. If children in the pilot school are learning to read by teachers using highly creative methods, then other teachers are faced with the pressure to have their children perform equally as well. The behaviors of teachers suddenly being held to a different standard may range from rising to the challenge to becoming repressed, angry and dogmatic. There may be frequent conflict about how much their school should change and how much they will be influenced by the pilot school.

Confronted with a controversial new idea, any group can enter a period when lines of communication break down, feelings and emotions are denied, and tensions build. Such tensions quite often are released through hostility directed toward other members, thus creating further points of stress.

Some groups never develop the feedback channels or problem-solving mechanisms that allow them to mature and function smoothly. Such groups remain predictably volatile or passive, trapped in a nonproductive pattern without the tools to extricate themselves. In most such groups, members realize that things are not "right" but may be unable to ask the tough questions necessary to gain perspective. Where this is the case, groups (perhaps like in the schools in our example) simply muddle along in their daily routines with little hope for growth or significant improvement.

It is not a sign of group immaturity that such tensions develop, but the degree of maturity is revealed in how effectively the group is able to cope with these very natural problems. A new, influential person being added to the group will be a threat to some members' security, for some a potential ally, and for others a competitive rival for leadership in the group. Because personal needs as well as various levels of the group's working relationships are involved, conflict is inevitable. Too many groups deny the various reasons for the increased tensions, assume conflict is destructive, and attempt to proceed as though nothing has happened. This denial begins to undermine existing levels of trust. A mature group will stop the deteriorating cycle of events by openly exploring the possible causal factors and then providing at least temporary solutions during the period of adjustment. Confronting the issues that tend to debilitate the group reinforces a norm of positive and constructive problem solving, and this will reduce the length and intensity of the regressive cycle.

Groups, like people, can become immobilized at certain levels or stages of their development. Some individuals can never break away from dependency on their parents, and it carries into nearly every other relationship they have. Others fail to resolve their own need to fight authority. Still others cannot tolerate conflict and the fear of being rejected. In a similar manner, some groups never move beyond a particular stage of development because of various unresolved issues among the members or external factors beyond their control. Whatever the reason, such groups find it difficult to reach an adequate level of functioning. For example, many groups develop a norm that inhibits the expression of anger. As a result, many emotions are bottled up, and the group remains at an artificial level of interaction where harmony inhibits the development of authenticity. Similarly, compromise may become a mechanism for escaping the true resolution of issues. Instead of tensions being reduced, they are increased by the passive behaviors used to cope with individual feelings of anger and aggression.

The concept of *situational leadership* (see Chapter 5) has particular relevance in such circumstances. A situational leader might, for instance, identify the factors impeding a "stuck" group and intervene in its process to enable growth and development to occur. Maturity evolves from the group's skill development, practice, and ability to provide itself with the support and experience required at the time. If the leader fails to view the group developmentally and situationally, the group may lose the opportunity to mature by these means (Carew, Eunice, and Blanchard, 1986).

Other Views of Group Development

Forming, Storming, Norming, Performing, and Adjourning

On the basis of a twenty-year review of the literature related to group development in therapy, natural, self-study, and laboratory groups, Tuckman and Jensen (1977) concluded that task groups, like all others, go through five basic stages of development that are rather predictable.

A first stage, *forming,* incorporates all the discomfort found in any new situation in which one's ego is involved in new relationships. This initial period of caution is followed by a period of predictable *storming,* as individuals react to the demands of what has to be done, question authority, and feel increasingly comfortable being themselves. A third stage is defined as *norming,* in which the rules of behavior appropriate and necessary for the group to accomplish the task are spelled out both explicitly and implicitly, and a greater degree of order begins to prevail. Next comes a period of *performing,* in which people are able to focus their energies on the task, having worked through issues of membership, orientation, leadership, and roles. The group is now free to develop working alternatives to the problems confronting it, and a climate of support tends to remain from the norming stage. Finally, with the task nearing completion, the group moves into what is called the *adjourning* period, in which closure to the task and a changing of relationships is anticipated.

Although some believe it is most difficult to consider the development of a group without stressing the interdependency of task and maintenance or process functions, Tuckman and Jensen found it helpful to view each of the stages from two points of view. The first is that of interpersonal relationships. Thus the group moves through predictable stages of testing and dependency (forming), tension and conflict (storming), building cohesion (norming), and, finally, establishing functional role relationships (performing) before it adjourns. Each of these substages focuses on the problems inherent in developing relationships among members.

At the same time, the group is struggling with the problems of the task. In light of this, the initial stage focuses on task definition, boundaries, and the exchange of functional information (forming), followed by a natural emotional response to the task (storming), a period of sharing interpretations and perspectives (norming) before a stage of emergent solutions is reached (performing).

A Task View of Group Development

Paul Hare and David Naveh (1984, pp. 299–318) spent years researching crucial and predictable stages in the development of small groups. According to Hare, in every problem-solving group there are four identifiable stages (Hare and Naveh, 1984, 68–69). The first phase, called L, stands for *latent* pattern maintenance and tension reduction. It is marked by the group's natural need to reach agreement as to its purposes, work methods, expectations, and participant obligations. This agreement reduces the inevitable tensions surrounding the group's direction, priorities, and maintenance in the problem-solving process.

The second phase, A, involves what Hare refers to as *adaptation*. During this phase, the group generates critical information necessary to solving the problem at hand. It lays out facts and identifies the necessary skills and resources required for eventual solution. Also, participants identify and take on essential roles that are key to the problem-solving effort.

Integration (I) is the focus of the third phase. This phase requires flexibility, reassessment, and innovation on the part of members and leaders alike as they struggle to compromise and create the alternatives necessary to move the group into the final phase—*goal* attainment (G).

The whole process—LAIG—is the pattern of expected development in a successful problem-solving group. In describing this pattern, Hare noted that the phases are not necessarily linear but rather may recur at different points and may also incorporate significant subphases.

Hare and Naveh tested this paradigm against the 1978 Camp David Summit, during which the presidents of Israel and Egypt, with the help of President Carter of the United States, forged the Camp David Accords. The four-phase pattern of group development did indeed occur at Camp David, according to the investigators' careful documentation of events. As Hare and Naveh described the summit, President Carter was able to facilitate agreement between President Sadat and Prime Minister Begin because of his intuitive understanding of the process of group problem solving and the interventions necessary to move the group through its natural stages. There is some evidence that both Sadat and Begin probably believed the talks would collapse and that each was prepared to repudiate the other side. When, however, a draft proposal resolved the major differences, the role of the key leaders had to change to support the peace process in deed and not just word. This became the crisis that Hare called "the revolution within the revolution" of the third, or integration, phase.

Leaders who understand the theory of group development, especially in task groups, can visualize the process as predictable and "normal" and respond to resistance by developing new alternatives rather than meeting it with ignorance and defeatism. Recent work by Fisher and Stutman (1987), in which critical "break points" were identified and a process described for moving a group through natural points of resistance, supported the kinds of intuitive interventions Carter made in facilitating the negotiation process. Future research into this area will be welcomed.

FIRO: A Theory of Interpersonal Behavior

William Schutz (1966) developed a theory of interpersonal behavior derived from a psychoanalytic orientation. The theory is called fundamental interpersonal relations orientation (FIRO). As the name indicates, the theory attempts to explain interpersonal behavior in terms of orientation toward others. The theory holds that people orient themselves toward others in certain characteristic patterns that are major determinants of interpersonal behavior.

According to the theory, each individual has three interpersonal needs. The first is *inclusion:* a desire to belong, to be involved, to be part of, *or* the opposite—a desire to be left alone, to be overlooked. The second need is for *control:* a desire to dominate, to be influential, to lead, and to persuade, *or* the opposite—a desire to be led, directed, to be guided, to follow. The third interpersonal need is for *affection:* a desire to be intimate, to form close interpersonal attachments, to express warmth and attachment, *or* the opposite—a desire to be distant, to be aloof, or to dislike. Each individual possesses a certain configuration of these needs and behaves in a manner that enhances her or his satisfaction of them.

A group develops in phases that repeat individual needs. In the first phase, *inclusion,* the question is how involved individuals will be, how prominent. What will the relationship with the leader be? How dependent? What are the group boundaries? Who's "in" and who's "out"?

The next phase is about *control* (power and influence). Now the group encounters a stage of conflict as it deals with issues of interpersonal dominance. Issues that come to the fore involve leadership, competition, and the amount of structure. How will decisions be made? If in phase one the issues can be thought of as "in or out", in phase two the issues center on "top or bottom."

In the third phase, *affection,* the group becomes increasingly concerned with intermember harmony, while intermember differences recede in the service of group cohesiveness. In this phase there are expressions of positive feelings, emotional support, extensions of friendship, and close personal attachment. For some, this is smothering. Within the group each person looks for a comfortable position in terms of the extent of giving and receiving affection. The third phase is characterized by concern about "near or far." The primary anxieties have to do with being liked, with being close enough to people or being too close.

Much later, the mature group emerges. It exhibits by high cohesiveness, considerable interpersonal investigation, and a full commitment to the primary task of the group and to each of its members. (Yalom, 1985).

The phases are not distinct. Schutz uses the metaphor of replacing a wheel on a car: one tightens the bolts one after another, just enough so that the wheel is in place. Then the process is repeated, each bolt being tightened in turn, until the wheel is entirely secure (p. 170). In a similar way, phases of a group emerge, come to the fore, and then recede only to have the group return later to deal with these same issues again at greater depth.

Schutz says that at termination of the group, the phase process recurs but in reverse. There is less involvement with closeness and intimacy, then a reduction in concerns of control and dominance, and finally diffusion of boundaries and cessation.

This model is frequently used in therapy groups.

Phase Movement of Groups

There are essentially two approaches to how groups change over time. One approach, which might be called a *sequential-stage* theory, specifies the typical order of phases. The Tuckman and Hare theories are such theories.

Yet another approach is that of *recurring phases*. Such theories specify issues that dominate group interaction and recur again and again.

Robert F. Bales (Bales, 1950, p. 195); (Borgatta and Bales, 1953) developed the first really effective system for observing group interaction directly. Bales developed a system of interaction process analysis (IPA) that combined a structured set of categories for observation and a set of theoretical concepts underlying these categories.

The underlying idea of IPA is that problem-solving groups (groups with a purpose, goal, or task) are continually faced with two related but distinct concerns: task-oriented concerns associated with the effort to accomplish the group task and socio-emotional concerns related to the relationships among members. Both of these areas of concern operate continually. The group's devoting attention and effort to one of these may produce strain on the other. Spending time on member relationships takes time away from the task. Time invested in the task takes time away from members' interpersonal "work."

According to Bales's theoretical structure, there is an orderly series of phases involved in the task-oriented activities of problem-solving groups, and a parallel cycle of phases characterizes socio-emotional behavior.

There are three problem-solving steps: orientation (gathering information and clarifying what the task is), evaluation (assessing that information), and control (deciding what to do). As the group moves through its task efforts, it follows a predictable pattern. Orientation is highest at the beginning and declines as the session progresses. Evaluation (opinions, thoughts, wishes) rises from the beginning to the middle of the session, then declines. Control (decision making) is low at the beginning and rises to its highest at the end of the session.

At the same time, in the continuing task/socio-emotional equilibrium process, there is a phase process in the socio-emotional level. There is less emotion on the orientation level, it increases during the evaluation stage, and it is most dominant, with the greatest tension, when the group is in the control phase. This increased strain is reflected in an increase in negative reactions. Efforts to deal with this strain bring an increase in positive reactions through the course of the session.

As a consequence, both positive and negative reactions increase from beginning to end, though they still account for a smaller proportion than task-related acts. Both positive and negative reactions reach their highest level in the last phase, but positive reactions in the form of tension release and expressions of solidarity predominate at the very end in successful problem-solving groups.

The Bales system has been especially effective, because the theory can be confirmed in observing a group over a session and over time and by analyzing the group in terms of its phase movement and its problem-solving success.

◆ Reader Activity

Like individuals whose lifestyles become routinized, groups too can become predictable. Instead of moving through certain developmental stages, members of a group will find themselves caught in one stage and unable able to move beyond it.

Can you think of a group of which you are a member that is stuck in a particular developmental phase and for some reason is not able to move ahead? What is the cost to the group of being immobilized?

In contrast, are you aware of a group that is not stuck—that is active and evolving? What makes it different from the first group? What are the factors that allow it to grow and develop? Is there any chance that it may become blocked like the first?

What are you doing as a member of the first group to help sustain its inertia? What can you and others do to move it to a more productive level of activity?

◆

The Family: A Microcosm

In recent years, systems theory—discussed in detail in Chapter 6—has provided a window into how groups evolve. And the most productive area of work has originated in family therapy. Nowhere has the emphasis moved more dramatically and more conclusively away from the simplistic cause–effect relationship.

Over the last 25 years, a wealth of theories and practices have yielded creative insights into the most common of all groups—the family.[2] Goldenberg and Goldenberg (1980, p. 9) sum up the relationship between the individual and the system as follows:

> Family therapy offers a broader view of human behavior than does individual therapy. The "identified patient," the person sent initially for help, does not remain the central focus of therapy for long. Rather, the family begins to understand that his or her problems or symptoms are an expression of the entire family's system. Problems get related within a family framework as relationship difficulties. Within such a system's prospective viewpoint, the locus of pathology is not the individual but rather the individual in context, and the individual's experiences and subsequent behavior patterns begin to change. The focus of family therapy is in changing the system—the family's characteristic pattern of interacting with one another, their style and manner of communication, the structure of their relationships—so that each member experiences a sense of independence, uniqueness, and wholeness while remaining within the context and security of the family relationship.

It is possible to learn much about small groups in general by looking at the family. Most of us are naturally fascinated by families because most have been part of these intense nuclear groups and can readily perceive their impact on ourselves and others close to us. The bridge from family systems to those of groups we encounter in business, education, and religious and social organizations is a short one.

The Ultimate Small Group

Our responses to the dynamics of virtually any group originate in our personal family experiences. In other words, our attitudes about leaders, co-workers, partners, and subordinates are shaped by our attitudes about and behavior toward our parents, siblings, spouses, and children. Sadly, just as parents are ill trained in understanding the enormous complexities of family development, so leaders are often ill equipped to understand their own groups as they evolve.

Further, how group members, both leaders and nonleaders, cope with the process of family life will have direct implications on how they go about solving problems in other groups. For example, the ability to handle conflict among our children, plan a trip, conduct a family meeting, or deal with in-laws whose values diverge from our own, and our ways of budgeting our time, handling financial problems, dealing with religious differences, and developing social relationships are all re-

2. A sample of these authors and their work includes Ackerman (1958, 1970), Beavers (1977), Bell (1978), Bodin (1969), Foley (1974), Friesen (1985), Goldenberg and Goldenberg (1980), Haley (1976), Minnchin (1974), and Satir (1967).

flected in our ability to handle related issues within the work place. For this reason, in the following subsections we will compare dysfunctional and functional family groups and explore their implications for other group settings. From a systems perspective, we are seeking to determine what throws a family or other group out of homeostatic equilibrium. Thus some of the problems that dominated family therapy a few years ago, such as infidelity, the acting-out child, sexual impotence, and the abused child or spouse, have come to be treated as elements of a more comprehensive exploration of the family scene. In a similar fashion, strikes, low quality and productivity, absenteeism, low morale, and even sexual harassment tend to be symptoms of larger, more complex problems that can block the development of a business or educational system.

Natural Cycles and Blocks to Development in Families

Previously, in our study of systems theory, we analyzed an organization that had been created to develop new products and, in the process, indicated that it would like to become an ideal company. It all sounded good on paper—like two lovers expressing goodwill, affection, and harmony along with values of cooperation, sharing, and honesty. Who would possibly deny these? Yet, in spite of goodwill and the most positive of intentions, the new business system had neither the skills nor the self-understanding to pull off its dream.

Despite their plans for a happy future, many couples lack the skill and understanding to realize their dreams. The need for conflict-resolution skills usually surfaces with recognition that the individuals hold values and expectations that differ greatly despite their love for each other and their mutual desire for a perfect relationship. How the two resolve the differences that arise in the formative year of their relationship will set the tone and often the structure of the entire relationship.

The excitement of creating a new small business is analogous to that suffusing the beginning of a love affair. The impatience to get on with building the product and seeking profits is overwhelming, and it is easy to overlook the norms, roles, and expectations developing in those early days. As in the love relationship, early problem-solving efforts will affect the success of the organization profoundly. Taking time for true collaboration, for developing two-way communication, and for insuring that proper mechanisms for feedback exist can help determine later degrees of success or failure. But poor problem-solving skills and early failures will have more immediate consequences in the next natural developmental stage in the family- or group-development cycle.

Expanding the Family Unit

For many couples, having a child may seem to be an "enabling" experience that allows the full expression of marital respect, sharing, cooperation, and all the other family virtues. More often, however, this period represents a major trauma, a disturbance of the sensitive balance created in the earliest stage of the relationship. Suddenly, all the carefully developed rules change again, and the new third party puts stress on the fundamental relationship of the couple. How this stress is handled becomes critical. Good problem-solving skills may well turn the imbalance into a chance for growth and self-discovery, but weak problem-solving skills can lead to serious schisms.

If the family system is open to new ideas, positive energy, and feedback, and if clear channels of communication exist, then the arrival of the new baby will stimulate the system to new levels of effectiveness (steady state). But if, as often happens, communication breaks down, then new ideas are shut out, problem solving becomes entangled with issues of power and influence, and issues of membership (usually never articulated) arise. Any discord that originated in the formative stage will widen, and the family's overall vulnerability will increase. In each of these eventualities, the analogy between family and small group holds true.

Further Disruption

Clearly, critical events in the life of the system, be it family or small group, disrupt the temporary balance and force members to change. How they adapt to changing demands will determine whether an event will initiate a stimulating and engaging stage of growth or result in a divisive and debilitating response. Any organization consciously aware of a critical impending event would be misguided not to give time and attention to potential consequences. Such a proactive approach will stimulate growth and differentiation of the family group. Yet people often sit back and avoid asking the hard questions and anticipating the consequences of predictably traumatic events. This almost always ensures some degree of failure because the resulting "crisis reactive" approach to change inevitably reduces choices and contributes to later problems.

Certainly parallels exist in other groups where a decision to expand (the arrival of new staff/children, issues of membership, roles, goals), the appearance of a new CEO on the scene, the reorganization of a business, the death of a critical employee, or a strike action can affect every part of the organization. These major events generate life energy of their own and can have long-lasting implications for the group. Simply trying to muddle through and acting as though such powerful occurrences were "business as usual" is to give in to the forces that can break a group apart from within.

The Development of a Healthy Family System

Trying to define an "ideal" or "perfect" group is to walk on very thin ice. Nevertheless, it is worth the risk, because it allows us to explore certain dimensions of group behavior that can result in a productive work climate where both emotional and task needs are addressed. Further, such a discussion can, at the very least, yield a basis for comparison in the evaluation of working groups. Special circumstances and particular demands apply to specific groups, but certain conditions appear to operate in *all* successful groups.

In families in particular, because they are so diverse and complex in their backgrounds, any qualities that can be isolated as characterizing health and good function are important. And, again, such characteristics have value in the analysis of other small group systems.

In 1986, Stinnett and Defrain published their book *Secrets of Strong Families.* They began by identifying 130 families, recommended by state extension agents, who scored high on the Family Strengths Inventory. These were families who scored high on "marital happiness" and on good parent–child relations. After the pilot group, 3,000 additional families were studied, 10 percent extensively. The study included a wide range of economic and educational levels; many religions; blacks, Hispanics, and Caucasians; and persons ranging in age from the twenties to the mid-sixties.

What are strong families? The authors explain that family strength is "more than being without problems; strong families have problems. It is the presence in the family of important guidelines . . . and the ability as a family to surmount life's inevitable challenges when they arise."

As might be expected, the researchers did not isolate any single quality as more important than any other. Rather than a "single thread," the authors suggested a tapestry of qualities that distinguish strong families. The same qualities are equally useful in describing any well-functioning small group or organization. The following are the distinctive qualities in the "tapestry":

Commitment   Members of strong families are dedicated to working together and promoting each other's welfare. In a group, this means working cooperatively to achieve a goal and recognizing each person as having resources that contribute to the group.

Communication   Members have good communication skills and spend a lot of time talking to each other. This means, at a group level, talking about interpersonal matters as well as task issues. It means the open sharing of information in a direct and specific manner. Differences of opinion seem welcomed, and bringing clarity to these differences seems crucial.

Appreciation   Members show appreciation and support of each other. Members are encouraged to express their feelings and emotions, and this authenticity and supportiveness are important.

Coping Ability   Members view stress and crisis as opportunities to grow. They see something positive in the crisis and focus on the positive elements. They unite to face the challenges of a crisis and ask how they can help. They work to minimize fragmentation, set priorities, and simplify. Groups too must cope with challenges, stressors, and problems. Working together to achieve the goal or overcome the obstacles can generate new energy and forge a stronger group. People are working as part of a whole while maintaining their individuality.

Other studies (Lewis, Beavers, Gossett and Phillips, 1976) of healthy families add that parents (leaders) model clear roles of authority, although their "power" is not used in an arbitrary or rigid manner. Quite the contrary: they solicit the ideas and opinions of other family members, and a healthy sense of negotiation and compromise emerges as members share their interests and concerns. In dysfunctional families, by contrast, there is less differentiation among individuals, less flexibility, and a greater sense of control for its own sake. In functional families, family members share responsibilities, individuals have a relatively clear understanding of their places in the family community, and both authority and individuality are honored.

In general, strong families express warmth, caring, and commitment to working together and dealing with problems. They have stress and conflict, but they tend to deal with these experiences openly and promptly, looking at alternatives and solutions that make sense to all members.

It is evident from the many views we have outlined that group development is a complex process. The precise nature and sequence of development vary with the kind of group, the context in which the group functions, the goals of the group, and other factors. It is not surprising, then, that different theorists see varying numbers of stages, attach different labels to similar processes, and emphasize different aspects of the group. Despite these differences, there are basic similarities across groups. In most groups, there is a period of orientation (deciding what the group is about and how it will function), followed by a period of conflict related to personal and authority issues among members. These are then resolved, and the group achieves a productive state in which the energies of group members are channeled into goal attainment. The length of time each stage lasts may vary, stages may recur, and some groups may not be able to resolve their difficulties, but an understanding of the general process is essential in working effectively with groups.

◆ Reader Activity

Take 30 minutes (not more, despite the natural temptation) to ask your father, mother, or both the following questions:

1. When you were married, what were the greatest adjustments you had to make in order to maintain a balanced and happy relationship? How difficult was it? What did you learn?

2. Once your first child came, what problems of adjustment did you experience? What were your strongest feelings and what changes occurred in your relationship?

3. Think back over your family life. What other major events forced changes of significant proportions in your relationship? Would you respond differently now?   ◆

Facilitating Group Success

Whether you are a member of a group or are in a position of leadership, it is your responsibility to help the group function effectively and accomplish its goal. Being aware of factors that influence the successful development of a group will put you in a better position to make an effective contribution. Each of the methods for viewing the development of a task group can arm you with the questions to ask in order to understand what is happening, what is needed, and how to help the group. Thus it is essential to be aware of how the group is developing, to know where deviations are occurring, to realize what tensions can be expected, and to understand what might facilitate the group's passage through a particular stage.

Similarly, it is important to consider the implications of critical incidents that may influence the development of the group. This information, as well as insight into essential group needs, will provide anyone with the essential tools for understanding. It will provoke useful questions for gathering data and testing personal hypotheses. At this point, as a member and/or leader, you will be aware of alternatives and begin to sense your own ability to influence the group. Individuals who feel impotent or victimized as members of a small group seldom have a framework for looking at and conceptualizing the group as a developing entity. Obviously, it requires some skill to translate theory into constructive action, but understanding the theory is the first critical step (Gist et al., 1987).

◆ *Reader Activity*

Pick a group in which you participate and pay attention to the process of one meeting during which the whole group is present. How do people talk? Who talks? What is the emotional tone of the conversation? From the way group members interact, can you determine what theme—anxiety, power, norms, interpersonal relationships, personal growth—is in the foreground? Can you determine what stage—forming, storming, norming, performing, adjourning—the group appears to be in? What in the process of the group leads you to your conclusions? Do these interpersonal issues appear to be inhibiting the group's effort to accomplish its goals? If so, what do you think the group should do to manage these issues productively?   ◆

Seeking the Ideal

As we have suggested throughout this section, the qualities of a functional family characterize small work groups of any sort. The community-building retreat described in Chapter 1 is a good example. One of the first tasks each group on retreat tackles is defining the elements of an ideal community. Among the 24 members of the most recent group were a bank president, a student from China, an actress, an environmental educator, an author, a secondary school teacher, an athletic director, a doctor, a therapist, a carpenter, a homemaker, and a social worker. To their surprise, the participants were able to come to an agreement in a mere 30 minutes. These are the qualities they agreed their ideal community would have:

- shared leadership
- the open communication of all relevant information
- channels for listening and being heard
- the soliciting of feelings and ideas
- a sense of equality among all members
- a climate of openness and trust
- collaborative problem solving—especially involving those having to live with the decisions
- shared labor in menial tasks
- respect for nature and the environment
- opportunities for play and celebration
- ways of dealing with conflict when it arises and before it builds
- the willingness to provide personal feedback to members of the community
- the valuing of personal growth and development
- time to be alone

The challenge for the group would lie not in agreeing on the characteristics of an ideal community but in evolving to a state where such ideas could take precedence over personal needs, biases, and vested interests. This community, after all, would be built on individual differences and egos, interpersonal conflict, differing goals and priorities, varying standards and levels of need, and a hundred unanticipated variables that could create system dysfunction. The group found that it needed patience, discipline, and care to resolve problems so that the common ideals could eventually be experienced.

Most work groups and families only glimpse the possibilities outlined by the retreat group. They are either unskilled in creating a functional and responsive group or unwilling to devote the time required to do so. Without the tools (skills) or time to deal with issues that arise, the members are unable to stop the inevitable "noise" or entropy (See Chapter 6 on systems) because the necessary problem solving does not occur. Typical groups collude in not spending the necessary time or in not dealing with the conflicts that arise (Obert, 1983). Further, they collude not to agree on goals, communicate on issues of membership, or share in problem solving. The result of such agreement *not* to agree is disharmony and eventual dysfunction. Building a functional group does not require expert knowledge or a college degree, but it does require the desire and discipline to look beyond one's self to analyze events and to follow the basic rules of productive human relations (Allcorn, 1985).

Positive Structured Interventions

An increasing body of research confirms the belief that carefully designed interventions into a working group can alter levels of problem-solving effectiveness, cohesion, risk taking, and productivity (Bednar and Battersby, 1976; Evensen, 1976; Hall and Williams, 1970; Stogdill, 1972). Although much of this work is in the formative stages and there are still more questions than answers, it seems appropriate to explore some of the tentative findings here.

In one series of studies exploring the impact of structure on self-study groups, it was noted that "empirical evidence supports structure as a robust variable which positively affects interpersonal behavior, group attraction and client improvement" (Evensen, 1976, p. 152). Thus, in groups whose purpose was to explore the nature of group behavior and interpersonal relationships, effectively placed structural interventions by leaders allowed various group goals to be attained more rapidly, even though leaders in such groups traditionally are a focus of group attention, anxiety, and frustration. More specifically, it was found that providing more structure encouraged members to risk more and be more disclosing of feelings and attitudes and, as a result, increased the level of measured cohesion in the group. Apparently, the structure gave members legitimate permission to say what was on their minds. This is particularly promising because individuals measured as low risk takers were consistently nudged toward greater participation and involvement. The lack of structure in groups can be destructive because it activates individual regressive trends, which can result in less productive and less mature behavior (Kernberg, 1980).

There is further corroboration for small group structure being helpful, in this case, in aiding students. Harvard conducted a five year study on what constitutes effective teaching and learning (*The New York Times*, 1991). One of the major findings of the study was that students learned more effectively when they worked in small groups in classes and that they were more successful at retaining and integrating what they had learned when they studied in small groups.

Finally, there is increasing evidence that groups given specific training in problem solving tend to be more effective. A study by Hall and Williams (1970) implies that groups can translate such learnings directly into their work efforts. Thus large numbers of working groups performed work of higher quality on new tasks of a similar nature after training in a rational approach to problem solving. This simply supports what many group facilitators have learned from experience. Groups that are provided appropriate structure, models for work, experience in problem solving, and guidelines for maintaining their own process tend to perform with less tension and with greater productivity than groups that do not receive such support (Reddi, 1983).

Maximizing the Group's Potential

The effective group leader or member tends to have an awareness of the group, its needs, and its present level of development. Just a few probing questions, a structure for observing, and the willingness to look carefully at what is happening are all that one needs to contribute to the group's effectiveness. Understanding the stages of development, group needs, and critical events that may occur in any working group increases the possibility of responding in appropriate and constructive ways that may facilitate or unblock a group and help it be more effective. The most frustrated members of groups are those who fail to understand what is happening and feel victimized by what may be a predictable course of events. Knowledge of developmental trends allows for a proactive rather than a defensive response and brings some modicum of control back to those privy to such insight.

Few people have ever experienced the ideal working group, with the participative approach outlined earlier in the discussion of the conditions facilitating people's involvement in groups. Nevertheless, knowledge of these qualities provides a basis for comparison as well as ideas for improvement. Developing such a working climate is rare indeed, because ignorance rather than awareness of effective group process is the rule, not the exception. It can be likened to being in a foreign country where everything appears to be familiar but it seems next to impossible to communicate effectively. Most of us are used to strong leaders who control rewards, establish the ground rules of a particular task, and provide the necessary push to get the job done. We expect to be directed, motivated, intellectual, impersonal, and rational in our approach to problem solving.

As a result, we tend to see ourselves as alienated from the group, often competing with other members for recognition and responding to authority rather than to member peers. Such a climate is not conducive to establishing free and open communication, role flexibility, and a truly nonpunitive atmosphere. It is this kind of atmosphere that helps predetermine the kind of development possible for a group. We are used to being dependent and, even if we do not like it, often demand behaviors from those in control that insure our dependence. Even when a work group is responsive to democratic principles, members too often become the victims of the majority vote—the conflict-reducing option that, if used indiscriminately, may polarize a group and erase the vital thread of compromise on which the effective decision-making group must be based.

If a group has never had experience outside the confines of a rigid time schedule, agenda, and parliamentary procedure, it is doubtful that it will ever develop the trust necessary for processing its own behaviors or the interdependence necessary to see issues as other than politically expedient and strategic. Certainly decisions will be made and groups will function, sometimes in an extraordinarily efficient manner. The price paid, however, may be in terms of participant involvement, interest, cooperation, and member accountability. Staw, Sandelands, and Dutton (1981) report the rigidity effects on a small group from an external threat. They identify a restriction in information processing and a constriction of control when the group experiences a threat. The interpersonal needs for involvement and influence are downplayed in such incidents. Like a growing child, the group responds best to patience, freedom within limits, concerns from others, and a climate that encourages spontaneity and authenticity. It is a mixture that varies from group to group, and intangibles often spell the difference between success and failure. Yet, more and more success can be insured if the leader–facilitator is able to formulate the necessary questions to help him or her understand the group with which he or she is to work. This, added to a familiarity with diagnostic techniques and a few basic approaches to working with the task and emotional problems that inevitably face any working group, is essential. Much more than the use of gimmicks and techniques, success seems geared to how effectively the group is able to respond to its very human needs in a manner that exploits no one and maximizes its own potential.

We are becoming increasingly familiar with the value of positive, structured interventions into the life of a working group that can facilitate its development, improve cohesion, open communication, and reduce the threat of participant risk taking while improving the quality of problem solving. The biggest drawback now is convincing those individuals who are stuck in ineffective patterns of leadership that both they and the group will benefit from the adoption of these new approaches.

◆ ◆ EXERCISE 1

Creating a Theory of Group Development from Experience

Objectives

- To explore the developmental aspects that seem to occur in most groups
- To help the participants think conceptually and organize their learnings into a meaningful and systematic analysis of groups and their development

Setting

This activity will be explained in terms of (a) an ideal and (b) the average or common situation.

Ideal The study of groups should ideally be done over a period of time that allows individual participants to internalize their insights from experience and practice within a developing conceptual framework. Learning about groups is often facilitated when individuals are placed with members they do not know and, over a period of weeks, are asked to participate in various tasks. Given time and a variety of experiences together, a certain pattern of development begins to be evident. This is especially true if the group is expected to work toward goals that they must decide, to make decisions in light of the decision-making procedures they create, to generate participant roles as a result of the changing needs of the group, and to establish patterns of communication and leadership that reflect these changing needs. Such leaderless groups are able to develop important understandings about group process if a facilitator is available occasionally to help them look closely at a particular issue or concept that they might not naturally focus on without assistance. Thus a few hours a week over a period of several months can be most helpful in developing a clear perspective on group development. This, of course, is not to say that intensive time blocks together are not also valuable, only that it is difficult to grasp the significance of all that is happening in a short time period.

Average   Most often it seems that groups do not have the time to gain a conceptual understanding of how groups operate. They are usually brought together for a short (perhaps intensive) period, and it is hoped that they "get something out of it."

This particular exercise is aimed more particularly at groups that have had the opportunity to work and learn together and those that have some understanding of what to look for in terms of the process of working groups. For the purpose of this example, it is assumed that three small groups have worked together over a period of weeks, both as a single large group and as individual work groups of perhaps seven to nine members.

Step 1. Three new groups from seven to nine participants are created. They are composed of from two or three members from each of the old working groups. The facilitator gives the three groups the following task:

As a group, look over your experiences of the past several months (weeks, days) and develop a theory of group development that may be applied to many new groups as their members work over a period of time to become effective problem solvers. Are there particular stages of development that most new groups seem to move through? Can certain behaviors be expected from the members? You will have 60 to 90 minutes to build your group development theory and present it to the total group (all three groups in this case) in some graphic manner. For example, you may wish to present your ideas using pictures, develop a skit, or design another method for transferring your ideas to the other participants.

Note   It is very important that the groups have enough time, because the tendency is to spend considerable time discussing what has happened to them in their own groups and little time attempting to integrate it into a theoretical framework. Thus, at the end of 45 minutes, the groups should be warned that they have only about 20 or 30 minutes to complete their task and be ready to make their presentation. This usually leads to the same kinds of problems that arise in most decision-making groups under pressure—forced decisions and reduced participation.

Step 2. At the end of an hour to an hour and a half, the groups are asked to make their presentations. It is important to keep the presentations to no more than ten minutes and preferably closer to five. (The groups should be made aware of this during their planning because it pressures them to make a more precise presentation.) At the end of this time, it is most helpful for the facilitator to integrate many of the ideas presented and supplement them with theoretical concepts about development with which he or she is familiar and that seem appropriate to the discussion.

Step 3. The three groups that started the day and from which the three theories were generated are reconvened. They are given 30 minutes to process their own work together. The group discusses what they saw occur and how they feel about it. They also may wish to analyze what happened in terms of the theory developed from the total resources of the three groups. They are asked to compare the new groups with the performance of their old groups.

Step 4. Briefly, the three groups are asked to share with all the groups any learnings they gained from the last discussion. The facilitator may wish to explore how many of the characteristics of long-term group development can be seen in the initial phases of a new group in a problem-solving situation.

Variation

With a group that is interested in group process but has not worked together before, it is possible to give the same instructions, suggesting that they look at groups with which they have worked in the past. Such experiences too hold keys to useful theory, and they will also generate important data that can later be analyzed in terms of the theory that is developed.

◆ ◆ EXERCISE 2

Maslow's Hierarchy of Needs[3]

Objectives

- To help a group begin to understand the kinds of restraints inhibiting individual members
- To focus on the emotional aspects of group process
- To provide a theoretical framework of reference for understanding the group process
- To create open communication and feedback in a group

3. Adapted from Maslow, 1954.

Rationale

According to A. H. Maslow, individuals tend to pass through certain stages of development, and the focus of their needs tends to change. How a person acts in a given situation depends partly on the demands and uniqueness of the moment and partly on the general developmental level at which the individual is functioning. It is not that we ever are able to satisfy all of our needs; in fact, even as mature adults many are still unsatisfied. The point is that as we mature developmentally, from childhood through adulthood, the focus of our needs and our ability to see beyond them change. Thus the first year or so of a baby's life is dominated by physiological needs. But even though a preoccupation with such things as food, water, and sex are brought under rational control, there are times when even the most mature individuals feel the overpowering push of some physiological need. Similarly, the growing child is often overly concerned about the safety of his or her environment. Whether he or she is safe from harm or threat can prove to be a dominant theme in his or her developmental system of needs. For the adult, however, familiarity and experience have provided the feeling of safety except in unusual crisis situations. Actually, it is the higher-order needs such as love and self-esteem that seem most difficult for people to handle. If these needs were met to a satisfactory degree, people would no longer have to expend a great amount of time fulfilling them at a period in their lives when they should be able to accept themselves as they are and concentrate on developing their own potentials. Included with this exercise is the well-known Maslow diagram of hierarchical needs.

Theoretically, a person moves upward with a tendency to satisfy one level of need before tackling the next. It is a rare person who feels fulfilled in the areas of love and self-esteem. How few are the people who are able to give and accept love and feel unconditionally accepted. Even fewer have resolved the needs to dominate and control, to achieve and be important.

Setting

In any group there are individuals who are controlled to some degree by their own needs in one of these areas. The person who blatantly says, "Why can't we be open here and just say what we really feel?" is either completely unaware of the forces restricting an individual's ability to be open or is sending up a smoke screen to hide his or her own apprehensions. Personal needs act as an important inhibiting factor in the communication and development of any group. This in itself is neither good nor bad, merely an important reality. When individuals within a group push too rapidly for openness, being personal, and freely giving feedback, it may lead to considerable pain as the group struggles to protect itself from itself. People do not wish to be rejected or to fail in a particular task. Thus most will play it relatively safe. Sometimes it is important to help a group gain new respect for the various levels at which people operate. If such is the case, this exercise may provide some insights. This particular activity assumes that the facilitator is in some sort of authority role and wields considerable influence. It also assumes that he or she is willing to be open about his or her own role and willing to alter his or her own behavior if it will benefit the functioning of the group.

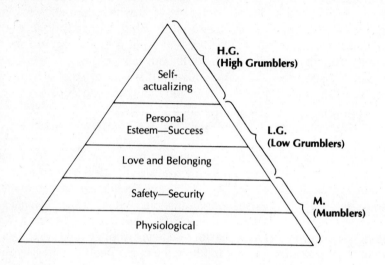

Action

The group is broken into trios to discuss specifically the role of the facilitator, his or her strengths and limitations (with examples), and how he or she might improve his or her role in ways that would facilitate the working of the group. After the initial groan, an unusually loud and animated discussion usually takes place with nearly everyone participating and sharing ideas. There is no doubt that they are dissecting the facilitator and probably enjoying it. It is essential to remind them that they need to be specific on all counts. After 10 or 15 minutes (that *should* be enough), the facilitator stands by the board and asks the group to list the limitations that were being discussed with such zest. It is quite possible that no one will volunteer. Those comments that are made will tend to be rather vague and indirect unless the facilitator's rapport with the group is unusually good. Even when the facilitator is asking for good points or ways in which his or her performance could meet the group's goals, the discussion will probably drag, with few individuals participating.

Discussion and Reference to Maslow's Theory

It is important to reaffirm the significance of the discussion and the data presented (the facilitator should take notes and expand on them). But it is also clear that the discussion lacked something vital that was present during the discussions in the trios. If possible, the group should develop reasons for the obvious change in spontaneity and involvement. There are many possible reasons: fear of being evaluated by the facilitator or other members, discomfort in making direct criticism (for fear of getting it back), the leader–subordinate relationship that exists, and perhaps the fact that it is easier to be candid with two or three than with the whole group.

At this point it is helpful to give a brief description of Maslow's theory of needs and how it is related to the behaviors that people are willing to exhibit. It seems to be true of most groups that when individuals do not like something about how the group is being conducted, sense becomes the better part of valor, and a disgruntled "mumble" is the most that rises to the surface. Some individuals will "grumble" to another person or to the group about what is happening, but it is the rare person who will take the bull by the horns and do something about the situation. This condition is particularly obvious in many classrooms where a teacher may be ineffective or is not meeting the needs of the students, yet nothing is said or done. The same is true with the boss. To say something places the person in jeopardy of losing the boss's goodwill and losing his or her own esteem because of reaction in the job (an even lower-level need). As a result, people tend to mumble (see M. on the diagram) or grumble (L.G. = Low Grumble), but few are willing to pay the potential price and speak bluntly (H.G. = High Grumble). High grumblers in a group are usually either those who have worked through their own needs and feel accepted and secure (self-actualizing level) or individuals who are striving for personal recognition (often need for esteem). The two types are easily recognized by the group. The theory raises an important question: How can a group climate be developed that minimizes the threat to personal needs and helps set the stage for a free expression of opinions and ideas? The facilitator may wish to explore this question in a variety of ways, or he or she may choose to let the implications go for a future discussion.

◆ ◆ *EXERCISE 3*

Tower Building[4]

Objectives

- To help a group focus on the aspects of helping within the context of a particular task
- To alert a group to the problems that may develop when they are working under severe pressures (in this case, time and competition)
- To deal directly with the inhibiting norms, roles, and leadership practices that can minimize the use of the group's resources

---

4. The idea for this exercise was originally developed by Clark Abt in his simulation activity "An Education System Planning Game," originally played in 1965 at Lake Arrowhead, Calif.

Setting

This exercise is as close to real life as one can get and still remain "in the laboratory." It involves all the important aspects of group planning and decision making, such as the allocation of human and material resources, working against deadlines, altering strategies in the face of unexpected crises, and seeking the problems inherent in negotiations. It provides an opportunity to view the evolution of conflict and compromise as they exist in many working groups, particularly groups that have not developed skills in group problem solving.

From two and a half to three hours should be allowed for this exercise. It can be undertaken with as few as 12 participants divided into two groups (two observers and two groups of five). However, the activity generates greater excitement and involvement among the participants if there are four or six groups with from seven to nine members and an observer or two in each group. It should be noted that, given space, materials, and an effective communication system, virtually any even number of groups can participate (on one occasion, the authors witnessed 20 groups with 200 students and teachers enthusiastically involved for three and a half hours). As in many of the other exercises that focus on the dimensions of group process, it may prove interesting and enjoyable for groups unsophisticated in group analysis, but many of the potential learnings will pass them by. Participants with at least an understanding of basic group concepts will gain considerably more from the exercise. The following description is based on four groups of seven members each, with an observer in each group. The room should be large enough for each group to meet with some privacy. In most cases heterogeneous groups seem to be especially effective.

Action

After the large group has been divided into four groups of equal size (some stratification may be necessary if groups are to be truly heterogeneous), the facilitator says

You are a group of architects (each group) who have won one of four contracts to build a tower. Although your tower will be built independently of the other three, it is to be judged in competition with the others. There is to be a planning deadline and a construction deadline. The criteria to be used in judging the four towers include height, beauty, strength, and message [symbol or motto and so forth]. A prize will be distributed to each of the three best towers. Independent judges will appraise the towers, and their decisions will be final.

Your groups now have 30 minutes to develop a diagrammatic plan of the tower you are going to build. You should know that you will have to plan in terms of certain materials that will be made accessible to you only during the building phase. The judges will also be asked to consider the completeness of this initial plan in their overall judging. The materials available for building will include the following for each group:

   2 rolls of masking tape (1" wide)

   2 rolls of colored streamers

1 pair of large scissors

1 ruler

1 roll of colored toilet paper

150 sheets of medium newsprint (36")

4 felt-tip markers (different colors)

12 large sheets of construction paper (different colors)

It may be possible to negotiate with other groups for certain additional materials. Also, other personal materials of the participants may be used; however, no artificial bases—for example, from chairs, wastebaskets, and the like—may be used. The tower must stand alone on its own support—it may not be attached to the ceiling.

You may begin your planning. Because this is a competitive situation, no additional directions will be given during the planning period.

After 25 minutes of the planning period, the following announcement is made to the four groups:

We are disappointed to have to announce that because of the existing crisis in government funding, we have not been allocated all of the materials we originally anticipated. As a result, there are only enough materials available for building two towers. We are extremely sorry for this inconvenience. Rather than selecting two groups from the plans developed at this stage, we have decided to allow two groups to merge, decide on one plan, and build a tower together. Thus there will be two towers, each constructed by two teams fr_m a plan on which they both agree. You will have an additional 30 minutes of planning time to integrate your ideas or to come up with a new plan. Remember, both teams must agree on the final plan (the facilitator will select the teams that are to join forces).

After 30 minutes, the following announcement is made:

You now have 30 minutes to build your tower. It must be completed by _____ , at which time the judging will take place. Remember the criteria of height, beauty, strength, and message. The judges will also circulate among the groups to make certain that all regulations are being followed. Good luck.

Observation and Data Collection

Four major sources of information will be discussed with the participants:

1. Information is gained by the observer during the initial planning phase. He or she will find it most useful to focus on a few salient features of the groups, such as (a) communication pattern (who to whom), (b) leadership styles exhibited, and (c) specific behaviors that seem to inhibit or facilitate the group during the planning.

2. The second planning session provides another distinct period of observation. One of the observers should collect the same type of data gathered during the first observation period, except now on the combined groups. The other observer should turn his or her attention to the developmental aspects of the new combined group. This should be carried through the actual construction

period. For example, he or she might ask the following questions as he or she observes the groups:

a. How is the potential leadership conflict either resolved or not resolved?
b. What norms are developing within this group, and are they different from those that existed in the original smaller group you observed?
c. Have individuals with certain roles in the first group taken new ones in the larger group, and if so, what is their reaction to this state of affairs?
d. How is the decision-making process developed in this second planning session? Is consensus actually reached, or is one plan forced on the total group? What are the responses of the group members? How is resistance exhibited (actively or passively)?
e. Is there a real attempt to involve members from both groups through the allocation of responsibility during the building phase? How?

3. During the actual building phase, both observers should concentrate on the question in *b* above. Special attention should be given to the quality of participation of the various group members. Is there any difference in the quality of participation among those in leadership (control) roles and those less involved in the planning? Are there signs of withdrawal and resistant behaviors by certain members? Can these behaviors be explained as a result of the historical development of the two groups—that is, the merger? Do the two groups tend to work together as one, or are the original relationships developed before the merger still the basis for most communication and participation during the building stage?

4. The final source of data is collected from a reaction sheet handed to all participants at the time the tower is finally completed. Information from this instrument will be used by the facilitator in a summary of the activity. This may provide a wide range of data. The following questions might be useful for a summary discussion.

1. Please note the letter of the original planning group you joined:
   A   B   C   D

2. My opinions were valued and solicited in the first planning group. (circle one)

1	2	3	4	5	6	7
Not at all			Somewhat			Completely

3. My opinions were valued and solicited in the second planning group.

1	2	3	4	5	6	7
Not at all			Somewhat			Completely

4. If there was a difference in the problem-solving climate that developed in one group, briefly explain why.

5. How satisfied are you with the product of your merged group?

1	2	3	4	5	6	7
Not at all			Somewhat			Completely

6. What specific behaviors hurt your (merged) group's efforts to work together and be as successful as it might have been?

7. What behaviors were facilitative as the two merged groups attempted to work together?

Judging and Discussion Period

Immediately after the towers have been completed, take a period of about 20 minutes to (a) have participants complete the brief reaction sheet, (b) have about a 10-minute break, and (c) have the judges (a team of three) decide on the winning tower. The winner and prize are not announced until after the discussion period.

JUDGE'S EVALUATION SHEET

On a scale of 1 (low) to 7 (high), rate the towers on the following criteria.

	Height	Beauty	Strength	Message	Total
Team 1 (A & B)	____	____	____	____	____
Team 2 (C & D)	____	____	____	____	____

After the break, each merged team (A & B and C & D) meets together to discuss what happened. It is assumed that during the break the two observers compared notes and have agreed on a procedure for processing what occurred during the planning session prior to merging as well as the one after the two teams had to join forces.[5] If the group is helped with stimulating questions about what happened as the participants worked together, the discussion should require at least 45 minutes. Special attention should be given to the behaviors or situations that helped or did not help the two groups merge into a working team.

---

5. If time allows, it is usually very helpful for the facilitator to spend as much as 30 minutes prior to the exercise with the observers, giving them the sequence of events and explaining their role in the postsession processing. It is important that they interject their process data as a stimulus for further discussion and underline a point being made in the group. They should not simply report data and await a reaction.

Summary

During this discussion, the facilitator should be organizing the data from the participant reaction sheets. His or her 10- or 15-minute presentation of these data should underline the learnings being discussed in the two groups. He or she should be free to draw both inter- and intragroup hypotheses from the data and should then be willing to ask for confirmation or denial of his or her views. This type of presentation and discussion can help demonstrate the importance of reaction sheets and process periods after a time of problem solving and group involvement.

Conclusion

A natural end to the exercise is to report the judges' results. This can be done with humor and zest. If possible, the winning team can be given a prize that is easily divided (soft drinks, for instance) and the losers a booby prize that can also be divided (perhaps a large candy bar). Occasionally, this award period offers new information for discussion.

◆ ◆ *EXERCISE 4*

The Bag or the Box: The Stress of Ambiguity on the Development of a New Group

Objectives

- ■ To demonstrate the impact of an ambiguous and potentially threatening environment on a developing group
- ■ To observe the building of tension-reducing mechanisms within a climate of heightened anxiety

Rationale

Individuals or groups, when placed in unfamiliar surroundings and faced with unpredictable variables, tend to become disoriented. They then organize that environment in a manner that is safest for them at that moment. Under these conditions, leadership behavior becomes exaggerated and dependency magnified as the group struggles to bring order and predictability to the situation. It is rare that we are in a position to stand back and observe a group under such stress— usually we are too involved to even recognize what is happening. Once having observed it in others, we have a tendency to become more aware of similar conditions developing and of our responses to them.

Setting

This is one of the few exercises that require special physical conditions. It is included because of its increasing availability and the willingness of facilitators to use it. Of first importance is an observation room with a one-way viewing mirror. This room should be large enough to hold 15 or 20 people. Also, the participants' room should be large enough to allow movement. (In most cases this would rule out observation rooms used by counselors.) A small circle of seven to ten chairs is placed at one end of the room. If possible, the participants should be a group of from seven to ten students (preferably boys and girls) between about nine and twelve years of age.[6] Although it is not necessary that the children be acquainted, it is best that there be some heterogeneity in the group and that relationships be, to some degree, still evolving.

Action/Directions

The students are met outside the observation room and told simply that they are to enter the room and work as a group for the next 30 minutes. They are requested not to leave the room.

When they enter the room, they find a variety of conditions that will tend to be disorienting. First, there will be no authority figure to give them directions or specific written directions to follow. Second, there will be the one-way mirror and the suspicion that they are being observed. Finally, there will be an object in one corner (at some distance from the circle of chairs). The object will be either a large canvas bag with a person in it (covered) or a blanket with a person under it. The person does not move or make any sound. On other occasions a large box made to resemble a cage may be used. In it sits a person (apparently unable to get out) who does not speak or move. A sign on the cage reads only, "Do not move."

Directions to Observers

As in many groups or in ongoing groups faced with an anxiety-producing situation, the developmental process will be influenced and a certain amount of regression is predictable. Those observing should note the specific tension-reducing behaviors used by individuals within the group and by the group as a whole. Questions such as the following may be helpful to the group as it observes the unfolding events:

1. How is the potential leadership in the group identified?
2. How do these leaders orient themselves to (a) the lack of structure, (b) the bag, and (c) the mirror?

6. Note that children are suggested for this exercise because they are so spontaneous with their responses. Adult participants respond similarly, but less dramatically and less overtly. The young students also provide an interesting change of pace for the usually adult-centered groups and give a new perspective on group development.

3. How do they orient themselves to the group?
4. What conflicts seem to arise because of the uncertainty of the situation?
5. How are these conflicts resolved or at least reduced?
6. What various individual and group roles tend to develop as the participants attempt to cope with the anxiety-producing situation?
7. Are particular rules of behavior perceived as acceptable by the group (norms), and do these change during the 30-minute observational period?
8. Does the group move through definable stages as it attempts to cope with the ambiguity and make sense out of the unfamiliar environment?

Interview

Following the 30 minutes, the children should be given an opportunity to move into the observers' room and watch the observers as they move into the room with the bag. Perhaps with soft drinks and in the most relaxed and informal atmosphere, groups of observers and children may discuss what happened. The participants are bound to have many feelings, and it takes skill, patience, and real interest to draw these out. Many of the questions the observers have been asking themselves can now be broadened to include the perspective of the children. It is important to note, however, that the children may have many questions of their own and it may be helpful to give them a chance to ask them so that the process becomes one of exchanging ideas and less like the typical adult–student interrogation. The "bag" should also respond to questions from the students as a means of breaking the ice during the interview period. This person should emerge from the bag and participate.

Postsession Analysis

Following the departure of the children, the observers should (perhaps in clusters of three or so) summarize their learnings in relation to parallel situations in other groups, particularly in terms of the process of group development. The sharing of these ideas based on concrete examples can be most stimulating.

◆ ◆ EXERCISE 5

Tinker Toy Exercise

Objectives

- To help the group focus on the importance of nonverbal communication in its developmental process
- To familiarize the group with how easily the group climate is influenced by particular behaviors of the participants

Setting

As in many of the other exercises, competition between groups can be used as a means of bringing a sense of reality to a particular task. How individuals behave and what their impact is on a group tend to be characteristic of other situations that stimulate, annoy, challenge, or bore them. In this example, it is assumed that there are two groups of randomly selected participants with from seven to ten in each group. (Note: if the group has been working together for some time, an interesting dimension may be added by assigning the individuals who tend to verbally dominate a group—gathered from previous data—into one subgroup and those who are less active in the other.)

Each group is placed around a table (no chairs). The two tables are close enough so that each group can see what the other is doing (about 10 to 15 feet apart). There is nothing on the table. All are told to await instructions.

Materials

One can of Tinker Toys is needed for each group.

Action

The groups are told that they will have 45 minutes to develop the best possible product from the materials distributed to them. It is important that the product represent a group effort. The groups may begin as soon as they have the assigned materials, but the members may *not* speak to one another during the exercise.

At this point, the Tinker Toys are spread on the center of the table. The can and all instructions are taken away. The participants must use *all* of the materials in their project. They may also use any materials they have brought with them, although they may not leave the table to obtain such materials.

Observation of the Task

It is assumed that the observers have some skill and experience in observing groups. If there are three for each group, they should have 15 minutes prior to the beginning of the exercise to decide what observation procedures will give the participants the best picture of what actually happened. The following questions may help the observers in selecting their observational instruments and strategies.

1. How do individuals in the group arrange themselves around the table (randomly, in friendship subgroups, and so forth)?
2. At the end of the task, how has this initial ordering been changed? In front of whom is the final product? Why? Has this person the most skill? Is he or she the best organizer? Is he or she the most popular? Does he or she have the most power?
3. To which people in the group was most of the nonverbal communication directed? Were others encouraged to share their ideas in some manner?

4. Did members "jump" on one of the first ideas communicated or did they seek to explore alternatives? Did all the participants really understand what they were building when they started, and did they seem to agree with the idea?
5. How were tasks distributed during the work period? Was there any organization of labor or did individuals just do what came naturally?
6. Were particular roles (facilitating and inhibiting) identified within the group?
7. What did individuals who obviously were not directly involved in the decisions or perceived as resource people do to compensate for feelings of noninvolvement, impotency, or even inadequacy in this particular group?
8. Did particular behaviors by individuals create defensive responses in other members? (No names are necessary, but it is helpful if the group can accept direct feedback.) Responses should be specific about the action and reaction parts to this question.
9. How did the group respond to the pressure of time and to the pressure of the group working next to them?
10. What norms developed as the group began to work together? Did these change as the task progressed?
11. What types of leadership were exhibited within the group and what impact did these have on the developing group climate?

Other observations related to membership, subgrouping patterns, tension release, reward, and punishment in the group may be explored. It is also important to observe how the two groups use each other as outlets for their own feelings.

Follow-up and Discussion

Depending on the particular objectives of the facilitator, there are a number of possible interventions that may be used following the action phase of the exercise.

Option 1 Still within the nonverbal framework, each group is asked to move to an opposite end of the room and, in a relatively open space (ideally, about 15 by 15 feet), form themselves into a "group shape" that should symbolically represent a picture of how the individuals within the group feel about their own participation and the product of the group. They should try out as many shapes as they feel are necessary until they can all agree on one. Again, this activity should be observed in terms of group pressure, decision making, leadership, and so forth. Do the members really have the courage to represent the feelings generated during the activity? Once the shape is formed, the members sit down where they are and discuss the implications of their shape and how it reflects the process of their work together. After this discussion, the observers may wish to bring the group into a circle and share with them some of the most useful data (again, there may be a tendency to overwhelm them with too much information). They should help draw the participants into the discussion and have them, using their own experience from participation, respond to the questions the observers were asking. Observers are most effective when they are used to supplement the insights of the participants themselves.

Option 2   The facilitator announces that the group will now have an opportunity to present their products to the other group. Each group will be asked to explain briefly what the product is and how the idea was arrived at. Then they will be asked to make a number of observations about their work together. The observers should carefully note who responds for the group, how this was decided, and how accurate the description is in terms of what actually happened. Also, it should be noted which behaviors occur while one group is listening to the other and while participants in the group being described hear their representative's version of what happened. Often the product is not what some of the participants thought, nor is the description of what happened the same as their own. After both groups have presented their product to the other group, each group meets to discuss the observers' data and explore what happened during (and after) the activity.

Summary

It is quite possible that the discussion period after either of the two options may take as much as an hour, but it can take much less if there is a more systematic presentation of the data and discussion is minimized. Time should be allowed at the end of the program so that each group can share with the total group specific learnings that seem to have developed out of the particular activity. Special emphasis should be placed on those behaviors that are characteristic of most groups as they develop during a specific task.

Other Possible Materials

The same basic design can be used with a wide range of materials. If the group is outdoors and near a wooded area, it is possible to build interesting products from what is available in nature. Or a brief trip to a dime store or supermarket can result in a seemingly endless supply of materials that could be distributed to the groups (clothespins, tape, paper, plastic hair curlers, hairpins, rubber bands, crayons, pipe cleaners, and so forth). The main thing is to give the group enough so that decisions must be made as to the allocation of materials, but the materials should be different enough so they do not naturally form a product.

References

Ackerman, N. W. *The Psychodynamics of Family Life.* New York: Basic Books, 1958.
Ackerman, N. W., ed. *Family Therapy in Transition.* Boston: Little, Brown, 1970.

Allcorn, S. "What makes groups tick?" *Personnel,* 62, No. 9 (September 1985), 52–58.

Bales, R. F. *An Interactive Process Analysis: A Method for the Study of Small Groups.* Reading, Mass.: Addison-Wesley, 1950.

Beavers, W. R. *Psychotherapy and Growth: Family Systems Perspective.* New York: Brunner/Mazel, 1977.

Bednar, R. L. and Battersby. "The Effects of Specific Cognitive Structure on Early Group Development." *Journal of Applied Behavioral Science,* 12 (1976), 513–522.

Bell, J. E. *Family Therapy.* New York: Jason Aronson, 1978.

Bennis, W., and H. Shepherd. "A theory of group development." *Human Relations,* 9 (1956), 418–419.

Bion, W. R. *Experiences in Groups.* New York: Basic Books, 1961.

Bodin, A. M. "Family therapy training literature: A brief guide." *Family Press,* 8 (1969), 729–779.

Borgatta, E. F., and R. F. Bales. "Interaction of individuals in reconstituted groups." *Sociometry,* 16 (1953), 302–320.

Brzezinski, Z. *Power and Principle.* New York: Farrar, Straus, and Giroux, 1983.

Carew, D. K. P.-C. Eunice, and K. H. Blanchard. "Group development and situational leadership: A model for managing groups." *Training and Development Journal,* 40, No. 6 (June 1986), 46–50.

Carter, J. *Keeping Faith.* New York: Bantam Books, 1982.

Cattell, R. B., D. R. Sanders, and G. F. Stice. "The dimensions of syntality in small groups." *Human Relations,* 6 (1953), 331–336.

Cissna, K. N. "Phases in group development: The negative evidence." *Small Group Behavior,* 15, No. 1 (1984), 3–32.

Cohen, A. M., and R. D. Smith. *Critical Incidents in Growth Groups: Theory and Techniques.* La Jolla, Calif.: University Associates, 1976.

Cooley, C. H. *Social Organization.* New York: Charles Scribner's Sons, 1909.

Davies, D., and B. C. Kuypers. "Group development and interpersonal feedback." *Groups and Organizational Studies,* 10, No. 2 (June 1985), 184–208.

Dayan, M. *Breakthrough: A Personal Account of the Egypt–Israel Peace Negotiations.* London: Weidenfeld and Nicholson, 1981.

Eagle, J., and P. Newton. "Scapegoating in small groups: An organizational approach." *Human Relations,* 34 (1981), 283–301.

Erikson, E. *Childhood and Society.* New York: W. W. Norton, 1950.

Evensen, P. E. *Effects of Specific Cognitive and Behavioral Structures on Early Group Interactions.* Louisville, KY: University of Kentucky Press, No. 76-20 (1976), 152.

Fisher, B. A., and R. K. Stutman. "An assessment of group trajectories: Analyzing developmental breakpoints." *Communication Quarterly,* 35, No. 2 (Spring 1987), 105–124.

Foley, V. D. *An Introduction to Family Therapy.* New York: Grune & Stratton, 1974.

Friesen, J. D. *Structural Strategic Marriage and Family Therapy.* New York: Gardner Press, 1985.

Gist, M. E., E. A. Locke, and S. M. Taylor. "Organizational behavior: Group structure, powers and effectiveness." *Journal of Management,* 13, No. 2 (Summer 1987), 237–257.

Goldenberg, I., and H. Goldenberg. *Family Therapy: An Overview.* Monterey: Brooks Cole Publishing, 1980.

Haley, J. *Problem Solving Therapy.* San Francisco: Jossey-Bass, 1976.

Hall, J. and M. S. Williams, "Group Dynamics Training and Improved Decision Making." Journal of Applied Behavioral Science, 6 (1970), 39–68.

Handfinger, R. "A theoretical tool for practitioners in the behavioral sciences." *Small Group Behavior,* 15, No. 3 (August 1984), 375–386.

Hare, P., and D. Naveh. "Group development at the Camp David Summit," *Small Group Behavior,* 15, No. 3 (August 1984), 299–318.

Homans, G. C. *The Nature of Social Science.* New York: Harcourt, 1967.

Kernberg, O. "Regression in Groups: Some Clinical Findings and Theoretical Implications." *Journal of Personality and Social Systems,* 2 (1980), 51–75.

Kuypers, B. C., D. Davies, and A. Hazewinkel. "Developmental patterns in self-analytic groups." *Human Relations,* 39, No. 9 (September 1986), 793–815.

Lacoursiere, R. *The Life Cycle of Groups.* New York: Human Sciences Press, 1980.

Lewis, J. M., W. R. Beavers, J. T. Gossett, and V. A. Phillips. *No Single Thread: Psychological Health in Family Systems.* New York: Brunner/Mazel, 1976.

Lundgran, D. C. "Developmental trends in the emergence of interpersonal issues in T-groups." *Small Group Behavior,* 8, No. 2 (1977), 179–200.

Mabry, E. A. "Exploratory analysis of a developmental model for task-oriented small groups." *Human Communications,* 2, No. 1 (1975), 66–74.

Mann, R. D. *Interpersonal Styles and Group Development.* New York: Wiley, 1967.

Maslow, A. H. *Motivation and Personality.* New York: Harper & Row, 1954.

Minnchin, S. *Families and Family Therapy.* Cambridge, Mass.: Harvard University Press, 1974.

McGrath, J. E. "Group Interaction and Performance." Englewood Cliffs, N.J.: Prentice Hall, 1984.

The New York Times, November 6, 1991, p. B–9.

Obert, S. L. "Developmental patterns of organizational task groups: A preliminary study." *Human Relations,* 36, No. 1 (January 1983), 37–52.

Parsons, T. *The Social System.* Glencoe, Ill.: Free Press, 1951.

Reddi, M. "Team development: A review." *ASCI Journal of Management* (India), 13, No. 1 (September 1983), 57–75.

Redl, F. *When We Deal with Children.* New York: Free Press, 1966.

Satir, V. *Cojoint Family Therapy.* Palo Alto, Calif.: Science and Behavior Books, 1967.

Schutz, W. *The Interpersonal Underworld.* Palo Alto, Calif.: Science and Behavior Books, 1966.

Staw, B., L. Sandelands, and J. Dutton. "Threat-rigidity effects in organizational behavior: A multilevel analysis." *Administrative Science Quarterly,* 26 (1981), 501–524.

Stinnett, N., and J. Defrain. *Secrets of Strong Families.* New York: Berkley, 1986.

Stogdill, R. M. "Group productivity, drive, and cohesiveness." *Organizational Behavior and Human Performance,* 8 (1972), 26–43.

Theodorsen, G. A. "Elements in the progressive development of small groups." *Social Forces,* 31 (1953), 311–320.

Tuckman, B. W. "Developmental sequence in small groups." *Psychological Bulletin,* 6396 (1965), 384–399.

Tuckman, B. W., and M. A. C. Jensen. "Stages of small-group development revisited." *Group and Organizational Studies,* 2, No. 4 (1977), 419–427.

Vance, C. R. *Hard Choices: Four Critical Years in America's Foreign Policy.* New York: Simon and Schuster, 1983.

Wanous, J. P., A. E. Reicheri, and S. D. Malik. "Organizational socialization and group development: Toward an integrative perspective." *Academy of Management Review,* 9, No. 4 (October 1984), 670–683.

Weizman, E. *The Battle for Peace.* New York: Bantam Books, 1981.

Yalom, I. D. *The Theory and Practice of Group Psychotherapy.* 3rd ed. New York: Basic Books, 1985.

◆ *11* ◆

Small Group Processes: Three Contemporary Applications

This chapter examines three kinds of small groups: self-help groups, quality circles, and focus groups. It uses the group process concepts covered in previous chapters to investigate how these groups function. The goal of this chapter is to illustrate the application of group processes in small groups.

Self-help groups, quality circles, and focus groups were chosen as examples of small groups because of their increasing prevalence and their ability to address the needs of individuals for identity and empowerment. Since World War II, people in our industrial society have often found their lives fragmented and isolated. People frequently experience the structures associated with large businesses, communities, and governments as dehumanizing or unresponsive to their personal and social needs. This sense of alienation and lack of control over one's immediate social environment creates feelings of stress and apathy. As a result of rapid social change and increased social mobility, the traditional supports of the extended family, religion, and the community have diminished. In contemporary society people seek stability, connection, faith, and a sense of empowerment in small groups.

Self-help groups offer emotional anchors and sources of identity and meaning for many individuals struggling with the ups and downs of daily life. At work, quality circles provide opportunities for employees to influence their environment and develop a greater sense of self-satisfaction. Focus groups help us understand how people view controversial issues. They enable participants to express themselves more personally and idiosyncratically than do surveys and questionnaires. Self-help groups and quality circles empower their members by helping them to cope with emotional stress, to solve problems, and to improve their work environment. Focus groups give people a voice in decisions that affect issues from the mundane to the international. Small groups that provide people with a sense of identity, a way to assert themselves and their values, and a sense of empowerment have become essential to the lives of increasing numbers of people.

Self-Help Groups

A number of chairs stand around a long conference table in an otherwise empty room. Within a few minutes, people begin to walk into the room, serve themselves coffee, find seats, and make themselves comfortable. It is clear that some people know one another; greetings are exchanged and certain people sit together. It also looks as though some individuals are new and awkward in the situation. They pick unobtrusive seats, fidget, and do not meet anyone else's gaze. The room fills quickly; soon all the seats are taken, and latecomers sit on the windowsills or stand against the walls. At the designated time, a young woman stands up and welcomes everyone to the meeting. The leader continues by leading the group in a short prayer and then introduces the speakers for the evening. Each one stands, introduces himself or herself, and tells his or her story of alcoholism—the pain, the depths of despair, and the long road toward sobriety. Every person in attendance is a recovering alcoholic, and the members of this group have joined together in their individual and collective struggle to live as sober, productive members of Alcoholics Anonymous (AA).

This scenario is repeated thousands of times each day. It is estimated that there are more than 500,000 self-help groups and 15 million members in the nation (Riessman, 1984, p. 661). The self-help movement extends much further than AA meetings; its scope and functioning will be examined in this chapter. Who joins these groups and for what reasons? How do groups get started, who leads, and who follows? How long have self-help groups been around, and what purpose do they serve?

Definition of Self-Help Groups

Self-help groups are voluntary gatherings of peers who share needs or problems that are not being addressed by existing organizations, institutions, or other types of groups. The broad goals of a self-help group are to bring about personal and/or social change for its members and society. All of these groups (and there is an almost overwhelming variety) emphasize face-to-face interaction among members and stress a set of values or ideology that enhances a member's personal sense of identity (Katz and Bender, 1976).

In the example of an AA meeting, members attend the meeting because they think it will be helpful, not because of outside coercion or pressure. The group described has 50 regular members. Although this makes for large meetings of 20 to 30 people, it is within the limit that allows for interpersonal contact. Everyone in AA is there because of a drinking problem; there are no mental health professionals dispensing treatment. In short, AA provides a set of values (one day at a time, the serenity prayer) and a structure that help a group of people help themselves stop drinking.

Generally, self-help groups start from a position of powerlessness, in that their initial resources of money, influence, and status are limited, and their objective is not to amass power. This position and the fact that self-help groups fill a gap in existing services distinguish self-help groups from other voluntary group experiences. Think about groups in our culture that you consider powerless or disenfranchised. Certainly former mental patients, people of minority ethnic background, families living in poverty, and individuals with a debilitating illness are among those who usually lack access to traditional forms of power. Hence self-help groups differ from traditional service organizations or political parties in their narrow power base and the alienation that group members may feel about their place in the social world. In addition, self-help groups differ from other activity, craft, or social groups because the goal of personal growth carries deep emotional sustenance, something not usually provided in other groups.

Ecological Niches   To enhance our understanding of self-help groups, some theorists have likened the meeting place of these groups to the "niche" sometimes located in a kitchen or stairwell, where it provides extra space for valued mementos, art objects, or a flower-filled vase. The notion that the space occupied by self-help groups conceptually resembles a niche also evokes ecological niches, or alternative social environments. Members may occupy these niches while responding to their common need (Levine, 1987). The importance of the "niche" simile lies in its implication that a niche is not disconnected from the rest of the environment; it is a solid recess in a wall with an opening to the rest of a kitchen or stairwell. The opening signifies a connection to the rest of (the larger environment of) the house.

The "niche" perspective has influenced the course of research on self-help groups. Instead of studying these groups as separate and independent entities, apart from the total environment in which the group members live, work, and play, research has adopted the ecological viewpoint: research on self-help groups has expanded to include the environment of which the members are a part. Applying the concept of ecological niches, Maton et al. (1989) viewed self-help groups as entities housed under the roof of larger entities, such as the community and the health care/human services system. In short, self-help group dynamics extend to a larger environment than the group itself.

History of Self-Help Groups

Self-help or mutual aid groups have a long history. The idea of cooperative groups or societies was traced to prehistoric times by Kropotkin (1955), who found that the most viable groups had rudimentary mutual aid practices, such as food gathering, child rearing, and common defense. Medieval city–states evolved from such cooperative roots. The Freemasons became one of the best-known examples of a self-help group when, after the Black Death decimated much of Europe, the organization provided an essential social anchor during devastating upheaval.

In more recent times, cooperative societies have flourished in both Europe and America to help members with anything from a financial crisis to livestock and grain management. The utopian communities of the 1800s were based on cooperative principles and were formed in response to the ills brought on by the urbanization of the Industrial Revolution. Today, trade unions and worker-organized businesses share a strong commitment to peer-organized structures that address a common need.

Self-help or mutual aid groups have also evolved steadily and flourished in the field of health and human services. With a growth rate of 9 percent a year (Maton, et al.), self-help groups have gained respect and recognition as viable groups. They promote individual feelings of self-satisfaction derived from awareness that individuals are valued, are not powerless or disenfranchised, and are bound by a common need that allays their sense of isolation.

Types of Self-Help Groups

Social scientists have developed a number of ways to categorize the types of self-help groups. Because the incredibly rapid growth of self-help groups is in itself a phenomenon worth examining, we can start by looking at how people have classified self-help groups in the context of social movements. Blumer (1951) differentiated three types of social movements. *General* movements refer to groups organized around a large issue such as peace, women's rights, or the environment. The goal is to change members' and the public's values. This type of movement often lacks established leaders, and membership and group structure are flexible and rapidly changing. The second type is a *specific* movement that has well-defined objectives and a recognized leadership and membership, as well as established rituals, traditions, and a status hierarchy. Groups such as welfare rights organizations, Black Muslims, and the Industrial Workers of the World during World War I are examples of this type. The third type is labeled *expressive* and includes Alcoholics Anonymous, groups for people with AIDS, National Mental Health Consumer's Association (for former mental patients), and Compassionate Friends (for parents who have lost a child). The emphasis is on intimate interactions and personal support and change.

Another way to classify self-help groups is to assess whether their goals and activities support the status quo of society or challenge established societal norms (Katz, 1972). Groups such as AA, Parents Without Partners (PWP), Recovery, Inc., and Take Off Pounds Sensibly (TOPS) do not challenge widely held values but rather focus on helping their members develop a comfortable existence within societal norms and values. Other groups, such as gay rights organizations, women's rights groups, and Little People of America, are interested in changing existing prejudices.

Sagarin (1969) looked at self-help groups composed of deviants and analyzed the ways the public perceives these groups, as well as the way group members think about themselves in relation to established institutions and cultural expectations. He found that stigmatized people—that is, people who do not conform to accepted norms—join self-help groups for two reasons: either to conform more easily to social norms or to create new standards that will accommodate their "deviant" behavior.

Certain groups come together for both support and information. For example, many divorced women who have young children find self-help groups a means of learning how to be a single parent, how to find acceptance for a family headed solely by a mother, and how to integrate child rearing and career building. Many such women have gained sufficient support from their groups to campaign for more and better child care, tax deductions for child care, and legislation to enforce negligent fathers' payment of child support.

As you can see, we can organize this diversity in a variety of ways. Many categories overlap, and many groups have similar dynamics, despite the fact that they address different problems or needs. In the next section, we will look at what makes self-

roups tick, using the group concepts we discussed in the previous chapters. The emphasis will be on expressive self-help groups that lend themselves readily to analysis of their dynamics from a small group perspective.

Levy (1979) classified self-help groups in accordance with group composition and purpose. His four categories were (1) behavioral-control or conduct-reorganization groups; (2) stress-coping and support groups; (3) survival-oriented groups; and (4) personal-growth and self-actualization groups.

Behavioral-control groups and conduct-reorganization groups consist of members who are trying to eliminate or control some problematic behavior. This desire is often the only requirement for membership, because the group's sole purpose is to help members control the problem common to them all. Groups in this category include Alcoholics Anonymous, Gamblers Anonymous, and Weight Watchers.

Stress-coping and support groups are composed of members who share a status or predicament that entails some degree of stress. The goal of these groups is to alleviate the stress through mutual support and the sharing of coping strategies and advice. Members' status is accepted, so no attempt is made to change that status. Rather, the goal is to help members carry on with their lives despite their current status. Such support groups as Parents Without Partners and Make Every Day Count (for people with cancer or a serious chronic illness) are characteristic of this type.

Survival-oriented groups consist of people labeled by society—and discriminated against—as a result of their life styles, values, sex, sexual orientation, socioeconomic class, or race. The major concern of these groups is to help their members maintain or enhance their self-esteem through mutual support and consciousness-raising activities. These groups attempt to gain societal acceptance for their members through educational and political activities aimed at legitimizing their life styles and eliminating the stigma associated with them. Examples of this type include the National Organization for Women, gay activist groups, and various racial and ethnic activist and support groups.

Personal-growth and self-actualization groups are composed of people who share one common goal: enhanced effectiveness in all aspects of their lives, especially those involving their emotionality, sexuality, and capacity to relate to others. The shared belief that together the members can help each other improve the quality of their lives is the primary reason for such a group's existence. Examples include some professional women's groups, "creativity" groups, and sensitivity groups.

◆ Individual Experiment

Sit down with a copy of your school or community paper and look in the "Announcements" section. Count the number of self-help group meetings listed. Use the definition of self-help groups to distinguish between self-help and other kinds of group meetings. Are the self-help groups' focuses similar or widely divergent? If you do not know what a particular group does, give it a call and find out.

◆

Origins and Membership of Self-Help Groups

When we think about the issue of membership in self-help groups, we are concerning ourselves with those people who are considered formal members of the group. They perceive themselves and are seen by others as a bona fide part of the group.

Origins   These groups may originate in a variety of ways. Some of the earliest groups (for example, AA) were begun by strong, authoritarian people who recognized the need for such groups. These groups still have strong leaders. Other self-help groups originate, for example, in a hospital's concern for patients with a particular problem. Recognizing that the professional staff can have only limited impact, hospitals have been helpful in organizing and promoting self-help groups and setting aside space for their meetings. For example, Hahnemann University Hospital in Philadelphia has established a self-help group for young people with cystic fibrosis. Certain affiliates of the American Diabetic Association sponsor young-adult support groups. And many hospitals sponsor "new-parent support groups." Groups originated by a hospital or other organization may have a coordinator/leader, but members of the group are usually encouraged to take on leadership and develop their own meeting structure and style.

Some self-help groups are founded by individuals searching for people who have the same problem that afflicts them. For example, the Adoption Forum was founded by two adult adoptees who met and discovered they shared a need to explore the adoption experience with other adoptees. They ran ads making themselves known to such adults and began to develop strategies for searching for birth parents.

The potential focuses of self-help groups are so wide ranging, and the stress-reduction benefits so needed that today, groups even exist whose sole purpose is to form self-help groups. For example, the Health and Human Issues Outreach Department at the University of Wisconsin, Madison, has helped form self-help groups for Wisconsin farm families. This organization begins a group with a few initial members and then encourages the group to continue on its own course, developing according to the interests of those present.

Membership   Membership in self-help groups is voluntary. Because all of these groups are organized around a need, handicap, or problem that their members share, it is important to distinguish between having the "problem" and becoming a member of a self-help group addressing that problem.

For example, Mended Hearts is a self-help group composed of people who have had a heart operation. Along with regular meetings, one of their main activities is going to see other people in the hospital who are awaiting or recovering from surgery. Mended Hearts visitors give support and general information about what the patient can expect, and they serve as models of people who have successfully gone through the same experience.

What reasons do people give for joining a self-help group? There has been an almost endless flood of writing about alienation in the twentieth century. The finger has been pointed at the increasing complexity of life brought on by industrialization, urbanization, and bureaucratization. This leaves the individual feeling powerless to effect any change, frustrated, and helpless. This predicament is exacerbated by the deterioration of traditional support systems such as the family, neighborhood, and community. Many have looked to small groups to find support, emotional nurturance, and a sense of identity that is lacking in their lives.

Some self-help groups address the needs of those considered deviant by society: people with physical or psychological handicaps that limit their acceptance by society. Multiply the impact of being outside the mainstream of society by the sense of isolation felt by everyone, and you begin to get a sense of the compelling pull of self-help groups.

People who join self-help groups must define themselves as in need of help from others. They must affirm that they have a problem, need, or handicap rather than denying its existence. For example, people who join TOPS or Weight Watchers have admitted that their weight problem is just that, a problem. It is a problem that they cannot manage by themselves, either. Like other groups, self-help groups serve as reference groups for their members. Groups exert social pressure to influence members to abide by group norms. In weight control groups, for example, individuals are weighed at the beginning of a meeting. Individuals who lose pounds are cheered and applauded, whereas those whose weight is stable or who gain weight are admonished to do better.

By serving as reference groups with which members strongly identify, self-help groups facilitate changes in self-perception, which empowers the individual. Kahn (1985) has suggested that people not only empower themselves within the context of self-help groups and then extend this power to their lives but also extend their new power into the community by influencing organizations, institutions, and even society's development. For example, diabetic self-help groups have formed powerful lobbies for insurance coverage for blood glucose monitors and other health needs. MADD (Mothers Against Drunken Driving) started as a self-help group and has been instrumental in the passage of laws punishing drunken drivers in New Jersey.

A brief look at research on the effectiveness of self-help groups confirms the assumption that self-help group members gain empowerment. And further research is helping to determine which populations are most likely to be helped by group membership and under what conditions. One study investigated the impact of self-help group participation on people with scoliosis (curvature of the spine) and their families. The 245 participants in the study were divided into three groups: adolescent scoliotics, parents of adolescent scoliotics, and adult scoliotics. On a questionnaire, most members of the three groups reported considerable satisfaction with the self-help groups. However, it is important to note that being a member had no discernible impact on the psychosocial adjustments of the adolescent patients or their parents. It was a different story for the adults and those who had undergone demanding medical treatment. These populations seemed to benefit the most from the self-help groups (Hinrichsen et al., 1985).

A study on the impact of self-help groups on the mental health of widows and widowers found that presence at sessions alone was insufficient to produce positive changes but that significant positive changes occurred for those who participated actively (Lieberman and Videka-Sherman, 1986). And after examining whether self-help groups meet the needs of the bereaved, Cluck and Cline (1986) reported that such groups seemed more effective than traditional resources, such as family, friends, and professional help givers. Toseland and Hacker (1985), interested in whether social workers would use self-help groups as a resource for clients, reported that most of their subjects considered self-help groups a valuable but underutilized resource.

Katz and Bender (1976) outlined seven steps that self-help groups help their members to take.

1. Develop and sustain a coherent world view. Members share a rationale and common understanding of their problem.

2. Learn new, more gratifying behavior. Members benefit from learning better ways to manage their dilemmas.

3. Tap unconscious feelings.

4. Fortify self-image and pride. Members receive support and feedback that give them external validation when they change.

5. Achieve mastery by uncovering competence. With group support, members are encouraged to try new skills and discover previously unknown qualities and abilities.

6. Increase coping abilities through participation in group tasks of graduated difficulty. A self-help group is a good place for people to be challenged. Members are given more responsibility within the group as they progress.

7. Advance to new status within the group, then perhaps leave. Self-help groups demand that people give as well as receive help, commensurate with their abilities. Although some groups expect long-term involvement, many encourage leaving once the person is coping better with his or her problem.

In summary, self-help groups provide a cooperative climate for growth, frequent interaction of their members, and the opportunity for members to see successful senior members. All of these factors serve to support and reassure members and increase the attractiveness of such a group.

Self-Help Group Norms

All groups develop norms—rules, policies, and unwritten expectations—to control members' behavior. In self-help groups, many of the norms help members feel better about themselves and learn better ways of coping. In some groups, norms are quite formal, written documents that not only delineate an overall world view but also specify in detail the steps a member is to take in order to change. For example, AA has twelve steps that point the alcoholic in the right direction, as well as a host of other written material describing the problem of alcoholism.

Other norms may not be in black and white but are explicitly stated and consciously shared by the membership. At Eagleville, a rehabilitative facility in Pennsylvania, and other spin-off self-help groups for drug addicts, there are a variety of sayings that communicate strong normative expectations. "No pain, no gain" and "Remember, when you point your finger at someone else, there are three pointing back at you" both illustrate norms of accepting responsibility for your actions, being honest, and acknowledging that change is a difficult process that can be expected to be uncomfortable and painful.

Two group norms that serve as basic underpinnings for many self-help groups are mutual aid and activity as a means to solve one's problems.

Mutual Aid   Group members are expected to provide support and concern for other members. The idea that assistance is a reciprocal process is congruent with the basic belief that individuals can join together to help themselves without the aid of professionals. This also speaks to the expectation that members will be active participants in their own recovery or rehabilitation, not passive receivers of a service in which there is little expected from them other than "getting better." This type of self-help group provides an arena in which getting better has some specific, behavioral components. New members who are recipients of help become veteran members who are dispensers of help. AA states, "You have to give it away in order to keep it." "It" is personal learning and change for the better. By expecting that he or she will help others in need, the individual can reverse his or her established role from receiver to giver and then can feel more competent and receive approval from others.

Another dynamic that is set up is that more senior members become role models and referents for newer members. Every non-obese person who gets up in an Overeaters Anonymous meeting to tell his or her story not only is telling a tale of struggle but is also a living affirmation that it works!

Activity   Self-help groups support members, sharing their feelings and emotions, but there is a strong emphasis on activity. People are urged, supported, and advised to cope with their handicaps, problems, or needs and continue to function. In Recovery, Inc., members advise one another to act as though they are "normal," even when they hear voices or suffer from delusions. AA exhorts members to take it "one day at a time." Groups for bereaved parents, children, or spouses encourage their members to mourn, but they also share how people have resumed regular social engagements. Patients who have undergone mastectomy, colostomy, amputation, or other surgeries also have self-help groups that share information, resources, and personal experience about how to adjust to one's body and its demands. Constructive action toward shared goals is the hallmark of self-help groups.

Negative and Positive Group Norms   Interestingly, emerging data indicate that self-help groups in which negative norms evolve do not help members. For example, in some self-help groups for women on welfare, the longer people remained members, the more depressed they became. When women joined, they hoped to build contacts that might help them get jobs or gain tips on child rearing in neighborhoods with heavy drug use. But after listening to other members' stories about their difficulties in getting or keeping jobs and influencing their children to stay in school and remain drug-free, the initially hopeful joiners came increasingly to feel that their own situations were hopeless.

In another example, a professional woman who had been raped reported her experience in joining a self-help group for survivors of sexual assault. For her, the self-help group was a negative experience, because it caused her to relive the horror continually rather than integrating the rape experience into her life and getting on with daily living. Each new member recounted another horrible experience, reigniting her own memories. This particular woman found it more helpful to call a "hotline" counselor at moments when she was overwhelmed by negative feelings.

Finally, a successful accountant who was confined to a wheelchair as a result of polio reported joining a support group to hear how others coped with continuing physical disability. However, he found the norms of the group he entered to be doom, gloom, passivity, and depression. Two sessions convinced him that the group was not for him.

When their norms are positive, problem-solving, and encouraging, self-help groups can offer powerful and positive experiences. As with any other group, when the norms are negative and an atmosphere of defeat and futility prevails, self-help groups might actually be detrimental.

Some data suggest that the benefits of groups to members can be questionable even where norms are positive. For example, Peele (1984), in examining AA, identified a powerful group-socialization process—a kind of brainwashing. And Scheffler (1983), in her experience with members of Overeaters Anonymous, became concerned about the possible damaging effects of matching new members with sponsors, experienced members who serve as guides. She stated that the counseling from a sponsor can be a negative influence in some people's lives.

Similarly, some social scientists express concern about how self-help groups create change. Lieberman (1988) stressed that "to generalize that all self-help groups work because of social support would be utter nonsense." In a series of studies (1979), he found that those who had established "give-and-take" relationships with other members benefited from being in a self-help group more than those who had not developed this give-and-take relationship. But in another study, involving bereaved parents, he found that the give-and-take relationship produced no added benefits. In still other groups, he found that members showed no psychological improvement whatsoever. Lieberman noted that although studies with self-help groups are encouraging, it has not been determined how, why, and for whom such groups work. These questions are currently provoking much research and study.

Still, it is generally acknowledged that a way to increase the effectiveness of self-help groups is for members to be trained in leading groups, facilitating communication, understanding group norms, and helping groups create positive norms. Simultaneously, group members need training in dealing with typical group problems, such as people who monopolize sessions or who insist on their solutions to problems as the only ones worth considering. Small group training of this sort has been found to increase member participation and group longevity.

Self-help groups provide a small group experience that can support and enrich their members. This is one of the major trends in group development, in coping with social problems, and in small group research at this moment.

Group Structure and Norms   In order to establish and maintain positive norms, groups need structure so that mutual aid and cooperative support can continue throughout meetings. Basic to the structure is the norm that each member is valued. To establish this norm, facilitators should encourage each person to introduce himself or herself and to relate personal reasons for joining the group. Further, he or she should encourage each member to participate in every discussion and foster an atmosphere of receptivity and empathy. Members need to know that they can safely express their true feelings and that their honesty will be acknowledged and welcomed. Acceptance and a shared understanding of a previously hidden problem are central to the effectiveness of self-help groups in meeting members' needs.

Another positive norm is the free flow of information among members, especially information derived from personal disclosure. Fawcett and his colleagues (1988) listened to tapes to get a sense of the "anatomy of self-help groups" and were surprised to find that the predominant activity seemed to be information giving.

Leadership may be rotated throughout the membership, which reinforces personal involvement and responsibility. Authority is shared by peers; there are no designated leaders or healers or people with special expertise that sets them apart from others. Status is earned by furthering the interests of the group. Within a self-help group, it is possible to enter as a new member who has hit rock bottom and rise through the ranks to a position of authority and responsibility—something that would not be possible in more traditional groups. In group psychotherapy, no matter how good a client you are, you will never become the therapist.

Decisions in a self-help group are made by the group as a whole, usually through consensus with much discussion and sharing of thoughts and feelings. Although not everyone may agree with a decision, the process of reaching a decision is built on the group's commitment to give everyone an opportunity to be heard.

◆ *Reader Activity*

Think back to the last time you sat down with a group of people from school or colleagues from work. Identify the common experiences all of you share. You may never have talked about them with each other, but they still exist. Think about what the group did talk about. Were there shared problems or concerns that surfaced? Did people offer empathic support or advice to one another, or was there confrontation and conflict? How did you feel afterward?   ◆

Self-Help Group Goals

Individuals come to self-help groups with personal goals—perhaps to seek relief from an addiction, to regain a better body image, or to gain self-confidence despite a stutter. In order for a group to continue to function successfully, it must address each individual's needs. There is also a process of self-selection that takes place in self-help groups. Some people may initially be drawn to a particular group and then find that it does not suit them.

One of the goals of any self-help group is to assist its members. However, groups have many other goals too, which work in the service of the larger goal of filling a need. A self-help group has goals that focus on its own survival: Will members be committed and keep coming? How will we let other people know we exist so they can benefit? How will we manage when we have too many members for just one group? What will our relationship be with professionals who work with people having similar problems? Can they be a source of referrals or do we disagree with their methods and want them out of our hair? In order for a group to flourish, its members have to identify with the group's goals and be willing to commit themselves to seeing that the goals are accomplished.

Goals vary in duration and in breadth. For example, neighborhood self-help groups that develop to meet some terrible adversity such as a tornado or flood tend to focus on a narrow concern or problem. When the crisis is over, people go back to their normal routines and the group disbands. At the other end of the continuum is a self-help group such as AA. It is common for AA members to remain involved and active in the organization for a number of years after their initial decision to remain sober.

A Typical Self-Help Meeting

Although self-help groups such as AA have a particular belief system that is actually written out and expressed in various prescribed activities, many others have no such ideology. Others, such as the Adoption Forum, widow and widower groups, young-adult diabetic groups, and Compassionate Friends, achieve their results through a relatively simple cluster of social psychological processes: mutual identification, confession, catharsis, the removal of stigmatized feelings, and mutual support in problem solving. In this process, the "I" feeling is replaced with a "we" feeling, the individual gains a sense of belonging, and together members redefine certain norms of behavior.

A typical self-help meeting is usually set for a certain day of the week. Often, meeting times are listed in the local paper. The meetings usually last an hour or two, and sometimes juice or coffee is served before or after the meeting. In some meetings, no refreshments are served and members may go out together to do their socializing.

Meetings start fairly promptly. Members enter and sit in a circle. The person who is the leader (almost always a volunteer) begins the meeting by asking those present to introduce themselves and briefly describe their situations. For example, at a meeting of Compassionate Friends, a self-help organization for bereaved parents, members state their names, give the names and ages of the children who died, and briefly recount how the deaths occurred. Usually, new members speak first and then the older members recount their experiences. Members listen attentively, ask questions, and give affirmations of support. After both old and new members have spoken, the meeting may go in one of two directions. An expert guest speaker—a psychologist, physician, or social worker, for example—might open the discussion, addressing a particular aspect of the grieving process. The speaker delivers prepared remarks and then invites members to express their feelings or share their particular methods of dealing with the phase under discussion. The other option is to hold a general discussion on a particular topic. For example, in the Compassionate Friends meeting, the discussion of the evening might center on the topic of guilt. Members speak of their own feelings and experiences, and the leader brings the discussion to a close perhaps 15 to 20 minutes before the end of the session. There might then be a "go-around," in which each member responds to a question posed by the leader—for example, "What was most helpful to you in tonight's meeting?"

The last few minutes might be taken up with business, such as setting up the next meeting and selecting the next volunteer leader. There might also be announcements of an upcoming lecture or other event of particular relevance to the members. Often, once the meeting is adjourned, members stay on to talk with each other about issues raised during the evening. Also, at this time, newcomers might be asked to sign the mailing list, dues or contributions might be collected, and literature might be circulated or laid out for the perusal of members.

The norms at a typical meeting support open communication. Members are encouraged to speak up about their own experiences. Others are encouraged to listen and support those who tell their stories. Those who have been in the group for a time encourage and affirm new participants in their self-revelations and, at the end of a meeting, make a point of personally welcoming them, thanking them for coming and sharing their experiences, and asking them to return. Tears, sadness, and anger are all acceptable within the group. Members are encouraged to explain how they coped with difficult situations and to recount both successes and failures. The prevailing climate might be summed up this way: "We've all been there. *We* especially understand the problems, and therefore we can help each other."

Stages of Development of Self-Help Groups

Groups, like people, have different needs at different times in their life cycle. Growth always involves change and a certain amount of tension between past experience and goals for the future. Even healthy, functional change incurs stress and conflicts, so it is no surprise that self-help groups struggle with certain dilemmas as they grow and mature. Each group is unique, but it is possible to outline a normative path of growth that can serve as a map for self-help groups.

Katz (1970) has outlined a developmental model for self-help groups.

1. *Origin.* The hallmark of this beginning stage is the presence of a founder—someone who assumes responsibility for getting people together. In many groups, this person is a professionally trained individual, such as a psychologist, minister, or physician. He or she may be in disagreement with the accepted treatment or service for a problem, seeing the gaps that are unaddressed or being aware of groups of people who lack adequate service. Typically, this perspective leads the professional to a different vision of how the problem can be rectified. In the case of Recovery, Inc., Abraham Low, a psychiatrist, saw a need for some sort of continued support for people leaving a mental hospital (Low, 1950). A cardiologist and founder of Mended Hearts, Dwight Harken, saw the potential benefits that peer support could offer heart patients. Founders, whether lay or professional, share one characteristic: they all have a charismatic presence that allows them effectively to organize a group of people burdened with a common concern or problem. Their personal energy and drive help mobilize potential members to begin to meet, and they provide a vision of how to help, as well as initial guidelines.

2. *Informal organizational stage.* Few hard and fast rules govern the group as it continues to meet. People join and continue their membership in the group because they get emotional sustenance and a sense of identity. People informally share the responsibility for running and organizing activities of the group; its small size and lack of complexity readily allow this to happen. Also, the role of the founder typically is reduced and his or her responsibility is diminished.

3. *Emergence of leadership.* As the beginning group develops cohesion and new members are added, new leadership emerges from within the group. The self-help group's norm of mutual aid and personal responsibility propels individuals into leadership roles. As the group continues to flourish and increase in size, there is a need to establish rules and structures so that the group can still function. At this point, natural leaders provide direction and help clarify the group's needs.

Most social scientists would agree that the first three stages characterize most self-help groups (Caplan and Killilea, 1976; Lieberman and Borman, 1979). After leaders have emerged from the membership, there are a number of different paths for self-help groups to take. Some continue through the next two steps that Katz presented. Others maintain their growth and continue at the same level, and still others become affiliated with more traditional institutions while retaining their independence. Katz's model follows the theory that organizations become more bureaucratic the longer they exist.

4. *Beginnings of formal organization.* Often, when a group continues to grow in size, it also grows in complexity. Not only does it start to serve as a self-help group, but it also must consider how it recruits new members, supports itself financially, locates space for meetings, charters new chapters, and expands its audience to include people with different yet related problems. In organizational terms this is called specialization: one part of the group attends to one piece of business, and others do other tasks. The organization becomes more defined and rigid in order to get the jobs done.

5. *Beginnings of professionalism.* In this last stage, professional fundraisers, accountants, managers, and others are hired to do the work of the organization. The self-help group has expanded to many, many chapters with a multitude of concerns, only one of which is the original face-to-face interaction of its members in small supportive groups. Obviously, the norms of the organization must shift to accommodate a nonvolunteer staff before any group can successfully negotiate this final stage. The National Association for Retarded Citizens is one such group that began as a self-help group for parents of retarded children. It has grown into a national organization that serves as a source of education and information for parents, as well as engaging in many other activities that advance the retarded individual's status and mobility in society.

One way to increase the effectiveness of self-help groups is for members to receive instruction in group leadership and communication, creating and understanding positive group norms and dealing with group issues such as sharing session time and realizing that problems often have more than one possible solution. Training in working with small groups has been found to increase member participation and the likelihood of group continuance.

Self-help groups provide a small group experience that supports and enriches their members. The next section focuses on a small group application in the workplace: total quality management, or TQM. This type of management technique utilizes small groups in the form of "teams" that share some characteristics with self-help groups yet also differ greatly in function.

Total Quality Management (TQM)

Since the first edition of this text was published in the late seventies, the use of groups as working units has increased fivefold. Twenty years ago it would have been unheard of to incorporate any kind of cooperative system into the workplace. Today, we find many different kinds of small group applications in this very area, from the problem-solving strategies of the quality circle to self-managing work teams responsible for the production of a whole product (Lawler, 1990). The use of teams to improve the quality of a business or institution has been part of a growing trend toward participative management and improvement in quality. One reason for this trend may be that extreme competitiveness, which was once thought to lead to higher performance and achievement, is now often thought to interfere with achievement (McGarvey, 1992). Perhaps the most talked-about method of using small groups in the workplace this decade is TQM: total quality management. This portion of the chapter will briefly trace the history of the TQM process, show how it fits in with the scheme of small group processes, and suggest some of its practical applications and potential pitfalls.

History of TQM

Japanese Influence   Total quality management began as an offshoot of total quality control, a management policy developed in Japan after World War II. At that time, Japan was in the process of rebuilding its industry and trying to establish itself in the world market. The Japanese Union of Scientists and Engineers, in an effort to improve the quality of Japanese products, sponsored lectures by several U.S. industrial specialists, including W. Edwards Deming. Deming presented a statistical method for controlling quality that had received little attention in the United States but was enthusiastically embraced by Japanese industry and government. By the early 1960s, Japan had implemented these ideas in the form of quality control circles. The circles were composed of five to ten workers from the same work area who, using statistical control methods, identified and developed solutions for a variety of problems that negatively affect the quality of industrial products. The quality control circle was one manifestation of an overall quality improvement effort.

Several factors existed in Japan at the time TQM was developed that made TQM particularly suitable. Japan was notorious for producing cheap, poorly made industrial products, and in order for it to compete internationally, quality and productivity had to be dramatically improved. Japan was reliant on its people as critical resources, because there was both a labor shortage after the war and a shortage of technology and industrial resources.

Japan also had an industrial policy that focused on "people building," which included an emphasis on lifetime employment, training and educational programs, and expenses for housing, medical, and recreational needs. The Japanese company was viewed as an extended family, in which employees remained for long periods of time—sometimes their entire careers—and developed close personal relationships with co-workers and superiors. All these factors made Japan fertile ground for the emergence of a team-oriented quality control effort such as TQM (Watanabe, 1991; Dumas et al., 1989; Axline, 1991).

Quality Circles in the United States   Quality circles were introduced in the United States in 1974 at the Lockheed Missile Corporation. At Lockheed conditions were favorable for quality circles because the labor force was highly skilled and success was highly dependent on quality. Lockheed reported saving three million dollars by introducing quality circles. The types of projects that quality circles took on included developing a plastic mold assembly that required fewer operations, improving the defect rate in producing circuit boards, and testing and choosing a more effective method for identification of parts. Several managers involved in introducing quality circles at Lockheed left the corporation and began a consulting firm for establishing quality circles in other companies. In 1974 Honeywell Corporation also introduced quality circles and reported considerable savings. Since then quality circles have blossomed in many diverse companies.

Three Components of TQM: Participative Management, Continuous Process Improvement, and the Use of Teams

According to Joseph R. Jablonski, writing in *Implementing Total Quality Management: An Overview,* TQM is "A cooperative form of doing business that relies on the talents and capabilities of both labor and management to continually improve quality and productivity using teams" (Jablonski, 1991). Implicit in this definition are three ingredients that are essential for the TQM process to take place: participative management, continuous process improvement, and the use of teams. It is the latter element that makes TQM an interesting contemporary application of small group processes. The second element follows directly from the idea that TQM is indeed a process, a continual transformation of the way management or an administration utilizes the knowledge and abilities of its employees (Walton, 1990). In the following pages, each of these elements is discussed in more detail.

Participative Management   TQM in the United States has become part of a trend toward increased employee involvement in a variety of work decisions and concerns that traditionally have been the domain of management. *Participative management* is a generic term for a broad range of innovations of this type. It has developed as a result of several factors, including the voice of the labor force expressed through unions; theories about human nature, motivation, and work; and many other changes that have evolved in the workplace over the last 50 years.

Over the years, a rising level of employee dissatisfaction and a decline in worker productivity have given additional impetus to acceptance of a participative management philosophy. According to social scientists, worker dissatisfaction, apathy, and alienation—all critical factors in slumping productivity—have been associated with increased task specialization of work and increased bureaucratization of organizations. Employees are segregated and have specialized work tasks that isolate them from peers and from completion of the products they work on. Jobs have become dull and routinized to the point where workers, despite higher pay and better work conditions, lack motivation and job satisfaction. They have limited contact with authority and little ability to affect their immediate work environment (Sashkin, 1984).

According to Johnson et al. (1991), behavior analysts have often suggested that "participation by the consumers of behavioral intervention will enhance cooperation and maintenance." If this is true, taking part in decision-making processes will boost employee interest in work-related tasks. Several social scientists have also proposed theories concerning individual behavior at work that support participative management. Maslow (1954) developed a theory of motivation that emphasized the human desire to work and function to one's capacity and potential. Hackman (1975; Hackman and Suttle, 1977) demonstrated that employee motivation and satisfaction results from the job itself, as well as from the work environment. He suggested that employees would be motivated by a job in which they had some degree of autonomy, were able to perceive results of their work, and obtained feedback about their job performance.

Work experiments in various countries have further shaped the trend toward increased employee participation. For example, there are a large number of self-managed plants in the countries that formerly constituted Yugoslavia. Volvo, in Sweden, organizes work to be completed by teams rather than the traditional assembly lines. Autonomous work groups have been formed in a number of British coal mines (Ellerman, 1984; Kelly and Khozan, 1980; Trist, 1981). In the United States, General Motors Corporation and Donnelly Mirror Company, among others, have developed similar innovations ("Participative Management at Work," 1977; Walton, 1979). These experiments expand the influence and responsibility of rank-and-file employees and attempt to incorporate a consideration of human social needs into the organization of work (Bernstein, 1982; Burck, 1981; Main, 1981).

Total quality management represents a workplace experiment that emphasizes employee involvement through the use of teams designed to analyze the process in which a systemic problem is occurring and then to solve the problem. Before we describe in more detail the functioning of those teams, we must further explore the concept of continuous process improvement, the second essential element in TQM.

Continuous Process Improvement   According to Ellen Earle Chaffee of North Dakota University, "quality is a verb, not a noun" (Sherr and Teeter, 1991). It follows that TQM is something that an organization actively engages in, and it is anything but random. Many people have tried to explain exactly what continuous process improvement entails, but probably the simplest yet most revealing definition comes from the Japanese in the form of one word: *Kaizen. Kaizen* means "constant improvement and incremental growth from taking very small risks each day" (Lagana, 1989). Kaisen is associated with a quality control that is not concerned simply with "product quality or productivity improvements" but with improvements in general organizational activities. In other words, the entire system needs constant reevaluation (Watanabe, 1991).

If an organization can control its processes—the way it does business or conducts itself generally on a daily basis—it is well on the road to quality improvement. Many companies have reported that "up to 80 percent of low-quality and organizational performance problems are traceable to processes, not employees" (Axline, 1991). In fact, a direct link has been found between quality and productivity. For example, when Bell of Canada began monitoring the speed of its operators as a group rather than individually, not only did productivity stay up but the operators themselves also claimed both that their services improved and that they liked their job more (Bernstein, 1991). All of which leads us directly into our next element: how the continuous process of improvement gets implemented. The vehicle for change in the previous example, as with the entire TQM process, is the work team.

The Use of Teams   The use of teams, or small groups, to solve problems in the workplace is another aspect of total quality control. It is estimated that problem-solving teams called *quality circles* are used by more than half of all large corporations. On the other side of the coin is the use of self-managing work teams that are responsible for producing a whole product or providing a complete service within a large work environment wherein all team members are expected to know, thoroughly, all aspects of each of their teammates' jobs as well as their own. Although this type of team has gained popularity, less than 10 percent of the workforce utilizes them (Lawler, 1990). Each of these kinds of teams represents an extreme, as we shall see.

The purpose of using teams in the TQM process is so that the best cross section of individuals who work within a given process are brought together to change and improve that process. The process could be the regular functioning of a university staff or the production of automobiles. In the former case, the teams might include administrators, professors, office personnel—whoever is deeply enough involved in the process to recognize opportunities for improvement (Jablonski, 1991). In the latter case, the teams might include everyone on a given production line, as well as the engineers and upper management—again, anyone who would recognize, at any level, an opportunity for improvement. Because so many problems in an organization are interdepartmental, they are often difficult to solve. What the TQM process suggests is that an organization becomes "seamless" by dissolving interdepartmental divisions so that problems can be addressed without the barriers that often prevent an organization from moving forward (Leebov and Scott, 1990). The teams must therefore be composed of employees from all levels of management, as well as the "frontline" workers. Membership depends not on status or placement but on proximity to the process or problem under consideration.

Quality circles were initially viewed as a major step to increased worker involvement. By using this method, groups of workers could examine problems of their department (or assigned problems), and as a group, recommend solutions based on their intimate knowledge of the work organization. The group was free to analyze problems as it wanted; it was not directed to reach specific, desired solutions by management. The reports on quality circles were very positive at first. However, after greater experience with the method, the outcomes raise many questions about why some have greater success than others.

Why Some Quality Circles Succeed and Others Fail

The functioning of a quality circle, just like that of any small group, depends on a variety of internal factors that the circle leader and members must manage. The circle must have a task and goal for which members have sufficient skill and access to resources to succeed. The membership of the circle must be relevant to the task, and vice versa. The group must be able to translate circle values into norms that successfully guide group behavior. The leader must establish procedures for decision making and conflict resolution that enable the group to reach its goals and manage its interpersonal and emotional needs. In addition to the group process issues we have discussed, the "fit" of the circle into the larger organization is a critical factor in determining the circle's success or failure.

Supporters of quality circles claim that the circles have the potential to do anything, that they give workers opportunities to identify and solve real problems of any type. They consider circles' solutions superior to solutions reached by other means and argue that because workers participated in finding those solutions, workers in general are highly committed to their implementation. But others consider quality circles a fad, an easy-to-implement package that calls for little administrative commitment. These critics point out that more than 60 percent of the quality circles in American organizations have failed (1986).

Two recent studies shed some light on the debate over the value of quality circles. Marks and his colleagues (1985) and later Marks alone (1986) examined the claims that quality circles improve the quality of work life and job performance of participants. These researchers worked in a manufacturing department and collected data over a thirty-month period beginning six months before a quality circle program began. They found that participation in the quality circle did indeed have a strong impact on areas of participants' lives that were directly related to quality circle activity—for example, decision making, group communications, and job advancement. But participants themselves did not change in their attitudes about the organization or in their feelings about organizationwide communication, job challenge, personal responsibility for getting work done, and overall job satisfaction. Among machine operators, participation in quality circles raised productivity and reduced absenteeism but did not increase satisfaction with the work situation.

In another study, Lawler and Ledford (1986) examined nine separate units of a large conglomerate that varied greatly in employment criteria and the amount of training provided. The researchers found that certain quality circles did succeed in changing the organization and that these shared several characteristics:

1. Sufficient training of members, including efforts to improve members' understanding of group dynamics and ways to work effectively in groups
2. Both inside and outside the circles, good access to useful information
3. Accurate record keeping, including the establishment of measurable goals for the quality circle
4. The creation of the circles themselves from intact work teams

These researchers found little evidence, however, that quality circles change corporate culture or improve individual work satisfaction and productivity. The general conclusion was that the quality circle technique was not strong enough to promote real organizational change.

Since quality circles were introduced in the United States in 1974, their goals have been to increase productivity and improve the quality of work life. Although quality circles have been successful in Japan, in the United States they have yielded mixed results. Current research on U.S. quality circles has uncovered some of the factors responsible for the failure of quality circles to meet their goals fully. Gmelch and Misking (1986) identified one of these factors as the inability of American companies to recognize and react to circle members' need to coordinate their efforts. The basis for this inability seems to be a conflict between widely held ideas and the basic notions on which quality circles are founded. Ferris and Wagner (1985) identified three notions that support quality circles:

1. Group performance is superior to individual performance.
2. Workers desire participation.
3. Participation improves productivity.

However, these researchers' analysis of the differences between workers' perspectives on work in the United States and in Japan suggest that the workers in most U.S. companies do not subscribe to these ideas. U.S. workers have an individualistic orientation toward work, whereas Japanese workers have a collectivistic orientation. The concepts that Ferris and Wagner identified conflict sharply with the embedded U.S. ideology. Thus, for the typical U.S. worker, quality circles themselves go against the grain.

Another factor responsible for the failure of quality circles in the United States is the relative lack of problem-solving skills among U.S. workers and of team-building skills among U.S. leaders (Gmelch and Misking, 1986). Two other factors are a lack of receptiveness to circle members' ideas and a failure of commitment to the basic idea of the circles among managers (Werther, 1983). The success and longevity of quality circles depend on management's receptivity to solutions proposed by the circles and a willingness to implement them. When their solutions languish, circle members lose interest and energy.

Nevertheless, in studies by Mohrman and Novelli (1985), Lawler and Ledford (1986) and Lawler and Mohrman (1985), the researchers concluded that quality circles can succeed at three kinds of tasks. First, quality circles can operate to suggest ways of improving work group communications and increasing awareness about quality and employee productivity. Second, quality circles can be useful in special short-term situations—for example, introducing a new technology or solving a major quality problem. Finally, quality circles can perform a bridging function when a company changes over from a traditional hierarchical organization to a more participative one.

The culture and management style of the organization must allow and actively support the participative approach of quality circles. A parochial, unyielding, autocratic management style will not respond to the participative input of a circle. Often circles fail because management did not assess the readiness and preparation of the organization before instituting a quality circle program. Organizations underestimate the attitudinal and organizational changes that occur when a participatory program such as quality circles is implemented.

A successful quality circle program necessitates visible support from both top and middle management. Where they are present, unions must also be involved in the planning and implementation stage to insure their support. In a study to determine why quality circles failed in five U.S. companies, the results suggested that the success of quality circles ultimately depended on continued support from trade unions (Dale and Hayward, 1984).

Management must fully understand the circle program and its values and be prepared to respond positively to the input from circles. Not only must the changes suggested by quality circles be compatible with the organization (Steel and Shane, 1986), but managers, supervisors, and workers must truly subscribe to the basic notion of voluntarism upon which quality circles rest (Meyer and Stott, 1985).

Middle managers, to whom quality circles' solutions are usually presented, often resist these solutions, probably because (1) they are reluctant to accept ideas from subordinates, and (2) they are uncomfortable with the problem-solving process characteristic of quality circles. Moreover, middle managers have no direct involve-ment until they are called on to approve or implement a quality circle suggestion, which increases their distance from the solution.

This resistance to quality circles on the part of middle managers has been a major concern to those who would expand the use of quality circles. One suggested means of overcoming this resistance (Bushe, 1987) was to involve middle managers in problem-solving groups of their own, on the assumption that such involvement would produce attitude differences in them. In a study of 415 middle managers in the United States automobile industry, managers in permanent quality circles had the most positive attitude toward the circles themselves. Those in temporary groups, however, had the most negative attitudes toward the circles—even more negative than managers with no group experience at all. It would seem, then, that a commitment to a quality circle grows over time.

Training is often a key element in the success of circles. The entire organization, not only those who volunteer to be in circles, needs training in the basic principles and functioning of quality circles. The circle leaders and members need sufficient training to develop the skills necessary for team problem solving.

There is an increasing emphasis on the training of quality circle leaders and participants in communication, group dynamics, and team decision making. Certain monographs, such as that of Blaker (1982), present detailed information on quality circle training. Still, companies that hope to use quality circles as quick-fix solutions will find the effects similar to those of aspirin—they treat symptoms and provide some immediate relief but don't touch underlying issues, such as management–employee tension and the underutilization of workers, that caused problems in the first place.

Companies that try to cut corners by limiting the planning and training stage inevitably run into difficulties down the road.

In some organizations, circles are inadequately implemented because manage-ment is not truly interested in or prepared for employee participation or is not committed to the "people-building" attitude necessary for successful circles. Man-agement can sabotage the circle in endless ways, including overcontrolling the circle, not providing an adequate budget, not allowing access to necessary infor-mation or resources, setting restrictive deadlines, focusing too narrowly on the financial return, providing an autocratic leadership style disguised as participative, repeatedly rejecting circle recommendations, and not building in avenues of rec-ognition for the circle's accomplishments. Setting unreasonably high expectations for a circle program can also set it up for failure and disillusionment. Many people, especially organized labor, distrust the labor and management cooperation inher-ent in a quality circle program. They fear that circles will be used as another guise for production speed-ups and believe that workers should get a financial share of the profits generated by the circle.

It has become increasingly evident that the quality circle is not a panacea for all the problems associated with productivity, quality, and employee dissatisafaction. If a company institutes a circle program to cure or resolve a poor labor–management relationship, the circle is destined to fail. If a company has been mismanaged, lacks sufficient critical resources, or has an ineffectual administrative structure, a quality circle program will not make up for these failures. But quality circles can succeed in an organizational environment in which participation is encouraged, employees can have an impact in areas of quality and productivity problems, and the company perceives its employees as a valuable resource.

Some Current Examples of TQM

What we shall see in the next few pages are some real world examples of the TQM process in action. Although the organizations involved are quite different, the theory behind all these applications of TQM is the same, and the problems that arise in its implementation are strikingly similar as well.

TQM in the Public Sector   The issue of quality in the public sector is especially problematic because it often must be achieved in the environment of increasingly scarce public resources. Like many troubled organizations, government offices must continuously evolve and implement new management policies if improvement in the quality of their services is to occur (Milakovich, 1991).

When Joseph Sensenbrenner became mayor of Madison, Wisconsin, in 1983, he decided that his organization, the city government, would have to create a "culture of quality" rather than allow the "we'll fix it downstream" mentality that is so pervasive in our culture to continue to gnaw away at the city's infrastructure. Sensenbrenner knew this would be a difficult task, given that "government invented the status quo."

What Sensenbrenner found to be one of the most difficult things to accomplish—and indeed what Deming himself presented as one of the most important points in achieving the TQM transformation—is the process of driving the fear out of an organization. What Michael Milakovich, associate professor of political science at the University of Miami, says is that there is such a fear of change in the public sector that great productivity losses may occur merely as a result of "chronic anxiety." These feelings are often not unfounded; the old school of management has always held that the use of fear is the only way to insure employee loyalty and increase job performance (Milakovich, 1991). For TQM to be successful, managers must relinquish power and loosen the stranglehold of fear on their workers.

Another thing Sensenbrenner found was that his departments were "too self-contained to be useful to one another" and that the very concept of being helpful was something completely out of his workers' realm of experience. What the city needed, and ultimately got, was a "quality army" comprising managers and frontline employees who would lead the way in taking "responsibility for risk as well as sharing credit for success" within his organization. He found that consulting and enlisting frontline employees in the team problem-solving and improvement processes enormously improved both morale and productivity (Sensenbrenner, 1991).

A similar story is that of the Parkview Episcopal Medical Center in Pueblo, Colorado. Another publicly funded institution, Parkview had to be very careful not to increase quality at the expense of its clientele. And, like the city of Madison, it found one of the major barriers to success to be managers who were afraid to stand up and say what they thought instead of trying to figure out what the boss wanted them to think. Once Parkview's employees overcame their fear, teams made up of surgeons, technicians, nurses, and scheduling managers were able to examine more easily the problems they faced and identify places where improvement could be achieved (Koska, 1990). Although garnering the support of all levels of the staff is often a lengthy process, no less is required for the TQM process to work. As we shall see, these are problems and solutions that are not unique to the public sector.

School-Based Management: TQM in Education   One very controversial application of the TQM process is that of school-based management, an obvious descendent of the participative policy of management. Just as in the public sector, years of top-down management have created deep wells of mistrust and suspicion. Thus, what should be an ultimately collaborative process whereby teachers become involved in the process of managing their own school is often perceived by teachers as another demand by an insensitive administration that hasn't done its own job. The training required to learn the skills and tools associated with turning the responsibility—and ultimately the rewards—over to the teachers and administrators as a working team is not to be taken lightly. It is very easy for middle managers, or their equivalents, in an attempt to regain control and consolidate authority, to abandon collaborative principles early. This, of course, is recognized by the faculty as exactly what they expected, and it generates predictable resistance.

School-based management can be viewed as a partial remedy to the deteriorating performance, bankruptcy, and despair so frequently found throughout our public schools today. In implementing the process, however, administrators must take care not to sacrifice training to save money and, even more important, not to undermine the level of risk taking that is required for such a system to work (Lagana, 1989). In the end, once again, involving individuals in the decision making, makes those decisions more durable and acceptable—an important outcome for an education system whose participants are growing ever more alienated and isolated (Hansen, 1990).

TQM in the Private Sector: Where it All Began   In today's global economy, businesses of all types are seeking methods that not only provide profitability but also create a much more particularized customer evaluation because of the availability of that world market. This is exactly what Deming designed TQM to do: to take advantage of the excellence within a company by putting the responsibility for quality into the hands of all who can potentially control it. It has worked for the Japanese, but businesses in the United States seem to have had more of a struggle. For many of the same reasons we cited when we discussed its applications in the private and educational sectors, TQM may fail in the business arena.

One important factor that often spells failure when private industries try to implement the TQM process is the high level of competitiveness that exists not only between companies but also among workers within a company. According to Harvard Business School professor Rosabeth Moss Kanter, "A sure sign of competitiveness gone awry is when the players pay more attention to beating their rivals then to performing the task well" (McGarvey, 1992). If TQM depends on the use of teams, how do we engender a team attitude in a market characterized by competition? How do cooperative attitudes become a part of a business world where quality has rarely been made a priority? The answer is that it must become a priority. American businesses are slowly learning that it pays off in the end. The Ford Taurus is an excellent example of how some of the ideas in TQM theory become a success story. Not only did Ford create a vehicle that was built well but its features were determined by teams of researchers and employees who ultimately had the greatest familiarity with both the process and the product.

In another success story, Federal Express learned that because it began by putting quality ahead of quantity or profitability, in time, both quantity and profitability followed. Just as in the public sector, however, none of this can be achieved without careful consideration of and protection against the problems inherent in the TQM strategy. One employee in a midwestern factory likened his situation to being afraid of "pushing the button" and stopping production in order to allow "impromptu work teams to whirl into troubleshooting activities." The problem is that he then must take responsibility for the lost time, even if, in the long run, more problems are avoided through his conscientiousness (Dumas et al., 1989). In short, the temptation to maintain the status quo is pervasive throughout our society and is one of the greatest inhibitors of the success of TQM, whether it is applied in the business, government, health care, or educational arenas. The last section in this part of the chapter deals with this and other common problems encountered by organizations attempting to implement TQM, as well as some suggestions for overcoming them.

Total Quality Management: The Ultimate Challenge

We have seen that the process of total quality management is one that might be profitably applied to many different sectors of our society. In fact, one of the greatest barriers to innovation using the TQM process is social rather than organizational. If businesses, institutions, or organizations of any kind continue to ignore whole categories of people as sources of ideas, they will certainly stifle innovation. Many organizations that have "jumped on the quality bandwagon" in the last few years have found that their shortcomings exist not "within existing organizational lines" but at the boundaries between work teams (Kanter, 1982). Problems arise as a result of a dilemma faced by middle managers, who must juggle the demands of subordinates who are dealing with their own increased responsibilities and those of top managers who are pushing for results (Schlesinger, 1984).

The solutions are not simple. From the top down, upper managers must learn to engender a high level of trust among all organizational members. As a result, middle managers will be able to focus on giving the necessary support and attention to the frontline workers. This will afford all those who have access to the process an area in which they can "dare to look for improvement." According to Susan Leddick, "managers need definition to help them behave . . . supportively toward their subordinates [who are] working on quality improvement" (Leddick, 1990).

In many ways, the ability of managers to relinquish their traditional source of power and authority can be considered the "foundation for the future success or failure of a new work system" such as total quality management (Manz et al. 1990). The new management role, as "facilitator" of work processes, requires extra training and consideration. Here team leaders coach rather than control (Milakovich, 1991).

TQM, then, requires three essential elements to survive: trust, support, and training. There's a world of potential for implementing the TQM process, but the process is doomed to fail unless some of the same qualities inherent in any successful group are exaggerated in the work teams using TQM.

Focus Groups

Imagine that you are an advanced Mass Media Communications student and that the final project of your course work is to produce a radio talk show to be broadcast by the university's radio station. After many hours of planning, writing, and re-arranging the radio program's content, you are ready to go on the air. Besides transmitting the program to college students, you have also recruited an audience, some of them your classmates, for the studio. The introductions are over and the talk show host announces the topic: sexual harassment at the workplace. As the host interviews a panel of three men and three women, graphic descriptions of what the panelists deem sexual harassment are given, some not without teary eyes, expressions of disbelief, and embarrassed giggles.

While you are anxiously watching and listening, the host questions one of the men about his harassment experience: "So, what did your boss do to embarrass you?" The panelist replies, "She'd sneak up behind me, pat my buns, and try to reach further." A noisy commotion comes from the audience: some women look shocked, others stifle their giggles, and some men hoot and cheer. All these re-actions are expressed and gone in a flash.

To you, the audience's liveliness perhaps signals the success of your show. To the social scientist, however, it tells a different tale: gender differences in evaluation of sexual experiences. To learn what these differences are, the social scientist would conduct in-depth interviews with some of the members of the audience—not individually, but in a group. The rationale for this type of interviewing is the assumption that in a group, people tell more or give a deeper understanding of what they think or feel about a specific topic. Social scientists have always been curious about exactly what type of behavior or event evokes negative or positive responses to a given social situation, and why. As they studied the audience responses to radio programs, films, advertisements, and government decisions (both domestic and foreign), the method they used to extract information during the in-depth interviews became known as group depth interviews, or focus groups.

History of Focus Groups

Originally, the focus-group-interview technique, or the focus group, grew out of Lazarsfeld and Merton's efforts to glean an understanding of how radio audiences evaluate radio programs and the reasons for their judgments (Stewart and Shamdasani, 1990). Shortly after the outbreak of World War II, their research subjects consisted of studio audience members who, while listening to a radio program, were asked to push a red button when they heard anything that provoked their anger, boredom, or disbelief. They were asked to push a green button whenever their responses were pleasant, amusing, or thought-provoking. After recording their responses, members of the audience were invited (on a voluntary basis) to discuss and explain their responses. These spontaneously recorded reactions functioned as guidelines by giving the discussion a firm and structured focus while it delved into discourse geared to unearth the emotional/logical underpinnings of the choices. The focus group, as a research tool, took on the dimension of gathering information not via surveys, questionnaires, or individual interviews that distance the respondents from the researcher, but via a person's repertoire of perceptions, ideas, assumptions, opinions, and beliefs expressed in the presence of the researcher.

During World War II, the focus-group-interview technique was applied to populations other than radio audiences. For the research branch of the United States Army Information and Education Division, Merton applied his technique to the study of the Army personnel who had watched training and morale-booster films (Merton, Fiske, and Kendall, 1956). His research findings, gathered during the war and later at Columbia University, laid the groundwork for *Mass Persuasion,* which focused on the persuasive impact of mass media (Merton, Fiske, and Curtis, 1946). Soon the focus-group interviews, known as focus groups, developed and expanded into such fields as marketing, advertising, program evaluation, communications, and public policy.

Like any type of research on humans, focus-group research has its limitations: each focus group represents data derived from the group members as they respond to the group. In other words, each group member is affected and influenced by the others and by the interviewer's questions, probings, reactions, and over-all demeanor. Still, the information that social scientists have gathered by applying the focus-group technique has contributed to our knowledge about how people think, form ideas, beliefs, opinions, and judgments, and how they explain them.

The Focus Group Defined

Suppose you have just come home from the mall where you happily found and purchased a battery-operated mobile for your sister's first child. Anxiously, you look at the clock: 3:55 P.M. Still in your coat, you flick on the television, press the Channel 6 button, and sink into the couch cushions while taking your coat off. The theme music of your favorite program seeps into your consciousness. Then you see her: Oprah Winfrey. You know the topic of her show—unusual sexual and behavioral habits—because you saw it advertised the day before.

As you watch, your curiosity peaks, but the telephone rings. Reluctantly you answer. A man asks whether you have watched the Oprah Winfrey program and how often. You tell him that you have seen it at least three or four times a week for the last two years and that you tape the shows you have to miss. Because you meet the criterion of watching Oprah daily, the man (a representative of a research company) selects you to participate in a study of the pros and cons of revealing intimate behaviors and thoughts via the mass media. After the caller answers your questions and satisfies you that the research is legitimate, he invites you to a one-time meeting to discuss intimate disclosures in public. A free trip and ticket to the Oprah Winfrey show are offered for your effort. Excited and flattered, you agree to attend the meeting. You are about to experience a focus group.

Focus groups are distinguished from others (therapy, advisory, assertiveness, training, and self-help groups and quality circles) by the following characteristics (Krueger and Patton, 1988):

1. Seven to ten voluntary members who participate in one meeting that last 1 to 1½ hours under the direction of a moderator. Members do not know each other.

2. Group members share a commonality, such as watching Oprah in our hypothetical case.

3. Group members generate data that are recorded and/or observed unobtrusively, through a two-way mirror.

4. The data generated are qualitative—that is, they proceed from in-depth, spontaneous, natural responses. The data are expressed in the respondents' own words and in the context of the question asked.

5. The in-depth discussion is focused in terms of the research interests of the sponsor of the study by the interviewer (who is referred to as the moderator in focus-groups literature). The moderator steers the discussion, probes selectively, and maintains the focus of the discussion.

Besides defining and setting focus groups apart, these features offer social scientists guidelines for conducting studies. Thus, although some variation may occur when the technique of focus-group interviews is applied to research, the basic characteristics are upheld and followed.

Preparing for the Summit: A Focus Group Application

In 1988, then President Reagan met with then Soviet leader Gorbachev—the first trip an American president had made to Moscow in fourteen years. President Reagan's preparation for the U.S.–Soviet summit entailed the extensive use of focus groups and " . . . all the care that Madison Avenue devotes to an advertising campaign for a new bar of soap" (Gerstenzang, 1988). The preparations for the U.S.–Soviet summit consisted to think tanks, experts on the Soviet Union, and focus groups made up of Americans living in a Philadelphia suburb. The focus, or topic for the focus group, was *how to achieve credibility and support for the upcoming summit from Americans.* Pollsters hired by the Republican National Committee met with blue-collar workers, professionals, and mothers of both parties. What they searched for were (1) words in which to express themes for the summit, words that the public would believe in, and (2) a message, containing those words, to the world that would convey the basic concerns of the American public.

After holding several focus-group sessions, it was concluded that "A brighter future and a safer world for all people" represented the American public's perception of what was important and needed to be conveyed to the rest of the world. Besides generating the message of a "brighter" future and a "safer" world, the focus groups also revealed that "people want to see more exchanges—people-to-people or student exchanges." In this case, the application of focus groups revealed the primary concerns and hopes of the American public: a future in a safe world, which hinges on the U.S.–Soviet treaty that bans ground-launched, medium-range nuclear missiles.

Uses of Focus Groups

Just as self-help groups and quality circles are not cures for all problems represented by, and reflected in, the purposes and goals of these groups, neither are focus groups. However, focus groups are a useful research tool with which to extract information from people who otherwise would have to report their thoughts, ideas, opinions, and judgments by either making a check mark or circling a number in a questionnaire. The exciting part about focus groups is that people, sitting together in a small group with a moderator, have a chance to explore their thinking about specific topics and thus contribute to the growing pool of knowledge about human behavior. Also, participating in focus groups seems to be invigorating; people report gaining enthusiasm and satisfaction from the experience. Focus groups instill in group members a sense of being important. What they have to say matters. This is especially appealing in a world where the common complaint—between bosses and employees, wives and husbands, parents and children, students and teachers, government leaders and their constitutents—is "You're not listening to me."

Some New Directions for Small Groups

In their most current applications, quality circles and focus groups are both being used at universities. Universities are confronted by a shrinking pool of students and by reduced financial support. They are realizing that their staff theoreticians and professors/consultants do not have a magic formula for attracting and retaining "customers." As a result, universities are now turning to industry to learn about quality, customer service, and focus groups.

University administrators are setting up total quality management programs. These programs are as much mindset as method. They require each department to define its customers, enhance activities linked to servicing these customers, and eliminate almost everything else.

TQM is a leadership philosophy that looks at each product and service from everyone's point of view. In 1990 more than 500 academics came to hear industry speakers at the first TQM symposium, hosted by the University of West Virginia.

The lessons of TQM are not easy to learn. TQM is not political, and academia is a political minefield. TQM is a team approach, and universities are not known to work well in teams. Universities deal with multiple customer groups: students who pay tuition, the companies who will hire the students, people who approve research grants, and the people who use the research. Universities are very bureaucratic. Many diverse types of people are involved in the "simple" process of collecting money for grant programs. There are faculty members, department chiefs, the head of the school, the office of research negotiation, and so on. There are hundreds of ways to make mistakes.

TQM breaks such problems into manageable tasks. The University of Pennsylvania carved a team out of each group in the process and charged it with reducing errors and lowering deficits. It designed new invoices, set out negotiation guidelines, and simplified communications and accounting.

Most universities are now trying this approach. TQM teams interview students, faculty members, recruiters—all sorts of "customers"—to see what they want done differently and how to do it. There is also talk of using TQM principles with the faculty. Suggestions include distributing a clear syllabus on day 1, having accessible office hours, and giving advance notice of when final exams will be.

After conducting focus groups with students, the University of Tennessee's College of Business Administration changed an arbitrary system of scheduled 15-minute sessions with counselors in favor of one that allots time in accordance with the complexity of the problem. On the request of participants in the advanced management program, it arranges follow-up visits by faculty members to company premises months after the course's end. To please other departments, financial affairs provides simplified accounting statements for department heads and more detailed ones for donors who want to see where their money goes.

Universities, then, are establishing and using adaptations of what were corporate quality circles and reaping the benefits of focus groups. It is not in business and industry alone that the effectiveness of small groups is being put to the test.

◆ ◆ EXERCISE 1

Creative Imaging of Self-Help

Objectives

- To better understand the meaning of "self-help"
- To learn more about leaderless groups
- To examine an abstract idea in a nonlinear, creative mode

Rationale

The concept of self-help groups is one that everyone is familiar with, but there is much discussion about what it really means. This exercise gives the class an opportunity to explore the idea of self-help within a small, leaderless group that replicates some of the same process issues found in self-help groups.

Materials

Sheets of newsprint or easel paper

Markers or crayons

Masking tape

Action

1. Divide the class into equal-sized groups of from four to six people.

2. Tell each group that it will be responsible for drawing a picture of "What does self-help mean to you?" (Post this question on the board.)

3. The finished product can be any type of combination of images; the only limitation is that it not include any writing or words.

4. Stress that there are no wrong or right answers and that the pictures will not be judged on artistic merit.

5. Make sure that each group has a place to work separately from other groups, such as a section of the room, the hallway, a lounge, or an adjoining empty room.

6. Give the groups from 20 to 30 minutes to plan and execute the picture.

7. Bring the class together as a whole and post the pictures. Have each

group present its picture and explain what the images or symbols mean and why they were chosen.

8. Discuss the pictures and the process of each group (30 to 50 minutes).

Questions for Discussion

Pictures

1. What common themes are portrayed in the pictures?
2. List the emotions that the pictures evoke. Caring? Compassion? Loneliness?
3. What are the five most important elements that these pictures of "self-help" communicate?

Group Process

1. How did each group decide what to draw? Was there a period of brainstorming or did one idea take hold immediately?
2. How did the group decide who would draw the picture? Was it the work of one member or were several involved?
3. Was there any conflict as the group worked? If so, what happened?
4. Did the group discuss maintenance issues (How will we do this?) or just task issues (What will we do?)?

◆ ◆ *EXERCISE 2*

Building Bridges

Objectives

- To experience different leadership styles
- To examine the impact of leadership style on group task
- To understand autocratic, democratic, and laissez-faire leadership styles

Rationale

Quality circles utilize a democratic style of leadership that involves explicit goal statements, joint participation in identifying, defining, and solving problems, and reliance on a high level of commitment and feedback. Problems with leadership often create major difficulties for innovations such as quality circles. When leaders attempt to change, they often swing to extremes: a previously autocratic leader may abdicate responsibility in a laissez-faire style rather than maintaining a balanced democratic approach. This exercise illustrates the impact of leadership style on work groups and gives students an appreciation of the values of democratic leadership as well as an understanding of the difficulties and complexities involved.

Materials

Miscellaneous items that can be used in building a bridge, such as blocks, Tinker Toys, cardboard tape

Action

1. Divide the class into three equal groups.
2. Select a volunteer from each group to be the group leader.
3. Instruct the leader to be either an autocratic, a democratic, or a laissez-faire leader. The autocratic leader should assign specific jobs to members, give step-by-step directions, and control the interaction among group members. The democratic leader should involve the group in joint decision making about how to proceed and should make decisions when the group gets stuck. The laissez-faire leader should give no direction to the group, explaining that they can do it any way they wish.
4. Hand out material and explain to the group that they have 45 minutes to build a bridge.

Questions for Discussion

1. How did the group function in response to the leadership style?
2. What were the students' experiences with their particular leader? Did he or she help the group function effectively? How comfortable or uncomfortable were students with the group's structure and decision-making process?
3. Did students feel acknowledged and utilized by the leader in the task? What did group members like and what did they dislike about the leadership style?
4. How involved did group members feel in completing the task?

◆ ◆ EXERCISE 3

Speaking Clearly in a Quality Circle

Objectives

- To experience some of the training given to quality circle members
- To distinguish between observation and inference
- To build observation and inference skills

Rationale

Building team leadership in a quality circle requires members to speak clearly and concretely. One common communication error is to present inferences as though they were facts. Inferences are actually interpretations, whereas facts are established by observing, hearing, touching, and smelling. For example, a person may say, "You are tired," presenting the observation as though it were a fact. The other may become angry at the speaker's audacity, while the speaker, unaware of his or her error, decides that the other is oversensitive. This problem in communication would have been avoided if the speaker had understood the difference between observation and inference.

Materials   One copy of the Observation-Inference Sheet

OBSERVATION-INFERENCE SHEET[1]

The statements that follow are either observation (left column) or inference (right column). Where there is an observation, you furnish an inference. Where there is an inference, you furnish the kind of data that might lead to that inference. Don't be concerned about "right" answers; the point of the exercise is simply to help you distinguish between data and interpretation.

Observation	Inference
1. I see my dog scratching.	
	2. Today must be a federal holiday.
3. My utility bill is 30 percent higher this month compared with last month's.	
	4. My friend was out late last night.
	5. My lover/spouse is in an amorous mood.
6. I see the hood of a car raised and someone has his head under the hood.	
7. My child received 1 C, 2 Ds, and an F on her grade report.	
	8. My companion enjoys Mexican food.

1. Blaker (1982). Reprinted by permission of Educational Quality Circles Consortium.

9. I see people around me
   looking up into the sky.
10. I've been waiting 40 minutes
    for a subway that runs on a
    15-minute schedule.

11. You don't love me
    anymore.
12. It is going to rain.

Questions for Discussion

1. How did you respond to each question? Compare your responses with those of the other participants.

2. What was your reasoning in coming to this decision?

3. What is the difference between observation and inference?

4. How can presenting inferences as fact cause difficulties in a group?

5. How would training like this be helpful for participants in quality circles?

6. How important do you think training would be?

Action   Members assemble in groups of three to four.

The facilitator distributes the sheets, announcing, "Before proceeding with this task, please read the introductory statement and follow the instructions there." Participants then fill in the sheets individually.

◆ ◆ EXERCISE 4

Being a Focus Group

Objectives

- To experience an in-depth discussion as in a focus group
- To experience being a moderator of a focus group
- To experience being a member of a focus group
- To understand the strengths and limitations of focus groups

Rationale

In a focus group, there is a subject of interest (for example, how mothers of small children feel about parenting in two-career families). The researcher is interested in learning how a variety of people in a similar situation feel about that subject. The group is led by a moderator who encourages each person to express his or her thoughts; to influence, and be influenced by, other participants; and to comment on each question or aspect of the discussion.

Preparation

One person will be the moderator. That person will select a topic and assume that she or he is conducting the focus-group discussion for a particular purpose. Here are a few suggestions for topics:

1. Should an ex-member of the Ku Klux Klan be allowed to run for public office (as was a recent candidate for governor in Louisiana)?

2. Should a family member be able to assist a husband/wife/mother/father, who has a terminal overwhelming illness and who wants to die, to take his or her own life?

3. Should homosexuals who teach in elementary schools be allowed to express who they are just as married teachers discuss their families in the course of their teaching?

4. Can an employer telling "off-color" stories constitute sexual harassment, or must it involve touching? What about an employer giving an employee unfavorable evaluations (or threatening unfavorable evaluations) upon being rebuffed?

5. Does watching violence on TV make children more violent with their friends? Does it make them use more violent language? Or encourage an attitude that war and winning at the expense of others is exciting?

6. Do you think there should be a National Health Care Act?

7. Do you think the best bargains at food stores are on the high shelves, whereas eye-level merchandise yields the biggest profit?

8. Should taxpayers provide housing for the homeless?

Here are some purposes for which the focus group might be convened:

An advertising campaign

In preparation for a political candidate deciding what issues she or he will address

A community tax dollar priority list

In preparation for formulation of a school board policy

In planning a new magazine

A series of newspaper articles

A projected radio or TV show

The moderator will select a topic, decide "for whom he is working," and develop a list of questions to ask.

The Group

Four to ten people volunteer to be participants in a discussion. All agree to represent one particular population, such as college students, parents of children under eight, or women in the labor force.

Observers

The others are observers. They do not participate. They take notes.

Action

The moderator invites members to participate in a discussion. Each is encouraged to express his or her thoughts, ideas, feelings. (The discussion continues for 20 to 30 minutes.) The moderator states the topics but does not reveal for whom discussion is being conducted. After a time, the moderator thanks everyone for their participation and assures them that their responses will be very helpful. The members "leave." Then the observers and the moderator talk about how they think the discussion went. They report their observations and discuss what the results mean for the "client" (the organization on whose behalf the focus group was convened). This analysis should take about 15 minutes.

Discussion

The entire group discusses the following questions:

1. How are focus-group data different from those derived from questionnaires or surveys?
2. What are the benefits of focus group?
3. How do focus-group members feel?
4. What are limitations of focus groups?
5. How would you assess the credibility of focus group?

References

Axline, Larry L. "TQM: A look in the mirror." *Management Review.* 80 (July 1991), 64.

Babbitt, R. "One company's approach to quality circles." Reprint. Cambridge, Mass.: American Biltrite, Inc., 1981.

Bean, M. "Alcoholics anonymous, part I." *Psychiatric Annals,* 5 (1975), 7–61.

Bean, M. "Alcoholics anonymous, part II." *Psychiatric Annals,* 5 (1975), 7–57.

Bernstein, A. *"Quality is becoming job one in the office, too."* *Business Week,* April 29, 1991, 52–26.

Bernstein, P. "Necessary elements for effective worker participation in decision making." In *Workplace Democracy and Social Change,* eds F. Lindenfeld and J. Rothschild-Whitt. Boston: Porter, Sargent, 1982.

Blaker, K. E. *Facilitation Skills in Quality Circles* (monograph). Redwood City, Calif.: Educational Quality Circles Consortium, San Mateo County Office of Education, 1982.

Blumer, H. *New Outline of the Principles of Sociology.* Ed. A. Lee. New York: Barnes and Noble, 1951, pp. 199–220.

Brockner, J., and T. Hess. "Self-esteem and task performance in quality circles." *Academy of Management Journal,* 29, No. 3 (1986), 617–623.

Burck, C. "Working smarter." *Fortune,* June 15, 1981, 68–73.

Bushe, G. R. "Temporary or permanent middle-management groups? Correlates with attitudes in QWL change projects." *Group & Organization Studies,* 12, No. 1 (March 1987), 23–37.

Caplan, G., and M. Killilea, eds. *Support Systems and Mutual Help: Multidisciplinary Explorations.* New York: Grune and Stratton, 1976.

Cluck, G. G., and R. J. Cline. "The circle of others: Self-help groups for the bereaved." *Communication Quarterly,* 34, No. 3 (1986), 306–325.

Cox, J., and B. G. Dale. "Quality circle members' views on quality circles." *Leadership & Organization Development Journal,* 6, No. 2 (1985), 20–23.

Dale, B. G., and S. G. Hayward. "Some reasons for quality circle failure: Part III." *Leadership & Organization Development Journal,* 5, No. 4 (1984), 27–32.

Dean, J. W. "The decision to participate in quality circles." *Journal of Applied Behavioral Science,* 21, No. 3 (1985), 317–327.

Deutsch, C. H., "Corporate lessons in campus quality." *The New York Times,* August 4, 1991.

Dumas, R., N. Cushing, and C. Laughline Zenger-Miller, Inc. Foundations for Company-Wide Quality Programs. Zenger Miller, M0066 (1/89).

Ellerman, D. "What is a workers' cooperative?" Reprint. Somerville, Mass.: Industrial Cooperative Association, 1984.

"Employee Involvement." Reprint. Belmont, Mass.: Northeast Labor Management Center, 1984.

Fawcett, S. B. In "Getting help from helping," by D. Hurley, *Psychology Today,* 22, No. 1 (January 1988), 63–67.

Ferris, G. R., and J. A. Wagner, III. "Quality circles in the United States: A conceptual re-evaluation." *Journal of Applied Behavioral Science,* 21, No. 2 (May 1985), 155–167.

Gerstenzang, J. "Shades of Madison Avenue seen in summit theme." *The Los Angeles Times,* 1988.

Gmelch, W. H., and V. D. Misking. "The lost art of high productivity." *Personnel,* 63, No. 4 (April 1986), 34–38.

Hackman, J. *Improving the Quality of Work Life: Work Design.* Washington, D.C.: Office of Research, ASPER, U.S. Department of Labor, 1975.

Hackman, J., and J. Suttle. *Improving Life at Work: Behavioral Science Approaches to Social Change.* Santa Monica, Calif.: Goodyear, 1977.

Hansen, J. M. "Site-based management and quality circles: A natural combination." *NASSP Bulletin,* 74, No. 528 (October 1990) 100–103.

Harken, D., G. Bond, L. Borman, E. Bankoff, S. Daiter, M. Lieberman, and L. Videka. "Growth of a medical self-help group." In *Self-Help Groups for Coping with Crisis,* ed. M. Lieberman and L. Borman, San Francisco: Jossey-Bass, 1979, 43–66.

Hatvany, N., and V. Pucik. "Japanese management practices and productivity." *Organizational Dynamics,* Spring, 1981, 5–21.

Hinrichsen, G. A., T. A. Revenson, A. Tracey, and M. Shinn. "Does self-help help? An empirical investigation of scoliosis peer support groups." *Journal of Social Issues,* 41, No. 1 (1985), 65–87.

Humphry, D. *Final exit. Hemlock Society,* (1990).

Jablonski, J.R. *Implementing Total Quality Management: An Overview.* San Diego, Calif.: Pfeiffer 1991, p. 4.

Jenkins, T. "Participative management: The new wave." *Management World,* May 1981, 8–10.

Johnson, S. P., T. M. Welsh, L. K. Miller, and D. E. Altus. "Participatory management: Maintaining staff performance in a university housing cooperative." *Journal of Applied Behavior Analysis,* 24 No. 1 (Spring 1991), 119–127.

Kahn, A., and E. I. Bender. "Self-help groups as a crucible for people empowerment in the context of social development." *Social Development Issues,* 9, No. 2 (1985), 4–13.

Kanter, R. M. "Dilemmas of managing participation," *Organizational Dynamics,* 11 (1982), 5–27.

Katz, A. "Self-help organizations and volunteer participation in social welfare." *Social Work,* 15 (1970), 51–60.

Katz, A. "Self-help groups." *Social Work,* 17 (1972), 120–121.

Katz, A., and E. Bender. *The Strength in Us: Self-Help Groups in the Modern World.* New York: New Viewpoints, 1976.

Kelly, J., and K. Khozan. "Participative management: Can it work?" *Business Horizons,* August 1980, 74–79.

Koska, Mary T. "Adapting Deming's Quality Improvement Ideas: A Case Study." *Hospitals,* July 5, 1990.

Kropotkin, P. *Mutual Aid: A Factor in Evolution.* Boston: Extending Horizons, 1955.

Krueger, R. A., and M. Q. Patton. *Focus Groups: A Practical Guide for Applied Research.* Newbury Park, Calif.: Sage Publications, 1988.

Lagana, J. F. "Managing change and school improvement effectively." *NASSP Bulletin,* 73, No. 518 (September 1989) 52–55.

Lawler, E. E., III, and G. E. Ledford, Jr. In Marks, M. L. "The question of quality circles." *Psychology Today,* 20, No. 3 (March 1986), 36–46.

Lawler, E. E., III, and Mohrman, S. A. "Quality circles after the fad." *Harvard Business Review,* 63 (January/February 1985), 65–71.

Lawler, E. E., III, "The new plant revolution revisited." *Organizational Dynamics* 19, No. 2 (Fall 1990), 5–14.

Leddick, S. "Teaching managers to support quality-improvement efforts." *National Productivity Review,* Winter 1990/91, 69–74.

Leebov, W., and G. Scott. *Health Care Managers in Transition.* San Francisco: Jossey-Bass, 1990, pp. 136–137.

Levine, M. "An analysis of mutual assistance." Invited address. Annual meeting of the American Psychological Association, New York, August 1987.

Levy, L. H. "Processes and activities in groups." In *Self-Help Groups for Coping with Stress,* ed. M. A. Lieberman, L. D. Borman, and Associates. San Francisco: Jossey-Bass, 1979, pp. 241–256.

Lieberman, M., and L. Borman, eds. *Self-Help Groups for Coping with Stress.* San Francisco: Jossey-Bass, 1979.

Lieberman, M. A., and L. Videka-Sherman. "The impact of self-help groups on the mental health of widows and widowers." *American Journal of Orthopsychiatry,* 56, No. 3 (1986), 435–449.

Likert, R. *New Patterns of Management.* New York: McGraw-Hill, 1961.

Likert, R. *The Human Organization.* New York: McGraw-HIll, 1967.

Low, A. A. *Mental Health Through Will-Training.* Boston: Christopher Publishing House, 1950.

Main, J. "Westinghouse's cultural revolution." *Fortune,* June 15, 1981, 74–93.

Manz, C. C., D. E. Keating and A. Donnellon. "Preparing for an organizational change to employee self-management: The managerial transition." *Organizational Dynamics,* 19, No. 2 (Fall 1990), 15–26.

Marks, M. L. "The question of quality circles." *Psychology Today,* 20, No. 3 (March 1986), 36–46.

Marks, M. L., P. H. Mirvis, F. Grady, and E. J. Hackett. "Employee participation in a quality circle program: Impact on quality of work life, productivity and absenteeism." *Journal of Applied Psychology,* 71 (1985), 61–69.

Maslow, A. *Motivation and Personality.* New York: Harpers, 1954.

Mazique, M. "The quality of circle transplant." Reprint. *Issues and Observations,* May 1981.

Maton, K. I., G. S. Leventhal, E. J. Madara, and M. Julien. "Factors affecting the birth and death of mutual health groups: The role of national affiliation, professional involvement, and member focal problem." *American Journal of Community Psychology,* 17 (1989), 643–671.

McGarvey, R. "The competitive edge." *US Air Magazine,* February 1992.

McGregor, D. *The Human Side of Enterprise.* New York: McGraw-Hill, 1960.

Merton, R. K., M. Fiske, and P. L. Kendall. *The Focused Interview.* New York: The Free Press, 1956.

Merton, R. K., M. Fiske, and P. L. Kendall. *Mass Persuasion.* New York: Harper & Row, 1946.

Metz, E. "The verteam circle." *Training and Development Journal,* 35 (1981), 78–85.

Meyer, G. W., and R. G. Stott. "Quality circles: Panacea or Pandora's Box?" *Organizational Dynamics,* 13, No. 4 (Spring 1985), 34–50.

Milakovich, M. E. "Total quality management in the public sector." *National Productivity Review,* Spring 1991, 195–205.

Mohrman, S. A., and L. Novelli. "Beyond testimonials: Learning from a quality circles programme." *Journal of Occupational Behaviour,* 6, No. 2 (April 1985), 93–110.

Ouchi, W. *Theory Z.* Reading, Mass.: Addison-Wesley, 1981.

"Participative management at work: An interview with John F. Donnelly." *Harvard Business Review,* 55 (1977), 117–127.

Pascarella, P. "Quality circles: Just another management headache?" *Industry Week,* June 28, 1982, 50–55.

Peele, S. *The Meaning of Addiction: Compulsive Experience and Its Interpretation.* Lexington, Mass.: Lexington Books, 1984.

"QCs—much more than rap sessions." *Training,* 20 (1983), 84–85.

Rafaeli, A. "Quality circles and employee attitudes." *Personnel Psychology,* 38, No. 3 (1985), 603–615.

Reiker, W. "The q.c. circle phenomenon." Reprint. Association for Quality Circles, 1979.

Riessman, F. "Self-helpers." *The Nation,* June 2, 1984, p. 661.

Sagarin, E. *Odd Man In: Societies of Deviants in America.* New York: Quadrangle Books, 1969.

Sashkin, M. "Participative management is an ethical imperative." *Organizational Dynamics,* Spring 1984, 5–21.

Scheffler, L. *Help Thy Neighbor: How Counseling Works and When It Doesn't.* New York: Grove Press, 1983.

Schleicher, W. "Quality control circles save Lockheed nearly $3 million in two years." *Quality,* May 1977, 14–17.

Schlesinger, L. A., and B. Oshry. "Quality of work life and the manager: Muddle in the middle." *Organizational Dynamics,* 13, No. 1 (Summer 1984), 5–19.

Sensenbrenner, J. "Quality comes to city hall." *Harvard Business Review.* March–April 1991, 64–69.

Sherr, L. A., and D. J. Teeter. *Total Quality Management in Higher Education.* San Francisco: Jossey-Bass, 1991, pp. 3–10.

Shipper, F. "Quality circles using small group formation." *Training and Development Journal,* 37 (1983), 80–84.

Sims, H., and C. Manz. "Conversations within self-managed work groups." *National Productivity Review,* 1 (1982), 261–269.

Sims, Henry P., Jr., and J. W. Dean, Jr. "Beyond quality circles: Self-managing teams." *Personnel,* 62, No. 1 (January 1985), 25–32.

Steel, R. P., and G. S. Shane. "Evaluation research on quality circles: Technical and analytical implications." *Human Relations,* 39, No. 5 (1986), 449–466.

Stewart, D. W., and P. N. Shamdasani. "Focus groups—Theory and practice." Newbury Park, Calif.: Sage Publications, 1990.

Toseland, R. W., and L. Hacker. "Social workers' use of self-help groups as resource for clients." *Social Work,* 30, No. 3 (May–June 1985), 232–237.

Trist, E. *The Evolution of Socio-technical Systems.* Toronto, Ontario: Ontario Quality of Working Life Centre, 1981.

Walton, M. "Deming management at work." *Soundview Executive Book Summaries,* 13 No. 2, Part 1 (February 1990).

Walton, R. "Work innovation in the United States." *Harvard Business Review,* 57 (1979), 88–98.

Watanabe, S. "The Japanese quality control circle: Why it works." *International Labour Review,* 130, No. 1 (1991).

Werther, W. B., Jr. "Going in circles with quality circles? Management development implications." *Journal of Management Development,* 2 (1983), 3–18.

Wilson, J. "Squaring the quality circle." *Chief Executive,* December 1982, 40–41.

Wood, R., F. Hull, and K. Azumi. "Evaluating quality circles: The American application." *California Management Review,* 26 (1983), 37–53.

Zemke, R. "Honeywell imports quality circles as long-term management strategy." *Training,* 17 (1980), 91–94.

◆ *12* ◆

Making Large Groups More Effective

Historically, large groups of over twenty-five or thirty people have generally been viewed as organized gatherings wherein people are drawn together to be told something, shown something, or educated about an idea or a method. In other situations such organized gatherings might be used to demonstrate politically, to incite people, to act out grievances (as in a strike), or sometimes to celebrate or create a climate of support. What such gatherings have in common is the effort to mobilize the thinking or feelings of a large group of people toward some preconceived end. Because size, Durkheim and Tonnier reported, is a key determinant of the nature and finality of relationships for members in a group (Wilson, 1978), it is essential to understand how such groups are similar to, and how they are different from, typical small groups.

Utilizing large groups of people in a more creative and productive manner is a very recent phenomenon. It was not until the 1950s and 1960s, spurred by the success that had been achieved working on management problems in the military during World War II (Galbraith, 1977), that social scientists began to show a real interest in group dynamics. Even then, attention was primarily focused on small groups. The development of specific skills and strategies for problem solving, learning, sharing, and team building was for many years reserved for smaller and more manageable groups. Although the intervening years have seen great progress in the small group arena, we are only beginning to understand the principles of managing large groups.

In an organizational setting, the vast majority of meetings with more than twenty or twenty-five in attendance are extraordinarily predictable and quite often focus on the narrow communication of information—the presentation of ideas, facts, and figures. One of the difficulties of utilizing a large group springs from the way it has been clinically defined: a large group is one that does not allow for "face-to-face interaction among all its members at any given time" (Morrison, Greene, and Tischler, 1985). It is common in large groups for overheads, videos, and flip charts to be used in order to engage the basically passive participants. Only rarely is an effort made to stimulate, challenge, or utilize the ideas of those present. Even though there is an increasing body of strategies and skills that can be applied to large groups and can dramatically increase their effectiveness, the shift to a more productive use of such large groups is just beginning to occur.

The Natural Resistance to the Use of Large Groups

Ironically, what has been learned about large group behavior far surpasses the understanding and courage of most of the group leaders who put such knowledge into practice. Leaders have for decades found large groups difficult to deal with for a variety of reasons. In many situations, an unstated rule of management has been to isolate subordinates from one another so that the potential power that lay in the group could not be actualized. There was (and still is) an abiding fear on the part of many leaders that simply bringing people together in a group environment will result in complaining or griping or will create in the minds of those present expectations that cannot possibly be realized.[1] Thus it is not difficult to understand why a leader might avoid such possibilities and simply not convene large group gatherings. These attitudes are strengthened by other biases suggesting that such groups gatherings might

- be inefficient
- take too much time
- be difficult to organize
- make people feel uncomfortable
- make the leader feel exposed and vulnerable

Not only this, but because few leaders had experienced the positive use of such groups in the past, there was always the chance that they would lose control of the group and that a blow-up or something unpredictable might cast a negative reflection on their leadership. Finally, powerful norms exist in many organizations defining specifically how groups and meetings are to be experienced. Any change represents a threat to the status quo regardless of the efficiencies or creative outcomes that might result. In addition, Allison and Messick (1985) suggest that members of large groups are not easily able to discern the effects of their behaviors on the resource pool, which decreases the efficiency of the large group.

It is little wonder, then, that large group gatherings have normally been used only in situations where strict control is insured. As we have noted, they are primarily used for communicating information or for telling and selling ideas.

Eight Designs for Improving the Effectiveness of Large Groups

During the last thirty years most organizational leaders have had at least some positive experience in small groups, and it is only natural that some of the methodologies should seem applicable to larger groups. Theoretically, a well-designed large group experience should save time, increase the quality of the desired outcomes, result in improved morale among the participants, reduce conflicts that might exist, and increase the participants' commitment to the organization itself.

However, our understanding of small groups reminds us that without an effective design, a meeting with ten or twelve people can easily be dominated by two or

---

1. It is possible that anxieties associated with large groups may be greater than in small groups because for the members, there is a greater fear of loss of ego boundaries, and for the leaders, there is a tendency to "experience a relative impoverishment of personal power" (Morrison, Greene, and Tischler, 1985, vol. 125, 601–611).

three individuals. This results in six to eight people participating minimally, contributing little, and feeling ineffective by the end of the session. Over time, participation in such groups will be relatively passive, as dependency rises along with resentment. And we can anticipate that the percentage of participation would decline as the size of the group increased. But research concerning social dilemmas has suggested that the negative effects of increasing group size may be overrated when the collective identity is high. In other words, the number of individuals in a group should become less relevant if the group is viewed similarly by its members (Brewer and Kramer, 1986). The critical question, in relation to either a large or a small group, becomes "How does one change the dynamic so that the skills, ideas, and energies of individuals are maximized—so that using the group has benefits that extend far beyond what might be expected?"

This chapter represents an effort to reveal the potential benefits of utilizing large groups in a wide variety of practical situations. Unlike other chapters in which practical activities and "designs" have been placed at the end, here we provide eight cases within the body of the chapter to show how theoretical concepts help explain the consequences of particular large group interventions. Many principles related to large group norms, membership, goals, and leadership are vividly displayed in these examples which are drawn from a wide variety of settings. What follows, then, are a number of specific, real-life cases in which large groups have been used creatively and productively in ways that were beneficial both to the organization and to the individuals involved.

Case 1: The Myth-Making Design

Setting: A Major American University

The Problem

The University had an enviable reputation. Though known for its exceptional School of Engineering, it had a broad curriculum and attracted student scholars from all across the country. In recent years, however, there had been signs of deterioration—not so much in relation to academics, although this was sure to follow—but from problems resulting from the use of drugs, drinking, and general rowdyism. Several incidents had gained regional and even national notoriety, and it had become clear that something had to be done. But what? As might be expected, along with the University's declining reputation, a certain apathy had developed. It was reflected in unwillingness on the part of both faculty and students to dedicate time and energy in service of the University. Some simply didn't want to be bothered; others believed nothing good would result from their efforts. Along with everything else, an anti-administration attitude had resulted from its previous heavy-handed attempts to "put out fires." This crisis-reactive approach seemed to focus on symptoms rather than on the more pervasive, underlying problems.

A well-known consultant with expertise in group and system dynamics—but not university life—was asked to help the administration create a climate of optimism that might enhance the success of a large-scale change effort. It was believed that a shift in attitudes might result in an enduring commitment to solving the serious problems at hand.

Thirty "movers and shakers" representing students, faculty, and administration throughout the University were identified. Everyone invited was a genuine stakeholder who represented a key University constituency. For example, there were deans, the leaders of all the fraternities and sororities, the head of the black caucus, and elected representatives of the faculty senate. All thirty leaders were told that the meeting was crucial but that they would be expected to attend only this one session. Even with dinner as an incentive, the reluctance to attend was obvious. Clearly, the challenge was to rekindle long-dormant pride and enthusiasm that had once been an important source of the University's reputation.

The Solution

After dinner, the participants were asked to divide themselves into four groups based on their number of years in the University. Those with over ten years came together in one group, five to ten years in another, three to five years in another, and finally, all those under three years. Each group was asked to develop a myth—a story that reflected their experience in the University and that had a plot, a clear beginning, and an ending. They were to bring into the story the language of mythology—of kingdoms, dragons, knights, and sorcerers.

Each group was given forty-five minutes to develop its myth in the most creative way possible. Then each was given the opportunity to tell its story. The stories were extraordinarily creative, humorous, and truthful. They differed in emphasis, but all had a common theme. In each the kingdom was in a state of decline and there was sadness and in some cases despair. The truth shone through in a vivid array of words that could not be denied.

The question placed before the group once the themes were understood was whether those present would be willing to work toward the changes necessary to alter the future course of the story and help reestablish the reputation and spirit of the University. The consultant said she would work with the group only if two-thirds agreed to commit themselves to a long-term view of change. A vote resulted in a 100 percent commitment.

Evaluation

The four stories had captured the group's imagination and had revived the latent idealism of those present. By not creating a climate of blame, by not preaching, by not selling, and by not being heavy-handed but rather allowing the concerns to evolve from those present, the administration had captured the commitment it so badly needed.

The creative design sparked concern, reestablished a sense of responsibility, and minimized a possible defensive response. Two years later the perceived impact was dramatic, and the University effort to improve itself was still developing in a positive and proactive manner.

Case 2: The News Conference Design

Setting: The Government of a Third-World Country

The Problem

Most large group meetings are utterly predictable and many are boring. One could estimate conservatively that most people are brought together in large groups simply to be given information that they already know or that could be provided in many other formats. Instead of being the primary focus, giving information should take up the smallest part of most agendas (see Chapter 9, on meetings). One study (Blythe, Gilchrist, Schinke, 1981) found that group intervention was a more effective approach than the group dissemination of information to helping to prevent adolescent pregnancies. Still, providing information of certain kinds to a large group of people gathered together, if done well, can afford the opportunity to praise, thank, support, celebrate, dispel rumors, and motivate. Because most people are not trained public speakers, they may be too terse, too rambling, or too dogmatic to have much appeal. The following large group design is challenging, is stimulating, and virtually never becomes boring. Rarely is it felt to be a waste of time. Although control of the meeting remains in the hands of the leaders, the design allows a wide range of freedom and participation on the part of a large and diverse group.

The situation was a day-long meeting of sixty cabinet-level ministers of a small third-world country. The government had, in the face of great odds, survived its first year in power. New crises arising on an almost daily basis had resulted in the President and Prime Minister centralizing authority further and further as they attempted to facilitate problem solving and decision making. They did this at a time when their ministers had an increasing need for autonomy and support as they attempted to tackle the huge problems facing each of them. The result was growing dependency, apathy, and resentment as the ministers grew reluctant to act without the consent of the key leaders.

At the same time, twelve-hour days left little room for communication downward to the ministers of the latest problems facing the government. Thus, the ministers felt isolated and impotent at a time when they needed greater support and information.

The problem: to design a meeting that would allow frustrations to be aired and information to be shared while insuring that an honest interchange would occur. Some individuals feared retribution. Others sympathized with the plight of the leaders and preferred to show them gratitude rather than give them grief. The tension in the room was enormous.

The Solution

In this case, the sixty participants were divided into groups of four or five, and each small group was asked to develop the three questions they felt were most important for the President and Prime Minister to answer. They were told that the written questions from each group would be redistributed throughout the large group so that anonymity would prevail. A three-minute time limit was to be imposed on the answering of any question, and a single follow-up question would be allowed in order to clarify or extend any response. This format insured that a wide range of questions would be asked and that no single question—or ensuing debate— could dominate a meeting in which information exchange and trust building were primary goals.

Evaluation

Too often, open periods of questions and answers promote defensiveness and justification on the part of the leaders, who may feel vulnerable to displays of anger, complaints, or even ridicule. Thus meetings intended "to motivate the troops" often leave people even more frustrated and demoralized than before. To be sure that this does not occur, leaders often squelch discussion by giving talks prepared in advance or answering questions submitted previously so that replies can be carefully rehearsed. Such transparent efforts to control a group seldom succeed, because in the long run, the participants feel manipulated and deprived of the very information they need. The results of this rather simple but elegant design was that

- all sixty members felt a direct sense of participation in the process
- all the critical questions of the group were raised
- the leaders had a rare opportunity to respond candidly to the most crucial concerns of those present
- there was little chance that control of the session would be lost
- a sense of trust evolved from the candor exhibited by the leaders

An obvious caution in such a design is that if the leaders are unwilling to be honest and forthright, the result will be further frustration and disillusionment rather than the hope and trust that were desired. In this case, the great majority of those present were seen as allies, and the goal was to be as candid as possible with questions and answers. Effective leaders tend to find the experience exhilarating. It creates a positive climate that they wish to replicate again and again.

◆ Reader Activity

Think of situations with which you are familiar wherein a large group is used and people feel "talked at" and uninvolved. What could be "designed" into the situation that would alter its negative aspects? How could the use of small groups breathe life into the situation, thus reducing the unpredictable boredom or indifference that often results?

_____

_____

_____

_____ ◆

Case 3: The Great Egg Drop Design

Setting: A Large Midwest Corporation

The Problem

One hundred and ten managers of the new-products division of a large midwestern corporation had come together with the hope of building a greater sense of team spirit and cooperation among the group. At the same time, the planners wanted those present to experience a day of fun and inspiration. Individuals representing product design, marketing, sales, and public relations were divided into eight 13-person, heterogeneous groups. A process observer was assigned each group to evaluate how it developed, planned, and executed the task it was given. The entire large group heard the following directions simultaneously, and the small groups were given one hour to complete the task.

Your team of thirteen has been asked to develop a new product in direct competition with seven other corporations (represented by the other seven teams of thirteen people).

The product is to be a device/machine for dropping an egg from a height of 10 feet without its breaking. You have available the following materials:

1. A roll of paper towels
2. A large number of small bar straws
3. Two large 7" × 6" ziplock bags
4. A roll of masking tape
5. Two large eggs

Entries are to be judged by a panel of judges who, in determining what is the best product, will weigh equally building and R&D costs, as well as creative marketing and public relations promotions for the device. This will include showing the value of the product to the consumer and its marketability. At the end of the one-hour development period, each presenting organization will have five to seven minutes to present to the judges (and the entire group of participants) all facets of the idea, including a demonstration of the device itself.

The cracking or breaking of an egg during the demonstration will lead to immediate disqualification. Cost factors will have to be itemized, and a total cost for the device must be estimated and provided the judges at the time of the presentation. Costs are to be based on the following list:

1. Each two-ply paper towel used, 5 cents
2. Each straw, 2 cents
3. Each ziplock bag, 10 cents
4. The cost of one practice egg, if used, 35 cents
5. The cost of the demonstration egg, 35 cents
6. The cost of masking tape per foot, 10 cents
7. The cost of any other materials or object utilized in the demonstration, 50 cents each

Finally, human contact with the egg may be made only at the point of the drop itself.

The groups were encouraged to utilize all the time available and to determine the best use of the human resources in the group. After the one hour of development and before the demonstration to the judges, the following events occurred:

■ The process observers assigned to each group debriefed their teams, and the teams were given the opportunity to assess their effectiveness in areas such as delegation, planning, utilization of time, idea generation, and the coordination of diverse tasks. (20 minutes)

■ They were encouraged to list things that occurred during the task development that mirrored the characteristic strengths and limitations of the larger organization. They were asked to submit two recommendations that might improve the mother company. (20 to 30 minutes)

■ At the end of the team debriefing period, all eight groups were called together and their identified strengths were posted, as were the factors that limited the process. Patterns were identified from across the various groups.

■ Finally, a summary of the recommendations to improve the larger company was identified and posted. There was an opportunity for comments to be made.

■ At this point, each group demonstrated its invention and presented its marketing and PR strategies to the entire community. The outcomes ranged from the mundane to the outrageous and from slightly humorous to hysterical. For an hour the participants laughed, cheered, jeered, and shouted at their own efforts and the efforts of their peers. Eventually all groups received recognition and prizes for their effort, and three groups were clearly acknowledged as winners of the first annual egg drop manufacturing competition. This was based on surviving the "drop" and on the criteria established at the beginning of the activity.

Evaluation

The approaches to planning and problem solving that were characteristically used in the company were clearly identified. The limited time allocated to the task exaggerated what appeared to occur normally within the organization during stressful periods of product development. For example, the tendency not to probe for consensus when planning and not to test certain ideas in advance was noted. Of particular interest was the fact that pride, not cost, was identified as the crucial variable that limited some necessary experimentation.

The assessments were found to be honest and not cluttered with defensiveness, because the participants had a good time and could see that they were not being singled out for criticism. Witnessing other intelligent human beings making what appeared to be similar errors—in short, being imperfect—seemed to create a climate that legitimized a positive learning process without blame or guilt.

Though some of the problems encountered were the result of ineffective leadership, it appeared that this kind of feedback was easier to hear because the tone of the entire day was positive, fun, and supportive.

The presentations themselves were nothing short of hilarious, as creativity and humor ran riot in clever promotions, songs, and TV pitches for the new device. Explosions of laughter echoed as eggs broke, cracked or (in three cases) remained whole as the various contraptions succeeded or failed.

Finally, as a result of experiencing such a positive initiative and witnessing the quality of the recommendations that were made, the participants had a clear sense of pride and success at the end of the 3½ hour session.

Three key conclusions can be drawn from this example:

1. Nonrelated tasks or initiatives often generate characteristic patterns of behavior that can inhibit group or organizational effectiveness. Identifying such patterns can prove to be of great benefit.

2. Because "owning" problems is as important as identifying them, interventions such as that described here can move the organization to the point of problem solving and solution without the use of unnecessary criticism or judgments.

3. Humorous events shared by large numbers of people can be "cultural benchmarks" for organizations and can become part of the collective memory of the group. Years later, a momentary recollection of the quite "ridiculous" contraptions may trigger laughter and reinforce the bonding effect of the historical/hysterical event. Many organizations spend very little time forging their own memorable histories, even though a wide variety of unique and creative events are possible. Increasingly, however, it is becoming clear that such occasions can have diagnostic, educational, and problem-solving value.

Case 4: The Interview Design

Setting: A Division of a Large Manufacturing Organization

The Problem

In recent years, strategic planning has become an integral part of organizational life. It represents the periodic and systematic review of how successful the organization is in achieving its mission, what progress it is making toward its vision, and how effectively it identifies and deals with operational problems. The process legitimately asks the following questions:

Is the organization reaching its goals?

Are operations effective?

What adjustments or changes need to be made to insure greater success in these pursuits?

Are the values implicit in the statements of vision and mission being reflected in the daily life of the organization?

Traditionally, strategic planning has tended to consist of a small group of key leaders reviewing the current financial numbers and the future projections and then assessing the viability of the current plan and determining whether, or even if, a new plan was needed. Strategic thinking was initiated and terminated from the top. It was biased by the hopes, dreams, and personal agendas of those present. Management by objectives (MBO) was middle management's response to the goals established at the top. Taking their cue from corporate goals, operational groups would define their own goals and specific objectives. Success for individuals would be determined by their ability to meet their objectives. Stebbins and Shani (1989) refer to this type of management as "The Mafia Model" and maintain that it relies on the diagnosis of a select few in an atmosphere where secrecy is critical and decisions often end in assassinations (the firing of individuals).

In recent years, however, many organizational leaders have recognized that it is often the individual with line responsibilities who can be most sensitive to both the realities of the marketplace and internal forces that reduce the ability of the organization to succeed. Enlightened management has increasingly been seeking cost-effective ways of tapping into the wealth of information available to them that might dramatically influence the planning process. The outcome would naturally be organizational goals that more faithfully reflect reality and, at the same time, a planning process that would give large numbers of workers a greater sense of ownership and empowerment within the organization. The human resources strategy proposed by Schuler and Walker (1990) suggests that human resource concerns be first seen as business concerns and then addressed as specific, people-related issues. Organizational priorities will then encompass people-related business concerns. This is achieved by bringing together line managers and human resource specialists to develop key issues that can be used as the focus around which "people-related" business concerns may grow.

This trend away from top-down, authoritarian management toward greater participation at all levels has unleashed a need for strategies that incorporate large groups of people into the envisioning, goal-setting, and problem-solving aspects of planning. Though it has always been possible to elicit ideas and attitudes by means of questionnaires, years of management insensitivity and limited response to this information have rendered this approach much less effective than it should be.

The Solution

Well-designed activities can increase the participation of people within a large group setting and can increase the quality of the information generated. Following is a large group intervention used with 65 managers and their bosses, who represented the strategic planning committee of an organization of 3,000 employees. The interview design described here offered a broad spectrum of middle managers an opportunity to influence the ultimate planning process of their organization.[2]

- Prior to the day-long meeting, individuals were requested to submit questions they believed the group should address at the outset of any strategic planning process. The questions could be general or as specific as desired. With the help of a consultant, a small, representative group selected the six most powerful and useful questions that they believed the total group of managers needed to address.
- Upon entering the session, the 72 leaders were requested to take a chair in any of the rows. What they saw were six groups of twelve

2. A modification of this design first appeared in Napier, R. W. and M. Gershenfeld *Making Groups Work* Boston: Houghton Mifflin Company, 1983, pp. 134–139. The design has been used successfully in a wide variety of group settings.

chairs, each consisting of six chairs facing six chairs. On each chair was a typed question, a note pad, and a pencil. The leaders were told that there were six different questions in their row and the same six questions in each of the rows in the room, although the rows were arranged so that a person with a different question was across from them.

When the design began, the people in Row A asked the people across from them in Row B their question. They were to probe with follow-up questions, attempting to gain as much information as possible. Seeking examples was essential. Each had approximately three minutes to do this and record their responses. A timer called time at the end of three minutes, at which point the individual across from the first interviewer had an opportunity to ask his or her question. Again, individuals had three minutes to respond. At the end of the allotted time, the round ended with all the individuals in both rows having answered a question and having asked a question. Now the people in Row A were asked to move one seat to their right (the first person rotated to the rear; see figure below). The people in Row B remained stationary. Thus each individual had another person to interview on her or his question and had the opportunity to *be* interviewed on another question. Again they had three minutes to question and three minutes to respond to the question from a new individual across from them. Eventually, everyone had the opportunity to answer their own question. The process continued for six-minute rounds until all the participants had gathered information from six people and had had an opportunity to respond to all six questions, including their own. And in the process, each individual had become somewhat of an expert on his or her own question.

Following are the six questions chosen to generate the information necessary for the initial phase of the strategic planning process.

1. What three operational factors most inhibit our present productivity and our ability to reach our organizational goals?
2. How, if at all, should our current mission be altered to insure the best use of our organizational resources while still maintaining our corporate values?
3. What currently inhibits management from being as effective as possible (structure, staffing, methods)?

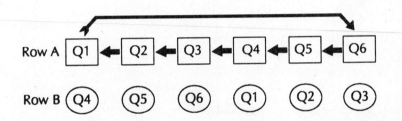

4. Considering our organization in ten years, what operational changes do you envision occurring in order for us to be increasingly successful?
5. What do we do that represents our greatest strength, which we should recognize and strive to maintain?
6. What values do we talk (act like we believe) but seldom walk in this organization?

- After the interviews were completed, fifteen minutes was allotted for individuals to organize their data into what could be called
  a. Statements of *fact*—four, five, or six people agreeing on an idea or response to a question
  b. *Trends*—two or three people agreeing on an idea or response
  c. *Unique ideas*—creative, original thoughts that warrant the attention of the participants
- At this point, all the people with Question 1 joined together in a group and were asked to discuss their data. The twelve people present selected a recorder to post the outcomes of their deliberations. They had one hour to complete two tasks. The first was to integrate their individual findings into a group consensus. Thus, they had to decide what information was worth bringing back to the total group as a fact or trend. In this case, at least eight of twelve would suffice to signify a fact. But a particular idea might be a fact for six people and a trend for six. If that occurred, the group had to reach consensus on the idea's significance. Similarly, the group had to agree on trends and any unique ideas they believed warranted the consideration of the total group.

The second task of the group of twelve was to take an idea or ideas that they believed the total group of 72 must hear *and never forget* and develop a memorable two-to-three-minute skit representing this fact or unique idea. This task is usually met with groans, yet it inevitably becomes the highlight of the experience as groups proceed to create an unforgettable event. The exaggeration of ideas in the vignette predictably results in gales of laughter. It not only reinforces the issue but also brings the group together in new and enjoyable ways.

- Each group then selected one or two presenters who had five minutes to present their data. The presentation of the data always followed the vignette.
- This entire diagnostic analysis took less than three hours. At a lunch break, the presenters (six people representing each question) and the facilitator/leader together decided which specific issues required the groups' attention as a natural next step in the strategic planning process. A participative problem-solving process to achieve those goals was then designed for the remainder of the day.[3]

---

3. See examples of these designs in the Exercise Section of Chapter 7.

◆ Reader Activity

Before reading ahead, write down what you believe are the five or six reasons why this particular large group "design" was successful. Try to be as concrete as possible and relate your ideas, whenever possible, to ideas you have encountered in your previous reading.

_____

_____

_____

_____

_____   ◆

Evaluation

There are a variety of theoretically sound reasons why this structured large group design works effectively with a variety of organizational goals.

1. The interviewing process is totally engaging. The participants are usually candid, because they realize that everyone else is answering the same questions and that their own responses have the potential to influence the outcome.

2. The fact that all have an opportunity to express their own views on each question is unique, and it yields a 100 percent sample during a forty minute activity. The process represents an extremely efficient use of both time and human resources.

3. There are usually a number of "facts" that arise from the integration and analysis of each question. A natural consensus evolves. People feel involved and empowered.

4. The process itself is difficult to manipulate even when one or two individuals bias their own note taking and interpretations of the data they gathered from their interviews. During the group discussion, the process itself is so public and consistent that individuals who might otherwise try to manipulate or influence the process are unwilling to compromise themselves in the face of such an open climate.

5. People feel "heard" even when their ideas don't make it to the status of fact, trend, or unique idea. The interview demands that each individual being interviewed receive 100 percent of someone's attention— a rare experience for many.

6. The effective use of time and people is so far superior to what occurs in most meetings that evaluations are predictably very high and comments inevitably suggest the desire for additional meetings of this kind.

7. Following negotiations by the creation of a skit is stimulating, fulfilling, and often humorous. This legitimizing of play in the context of a serious work situation is often registered as one of the most positive aspects of the day.

This particular design is effective in a wide variety of situations. One is the "future search" exemplified here. In another instance, the goal might be the resolution of specific problems. Questions would then be directed at finding solutions rather than being diagnostic. Groups of eight, ten, or twelve can be used.[4] In some cases, each individual is given two questions; this doubles the data available. The focus of the questions and the intent of the design itself must be absolutely clear if the true value of the technique is to be realized.

Case 5: The Video-Link Design

Setting: A Large Manufacturing Organization

The Problem

A 1,500-person division of a large manufacturing organization had been experiencing hard times. The credibility of the eight-person executive management group, which was spread over multiple locations, had been deteriorating rapidly. This management group's recent decisions seemed self-serving, and many believed the group was more interested in self-promotion than in the future of the organization. Some actually felt that commitment to the division itself had been lost and both trust and morale were at an all-time low. To make matters even more difficult, many within the organization did not feel that they knew or understood the key leaders, so many attitudes were being influenced by rumor and hearsay.

Management was convinced that its credibility could not be redeemed through typical friendly letters or memos "to the troops." Something dramatic was required that would shift opinions, reduce management isolation, and boost morale.

The Solution

The decision was to create a video link with each of the outlying locations, along with a phone hook-up to a central boardroom where the eight leaders would hold an open telephone forum for three hours. Witnessing an honest give and take among the eight would provide viewers with a close-up of the individuals behind the names and the rumors.

---

4. When an uneven number results, a person is added to the stationary row and simply works with the adjacent individual, sharing fully in asking questions and in responding to them.

Although the callers would not be anonymous, it was believed that a sense of privacy would be created and that tough questions would prevail, resulting in a much-needed opportunity for the leaders to be candid and to respond authentically.

Evaluation

With the creative use of television and the phone hook-up, the executives were able to create the turn-around desired. They achieved maximum visibility and a sense of openness and spontaneity as they fielded questions of both technical and emotional content. During the three hours, a thousand people witnessed the humor, unplanned responses, disagreement and (above all) sense of hope and optimism reflected in the attitudes of the leaders. The response was almost unanimously positive, and the program was later viewed as a "trigger event" that stimulated a period of increasing openness and positive relations. Apparently, as Drude and Lourie (1984) suggest, organizational design does, in fact, affect program outcomes.

Case 6: The Incoming Freshmen Design

Setting: An Eastern University

The Problem

National studies that reveal problems of discrimination or abuse are often discounted at the local level by individuals and groups, who rationalize that they are different from those in the study. Such denial has begun to be expected.[5] To combat this possibility, an eastern university replicated a national study that had revealed an unsettling amount of discrimination toward female students in the classroom. The replicated study affirmed the original findings and revealed, for example, that women, and most particularly, black women were much more fearful than men of volunteering or offering an answer. Thus, for example, when asked whether they would raise their hand if they had a correct answer,

> 90 percent of the men said yes
>
> 50 percent of the women said yes
>
> 90 percent of the black women said no

When the local results were released, there was an uproar on the campus as most parties—students and professors alike—denied the value of the study. In fact, nearly all forms of discrimination revealed in the study were denied. Obviously, acknowl-

---

5. Patricia Yancey Martin, a professor of sociology, suggests that organizations and institutions must become morally responsible for their effects on members (Martin, 1989).

edgement of a problem is necessary if there is to be any hope of changing the condition. It is also true that denial is a common defense in a situation where "owning" a problem could prove embarrassing (drug addiction, alcoholism, child or wife abuse, cheating, discrimination) or would have social or legal consequences. Because it was not feasible to have a thousand small group discussions or to "tell" (sell) the facts to a resistant audience, another approach had to be found that would influence the campus and promote acceptance of the information the study had revealed.

The Solution

Because the problem was seen as a long-term one, attention was focused on the least defensive and potentially most receptive group: incoming freshmen. The assumption was that dramatic changes in attitudes on the campus might occur over a four-year period. The key was to raise the level of consciousness among entering students. To do this, ten video tapes of simulated classroom situations were recorded in which subtle forms of discrimination were observable. The videos were shown in large groups of freshmen during the new student orientation week. Discussion in small mixed groups followed.

Evaluation

The discussions revealed that white students were much less sensitized to the discrimination than black students. Even in situations where discrimination was obviously "unintentional," the new students were willing to identify the problems. They had no vested interest in denial, because they were still "outsiders" and had no need to defend themselves. For their part the faculty members who were asked to help in the discussion were less defensive because of the use of the simulations. Distanced from personal scrutiny, they didn't have to defend themselves and their own classroom behavior.

Bringing the "learnings" from the small groups back to larger meetings provided the opportunity to legitimize the new understandings. In addition, students were given information about what they could do, in ways that would not alienate the professor or other students, when they experienced discrimination or saw others subjected to it in the classroom. An example of a learning generated by the small groups and shared in the larger meeting follows. This particular one became a focus for later study groups.

It was expressed that if people *wanted* to make others defensive and unable to accept the reality of a problem in which they were involved, they should be certain to shame them, blame them, "guilt them," criticize them, or make them feel ignorant or stupid in a public setting. Most of the participants could imagine how their own defenses would be raised in such situations. They could easily trace their reactions to early experiences with their parents, teachers, or other authority figures. Particular skill-based responses were then prescribed and practiced after the participants had generated some of their own strategies to reduce potential defensive responses.

Case 7: The Rebuilt School Design

Setting: An Inner-City Catholic Girls' School

The Problem

An inner-city Catholic girls school was known for its conservative, formal, and sometimes punitive approach to education. New teachers were appalled by the restrictive, uncreative, and controlled learning conditions. And they learned quickly that the "we've tried that before" syndrome was a powerful means of quelling their youthful enthusiasm and new ideas.

The older teachers, many of whom were once enthusiastic idealists, expended so much energy justifying their ways that initiating new ideas seemed a lost cause. A new principal wanted desperately to pull the faculty out of their lethargy and to instill new and useful methods into the classrooms. The assumption was that all the sisters and lay teachers had to have their idealism rekindled in a manner that would not force them to justify their present behavior. A key to discovering the benefits of new ideas had to be found.

The Solution

At one of the periodic in-service days, each of the 80 faculty members was asked to join a group of five that had to include veteran, youthful, and somewhat experienced teachers. And they had to be with at least three people whom they didn't know well. Their directions were as follows:

Imagine that we can build our old school across the street. The structure will be basically the same, but we will have no rules, traditions, or expectations. The teachers and administrators must remain the same. There is no money to expand, but things can be rearranged and walls can come down. Thus time, space, and rules are fluid. Your goal is to suggest visionary ideas that would make ours the best school possible—a place where you would be happy to send your talented and sensitive niece or good friend. Each group must—in a two-hour period—come up with from three to five concrete, specific recommendations the group agrees would work. Any idea is acceptable only if you include the "who, how, when, where" of the idea and its method of implementation. Ideas can deal with the physical structure, the curriculum, the students, or the administrative process. State regulations and codes cannot be altered. Please begin.

The noise in the room was deafening. People who for years had been restricted by negative norms that stifled creative thought were suddenly not only given permission but actually requested to bring forth their long-dormant idealism. Because solutions were the goal and they didn't have to worry about all the restrictions of the past, the ideas poured forth. People felt the excitement and enthusiasm in the room and wanted to create something.

At the end of two hours, every two groups were joined and instructed to negotiate consensus on their two or three best ideas. A person from each group was elected to represent that group's ideas to the whole gathering. At the end of three hours, eight groups presented a total of twenty ideas, all of which had the support of at least ten people diverse in age and experience. The ideas were simple and complex, practical and impractical. They drew oooh's, ahhh's, laughter, and shaking heads.

One suggestion was to create a roof garden and greenhouse for the study of botany and biology. Another was to bring experts in from the community to teach special courses. Another was to extend the teaching day so it could begin at 7:30 A.M. and end at 5:30 P.M., allowing a dramatically more flexible curriculum. Yet another included creating large classrooms by knocking down the walls.

The eight presenters were drafted into a steering group whose job was to classify the ideas, enrich them if necessary, and bring them to the faculty for a vote within a three-month period. This group would also weigh the possibility of each idea (on such bases as cost, legality, and available resources). Ideas receiving two-thirds of the vote of the faculty and again two-thirds of the vote a week later would be experimented with for one year. The double-vote method encouraged debate and tested the validity of the ideas in the crucible of the school's political and administrative realities.

Evaluation

Over the years, the faculty had slowly been disempowered and "nay-saying norms" had come into being. If an older teacher accepted the validity of a new idea, it had to be squelched or the older teachers would lose their credibility. Change was stifled not for lack of good ideas but because of the loss of pride of older members. Change often implies that what was before and is to be changed was necessarily negative. In this school, new ideas had to be attacked so that people could feel good about their years of personal investment in the old ways. To judge the old idea was to judge the individuals and "their" system of education.

To counter these sorry circumstances, the large group design

- reframed the school's physical structure, organization, and curriculum
- gave permission and encouragement to change
- rewarded the rekindling of idealism
- provided a clear, positive, and achievable task
- encouraged creativity
- mixed the groups so that they reflected the total community, thus improving the chance of success if a consensus ten individuals strong could be reached

- created a follow-up process that was led by elected leaders but was temporary in nature
- empowered the group to create change, yet made it experimental to lessen the fear of "forever"

Thus what appeared to be a simple, readily replicable design was based on a variety of assumptions and goals and on knowledge of the particular organization—its norms, history, and attitudes. Clearly, the experience of the whole group of 80 had huge benefits and resulted in the reawakening of the organization. The younger teachers saw stereotypes of older teachers crumble, and older teachers felt excited by new possibilities that could break the routine and predictability of old ways.

Case 8: The Nicaraguan Concertacion Design

Setting: The Nicaraguan Government

The Problem

Most national conferences are known for their structure, order, preplanned agendas, and limited ability to specify outcomes beyond general statements, board-based guidelines, and high-sounding platitudes. What follows is an extraordinary exception to this generalization and a fountain of information for any student of large or small group dynamics. Here we will briefly describe the background of the event, the Nicaraguan Concertacion[6] itself, and the learnings from the process that seem to have implications for large group management.

The powerful and often brutally repressive Somocista dictatorship in Nicaragua lasted for nearly three decades. It was characterized by exploitation of the working class and the establishment of an economic elite. For years it was supported by Western democracies who found right-wing repression tolerable as long as economic standards and Western investments were secure. The Somosa regime fell eventually in a classic workers' rebellion—a revolution of the oppressed representing a violent reaction to the years of exploitation as virtual slaves. The Sandinista revolution turned land and factories over to the party union. Plagued by lack of experience in the management of business and government and fettered by a counterinsurgency guerrilla war of the disenfranchised right (Contras), the enthusiasm of the "people's revolution" was dampened by serious economic and social problems. This included what was to become the largest international debt, per capita, of any third-world country.

---

6. The Concertacion was defined as a representative meeting of equals gathered to negotiate solutions to problems blocking government effectiveness.

In 1989, disillusioned by a decade of war, a stifled economy, and the horror of families killing their own, the people, contrary to all public opinion polls, elected the moderate right-wing candidate Violeta Chamorro to the presidency over the charismatic Daniel Ortega. Like that of the Sandinistas before, hers was to be a government of inexperienced officials. The well-intentioned technocrats chosen to run the government were professors and businessmen dedicated to rejuvenating the economy on a platform of peace and reconciliation. But they had little experience in local, national, or international politics. The Sandinistas responded with stunned disbelief and a sense of betrayal. Their formidable, well-organized opposition could derail even the best efforts because they still controlled the army, the police, and the courts and represented most of labor. The vote for peace left an incredible political morass.

Within the first thirty days of the new government, it became clear that something extraordinary would have to occur to launch a healing process and stop the deterioration of relationships between the still-powerful Sandinistas and those now guiding the country's future. As anyone can attest who has experienced the brooding hostility that follows a strike in an organization, it often takes years to reduce the alienation created by the striking and antistrike factions. In Nicaragua, the government was being rendered impotent. A "system intervention" of extraordinary proportions, which would literally involve the entire nation, was decided upon as a strategy to help move the long-embattled country forward.[7]

The Solution

The individual member of the government who was responsible for planning and executing such a complex "strategy" had no previous experience designing such a course of action. Though this was indeed a handicap, it also left him free to consider all possibilities. A course in small group facilitation had armed him with the necessary tools of group process. The underlying principle of all "design" interventions, he remembered, was that every act must be intentional because in almost all cases, predictable consequences can be hypothesized. Intervening in a large and complex system demands discipline. Attention to detail would be crucial: even a small error could result in an unanticipated consequence and rupture the fragile and highly volatile status quo that had made the attempt at reconciliation possible. With this in mind, let us systematically analyze each "action" of the design, the critical underlying assumption(s), and some of the consequences.

7. The 1991 Mid-East Peace Conference is another example of an attempt to bring about a change in the political order of a region under conditions where any action could result in a powerful reaction that could abort the entire process. Large egos and differing traditions, cultures, expectations, and political and social agendas confronted the peace brokers with a minefield of unpredictable consequences to consider.

Action	Assumption
1. The government created an invitation to the three critical sectors—the workers, the owners, and the government. A negotiation process among the various constituent groups representing each sector would determine what delegates would attend the Concertacion.	1. Those representing the three major sectors had to feel control over their own ability to choose their representatives. The government could not afford to be perceived as manipulating the choice of participants and, as a result, the potential outcomes. Many organizations attempt to influence eventual outcomes by controlling who can be heard, thus minimizing potential conflict and discord. In this case, however, it was assumed that conflict and disharmony were essential if authentic reconciliation was to occur.
2. The goals were explicit with potential benefits to everyone. They were to increase political, economic, and social stability; to increase production and productivity; and to increase economic growth.	2. Any effective design must have clear and compelling goals for each participating group.
3. A pre-Concertacion press campaign, along with wide TV coverage, was initiated. The entire process was to be a national media event from beginning to end.	3. It was essential that the public be brought into the process— to feel it was "their" Concertacion and to be engaged in an event that would reflect the openness of the new democracy and a willingness to deal with real problems and real conflict in public view.
4. An extravagant inauguration for the entire process was held. Participants included all branches of the government— legislature, judiciary, cabinet, church, and international or-	4. Increasing national and international attention and support would place great pressure on the delegates to act responsibly and to put the needs of the nation ahead of group interest.

Action	Assumption
ganizations (UN, AID, OAS, etc.), as well as the diplomatic corps.	Too, keeping the process open and visible insured that the government could not justly be accused of manipulation.
5. A clear definition of the rules and parameters of the Concertacion process was carefully laid out and explained at all levels. The unambiguous guidelines were found to be acceptable.	5. In a highly volatile situation where conflict is expected, people need to feel safe and to believe that all individuals will be treated fairly and equitably. Control is ensured through the "buying" of the rules by all parties. (For example, patients in a therapeutic community who are provided knowledge of clear rules and boundaries are more free to let down their guard and reveal strong feelings and opinions.) The Sandinistas entered the process feeling mistrust, because they had little control over the process. They needed the security offered by clear rules and boundaries, which were to be applied equally to everyone.
6. No boundaries were set on the time allotted for the process itself. (It lasted 37 days.)	6. If a commitment is made to reach agreement on outcomes such as national priorities, it is difficult to abort the process when the initial understanding is that participation will continue until the goals are reached.
7. Prior to the beginning of the negotiations and substantive work, two questions were asked: (a) What outcomes/expectations would you hope for from the meeting? (b) What concerns do you have?	7. It was assumed that all the participants would have the best interests of the country at heart. All sides included many idealists. Hearing similar expectations reported from the three different sectors (a small group synthesis design was used) was considered to be a

Action	Assumption
	very affirming process for the adversaries to experience. Similarly, to hear the same fears (we won't be heard, nothing will happen) expressed by everyone is always surprising. *This assumption proved to be totally accurate. Laughter and oh's were audible as old enemies had similar expectations and concerns revealed. When initial agreements are experienced even around nonsubstantive facts, a certain relief results, along with a dawning sense of optimism. This seemed to occur.*
8. An open-ended period was allowed for everyone to express all their feelings, frustrations, and fears. Old "baggage" was dumped unceremoniously on the group. There were no limits. People were allowed to say anything with as much passion as they chose. It was not a debate or a session to create ideas. The object was to exorcise demons, to blame, and to legitimize anger. It was also an opportunity to perform for "the folks back home" who were watching their representatives on television.	8. The televised catharsis, the emotional venting of anger and grief, hopes, and fear, was assumed to be necessary before people could begin to hear each other or to consider other ideas. It is well known that ideas pushed down deep will surface in resistance, anger, or other indirect ways that can block the progress of the group. The catharsis was seen as a necessary step toward healing and reconciliation. The United States is a nation where anger and pain are denied and where frustration is often internalized. Conflict is avoided until it is no longer possible to deny. Even then, it is often minimized and not dealt with authentically. The real anger submerges, only to surface later still unresolved.

Action	Assumption

In the Concertacion, the national catharsis lasted for seven days—seven days of shouting, taunting, name calling, blaming, and persuading. People talked and performed and eventually tired. Exhaustion set in as old stories were repeated. Eventually, the real process of negotiation and rebuilding began. The high-risk design intervention was successful.

9. An agenda was set forth by the government.

9. The assumption was that the agenda would be seen as a first effort to tackle the issues everyone had tacitly approved prior to the Concertacion. *This assumption was proved wrong. The Sandinista delegation walked out after the agenda was presented. It was not that the ideas were inappropriate, but the Sandinistas wanted representation in their creation. As is often the case, the "process" and not the product was creating tension and divisiveness. Agenda building by an empowered few is one of the ways people maintain organizational power. Individuals often feel manipulated but say little overtly, because to criticize the agenda is to attack directly those key leaders who have the ability to punish. In this case, the Sandinistas feared later biased manipulation by the government. The result was that an overseeing Board of Governors (two elected leaders for each of the worker, owner, and government sectors) created daily agendas that were open to input from the various delegations. Real participative*

Action	Assumption
	management began with an agenda and meeting process that solicited ideas from multiple constituencies and then created a means of dealing with them in an even-handed manner.
10. At this point an economic plan for the nation was presented as a point of departure in a plenary session (session of the whole). The government proposal was accepted as a stimulus for debate.	10. The plan was expected and was perceived as a starting point. The parties saw that the plan did not represent manipulation in favor of any special interest's agenda. In fact, the plan was seeded with a variety of acceptable compromises.
11. Representative work groups, or commissions, of thirty-six were created in four substantive areas to debate the implications of the economic plan and to frame issues for a National Agenda that would guide the government's activities over the course of the next year.	11. It was within these groups that the real work of the Concertacion occurred. Although debate by any individual was limited to five minutes, it was nearly four weeks before agreement was reached on the final issues. Land, safety, economic development, and finance were the focal points of the four commissions. Areas of contention that became blocks to the process were restored at the level of the board.

The Aftermath

One year later the Concertacion reconvened. This time most participants had a sense of trust in the process and the facilitator, and a much more efficient design was created to facilitate evaluation of the original issues stated in the National Agenda. Instead of thirty-seven days the process took one week.

Evaluation

- The plenary sessions were crucial to the success of the entire process. These sessions provided progress reports and communication across the commissions. They also allowed celebrations of successes to occur throughout the process, giving fragile hopes a much-needed reinforcement during some very difficult and tedious times.
- Of course, some structure was essential to the various meetings, but respect was shown for the subcultures represented in the various constituent groups, who differed in how and when they arrived, where they sat, and how they engaged the process. As acceptance of differences became more apparent, the need to express those differences became less important. Thus the outbursts of the Sandinistas subsided as they came to feel accepted and observed, at the same time, their disruptive behavior was having little effect on the proceedings.
- The facilitator noted in retrospect that with so many unpredictable contingencies, it was very important not to "possess" the process. Instead, it was important to remain flexible and adaptable to the changing needs and shifting levels of readiness apparent in the various commissions and among the represented constituencies. The initial catharsis during which participants were given permission to vent their feelings freely was a good example of this.
- Similarly, maintaining total objectivity in the facilitator role was crucial—and it was tested regularly. The facilitator's honesty and scrupulous attention to being fair were crucial to the success of the Concertacion.
- Opportunities for having external organizations of high social and political status applaud and reinforce the process through the press and the media were a necessary and ongoing part of the process. Pessimism and disillusionment were not allowed to take over. The participants felt the eyes of an expectant world focused on them.
- Maintaining a firm control over the proceedings, while still allowing shifts in format and structure to meet changing needs, was essential. People who doubt authority, or who tend to react against too much authority, respect leadership that is perceived as fair, firm, and still flexible. In this situation, imposing a fixed set of rules and norms would have sabotaged the program. Changes occurred in what were described as irregular states of progression and regression: two steps forward, one step back. The total process was treated as a grand experiment wherein adjustments were expected and necessary. Form and process blended, so structures and procedures were developmental in nature rather than static.
- Typically, when the various commissions reached an impasse, a smaller representative group was used to mold a compromise. Similarly, the

representative Board of Directors was used to break periodic log jams as well as to provide advice daily. The directors' wise and steady presence was regularly visible and fostered a sense of well-being. They were a necessary sounding board for clarifying problems and became an ongoing source of legitimacy for the facilitator. Without this group, the facilitator would have been the focal point of all discontent and blame. (In many workshops, a representative steering group is seen as an essential source of information and support for the leader.

- When conflicts arose, they were dealt with promptly and never allowed to fester. It was a strong expectation built into the working process of each commission that conflicts would be handled and resolved. Interpersonal issues were discussed and were separated from the substantive issues whenever possible.

- It was important to formalize outcomes and to create highly visible contractual commitments of all the key parties right in the public eye. The celebration of these outcomes enabled all the participants to walk away as winners. Without a strong and visible commitment, most efforts at changing systems falter and eventually break down.

- Finally, a follow-up evaluation was scheduled for one year later. It was to be a time of reviewing progress and planning the next steps that all of those present should take. Knowing that nothing that had been agreed to had to be "forever" enabled the participants to compromise and "experiment."

Final Thoughts on the Utilization of Large Group Interventions

The preceding cases in which designs were created for use with large groups were wide-ranging in scope. The following are a number of principles that can be drawn from these experiences and that constitute a natural summary to this chapter.

- Trust tends to increase across an entire large group after small groups formed within it and made up of representatives from all "factions" are able to share in a manner that is risk-taking, highly involving, and productive. The transfer of successful small group experiences is insured when a forum is created in which learnings, products, or other experiences can be shared with the larger group. According to Zander (1985), because bigger units are ordinarily more imposing than smaller ones, their purposes can be more powerful and important than smaller units. Obviously, boring, repetitive sharing can reduce the overall value, so designers should take that into account when planning the small group experience.

According to Cochran (1982), the use of a smaller group as a vehicle to improve the larger group enhances cohesive group decision making, the responsibility that all members assume for the large group's actions, and the representation of all levels of group membership.

- When small groups are used, it is often best to have a large room: the energy of many small groups working productively on a task is catching! Witnessing others being excited and positive often stimulates
  1. natural and often positive competition, especially when ideas are to be publicly shared later
  2. a tendency to be candid and to take more risks than might be anticipated because some will believe that "others" will probably be open so "why not them as well". Wilson reported that group members' personalities become more absorbed in the group because small groups require more participation on the part of the members (Wilson, 1978).
- A large group experience can be a "memorable" experience and can alter norms and enrich the organizational culture.
- Organizations need the opportunity to have fun and celebrate. Large group sessions provide an opportunity to celebrate ideas, individuals, or outcomes. Failure to "design" such opportunities into the life of the organization is most certainly an opportunity lost.
- The use of a representative group to follow up a large group session can allow an organization to experience ongoing benefits. Systematic progress continues on the basis of outcomes that originated at the large group event, and the participants continue to feel empowered. Thus the perennial tracking and communicating of progress is essential if the value of such large group activities is to be sustained.

References

Allison, S. T. and D. M. Messick. *"Effects of experience on performance in a replenishable resource trap."* *Journal of Personality and Social Psychology,* 49, No. 4 (1985), 943.

Blythe, B. J., L. D. Gilchrist, and S. P. Schinke, "Pregnancy-prevention groups for adolescents." National Association of Social Workers, 1981.

Brewer, M. B., and R. M. Kramer. "Choice behavior in social dilemmas: Effects of social identity, group size, and decision framing." *Journal of Personality and Social Psychology,* 50, No. 3 (1986), 544–545.

Carr, R. A. "Principal-centered preventive consultation." *Group and Organizational Studies,* 1 No. 4 (December 1976), 457.

Cochran, D. J., "Organizational consultation: A planning group approach." *The Personnel and Guidance Journal,* January 1982, 314–317.

Drude, K. P., and I. Lourie. "Staff perceptions of work environment in a state psychiatric hospital." *Psychological Reports,* 54 (1984), 263–268.

Galbraith, J. R. *Organizational Design.* Reading, Mass.: Addison-Wesley, 1977, p. 25.

Martin, P. Y. "The moral politics of organizations: Reflections of an unlikely feminist." *Journal of Applied Behavioral Science,* 24, No. 4 (1989), 468.

Morrison, T. L., L. R. Greene, and N. G. Tischler. "Manifestations of splitting in the large group." *Journal of Social Psychology,* 125, No. 5 (October 1985), 601–611.

Morrison, T. L., L. R. Greene, and N. G. Tischler. "Member perceptions in small and large Tavistock groups." *The Journal of Social Psychology,* 1984, Vol. 124, 209–217.

Napier, R. W. and M. Gershenfeld. *Making Groups Work.* Boston: Houghton Mifflin Company, 1983, pp. 134–139.

Schuler, R. S., and J. W. Walker. "Human resources strategy: Focusing on issues and actions." *Organizational Dynamics,* 19, No. 1 (Summer 1990), 5–19.

Stebbins, M. W., and A. B. (Rami) Shani. "Organization design: Beyond the 'Mafia model'." *Organizational Dynamics,* 17, No. 3 (1989), 18–30.

Weisbord, M. R. "Organizational diagnosis: Six places to look for trouble with or without a theory." *Group and Organization Studies,* 1 No. 4 (December 1976), 430.

Welsh, M. A. and E. A. Slusher. "Organizational design as a context for political activity." *Administrative Science Quarterly,* 31, No. 3 (September 1986), 389–402.

Wilson, S. *Informal Groups: An Introduction.* Englewood Cliffs, N.J.: Prentice-Hall, 1978, p. 17.

Zander, A. *The Purposes of Groups and Organizations.* San Francisco: Jossey-Bass, 1985, pp. 90–91.

Author/Name Index

Abraham, A., 7
Abrahamson, M., 235
Abse, D.W., 391
Abt, C., 507n4
Acion, Lord, 230
Ackerman, N.W., 493n2
Adams, J., 244
Adams, J.K., 325
Adams, P.A., 325
Adams, W.F., 237
Agazarian, Y., 301, 302, 308n2
Aggens, L., 460
Aiello, J., 65
Alderfer, C.P., 308n2
Allcorn, S., 500
Allen, F., 394
Allen, S.B., 399
Allison, S.T., 12, 567
Allport, F., 183
Altus, D.E., 561
Amidon, E., 441
Amir, Y., 90
Anderson, L., 351, 354, 366
Andreoli, V.V., 89
Antony, J., 428
Archer, D., 65, 231
Argyris, C., 150
Armelius, K., 328
Armstrong, S., 114
Aron, A.P., 91
Aronson, E., 88, 90, 91, 328, 329
Aronson, M.L., 89
Asch, S.E., 62, 107, 133, 134–135, 142
Atkinson, J.W., 197
Atlesk, F., 110
Auger, B.Y., 438
Aumann, R.J., 175
Axline, L.L., 538, 540
Azumi, K., 563

Babbit, R., 559
Back, K., 62, 79
Bader, G., 347
Bader, L., 446
Baer, J., 146
Bagnall, J., 341

Bailey, G.D., 237
Baird, J., 154
Baker, G.A., III, 253
Bales, R.F., 62, 83, 255, 390, 491
Bandler, R., 336n1
Bandura, A., 124
Bankoff, E., 560
Barlow, S., 243
Barnard, C.I., 199
Baron, P.H., 144
Baron, R.A., 147, 401
Baron, R.S., 144
Barrett, R.A., 175
Bass, B., 254
Bass, B.M., 179, 307
Battersby, 500
Baum, A., 65
Bavelas, A., 40
Bean, M., 560
Bear, J., 62
Beavers, W.R., 493n2, 497
Beavin, J.H., 20, 124, 158
Beckard, R., 432, 441
Becker, M.C., 428, 453
Bednar, R.L., 500
Begin, M., 489
Beishon, J., 320
Bell, J.E., 493n2
Bender, E., 523, 529, 561
Benne, K.D., 223, 255, 278n5
Bennett, E., 160
Bennis, W., 5, 6, 223, 252, 258, 260, 261,
    262, 263, 266, 481n1
Berelson, B., 39
Berg, I.A., 179
Berger, A.A., 398, 400n1, 402, 407
Berger, J., 153
Berger, R., 433
Bergum, B.O., 352
Berkowitz, L., 202
Berleson, B., 239
Bermant, G., 62
Berne, E., 6, 108
Bernstein, A., 540
Bernstein, M.D., 243
Bernstein, P., 539

Subject Index